A.J.P. TAYLOR

A Complete Annotated Bibliography and Guide to His Historical and Other Writings

A.J.P. TAYLOR

A Complete Annotated Bibliography and Guide to His Historical and Other Writings

CHRIS WRIGLEY

Senior Lecturer in Economic History,
Loughborough University

TEN YEARS HARVEST 1970 1980 FROM HARVESTER

THE HARVESTER PRESS · SUSSEX

BARNES & NOBLE · NEW YORK

First published in Great Britain in 1980 by
THE HARVESTER PRESS LIMITED
Publishers: John Spiers and Margaret A. Boden
16 Ship Street, Brighton, Sussex

and in the USA by
HARPER & ROW PUBLISHERS, INC.,
BARNES & NOBLE IMPORT DIVISION
10 East 53rd Street, New York 10022

British Library Cataloguing in Publication Data

Wrigley, C J
A.J.P. Taylor.
1. Taylor, Alan John Percivale – Bibliography
016.907′2′024 Z8861.2

ISBN 0–85527–981–8

Barnes and Noble
ISBN
0–06–497910–5

Printed in Great Britain by Redwood Burn Limited,
Trowbridge and Esher

CONTENTS

PREFACE

When reviewing a listing of 1,043 printed works by Moses Hess, A.J.P. Taylor commented that it was 'a staggering achievement'. The sheer volume of his own writings is even more staggering. My own feelings on discovering the extent of A.J.P. Taylor's writings were similar to those a sprint runner would experience if he found himself in the marathon. That A.J.P. Taylor has written much is well known – but I for one had not realised quite how much until I was some way into compiling this bibliography.

I was pleased to be asked to take on this task as I have a great respect for A.J.P. Taylor as a historian and as a person. I have always been fascinated by history, but I only really became *excited* by it when I first watched A.J.P. Taylor give a series of television lectures. The 'Men of the 1860s' really came alive. His lectures were captivating and his enthusiasm for the past was irresistible. I found myself wanting to know much more. A few years later, in October and November 1968, I attended his series of lectures, 'The Origins of the First World War' (a series close to his *War By Time-Table*), at University College, London, and again found him to be a supreme master in stimulating interest in history. At that time I was a postgraduate student. When I worked on the Lloyd George Papers at the Beaverbrook Library I was very impressed by the real interest he took in the research carried out there, both in the work of the newest of research students as well as that of the famous.

I have prepared this bibliography with historians primarily in mind. I hope it will be useful for anyone interested in A.J.P. Taylor himself, his writings, or in the topics about which he has written. I hope it meets at least one criteria of a good bibliography – that is, to use F. Bowers often quoted words, 'A good bibliography can be read as well as consulted.'

In the bibliography I have tried to find the right mixture of consistency and common sense. In dividing A.J.P. Taylor's writings into seven sections there have been inevitably some arbitrary decisions. However I believe these seven groupings are the most sensible ones for his material if the listing is to be done other than on a straightforward chronological basis. I hope the divisions are sufficiently clear-cut to make it relatively easy for the reader to find some particular work by A.J.P. Taylor. I have reproduced the headings of articles exactly as they originally appeared, even though the varying use of capitals in the original has made some entries appear inconsistent. I have not listed Book Club editions. From *The Origins Of The Second World War* most of A.J.P. Taylor's books have been issued by book clubs; and earlier, *From Napoleon To Stalin* was published, curiously enough, by the Right Book Club.

When he reviewed a new edition of J.L. Hammond's *Gladstone and the Irish Nation* in 1964 A.J.P. Taylor commented on the Hammond Papers in the Bodleian: 'Fortunately times have changed. Historians no longer write to each other. They do not take themselves seriously enough. At any rate, there will be no Taylor archive.' A.J.P. Taylor has kept very little indeed over the years, especially before he had the services of a secretary. Anyone intending to write a biography of him will need to rely on his published writings and any letters which individuals or bodies such as the BBC or his publishers have kept. Such material of his as there is will soon be available at the University of Texas in Austin.

In preparing this bibliography I have been greatly helped by A.J.P. Taylor. His aid has been invaluable. As already mentioned, except for his books (Section A and some of B), A.J.P. Taylor has not kept copies of his writings. The only exception to this is a book of clippings covering some of his pieces from the mid 1930s until just after the end of the Second World War. Unfortunately, many of these do not give the place or date of publication. I have been able to locate all but two of these (G58 and G259). Otherwise, I have been dependent on A.J.P. Taylor's suggestions for where to look and my own hunts through indexed and unindexed journals and newspapers. As A.J.P. Taylor has kept records of payments received for his articles I feel fairly confident that I have tracked down nearly all those pieces for which he was paid and which appeared in print. One will not have a full list of his contributions to *The Times Literary Supplement* until its records for the period when reviews were anonymous are made available; but the majority are listed here, and each of these has been fully confirmed. The other area of doubt is European newspapers. Some are listed; but there are almost certainly other pieces by him elsewhere. It could be a life time's work to hunt systematically through all possible European journals and newspapers.

Della Hilton's help has been particularly valuable. She has been a source of considerable encouragement. I am equally grateful to Jean Raymond. I am also grateful to Katharine Wheeler, Dr. Patricia Jalland, Hermione Hockliffe, Julia Eccleshare, Roberta Routledge, Professor Alfred Gollin, Professor Roger Louis, Arthur Crook, Roger Machell, Alistair MacDonald, Dr. Ian Keil, Michael Shuker and Nicholas Roe-Ely. Professors Dennis Swann and David Llewellyn have been generous to me with Departmental funds whilst I hunted down material for this book. Joyce Tuson has been remarkably patient in typing it. John Spiers and Gillian Orton of the Harvester Press have been equally patient.

I was delighted with the BBC Written Archives Centre at Reading, and I am very grateful to Jacqueline Kavanagh and her staff for their help. I am equally grateful to the staff of the British Library's newspaper collection at Colindale. My thanks also go to the staff of the libraries of Loughborough University, especially Eric Davies, Leicester University, Nottingham University, Magdalen College, Oxford, as well as the Bodleian and the British Library. I also wish to thank all those who have permitted me to cite material for which they hold copyright. In particular I am indebted to A.J.P. Taylor and the BBC.

INTRODUCTION

A.J.P. Taylor's main claim to fame is as a historian. Many would consider him the greatest living British writer of history. Few would doubt that he is the best known historian in Britain – and perhaps in the English speaking world. He writes with brevity, pungency, humanity and wit. Scholars who are shocked by the firmness of his judgments, judgments seldom surrounded by qualifications, still read him and praise his style.

A.J.P. Taylor has often commented that a historian has only carried out half his task when he has done his research and come to his conclusions. The other half is to present it in a readable style. From early on in his career Taylor has been very conscious of style and has been concerned to present his history in a lucid and attractive way. Thus, in 1936, he wrote:

> Macaulay claimed that his History has ousted the latest novel from the ladies' dressing table; no living historian, except Macaulay's nephew, Professor Trevelyan, can boast as much. The most important works of history often seem to the general reader rather dull and technical, while the popular successes usually merit the censure of the historian. It is no easy task to be both interesting and accurate. (G30)

To a great extent A.J.P. Taylor has succeeded in writing history which has a very wide appeal and yet is essential reading for the scholar. For the non-academic reader he brings history to life, painting vivid miniature portraits of the people of the past and making old controversies intelligible and interesting. For the academic he offers challenging interpretations, based on very extensive reading and a rare intuition. There is a very reasonable chance that his history will be read as long as that of Macaulay and other great British historians. It has the literary flair to sustain it.

In Britain his second claim to fame is as a radio and television personality. In the 1950s he was rarely long off the television screen, appearing both as an academic and as a 'controversialist'. In this period he was very much a household name. He appeared, week after week, with Michael Foot, Lord Boothby and W.J. Brown, discussing current affairs, first on BBC's 'In The News' programme and then on Independent Television's 'Free Speech'. He was the first person to deliver historical lectures, and he gave them as in a university lecture theatre, without visual aids. At the age of 70 and over, his series of lectures on BBC Television in 1976, 1977 and 1978, received on the whole warm acclaim from the television critics, who commented with admiration on his ability to give the lectures without notes, without visual effects and to end them exactly on time.

The third area where he has made his mark is journalism. This has always attracted him. In the 1930s he considered making a career in it. In 1945 he was keen to be *The Manchester Guardian's* special correspondent in Eastern Europe. In the later stages of the Second World War he wrote numerous leaders for *The Manchester Guardian.* Later he wrote regularly for the popular press, *The Sunday Pictorial*, then *The Daily Herald* and later *The Sunday Express*. This has shocked some academics. In addition he has reviewed for more highbrow newspapers, *The Manchester Guardian* and *The Observer*.

Fourthly, he has made some impact on politics. He is most famous as a leading figure in the Campaign for Nuclear Disarmament (CND). In the late 1950s, he toured Britain, addressing mass meetings, calling on the Government unilaterally to abandon nuclear weapons. In the 1930s he had also been very active, condemning appeasement and supporting the Labour Party. After the end of the Second World War he spoke out against the Cold War. In December 1946 an MP complained in Parliament of one of his broadcasts on foreign policy – and the talk was condemned by the Leader of the House of Commons. Although he has made his mark in politics at times, his political activities have been subsidiary to his scholarly work.

In all these areas A.J.P. Taylor's output has been astonishing, as this bibliography bears witness. Few historians produce more books than he has – or books of better quality. His include an international best-seller, *The Origins of the Second World War*, and two standard scholarly works, a volume in the Oxford History of Modern Europe and a volume in the Oxford History of England. His output of articles in the press, both historical and on current affairs, is immense. Most remarkable of all is his massive output of book reviews, over one and a half thousand, many of which are as weighty and stimulating as his essays.

Of course, A.J.P. Taylor the historian is not an isolated being from A.J.P. Taylor the caustic commentator on current affairs. Common assumptions pervade his history, journalism and utterances on radio and television. In this introduction I have provided an outline of his career, phase by phase, which I hope will illustrate how his basic attitudes have developed and have been expressed over the years.

* * *

Alan John Percivale Taylor was born on 25 March 1906 at Birkdale, Southport, in Lancashire. His father, Percy Lees Taylor, was a cotton cloth merchant in the firm James Taylor and Sons, founded by his father in the 1870s. The business was mainly concerned with exporting cotton lengths to India. Percy Taylor had joined the firm in 1890, and as eldest brother, was the senior partner in it before the First World War. Apart from one six month visit to the firm's Calcutta office he remained based at its headquarters in Manchester.

Percy Taylor was of nonconformist background. Before the First World War, he was a Lloyd George Radical. At the time of A.J.P. Taylor's birth the British cotton trade was enjoying what was to be a final burst of prosperity, nonconformity was at the zenith of its political power (after 1660 that is), and the Liberals had just won a landslide victory in the 1906 General Election. For one born at that time in that background Wordsworth's lines on the early days of the French Revolution are almost apposite: 'Bliss was in that dawn to be alive, But to be young was very Heaven! . . .' (*The Prelude*, Book XI). However such a background still provided a strong feeling of being an outsider in British society. It gave A.J.P. Taylor a strong sense of being different – of the industrial North of England not of the genteel South, of Dissent not of Established religion, of self-help not of everything being handed to him on a silver platter. Such a background encouraged sturdy independence, not a sense of deference to inherited position. From his background A.J.P. Taylor drew the moral, 'I am no better than anyone else, but no one is better than me.' (D41)

As a child he appears to have been happier with books than with children of his own age. 'I was always a 'loner', a solitary child', he has written, 'out of step in all sorts of ways, rarely influenced by others and learning by the painful process of trial and error'. (D41) Though he was not learning Greek at the age of three, as John Stuart Mill did, he was reading by then. At school he outpaced the other children, and did not form close friendships with any of them. He has recalled, 'I once asked another little boy to tea. He knocked over my toy soldiers, so I punched him on the nose and made it bleed. He never came back after that.'[1]

The person to whom he was closest and by whom he was most influenced was his father. He clearly loved and admired him deeply. A.J.P. Taylor shared many of his father's views – and strove hard to be worthy of him. When reviewing Kingsley Martin's *Father Figures* he quoted with approval Martin's words: 'His causes became my causes, his revolt mine'. A.J.P. Taylor then observed, 'I had much the same relationship with my father and I have derived nothing but strength from his example. Father-son hostility is a great waste of time . . . it prevents a dissenter from getting on with the real job which is to kick against the world.'[2] (G1095)

He received his secondary education away from home. He attended The Downs School, Colwall near Malvern, a Quaker preparatory boarding school, from 1917–19. There he gained a scholarship to Bootham, the Quaker public school at York, and was there 1919–24. He emerged from this education without a religious faith. He has written, 'The loss of faith is much like having a tooth out. The process is painful, but once it is over you hardly notice the difference'. (G556) However the Quaker upbringing has left its mark on him, and this is suggested by his various comments on

Christian churches. He often judges them and finds them wanting – yet on criteria stemming from his Quaker upbringing. As a child one of his favourite books was John Bunyan's *The Pilgrim's Progress*. This, too, has left its mark. He has a tendency to personify people or groups in a similar way. However with his loss of faith his sympathies went to Tom Paine and to the worship of Reason. For him modern times began with the French Revolution. Throughout his career, time after time, A.J.P. Taylor has quoted with approval Fox's comment of July 1789, 'How much the greatest event it is that ever happened in the World! and how much the best!'

However his schooling did strengthen his attachment to the causes of Dissent. Two of his early heroes were Richard Cobden and John Bright; indeed, men whom he has admired throughout his life. Bright, he admires in particular, for his splendid rhetoric against the Crimean War. This gave him his subject for his lecture at the John Rylands Library, Manchester. (C3) John Bright had attended Bootham's forerunner Walmgate in 1823–5, nearly a hundred years before A.J.P. Taylor. When Taylor was there, as he recalled in his lecture, 'there was an annual prize for a Bright oration, and I have heard his great speeches against the Crimean War recited a score of times in the school library which bears his name'. Cobden he particularly admires as the man who 'argued the Corn Laws out of existence'. (G789) Overall his sympathies for Dissenters, his identification with them, indeed the fact that he himself is in this tradition, gave him a subject close to his heart for his Ford Lectures. He has described the book of these lectures, *The Trouble Makers: Dissent Over Foreign Policy 1792–1939*, repeatedly as the one that has pleased him most.

His time at Bootham also encouraged his interest in history in other ways. In 1962 he wrote '... I can hardly believe that the past would have gripped me if I had not spent five years at school in York ... I spent much of my five years examining the parish churches; speculating on life in York from the Romans until the present day; and recording the results in notebooks, which I destroyed only last year.' (G930) Years earlier he had commented, with some feeling about Southport, 'I was born and brought up in one of the strangest and I'll say most hideous places ever created by men; and the stranger because it hadn't been created by man's poverty but by man's wealth . . . Even the churches were brand-new; and you had a feeling that the religion that was preached in them was also synthetic, made up of vague recollections from what had been taught in more traditional times.'[3] The passion for ecclesiastical architecture, especially Anglo-Saxon, which he acquired in York, has remained with him all his life.

The Quaker background instilled in him an attitude of high moral seriousness. At Bootham the boys were repeatedly exhorted to be concerned about social problems by Seebohm Rowntree and his associates. (G914) A.J.P. Taylor has always been aware of the dangers of a surfeit of moral earnestness. 'Quakerism' he has observed, 'has always been in danger of smugness, and is redeemed from it only by obstinate radicalism' (G597); a point he has made on several occasions.

Similarly in his historical writings there has been a strong moral strain. In some of his earlier reviews this is particularly marked. In dealing with Sir Francis Dashwood he gave the verdict that Dashwood's life was 'sheer futility from beginning to end'–and went on to moralise, 'rich young men will always be silly, and rich men who are idle all their lives will remain silly all their lives'. (G108) In reviewing in 1937 the life of Dreyfus by his son, his comments must have appeared as true milk of the gospel to many nonconformist readers of *The Manchester Guardian*:

> Injustice occurs in free states as in despotic states; and the attempt to right the wrong is as unpopular and dangerous in the one as in the other – as the case of Zola shows. The difference between free and unfree countries is that in the free country there are always men who will champion the unpopular cause at whatever the cost. It is this stage army of the good, with its slightly ridiculous reappearances which alone keeps our liberties alive. The Dreyfus case, at its outset, was a disgrace for France; but because of the struggles of a small minority it ended in bringing France more glory than all the campaigns of Napoleon'. (G41)

However he became aware that moral earnestness counts for little in the world of power politics. Thus, during the

Second World War, he observed of Greece's policy of neutrality that it was wrong, and argued, 'The object of policy is not to prove one's moral worth, but to succeed.' (G158) Similarly he had no compunctions in urging alliance with Soviet Russia to save Europe from Germany. In his history there often appears a battle between his two *persona*, the hard-headed realist and the nonconformist moralist.

* * *

In 1924 A.J.P. Taylor went up to Oxford to read history. He was an exhibitioner at Oriel College and his studies were within the School of Modern History. He read voraciously – but he did not gain much from the lectures. Indeed he has written, 'I did not go to any lectures except those of Sir Charles Oman and that only because Sir Charles, being very old, was a period piece.' (D41) The syllabus covered 55–1914 in English history and 1798–1878 in European history. At that time English history at Oxford was dominated by the medievalists. A.J.P. Taylor studied the reign of Richard II as his Special Subject, and received little tuition beyond 1688. In 1927 he graduated with First Class Honours.

He went to Oxford feeling very conscious of being an outsider. When he went there he was, like his father, a socialist; he has commented, he was 'more or less born into socialism'. (G641) After the First World War Percy Taylor had moved to the Left in politics and joined the Labour Party in 1919. Soon afterwards, in 1920, for health reasons he sold his interests in the family business. Percy Taylor was active in Preston Labour politics in the 1920s and 1930s; he was a member of the Trades and Labour Council, as a delegate of the General and Municipal Workers' Union, Gas Workers' branch (the nearest branch to his home); from 1925–31 and 1932 until his death in 1940 he was a Labour Councillor.[4] At home A.J.P. Taylor came into contact with many of his father's socialist friends. These included William Paul, author of the Marxist book *The State* and editor of *The Sunday Worker*.[5]

At Oxford A.J.P. Taylor immediately joined the Labour Club. He had joined the Independent Labour Party in 1921, when he was fifteen. However, at Oxford he went further than his father, and in 1925 joined the Communist Party as well. He saw this as a natural development; for, as he later wrote, 'I called myself a Marxist from the time I became a Socialist.' (D41) At that time the university's Communist Party was a small select group. He was, as he has often commented, Tom Driberg's rank and file. They had very little contact with the Party outside. He has written, 'We got our instructions from a Cowley worker, though I never carried them out.' (F445) When the General Strike took place in May 1926 A.J.P. Taylor was one of the relatively few Oxford undergraduates who took an active part on Labour's side in it. Hugh Gaitskell was another. A.J.P. Taylor went back to Preston, where his father was the finance member of the strike committee. There he gave his services as a driver. His experiences in the General Strike disillusioned him with the Communist Party. 'My experiences in the General Strike', he wrote in a 50th anniversary article, 'cured me of communism . . . I decided that the Communist Party was not for me and quietly lapsed, thus escaping the soul torments that troubled so many intellectuals during the 1930s.' (E94) In truth he has been too much of an individualist and sceptic to follow a strict party line. He has remarked, 'Like Johnson's friend Edwards, I, too, have tried to be a Marxist but common sense kept breaking in.' (D41)

After leaving Oxford he spent six months from October 1927 in London as a solicitor's articled clerk, before returning to history. He worked for one of his uncles, his mother's brother Harry. During this period he sustained his voracious appetite for books. A.J.P. Taylor has kept a list of books he has read month by month. In 1927 he read at least 303 books. The 154 in the second half of the year included books by Bucharin, Harold Nicolson, Upton Sinclair, G.O. Trevelyan, Anatole France, George Moore, Aldous Huxley, Somerset Maugham, Charles Dickens and six by Thomas Hardy. His first book review was published in *The Saturday Review* in June 1928. (G1) He met the editor, Gerald Barry, through an uncle and was invited to write a review. He offered to write one of John Forster's *Life of Dickens* which had just been reissued, and the offer was accepted. A.J.P. Taylor did not follow up this opening. His efforts were now directed to research in the Staatsarchiv, Vienna.

* * *

A.J.P. Taylor went to Vienna in 1928 to study under Alfred Pribram. He intended to study the impact on British radicalism of the 1848 revolutions in the Habsburg Monarchy. However this proved to be an unrealistic research project, and instead Pribram set him off on Anglo-Austrian relations 1848–60. Once working in the archives A.J.P. Taylor soon devised his own research area, a study of European diplomacy concerning Northern Italy in 1848. He was awarded a Rockefeller Research Fellowship for 1929–30.

Interest in diplomatic history was at its height in the inter – war period. After the Paris Peace Conference of 1919 there was a vigorous debate as to who was 'guilty' for the outbreak of the First World War. Later, with the arrival of Hitler, the boundaries of European states came under increasing scrutiny and European diplomatic affairs came to the forefront of current politics. As A.J.P. Taylor has written of the period, 'Men wanted to understand the contemporary world; and historians answered them that they could do so if all diplomatic secrets were 'revealed'.' (D18) In May 1939 he championed diplomatic history, observing that 'diplomatic history deals with the greatest of themes – with the relations of States, with peace and war, with the existence and destruction of communities and civilisations'. (G99)

The specific period of his research was one with obvious attractions for him. 1848 had a special appeal for him as a radical and socialist. He has written of his undergraduate studies, 'I cultivated the revolutions of 1848 after reading Marx's *Eighteenth Brumaire of Louis Napoleon*, the book of his – apart of course from the Communist Manifesto – that I most admired.' (D41)

A.F. Pribram did not have a great impact on him. A.J.P. Taylor made his own way in the archives – and mostly saw Pribram only socially, at gatherings at Pribram's house. However, Pribram did recommend Taylor to Professor Ernest Jacob, head of the history department at Manchester University, for a post teaching modern European history.

So in 1930 A.J.P. Taylor returned to Lancashire, and began his university teaching career, lecturing on European history from 1494 to 1914. When he started he asked who had lectured over this long time span before him. He received the answer, 'Oh Tout. He said that modern history was not a serious subject and anyone could lecture on it.' (F441)

The following year Lewis Namier took the chair of Modern History in the Department. Namier did influence A.J.P. Taylor's career in several ways – but he did not influence his approach to history to the extent which commentators on A.J.P. Taylor and his writings have suggested. The arrival of Namier provided A.J.P. Taylor with a stimulating colleague, who could talk about East European history authoritatively – and this, no doubt, must have encouraged Taylor in developing his interests in that direction. He also gained one or two tips about style from Namier, notably that articles should have a striking beginning to catch the reader's attention. In preparing this bibliography I read many anonymous reviews in *The Times Literary Supplement* to try and detect those by A.J.P. Taylor. This piece at the start of an 1848 centenary review seemed a very likely possibility for inclusion:

> The men of 1848, victorious in Paris, Vienna, and Berlin stood amazed at their own success and moderation. A revolution had swept over Europe, wider than any before it, but eminently humane in its principles and practice. It had its dead but no victims; it made refugees but no political prisoners. Louis-Philippe crossed the Channel – not the first French ruler nor the last to take to that route. The other sovereigns remained, shaken but not overthrown.

In fact it is by Lewis Namier.[6]

Lewis Namier's reluctance to undertake certain tasks also influenced A.J.P. Taylor's career. Namier reviewed books for *The Manchester Guardian*, but he was not enthusiastic about it nor very quick at sending in his reviews. Namier was particularly slow to review a life of Robespierre. A.J.P. Taylor taught at Manchester a course on French History 1789–1914 and Namier suggested that he should do the review. A.J.P. Taylor wrote it (G2) and asked the newspaper's literary editor for more. As he possessed the rare combination of abilities of writing well and quickly, he increasingly received more and more to review. Later, at A.P. Wadsworth's invitation, he wrote leader-page articles on historic parallels with current events, and on anniversaries of famous people or events. When Harold Macmillan wanted a brief account of the Habsburg Monarchy he asked Namier; and on his refusal, A.J.P. Taylor took on the task.

A.J.P. Taylor's first book, *The Italian Problem in European Diplomacy*, published in 1934, stemmed from his research in Vienna and subsequent work in archives in London and Paris. This was the first of a line of diplomatic and European studies of his which were published over the next twenty seven years. Much of the diplomatic history of the inter-war period fell into one of two types. One was polemical or near polemical – and involved the investigation, back into the past, of 'guilt' for the First World War. The other was very detailed accounts of foreign policy, document by document; works of dull prècis, often without a spark of humanity. A.J.P. Taylor's first book was a detailed study, including heavy use of footnotes. But in it he did try to point to the broad outline of the forest, and not just itemise the individual trees. At the start of the introduction he boldly proclaimed:

> At first sight the European diplomatic system appears to proceed in the most haphazard way . . . But, on a closer view, there emerge more and more clearly certain principles, until the petty struggles of day to day diplomacy take on the appearance of a battle of Platonic Ideas . . . the course of national policy is based on a series of assumptions, with which statesmen have lived since their earliest years and which they regard as so axiomatic as hardly to be worth stating. It is the duty of the historian to clarify these assumptions and to trace their influence upon the course of every-day policy. (A1, p 1)

The book, on the whole, was not polemical. He dealt with the Habsburg Monarchy in a milder manner than he was to do later. In it Metternich was depicted as an able conservative, who was restricted by the system from applying any remedies. However his sympathies clearly were more with Palmerston. He was portrayed as a skilful diplomat who was a realist, more interested in peace than imposing Whig ideals on others. 'Palmerston was the hero of England because he deserved to be.' (p 31)

Despite the often lengthy footnotes, it was not dull. Already Taylor's wit and sparkling style were in evidence. In it characters were drawn vividly. He often used striking metaphors to make his points with brevity. Thus in describing Minto's efforts to offer conciliation in Italy before the 1848 revolutions, he wrote: 'Minto was a consulting physician and by this time Italy needed a surgeon.' (p 68) Also, however, he displayed his penchant for controversial comparisons, which would enrage reviewers; for instance, writing about Napoleon, he stated that in 1815 the 'nations of Europe had just succeeded . . . in freeing themselves from the worst (because the most extensive) tyranny Europe had suffered since the time of Attila'. (p 9)

His next two major publications were in a series edited by Lewis Namier. The first was a translation of the great Austrian historian Heinrich Friedjung's book *The Struggle for Supremacy in Germany 1859–1866*, which he did in collaboration with his friend William McElwee. (B1) In this he was dealing with a major turning point in German history. As he noted in his introduction to it, there was no longer a chance of Germany being united under Austria: 'the leadership of Germany passed irrevocably to Prussia . . . ' A.J.P. Taylor had gone to Vienna with great faith in Austrian radicalism, both past and present. He concluded his introduction to Friedjung's book with speculation about the possibility of the existing Austria becoming part of a new Danubian grouping, providing the Austrians would recognise the Slavs as equals.

His second publication at this time was his *Germany's Bid For Colonies 1884–1885. A Move in Bismarck's European Policy*. This was a brief monograph, written to the theme of its subtitle. In it he had a clear thesis and he pushed it hard, understating other factors which influenced Bismarck in acquiring these colonies. A.J.P. Taylor made his case lucidly and wrote well.

When he had gone to Vienna, Pribram had been working on the origins of the First World War. This area had not attracted A.J.P. Taylor then, as his undergraduate studies of European history had ended with the Congress of Berlin. At Manchester A.J.P. Taylor did move on to studying and teaching European diplomatic history before the First World War. Namier wanted a Special Subject taught in this area and being too busy to do it himself, he passed it on to A.J.P. Taylor. This involved him in studying the published German, French and British foreign policy documents of the period. Hitherto he had accepted the view that Germany had been blameless of 'war guilt', indeed had been the innocent party. He now changed his views. It was his teaching of the Special Subject 'England and the Making of the Ententes 1898–1907' and his growing interest in the diplomacy preceding the First World War that attracted the attention of Llewellyn Woodward at Oxford. Woodward helped him gain a fellowship at Magdalen College. So he moved from Manchester back to Oxford in the autumn of 1938, a year before war broke out in Europe.

During his time at Manchester A.J.P. Taylor maintained his interest in politics. Indeed, apart from his time as a speaker for the Campaign for Nuclear Disarmament (CND), the period 1933–6 was the most politically active time of his life. He has never been interested in standing for Parliament. Once he was approached to be a candidate. He had supported the Labour candidate for Macclesfield, a Conservative seat, in the 1935 general election. When that candidate withdrew after the election, A.J.P. Taylor was approached to be the Labour candidate, but declined.

He also took an active interest in current international affairs. In December 1935 he took a prominent role in Manchester in condemning the Hoare-Laval plan, which would have carved up Abyssinia. The revelation of the details of the plan unleashed a moral outcry in Britain; 'the greatest explosion over foreign affairs for many years, perhaps the greatest since the campaign against the 'Bulgarian horrors' in 1876', he wrote later. (A14, p 385) On 17 December he was the speaker at a meeting at Manchester University, chaired by Professor J.L. Stocks and convened by the University League of Nations Society, the Liberal Association, the Socialist Society, the Anti-War Group and the Student Christian Movement. He made the traditional radical plea that it was 'a matter of great moment that the reputation of this country as a country prepared to see just treatment for small nations should be maintained'. He then went on to ascribe the policy to British imperialism: 'It is no accident that the one bit of Italian territory to be surrendered to Abyssinia is Assab; because Assab, a fortified port, would be a great menace to Aden . . . This Government has pursued a policy of buying Italy off in order to pursue its own imperialist aims.' The meeting condemned the plan by 234 votes to 2.[7]

From the time of the German reoccupation of the Rhineland in 1936 A.J.P. Taylor vigorously opposed appeasement. He has written, 'I was one of the few people outside London who addressed meetings against appeasement at the time of Munich, and very rough they were.' (D41)

* * *

In the 1940s A.J.P. Taylor came to the fore as a commentator on current affairs. During the Second World War and its aftermath he became a regular broadcaster on the BBC's radio networks. In the later stages of the war he frequently wrote leaders for *The Manchester Guardian.* In the Second World War his view on Germany being a permanent threat to the rest of Europe hardened – and he became a vigorous advocate of Anglo-Soviet accord.

During the Second World War he remained in Oxford. He was a member of the Home Guard – and spent many nights guarding the Oxford Gas Works against German paratroopers. He spent much time travelling around the Oxford area giving monthly lectures on the development of the war. His views were sufficiently controversial for Quintin Hogg, then MP for Oxford, to complain in the House of Commons in October 1940 of 'a public speech in Oxford by Mr. A.J.P. Taylor, a member of the local Information Committee appointed by the Ministry of Information, to the effect that a withdrawal from Egypt would not be a major disaster'.[8] A.J.P. Taylor went on to give his views on the war on the radio. In the spring and early summer of 1942 he appeared several times on the programme 'The World at War – Your Questions Answered' on the Forces network (a national network, the precursor of the BBC Light Programme and now Radio 2).

Before the outbreak of war he had nearly completed *The Habsburg Monarchy*. The book brought out, amongst other things, the tensions between the 'historic' nationalities, the Germans, Magyars, Poles and Italians, and the 'submerged' nationalities, the Czechs, Serbs, Romanians and Little Russians. A.J.P. Taylor observed, 'The German penetration into eastern Europe and the conflict of nationalities which this created is one of the most fundamental processes of modern European history, and cannot be too often studied.' (G114) The war focussed his attention on the 'German problem'. For him this involved more than just a study of Nazi Germany or inter-war Germany. Thus in reviewing G.P. Gooch's *Studies in Diplomacy and Statecraft*, A.J.P. Taylor commented that Gooch's views on the diplomacy before the First World War influenced informed opinion more than any other writer. 'Dr. Gooch was a pupil of Acton and a Liberal member of the 1906 Parliament; in both capacities he was convinced of the civilised character of Germany and this influenced all his scholarship. Germany appeared to him a power like any other, with some faults, but more grievances . . . ' However, now this view appeared to be bankrupt. A.J.P. Taylor concluded, 'The new generation of historians has now the obligation to make a new analysis of the underlying forces in Europe which will be closer to reality and so prepare a British policy which will suffer from fewer illusions and make fewer mistakes.' (G168)

A.J.P. Taylor's analysis of German history, which argued that Hitler and the Nazis were not a dramatic break with past German history, proved too dismal for the British authorities. The Political Warfare Executive asked him to provide a chapter on the Weimar Republic for a handbook for British officers who would administer Germany after the war – but they found it too anti-German and did not use it. Similarly he was soon replaced by E.J. Passant in giving outline lectures on German history to the officers.[9] A.J.P. Taylor turned his views into a book, *The Course of German History*, which he completed in September 1944. He informed a BBC producer, with relish, that the book 'is as hot as can be – a good thing that it doesn't have to pass your censorship'.[10]

His interpretation of German history emphasised Germany's continual drive to dominate central and eastern Europe – and her determination to crush the Slav peoples. He argued that nearly all Germans – Junkers, Liberal industrialists, and socialists – had been committed to a Greater Germany. Germany's expansionist policies and lack of freedom internally were related, in his view, so the guilty were not just the militarists and Nazis: '. . . the rest of the world had to pay the penalty for the political incompetence and timidity of the German middle class. The failure of the 'good Germans', not the ranting of the 'bad' ones, was the real crime of Germany against European civilisation.' (A4, p 166) For Taylor the true test for Germans was to oppose expansionary foreign policies. Thus in a letter of November 1944 he observed, '. . . no one would deny that many, perhaps most, Germans dislike the ruthlessness and barbarity of Nazi rule when applied to themselves; but these same lovers of liberty support a line of action in foreign affairs which can only be attained by Nazi methods'.[11] In an earlier letter he had asked '. . . how many German refugees, living securely in this country, are prepared to recognise the full national independence of the east European peoples, and to renounce for ever all prospects of a European system under German leadership?'[12]

Hitler was not an aberration. 'In reality', he wrote in a review, 'Hitler did not argue with the German people, but expressed, in somewhat violent form, their outlook and wishes.' (G219) Therefore A.J.P. Taylor gave warnings of the dangers of allowing Germany a third bid for European supremacy. In 1947 he was still urging '. . . whoever offers the German people unity will command their support . . . the problem of the Great Powers is whether they shall renew the French policy which gave Europe security for centuries or whether they shall be humbugged into believing that Hitlerism was not a democratic movement, and stand approvingly by while the German people renew the unity which was achieved in 1938'.[13]

The policy he advocated was Anglo-Soviet accord. Before the war he had deplored suggestions that Czechoslovakia and Russia should be left to fend for themselves against

Germany (for example G48). During the war he pronounced that Anglo-Russian estrangement was 'the most profound cause of the present war' (for example G188). After Hitler invaded Russia, A.J.P. Taylor strove hard to put Russia's point of view. In 1941 and 1942 he argued that there must be no return to 'Great Poland', in which Polish landlords ruled over Lithuanians, Little Russians and White Russians. (G144) He stated that 'the heart of the Russo-Polish conflict' was 'the determination of Russian Governments, past and present, to free Russian peoples from their Polish lords'. (G163) He also insisted that 'Russian policy has a single object, security, and she regards the frontiers of 1941 as essential to this object'. He went further, and suggested that Europe should be carved up, in effect, into two spheres: 'The peoples of Europe can enjoy freedom only under the joint protection of England and Russia; and just as we postulate a group of friendly states in western Europe with similar social and political systems to our own, so does Russia in eastern Europe.'[14] (G169) These views, expressed in a *Time and Tide* book review, caused a furore – and soon ended his connection with that journal. In writing *The Course of German History* he stressed the theme that Europe must either divide Germany or be ruled by Germany. The first edition ended on a triumphant climax on 22 June 1941, 'the day of Germany's doom'. 'For on that day, by the greatest act of statesmanship of the century – say rather, of modern times – Winston Churchill proclaimed the alliance of England and Russia. There were no folded hands in England for the renewed *Drang nach Osten*.' (A4, p 260)

In 1942 A.J.P. Taylor was advocating drastic measures to remake Europe after the war. He had an exaggerated sense of the thoroughness of German economic planning in Europe. He argued repeatedly that summer: 'Unfortunately the Nazis have by now carried through their schemes of economic conquest so thoroughly that if private capitalism survives in Europe, German hegemony will survive with it; public ownership of industry is the only way of avoiding the ownership of Europe by the Germans and their agents.' (F1) He also felt that the nationalities problems would have to be solved. 'The existence and compelling reality of national communities is the fundamental, inescapable fact of European politics, both past and present.' (G149) In the case of Poland, Russia would keep the 1941 frontiers. In the case of Czechoslovakia, German minorities would have to move. Thus in a review in May he wrote: 'To remake Czechoslovakia will demand as much ruthlessness, foresight and energy as the Germans brought to its destruction; it will involve as much suffering, though not by the same people. But unless Czechoslovakia is remade with complete political and economic independence Germany will have won the war . . . ' (G155)

Czechoslovakia was one of A.J.P. Taylor's central European causes in the war.[15] He found Czechoslovakia to be the symbol of what he most admired in the contemporary world. It combined the best of Western democracy and of the Slavic world, unlike Germany which combined the worst. Thus, in a lecture at the Czechoslovak Institute in London, chaired by Jan Masaryk, he declared of the country in the inter-war period.

> In Czechoslovakia alone there really existed the conceptions of individual liberty, of the security of the individual, of the process of law which we identify with Western, and particularly with British, democracy. The things an Englishman understands by constitutional rights for the individual, things which are essential for a secure civilised State, these things existed as a full grown reality in Czechoslovakia. At the same time . . . nowhere did the Slav sense of community, which is, after all, the basic underlying reality of the Soviet Union, a community of people living together and enjoying a social freedom on a basis free from a hierarchy of of class, nowhere did this exist so far west as in Czechoslovakia. (C1)

In A.J.P. Taylor's eyes, the Czechs had one further golden attribute: 'There is probably no other people in Europe where national sentiment has passed so successfully from the intellectual minority to the broad masses of the nation.' (G215) For him Czechoslovakia would play a crucial role in the post-war world. He argued that it and Yugoslavia were 'the two key countries . . . the essential links between England and Russia, geographical and still more spiritual links'.[16]

In the case of Yugoslavia the main issue in 1945 was Trieste. The question was whether it should go to Italy or to Yugoslavia or be a Free City. A.J.P. Taylor championed the Yugoslav case. He urged in one article in December 1944 that Trieste could have similar merits to Czechoslovakia: 'Here the Slav world and the world of Western democracy can overlap and combine.' He argued the case for Yugoslavia on grounds of historic and national justice, in the press and in a pamphlet published by the Yugoslav Government.[17] He also argued that giving it to Yugoslavia would improve relations with Russia – 'we can be more confident of the future of the Anglo-Soviet alliance when we have learnt to think of Trieste as Trst'. (F7)

A.J.P. Taylor's advocacy on the radio of the Yugoslav case for Trieste involved him in his first row with the BBC. From October 1944, when he chaired a discussion on the future of Germany, he had made frequent appearances on BBC home and overseas radio programmes, usually as a commentator on foreign affairs. The BBC producers fully recognised that he was likely to be highly controversial. Thus, in March 1945, one producer, Trevor Blewitt, when discussing a proposed short discussion programme which would be between A.J.P. Taylor and Barbara Ward, wrote to him in cautioning terms: 'I do not think we can or need aim at a pyrotechnic display in so short a time as fifteen minutes, or violent controversy; what we should strive at is a sober statement of the facts with contrasting interpretations of what these facts mean and how they are likely to work out; in a word, a balanced commentary from a rather wider viewpoint than could be given by a single speaker.'[18] However, the row over his comments on Trieste in September 1945 seem to have been due more to the fact he had written the pamphlet on it than to what he actually said.

The most significant complaints to the BBC came from the Government. Mr. Grubb of the Ministry of Information asked the controller of discussion programmes on the radio if the scripts of such talks had been cleared with the Foreign Office. The controller commented in his memorandum on this query, 'It appears that some concern has been expressed in some other Government office that a man with known views on the Yugoslav question should be speaking on this subject at a time when it was about to be decided upon.'[19] Victor Cunard of PIB, in consultation with the Foreign Office, formally complained of A.J.P. Taylor talking on the radio about Trieste – on the grounds that he was well known to be committed to the Yugoslav cause. He reported that 'Taylor at a dinner party the night before had expressed himself unwisely as regards to the use he might make of his broadcasting to favour the Yugoslav case' – though he agreed that in the talk A.J.P. Taylor had not gone in for propaganda.[20] The Controller and George Barnes interviewed A.J.P. Taylor and discussed the matter. A.J.P. Taylor assured them that he was primarily an academic – and commented that he 'would have preferred that the Trieste pamphlet which expressed entirely his own views, and was not touched by the Yugoslav Government, should have been published independently, but it was only in this way that he was able to get paper'. He left them satisfied. The Controller noted, 'Barnes and I were impressed by his candour and good sense, and his appreciation of our problems in this field.'[21]

A.J.P. Taylor continued to press for Anglo-Soviet understanding during the Cold War. He has always deplored the Cold War, often commenting, as in a review in 1966, 'The Cold War has been the greatest obstacle to rational thinking in my lifetime.' (G1113) His constant theme at the end of the war was that the old assumptions on which British foreign policy had been based had been swept away by the upheavals brought about by the Second World War. He argued that the Balance of Power on the continent of Europe had gone, leaving only Russia as a Great Power, and that Britain's naval supremacy was a thing of the past.[22] He felt Britain was still a Great Power, but 'we cannot afford to make any more mistakes; the others can . . . ' (F19) He also felt Britain was a major force for peace, commenting on one occasion that 'we are the only Power whose interest in the *status quo* is world wide'.[23] As to the Russians, as he wrote in a letter in February 1946, they also 'want peace and prosperity, not to conquer the world; they are hesitating whether to get it by spheres of influence or by co-operation. Therefore we have to go on trying to co-operate.'[24] During and in the immediate aftermath of the war he continued to look for areas of co-operation between Britain and Russia, and not just on the mainland of Europe. He argued for such agreement in Persia, Turkey and the Straits, and the Middle

East generally. So, for A.J.P. Taylor in this period, Britain's foreign policy should have been based on continuing the Anglo-Soviet alliance. In April 1945 he wrote, 'In the near future, say the next twenty years, the Soviet Union is our natural ally.'[25]

With the deterioration of Anglo-Soviet relations in the post-war period A.J.P. Taylor increasingly found himself out on a limb. His championing of the Anglo-Soviet alliance became unacceptable to *The Manchester Guardian*. He ceased writing leaders for it after one on the Cold War, commissioned by A.P. Wadsworth, was not used. In fact Wadsworth had continued to commission foreign policy pieces from A.J.P. Taylor long after their views had differed. Their relationship remained very good, despite this break over the Cold War. In mid-1946 his series of talks on foreign affairs on the radio were terminated. The producer wrote in his memorandum on why A.J.P. Taylor was not going to be used again for 'World Affairs': 'Not so much because he is a cause of anxiety every time we put him on, but because I think his admirable qualities (courage, intellectual brilliance, if not profundity, ability to avoid the clap trap of the age, whether from Right or Left, vigour) are vitiated by a certain cynicism which is out of place in an objective and ultimately educational series for the ordinary listener!'[26] At the end of 1946 A.J.P. Taylor gave a series of talks on the radio on British Foreign Policy. The second dealt with Britain's relations with America. An MP complained about it in the House of Commons – and Herbert Morrison gave his verdict that 'the broadcast was anti-British, anti-American and not particularly competent. And that is all I can say about it.'[27]

A.J.P. Taylor's advocacy of the Anglo-Soviet alliance long after it had ceased to be a popular cause in Britain made him seem an ideal Englishman to be invited to the Congress of Intellectuals at Wroclaw in August 1948. The Poles held it in Wroclaw to emphasise the Oder-Neisse Line, and expected those at the Congress to praise the Soviet Union and condemn America. However A.J.P. Taylor was not a fellow-traveller. His attitudes in the war had been based on radical precepts, including a fervent belief in nationalism, not on dogmatic Marxism. As he put it, in a letter on a proposed radio talk on Soviet affairs in 1946, his attitude was not 'pro-Bolshevik, except in the sense that I am always pro-Russia, i.e. I have no sympathy with anti-Russian hysteria and think that we should judge Soviet affairs with the same critical, but friendly, detachment with which we judge American affairs'.[28] A.J.P. Taylor has always been an individualist. He has always been a fervent believer in democracy. He expressed in 1941 sentiments that he has often repeated: 'Without democracy Socialism would be worth nothing, but democracy is worth a great deal even when it is not socialist.' (G137) Just before going to Wroclaw he stated on the radio 'I care for liberty above all other causes ... ' (E19) Thus it was not surprising that he upset the conference organiser's plans.

At Wroclaw A.J.P. Taylor courageously argued that the intellectual's paramount duty was to be intellectually honest. 'In demanding freedom of thought', as he wrote in a subsequent letter to *The Times*, 'the intellectual ... is making his greatest contribution to the cause of peace.'[29] In his speech to the Congress he denounced the use of such a Congress for crude propaganda. 'Some people in England, and more in America', he was reported by Kingsley Martin as saying, 'now said that the Soviet Union and Nazi Germany were indistinguishable. As intellectuals ... it was our business to refute such assertions. It was equally the business of the intellectuals at this conference to reject, instead of repeating, wild slogans about American Fascism. He had come to the conference in order to look for ways of peaceful co-operation ... (He) declared that he hated all authoritarian interference, whether from Wall Street or the Kremlin. He ended with a plea for intellectual honesty, tolerance, love and the pursuit of truth.' Kingsley Martin's report ended with the observations, 'These remarks were made with a stern ferocity which no Communist delegate could have bettered ... He looked at the rostrum like a British bull terrier challenged to fight by a Russian wolf.'[30]

By the end of the 1940s, A.J.P. Taylor was disillusioned about Russia's policies. In a review of a book by Basil Davidson in April 1950, he wrote:

Mr. Davidson thinks that the Russians will co-operate with us, if only we will co-operate with them. I don't share his belief in Russian good faith, just as I don't share the Foreign Office belief in American good faith; though I am inclined to think that there are more good intentions mixed with stupidity in American than in Russian policy. But both Russia and America are instruments for power; and it is their nature to pursue more power. American policy is tinged with idealism, Russian is not; this probably does not make much difference. (G374)

But, he never became a Cold War Warrior. He saw America, by far the most powerful country in the world, as the greatest threat to national freedom. (G334)

A.J.P. Taylor now argued for a British foreign policy, independent of the United States, which would encourage other communist states to be independent of Russia and which would help underdeveloped countries. On such issues as Formosa, he urged appeasement. The use of this word was deemed sufficiently provocative in a talk he prepared for the radio series 'As I See It' in July 1950, that the talk was vetoed by the BBC. He wrote his views in a letter to *The Times*:

If there is to be any hope for peace in the world, it depends on Communist Governments becoming independent of Russian control. To refuse Formosa to the Chinese Communists is, instead, to force them into Moscow's arms.

If we are bent on launching a third world war or think . . . that it has already started, then certainly we should line up with America on every issue, regardless of its rights and wrongs. If we intend to live in the world alongside Soviet Russia and other Communist Governments, then we must think in terms of negotiation and not of 'unconditional surrender'. For appeasement is still one of the noblest words in the language, in spite of its abuse twelve years ago; and appeasement should be at all times the object of an enlightened diplomacy.[31]

He urged Western withdrawal from Asia by agreement, rather than being expelled in due course by force. His arguments were based on the old tenets of Radicalism. Thus, as he put it in one article, 'As in our domestic affairs the ultimate solution is to be found in a policy of equality, of fair shares, and not in the maintenance of privileges which have lost all moral justification.' (F43)

* * *

In the 1950s A.J.P. Taylor was a national figure, recognised quite literally by the man in the street. He appeared on television weekly for much of that period, discussing current affairs with Robert Boothby (Lord Boothby), W.J. Brown and Michael Foot. He continued to broadcast frequently on the BBC radio networks. As well as writing articles and reviews for 'high-brow' newspapers and journals he was also a weekly columnist for *The Sunday Pictorial* and then *The Daily Herald*, and thereafter contributed regularly to *The Sunday Express*. Whilst doing all this, he continued to write major works of history and to lecture on history at Oxford.

The BBC television programme 'In The News' really made him a household name. The programme was started after the 1950 General Election. It was a current affairs discussion programme, with a regular team of four speakers. The speakers were intended to be politically balanced. There was a Labour backbencher, Michael Foot, and a Conservative backbencher, Robert Boothby, W.J. Brown, a former Independent MP, and A.J.P. Taylor. The programme was a great success, with huge numbers of people watching it every week. Dingle Foot has written of his brother Michael, 'He was the first political leader who owed his advancement to television.'[32] However its very success soon proved to be its undoing.

The leaders of the political parties did not like mere backbenchers, indeed political mavericks, to have so much attention focussed on them. By early 1951 the Director of Television was under pressure from the political parties to see that 'on occasion representatives of the main core of opinion in the two parties' appeared on the programme. There was even more pressure when, in April 1951, Aneurin Bevan resigned from the Labour Government, and the continued appearance of Michael Foot, a Bevanite, could have been construed as giving support to the Bevanite wing of the Labour Party. By the end of the year the Director was consulting the Conservative Chief Whip, for possible Conservative MPs to take part in the programme. In due course the programme was castrated by having different panels of speakers, and the old team was only allowed to appear once a month.[33]

However, with the coming of commercial television Boothby, Brown, Foot and Taylor were given a weekly appearance again in a similar programme, 'Free Speech'. The success of this team was precisely that they were not solid party men, but lively individualists. Grace Wyndam Goldie has written of them, that they 'seemed, in combination, to provide a remarkable effervescence of wit, common-sense, intellectual honesty and political passion. Week after week matters in the news were discussed by intelligent men who seemed to be thinking independently, not merely mouthing the clichés of routine party politics.'[34] The discussions often got very heated, especially at the time of Suez. Maurice Richardson, *The Observer's* television critic, observed of one programme that the 'team seemed to be not only on the verge of, but actually, losing their tempers with each other over the desirability or otherwise of the House of Lords. Boothby boomed, Foot fumed, Taylor trephined, with apparent real malice ... Anyway it was first-class television.'[35]

A.J.P. Taylor gained a reputation for being a fiery and ferocious speaker in the programmes. Randolph Churchill went as far as to write on one occasion, 'He has only to see a television camera in order to lose resemblance to a human being. He then becomes an angry mountebank and buffoon.'[36] When accused of being cantankerous, Taylor replied, 'Am I cantankerous? I don't think so. Assertive, yes, and ready to hit back if anyone attacks me. But without malice or bad temper.'[37] In one of the 'In The News' programmes, when he took part with 'main core' party politicians (including James Callaghan) and not the regular team, he erupted and refused to take any further part in the discussion of controlled rents as he felt it to be merely an exchange of party dogmas, and not an open-ended discussion. He remained seated and silent until the end of the programme, the television camera now and then showing him sitting aloof from the discussion. He was not invited back until ten months later. (F108)

A.J.P. Taylor's appearances on 'In The News' opened up popular journalism to him. In January 1951 he began a weekly column in *The Sunday Pictorial*. This was first captioned 'A million people see and hear this man on Friday nights'. From 10 January 1953 he wrote a weekly column in

The Daily Herald. In the issue of 1 January his forthcoming column was advertised on the front page. Naturally the blurb included references to him as a television star: 'A.J.P. Taylor, the blunt spoken Oxford don who was sacked from television's 'In The News' is to write a weekly commentary . . . Viewers know that Taylor says what he thinks – and it is always forthright, provocative and original.' In his columns in the popular press he maintained his image of being provocative and unpredictable. *The Daily Herald* frequently headed his columns with captions such as 'The Man of Independent Mind', 'I Say What I Please' and 'Alan Taylor is out of step again'. From 1957 he became a regular contributor to *The Sunday Express.* His pieces for this paper were increasingly populist, championing people's pleasures and traditional ways against bureaucracy, intellectuals and anyone else who took it upon themselves to dictate to 'ordinary people'. Earlier, for example, he had favoured subsidies to the arts. Now, in such articles, he condemned the subsidisation of 'high-brow' culture out of the taxes of the many.

Among Left-wing intellectuals A.J.P. Taylor was out of line in being in favour of commercial television. In view of his experiences with the BBC over various radio programmes and their television programme 'In the News' it is hardly surprising that he held such views. George Barnes once went so far as to remark that without 'In The News' there would never have been commercial television. A.J.P. Taylor condemned the BBC as a monopoly, run by and for the Establishment. On one occasion he wrote of the BBC's Controllers, 'Their task is to stop things going out, or rather to see that everything which goes out is innocuous. Their attention is focussed on possible complaints, not on pleasing the public.' (G544) Later, when he was giving lectures on Independent Television, he wrote, 'If I had ever persuaded the BBC to televise history lectures, I know what would have followed: endless debate about whether I had chosen the right subjects, and insistence that every word should be approved beforehand. Some 'controller' would have claimed to know more about history than I do and would have been for ever correcting my facts when he was not condemning my ideas.' (F249) He also favoured commercial television as he felt it would be much more receptive to popular taste. In one letter to *The New Statesman and Nation*, he accused Labour of still being Puritan, and of being against entertainment. 'In my opinion' he wrote, 'it is possible to be a Socialist and still to believe in freedom. And freedom means letting people have what they want, not what I think is good for them – nor even what you do.'[38]

A.J.P. Taylor was delighted when Independent Television invited him to give a series of lectures in 1957. He was pleased because these were the first straight lectures on British television. He was even more pleased that they were on commercial television, because such lectures would only continue if people wanted them. 'If these lectures had been screened elsewhere', he commented, 'it would have been because some high-up considered they were 'good for the viewer, and he must stick it out even if it is way above his head'.'[39] John Irwin, the producer of the series, went to Oxford, unannounced, and attended one of A.J.P. Taylor's lectures. He reported that his lectures were packed and added, 'I've seen nothing like it. That audience was hypnotised by Taylor's dynamic personality, his passionate sincerity, his wit, his command of words, his brilliant sense of timing, and his complete mastery of the subject – without a single note.'[40]

A.J.P. Taylor was very conscious of the problems of conveying history on television and radio. Before his first television series, on the Russian Revolution (C4), he observed, 'It's not only me on trial but the whole idea of lecturing on TV.' He expressed his optimism about informative programmes having a big audience. 'I do believe', he wrote, 'that the British public has an appetite for things which are intellectually interesting and stimulating to the mind'; and he predicted, 'I expect we shall have a tremendous university of the air in no time.'[41]

Earlier he had been a pioneer in presenting history on the radio. In September 1946 he had written to George Barnes to congratulate him on the start of the BBC's Third Programme. He added, 'I am anxious to escape from the controversies of political commentary into the more serious tasks of history and I think I have some suggestions that might appeal to you.'[42] He marked the outstanding lectures on an Oxford lecture list for 1946, including Asa Briggs on Bright, J. Steven Watson on Disraeli and Robert Ensor on Gladstone. He suggested that the Third Programme should do a series on Prime Ministers.[43] This was taken up, and A.J.P. Taylor acted as general editor for the series. However the critical response to the series was not very good. George Barnes expressed his disappointment in a letter to Taylor in which he aired his doubts about history lectures as such on the radio. Barnes wrote that the talks:

> . . . contributed nothing, in my opinion, to the very difficult question of how to treat history over the radio . . . these talks did not make me alter my opinion that a lecture, however skilfully potted, will never obtain the interest of the critical listener in history. A lecturer in a university or with a WEA class can stimulate the interest of his audience by paradox or any other device, knowing that its members will form their opinions not only from what he says but from reading the books set for the course or the examination. The radio audience is different. It is made up of people with widely differing knowledge who listen for widely differing purposes. A provocative talk about Pitt *may* send the listener to check his impression with Rosebery or Holland Rose but it is more likely, if he is ignorant, to foster a prejudice. History is surely not a matter of snap judgements and if radio listening is to contribute anything to the critical evaluation of historical events there is a lot of hard thinking to be done about the method first of all.

A.J.P. Taylor naturally felt that this was too dismal a view of the possibilities of history on the radio. His reply to the letter is especially interesting in that it makes explicit the assumptions behind his two talks in the series (E12 and E13):

> I had hoped . . . that my talk would succeed in starting people off thinking about the subject, and my aim . . . was to stimulate by new thought not merely by provocation. As you say, a fool can be provocative; and I try not to be a fool. My effort on Salisbury was meant as a serious attempt to understand Victorian Conservatism at its moment of transition; and for that matter Russell was meant to be a study of the transition from Whiggism to Liberalism. I assumed that I must aim at the same level as, say, Huis Clos or Les Noces; and I don't honestly see what other assumption one can make when writing for the Third Programme.[44]

A.J.P. Taylor felt that television was a better medium than radio for presenting history. However his presentation of history on television has not depended on use of old film, old photographs or prints, or visits to historic locations. Although he has dubbed television talks using these 'glorified magic-latern lectures', he has urged producers to think more in terms of personality and less of pictures. Thus, whereas radio can use someone's voice only, television can present 'the whole man'. So television, for him, has the same justification as the university lecture: 'the interpretation, the illumination, need the human being'. (F264)

Over the years A.J.P. Taylor has kept to the simple format of the formal lecture. He has faced the television camera with no visual aids. In his first series the producer put shots of the audience in; but this practice was felt to be a distraction and was dropped. In his television lectures he holds attention by his personality, by his narrative skill. Reviewing his 1978 series 'Revolution' one critic wrote, 'The background is black, the clothes are neutral, the body is still, the visual display consists only of his attention – demanding right eye balanced by his gesticulating left hand, sometimes signalling the shovelling of parenthesis and sometimes pointing the pedagogical finger.'[45] A larger part of the success of his television lectures stems from the obvious pleasure he gains from talking about his subject. Part way through such lectures a glint comes into his eyes and he speaks with real joy and enthusiasm; the people and events really matter to him – and his evident fascination with them brings history alive to the viewer. His ability to convey this enthusiasm is, on the whole, helped by the fact that he gives the talks without notes or autocue. In 1957 his lecture series were live because they had to be. Twenty years later he lectured in the same manner, with the lecture recorded for television in one take.[46]

His first television lecture series was screened early in the evening at 6 p.m., a time when many English families would have been watching television while having a meal. In an interview before giving the lectures A.J.P. Taylor commented, 'I shall try to make these lectures intellectual entertainment. They won't be frivolous, but I do hope they will help to make minds lively.'[47] ATV issued audience viewing figures of 750,000 for the follow up series 'When

Europe Was The Centre of the World', which began a month after those on the Russian Revolution. These were the first of many successful series of television lectures. From 1962 he also gave lectures on BBC television. His approach to them was much the same as the earlier ones. As he wrote, when introducing the first BBC series 'The Twenties', 'These lectures are intended as serious history or as serious as I can make it. They are generally like lectures which I give at Oxford University except that they are shorter and rather faster. I sometimes add a date or a word of explanation.' Overall, he observed, 'History is of interest. At least I find it interesting; and my aim is to make it interesting for others.' (E60)

During the 1950s, he continued to publish major works of history. The most substantial book was *The Struggle For Mastery In Europe 1848–1918* (1954), an authoritative volume, written for the Oxford History of Modern Europe. This was the outcome of his years of research, reviewing and teaching diplomatic history. In it he sketched the long term trends behind the history of Europe of that period, and then expounded in detail the diplomatic history. Writing later he observed of the book that he had difficulty in reconciling '*les forces profondes* with the play of accident that determines the day-to-day course of events . . . when you look at details, individual men affect even the greatest events'. (D41) Bismarck naturally was a major figure in the book. After Bismarck's disappearance from the scene Germany's unrestrained drive for hegemony became the threat to peace; a theme he had earlier developed in *The Course of German History*.

His interest in Bismarck developed in spite of his initial prejudices. In reviewing a book by Michael Foot in 1957 he wrote that Foot had been 'suddenly captived by events and swept into unexpected waters'. A.J.P. Taylor went on, 'Historians often have this experience, and very exciting it is, though frightening if you are not used to it. The facts get up, hit the historian on the head, and make him go where he did not intend to go at all. I remember well my embarrassment at discovering that I was presenting Bismarck as a moderate, pacific statesman and an attractive character.' (G760) In the summer of 1954, whilst staying with his family on the Isle of Wight, he wrote a sparkling brief biography of Bismarck, which was published the following year. Bismarck, like the revolutions of 1848, has remained one of his favourite topics.

From the mid 1950s his interests increasingly turned to British history. This was encouraged by two surprise invitations; one to deliver the prestigious Ford Lectures at Oxford, the other to write the 1914–45 volume of the Oxford History of England. His Ford Lectures developed a theme close to his heart, 'Dissent over Foreign Policy 1792–1939'. In it he resurrected the reputations of the dissenters of the past. He could identify with their struggles. Thus he proclaimed, 'Conformity may give you a quiet life; it may even bring you to a University Chair. But all change in history, all advance, comes from the nonconformists. If there had been no trouble makers, no Dissenters, we should still be living in caves.' The subject matter of the lectures was outside the mainstream of 'respectable' history. In putting the emphasis on the ideas of those who dissented from official policy, his lectures were something of a challenge to established historians of the day, especially those studying the eighteenth century. He explicitly criticised Namier's History of Parliament project and observed that the men of the past 'persist in having ideas and ideals, despite the exhortations of Mr. Trevor-Roper, and Professor Pares and Sir Lewis Namier. Historians have to take the past as they find it, not as they would like it to be; and our political past was shaped by the clash of argument as well as by family connections and systems of land tenure.' (A10, p 14) All in all *The Trouble Makers* displayed A.J.P. Taylor at his most irreverent, most iconoclastic; it was his academic equivalent to arguing his corner, with vigour and wit, on 'Free Speech'. The respectable and staid, if they were as unwary as to attend his first lecture, must have been suitably shocked. Taylor wrote in the published form of the lectures that the book was 'a gesture of repentance for having written recently a substantial volume of what I may call 'respectable' diplomatic history' (A10, p 12); and ever since, with characteristic pertinacity, he has deemed it to be 'by far my favourite brainchild'.

As well as these books, three volumes of his essays were published in the early 1950s. The publication of these, which contained many otherwise ephemeral newspaper centenary pieces and book reviews, was frowned on by many of the academic 'establishment'. However, as with broadcasting history on television, other eminent historians were not slow to follow his lead.

What the academic 'establishment' could not take was his role as controversialist in the popular press and on television. A.J.P. Taylor himself thoroughly enjoyed this and had no intention of giving it up. When the Regius Chair came up at Oxford Hugh Trevor Roper, not A.J.P. Taylor, got it. A major part of the reason for A.J.P. Taylor's elimination was his refusal to give up these aspects of his life. However honours did come his way. In 1956 he was elected to the British Academy. As well as the Ford Lectures he was invited to give the Raleigh lecture on history at the British Academy in 1959 (C7) and the Leslie Stephen lecture for 1961 at Cambridge. (C8)

Amongst the topics A.J.P. Taylor had been immersed in whilst preparing the Ford lectures was the Anti-Corn Law League. He felt that the League's orators, notably Cobden, had argued the Corn Laws out of existence. Reason, vigorously expressed, had triumphed against vested interests. Taylor himself stumped the country in 1958 in an effort to persuade the British people to demand a change in policy at that time. As he put it in a pamphlet, 'There can be no harm in trying morality for a change.' (C5) His cause, which he later deemed to be the most worthy of his life, was to get the United Kingdom unilaterally to abandon the nuclear bomb.

A.J.P. Taylor was a member of the executive committee of CND from virtually the start. The central group of CND sprang from a party in Kingsley Martin's London flat, a party given when Walter Lippman came over to Britain in 1957 on one of his periodic visits. J.B. Priestley and others present constituted themselves into an executive committee – and A.J.P. Taylor joined it a couple of days later.[48] The group gained prominence after articles by J.B. Priestley and Bertrand Russell in *The New Statesman* had created much interest. Thereafter other groups which had been campaigning against nuclear weapons in the mid-1950s came together under the banner of CND.

The morality of using the bomb had been discussed amongst intellectuals since 1945. A.J.P. Taylor himself had taken part in a radio discussion on the subject, with Professor J.D. Bernal and two members of Parliament, in September 1945. He had argued then that 'you can't frighten people into an international order with the atomic bomb' and had spoken in favour of setting up 'some sort of international centre for research and not to have secrecy'. However in the discussion he used the issue, as he did most issues at that time, to urge co-operation with Russia. He observed, 'I would tell the Russians about it without any strings being tied to it. I would do so for two very good reasons. First, because they will find out very soon in any case; you gain nothing by secrecy. Secondly, we know the Russians are already working on the other problem of applying atomic energy to peace-time use, and they might easily have something to swap for it to us.'[49] During the early 1950s he frequently expressed his concern about the atomic bomb. In *The Daily Herald* in April 1954 he called for Britain unilaterally to renounce it: 'Even if this makes it certain that London or all England will be destroyed, we will not plan to blow up a million people in Moscow or Warsaw.' The issue, he declared, was 'a question of morals'. (F134)

A.J.P. Taylor was one of the speakers at CND's inaugural meeting at the Central Hall, Westminster. There he gave a fiery speech, in which he described the effects of nuclear explosions on human beings and concluded by urging his audience to emulate the suffragettes and disrupt Ministers' public meetings, but with the cry of 'Murderer'. Soon A.J.P. Taylor was involved heart and soul in the movement. Kingsley Martin referred to him as 'one of the most effective missionaries of the campaign'. Beaverbrook was highly laudatory about his speaking skills, observing 'For clarity, wit and polish his speech was equal to the matured orations of Winston Churchill, and with the fire and enthusiasm of

Lloyd George at the height of his powers.'[50] A.J.P. Taylor was one of the few leading figures of CND who would speak all round the country. Thus, in the early summer of 1958 he spoke at the Sandown Pavilion, Isle of Wight (23 April), the Congregational Hall, Guildford (5 May), the Town Hall, St. Pancras (11 May), the Town Hall, Birmingham (12 May), the City Hall, Sheffield (16 May), the Town Hall, Cheltenham (19th May), the Free Trade Hall, Manchester (21 May), in Southampton (30 May), the Central Hall, Bristol (2 June), the Wesley Central Hall, Portsmouth (6 June), the Co-operative Hall, Leicester (9 June), the Guildhall, Salisbury (26 June) and the Dome, Brighton (9 July).[51] He had audiences of two or three hundred at the smaller venues, and two or three thousand in the big cities. (F 253) The Birmingham meeting gave him special pleasure, as he later recorded: 'My best evening came at Birmingham Town Hall where I spoke precisely a hundred years after Bright delivered there his great speech on British foreign policy – 'a gigantic system of out-relief for the British aristocracy'.' (D41)

A.J.P. Taylor, like J.B. Priestley, campaigned for Britain unilaterally to renounce nuclear weapons. He felt that to campaign for general nuclear disarmament was too Utopian. Throughout his campaigning he referred back in time to the activities of the Anti-Slavery campaign and the Anti-Corn Law League. With CND he aimed to win by argument, just as the nonconformists of the past had done. He remained with the main body of CND – and did not support Bertrand Russell and the Committee of 100 in defying the law.

A.J.P. Taylor argued for the renunciation of the bomb by Britain both on practical and moral grounds. He argued that turning Britain into an island aircraft carrier for America made Russia more likely to attack her, not less. In arguing this he still held to his interpretation of Russian foreign policy, that it was dominated by defensive not aggressive motives. He dismissed as nonsense the arguments of Aneurin Bevan and John Strachey that an independent nuclear weapon would enable the UK to hold the balance between America and Russia. He urged that the abandonment of the bomb would make Britain more prosperous, and leave more resources for defensive weapons.[52]

He was an ardent missionary of the moral case. He continued to argue that to unleash the bomb on the citizens of Russia or anywhere else was unthinkable. He also urged that a moral lead by Britain might be followed elsewhere. He wrote in a pamphlet, 'I believe that this will have an effect in the world. Morality counts for something, though not for as much as we used to think. Ordinary people everywhere want to be free of this nightmare. . . . We might start general disarmament and general peace in the world.' (C5) In writing in *The New Statesman* about his experiences campaigning around the country, he regretted that appeals to morality received a poor response in modern Britain. He reflected on this ruefully:

> Sooner or later we shall have to win the younger generation back to morality. I wonder where they learnt that it was buncombe. Was it from contemporary philosophers or from the day-to-day behaviour of statesmen? This country of ours fought two world wars mainly for high principle; and the only lesson drawn from this by the young is that might is right. It now seems unbearably priggish to say that the country which went to war for the sake of Belgium and Poland must not, in any circumstances, drop the H-bomb. But it is true. (F253)

To be effective in Britain the Campaign needed to convert the politicians in London. In the same article A.J.P. Taylor urged that CND 'must never forget that ultimately we have to convert the Labour Party, just as the Anti-Corn League converted Sir Robert Peel'. He observed, 'I understand Labour hesitations and equivocations. The Labour Party backed unilateral disarmament and moral suasion in the Thirties when these turned out to be wrong; and now it shrinks from unilateral nuclear disarmament and moral suasion though they are the only hope.' He urged, 'We are not seeking to win it over. We offer it the moral leadership of the world.'

For the world to take much notice Britain would have had to be a first rate power. The post-war economic crisis and Suez shook some of these illusions. The 1960s were to see more shaken. In 1960 the Macmillan Government cancelled the Blue Streak missile, and Britain no longer had an 'independent deterrent' to renounce. In the Cuban missile crisis, 1962, Britain was not seriously consulted, her views no longer affected the issue of peace or war between America and Russia. A.J.P. Taylor feels that that crisis killed off CND.[53]

Whilst CND was A.J.P. Taylor's big cause in the 1950s, and the one he actively worked for, he also championed various other progressive causes. As a radical he championed nationalism wherever it might be found; and he condemned colonialism. At the time of the 1951 General Election he urged a 'Fair Shares For All' policy towards the Third World and called for independence for British Empire countries. With prescience he warned that the Conservatives 'would like to treat Persia and Egypt just as the Russians have treated Czechoslovakia and Poland'. (F60) Naturally he opposed the Suez expedition in 1956. Twenty years later he recollected:

> I addressed one of the first meetings on this affair, I think on 10 August 1956. At that time the Labour Party was treating the Suez Canal as an international waterway and calling on the UN to intervene against Nasser. For me the canal was Egyptian and the British, or rather Anglo-French threats against Egypt were not different from Hitler's threats against Poland. I told my audience that they had often sneered at the Germans for not resisting Hitler. Now was the time for us to resist a British government that was following the same wicked course. Kingsley Martin, who had just written for the *New Statesman* yet another article invoking the UN, was in the audience. The next day John Freeman, then assistant editor, said to me: 'Whatever did you do to Kingsley? He swept into the office this morning and said – tear up this leader. This is the Boer War all over again, and we are going to fight it!' (F436)

He was an advocate of nationalism in the Third World. He urged British governments to side with liberation movements and not with the colonial powers. Thus in 1954 he urged Britain to support the Viet Minh and not the French. (F137) Later he condemned American intervention in Viet Nam. He has always condemned colour prejudice – and in particular South Africa's racialist and repressive policies. In 1941 he wrote 'whatever the efforts at 'segregation', the fortunes of black and white in South Africa are inextricably mingled', and he added 'that one cannot prosper while the other is degraded'. (G141) In 1959 he was one of the intellectuals who supported Christian Action's Defence and Aid Fund for the thirty accused in the South African Treason Trial of that year.[54]

Russia was a great disappointment to A.J.P. Taylor. He described Russia as 'the greatest catastrophe in my lifetime', in 1954. 'Thirty years ago we all thought Russia was going to turn into the perfect Socialist State. We didn't like the dictatorship. But we thought it would get less. Instead, it got worse.' (F129) However, he did not turn on Russia, or on socialism, as many disillusioned intellectuals did in the 1950s. He continued to urge that Britain and the West should seek agreement with Russia, and at the end of the decade praised Khrushchev for genuinely seeking peaceful co-existence.

He remained deeply distrustful of Germany. He condemned talk of rearming Germany. In 1950 he warned, 'You will make them the bosses of Europe, which is what Hitler did, and they will protect Europe from the Russians.' But, he observed, "just think of the effect of rearming the Germans on the peoples of Western Europe who were occupied by the Germans. It would be disastrous ... ' (F40) He was not alone in his opposition to German rearmament. In 1954 it was an issue which divided the Labour Party; and at the 1954 Party conference the opponents were only narrowly defeated. Whilst the Labour Party division was not on Left/Right lines, the Bevanites were prominent in opposing it.[55] A.J.P. Taylor often found himself in line with the Bevanites, though he always rejected suggestions that he was a Bevanite. In 1959, still a vehement opponent of German rearmament, he commented that 'keeping them disarmed is about the only good thing that has happened since 1945'. (F267) Earlier in the year he had condemned the West for 'rearming the very Germans who nearly destroyed Russia not so long ago'. (F265) Some of his remarks in that article, in which he had urged friendship with Russia and had been especially hostile to the Germans, earned him the rebuke of Selwyn Lloyd, the Foreign Secretary. (F267)

* * *

It is highly ironic that one who had been so vehemently

anti-German as A.J.P. Taylor should be pilloried so mercilessly in 1961 and 1962 as an apologist for Hitler. It was a cruel irony, which might well have astonished Thomas Hardy. The publication of *The Origins of The Second World War* turned him into an international figure and plunged him into a long controversy.

In *The Origins* A.J.P. Taylor presented Hitler not as a far-sighted man acting on long-term plans, but as a man who proceeded one step at a time, taking advantage of each opportunity as it arose 'to make Germany the greatest power in Europe'. In line with his *The Course of German History*, Hitler's foreign policy was shown to be conventional German foreign policy, but carried out more ruthlessly. The book was no less hostile to the Germans than his earlier books. Less than three years before he had written in a newspaper article, 'We cannot be friendly with all Germans until the generation which served Hitler has passed away.' (F259) In *The Origins* he pressed his point that Hitler was being used as a scapegoat: 'With Hitler guilty, every other German could claim innocence.' (All, p 35) Many of his critics misinterpreted such an emphasis as an attempt to exonerate Hitler, a surprising verdict in view of A.J.P. Taylor's record on Germany.[56] However one reviewer of *The Course of German History* had given a forewarning of this: 'In the effort to make the Nazis, not in large measure the result of the anarchy, but a development quite to be expected of German history, Mr. Taylor nearly succeeds in making them respectable.'[57]

Despite the shock that was expressed when the book was published A.J.P. Taylor had aired many of the more controversial points long before, usually in book reviews. He had reviewed the various volumes of inter-war foreign policy documents, published by various Governments, since 1947. In these reviews he had developed most of the ideas that went into the book. However the first review he did in which he took up the idea that Hitler did not have detailed plans for war to start in 1939 was that of Namier's *Diplomatic Prelude*. In a broadcast on the BBC's Third Programme he praised Namier for ignoring the legends of what happened in the period before the outbreak of war. He observed, '. . . you can find in Namier the more humdrum truth, discreditable no doubt to both sides in the negotiations – not discreditable from wickedness or sinister intention, discreditable from short sightedness, vanity and ignorance'. At this time Taylor saw Hitler as a muddler: 'Certainly, Hitler aimed at German domination of Europe, but he too, went about this in the most blundering way and, as Namier shows, was quite taken aback at the end when he found that, against all expectations, Britain and France were really going to war.'[58]

With the publication of the diplomatic documents he continued to question the view of Hitler as a man with a detailed plan of action, and started a long process of formulating the views that were to be expressed in his book. Thus in December 1949, reviewing a volume of German documents, he wrote: 'Hitler intervened only on a sudden impulse, without plan or preparation. The editors reprint the Hossbach memorandum of November 5th 1937, in which Hitler expounded his aggressive designs. This is evidence that he was a violent and unscrupulous man; it is not evidence that he had any concrete projects, and his prophecy of events had no relation to what actually happened.' He concluded that the volume 'does not provide the evidence that there was a German, or even a Nazi conspiracy against peace, if by conspiracy it is meant a coherent objective plan. It provides the evidence that the Germans, and especially the German governing class, allowed a criminal lunatic to establish himself in supreme power; and that they were abetted by those in England and France who, from feebleness or fear of Communism, treated the lunatic as a sane man.' (G357) Later, his main modification to this interpretation was to avoid describing Hitler as a lunatic, especially in the pre-war period. When he reviewed the next volume of German documents in April 1950 he stressed again Hitler's opportunism. Thus, of 1938, he wrote, 'Still Hitler did not settle his course even at the end of May. British appeasement, not Czech resistance, made him decide to provoke a crisis before the autumn. Until the Runciman mission even Hitler could not believe that the British would carry their surrender so far . . . ' Also he expressed his views of continuity in German history and general German guilt more extremely than in his latter book:

> It would be a great mistake to regret Hitler's victory.[59] He differed from the generals and diplomats in method, not aim; indeed, since he was incapable of systematic thought, he had no aim except to take advantage of the moment. The old-stylers were infinitely more dangerous to the rest of Europe, since they were more skilful in method and clear as to their intentions. They meant to establish Germany as the dominant power of Europe; and they would have done it except for Hitler's pursuit of theatrical violence. We should therefore be very grateful that Hitler broke loose in 1938.[60] (G372)

Such reviews did not cause a storm of controversy at the time. At least not on these interpretations. The main controversy came over his review of the first volume of the British documents in 1947, and this was over his criticisms of the editing.[61]

A.J.P. Taylor came to write *The Origins* during a busy period of his life, when he had little or no time for research in the archives. He was Vice President of Magdalen College at the time of the College's quincentenary in 1958. So, in writing *The Origins* he relied on the printed documents; perhaps relied too heavily on them, as some critics have observed, who regret that he did not deal more with the societies involved. However, as usual, he took pains with his style, and presented what is one of the highest peaks of narrative history. The style, especially of the first hundred or so pages, is superb.

The uproar following the publication of this book surprised him. He has always taken criticism in silence, and shown no signs of resenting it. But when attacks have become personal he has been hurt. Thus when his series of talks on British Foreign Policy (F27–30) given in late 1946 were vigorously attacked, he complained to a BBC official, 'I daresay it did not occur to you or to others . . . looking after this programme that I had feelings to be hurt; but I have. I made these talks at the request of the BBC and was encouraged by you and others to make them lively.'[62] At the time of the storm over *The Origins* he had an opportunity to rebut on television the arguments of his main English critic, Hugh Trevor Roper, and he acquitted himself well; though for many watchers the debate did not live up to the pyrotechnic display that some had predicted.[63] He also had the considerable consolation that the book became an international best-seller.

However the period after the publication of *The Origins* marked the nadir of his standing amongst academic historians. When his university lectureship at Oxford ran out in 1963, it was not renewed. A.J.P. Taylor, without any doubt, had been one of the outstanding lecturers at Oxford. The attendance at his lectures was so large that he had to lecture in the Exams Hall, even though he lectured at the unpopular time of 9 a.m. His lecturing style was striking. He entered the lecture hall suddenly, looked at the clock and promptly began his lecture. He would stand at the front of the lecture hall, and, twiddling his bow-tie, just talk; sometimes he gave the appearance of holding a debate with himself, rehearsing all sides of an argument. The lectures were given without notes, save sometimes when he would produce record cards from his pocket (with dramatic effect) to give a lengthy quotation. As with his television lectures he timed himself impeccably, and left the lecture theatre as quickly as he arrived. He gave sparkling lectures which encouraged listeners to go to the library and find out more about the subject, not lectures which served only to provide the listeners with detailed notes for exam revision. Although his university lectureship was terminated, he remained a Fellow of Magdalen College. He was elected to a research fellowship, which he held from 1963 to 1976 (and since then he has been an Honorary Fellow). Thereafter, for some years, his only regular university lectures were given at University College, London, as a special lecturer.

However, as Roger Louis commented in 1972, 'The eclipse of his reputation was brief; it is probably accurate to say that he is now widely regarded as the doyen of English historians.'[64] His reputation was fully restored with the publication of his volume in the Oxford History of England series. *English History 1914–45* again demonstrated his high skills as a narrative historian. He wrote a sparkling account of the history of those years, in which he succeeded largely in welding together all aspects of the history of the period, unlike the other major histories of England, in which different topics had been confined to separate essays. The book, written before Government Papers for the period were released, as usual displayed his 'green fingers' in writing history – his uncanny instinct for sensing what had happened. In the book he worked his way through the history of the period challenging orthodoxy after orthodoxy; and most reviewers acknowledged that such extensive revisionism was fully necessary. This book is one of his two finest.

The other is his *Beaverbrook*, published in 1972. It is a massive study of Beaverbrook, based on lengthy research in primary archival sources. The book was a realistic appraisal of Beaverbook's importance in British politics in the first half of the twentieth century – and, as such, was a major contribution to the study of the period. It was written with skill, with great knowledge, and with affection. A.J.P. Taylor's feelings for Beaverbrook led him to make considerable allowances for Beaverbrook's less likeable personal characteristics and his embellishments to history; the fact that he realises this probably makes him undervalue his book.[65] However, this personal commitment, like Boswell's to Johnson, will help the book endure. As a study of Beaverbrook the man it has limitations, for he avoided dealing in any depth with Beaverbrook's family life.

Beaverbrook was a major influence in A.J.P. Taylor's life between their meeting in 1956 and Beaverbrook's death in 1965. Reading A.J.P. Taylor's review of his *Men and Power 1917–1918* (G693) gave Beaverbrook immense pleasure. On a radio programme Michael Foot commented to A.J.P. Taylor about this, 'It was one of the most thrilling days in his life. Your review changed the whole of his outlook about the writing of books, and it also changed the attitude of other people about his writing of books.'[66] After this Taylor and Beaverbrook met and became friends. Beaverbrook appears a strange friend for a radical nonconformist such as A.J.P. Taylor. Yet he was not alone amongst English left-wingers in being attracted to Beaverbrook; Michael Foot was also amongst his admirers. A.J.P. Taylor admired Beaverbrook's unorthodoxy, his drive and the radical vein in him. He could admire much of Beaverbrook's past record: his advocacy of full support for Russia in the Second World War, his vigour at the Ministry of Aircraft Production, his strong sympathy for Irish nationalism. Like him, Beaverbrook was not a good party man; he was usually out of step with the solemn and established. Also like A.J.P. Taylor, Beaverbrook had broken away from Puritan disapproval of people enjoying themselves. A.J.P. Taylor found Beaverbrook's company highly enjoyable, and in particular admired his zest for life and his sense of fun. Michael Foot commented of Beaverbrook that 'the thing that was most notable about him was his gaiety. He could make life gayer altogether than almost anybody I've ever met.'[67]

A.J.P. Taylor was not an uncritical admirer of Beaverbrook, either then or in his book. As he put it, he was captivated by him, but not bewitched. In the book hc avoided exaggerating Beaverbrook's role in British politics. He did not agrcc with much of his politics, a point he made in highly characteristic fashion: 'Lord Beaverbrook has often been wrong in political matters. In my opinion as often wrong as right. But he has been wrong for the right reasons. He has made his own mistakes, not copied the mistakes of others.' (E68) After Beaverbrook's death he became Honorary Director of the Beaverbrook Library, which opened its doors to scholars in 1967.

The Beaverbrook Library provided A.J.P. Taylor with a scholarly base in London. As well as an office, it also provided him with a secretary for the first time in his life. The library housed Beaverbrook's collection of papers – notably the main body of those of Lloyd George, Bonar Law and of Beaverbrook himself. It was an attractive collection for A.J.P. Taylor. He had done more than anyone else to resurrect Lloyd George's reputation.[68] Throughout his writings on English history he has been appreciative of Lloyd George's career. He warmly defended Lloyd George's achievements at the Paris Peace Conference of 1919; this support for the peace-maker's solutions being in line with his interpretation of German history in general and inter-war history in particular.[69] In 1961 he used the Leslie Stephen lecture to make a reassessment of Lloyd George; an essay which is one of the shrewdest pieces ever written about him, easily outclassing most of the books. In *English History 1914–45* Lloyd George appears as 'the greatest prime minister of this century' (A14, p 87), one of the very few politicians for whom he can find any enthusiasm.

A.J.P. Taylor made fruitful use of the Beaverbrook Library collections other than for his biography of Beaverbrook. He edited with considerable skill and judgment Frances Stevenson's diaries and her correspondence with Lloyd George, and also a selection of W.P. Crozier's interviews with prominent political figures of the 1930s. Also, whilst Director, he wrote and selected the photographs for his history of the Second World War. In it he again demonstrated his remarkable narrative skills in his coherent account of that war, in which he particularly successfully combined the events in the Far East with those in Europe. As with his fine pictorial history of the First World War, it was a major feat of writing to compress successfully so much into so little space.

The Beaverbrook Library also brought A.J.P. Taylor into contact with historians who were working on twentieth-century British history. He took a real interest in those using the archives, be they scholars of international repute or postgraduates just beginning their research. He instituted a series of seminars, from December 1968, at which researchers could present their findings and have them discussed. Sadly the Library was closed in March 1975. However he resumed chairing a research seminar on twentieth-century British history in the autumn of 1977, at the Institute of Historical Research. His Beaverbrook ties did not end with the Library. He has continued to work for the Beaverbrook Foundation, and was provided with a secretary and an office, first in the *Express* and then in the *Evening Standard* building until late in 1978. He still has a contract to write on current affairs for *The Sunday Express*.

In recent years his political pieces have continued to be populist. Thus he has condemned bureaucracy and those in authority who think they know best, and who do not trust the people's judgment. He has continued to champion nationalism, and in particular has condemned Britain's activities in Northern Ireland. He has opposed Britain's entry into the Common Market. He has become considerably disillusioned with the Labour Party. Indeed from 1963 to 1966 he was not a member of the Party, because of his disgust at its immigration policy.

With the British public at large he has come to personify History. For many years when radio or television producers have wanted a historical perspective given on some event, they have often turned to A.J.P. Taylor. He has been impressive in this role. The television critic Elkan Allen has written, '. . . he was telephoned the day Churchill died and asked to come into the studio that evening; four hours later, with drapes over the Ready Steady Go? set, he was delivering an elagaic and informative obituary which any other lecturer would have needed six weeks – and it all written out in front of him – to deliver'.[70] A.J.P. Taylor can always be relied on for incisive and provocative comments. In addition, of course, he has given several series of television lectures in recent years. His face has appeared on posters all over the country, on advertisements for *The Listener* as one of their four best known contributors. Similarly book clubs frequently include one or more of his volumes in their advertisements. Publishers know that the inclusion of an introduction by A.J.P. Taylor will help the sales of a book. He has produced much for the 'general reader', from contributions to 'part' works such as the highly successful *History of the Twentieth Century* (B9) to commentaries on collections of historic photographs, such as the interesting *The Russian War 1941–1945*. (B26)

At the same time his reputation is very great amongst professional historians, especially amongst those who graduated in the 1950s and after. The prestigious American *Journal of Modern History* paid him the very rare compliment of devoting its March 1977 issue to him. In Britain more academic honours have come his way. He has been awarded honorary doctorates by York and Bristol universities, to add to the earlier one from New Brunswick. He has been invited to give other prestigious lectures – the Creighton Lecture at London University, 1973, and the Andrew Lang Lecture at St Andrews, 1974. In 1976 he was appointed Visiting

Professor of History at Bristol University for two academic years.

* * *

Mr. Taylor is in the very first rank. He is among English historians today about what Mr. Evelyn Waugh is among English novelists, a rescuer of forgotten truths, a knight of paradox, a prince of story-telling, and a great, maybe the greatest, master of his craft.[71] (Sebastian Haffner, 1961)

In the last two decades A.J.P. Taylor has frequently been deemed the best known, and nearly as frequently the best, of living historians by writers in the British press, and increasingly by academics who are at present under the age of fifty. His books remain popular with students. Hugh Thomas' experiences were not exceptional when he recalled in an essay on the books which have influenced him: 'Alan Taylor I did find very exciting as an undergraduate. I must say I find today's undergraduates do so too.'[72]

A.J.P. Taylor's appeal does not lie in an original methodology or in his investigating some new area of interest, though he has not been afraid of fresh approaches to history. For example, he has welcomed statistical approaches to history, (G433), and he was quick to consider seriously the value of contemporary film to the study of modern history (A14, p 611 and C10). But it is not in such areas that he has made his mark. Indeed he has often been accused of being the last of the old guard of English historians. Thus in 1952 one reviewer wrote, 'The English school of history for the best part of the past 100 years has been the liberal, individualist school, the school that is more interested in men than movements, discusses causes and consequences, primarily in terms of moral judgements, and wants to know first and foremost – as Rosebery put it 50 years ago – whether Napoleon was a 'good man'. Mr. Taylor is not only a perfectly orthodox member of this school, but may not unfairly be called its leading diehard.'[73] There is some truth in such an appraisal, though in the case of *The Origins of the Second World War* quite clearly his interpretation was not primarily concerned with moral judgments. However his vivid pen portraits of historical figures gain much from his very real interest in the men and women of the past, and in sharply appraising them he often judges them by radical and moral standards. He has observed, albeit with some exaggeration, 'My taste in history is old fashioned and orthodox. I like narrative based on documents: no guesses, no psychological jargon, no attempt to turn history into anthropology.' (G337)

His supreme skill has been in writing brilliant narrative history. He has taken this form to its greatest height, avoiding the rhetorical flabbiness and general verboseness of many of the great narrative historians of the past. He has an incisive mind and he has written in a lucid, incisive style. 'The problem of the historian', he has written, 'is to write a book which shall be both accurate and interesting; the problem is not solved by writing a book that is accurate.' (G318) He has always taken great pains with his style, consciously writing with the reader in mind. He has been a skilled craftsman in his field, using paradox and irony to hold the interest of his reader, as he displays the happenings of the past with real enthusiasm and wit. 'The highest history', he has remarked, 'combines scholarship and art.' (G301)

His own scholarship is of a very high order. A.J.P. Taylor is a master of printed sources, foreign policy documents and the writings of other historians. He is skilled in working in archives, both for his earlier diplomatic histories and also for his later major works on modern British history. His remarkable output is a result of a very good memory and consistent hard work over the years. Unlike many academics he has kept office hours, indeed longer than office hours, and he has been doing this for the last fifty years. In recording his incredible output of book reviews my first thought was that it was sad so much energy had been misdirected; how much better, forty years ago, if he had produced a sparkling brief history of the French Revolution, than writing innumerable book reviews about it. Then I realised that his formidable volume of reviewing was the way he built up his huge reservoir of knowledge, and in most areas this had been tapped for later books. I realised, also, that he has had an unquenchable delight in reading the latest works of history; he has frequently written of the thrill that comes over him when a new package of books arrives to be reviewed. Whilst having this huge reservoir of knowledge, he has exercised moderation is using it. Unlike most scholars he has resisted the temptation to overfill his narrative. As he has put it, 'My own taste in history is for the book that simplifies and sharpens. I want to see the skeleton of the past and am not much interested in its flesh. One good epigram counts for more with me than pages of luscious description.' (G723)

Like many of the great historians of the past his work is unmistakeable. Not only has he perfected his own distinctive style, he has also developed his own historical personality. In his work he has been irreverent to those in authority, he has pulled the rug from under the pompous and powerful, and has applauded the unconventional and the rebellious. He has had unstinted faith in the common sense of ordinary people; indeed on one occasion he wrote, vividly, regretting that young people 'do not believe, as every democrat must, that the voice of the people is the voice of God'. (F210) Whilst he has shown considerable nostalgia for the politics of the past where there has been a clash of ideas – of Cobden and Bright against the landed interest, of Gladstone against Disraeli – sometimes he has been hard on the failed causes of the past. In his work he has displayed great warmth for the advocates of progressive causes and often querulousness to their opponents. A.J.P. Taylor is the most distinctive writer of history today. He himself has praised such distinctiveness. Thus he has asked, 'What is it that such individual authors as, say, Sir Lewis Namier, E. H. Carr and Hugh Trevor-Roper have in common? Great scholarship, of course; but also literary mastery and clear personal convictions. A work of history, like any other book that is any good, must bear its author's stamp. The reader should feel that no one else could have written this particular book in this particular way.' (G517)

A.J.P. Taylor has made a considerable impact on history in the English speaking world. He has played a major part in making contemporary history respectable. Not so many years ago universities and schools looked askance at any syllabus that came within fifty years of the present. A.J.P. Taylor has been at the fore in writing and lecturing on more recent history. In addition he has been a vigorous opponent of the British fifty, and later thirty, year restrictions on Government records.[74] Above all he has helped to avoid a major gap growing up between academic and popular history, as happened in France. He has been a warm supporter of moves to broaden and nurture interest in history; hence his strong support for the Historical Association in Britain and his warm words for the journal *History Today*.[75]

He has been a major influence on many other historians. Because, his style and approach is so individual, he has had no imitators and there is no 'Taylor school of history', but several of the most distinguished younger historians of modern Britain have been pupils of his. Roger Louis has commented 'that there is one aspect of Alan Taylor seldom mentioned in print. That is the encouragement he has given to younger scholars to get on with their own work in their own way. I happen to have benefited from his guidance. There are many others. Perhaps the greatest tribute to him is that he has profoundly enriched the scholarship of the next generation.'[76] A.J.P. Taylor has stimulated so many modern historians to challenge received ideas, to take nothing for granted. One could multiply tributes to him by prominent historians. Perhaps one by Alfred Gollin, whom A.J.P. Taylor has described as 'that prince of researchers' (G1071), is sufficient to make the point:

> In my opinion he is the most stimulating scholar in the field of recent British political history. One need not always agree with him – but he stimulates thought and reflection. His mind, in my opinion, works differently from other people's. The result is a novelty of approach and analysis that makes the rest of us think again. He reads the published works of other scholars and then produces new ideas and insights that provoke further reflection, and also discussion.
>
> I can give two personal reactions to his work. One is not really professional, but it counts – for me. When I first went up to New College, my tutor, Alan Bullock, was not especially pleased with my essays. He then assigned me a question on the Austro-Hungarians and a book he asked me to read for it was Taylor's *The Habsburg Monarchy*. At first I could not make head or tail of the book but I suddenly saw what Taylor was doing and re-read the whole thing. My essay, based on Taylor's book, was the first that

Bullock ever approved of. Bullock said: 'You have arrived, laddie.' I did not even know Taylor but, after that I looked out for everything he wrote. It was a personal touch, of consequence to me. As a young American I found the Oxford system rather strange and quite different. After this incident I began to see what was required of me there.
More seriously, I believe that pound for pound Taylor's Raleigh Lecture, 'Politics in the First World War', delivered in 1959, is a contribution of vital consequence. Although it is a brief composition I believe it opens up the entire subject in a way that has not been done by anyone else. The politics of the war are confusing. Tories support Liberals and other Liberals attack their fellow party members. I think Taylor has produced, in this lecture, the most brilliant insights. They help to explain what was previously inexplicable. Taylor wrote: 'The great underlying conflict was between freedom and organisation. Could the war be conducted by 'Liberal' methods – that is, by voluntary recruiting and *laissez-faire* economics? Or must there be compulsory military service, control of profits, and direction of labour and industry?' This was the underlying conflict that cut across party lines. These themes were already in the published literature. But Taylor has plucked them out and presented them in his own fascinating way.[77]

A.J.P. Taylor's chosen area of study, a large one, has been European history since the French Revolution. He has frequently remarked that to him all that went before that was pre-history. 'When we speak of the modern world', he wrote in 1954, 'we really mean the world that has rejected the notion of Original Sin, the world that believes in Progress and secular values, the world, in short, of liberalism.' (G557) Part of his historical *persona* has stemmed from the way he has championed liberal values in writing the history of the past two centuries. He has his clear heroes: men such as Charles James Fox, Richard Cobden, Abraham Lincoln, Garibaldi, Charles Bradlaugh and William Morris. He has been shocked when Left-wingers have expressed admiration for Disraeli and dislike of Gladstone. (G496) The moral issues of the past have always been very live matters for him. He has been on the side of the angels, fighting the good fight with the radicals of the past and present.

He had played a notable part himself in what he has always seen as a great tradition in Britain. 'British radicalism runs in a continuous history', he noted with pleasure in 1962, 'from Wilkes to Michael Foot.' (G934) He has been a friend of Michael Foot since the days of 'In the News' – and they were both prominent in CND. Like Michael Foot, A.J.P. Taylor is a socialist. Like him, he has often championed the freedom of the Press. A.J.P. Taylor believes very deeply in freedom and democracy. He has written, 'You cannot have genuine freedom without socialism . . . But you can have socialism without freedom – and then it becomes the most hated of tyrannies.' (F92) In fighting for his causes he has always been pugnacious. He has shown absolute faith in the rightness of his views – no 'ifs' and 'buts' or signs of philosophic doubt. Similarly in his history he has expressed few doubts about his interpretations. In his preface to *English History 1914–1945* he thanked Kenneth Tite, amongst other things, for having 'tempered the dogmatism of my style. He must take part of the blame if the word 'probably' occurs too often.' (A14, p vii) A.J.P. Taylor has always entered into controversy over current affairs and history with great gusto. G.D.H. Cole once teased him, 'All you like in politics is fighting.' (G1293) Beaverbrook dubbed him 'The Man Who Likes to Stir Things Up.'[78] The element of enjoying being mischievous is in A.J.P. Taylor's writings and in some of his public utterances; but this is only part of him. Alongside the mischievous streak there is one of high moral seriousness. Indeed his writings often have a moral tone which is uncommon today.

This is not the only dichotomy which is apparent in his writings. There is one A.J.P. Taylor who sees things getting better and better – and there is a pessimistic one who sees little future for mankind. In his optimistic writings he has pointed to a rising standard of living for ordinary people in the West. For Britain he has applauded the Welfare State, the ending of colonialism abroad, and the declining power of inherited privilege. However, he has also been a Cassandra, predicting a third world war over Germany's position in Europe and inevitable disaster for mankind from nuclear weapons. With hindsight it is easy for the historian to judge people to have overreacted. In the case of A.J.P. Taylor there are a number of occasions where this seems a fair comment on him. However, part of the reason for this is the vigour with which he states any point of view that he takes.

Pushing arguments to the limit makes for striking journalism. In a revealing comment A.J.P. Taylor has distinguished the prime aim of the historian from that of the journalist: 'The first aim of the journalist is to interest; of the historian it is to instruct – of course the good journalist and the good historian try to do both.'[79] A.J.P. Taylor has been very proud of his ability to earn a living from his journalism and his television appearances. His attachment to these marks another contrast in his character. He is a kindly, shy, sensitive man – yet he has enjoyed the opportunity to shine in public. He has often regretted the British love of amateurism and deep suspicion of intellectuals. The television discussion programmes of the 1950s put a premium on quick intelligent thinking. He wrote of such discussions, 'It is easy to think what to say next when you yourself are talking: one sentence leads on to the next . . . It is much more difficult to think what to say next when the other man is talking. You have to take in what he says; realise where it is leading to; not be surprised if it goes somewhere else; and marshal your own thoughts as well as your own answers.' In such programmes he was delighted, therefore, that: 'It is actually an advantage to be quicker, cleverer, more intellectual than the other man. In this way television is not at all like life and is indeed a serious disqualification for real life: television stupidity never pays.' (F264) He has always been remarkably aware of his own strengths and weaknesses, much more so than any other leading figure that I can think of, past or present. He wrote disarmingly of his own taste for publicity in one of his newspaper columns when he was off 'In The News' for several months: 'I used to take part in a discussion programme on television. At first I was surprised and a bit worried when people recognised me in the streets. But soon I was anxious and unhappy unless people waved at me and called me by my Christian name all the time I was out. Publicity became a craving worse than alcohol and more exciting. I had only a mild attack. Television sees me no more; and no one recognises me as I walk around. But it taught me that everyone who lives for publicity must be a bit crazy.' (F82)

However A.J.P. Taylor has always remained first and foremost a very dedicated historian. His application has been prodigious. He has always been an avid reader, deeming reading to be 'the best thing in life'. (F147) Indeed he has remarked on several occasions that, apart from his family, he prefers the company of books to people. Other than reading and writing his interests have been few. He enjoys music, especially chamber music. At one time he enjoyed growing vegetables. He has always been a keen walker, in recent years traversing most of the Pennine Way and Offa's Dyke. But his real passion in life has been history.

He has enraged some professional historians by repeatedly observing that history is not a utilitarian subject. As he put it in *The Trouble Makers*, 'In my opinion we learn nothing from history except the infinite variety of men's behaviour. We study it, as we listen to music or read poetry, for pleasure, not for instruction.'[80] (A10, p 23) In such pronouncements he is bestowing on it the value of many of the humanities – of enriching people's understanding of life and, probably, of themselves. In 1953 in an appraisal of Sir Lewis Namier's work he wrote, 'But history is more than scholarship, more even than a method of research. It is above all a form of understanding; and the general reader will not put a historian in the highest rank unless he has supplied a new version and a new vision.' (D10) He was even more explicit in a radio talk, 'How History Should Be Written'. Then he observed that:

> . . . history is the one way in which you can experience at second hand all kinds of varieties of human behaviour, and after all the greatest problem in life is to understand how other people behave, and this is what history enables us to do: to see people in all kinds of situations, in all kinds of walks of life . . . ; it makes the reader, and to a certain extent the historian too, aware of a fuller, much wider life than somebody could possibly have merely by his own private experience.[81]

Over the past half century A.J.P. Taylor has done much to make the study of the past enjoyable and stimulating for a very large number of people. In his hands history has never been a dead or a sterile subject.

NOTES

1 Interview, 'Atticus' column, *Sunday Times*. 14 Nov. 1976. p 32

2 See also G1150. In this review he denounced the Oedipus Complex interpretation of men, pointing out that many men have loved their fathers and have remained normal.
3 Script of 'I Speak For Myself' broadcast, 23 Oct. 1950; BBC.
4 His father was not his only relative to be involved in local politics. The *Preston Herald*, 21 Feb. 1936, described him as 'the grand-nephew of the late Alderman William Thompson'.
5 After the General Strike Paul offered A.J.P.T. some books on it to review for the *Sunday Worker*. I have been unable to find the review.
6 '1848: Seed Plot of History', *TLS*. 2396. 3 Jan 1948. pp 1–3
7 *MG*. 18 Dec. 1935. See also his comments in G1467
8 *House of Commons Debates*. 365, 1143. 24 Oct. 1940; cited in 'Journey to the Centre: Churchill and Labour in Coalition 1940–5', Paul Addison, in *Crisis and Controversy*, ed. A. Sked and C. Cook, London, Macmillan, 1976
9 Passant's lectures were also the basis of a book; for A.J.P.T.'s review of it, see G825
10 A.J.P.T. to Trevor Blewitt, (the man whom he had dealt with hitherto at the BBC), 23 Aug. 1944; BBC.
11 *NS & N*. 28, 716. 11 Nov. 1944. p 321
12 *Ibid.* 714. 28 Oct. 1944. 285. He also expressed this vigorously in a radio discussion with Lord Vansittart, Kingsley Martin and Barbara Ward, broadcast on 13 October. 'What Shall We Do With Germany?', *Li*. 32, 832. 19 Oct. 1944. pp 423–4, 436
13 Letter, *TLS*. 2367. 14 Jun. 1947. p 295. See also the second part of the radio discussion of October 1944, *Li*. 32, 824. 26 Oct. 1944. pp 459–60, 465
14 In 1944 he wrote of Latvia, Lithuania, and Estonia, 'Not as artificial sovereign states, manufactured by German Free Corps, but as autonomous Soviet Republics, the Baltic people can at last begin their national history.' For him then the lesson of Baltic history was that those states 'enjoy only a secure national existence only within the framework of the Soviet Union'. (F3)
15 He was particularly indignant when the Royal Institute of International Affairs published a pamphlet, *The Problem of Germany*, which failed to recognise that the Munich agreement had been repudiated by the British Government – and wrote to *The Manchester Guardian*. This lengthy letter was reprinted with approval in *The Central European Observer*. 20, 16. 20 Aug. 1943. p 242, a fortnightly review edited by Rennie Smith.
16 A.J.P.T. to T. Blewitt, 11 Oct. 1944; BBC.
17 As well as C2 see in particular a lengthy letter, *MG*, 19 Sept. 1945. p 4. Richard West, in a recent article on Trieste, deemed him to be the 'only distinguished outside supporter' of the Yugoslav cause. *Daily Telegraph*. 7 Mar. 1977. p 14
18 T. Blewitt to A.J.P.T., 9 Mar. 1945; BBC.
19 Memorandum by R.A. Rendall, 24 Sept. 1945; BBC.
20 Memorandum by George Barnes, 1 Oct. 1945; BBC.

21 Memorandum by R.A. Rendall, 30 Oct. 1945; BBC.
22 See especially F27
23 A.J.P.T. to T. Blewitt, 12 Apr. 1945; BBC.
24 A.J.P.T. to T. Blewitt, 14 Feb. 1946; BBC.
25 A.J.P.T. to T. Blewitt, 12 Apr. 1945; BBC.
26 Memorandum by T. Blewitt, 9 May 1946; BBC.
27 At which an M.P. interjected, 'Apart from that it was all right'! *House of Commons Debates*. 431, 11 Dec. 1946. p 1285. The complaint came from H. Strauss, MP for the Combined Universities, who read sizeable extracts of A.J.P. Taylor's talk to the House; *Ibid.* 1237–40
28 A.J.P.T. to T. Blewitt, 14 Feb. 1946; BBC.
29 *The Times*. 17 Sept. 1948. p 5
30 'Hyenas and other Reptiles', Kingsley Martin, *NS & N*. 36, 913. 4 Sept. 1948. pp 187–8. His speech was widely reported in the British and American press. For A.J.P.T.'s own account see A5. For the statement issued by him and the others of the British dissenting minority, see that journal's letter column, *Ibid.* p 195
31 26 Jul. 1950. p 7
32 'Brother Michael', *Sun Ex*. 29 Sept. 1974. pp 8–9
33 This paragraph is based on chapter 5 of Grace Wyndham Goldie's *Facing The Nation*, London, Bodley Head, 1977, pp 68–78
34 *Ibid.* p 70
35 *Obs*. 18 Dec. 1955. p 9
36 In the 'Critic for a Week' column, *Ev Stan*. 19 Dec. 1955. p 5. A.J.P.T. made a reply in his weekly column (F208)
37 'Alan Taylor's Own Big Rows', Anthony Davis, *TV Times*. 3 Dec. 1964. pp 8, 33
38 *NS & N*. 43, 112. 28 Jun. 1952. p 773. See also his letter, *Ibid.* 45, 1163. 20 Jun. 1953. p 734. The journal was vigorous in opposing commercial television. It published a cartoon of him as independent television's 'Don in the Window' and commissioned a counter book review to one by him on the subject; see G911
39 '(Un) Quiet Flows The Don: Alan Taylor starts a 'revolution' on ITV', *TV Times*. 8, 93. 9 Aug. 1957. p 12
40 'It's the great experiment – Taylor vision!', Fred Cooke, *Reynolds News*. 26 May 1957. p 8
41 '(Un) Quiet Flows The Don', *op cit*.
42 A.J.P.T. to George Barnes, 27 Sept. 1946; BBC.
43 A.J.P.T. to Harman Grisewood, 21 Oct. 1946; BBC.
44 G. Barnes to A.J.P.T., 16 May 1947; A.J.P.T. to G. Barnes, 17 May 1947; BBC.
45 Sean Day-Lewis, *Daily Telegraph*. 15 Jul. 1978. p 15. That day his column had the headline 'A.J.P. Taylor's skill is compelling'.
46 Generally critics have praised this spontaneity. See the previews for the 'How Wars Begin' series by W. Stephen Gilbert, *Obs*. 10 Jul. 1977. p 29 and Elkan Allan, *Sun Times*. 10 Jul. 1977. p 52. For a marked exception, see Peter Dunn, *Sun Times*. 30 Jul. 1978. p 39

47 '(Un) Quiet Flows The Don', *op cit.*

48 These points are drawn from A.J.P.T.'s talk on CND, given at the Twentieth Century British History research seminar at the Institute of Historical Research, 24 May 1978.

49 'San Francisco and the Atom Bomb', *Li.* 34, 873. 4 Oct. 1945. pp 367–8, 381–2

50 For Kingsley Martin's comment see 'Outlook for CND', *NS.* 62, 1605. 15 Dec. 1961. pp 915–6. For Beaverbrook's, see his piece in *A Century of Conflict 1850–1950*, ed. M. Gilbert, London, Hamish Hamilton, 1966, pp 3–5

51 This list is not necessarily comprehensive; it is drawn from CND advertisements.

52 His arguments are collected in his pamphlet 'The Great Deterrent Myth' (C5). He defended his point of view in numerous letters to the *New Statesman*. See *NS.* 56, 1425. 5 Jul. 1958. pp 17–18; *Ibid.* 1429. 2 Aug. 1958. p 145; *Ibid.* 1439. 11 Oct. 1958. p 492; *Ibid.* 58, 1498. 28 Nov. 1959. pp 748–9; *Ibid.* 1500. 12 Dec. 1959. p 839; *Ibid.* 61, 1557. 13 Jan. 1961. p 48. See also *The Times*. 11 Mar. 1958. p 11

53 CND talk, 1978; see above, 48

54 *NS.* 57, 1469. 9 May 1959. p 647. At the start of that decade, like many of the Left in Britain, he did not advocate the expulsion of South Africa from the Commonwealth, though he loathed its policies (F40)

55 See, for example, the Tribune pamphlet *It Need Not Happen: The Alternative to German Rearmament*, n.d. (?1954), by Aneurin Bevan, Barbara Castle, Richard Crossman, Tom Driberg, Ian Mikardo and Harold Wilson. As late as 1963 Harold Wilson was warning against German rearment; see his 'Danger! ... the German finger is reaching for the H-bomb trigger', *Sun Ex.* 13 Jan. 1963. p 16

56 For A.J.P. Taylor on this ambiguity see his remarks to Ved Mehta, in the latter's entertaining book *Fly and the Fly Bottle*, Boston 1963, (Pelican, 1965), pp 144–5. Also see Roger Louis' comments in *A.J.P. Taylor and his Critics*, pp 8–9

57 R. Birley, *Int. Affairs*. 22, 1. Jan. 1946. p 136

58 Script of 'An Exercise in Contemporary History', broadcast 13 Jan. 1948; BBC.

59 i.e. 1938.

60 Though he did remake this point later, apparently in letters to Pieter Geyl. See *Fly and Fly Bottle*, p 136

61 The editors protested that they were independent of the Government, *TLS.* 2360. 26 Apr. 1947. p 197. In the next issue it was stated that the reviewer 'withdraws the statement in the article that they had subordinated their independence to a Government department', *ibid.* 2361. 3 May 1947. p 211. He later recalled, 'The review ... caused a terrible row and blew Morison out of the editor's chair', A.J.P.T. to C.J.W., 12 May 1978.

62 A.J.P.T. to Harman Grisewood, 4 Jan. 1947; BBC.

63 In fact the BBC's staff was more acute in its assessment of the book than many academics. C.F.O. Clarke wrote to the Chief Assistant, Current Affairs on 22 Jun. 1961: 'Taylor's theme is less controversial than it has been made out to be and does not lend itself to a discussion on whether he was right to white-wash Hitler, because in fact he did not do so'; BBC.

64 R. Louis, *op. cit.* p 8

65 He was given a hard time over his attitude to Beaverbrook's embellishments to history by Richard Crossman on television. 'Crosstalk', *Li.* 89, 2288. 1 Feb. 1973. pp 148–9

66 'The man who wanted to get things done', *Li.* 88, 2259. 13 Jul. 1972. pp 44–7

67 *Ibid.*

68 A point well made by Stephen Koss in A. Sked and C. Cook, *op cit.* pp 68–9

69 Thus in *The Trouble Makers*, he wrote, 'Keynes, I am told, was a very good economist, but there can be few examples in history of a judgement that went more astray than his condemnation of the peace settlement.' (A10, p 174)

70 *Sunday Times*. 9 Jul. 1978. p 52

71 'Mr. Taylor's masterpiece', *Obs.* 16 Apr. 1961. p 30

72 *Bookmarks*, ed. F. Raphael, London, Jonathan Cape, 1975, pp 152–3. In January 1977 I invited two groups of undergraduates to list the names of any historians, living or dead, they could remember. They were unable to see each other's lists and were completely unaware of my interest in A.J.P. Taylor. I was curious as to which historians are best known amongst students today – A.J.P. Taylor headed the list, being named by 39 of 62 students with, curiously, Winston Churchill second, being named by 29. 18 of 22 assorted social sciences second year students named Taylor, 12 naming him first and four others had him in their first five. 21 of 40 economics first year students named him, 12 naming him first and all the others in their first five. Excluding the authors of their economic history textbooks, the runners up were Christopher Hill, 14, G. R. Elton and G. M. Trevelyan, 12, H. Trevor Roper, 10, and Asa Briggs, Antonia Fraser and Eric Hobsbawm, 9.

73 'History and Journalism', *TLS*. 2655. 19 Dec. 1952. p 847

74 He was very critical of the 50 year rule in his reviews of the volumes of documents on British Foreign Policy, in A10, 22 and in various letters to the press, e.g. *The Times*. 6 and 14 Aug. 1952. p 5. He has not been satisfied with the current 30 year rule; see for example, his comments in a discussion on political memoirs with Roy Jenkins and Lord Butler, *Li.* 85. 4 Mar. 1971. p 272.

75 He has been generous with his time on behalf of the Historical Association. He has lectured to branches all round the country, and attracts packed meetings. The Association's *Branch Reports 1976* includes six reports; two giving audience figures of 250 and 350. For a report of his lecture 'The War Lords of the Second World'

at the Association's 1977 conference, see *The Times Higher Educational Supplement*. 22 Apr. 1977. p 4. See also his eulogy on the Association, F213

76 Roger Louis to C.J.W. 4 May 1977

77 Alfred Gollin to C.J.W. 4 Feb. 1977

78 M. Gilbert ed. *op cit*. pp 3–5

79 Script of 'An Exercise in Contemporary History', broadcast 13 Jan. 1948; BBC.

80 For Arthur Marwick's discussion of his views on history, see *The Nature of History*, pp 190–3. See also J.H. Plumb's interesting essay 'The Historian's Dilemma' in *Crisis in the Humanities*, ed. J.H. Plumb, Harmondsworth, Penguin, 1964, pp 24–44

81 Script of 'How History Should Be Written', broadcast 16 Jul. 1950; BBC.

SOME BOOKS AND ARTICLES ON A.J.P. TAYLOR

Anon. 'The Seventh Veil', *NS*. 54, 1385. 28 Sept. 1957. pp 376–7

Anon. 'A.J.P. Taylor', *Obs*. 30 Apr. 1961. p 24. An 'Observer Profile', written in the calm just before the storm over his *Origins of the Second World War*.

Anon. '(Un) Quiet Flows The Don: Alan Taylor starts a 'revolution' on ITV', *TV Times*, 8, 93. 9 Aug. 1957. p 12. In it A.J.P.T. discusses his coming television lectures and his attitude to politics.

Briggs, Asa *The History of Broadcasting in the United Kingdom, Vol. 4: Sound and Vision*, Oxford U.P., 1979. Especially interesting on 'In The News' and the ban on the broadcasting of matters soon to come before Parliament.

Boyer, John W. 'A.J.P. Taylor and The Art of Modern History', *JMH*. 49, 1. Mar 1977. pp 40–72. He is shrewd on A.J.P.T.'s writings but exaggerates the impact of Pribram and Namier on him.

Burn, Gordon 'A Life in the Day of A.J.P. Taylor', *Sun Times*. 23 Oct 1977. *Magazine*. p 110. One of a series with this title; in it A.J.P.T. comments on his daily routine.

Cole, C. Robert 'A bibliography of the Works of A.J.P. Taylor', 2 parts, *Bulletin of Bibliography and Magazine Notes*. 33, 4 and 5. Jul.-Sept. and Oct.-Dec. 1976. pp 170–7, 181, 212–225. A major listing – but is far from being comprehensive, it is not annotated and suffers from numerous printing errors.

David, Anthony 'Alan Taylor's Own Big Rows', *TV Times*. 3 Dec. 1964. pp 8, 33. A brief survey of academic, political and television rows involving A.J.P.T. At the end of it there is a brief reply by A.J.P.T.

Dray, W.H. 'Concepts of Causation in A.J.P. Taylor's Account of the Origins of the Second World War', *History and Theory*, 17, 2, 1978. pp 149–74

Fieldhouse, H.N. 'Noel Buxton and A.J.P. Taylor's *The Trouble Makers*' in M. Gilbert (ed) – see below.

Foot, Michael 'The History of Mr Taylor', *Radio Times*. 30 Jul. 1976. p 6

Gilbert, Martin (ed) *A Century of Conflict 1850–1950: Essays for A.J.P. Taylor*, London, Hamish Hamilton, 1966. A *festschrift* to mark his 60th birthday.

Goldie, Grace Wyndham *Facing The Nation: Television and Politics 1936–1976*, London, Bodley Head, 1977. In chap. 5 she discusses the programme 'In The News' and why it was ended.

Haraszti, Eva 'A.J.P. Taylor at 70', *New Hungarian Quarterly*. 17, 61. Spring 1976. pp 129–32

Harrison, Brian 'Oral History and Recent Political History', *Oral History*. 1, 3. 1973. pp 30–48. This article includes comments on Beaverbrook by A.J.P.T.

Hauser, Oswald 'A.J.P. Taylor', *JMH*. 49, 1. Mar. 1977. pp. 34–9

Louis, W. Roger (ed) *The Origins of the Second World War: A.J.P. Taylor and his Critics*, New York, John Wiley and Sons, 1972

Marwick, Arthur *The Nature of History*, London, Macmillan, 1970. The sixth chap. 'The Contemporary Scene', contains a discussion of A.J.P.T.'s writings, pp 187–93. The seventh chap. 'Problems in History', has a section devoted to *The Origins of the Second World War*, pp 235–9.

Mehta, Ved *Fly and the Flybottle: Encounters with British Intellectuals*, Boston, Little, Brown, 1962

Segel, Edward B. 'A.J.P. Taylor and History', *Review of Politics*. 26. Oct. 1964. pp 531–46. Repr. in W.R. Louis (ed), *op cit*. pp 11–25

Sked, A. and Cook, C. *Crisis And Controversy: Essays in Honour of A.J.P. Taylor*, London, Macmillan, 1976. A *festschrift* to mark his 70th birthday.

Vincent, John 'Criticising Taylor', *NS*, 72, 1863, 25 Nov. 1966. pp 800–1

Watt, D. C. 'Appeasement. The Rise Of A Revisionist School?', *Political Quarterly*. 36, 2. Apr. 1965. pp 191–213

'The Historiography of Appeasement' in Sked, A. and Cook, C. (ed), *op cit.* pp 110–29
'Some Aspects of A.J.P. Taylor's Work As Diplomatic Historian', *JMH.* 49, 1. *Mar.* 1977. pp 19–33

Weintraub, Bernard 'A.J.P. Taylor, the Historian, Reflects on Europe, the British and the World', *New York Times.* 16 Jun. 1976. p 2. A.J.P.T. also comments on his two best selling books.

Williams, H. Russell 'A.J.P. Taylor' in *Historians of Modern Europe*, ed. Hans A. Schmitt, Louisiana State U.P., 1971. pp 78–94

ABBREVIATIONS

Am.Hist.Rev.	*American Historical Review*
BD.	(British Documents). *Documents on British Foreign Policy 1919–1939*, ed. Rohan Butler and Sir E. L. Woodward
Crit.	*Critique*
D.Her.	*Daily Herald*
EHR.	*English Historical Review*
En.	*Encounter*
Ev.Stan.	*Evening Standard*
FD.	(French Documents). *Documents diplomatiques francais 1871–1914*
GD.	(German Documents). *Documents on German Foreign Policy 1918–1945*
Gdn.	*Guardian*
Hist.	*History*
Hist Today.	*History Today*
HJ.	*Historical Journal*
ID.	(Italian Documents). *I documenti diplomatici italiani 1861–1943*
Int.Affairs.	*International Affairs*
JMH.	*Journal of Modern History*
Li.	*Listener*
MG.	*Manchester Guardian*
MGW.	*Manchester Guardian Weekly*
NR.	*New Republic*
NS.	*New Statesman*
NS & N.	*New Statesman and Nation*
NYRB.	*New York Review of Books*
Obs.	*Observer*
OM.	*Oxford Magazine*
P & P.	*Past and Present*
Rev.His.	*Revue Historique*
Sp.	*Spectator*
Sun.Ex.	*Sunday Express*
Sun.Pic.	*Sunday Pictorial*
T & T.	*Time and Tide*
TLS.	*Times Literary Supplement*

A: BOOKS

A1. *The Italian Problem in European Diplomacy 1847–1849*, Manchester, Manchester U.P., 1934 (Pub. of the Univ. of Manchester, 232, Historical Series, 67), viii, 252 p

A detailed narrative study of the diplomatic moves of Austria, France and Britain in response to the North Italian issue; based on archival material in Vienna, Paris and London.

He takes the theme that underneath the personal likes and dislikes of diplomats and the accidental issues which arise now and then, diplomatic history rests on the long term interests of the countries involved. Austria was afraid of French intervention in Italy. France, in the last analysis, was afraid of the emergence of a strong kingdom of Northern Italy on her frontier. Britain favoured such a development if it helped maintain the Balance of Power (and thereby her basic interest of peace). Palmerston, a very skilful diplomat, was more committed to the maintenance of peace than to Italian nationalism.

(a) Repr. Manchester, Manchester U.P.; New York, Barnes and Noble, 1970

Reviews

(i) 'A Study in Diplomacy', *TLS*. 1720. 17 Jan. 1935. p 27

'. . . this most interesting study . . . a valuable contribution to our knowledge of the interplay of influences and forces outside Italy by which the issue of revolution was largely determined. But it is more than this; it . . . reveals the broad principles which in the end always determine national policies in spite of the haphazard way in which diplomacy seems to function.'

(ii) J.P.T.B. (Bury), *Cambridge Review*. 56, 1380. 3 May 1935. p 351

'A synthesis which usefully fills a gap in diplomatic history.' But he criticises it for not considering Russia and Prussia, for not considering the economic aspect of British policy, and for having footnotes which are not digested into the text.

(iii) D.W.B. (Brogan), *OM*. 53, 17. 2 May 1935. p 553

'References to the Napoleonic empire as 'the worst (because the most extensive) tyranny since the time of Attila . . . ' are not encouraging, but once Mr. Taylor has unburdened his soul in this fashion, he sets to work to tell his story with great skill and original learning. The result is a really important contribution to our knowledge of the *Risorgimento*, of the doom of Austria and of the methods of Lord Palmerston.'

(iv) W.K. Hancock, *Hist*. 20, 77. Jun. 1935. pp 82–3.

'It gets away from egocentric nationalism and treats Italy's *Quarantotto* as a problem of the European order.'

(v) Kent Roberts Greenfield, *Am.Hist.R*. 41, 3. Apr. 1936. pp 539–40

He regrets that it does not deal with Russia or Prussia and that it is written without research on Italy; hence it does not cover European diplomacy. 'What it actually contains is a fresh and sometimes brilliantly illuminating study of the policies followed by the British, French and Austrian governments . . . ' in dealing with the Italian question. 'Unsatisfied with the usual account of 'day-to-day diplomacy', Mr. Taylor constantly refers the action of the diplomats to the deep persistencies of interest which to the thoughtful give to international relations 'the appearance of a battle of Platonic ideas'.

A2. *Germany's First Bid For Colonies 1884–1885. A Move in Bismarck's European Policy*, London, Macmillan, 1938 (Studies in Modern History; general ed. L.B. Namier), v, 103 p

A detailed narrative study of Germany's diplomatic

moves at this time, which he argues were intended to bring about a Franco-German alignment on the grounds of common hostility to Britain. It is based on the printed British, French and German foreign policy documents and also on the British Foreign Office and the Granville Papers.

He argues that Bismarck's demands were not the result of domestic pressures on him but were part of his foreign policy. 'The German colonies were the accidental by-product of an abortive Franco-German entente'. (p 6) Bismarck is depicted as the rare statesman who has elaborate deep laid plans. These he pursued by unscrupulous means; but unlike his successors who lacked his genius, Bismarck's aggressive actions did not lead to disaster.

(a) Repr. New York, Archon Books, 1967

(b) Pub. in pbk. in 'The Norton Library', New York, W.W. Norton, 1970

A.J.P.T. in reviewing Eric Eyck's *Bismarck*, Vol. 3 (*see* G275) in 1947 observed that Eyck 'agrees with my interpretation . . . that, insofar as the colonial demands had any purpose in foreign policy, their object was to improve relations with France by a trumped-up dispute with England; but he is of course right to insist that they were directed against the German Left even more than against England; and I recant anything of mine which may have obscured this'. (*see also* A8, pp 215–8)

A.J.P.T. in reviewing the *festschrift* to Harry Rudin in 1969 (*see* G1235) observed of an essay by H.R. Turner: 'He rejects the attempt which I made years ago to fit this conversion into Bismarck's diplomacy and argues that Bismarck was acting mainly from fear of otherwise being left out. Colonialism was thus part of the change to protective tariffs. There is some evidence in favour of this view. I now incline to believe that the principal explanation lay in Bismarck's bad temper, when the British government failed to do what he wanted. This explanation sounds trivial, but there is more evidence for it than for any other.'

Reviews

(i) 'Germany's Colonial Empire: An Accident of Policy', *TLS*. 1885. 19 Mar. 1938. p 178

'A brilliant study . . . fulfills the highest standards of scholarship . . . His narrative powers and pleasantly ironic style at once arouse his readers' interest and retain it to the close.'

(ii) 'How Germany Obtained Colonies', E.L. Woodward, *Sp*. 5726. 26 Mar. 1938. pp 537–8

'A model of the way in which diplomatic history should be written . . . To a certain extent, perhaps, Mr. Taylor overstates the case . . . Mr. Taylor might have given a little more space to an estimate of the strength of the colonial movement in Germany . . . '

(iii) R.P. (Richard Pares), *OM*. 56, 20. 19 May 1938. pp 652–3

'Mr. Taylor accepts, and even exaggerates, the fairly probable opinion that Bismarck was hardly interested at all in the subject-matter of his colonial disputes with England, but worked them up in order to obtain the advantage of a common diplomatic alignment with France (Mr. Taylor attributes to 'the German mind' the idea that it was necessary to quarrel with England in order to make friends with France; but it was, in fact, a sound and pretty old established trick of diplomacy)' . . . 'Diplomatic historians – even believers in 'pure' diplomacy like Mr. Taylor – ought to know that their explanations of history must be barren and will probably be mistaken if they will not attend to the subject-matter of diplomacy. It cannot be dismissed with undergraduate levity.'

(iv) W.K.H. (Hancock), *Int.Affairs*. 17, 4. Jul-Aug. 1938. p 558

'Mr. Taylor has already won for himself a foremost place amongst the younger diplomatic historians . . . The reader of this volume is probably expected to conclude that something very similar is true today. The book will also suggest that the student of world politics should draw for their rules of interpretation rather less on Marx and rather more on Machiavelli.'

(v) Gavin B. Henderson, *Hist.* 23, 91. Dec. 1938. pp 276–7

'Dr. Taylor's thesis that "the German colonies were the accidental by-product of an abortive Franco-German entente' will not bear examination . . . What should have been a most tentative hypothesis is described throughout the book – in the title, the text, and even the index – as unassailable fact.'

(vi) Mary E. Townsend, *Am.Hist.R.* 44, 4. Jul. 1939. pp 899–901

'He presses his thesis somewhat too far when he claims that Bismarck's foreign policy is the sole explanation of the origin of Germany's colonial empire.'

A3. (A) *The Habsburg Monarchy 1815–1918: A History of the Austrian Empire and Austria-Hungary*, London, Macmillan, 1941, xii, 316 p

A narrative history of the Habsburg Monarchy, focussing on 'the imperial organisation, with its weaknesses, its difficulties, its successes, and its final failure'; with discussion of economic and social changes and foreign policy very much subordinate to this. The book brings out the tensions between the 'historic' nationalities of the Empire – the Germans, Magyars, Poles and Italians – and the 'submerged' nationalities – the Czechs, Serbs, Rumanians and Little Russians.

In the preface he comments, 'The story has no moral, except the banal moral that people can live happily, either as individuals or in communities only on the basis of mutual tolerance and respect . . . I have not pretended that the victory of the new nationalities was more than a reversal of the previous order. The legacy of history is such that there is no conceivable settlement of Central Europe which will not involve injustice to some of those living there; this is no excuse for tolerating the maximum of injustice, but all the same it would be romantic to deny or conceal it.'

He also notes in the preface that the first draft of the book was virtually completed by the outbreak of the Second World War in Europe. The book (like the 1948 version) has the dedication, 'To L.B. Namier, This Token of Gratitude, Affection and Esteem.'

Reviews

(i) 'Dynasty in Fetters: Why The Habsburg Monarchy Fell', *TLS*. 2038. 22 Feb. 1941. p 88

'It is a work of 'book learning'. He has read widely and understood much ... If he has not mastered the essay form – the form usually employed by the one or two Austrian writers who had real insight into Habsburg affairs – he has written a book by no means unreadable and fairly accurate.'

A.J.P.T. replied, in *TLS*. 2039. 1 Mar. 1941. p 103, to the criticism in the review that his book was not based on 'first-hand observation' by observing that Gibbon and Macaulay had been similarly handicapped.

(ii) 'Austria of the Past', F.M. Powicke, *MG*. 28 Mar. 1941. p 6

'A very able book. He is not only a master of his subject: he knows how to present it, and he is thorough. ... It is the work of a good scholar who, without pose or effort, beats the men of words at their own game. He is, in short, a very intelligent man who knows what he is writing about.'

(iii) 'Austrian Empire', J. de C. (Courcey), *Free Europe*. 3, 37. 4 Apr. 1941. p 227

'We can well be grateful to him for expounding in considerable detail the elements of the vast problems which faced the Austrian Empire in the nineteenth century, even if we cannot accept his conclusion that there is no place for the Habsburgs any more in Europe.'

(iv) Louis Einstein, *Hist*. 26, 101. Jun. 1941. pp 83–4

He 'is generally fair in his judgement. He writes with intelligence, and his opinion is often shrewd. But after having breathed the close atmosphere of Austrian distortions and quarrels, even an Oxford scholar cannot escape altogether from the miasma of hatred which poisoned the political life of the Dual Monarchy.' Objects to the treatment of King Peter of Serbia (p 259), of Italy (p 268) and of the Italian troops at Vittoria Veneto (p 300). Doubts if he 'has sufficiently appreciated the architectural structure of the Habsburg Monarchy or is fair to its accomplishment.'

(v) R.W. Seton-Watson, *EHR*. 57, 227. Jul. 1942. p 389–92

'Scholarly, well proportioned and realistic', 'Mr. Taylor's judgements are acute, balanced and admirably fair, even when he reveals very definite sympathies.'

(vi) A.F. Pribram (source not identified)

'A clear and concise account.' 'Little attention is devoted to foreign policy, and this seems to me a defect of the book. The connection between external and domestic policy is close in all states, but nowhere closer than in the Danubian Monarchy. It can be shown that all the important events in its domestic policy from the Vienna Congress till the collapse of the Empire were determined by successes or failures in the field of foreign policy.'

(vii) Oscar Jaszi, *JMH*. 14. 4 Dec. 1942. pp 538–40

'He has accomplished his task not only skilfully but brilliantly.' He is 'successful in penetrating into the real spirit of this strange experiment. Few foreigners have understood the complication of this problem as clear as this author . . . He belongs to that rare class of historians who are able to supplement the factual evidence with a high grade of psychological insight and artistic imagination . . . What we read in his book is not dead history but an often thrilling analysis of personalities and mass psychological insights.' He has 'a highly individualistic style, a quick wit compressing the essence of personality or of a period in a few admirably formed phrases – a quality reminding us of some of the best essayists'. However feels he is too critical of Kossuth, too appreciative of Deak, and regrets the omission of Koloman Tisza.

(viii) Robert J. Kerner, *Am.Hist.R.* 48, 2. Jan. 1943. pp 334–4

'The best thus far written in any language in fundamental analysis, in keen penctration, and in literary style. It abounds in pungent descriptions and in expressions demonstrating remarkable insight, even if at times there is a touch of the facetious or even the flippant concealed within.'

(B) *The Habsburg Monarchy 1809–1918: A History of the Austrian Empire and Austria-Hungary*, new edn., London, Hamish Hamilton, 1948, repr. 1951, 1952, 1955, 1957, 1960, 1961, 1964, 1972, 279p

In the preface he states that the book is 'an entirely rewritten version'. The manuscript was completed in November 1947. He observes that one of the main changes is a more full treatment of foreign policy. 'The Habsburg Monarchy, more than most great powers, was an organisation for conducting foreign policy; and its fate was determined quite as much by foreign affairs as the behaviour of its peoples.' He states that the other principal change was to remove 'the liberal illusion' that the Habsburg Monarchy could have survived if people had been more sensible in some of their actions. 'These regrets are no part of the duty of a historian, especially when the story which he tells makes it clear, time after time, that there were no opportunities to be lost. The conflict between a super-national dynastic state and the national principle had to be fought to the finish; and so, too had the conflict between the master and subject nations . . . The national principle, once launched, had to work itself out to its conclusions.'

The 1941 version has passages such as: 'It was a disaster for the Empire that its forceful statesmen were never conciliatory, and its conciliatory statesmen were never forceful', (A, p 175), which indeed are removed from thc 1948 version; and the later version has additional passages vigorously dismissing 'the Austrian idea' (e.g. B, pp 234–5). The later version has a more lively style. For example, Chapter 2 starts as follows in the two versions:

'There has never been an Austrian people, only the peoples over whom the House of Austria ruled. Austrian meant an inhabitant of the Empire, or, more positively, one who was loyal to the dynasty . . . ' (A, p 16)

'Francis I, told of an Austrian patriot, answered impatiently: 'But is he a patriot for me?' The Emperior was needlessly meticulous. Austria was an Imperial organisation, not a country; and to be Austrian was to be free of national feeling – not to possess a nationality.' (B, p 25)

The 1948 version is also marked by comparisons with Russia's role in the Second World War, a tougher attitude to the Germans, and it tones down a eulogy to Masaryk.

(a) Pub. Harmondsworth, Penguin Books in Association with Hamish Hamilton, as Peregrine pbk. Y41, 1964 (repr. 1967, 1970 and 1976); New York, Harper, 1965; Chicago U.P., 1976, 304p

(b) Trans. into Slovene, including 'Spremna beseda' by Fran Zwitter (pp 325–334), Ljubljana, 1956, 335 p

Reviews

(i) 'The Austrian Empire', *TLS*. 2456. 26 Feb. 1949. p 132

Comments that foreign policy is dealt with somewhat more adequately but feels that in removing 'the liberal illusion' he has become more dogmatic: 'It is not easy to resist the impression that in rewriting his book Mr. Taylor has indulged a dogmatic temper at the expense of a well-considered appraisal of men and things.' Overall the reviewer finds it 'fuller and more detailed, though less easily readable than his original volume'.

(ii) 'The Habsburgs', F.W. Deakin, *MG*. 4 Mar. 1949. p 3 Repr. *MGW*. 60, 10. 10 Mar. p 10

'The new version is coloured by an acid realism and a professed belief in the fatal inevitability of the events which pass under review.'

(iii) C.A. Macartney, *Hist*. 37, 125. Oct. 1950.

pp. 273–4

'... this edition, like its predecessor, contains much that is brilliant and much that is only flashy ... Mr. Taylor's merits as a historian are considerable. They include acute perception, ability to find a way through tangles, and great skill in making short *précis* of long sources ... His weaknesses, which unfortunately have grown perceptibly since the *Habsburg Monarchy* was first issued, include cock-sureness and a complete intolerance of those whom he disapproves, whether living or dead. Everybody has to be scored off, and with very few exceptions, almost everyone who figures in his pages is a villain, an imposter or, more frequently still, a fool.'

A4. *The Course of German History: A Survey of the Development of Germany Since 1815*, London, Hamish Hamilton, 1945; New York, Coward-McCann, 1946, 229 p, 4 maps

'1848: the Year of German Liberalism', chap. 4, pp 68–89, repr. in *1848 : A Turning Point?*, ed. Melvin Kranzberg, Boston, D.C. Heath, 1959, pp 24–39

A narrative history of Germany from 1792 to the Anglo-Soviet alliance of 1941; with the first chapter providing a brief survey from Charlemagne's time to the French Revolution. The manuscript was finished in September 1944 and it was published in July 1945.

His interpretation emphasises Germany's continual drive to dominate central and eastern Europe. English and French liberals failed to see this brutal side of Germany – 'her eastern face, the face which she wore towards the Slavs, the face of the intolerant exterminator and overlord'. (p 125) He condemns the 'good Germans', liberals and socialists, for not wresting power from the old ruling class – and so allowing militarism and Nazism to endanger European civilisation. (p 166) Indeed he argues that nearly all Germans – liberals and socialists as well as Junkers and industrialists – were committed to a Greater Germany. The German liberals whom he admires are those 'who saw in Switzerland, and not in the militarist Reich, the true model of German political civilisation, and who dreamt of transforming Germany into an association of free Swiss States'. (pp 210–1) He sees the expansionist foreign policies and lack of freedom internally to be profoundly linked; thus of inter-war Germany he writes, 'Only by renouncing foreign ambitions could Germany become a democracy'. (p 247) He also argues that Europe must divide Germany or be ruled by her, and blames France, Russia and Britain for allowing a united Germany repeatedly to try to dominate the continent. The final paragraph of the 1945 edition applauds 'the greatest act of statesmanship of the century – say, rather of modern times – (when) Winston Churchill proclaimed the alliance of England and Russia'.

(a) Repr. London, Hamish Hamilton, 1946, 1951, 1954, 1956, 1959, 1963, 231 p

The last paragraph in the 1945 edition, after praising the formation of the Anglo-Soviet alliance, ended: 'The 'many great nations', whom Bismarck had dismissed with scorn, at last awoke. Germany owed her unity and success to the disunion of her neighbours. That was now at an end. There will be no German 'New Order' in Europe. Instead there will be a 'New Order' in Germany which will owe nothing to German efforts. It will be imposed by the united strength of England, Russia, and the United States; and it will prove impermanent unless these three powers remain as united in peace as they have been in war.' Subsequent editions have omitted this and added two extra paragraphs taking the story to the Potsdam Conference, July 1945.

(b) Pub. in pbk. London, Methuen in University Paperbacks, U.P. 37, 1961, repr. xi, 271 p, 4 maps

This edition has a preface (pp vii–xi), in which he discusses the history of the book and also his attitude to Germany.

(c) Pub. in pbk. New York, Capricorn Books, 1962

(d) Trans. into Italian by Alberto Aquarone and

pub. as *Storia della Germania*, Bari, Editori Laterza, 1963, Vol. 579 in their Biblioteca di cultura moderna, 407 p

Repr. Milan, Longanesi, 1971, vol. 281 in their I Libri Pocket series, 289 p

(e) Trans. into Hebrew by Chaim Isaak, Tel Aviv, Machbarot Lesifud Publishing House, 1974, 264 p

Reviews

(i) 'Dream-Play of the German Century: Power For Power's sake', *TLS*. 2278. 29 Sept. 1945. pp 457–9

'Years of study, usefully recapitulated in lectures and tutorials, have equipped him for the task . . . a rough realism and independence, blended with a quick and lively spirit, debar him from the abstract and ponderous, systematic and yet vague thinking of the German. Still his combination of ruggedness and impressionable vivacity renders him also impatient of the careful labour of perfecting and polishing – he discovers precious stones by the handful, and puts them half-cut into circulation . . . The basic ideas of Mr. Taylor's book are sound, but would have profited by further careful examination and unfolding . . . the book should prove of high value in the study of the German problem.'

This review by L.B. Namier repr. as 'The Course of German History', in his *Facing East*, Hamish Hamilton, 1947, pp 25–40

(ii) R. Birley, *Int. Affairs*. 22, 1. Jan. 1946. pp 136–7

Praises the main part of the book, 1815–1919, but observes that 'It is too facile an attempt to discover some continuity in German history which can compare Charlemagne with Hitler' and he objects to the treatment of the inter-war period, 'The economic crises of the late nineteen-twenties is minimised. In the effort to make the Nazis, not in large measure the result of this anarchy, but a normal development quite to be expected, of German history, Mr. Taylor nearly succeeds in making them respectable.'

(iii) Sigmund Neumann, *Am.Hist.R.* 52, 4. Jul. 1947. pp 730–3

'... a challenging essay, packed with substantial summaries and spiced with brilliant observations, reflecting his scholarly maturity, his lucid mind and his Vienna training under Pribram and the Austrian school of Friedjung and Redlich ... An answer to a burning query, it is an impatient book, vivid and tempestuous, pointed and pugnacious, concise and overzealous, severe and sarcastic, ambitious and angry. Grandiose in style it often overshoots its mark. The profound is mixed with the wisecrack. It has the shortcomings of its virtues. It will shock the scholarly reader but it must challenge him too. A returning American scholar reports that it challenges equally German historians, some of whom admit that it will make them rethink their modern national history.'

A5. *From Napoleon to Stalin: Comments on European History*, London, Hamish Hamilton, 1950, repr. 1953; New York, British Book Centre, 1950, 224 p

A collection of centennial essays, review articles and contemporary pieces plus a pamphlet and the introduction to a book of essays by other authors. It includes one piece, The Austrian Illusion, not previously published.

In the Intro. he writes that the underlying theme is the one which has run through European history since 1789 – 'the search for stability in an unstable world. The great revolution destroyed tradition as the basis for society; ever since men have been seeking for something to take its place.'

Contents

Part One : Historical

1. Napoleon: (1) On Himself (Sept. 1948. *see* G294, A15 *and* A17)
   (2) The Verdict of History (Feb. 1949. *see* G317 *and* A15 *and* A17)
2. Napoleon and Gentz (Dec. 1946. *see* G258 *and* A15)

3. 1848: (1) Year of Revolution (Jan. 1948. *see* E14, A15 *and* A17)
   (2) The French Revolution (Feb. 1948. *see* E15, A15 *and* A17)
   (3) Vienna and Berlin (Mar. 1948. *see* E16, A15 *and* A17)
   (4) The Slav Congress (Jun. 1948. *see* E18, A15 *and* A17)
4. 1848: Opening of An Era (1948. *see* B2, A15 *and* A17)
5. De Tocqueville in 1848 (Nov. 1948. *see* G303, A15 *and* A17)
6. Francis Joseph: The Last Age of the Habsburgs (Dec. 1948. *see* E23, A15 *and* A17)
7. Bismarck: The Man of German Destiny (Jul. 1948. *see* E20 *and* A17)
8. The Ruler in Berlin (Dec. 1948. *see* G304, A15 *and* A17)
9. German Unity (Mar. 1944. *see* E7, E8 *and* A17)
10. French North Africa: Creation of a Century (Nov. 1942. *see* E5)
11. Fashoda (Sept. 1948. *see* E21 *and* A15)
12. The Entente Cordiale (Apr. 1944. *see* E9, A15 *and* A17)
13. The Secret of the Third Republic (Feb. 1948. *see* G284, A15 *and* A17)
14. Tangier in Diplomacy (Jul. 1945. *see* E11)
15. Two Prime Ministers: (1) Lord John Russell (Mar. 1947. *see* E12 *and* A21)
   (2) Lord Salisbury (Apr. 1947. *see* E13 *and* A21)

Part Two: Contemporary

1. M. Flandin and French Policy (Jan. 1948. *see* G280 *and* A17)
2. Munich Ten Years After (Oct. 1948. *see* E22 *and* A17)
3. The Diplomacy of M. Bonnet (Nov. 1946 and Jun. 1948. *see* G256, G290 *and* A17)
4. General Gamelin: Or How To Lose (Mar. 1947

and Oct. 1948. *see* G266, G299 *and* A17)
5. The End of the Third Republic (Aug. 1947. *see* G276)
6. Dr. Schact's Defence (Jan. 1949. *see* G307)
7. Jackal Diplomacy (Dec. 1948. *see* G305)
8. The Supermen: Hitler and Mussolini (May 1949. *see* G325, A15 *and* A17)
9. The Springs of Soviet Diplomacy (May 1948. *see* E17 *and* A17)
10. A Vanished World: The Memoirs of Cordell Hull (Nov. 1948. *see* G300)
11. The Austrian Illusion (Written for *MG*. but not pub. *see also* G298 *and* A17)
12. Trieste (1945 *see* C2). It is reprinted here with a postscript (1949).
13. Tito and Stalin (Jan. 1949. *see* F37)
14. Two Congresses: (1) The Paris Congress of the History of 1848 (Apr. 1948. *see* F34)
    (2) The Wroclaw Congress of Intellectuals (Sept. 1948. *see* F35)

Reviews

(i) 'The Brighter Side of History', Leonard Woolf, *NS & N*. 39, 1004. 3 Jun. 1950. pp 836, 838

'He never fails in his effort both to amuse and instruct his reader . . . the dullness of facts, the stupidity of the human race, the tragedy of European history brightened up by the epigram, the bon mot, the scintillating quip . . . His essays are . . . better when they deal with persons than with events.'

'The truth can never be wholly black or completely white as Mr. Taylor so often represents it in his clever and uncompromising sentences . . . The truth is either a kaleidoscope of different colours or a dirty grey; that is why it can so rarely be stated epigrammatically.'

(ii) 'An Unstable World', Elizabeth Wiskemann, *Sp*. 184, 6364. 16 Jun. 1950. pp 830, 832

The review is very critical of the volume, regretting that the essays have not been revised and that the volume does not live up to its title. 'All this is very disappointing because Mr. Taylor very often is brilliant and very often states unpopular facts which it would be of major importance that the British public, or a larger section of it, should grasp.'

(iii) 'Comments on Modern Europe', *TLS*. 2527. 7 Jul. 1950. pp 413–4

The 'volume is valuable for such intermittent flashes of insight lighting up a whole period rather than for any systematic presentation . . . While it would probably be fair to sum up the volume . . . as an obituary of Liberalism, Mr. Taylor's own deepest roots are in the liberal tradition. His inherent tendency to believe that God is on the side of the small battalions is well illustrated . . . (e.g. Part 2, 13 and 14 (2)).'

(iv) 'From Napoleon to Stalin', R.T. Clarke, *MG*. 18 Jul. 1950. p 4

'Read as a collection the essays suggest a constant trailing of the coat, and the piling up of audacious opinion produces the effect of a firework display that has gone on too long.

. . . Mr. Taylor can sketch a character in which many of the details are wrong and yet make the whole true as well as convincing; he can appreciate opposites without being catholic in his sympathies, and above all give dry facts life.'

(v) Dwight E. Lee, *Am.Hist.R*. 56, 4. Jul. 1951. p 938

'Taylor writes smoothly and brilliantly – sometimes too brilliantly. . . . There are many well-coined phrases which anyone might wish he had made himself . . . But there are just as many questionable generalizations . . . Such aphorisms and half-truths shake serious students out of thought-ruts but are pitfalls to the unwary. While these essays whet the appetite, they fail to satisfy.'

A6. *Rumours of Wars*, London, Hamish Hamilton; New York, British Book Centre, 1952, viii, 262 p

A collection of historical essays, book reviews and contemporary articles. It includes two pieces published for the first time: Bismarck and Europe and The Traditions of British Foreign Policy. The book is dedicated to Robert Boothby, W.J. Brown and Michael Foot, who regularly appeared with him on the BBC television programme 'In the News' (*see* Appendix) and then on Independent Television's 'Free Speech'.

Contents :

1. History in England (Aug. 1950. *see* D4)
2. History Without Morality (Nov. 1951. *see* G456)
3. Tory History (May 1950. *see* G378 *and* A21)
4. *Democracy in America* (Sept. 1951. *see* G443)
5. The Man of December (Dec. 1951. *see* E30, A15 *and* A17)
6. Crimea: The War That Would Not Boil (Feb. 1951. *see* D5, A15 *and* A17)
7. Bismarck's Morality (Aug. 1950. *see* G390, A15 *and* A17)
8. Nietzche and the Germans (Jun. 1951. *see* G435 *and* A17)
9. Bismarck and Europe (approx. 1951. Not previously published. *see* A15 *and* A17)
10. The Failure Of The Habsburg Monarch (Apr. 1951. *see* G424, A15 *and* A17)
11. Thomas Garrigue Masaryk (Mar. 1950. *see* E27, A15 *and* A17)
12. The Traditions of British Foreign Policy (Jan. 1951. *see* Appendix (a), 34 *and* A17).
13. Prelude to Fashoda: The Question of the Upper Nile, 1894–5 (Jan. 1950. *see* D2 *and* A21)
14. British Policy in Morocco, 1886–1902 (Jul. 1951. *see* D6)
15. The Jameson Raid (Jan. 1952. *see* G460 *and* A21)
16. The Boer War (Oct. 1949. *see* E26 *and* A21)
17. "Joe" at his Zenith (Jun. 1951. *see* G430 *and* A21)
18. Queen Victoria and the Constitution (Jan. 1951. *see* E29 *and* A21)
19. Northcliffe and Dawson (Apr. 1952. *see* G473)
20. Old Diplomacy – and New (Mar. 1951. *see* F47 *and* A17)
21. Spain and the Axis (Apr. 1951. *see* G422 *and* A17)

22. Full Speed to Munich (Sept. 1949. *see* G344 *and* A17)
23. From Munich to Prague: (1) British Version (Nov. 1950 and Aug. 1951. *see* G410, G439 *and* A17)
    (2) German Version (Dec. 1951. *see* G457 *and* A17)
24. Stalin and the West (Dec. 1950. *see* G414)
25. On the Eve (May 1952. *see* G480)
26. Thus Spake Hitler (Jan. 1952. *see* G458 *and* A17)
27. Another "Good German" (Oct. 1950. *see* G402)
28. France in Defeat (Apr. 1950. *see* G373 *and* A17)
29. De Gaulle: Triumph of a Legend (Nov. 1950. *see* G407 *and* A17)
30. America's War (Jun. 1950. *see* G382 *and* A17)
31. Can We Agree With the Russians? (Mar. 1951. *see* F45 *and* A17)
32. Is Stalin a Statesman? (Nov. 1951. *see* F62 *and* A17)
33. Mr. "X" Rides Again (Feb. 1952. *see* G465)
34. The Turn of the Half Century (Dec. 1950. *see* F41 *and* A17)
35. Up from Utopia: How Two Generations Survived Their Wars (Oct. 1950. *see* E28 *and* A17)

Reviews

(i) 'Mr. Taylor Rides Again', Asa Briggs, *NS & N.* 44, 1135. 6 Dec. 1952. p 698

'This is a brilliant book; almost every sentence crackles and there is often a whiff of fire and brimstone in the air.' However the reviewer does criticise 6, 'he is more intent in this case in manufacturing phrases than clarifying a particularly difficult problem in nineteenth century history' and concludes 'the morals he draws from the story are really the preconceptions with which he begins'.

(ii) 'History and Journalism', *TLS.* 2655. 19 Dec. 1952. p 847

The reviewer finds 2, 9, 13, 14 and 35 to be 'solid

contributions to historical thinking' and the remainder to be 'short, sparkling pieces' for the general reader. Of these, the reviewer writes, 'Generally ... Mr. Taylor shows a flawless mastery of the art of fitting subject to style and scope. Like every good journalist he knows that an effective article is built up, at the cost of much over-simplification, round one or two outstanding points; and he makes his points so competently and sharply that the critical reader will be conscious that he has been made to think the issue over again. This is a book which deserves the overworked epithet 'stimulating'.'

The reviewer deems him to be 'a historian of high quality – one of the outstanding British historians of today'; but feels that there is 'a certain lack of depth' in his writings.

(iii) 'Contentious But Creative', Martin Wight, *Sp.* 190, 6516. 15 May 1953. pp 639–40

'When Mr. Taylor is praised or disparaged for his brilliance, pungency, provocativeness and wit, it often means that the strength of his historical writing goes unrecognised. With the exception of Sir Charles Webster, he is our most distinguished international historian, the one who offers the most creative interpretation of the European balance of power and of tensions and limitations of diplomacy.' The reviewer praises the essays, but observes that they are 'peppered with half-truths and overstatements. It is the price of assiduous journalism ... '

'Mr. Taylor is distinguished from so many professional historians by possessing not only a trenchant style but also a historiographical personality. This is the reason why he is so readable and worth reading.'

(iv) Sidney B. Fay, *Am.Hist.R.* 69, 3. Apr. 1954. pp 590–1

'Mr. Taylor is a master of brilliant paradox, startling juxtapositions, and dogmatic brevity.'

A7. *The Struggle for Mastery in Europe 1848–1918* (1st vol. to be pub. in The Oxford History of Modern Europe; general ed. Alan Bullock, F.W.D. Deakin),

3 folding maps Oxford, Clarendon Press, 1954, (repr. 1957, 1960, 1963) and New York, 1954, xxxvi, 638 p, 18 maps incl.

Pub. in pbk. London, Oxford U.P., 1971 and New York, A Galaxy Book, Oxford U.P., 1971

Pp 518–3 repr. as 'The Outbreak of War' in *The Outbreak of the First World War: Who Was Responsible?* ed. D.W. Lee, Boston, D.C. Heath, 1958, revised edn. 1963

The book is a careful survey of European diplomatic history. A.J.P.T. later commented that his Ford lectures were 'a gesture of repentance for having written recently a substantial volume of what I may call 'respectable diplomatic history''. (A10, p 12)

He argues: 'Ever since the defeat of The French revolution Europe had conducted its affairs merely by adjusting the claims of sovereign states against each other as they arose. In 1914 Germany had felt strong enough to challenge this system and had aimed to substitute her hegemony over the rest.' (p 568) The volume ends in January 1918, with Europe ceasing to be the centre of the world and the future being between two world powers, the Soviet Union and the United States.

(a) Trans. into Italian by Emilio Bianchi and pub. as *L'Europa Delle Grandi Potenze: Da Metternich A Lenin*, Bari, Editori Laterza, 1961, 885 p

Repr. in pbk. in 2 vols. in their Universale Series, 848 p

(b) Trans. into Russian, intro. by M.N. Mashkin (pp 5–29), 644 p

(c) Trans. into Hebrew by A.D. Shapir, Israel, Hakibbutz Hameuchad Publishing House, 1963

(d) Trans. into Serbo-Croat by Milutin Drecun, Sarajevo, Vesilin Maslesa, 1968, 592 p

In a review in 1942 he wrote, 'It is strange that . . . the story of the Struggle for Mastery of Europe has never been attempted . . . It would be a superb opportunity for an English historian, if one could be found with real standards of scholarship and understanding'. (G172)

Reviews

(i) 'Before the Ball Was Over', Asa Briggs, *NS & N.* 48, 1235. 6 Nov. 1954. pp 586, 588

'Sometimes we need to rest and think three times about his brilliant epigrams; sometimes we pine for a closer study of the economic and social background of diplomacy . . . On more than one occasion we feel the necessity for applying microscopes as well as binoculars to the detailed scrutiny of particular problems and judgements. But whatever we do will be influenced by what he has done, for he has re-opened the nineteenth century rather than closed it down.'

(ii) 'European Diplomatic History', *TLS.* 2756. 26 Nov. 1954. pp 749–50

'Diplomatic history in the strictest sense . . . an infinity of patient detail . . . an outstanding book.' The reviewer feels that it is a corrective to W. Langer's volumes which are 'over-indulgent to German manoeuvres' as it 'leans on the other side' and observes, 'If Mr. Taylor would shed his distaste for ideas, recognise that history would not be worth writing or reading if it had no meaning and cease to give so many hostages to the assumption that the important explanations in history are to be found in the conscious purposes and foresights of the *dramatis personae*, he would stand in the front rank of living historians.'

(iii) 'Europe's Perpetual Quadrille', Gordon A. Craig, *Saturday Review.* 38. 16 Jul. 1955. p 28

'What makes this the best study of European diplomacy since W.C. Langer's volumes on the post-1870 period is his ability to keep the major developments of the period clearly before his readers, while at the same time providing them with circumstantial and absorbing accounts of the policies and ambitions of individual powers and statesmen, the changing diplomatic alignments, and the crises and wars which filled the period.'

(iv) Bernadotte E. Schmitt, *Am.Hist.R.* 60, 4. Jul. 1955. pp 880–2

He praises it, commenting that within the limits of an almost exclusively diplomatic history 'Mr. Taylor has written an admirable book. He has mastered the enormous quantity of new evidence published since 1919 . . . ' 'Throughout the book Mr. Taylor forms his own judgements and constantly challenges conventional opinions . . . He has a fine gift of making points by contrast.'

(v) Robert A. Spence, *Canadian Historical Review.* 36, 4. Dec. 1955. pp 364–5

'He has produced a brilliant book which will take its place as indispensable reading for every student of European history in the nineteenth century. It is characteristically mistitled. The 'struggle for mastery' is evidently the German quest for domination . . . '

(vi) C.W. Crawley, *Hist.* 61, 141–3. Feb-Oct. 1956. pp 263–4

'In working out this theme, not in itself novel, Mr. Taylor is original in keeping his eye relentlessly on the ball of power . . . and, in dismissing all else as irrelevant to his purpose, and consequently in his caustic judgements upon almost every actor on the stage . . . this is the work of a serious, acute and extremely well read writer, who stimulates more than he annoys and redeems his acidity by his zest.'

A8. *Bismarck: The Man and the Statesman*, London, Hamish Hamilton, 1955, repr. 1956, 1960, 1964, 1971, 1978; New York, Knopf 1955, 286 p, 6 illus. 1 map

A biography of Bismarck which focusses on broad sweeps of foreign policy and the political juggling of domestic policy. Bismarck is depicted as a very shrewd conservative who hoped to preserve Junker ascendency in Germany but who was led by events to accept German unification and other dramatic changes in policy. For A.J.P.T. the diplomatic reality in Europe was German strength in the centre of the continent. This could only be contained by Russia and England, whilst 'a war between England and Russia would give Germany the effortless mastery of Europe'. (p 219) In Bismarck's later career 'his only object was to maintain the peace of Europe'. (p 227) Bismarck's attitude to Parliamentary majorities is compared with that of Sir Robert Peel's over the Corn Laws; his attitude to foreign policy 1871–8 compared with that of Gladstone 1868–74; and more generally his outlook is compared with that of Disraeli.

His treatment of the German colonies (pp 215–8, also pp 197–8) modifies the views in A2 to take more account of domestic politics; though he still suggests that 'perhaps . . . this had been a secondary consideration all along.' (218) His treatment of the monarchy and its powers in Germany modifies that in A4.

(a) Pub. as a Grey Arrow pbk. (*G66*), London, Arrow Books 1961; in pbk. London, Hamish Hamilton (minus illus. and map) 1965; and as a N.E.L. Mentor book, London, New English Library 1968

(b) Trans. into German by Willie and Barbaba Klau, Hamburg, Stuttgart, 1961

Pub. in pbk. Munich, R. Piper, 1962, p 278

This has an intro. by A.J.P.T. (pp 7–9) in which he explains that as a nineteenth – century historian he had to find out what Bismarck really did and to explain his successes, mistakes and failures. He states that the book is based exclusively on printed sources; that he has never seen an original document in Bismarck's handwriting or visited Friedrichsruh or Varzin. He also gives his view that history can do no more than give us a better understanding of the past. Although he is an English radical and a socialist in private life, as a historian his only aim is to discover the truth about the past.

(c) Repr. in pbk. New York, Random House, 1967 and in pbk. as a Vintage Book (V387), New York, Vintage Books, 1967. These have an additional page at the end, giving biographical details of A.J.P.T.

In his revised bibliography to his Bismarck entry in *The New Encyclopedia Britannica, Macropaedia,*

Vol. 2, (*see* D15) he notes of this book that it is 'largely an expansion of the present article'.

In reviewing the first volume of Eric Eych's life of Bismarck in 1943 (*see* G178) he wrote, 'To write a life of Bismarck within reasonable compass would be one of the greatest of historical achievements; but perhaps it is impossible. The material is overwhelming; and to make matters worse, Bismarck himself has left, in speeches, conversations or his reminiscences, versions of all the principal events usually deliberately misleading.'

In reviewing Eric Eyck's *Bismarck and the German Empire*, 1950, (*see* G388) he wrote, '... the time is coming when a truly historical approach to Bismarck can be attempted, without worrying whether what he did was right or wrong'.

Reviews

(i) 'The Iron Chancellor', Harold Nicolson, *Obs.* 3 Jul. 1955. p 11

'Mr. A.J.P. Taylor is the type of don whose thought and method are those of a scholar and whose feeling that of an adolescent. This dichotomy is welcome and familiar ... I enjoy his irreverence and the sharp snaps of paradox.' The book 'sheds light into obscure corners, sets up fresh ideas crossing and recrossing in the passages of the brain, combines scholarship with enthusiasm, and possesses such rare charm that the temperature of our interest rises to zest'.

(ii) 'The Iron Chancellor', Michael Howard, *NS & N.* 50, 1270. 9 Jul. pp 47–8

'Mr. Taylor carries out his revaluation in the clear, sharp, epigrammatic prose which makes all his work as stimulating as champagne – and which makes one wonder, sometimes, whether it was all really as simple as that. His mind is a convex mirror in which events appear brilliantly coloured, brilliantly distinct, and sometimes a little distorted. He has many of the virtues of Macaulay, and one or two of his faults. The pattern is too sharply etched; the epigrams are too neat;

the judgements are too final: but how refreshing it is to read a historian who is not afraid of patterns, epigrams and judgements!'

(iii) 'Maker of an Empire', *TLS.* 2785. 15 Jul. 1955. pp 389–90

'Mr. Taylor has performed the difficult task of compressing the most earth-shaking career between Napoleon and Hitler into fewer than 300 pages with conspicuous success.'

(iv) 'Devoted Opportunist', Gordon A. Craig, *Saturday Review.* 38. 19 Nov. 1955. p 35

'. . . A.J.P. Taylor does two things excellently. He provides a long needed account in English of the main facts of Bismarck's career, an account which is at once readable, up to date . . . and balanced . . . In the second place, he points a fascinating portrait of one of the most complicated personalities in an age which was filled with gifted and original minds . . . (The) chapter on the corrosive effects of the Bismarckian tradition in Germany's intellectual development is not the least interesting part of this highly provocative study.'

(v) 'Some Recent Books on German History', Robert A. Spencer, *Canadian Historical Review.* 37, 2. Jun. 1956. p 172

'. . . It is by no means a rival to Erich Eyck's three volume (work) . . . What Mr. Taylor has done is to write . . . a brilliant and provocative interpretive sketch, in which Bismarck the man is skilfully integrated with Bismarck the statesman . . . (It) is written in his accustomed witty and incisive style, but sometimes phrases run away with the facts.'

A9. *Englishmen and Others*, London, Hamish Hamilton, 1956, vii, 192 p

A collection of historical essays and book reviews.

In the Preface he writes, 'I am not a philosophic historian. I have no system, no moral interpretation. I write to clear my mind, to discover how things happened and how men behaved. If the result is shocking or provocative, this is not from intent, but solely because I try to judge from the evidence without being influenced by the judgements of others.'

Contents

1. Prophets of Man (May 1954. *see* G565)
2. William Cobbett (Aug. 1953. *see* G524 *and* A21)
3. Ranke (May 1950. *see* G379 *and* A17)
4. Macaulay and Carlyle (Jul. 1953. *see* E31 *and* A21)
5. Metternich (Jan. 1954. *see* G548, A15 *and* A17)
6. Cavour and Garibaldi (Apr. 1954. *see* G562, A15 *and* A17)
7. Palmerston (Jul. 1951. *see* D7 *and* A21)
8. John Bright and the Crimean War. (1954. *see* D13, C3, *and* A21)
9. Dizzy (Jan. 1955. *see* G 606 *and* A21)
10. The Use of Monarchy (Aug. 1952 *see* G486 *and* A21)
11. Economic Imperialism (Mar. 1955. *see* E36, *and* A21)
12. The Rise and Fall of Diplomatic History (Jan. 1956. *see* D18 *and* A17)
13. The Conference at Algeciras (Oct. 1952. *see* D8 *and* A15)
14. Holstein: The Mystery Man (Jul. 1955. *see* G627 *and* A17)
15. The Second International (Apr. 1956. *see* G666 *and* A9)
16. The Outbreak of the First World War (Aug. 1954. *see* E34, A15 *and* A17)
17. Marx and Lenin (May 1954. *see* G567, A15 *and* A17)
18. Trotsky (Feb. 1954. *see* G553, A15 *and* A17)
19. The German Army in Politics (Sept. 1955. *see* G640 *and* A17)
20. Hitler's Seizure of Power (1955. *see* D16 *and* A17)
21. The Appeasement Years (Jul. 1953. *see* G520)
22. The Alliance That Failed (Sept. 1952, Oct. 1953 and Sept. 1954. *see* G489, G532, G584 *and* A17)

23. From Isolation to World Power (Apr. 1953. *see* G509)
24. Stumbling into War (Nov. 1953. *see* G543 *and* A17)
25. Man of an Idea (Oct. 1955. *see* G649 *and* A17)
26. The Twilight of the God (Aug. 1954. *see* G580 *and* A17)
27. Democracy and Diplomacy (Dec. 1954. *see* F162 *and* A17)

Reviews

(i) Philip Toynbee, *Obs.* 21 Oct. 1956. p 17

'. . . if it had been true that Mr. Taylor eschews moral interpretations he would surely have been a much duller historian than he is. . . . The fact is . . . that Mr. Taylor is a man of strong and pugnacious moral feeling who is never so happy as when he is attacking cruelty, pomposity and dishonesty.' However he criticises him for his tendency to mix historical judgement with personal views – 'in his role of popular historian he ought to make it plain that he is expressing his own odd opinions here and not speaking from the top of a historian's Olympus'. 'I like the tough radicalism which is the fundamental attitude expressed here. I like the freshness of Mr. Taylor's mind.'

(ii) 'Englishmen and Others', Charles Wilson, *Sp.* 197, 6697. 2 Nov. 1956. pp 614–5

'Some of these essays . . . and notably those on John Bright, on Marx and Lenin, on Trotsky, on Macaulay and Carlyle, maintain his best standard.'

However he is critical of certain features of his writing. 'The real trouble is that Mr. Taylor, like Cobbett (whom he admires) and other kindly men who enjoy a reputation for irascibility, cannot contain his impatience with the amiable virtues of those nearest to him socially and intellectually . . . Contrariwise, he puts his trust in the occupants of the public bar and their collective wisdom. The cult of the pub is a harmless enough affectation in dons revolting against the senior common room or the Athenaeum. But to rest one's political judgements on the dogma that the more educated are always wrong and the less educated always right is nihilism not progress.' The reviewer then comments on popular support for Hitler, Mussolini and Joseph McCarthy.

(iii) 'Rogue Elephant', Ralph Partridge, *NS & N.* 52, 1338. 3 Nov. 1956. pp 560–1

'These ... essays ... exhibit Mr. Alan Taylor's wide range as critic and historian, together with his wit, his power of reaching simple conclusions from complicated facts, his downright common sense and his delight in exposing stupidity and error ... When not posing in a Preface Mr. Taylor is quite ready to admit his own cantankerous individualism ... That a historian with such an acute mind should be content to roam the jungles of history like a rogue elephant, bowling over all comers with slashing generalisations, is a source of grievous disappointment.'

(iv) 'History Without a Philosophy', *TLS.* 2857. 30 Nov. 1956. p 706

'They all have the quality of suspense – the suspense of wondering, not what is going to happen next, but what Mr. Taylor is going to say next; and this gives them a readability which many other historians will secretly envy Mr. Taylor even when they criticise him.' Points to inconsistencies of judgment in the essays. Observes that his 'best work, when he gives himself the time and trouble to think, matches that of any other living historian in penetration and originality'. Feels that only 8 is an example of his best work, 13 is 'a competent and useful contribution to diplomatic history', half the rest 'make suggestive points' and the other half 'were scarcely worth preserving'.

(v) E. Malcolm Carroll, *Am.Hist.R.* 63, 3. Apr. 1958. p 722

'If there is much that is provocative ... not to say controversial, this largely results from pet phobias in regard to the British ruling classes and professional diplomats. Here Taylor is a born dissenter ... He prefers pub conversations . . . to the advice of the Foreign Office experts as the basis for deciding what the aims of foreign policy should be . . . There is, of course, not a dull page in the book.'

A10. *The Trouble Makers: Dissent Over Foreign Policy 1792–1939*, The Ford Lectures Delivered In the Univ. of Oxford in Hilary Term 1956, London, Hamish Hamilton, 1957, repr. 1964, 1969; Bloomington, Indiana U.P., 1958; Toronto, Copp; 207 p

A survey of the views and activities of those who vigorously opposed British foreign policy from the time of the French Revolution to the outbreak of the Second World War. He writes, 'A man can disagree with a particular line of British foreign policy, while still accepting its general assumptions. The Dissenter repudiates its aims, its methods, its principles. What is more, he claims to know better and to promote higher causes; he asserts a superiority, moral or intellectual.' (p 13) He also observes, 'Every historian loves the past or should do' (p 14) – and in this book he enjoys himself discussing his nonconforming heroes from Paine and Fox onwards; though in so doing, he is not blind to their faults and to their frequent lack of realism. His greatest praise goes to Cobden, whom, he deems to have been 'the most original and profound of Radical Dissenters.' (p 50)

The book is also something of a declaration of faith, or even of self – justification. 'Conformity', he writes, 'may give you a quiet life; it may even bring you to a University Chair. But all change in history, all advance, comes from the nonconformists. If there had been no trouble-makers, no Dissenters, we should still be living in caves.' (p 14) He also gives his characteristic views on history in it – including 'we learn nothing from history except the infinite variety of men's behaviour. We study it, as we listen to music or read poetry, for pleasure, not for instruction.' (p 23)

He repeated these lectures as 'The Other Foreign Policy' for a series of radio broadcasts on the BBC Third Programme. These were broadcast on 4, 11,

18, 25 April and 2 and 9 May 1956 and repeated on 9, 16, 24, 30 April and 7 and 15 May 1956. (*see* Appendix)

(a) Pub. in pbk. London, Panther, 1969, 190 p

A.J.P.T. has repeatedly described the book as his best book. In '*Accident Prone*' (*see* D41) he writes that Alan Bullock suggested the theme to him – and the outcome was the book which is 'by far my favourite brainchild and the one I hope to be remembered by'.

Reviews

(i) 'Dissenters', Kingsley Martin, *NS & N.* 53, 1369. 8 Jun. 1957. pp 740–1

'A.J.P. Taylor is this generation's Bernard Shaw, at once its unrelenting preacher and its irrepressible debater. Every subject has its moral and every moral its refutation. No one, including himself, is allowed to get away with anything. From every opinion there is Dissent; from every Dissent there is another Dissenter.'

'Mr. Taylor's lectures delivered brilliantly, staccato, without notes, make such points; but they retain their epigrammatic, rather inconsequential, quality in book form.' Martin criticises in detail the fifth chapter (on E.D. Morel).

(ii) 'Honest Mr. Taylor names the guilty men of the Left', George Malcolm Thomson, *Ev. Stan.* 16 Jun. 1957. p 12

'the main impression it leaves is that of men, muddled in motives, blinded by prejudices and stumbling towards disaster. For the troublemakers . . . stand exposed as the men who helped to bring the war in 1939.'

(iii) 'Political Dissent', *TLS.* 2886. 21 Jun. 1957. p 382

A.J.P.T. is 'very nearly an ideal general reader's historian. He tells them exactly what they want to know, briefly, wittily and often wickedly . . . It was at first an amusing trick to invent that *enfant terrible* (which may perhaps be anglicised as an intellectual teddy-boy) to serve as the serious historian's *alter ego*; but the trick can well become an obsession, and the obsession can become involuntary and irreversible.'

The reviewer criticises the construction as 'slapdash'. Observes that A.J.P.T.'s range is 'from Charles James Fox to the almost unidentifiable specimens of the late 1930s, of whom perhaps Mr. Taylor himself is to be counted as the only known survivor'. Concludes by observing, 'If he believes, as the dust-cover suggests, that an invitation to deliver the Ford Lectures is the highest honour which an English historian can receive, one could wish that he had been more thoughtful about returning the compliment.'

(iv) 'The Dissidence of Dissent', Lord Attlee, *Sp*. 198, 6731. 28 Jun. 1957. p 836

'Mr. Taylor has a lively style and has written an interesting book, though I think that he tends to over-stress the importance of the intellectuals as is natural in an academic writer.' Amongst his comments on the book, the reviewer observes that many men of the Right deserve as much attention – from Lord Chatham to Winston Churchill in the period before the Second World War.

(v) W.L. Burn, *Hist*. 63, 147. Feb. 1958. pp 61–3

'This is a rolicking book.'

(vi) William L. Neumann, *Am.Hist.R*. 63, 3. Apr. 1958. p 723

'As the 'Peck's Bad Boy' of British historians Taylor is ever ready to stick a deflating pin in his more pompous colleagues or to tip over the tribal idols of his profession . . . conventions of sobriety and cautious generalization are cast aside as Taylor, in the tradition of dissent, strikes out at the 'Establishment' of his profession. The result is a volume which will infuriate or delight the reader, according to his tastes. The reviewer recommends its brilliant half-truths and suggestive paradoxes.'

(vii) 'Some Recent Books in British History', H.W. McCready, *Canadian Historical Review*. 39, 2. Jun. 1958. pp 149–50

The subject 'is rather peripheral to say the least, whether regarded as a contribution to the history of British foreign policy or to that of British domestic politics'. The reviewer argues that the Dissenters 'were ... largely without influence on events ... It is also plain that Mr. Taylor's heroes tended, like all impotent minorities, to nag and complain for want of anything better to do, to oppose for the sake of opposing and to see sinister motives behind every move by those in responsible office.'

A11. (A) *The Origins of the Second World War*, London, Hamish Hamilton, 1961, 3 repr. 1962 in this imp. Ontario, Collins; 296 p, 2 maps

A narrative diplomatic history of 'the origins of the second World War, or rather of the war between the three Western Powers over the settlement of Versailles; a war which had been implicit since the moment when the first war ended'. (p 336) It is based on the published primary sources – official foreign policy documents, private diaries and memoirs etc.

In the book he attempts to explain why the war in Europe started when it did. He writes that one can investigate the profound causes of all wars and also one can answer 'the question why that particular war happened at that particular time. Both inquiries make sense on different levels. They are complementary; they do not exclude each other. The second World War ... had profound causes; but it also grew out of specific events, and these events are worth detailed examination.'

In it he examines 'the German problem'. (p 48) He argues that in the inter-war period 'if this were settled, everything would be settled; if it remained unsolved, Europe would not know peace'. (p 66) Whilst he judges Hitler's internal policy to mark a major change, he argues that Hitler's foreign policy of wishing 'to make Germany the greatest power in Europe from her natural weight' was in fact the conventional German foreign policy. (p 97) He argues that Hitler did not have deep-laid plans, either in his internal politics or in his foreign policy. Like other statesmen he took one step at a time, and the next one followed on from it. Hitler was not planning for a European War to start in the autumn of 1939; the German economy and her armaments were not ready.

He draws a characteristic moral, 'Human blunders ... usually do more to shape history than human wickedness. At any rate, this is a rival dogma which is worth developing, if only as an academic exercise.' (p 265–6)

(a) Pub. in New York, Atheneum, 1962 with a 'Preface for the American Reader' (pp v–x), and a brief biographical outline at end, p 299

In this Preface he explains that he is dealing with the question 'why did Great Britain and France declare war on Germany?' not with the invasion of Russia or Pearl Harbor. As a result there is very little about US policy in it. He observes that 'until 1931 or thereabouts, the policy of the Western Powers ... met broadly with American approval', thereafter US concern for the Far East and Roosevelt's victory led to isolationism. American isolationism reinforced isolationism elsewhere – 'It supplied a strong argument for those who hesitated to make collective security a reality.'

He also rebutts charges that he had apologised for Hitler or the appeasers, 'Nothing could be further from my thoughts.' He points out that he had been an active opponent of appeasement, whilst 'my critics were confining their activity to the seclusion of Oxford common rooms'. He also points out that the US only entered the war when Hitler declared war on them.

Extracts (pp 9, 13–4, 71–2, 131–2, 195–6, 209–11, 215–6, 218–20, 250, 263–4, 268–9, 272–8) repr. as 'A Challenge To Nuremberg and Postwar History' in *The Outbreak of the Second World War: Design or Blunder?*, ed. John L. Snell, Boston, D.C. Heath, 1962

(b) Pub. in pbk. New York, Premier Books, 1963

(with the preface of (a)), xi, 286 p

(c) Trans. into French by R. Jouan, Paris, Presses de la Cité, 1961, 315 p

(d) Trans. into Italian by Luciano Bianciardi, and pub. in pbk., Bari, Editori Laterza, 1961 as Vol. 67 of their Libri del tempo, 419 p

(e) Trans. into German by Dieter Werner, intro. by Michael Freund (pp 7–11), Gutersloh, Sigbert Mohn, 1962, 383 p

(f) Trans. into Finnish by Keijo Kylavaara, intro. by Keijo Kylavaara (pp 3–4), Helsinki, Kirjayhtyma, 1962, 280 p

(g) Trans. into Dutch by H.J. Hofland, J.B. Charles and J. Vrijman, Amersterdam, Uitgeverij de Besige Bij, 1963, 311 p

(h) Trans. into Portuguese by Waltensir Dutra and pub. in pbk., Rio de Janeiro, Brazil, Zahar, 1963 in their Biblioteca de Cultura Historica, 278 p

(B) *The Origins of the Second World War*, new edn. with 'Foreword: Second Thoughts' (18 p unnumbered), London, Hamish Hamilton, 1963. Repr. 1965, 1971, 1972.

In this he points out that he was not trying to 'vindicate' Hitler but to show how Hitler came to take his various actions. As far as world war is concerned, 'He did not so much aim at war as expect it to happen, unless he could evade it by some ingenious trick . . . ' He argues that anti-semitism 'was the one thing in which he persistently and genuinely believed from his beginning in Munich until his last days in the bunker'. The moral he draws from this is a further condemnation of the Germans – 'His advocacy of it would have deprived him of support, let alone power, in a civilised country.' Of Hitler he concludes, 'He was in part the creation of Versailles, in part the creation of ideas that were common in contemporary Europe. Most of all, he was the creation of German history and of the German present. He would have counted for nothing without the support and co-operation of the German people.'

(a) Pub. in pbk. Penguin Books, Harmondsworth, 1964

(b) Trans. into Spanish by Luis del Castillo Aragon, Barcelona, Luis de Caralt, 1963, 373 p

(c) Trans. into Italian by Luciano Bianciardi and pub. in pbk. Bari, Editori Laterza, 1965 in their Universale series, 379 p

(d) Pub. in USA, Greenwich, Conn., Fawcett, 1966 as a Fawcett premier book, 304 p

(e) Trans. into Norwegian by Jens Reinton and Jan Gjerde and pub. in pbk. Oslo, Pax, 1967, 296 p

(f) Trans. into Danish and pub. in pbk. Denmark, Jorgen Paludans, 1968, 282 p

(g) Trans. into Swedish, Stockholm, Ratren and Sjogren, 1968, 295 p

(h) Trans. into Sinhalese, with an intro. which discusses the topic and A.J.P.T. (pp 1–22), Columbo, Ceylon, Ratna Kara Book Depot, 1969, 374 p

The 'Foreword: Second Thoughts' repr. as 'Erneute Betrachtungen' (pp 29–51) in '*Kriegsbegsinn 1939: Entfesselung oder Ausbruch des Zweiten Weltkriegs?*', ed. Gottfied Niedhart, Darmstadt, Wissenshaftliche Buchgesellschaft, 1976

Reviews

The book caused a furore – and became a best seller. The reviews went to extremes, as the two following examples illustrate:

(i) 'Mr. Taylor's masterpiece', Sebastian Haffner, *Obs.* 16 Apr. 1961. p 30

'This is an almost faultless masterpiece, perfectly proportioned, perfectly controlled. Bitterness has mellowed into quiet sadness and even pity ... ; fairness rules supreme and of all passions only the passions for clarity remains ... In spite of all this, it will probably become his most controversial book.'

(ii) 'A.J.P. Taylor, Hitler and the War', H.R. Trevor Roper, *Encounter*. 19, 1. Jul. 1961. pp 88–96

'In spite of his statements about 'historical discipline', he selects, suppresses, and arranges evidence on no principle other than the needs of his thesis; and that thesis, that Hitler was a traditional statesman, of limited aims, merely responding to a given situation, rests on no evidence at all, ignores essential evidence, and is, in my opinion, demonstrably false.'

A.J.P.T. replied to his critics not only in his 'Foreword: Second Thoughts' but also in:

'How to Quote: Exercise for Beginners' (Sept. 1961; *see* D29) in which he suggests that H.R. Trevor Roper's quotations from the *Origins* are unfairly selective; and

'War Origins Again' (Apr. 1965; *see* D31), in which he responds to 'Some Origins of The Second World War' by T.W. Mason, *P & P*. 29. Dec. 1964. pp 67–87

In this he observes that he misinterpreted the Hossbach Protocol as a move against Schact and that he overreacted to exaggerations of German rearmament; however he reaffirms that there would have been a 'German problem' even if Hitler had not emerged.

The more important reviews and articles stemming from this book are reprinted in:

The Origins of the Second World War, ed. Wm. Roger Louis, New York, Wiley, 1972. (This book includes an interesting letter by A.J.P.T. to Edward Segel, 21 Sept. 1964. pp 26–7, on A.J.P.T.'s approach to history); and

The Origins of the Second World War, ed. Esmonde M. Robertson, London, Macmillan, 1971

As a 'revisionist' A.J.P.T. appears very moderate indeed when one is confronted by Harry Elmer Barnes' pamphlet, *Blasting The Historical Blackout: Professor A.J.P. Taylor's The Origins of The Second World War: Its Nature, Reliability, Shortcomings and Implications*, May 1963!

A12. *The First World War: An Illustrated History*, London, Hamish Hamilton, 1963, repr. 1976. Issued in U.S. as *Illustrated History of the First World War*, New York, Putnam, 1964, 224 p, illus. maps

A narrative survey of the First World War. It is

well illustrated with many witty captions to the photographs. In his Preface he writes, 'I have tried to explain what the war was about; particularly, to resolve the paradox that men were passionately engaged in the war and hated it at the same time.' He has a hero – the Unknown Soldier. And, out of character, he offers a moral – 'Maybe, if we can understand it better, we can come nearer to being, what the men of that time were not, masters of our destiny.'

His analysis that war came unplanned has a moral dear to the heart of a supporter of CND.: 'The deterrent on which they relied failed to deter; the statesmen became the prisoners of their own weapons. The great armies, accumulated to provide security and preserve the peace, carried the nations to war by their own weight.' (p 13) In looking at the Western Front he offers the generalisations that it was surprise that worked, not standard practice, and that it was taking offensives that brought disaster on armies.

(a) Pub. in pbk. Harmondsworth, Penguin Books, 1966. This edition repr. 1967, 1970, 1972, 1974, 1976 and 1977

(b) Trans. into Italian by Piero Pieroni, Firenze, Vallechi, 1967 (this ed. has additional material on Italy's role in the First World War and different illus.), 213 p

(c) Trans. into Swedish by Hans Dahlberg, Stockholm, Prisma, 1967, 286 p

(d) Trans. into Norwegian and pub. in pbk. Norway, J.W. Cappelens, 1968, 286 p

Reviews

(i) 'History: Instant or Interpretative?', Alan Clark, *Sp.* 211, 7063. 8 Nov. 1963. pp 604–5

The reviewer, in his general review, observes that this book 'is a masterly omnibus of generalities, every one of which, taken individually, will stand the most critical dissection . . . Every aspect of the Great War is uncovered, discussed, dismissed – in a manner which stimulates the intellect rather than oppressing the memory.'

(ii) 'Historians View of A War', *TLS*. 3223. 5 Dec. 1963. p 1013

'A study which will astonish his many admirers as well as his critics, a formidable total. Both parties will surely find the experiment extremely interesting.' Criticises some military details but overall praises his illuminating judgments.

(iii) 'Goodbye to All That', Geoffrey Barraclough, *NYRB*. 2, 7. 14 May 1964. pp 3–4

The reviewer, in discussing several books, warmly praises this one, observing that A.J.P.T.'s book is short and incisive and clarifies the key issues.

A13. *Politics in Wartime : and other Essays*, London, Hamish Hamilton; New York, Athenaeum, 1964; Ontario, Collins; 207 p

A collection of reprinted essays and reviews, including his Raleigh Lecture, 1959, and his Leslie Stephen lecture, 1961.

In his Preface (p 7), he writes, 'Some historians, it has been said, produce rich plum puddings; some produce dry biscuits. I produce dry biscuits, I hope with a pronounced flavour. I hope, too, that the flavour has improved with keeping.'

Contents

Part 1

1. Politics in the First World War (1959. *see* D26, C6 *and* A21)
2. The Man in the Cloth Cap (Aug. 1956. *see* E39 *and* A21)
3. The Anglo-Russian Entente (Aug. 1957. *see* E42 *and* A21)
4. 'We want eight, and we won't wait' (Feb. 1959. *see* E52 *and* A21)
5. Agadir: the *Panther*'s Spring (Jul. 1961. *see* E58)
6. The Schlieffen Plan (Nov. 1956. *see* G697)
7. How a World War Began.

(1) Murder At Sarajevo (Nov. 1958. *see* E49)
(2) A Dead Man's Battle Orders (Nov. 1958. *see* E50)
(3) Great Britain on the Brink (Nov. 1958. *see* E51)

8. The War Aims of the Allies in the First World War (1956. *see* B5)
9. Lloyd George: Rise and Fall (1961. *see* C7 *and* A21)
10. The Chief (Jun. 1959. *see* G836 *and* A21)

Part 2

11. Cromwell and the Historians (Sept. 1958. *see* E47 *and* A21)
12. Charles Jamex Fox (Sept. 1956. *see* E40 *and* A21)
13. Metternich and his 'System' (Jul. 1959. *see* E53)
14. Genocidc (Nov. 1962. *see* G966 *and* A21)
15. Who Burnt the Reichstag? (Aug. 1960. *see* D27)
16. Unlucky Find (Dec. 1961. *see* G927 *and* A21)
17. Dictator without a Cause (Jan. 1962. *see* G931)
18. Spam on a Gold Plate (Oct. 1958. *see* G804 *and* A21)

Reviews

(i) 'Lloyd George's Hour', Geoffrey Barraclough, *Obs*. 20 Sept. 1964. p 24

He sees Lloyd George as the hero of the volume: 'perhaps it is natural that the great 'rogue' of English political life should appeal to the great 'rogue' of English history'. The essays 'have all the gusto we expect of Mr. Taylor . . . Those he debunks deserves debunking; there are others to whom he doffs his cloth cap.'

(ii) 'Taylor's Germany', George Lichtheim, *NS*. 68, 1750. 25 Sept. 1964. p 454

The reviewer warmly praises 1 and 7, but observes: 'When he turns to other countries, the note of authority vanishes, and what we get is mere assertion: confident, cockshure, misleading.'

(iii) 'Soldiers and Politicians', *TLS*. 3267. 8 Oct. 1964. p 911

The reviewer finds the pieces on the First World War most interesting but feels that many of the short book reviews were hardly worth reprinting. The reviewer feels that 6 and 7 have become outdated with the publication of Fritz Fischer's work.

(iv) 'The History of A.J.P. Taylor', F.H. Hinsley, *NYRB*. 4, 7. 6 May. 1965. pp 24–6

The reviewer observes that A.J.P.T. 'is the most prominent living historian' and the most controversial, but 'it is not the universal opinion that he is among the most distinguished'. He then assesses A.J.P.T.'s approach to history in depth. He observes, 'It is difficult to believe that he could slip into so limited and distorted an account of the Sarajevo crisis were it not the case that his mind is fundamentally one that is absorbed in the what and how of history and uninterested in the why. If his weakness as a historian is that he neglects 'the profound causes' – and this is his phrase – he will not correct it by jumping from his own extreme of concentrating entirely on the detailed reconstruction of historical episodes to that other.'

A14. *English History 1914–1945* (The Oxford History of England, Vol. 15, ed. Sir George Clark), Oxford, Clarendon Press, and New York, Oxford U.P., 1965, repr. with minor corrections, 1966, xxvii, 709p, 8 maps, 7 graphs

A narrative history, based on printed sources. It skilfully blends social, economic and political history into the narrative.

If it has a hero it is Lloyd George 'the greatest prime minister of the century'. (p 87, f. 1) If the early part has a villain it is Asquith. (p 70) Baldwin and Ramsay MacDonald are rehabilitated. A.J.P.T. appears a whole-hearted Keynesian in economics. He restates his views on the origins of the Second World War (p 424, f.1) and on British bombing. (p 518) He concludes on an optimistic note: 'Imperial greatness was on the way out; the welfare state was on the way in.

The British empire declined; the condition of the people improved.' (p 600)

(a) Pub. in pbk. as a Pelican book, Harmondsworth, Penguin Books, 1970, 875 p

Repr. 1973 and with a revised bibliography, 1975

(b) Pub. in pbk. New York, Oxford University Press, 1970, xxvii, 713 p

(c) Trans. into Italian by Lucia Biocca Marghieri and pub. as *Storia Dell' Inghilterra Contemporanea*, Bari, Laterza, 1968, vii, 823 p

Repr. in their Universale series, 2 Vols. 1975, vii, 823 p

(d) Trans. into Japanese by Misuzu Shobo and pub. in 2 vols. Tokyo, Oxford University Press, 1968, 3, 308 p; 258 p, 31, ix

In reviewing *The New Cambridge History*, Vol. 12 (*see* G877) in July 1960 A.J.P.T. wrote of the problems of writing such histories as this and the Oxford History of England: 'Political history provides the acts of drama; and the rest – culture, economics, religion and so on – are refreshing interruptions, like drinks at the bar during the intervals. Even Macaulay did not solve this problem: his wonderful third chapter has no association with the rest. One day a historian of genius will find the answer. He will paint the picture of society binding the strands together instead of laying them out separately, as we all do at present.'

In one of his 'London Diary' pieces in 1976 (*see* F438) he wrote: 'When I wrote *English History 1914–1945* I believed that victory and the Attlee government made a triumphant conclusion. Now I feel differently. The incompetence of an arrogant governing class has led the country to decay and ruin.'

'Comment' by A.J.P.T. *JMH*. 47, 4. Dec. 1975. pp 622–3

In this he defends his Preface in which he argues the case for using 'England' not 'Britain'. (*see* D40)

Reviews

(i) 'England from Asquith to Attlee', Alan Bullock,

Obs. 24 Oct. 1965. p 26

'Mr. Taylor has brought off a double: a masterly account of the most difficult (because the most recent) period of English history, and at the same time a book so well written that it is compulsive as well as compulsory reading.' He feels most historians would feel such a venture would be the quickest way to lose their reputations, but with A.J.P.T. 'the danger lay in . . . that he would be tempted by his love of paradox and his fondness for knocking down accepted opinions into writing a book which was too clever by half and would confirm the opinion of the disapproving that he is a brilliant television performer and journalist but no longer a serious historian'.

He regrets that he give little attention to intellectual history, and wishes that there was more political and social history. Observes 'He is a born revisionist. 'Simply as a piece of literary craftsmanship, this is a *tour de force.*'

(ii) 'Historian of the People', Noel Annan *NYRB.* 5, 9. 9 Dec. 1965. pp 10, 12

'He is in fact a figure well known in America, but rare in England – a Populist. Taylor believes that the people are not just equal with their rulers, but are better than them.'

After a number of reservations the reviewer concludes: 'Nevertheless his volume is an astonishing *tour de force*. It not only deserves, like Macaulay's history, to supersede for a few days the last fashionable novel on the table of young ladies. It will also be a set book for research students who, as they pounce on misjudgements, will be brought up sharp by the inconvenient contingencies with which Taylor will confound their theories.'

(iii) 'History Taylor-made', *TLS.* 3329. 16 Dec. 1965. pp 1169–70

'He has at least produced a book which is as zestful as any of his previous works. (It) . . . must be the most readable book of its size that we have been given for many a day.' The reviewer feels that 'he has . . . deployed a quality of judgement in which ... his earlier work has been deficient'. Overall it is 'a book in which his undoubted talents as a technical craftsman of wide learning are at last happily yoked, not only with his accustomed brilliance as a stylist, but also with the balance and the sensibility of a mature historical mind'.

(iv) 'Taylor's England', Henry Pelling, *P & P.* 33. Apr. 1966. pp 149–58

After critically discussing the structure of the book he observes: '... Mr. Taylor's unwillingness to allow for the strength of social and political forces outside Whitehall and Westminster ... constitutes the chief weakness of his book'. He provides a lengthy list of factual errors in the book. Overall he comments that reading the book is 'a very rewarding experience. The narrative, which is exceedingly skilfully woven, never fails to keep up its pace from the first page to the last.'

(v) 'England In The Twentieth Century', C.L. Mowat, *Hist.* 51, 2. Jun. 1966. pp 188–96

'Here is the history of a generation, comprehensive and comprehensible, well proportioned, seldom rushed, and never flagging in interest.' The reviewer lists many points he finds doubtful, including the comment on the early pages that they 'contain some of his most far-fetched and unsupported observations, as though he must emulate Gibbon not only in pungency but in naughtiness'. 'Yet the main impression the book makes is of comprehensiveness and sanity, not of omissions and idiosyncrasies.'

(vi) David Owen, *Am.Hist.R.* 71, 4. Jul. 1966. pp 1352–4

'... for many years Mr. Taylor has been writing history that is meant to be read. When he settles down ... to do a professional job, the result can be a noteworthy achievement – well informed, critical, brilliantly written, and contentious enough to exercise the curse of learned dullness. This study finds him in top form ... Still, with its occasional perversities – in part, because of them – this is vintage Taylor.'

(vii) P. Stansky, *JMH*. 39, 3. Sept. 1967. pp 329–31

Finds the weakest aspect is the treatment of literature 'where his accounts are so compressed as to be perfunctory and are sometimes philistine'.

'He is by temperament and reputation a revisionist, and here, at least, the habit is valuable, directed to so much material that has been allowed hitherto to go unexamined. On occasion, there is a sense of strain, and the reader feels that a new paradoxical interpretation is being offered for its own sake. But it is rare that it has not been fruitful to question received opinions.'

(viii) Maurice Shock, *EHR*. 82, 325. Oct. 1967. pp 807–12

'The style is a perfect model, hard and vivid, the sentences short but with few failing to carry a point and a punch of their own. There is not a dull page in the book. But the style is only a reflection of the method which essentially consists of bringing before the reader a rapid succession of events, each of which is caught momentarily, but sharply, under the microscope. It is this skill which makes Mr. Taylor such a master of the condensed narrative.'

'This is a very personal book. What it describes and analyses is Taylor's England with an idiosyncratic choice of what was to be included or left out, spotlighted or diminished . . . It is certain that any future general history of the period will contain much more economic history, and less political, than his.'

A15. *From Napoleon to Lenin: Historical Essays*, Harper Torchback, New York, Harper and Row, 1966, vii, 174 p

A collection of essays on European history from the time of Napoleon to the First World War, selected from the British published collections (A5, A6, and A9).

There is a note by Fritz Stern (p vii) which states that this is the first of three projected volumes; the second projected volume would contain essays on recent history and contemporary essays, and the third, essays on English history and on historiography.

Contents

1. Napoleon (1) on himself (Sept. 1948. *see* G294, A5 *and* A17)
   (2) The Verdict of History (Feb. 1949. *see* G317, A5 *and* A17)
2. Napoleon and Gentz (Dec. 1946. *see* G258 *and* A5)
3. Metternich (Jan. 1954. *see* G548, A9 *and* A17)
4. 1848 (1) Year of Revolution (Jan. 1948. *see* E14, A5 *and* A17)
   (2) The French Revolution (Feb. 1948. *see* E15, A5 *and* A17)
   (3) Vienna and Berlin (Mar. 1948. *see* E16, A5 *and* A17)
   (4) The Slav Congress (Jun. 1948. *see* E18, A5 *and* A17)
5. 1848: Opening of an Era (1948. *see* B2, A5 *and* A17)
6. De Tocqueville in 1848 (Nov. 1948. *see* G303, A5 *and* A17)
7. Crimea: The War That Would Not Boil (Feb. 1951. *see* D5, A6 *and* A17)
8. Cavour and Garibaldi (Apr. 1954. *see* G562, A9 *and* A17)
9. The Man of December (Dec. 1951. *see* E30, A6 *and* A17)
10. Bismarck's Morality (Aug. 1950. *see* G390, A6 *and* A17)
11. Bismarck and Europe (Approx. 1951. *see* A6 *and* A17)
12. The Ruler in Berlin (Dec. 1948. *see* G304, A5 *and* A17)
13. Francis Joseph: The Last Age of the Habsburgs (Dec. 1948. *see* E23, A5 *and* A17)
14. The Failure of the Habsburg Monarchy (Apr. 1951. *see* G424, A6 *and* A17)

15. Fashoda (Sept. 1948. *see* E21 *and* A5)
16. The Entente Cordiale (Apr. 1944. *see* E9, A5 *and* A17)
17. The Secret of the Third Republic (Feb. 1948. *see* G284, A5 *and* A17)
18. The Conference at Algeciras (Oct. 1952. *see* D8 *and* A9)
19. The Outbreak of the First World War (Aug. 1954. *see* E34, A9 *and* A17)
20. Thomas Garrigue Masaryk (Mar. 1950. *see* E27, A6 *and* A17)
21. Marx and Lenin, (May 1954. *see* G567, A9 *and* A17)
22. Trotsky (Feb. 1954. *see* G553, A9 *and* A17)

A16. *From Sarajevo to Potsdam* (History of European Civilisation Library, ed. Geoffrey Barraclough), London, Thames and Hudson, 1966, repr. 1975; New York, Harcourt, Brace Janovich International, 1966; Toronto, Nelson 216 p, 116 illus. incl. 2 maps

An illustrated narrative survey of European history 1914–1945. 'European civilisation is whatever most Europeans as citizens were doing at the time. In the period covered by this book they were either making war or economic problems . . . I think that many of the things which civilised people did were highly barbarous, but this is a personal whim which I have tried to keep out of the text.' (p 8)

One theme is that ordinary people generally have shown sense in the period, whereas most intellectuals have been foolish. Thus in dealing with the period after the First World War, 'Civilisation was held together by the civilised behaviour of ordinary people . . . in reality the masses were calmer and more sensible than those who ruled over them.' (p 62) Stalin appears as the pragmatist who carries out practical measures; he disregards Marxist dogmas as he realised 'that these dogmas were leading to disaster'. (p 125) Hitler 'was the Unknown Soldier, the little man of Chaplin's inspiration, come to life and turned sour'. (p 131) He was the product of German history – in particular 'he was the end-product of a civilisation of clever talk and helped to shake that civilisation by taking the talk seriously'. (p 134)

There are familiar A.J.P.T. attitudes to the outbreak of war in 1914 (pp 20, 22), Stresemann (p 80), Britain in the Second World War (p 172), bombing (p 174), America and Russia's attitude to Europe after 1945 ('they merely wanted Europe to leave them alone', p 196) and other topics.

(a) Trans. into French by Simone Darses and pub. in pbk. Paris, Flammarion, 1968, 216 p

(b) Trans. into Swedish by Christina Monthan – Axelsson and pub. in pbk. (with a limited number of illus. printed together in the centre of the book), Stockholm, Wahlström and Widstrand, 1968, 122p

Reviews

(i) 'Taylor's Europe', C.L. Mowat, *NS*. 72, 1863. 25 Nov. 1966. p 799

As a brief outline 'the book is a success, if not quite vintage Taylor'.

(ii) 'Picture Past', *TLS*. 3381. 15 Dec. 1966. p 1163

'Mr. Taylor has had a fine romp . . . There is the familiar combination of non-fact and debatable statement which irritates the professional historians – but there is also the striking probe, the brilliant summation and the arresting choice of word and phrase which will always excite their envy and admiration . . . This is the kind of book Mr. Taylor can now write with his left hand.'

(iii) 'Plus ca Change', D.C. Watt, *Sp*. 217, 7226. 23 Dec. 1966. pp 818–9

'As always with Mr. Taylor, what the reader is faced with is a far cry from the 'scientific history' beloved of academic historians. The reader faces a piece of historical vision, a dramatised construction, a personal vision, as he does when embarking on Macaulay, Froude or Carlyle.'

The reviewer finds the main weakness to be the

treatment of civilisation. 'Mr. Taylor's vision does not really comprehend the writers, composers, artists and architects of the time.'

A17. *Europe : Grandeur and Decline*, Harmondsworth, Penguin, 1967, 378 p

Essays and book reviews selected from earlier collections (A5, A6 and A9)

In the Preface he comments on how his views on the origins of the Second World War changed during the period he wrote these pieces. He also argues that Soviet Russia only asked of Europe to be left alone. 'Anyone who claims to learn from history should devote himself to promoting an Anglo-Soviet alliance, the most harmless and pacific of all combinations.'

Contents

1. Napoleon (1) On Himself (Sept. 1948. *see* G294, A5 *and* A15)
   (2) The Verdict of History (Feb. 1949. *see* G317, A5 *and* A15)
2. Metternich (Jan. 1954. *see* G548, A9 *and* A15)
3. 1848 : (1) Year of Revolution (Jan. 1948. *see* E14, A5 *and* A15)
   (2) The French Revolution (Feb. 1948. *see* E15, A5 *and* A15)
   (3) Vienna and Berlin (Mar. 1948. *see* E16, A5 *and* A15)
   (4) Slav Congress (Jun. 1948. *see* E18, A5 *and* A15)
4. De Tocqueville in 1848 (Nov. 1948. *see* G303, A5 *and* A15)
5. 1848: Opening of an Era (1948. *see* B2, A5 *and* A15)
6. The Man of December (Dec. 1951. *see* E30, A6 *and* A15)
7. Crimea: The War that would not Boil (Feb. 1951. *see* D5, A6 *and* A15)
8. Francis Joseph: The Last Age of the Habsburgs (Dec. 1948. *see* E23, A5 *and* A15)

9. Cavour and Garibaldi (Apr. 1954. *see* G562, A9 *and* A15)
10. Bismarck: The Man of German Destiny (Jul. 1948. *see* E20 *and* A5)
11. Bismarck's Morality (Aug. 1950. *see* G390, A6 *and* A15)
12. Bismarck and Europe (Approx. 1951. *see* A6 *and* A15)
13. Ranke (May 1950. *see* G379 *and* A9)
14. German Unity (Mar. 1944. *see* E7, E8 *and* A5)
15. The Failure of the Habsburg Monarchy (Apr. 1951. *see* G424, A6 *and* A15)
16. Marx and Lenin (May 1954. *see* G567, A9 *and* A15)
17. The Second International (Apr. 1956. *see* G666 *and* A9)
18. The Entente Cordiale (Apr. 1944. *see* E9, A5 *and* A15)
19. The Secret of the Third Republic (Feb. 1948. *see* G284, A5 *and* A15)
20. Holstein: The Mystery Man (Jul. 1955. *see* G627 *and* A9)
21. The Ruler in Berlin (Dec. 1948. *see* G304, A5 *and* A15)
22. The Rise and Fall of Diplomatic History (Jan. 1956. *see* D18 *and* A9)
23. Trotsky (Feb. 1954. *see* G553, A9 *and* A15)
24. Thomas Garrigue Masaryk (Mar. 1950. *see* E27, A6 *and* A15)
25. The Outbreak of the First World War (Aug. 1954. *see* E34, A9 *and* A15)
26. The German Army in Politics (Sept. 1955. *see* G640 *and* A9)
27. Nietzsche and the Germans (Jun. 1951. *see* G435 *and* A6)
28. Thus Spake Hitler (Jan. 1952. *see* G458 *and* A6)
29. Hitler's Seizure of Power (1955. *see* D16 *and* A9)
30. The Supermen: Hitler and Mussolini (May 1949. *see* G325 *and* A5)

31. Spain and the Axis (Apr. 1951. *see* G422 *and* A6)
32. M. Flandin and French Policy (Jan. 1948. *see* G280 *and* A5)
33. The Traditions of British Foreign Policy (Jan. 1951. *see* A6)
34. Full Speed to Munich (Sept. 1949. *see* G344 *and* A6)
35. The Diplomacy of M. Bonnet (Nov. 1946 and Jun. 1948. *see* G256, G290 *and* A5)
36. The Alliance That Failed (Sept. 1952, Oct. 1953 and Sept. 1954. *see* G489, G532, G584 *and* A9)
37. The Springs of Soviet Diplomacy (May 1948. *see* E17 *and* A5)
38. From Munich to Prague (1) British Version (Nov. 1950 and Aug. 1951. *see* G410, G439, *and* A6)
    (2) German Version (Dec. 1951. *see* G457 *and* A6)
39. Munich Ten Years After (Oct. 1948. *see* E22 *and* A5)
40. General Gamelin (Mar. 1947 and Oct. 1948. *see* G266, G299 *and* A5)
41. France in Defeat (Apr. 1950. *see* G373 *and* A6)
42. De Gaulle: Triumph of a Legend (Nov. 1950. *see* G407 *and* A6)
43. Stumbling into War (Nov. 1953. *see* G543 *and* A9)
44. Man of an Idea (Oct. 1955. *see* G649 *and* A9)
45. America's War (Jun. 1950. *see* G382 *and* A6)
46. The Twilight of the God (Aug. 1954. *see* G580 *and* A9)
47. The Austrian Illusion (Autumn 1948. *see* A5)
48. Up from Utopia: How Two Generations Survived Their Wars (Oct. 1950. *see* E28 *and* A6)
49. Is Stalin A Statesman? (Nov. 1951. *see* F62 *and* A6)
50. Can We Agrce with the Russians? (Mar. 1951. *see* F45 *and* A6)
51. Democracy and Diplomacy (Dec. 1954; *see* F162 *and* A9)

52. Old Diplomacy – And New (Mar. 1951. *see* F47 *and* A6)
53. The Turn of the Half Century (Dec. 1950. *see* F41 *and* A6)
    (a) Trans. into Japanese, Tokyo, 1975, 479 p, viii

A18. *War By Time-Table: How the First World War Began* (MacDonald Library of the Twentieth Century, general ed. John Roberts), London, MacDonald; New York, American Heritage Press, 1969, 128 p, 90 illus. incl. 1 map

An illustrated account of the run-up to the First World War and the opening campaigns of the War. He argues that war was no likelier in 1914 than earlier. He examines the military Powers' plans, showing that they depended on speed and once put into operation they were extremely difficult to halt because of the complexity of moving armies by rail. However all the plans, 'even that of the Germans, were designed to win a war if one happened, not to bring one about'. (p 32) The one country whose mobilisation was decisive was Germany; her mobilisation involved taking the offensive. He discusses decision making in Vienna, Russia, Berlin and London, emphasising the haphazard nature of it and the general unwillingness to take decisions.

He concludes, 'When cut down to essentials, the sole cause for the outbreak of war in 1914 was the Schlieffen plan – product of the belief in speed and the offensive.' In 1914, 'The deterrent failed to deter .... There is a contemporary moral here for those who like to find one.' (p 121)

(a) Trans. into Spanish by Sara Estrada and pub. in pbk. Barcelona, Nauta, 1970, 128 p

(b) Trans. into Dutch by J.F. Kliphuis, Leiden, A.W. Sijthoff, 1971, 128 p

(c) Trans. into French ('*La Guerre des Plans*'), with the subtitle '1914: Les Dernières Heures de l'Ancien Monde', by M. Fougerousse, Lausanne, Editions Rencontre, 1971, 128 p

(d) Trans. into Swedish by Richard Matz and pub. in pbk. Katrineholm, Ratren and Sjogren, 1971, 128 p

A19. *Beaverbrook*, London, Hamish Hamilton, 1972; New York, Simon and Schuster, 1972, xvii, 712 p 25 illus.

Pub. in pbk. as a Penguin, Harmondsworth, Penguin Books, 1974

A biography of Lord Beaverbrook which sets him clearly in the politics of the period and discusses how he made his fortune, ran his newspapers and wrote history books.

In the Introduction (pp ix–xvii) A.J.P.T. frankly declares that 'this old man was the dearest friend I ever had'. (p xvi) 'Beaverbrook's friendship enriched me. The joys of his company are beyond description . . . I loved Max Aitken, Lord Beaverbrook, when he was alive. Now that I have learnt to know him better from his records I love him even more.' (p xvii)

Reviews

(i) 'In the Sight of the Lord', Tom Driberg, *NS*. 83, 2154. 30 Jun. 1972. pp 908–9

'This biography does not pretend to be objective. As such phrases as 'romantic story' and 'admirable embellishments' suggest, Alan Taylor is prepared to make excuses for his hero's waywardness . . . (As a devoted admirer) It is the more to his credit that he has not suppressed some things which might be thought to show Beaverbrook in a less than favourable light.'

It 'is a massive achievement . . . It is also 'wonderfully entertaining' . . . His is a much richer and, obviously more comprehensive book than mine – though, so contradictory was the character that he portrays, he still leaves in some perplexity those of us who are neither so adoring as he nor so hostile as, say, the aristocrats of the Establishment whose arrogance Beaverbrook resented.'

(ii) 'The great fixer', *TLS*. 3670. 30 Jun. 1972. pp 747–8

Describes the author as 'one of the few really original

intellects in contemporary historiography – often idiosyncratic, frequently iconoclastic, sometimes wrong-headed, occasionally very wrong indeed, but always interesting, always provocative and always exciting'. Praises the biography as a work of art – in particular the author's 'refusal to offer simple solutions, and . . . his determination to cover all aspects of his subject's life and personality with thoroughness and sympathy . . . '

(iii) 'Eager Beaver', Ronald Blythe, *NYRB*. 20, 3. 8 Mar. 1973. pp 29–30

' . . . a full, affectionate, brilliantly written, and highly readable case for him. Though the book is intended to be a monument it is not an entirely polite one. Much of it is a kind of secular hagiography in which the virtues of the subject constantly come up against the reader's resistance; but it holds one's attention throughout by its expert marshalling of a vast amount of material.'

(iv) Kenneth O. Morgan, *Hist*. 58, 194. Oct. 1973. pp 475–6

'Only a biography of extraordinary quality could recapture the zest and fascination of this contradictory man; but that is the achievement of this compelling book by our greatest living historian . . . The supreme value of Mr. Taylor's book for historians lies in the important evidence from the Beaverbrook archives for British politics in the two world wars. Here, like his subject, Mr. Taylor attains full stature.'

A20. *The Second World War : An illustrated history*, London, Hamish Hamilton, 1975; New York, Putnam, 1975, 238p, 169 illus. 23 maps

Pub. in pbk. as a Penguin, Harmondsworth, Penguin Books, 1976

It is a concise narrative history, which blends together the war in Europe and that in the Far East. He concludes, 'Despite all the killing and destruction that accompanied it, the Second World War was a good war.' (p 234)

In the Preface (p 10) he observes, 'I have been composing this book for more than thirty years.

During the war I gave monthly commentaries in Oxford and other towns, surveying the events of the previous month and sometimes speculating on what was likely to happen next. At the end of the war I summarized its history in a series of radio talks for the Danish service of the BBC . . . ' (*see* Appendix (b), 2–13). 'Thirty years afterwards is about the right time to look at the Second World War with detachment.'

The substance of the first chapter of the book was given at London University as the Creighton Lecture for 1973 (*see* C13). The book is dedicated to Len Deighton.

Reviews

(i) 'World War II in perspective', C.M. Woodhouse, *Obs*. 13 Apr. 1975. p 29

'Three things distinguish his work from any other account of the war: his unfailing grasp of the details on every front, the marvellous succinctness of his narrative, and his acute use of anecdotes to concentrate attention on the crucial turning-points.'

' . . . Mr. Taylor's writing has an impeccable precision. Not a word is wasted, not a sentence without point; and the composition is a work of art.'

(ii) 'Pot Shots', Mark Arnold-Forster, *NS*. 89, 2300. 18 Apr. 1975. pp 416–7

He comments that A.J.P.T. 'has so triumphantly overcome' the problems of condensing the whole war into a brief space. 'He has written a sequential story which describes all the major events and developments in chronological order', without clumsiness. 'Taylor's great gift, which shines through this book, is to show how events, mistakes and decisions which must now seem amazing were actually inevitable.'

(iii) Hugh Thomas, *Li*. 93, 2403. 24 Apr. 1975. p 537

'The style of the book suggests the moral. Mr. Taylor's prose is well adapted to a view of history which concludes that everything happens by accident

... Practically no-one has any idea of what they are doing ... This is, of course, the reverse of Marxist history. The result is that the book is unfair to all in authority.'

(iv) C.J. Bartlett, *Hist.* 61, 203. Oct. 1976. pp 474–5

'There is much to admire in this book, especially the skill with which so complicated a story is told ... There is a continuing retreat by Taylor from his earlier portrayal of Hitler as a politician with no serious long-term plans, although elsewhere he is able to develop to good effect his argument that politicians and generals were more often the victims than the makers of events.'

(v) "The Good War", Neal Ascherson, *NYRB*, 23, 21–2, 22 Jan. 1976, pp 14, 16

'The whole book is perhaps masterful rather than masterly. Gaudy beads of anecdote roll about among the hypotheses ... The text is brilliant and the pictures nothing very special, intelligently selected but ancillary to the writing.'

A21. *Essays in English History*, London, Hamish Hamilton, 1976, 335 p

Pub. in pbk. as a Pelican, Harmondsworth, Penguin Books, 1976

Essays and book reviews mostly selected from earlier collections (A5, A6, A19 and A13). Items 1, 4, 25, 30 and 31 are collected in a book of essays for the first time. A.J.P.T. introduces each essay, often just indicating why it was written and in what publication, sometimes giving anecdotes about it or giving up to date information on the topic. Thus of 26, he writes that Lord Stansgate had been in the audience for the lecture and had commented to A.J.P.T. 'I had no idea it had been like that'; and for 31 he reflects on changes in Manchester over the twenty years since he wrote the piece. There is a very brief Preface. (p 7)

Contents

3. Cromwell and the Historians (Sept. 1958. *see* E47 *and* A13)
4. Conquerors and Profiteers (1973. *see* D37)
5. Charles James Fox (Sept. 1956. *see* E40 *and* A13)
6. William Cobbett (Aug. 1953. *see* G524 *and* A9)
7. Macaulay and Carlyle (Jul. 1953. *see* E31 *and* A9)
8. Queen Victoria and the Constitution (Jan. 1951. *see* E29 *and* A6)
9. Lord John Russell (Mar. 1947. *see* E12 *and* A5)
10. Genocide (Nov. 1962. *see* G966 *and* A13)
11. John Bright and the Crimean War (1954. *see* D13, C3 *and* A9)
12. Palmerston (Jul. 1951. *see* D7 *and* A9)
13. Dizzy (Jan. 1955. *see* G606 *and* A9)
14. Lord Salisbury (Apr. 1947. *see* E13 *and* A5)
15. Prelude to Fashoda: The Question of the Upper Nile 1894–5 (Jan. 1950. *see* D2 *and* A6)
16. Economic Imperialism (Mar. 1955. *see* E36 *and* A9)
17. The Jameson Raid (Jan. 1952. *see* G460 *and* A6)
18. The Man In The Cloth (Aug. 1956. *see* E39 *and* A13)
19. The Boer War (Oct. 1949. *see* E26 *and* A6)
20. 'Joe' at his Zenith (Jun. 1951. *see* G430 *and* A6)
21. The Chief (Jun. 1959. *see* G836 *and* A13)
22. The Anglo-Russian Entente (Aug. 1957. *see* E42 *and* A13)
23. 'We Want Eight, and We Won't Wait' (Feb. 1959. *see* E52 *and* A13)
24. The Use of Monarchy (Aug. 1952. *see* G486 *and* A9)
25. A Patriot for One Ireland (May 1973. *see* G1349)
26. Politics in the First World War (1959. *see* D26, C6 *and* A13)
27. Lloyd George: Rise and Fall (1961. *see* C7 *and* A13)
28. Spam on a Gold Plate (Oct. 1958. *see* G804 *and* A13)
29. Unlucky Find (Dec. 1961. *see* G927 *and* A13)

30. Daddy, What Was Winston Churchill? (Apr. 1974. *see* E93)
31. Manchester (Mar. 1957. *see* D19)

A22. *The War Lords*, London, Hamish Hamilton, 1977; New York, Atheneum, 1978, 189 p, 162 illus.

Pub. in pbk, Harmondsworth, Penguin, 1979 (dated 1978 but not issued until early 1979).

The six lectures given on BBC television in 1976 (*see* Appendix (c), 96–101). In the Preface (pp 13–14) he observes that he gave the lectures without notes and so 'I have tidied up the text for publication, removing occasional muddles or false starts.' He comments of the five War Lords, 'They provided the springs of action throughout the years of War. This was an astonishing assertion of the Individual in what is often known as the age of the masses.'

Trans into Dutch by Jan Stoof, with intro. by Dr. H.W. Tromp (pp 2), Ede, I.J. Veen, 1978.

A23. *How Wars Begin*, London, Hamish Hamilton; New York, Atheneum, 1979, 192 p, 150 illus.

(i) 'Making historians sit up', John Terraine, *Daily Telegraph* 5 Jul., 1979, p. 15

Suggests that A.J.P.T.'s thought provoking remarks are sometimes valuable, sometimes likely to cause other historians 'rage and anguish'.

'On the television screen, A.J.P. Taylor has a quite extraordinary skill at gripping an audience with unscripted historical discourse. Unfortunately ... what may pass for profundity on screen has a way of looking rather less so in the cold light of print'.

B: BOOKS EDITED OR INTRODUCED BY A.J.P.T.

B1. *The Struggle for Supremacy in Germany 1859–1866*, Heinrich Friedjung, London, Macmillan, 1935; New York, Russell and Russell, 1966 (Studies in Modern History; general ed. L.B. Namier), trans. A.J.P. Taylor, W.L. McElwee, intro. A.J.P. Taylor, xxxi, 339 p, map

The book is an abridged trans. from the 10th ed. (1916–17) of the 2 vol. work by Friedjung, first pub. in 1897

Translators' note (pp v–vi). 'Our general principle has been to preserve in full the political and diplomatic matter, but to keep only so much of the military history as is necessary for an understanding of the general account.' They added translators' notes to take account of new material stemming from the opening of the Austrian archives after the First World War.

Intro. (pp ix–xxxi). It is dated 3 Jan. 1935. It appraises Friedjung's career against the background of the history of Austria 1866–1918 and in particular against the position of German Austrians in Austria in that period. He deems Friedjung to be 'the greatest of Austrian historians' and this to be his greatest work. 'His account is impartial . . . it springs from the fact that Friedjung sympathised with both sides, as he was both an Austrian and German.'

B2. *The Opening of An Era: 1848. An Historical Symposium*, ed. Francois Fejtö, London, Allan Wingate, 1948, with an intro. A.J.P. Taylor, xxviii, 444 p

Intro. entitled 'The Opening of An Era: 1848' (pp xv–xxviii). It surveys the revolutions of 1848 in Europe. 'Movement, and a conviction that Utopia could be reached, were the essence of 1848: underlying these was a faith in the limitless goodness of human nature.' 'Reason took the place of respect; and self-interest the place of tradition.'

Repr. omitting the final section (pp xxv–xxviii, which introduces the essays in the symposium) in A5, pp 47–60; A15, pp 40–53; and A17, pp 46–59

B3. *A Select List of Books on European History 1915–1915*, ed. for the Oxford Recent History Group by Alan Bullock and A.J.P. Taylor, Oxford, Clarendon Press, 1948, 72 p

The Preface has the comment, 'It is limited to secondary works and takes no account of collections of documents, memoirs or other historical sources.' It also excludes books on British history and those in Dutch or in Scandinavian and East European languages.

2nd edn. 1957 (with a new preface in addition to that of the 1st edn. and a thorough revision of the list), 80 p

B4. *British Pamphleteers. Volume Two: From The French Revolution To The Nineteen Thirties*, ed. Reginald Reynolds, intro. A.J.P. Taylor, London, Allan Wingate, 1951, 302 p

Intro. (pp 7–15). In it he praises the pamphlet as a form of literature ('the Hyde Park corner of the written word'). He then argues that in recent times rebels have been feted by society. 'All the authors in this book are individuals for whom rebellion has paid big dividends.' He concludes by discussing freedom. '. . . I care for intellectual freedom very deeply; and can think of nothing else which can make existence tolerable'.

Ack. (p 16) includes a paragraph noting 'the complete disagreement between the views' of A.J.P.T. and Reginald Reynolds.

On a comment in his Intro. which might have been construed to suggest that H.N. Brailsford felt that Belgium would be better off under German rule, A.J.P.T. wrote in a letter to *The New Statesman and Nation* 'I withdraw the remark unreservedly and regret that it was made.' (*NS & N.* 43, 1090. 26 Jan. 1952. p 99)

B5. *Essays Presented to Sir Lewis Namier*, ed. Richard Pares, A.J.P. Taylor, London, Macmillan, 1956; New York, St. Martin's Press 1956, Books for Libraries Press, 1971, viii, 542 p

The Preface (pp v–vi) gives a brief outline of Namier's career.

The volume includes an essay by A.J.P.T. 'The War Aims of the Allies in the First World War' (pp 475–505). This is a major essay which discusses the evolution of war aims in some detail.

Repr. in A13, pp 93–122

B6. *The Reichstag Fire. Legend And Truth*, Fritz Tobias, trans. from the German by Arnold J. Pomerans, intro. A.J.P. Taylor, London, Secker and Warburg, 1963; New York, Putnam, 1964, 348 p

Intro. (pp 9–16). In it he gives a brief sketch of the historical background and praises Tobias' research. A.J.P.T.'s main pleasure in it is that it destroys one accepted case of Nazi planning. 'It . . . set the pattern for explanations of all Hitler's later acts. We saw at every stage – over rearmament, over Austria, over Czechoslovakia, over Poland – the same deliberate and conspiratorial cunning which had been first shown on 27 February 1933.'

See also D27 and Appendix.

B7. *The Abdication of King Edward VIII*, Lord Beaverbrook, ed. A.J.P. Taylor, London, Hamish Hamilton, 122 p; New York, Atheneum, 1966 (American edn. has a biographical outline of Lord Beaverbrook, p 123); Ontario, Collins.

Foreword (pp 7–11) by A.J.P.T. He discusses how Beaverbrook composed his historical works and how reliable they are. He deems this book to be 'Beaverbrook at his most sparkling' and discusses what new information it provides.

B8. *The Communist Manifesto*, Karl Marx and Friedrich Engels, intro. A.J.P. Taylor, Pelican pbk. Penguin

Books, Harmondsworth, 1967, repr. 1968, 1969 (twice), 1970, 1971, 1972, 1973, 1974, 1975, 124 p

Trans. Samuel Moore, first pub. 1888. As well as the intro. A.J.P.T. supplies a bibliography (pp 48–9) and notes (pp 123–4)

In the Intro. (pp 7–47) he puts Marx and his ideas into their historical context (thus he argues strongly that the *Manifesto* is very 'deeply . . . rooted in the circumstances of the time'). He presents a critique of Marx's theories, which is an irreverant and sceptical appraisal, witty but often unfair to Marx.

B9. *History of the Twentieth Century*, 6 Vols. editor-in-chief, A.J.P. Taylor; general ed., J.M. Roberts, pub. in parts in magazine form, London, Purnell, 1968–70, 2688 p

This includes the following contributions by A.J.P.T.:

(a) 'Uneasy Splendour: British Empire to 1902', Vol. 1, pp 6–12. This is a brief survey, which includes the view that in 1902: 'Isolation might be a little tarnished. There might be uneasy moments. It remained splendid all the same.'

(b) 'Entente-Cordiale: Great Britain and France 1893–1904', Vol. 1, pp 86–9

(c) 'Joseph Chamberlain', Vol. 1, p 112. 'Chamberlain brought a new bitterness into British politics. He was unsparing in victory and savage in defeat.'

(d) 'War By Time-Table: European Crisis, July-August 1914', Vol. 1, pp 443–8. 'Though there were, no doubt, deep-seated reasons for disputes between the greatest powers, the actual outbreak of the First World War was provoked almost entirely by the rival plans for mobilisation.'

Repr. in B19, pp 25–28

(e) 'War Weariness and Peace Overtures: 1916–1918', Vol. 2, pp 815–9. 'No doubt the people ought to have demanded an end to the war. In fact fiercer war was from first to last the popular cause.'

Repr. in B19, pp 149–53 and another compilation from this project, *History of the Twentieth Century*, intro. Alan Bullock, London, Octopus Books, 1976, (hereafter "1976 compilation"), pp 113–7

(f) 'Lenin: October and After', Vol. 3, pp 1026–30. 'He was a very great man and even, despite his faults, a very good man.'

(g) 'The Myths of Munich', Vol. 4, pp 1627–30

(h) 'Europe on the Brink of War: Europe 1938–9', Vol. 4, pp 1647–52

Repr. in B20, pp 19–24 and 1976 compilation, pp 219–25

(i) 'The Outbreak of War: Europe, August-September 1939', Vol. 4, pp 1655–7

Repr. as 'The Storm Breaks' in B20, pp 29–31 and as 'The Outbreak of War' in 1976 compilation, pp 230–3

(j) 'The False Alliance: The Soviet Union and Germany, August 1939 – June 1941', Vol. 5, pp 1795–8. '. . . Soviet Russia was thrown into the most terrible war ever fought by a civilised power. She was saved more by the heroism of her own people than by the abilities of her rulers.'

(k) 'To Be Continued?', Vol. 6, pp 2682–3. In this he takes a gloomy view of the rate of growth of population in the world in the future and of the nuclear arms race.

B10. *Churchill Revised : A Critical Assessment*, A.J.P. Taylor, Robert Rhodes James, J.H. Plumb, Basil Liddell Hart, Anthony Storr, New York, Dial Press, 1969, 282 p; pub. in Great Britain as *Churchill : Four Faces and the Man*, London, Allen Lane, 1969, 252 p

Pub. as a Pelican pbk., Harmondsworth, Penguin Books, 1973

His contribution is the essay 'The Statesman' (pp 9–51) in which he shrewdly surveys Churchill's career, putting most emphasis on the Second World War. 'From the beginning Churchill was a statesman rather than a politician.'

The last part of the essay, dealing with the Second World War was published as 'The Price of Victory', *Obs.* 13 April 1969, p 23

B11. *The History of the English Speaking Peoples*, Sir Winston Churchill, ed. Christopher Falkus, Christopher Humble; editorial board, Sir Mortimer Wheeler, Hugh Trevor-Roper and A.J.P. Taylor, 7 Vols. issd. in magazine form in 112 parts, London, Purnell for BPC Publishing, 1969–71, 3598 p

Based on Sir Winston Churchill's book, it amplifies many themes with articles by various writers. It includes the following two contributions by A.J.P.T.:

(a) 'Lament for a Commonwealth', Vol. 1, pp 12–13. In it he argues that for Britain the Second World War was an Imperial war ('It was fought by the British mainly in the Imperial zones of the Mediterranean and the Far East') and regrets that Britain has turned to Europe in recent years.

(b) 'A Troubled Legacy', Vol. 7, pp 3592–8. A survey of British history from the death of Queen Victoria, which observes that 'the problems which baffled the Victorians were solved by their successors' and optimistically suggests that the same will be true in the future.

B12. *Lloyd George: Twelve Essays*, ed. A.J.P. Taylor, London, Hamish Hamilton; New York, Atheneum, 1971, xiv, 393 p

A collection of twelve essays stemming from some of the earlier Beaverbrook Library research seminars, which A.J.P.T. organised and chaired. (The seminars were started in December 1968 and held in university vacations from then until the Library closed in 1975).

Introduction (pp v–vii) by A.J.P.T. It contains a brief apraisal of Lloyd George ('the most dynamic figure in British politics during the first part of the twentieth century'), a brief account of the history of the Lloyd George Papers under Beaverbrook's ownership and of the holdings of the Beaverbrook Library.

B13. *Lloyd George. A Diary by Frances Stevenson*, ed. A.J.P. Taylor, London, Hutchinson; New York, Harper and Row, 1971, xiv, 338 p

Preface (pp ix–xiii) by A.J.P.T. In this he discusses

the significance of the diary, its value and its shortcomings. 'The Diary is a unique document – a claim often made but rarely with as much justification as in this case.'

Extracts from it were serialised on pp 8 and 9 of *The Sunday Express* on 14 and 21 February 1971 under the title 'My Darling Pussy. The Diary of a Prime Minister's Mistress'.

B14. *My Youth in Vienna*, Arthur Schnitzler, trans. Catherine Hutter, London, Weidenfeld and Nicolson, 1971, 304 p

Foreword (pp ix–xiv) by A.J.P.T. In it he gives an outline of the political significance of Vienna and its cultural development in the second half of the nineteenth century. 'Schnitzler's autobiography describes the last years when Vienna was still living in the present.'

B15. *White Eagle, Red Star : The Polish-Soviet War 1919–20*, Norman Davies, London, MacDonald; New York, St. Martin's Press, 1972, 318 p

Foreword (pp ix–x) by A.J.P.T. In it he consider the importance of the war – 'It largely determined the course of European history for the next twenty years or more.' He commends the book without any reservations.

B16. *The Dictionary of World History*, general ed. G.M.D. Howat; advisory ed. A.J.P. Taylor, London, Nelson, 1973, 1720 p

Foreword (pp xxi–xxii) by A.J.P.T. In it he discusses 'facts' in history, what has survived and how significant it is. He also discusses the nature of history and the role of the historian. '... the true historian is not a chronicler. In a sense he 'makes' history. He creates a version that satisfies contemporaries until a better one comes along.'

Contributions by A.J.P.T.: Beaverbrook, pp 157–8; Sir Richard Stafford Cripps, p 403; The First World War, pp 535–6; Lloyd George, p 886; and The Second World War, pp 1360–1

B17. *Off The Record. Political Interviews 1933–1943*, W.P.

Crozier, ed. and intro. A.J.P. Taylor, London, Hutchinson, 1973, xxiv, 397 p

Intro. (pp xix–xxiv). He discusses Crozier's place in the history of *The Manchester Guardian* and the nature and purpose of these interviews.

Extracts from the book were published in *The Guardian*, 25 July 1973. p 14

B18. *British Prime Ministers*, general ed. A.J.P. Taylor. A series of brief biographies, each with a short intro. by A.J.P. Taylor, London, Weidenfeld and Nicolson, 1974–6;

Pitt, New York, Scribner, 1974, *Eden*, New York, St. Martins Press, 1977

(a) *Pitt The Younger*, Derek Jarrett, 1974. In his Intro. (pp 9–10) he observes, 'It is a career in which I find much to admire, if, personally, little to like.'

(b) *Lloyd George*, Kenneth O. Morgan, 1974. In his Intro. (pp 7–8) he briefly discusses Lloyd George's character and achievements, and concludes, '... Lloyd George was the greatest ruler of England since Oliver Cromwell.'

(c) *Palmerston*, Dennis Judd, 1975. In his Intro. (pp vii–viii) he deems him to be 'a sort of nineteenth-century Churchill' and observes, 'He was in politics for fun, and no prime minister has provided it so abundantly.'

(d) *Lord Melbourne*, Dorothy Marshall, 1975. In his Intro. (pp vii–viii) he finds him 'a mysterious figure', delightful to read about but he wonders 'what does he tell us about the political world in which prime ministers are supposed to rule supreme?'

(e) *Sir Robert Walpole*, Betty Kemp, 1976. In his Intro. (pp ix–x) he observes that Walpole 'was just as much the first modern Prime Minister we should recognise as Adam was the first man'.

(f) *Sir Anthony Eden*, Sidney Aster, 1976. In his Intro. (2 p unnumbered) he roundly condemns Eden over the Suez crisis, observing, 'Eden, if anyone, not Nasser, was the Hitler of 1956 with the same cloud of words and the same unscrupulousness of action.'

(g) *Neville Chamberlain*, H. Montgomery Hyde, 1976. In his Intro. (pp ix–x) he observes, 'Where he failed was in inspiration . . . In a crisis good will and efficiency are not enough.'

(h) *Stanley Baldwin*, Kenneth Young, 1976. In his Intro. (pp ix–x) he discusses Baldwin's character and achievements. He finds that 'Behind his rustic exterior there was a man of infinite guile', but concludes, 'In the last resort, Baldwin was a good man. He left maybe a legacy of neglect. But he also preserved and enhanced the civilised values that have distinguished British politics and the British people.'

B19. *History of World War I*, editor-in-chief, A.J.P. Taylor; comp. S.L. Mayer, London, Octopus Books, 1974, 286 p

A compilation from B9, including pieces (d) and (e) by A.J.P.T.

B20. *History of World War II*, editor-in-chief, A.J.P. Taylor; comp. S.L. Mayer, London, Octopus Books, 1974, 286 p

A compilation from B9, including pieces (h) and (i) by A.J.P.T.

B21. *My Darling Pussy. The letters of Lloyd George and Frances Stevenson 1913–41*, ed. A.J.P. Taylor, London, Weidenfeld and Nicolson, 1975, xi, 258 p

Intro. (pp vii–xi). He discusses the relationship between Lloyd George and Frances Stevenson and the value of the letters to the historian.

He introduced a selection from the correspondence in a programme ('My Darling Pussy') on BBC Radio 4 on 30 Jan. 1977, 2215–2300 hours

B22. *The Last of Old Europe: A Grand Tour With A.J.P. Taylor*, London, Sidgwick and Jackson; New York, Quadrangle Books/New York Times Co., 1976, 225 p

'A Photographic Panorama from the 1850s to 1914'. The photographs were not selected by A.J.P.T.

Intro. (pp 6–29) by A.J.P.T. He surveys European history in the period, starting with a discussion of the significance of the 1848 revolutions. He considers such themes as nationalism, the impact of technological innovation, and the position of women in society and their treatment in history books.

B23. *The Bedside Guardian : 25 : Selections from the Guardian 1975–1976*, London, Collins, 1976

Intro. (pp 5–7) by A.J.P.T. He discusses what *The Manchester Guardian* has meant to him in the past and contrasts its past with what it is today.

B24. *Ten Days That Shook The World*, John Reed, pbk. edn. in Penguin Modern Classics, Harmondsworth, Penguin Books, 1977, xix, 351 p

Intro. (pp vii–xix) by A.J.P.T. It is prefaced by A.J.P.T. explaining that it was written for Penguin Books in 1964. Then the copyright, which was held by the Communist Party of Great Britain, had not expired. Major objections were made to the introduction – and Penguin Books then published the book without any introduction, rather than have someone else write an introduction acceptable to the copyright holders.

He praises Reed's book as a classic, but warns that it 'is not reliable in every detail. Its achievement is to recapture the spirit of those stirring days.' In particular he disagrees with Reed's belief that the Bolshevik leaders knew precisely what they were doing. He provides his own sketch of events in Petrograd between March and November 1917.

B25. *Fighter. The true story of the Battle of Britain*, Len Deighton, London, Jonathan Cape, 1977, intro. A.J.P. Taylor, 304 p. In paperback, London, Granada, 1979.

Intro. (pp 11–18). He praises Sir Thomas Inskip for getting more fighter 'planes built – 'he deserves some credit as the man who made British victory in the Battle of Britain possible'. (p 13) He also praises Dowding and Beaverbrook. He discusses the significance of the Battle of Britain and its consequences.

B26. *The Russian War 1941–1945*, ed. Daniela Mrázková and Vladimir Remes, text A.J.P. Taylor, Jonathan Cape, 1978 (first pub. in Czechoslovakia, 1975), 143 p

Preface (p 7) and intro. to each section by A.J.P.T. He observes at the start of the first chapter, 'A People At War', 'In the Second World War the camera came of age as an instrument of information and propaganda.' (p 9) He comments that the Cold War was 'the greatest disaster in our lifetime' and, 'If this book does something to dispel western suspicions of the Soviet Union it will have achieved its purpose and I shall have achieved my humbler purpose in writing this introduction.' (p 11)

Some of the photographs and part of A.J.P.T.'s intro. to the first section were repr. as 'Classic Images Of The Russian Front', *Sun. Times*. 23 Apr. 1978. Magazine, pp 24–34

C: PAMPHLETS

C1. *Czechoslovakia's Place in A Free Europe*, London, Czechoslovak Institute in London, 1943, 20 p

'. . . the substance of the lecture given by A.J.P. Taylor . . . at the Czechoslovak Institute in London on April 29th 1943. Jan Masaryk, Czechoslovak Minister for Foreign Affairs and Deputy Prime Minister, was in the Chair.'

In it he outlines themes developed more fully in A3 and A4. He argues that the Habsburg Monarchy had been a bulwark against the Turks and then against German expansion (up until 1867). 'The vast German power has threatened for a century to destroy the balance of force which secures the liberties of Europe. . . .' (p 9) However the Habsburg Monarchy was doomed as it was organised 'not merely on the basis of a landed aristocracy but with ideas derived from a landed aristocracy'. (p 10)

Czechoslovakia's function is to be a barrier against Pan-German expansion. It is also to be a meeting point between the Western democracies and Russia; she should 'be the interpreter of the Slav spirit in England and America and the missionaries of democracy among the Slavs'. (p 20) Czechoslovakia combines the best values of Western society and also of Slav society (p 14); in contrast, 'Germany has accumulated inside itself all the vices of both West and East.' (p 15)

C2. *Trieste*, London, Yugoslav Information Office, 1945, 32 p map

Repr. A5, pp 179–207, with a Postcript (1949), pp 207–8

In the Postcript (1949) he writes 'This essay was written as a pamphlet in 1945 at the request of the Yugoslav Government. It originally ended with the plea that to recognise Slovene claims to Trieste would strengthen good relations between East and West. This ending was removed at Yugoslav suggestion . . . ' Publication by the Yugoslavs in 1945 was advantageous, as it ensured that paper was provided for the pamphlet.

In the pamphlet he argues that Trieste should be part of Yugoslavia not Italy. As a port it was essential for the Slovenes, of no importance for Italian foreign trade. Even if the majority of the population of Trieste called themselves 'Italian' they were not so by descent and did so 'rather as a mark of class distinction than of Italian patriotism'. The Treaty of Rapallo, 1920, gave Italy 600,000 Slovenes and Croats. He observes, 'Italian rule over these South Slavs had no parallel in Europe until the worst days of the Nazi dictatorship.'

C3. *John Bright and the Crimean War*, (*see* D13), repr. as a pamphlet, Manchester, The Librarian, John Rylands Library and Manchester U.P., 1954, 22 p

It was a lecture given at the John Rylands Library, Manchester. In his introduction to it in A21 he writes, 'The lecture was the only one I ever gave with a prepared script. It was an offshoot from *The Struggle for Mastery in Europe 1848–1918*. If I were to deliver the lecture again, I should be less critical of John Bright and more critical of British policy.'

Repr. A9, pp 45–64, and A21, pp 79–104

C4. *The Russian Revolution*, (ATV Library Series), London, Associated Television Limited, n.d. (in fact, early 1958), 30 p

It consists of three television lectures: (1) The End of the Tsars; (2) Russia Out of Control; (3) How the Bolsheviks Did It. These were transmitted on Monday evenings between 1800 and 1830 hours on 12, 19 and 26 Aug. 1957 as the first series of lectures on television, with the overall title of 'Challenge'.

This series was soon followed by another: 'Alan Taylor Lectures: When Europe Was the Centre of the World'. The first eleven of these were half hour broadcasts, at 1830 hours on Monday evenings; the last two were twenty minutes long, starting at 1840 hours on Mondays. The titles were: The Fall of the Bastille (23 Sept. 1957); Napoleon (7 Oct.); The Congress of Vienna (21 Oct.); The Revolutions of 1848 (4 Nov.); Cavour and Garibaldi (18 Nov.); Bismarck (2 Dec.); Francis Joseph of Austria (16 Dec.); Turkey: The Sick Man of Europe (30 Dec.); The Expansion of Europe (13 Jan. 1958); China (27 Jan.); International Socialism (10 Feb.); Liberal Civilisation (24 Feb.); The End of the Story: 1914 (10 Mar.)

The pamphlet's introduction mixes the two series together. It gives estimated audience for figures for the second series as 750,000.

The pamphlet publishes the Russian lectures with the order of (2) and (3) reversed. The End of the Tsars, pp 4–12. Russia Out of Control, pp 22–9. How the Bolsheviks did it, pp 13–21. Perhaps at ATV they felt the title 'Russia out of Control' must describe post revolutionary Russia!

These three lectures provide a popular account of the Russian Revolution. The first deals with the February Revolution and Lenin's return to Russia. In it he argues that 'the strain which broke down Russia was the strain of sending fodder to the millions of army horses. . . . ' (p 5); and, less surprisingly, that the February Revolution grew out of food riots and disillusionment with the established order. The second deals with the period between the February Revolution and the end of September 1917. In this Lenin is not depicted as 'the wise, confident all-seeing leader'; though he is seen as a single minded revolutionary. Kerensky is depicted as 'the great talker'. (p 24) The third deals with the October Revolution, one which he characterises as having 'had leaders and practically no followers', (p 13) in complete contrast with that of February. He also argues that it would be wrong to depict the Bolsheviks (other than Lenin) as knowing what they were doing or planning carefully in advance. He praises 'Trotsky's practical genius' (p 15) and finds that 'The real creator of the Bolshevik Revolution, the man who forced the Bolsheviks into action, was none other than Kerensky.' (p 17)

C5. *The Great Deterrent Myth*, London, CND, 1958, 8 p

The text is dated 3 Apr. 1958. A.J.P.T. was on the Executive Committee of the Campaign For Nuclear Disarmament.

He argues that there is no defence against H-bombs – and that possession of them does not deter the Russians from conventional war. 'Maybe H-bombs make a big war impossible. But reliance on them makes little wars easy – for the other side.' (p 2) Argues that the Russians would only attack Britain either as a pre-emptive strike in fear of American and British H-bombs in the country, or to acquire Britain's resources, or to turn the populace into communists. In the first case possession of the bomb would be Britain's undoing; in the latter there would be no point in their using H-bombs. He dismisses the idea that they make Britain independent of America.

He calls for the immediate abandonment of the H-bomb in the UK. It would make Britain more prosperous, remove the danger of nuclear attack and leave more resources for conventional defence weapons. In addition 'there is just a tiny chance that our example may spread. ... There can be no harm in trying morality for a change. Look what happened about the slave trade a century and a half ago . . . ' (p 7)

C6. *The Exploded Bomb*. London, C.N.D., n.d. (1959), 8 p

The pamphlet begins with the statement that C.N.D. started 'just over two years ago'. A.J.P.T. was on the Executive Committee at the time this pamphlet was published at the price of 4d.

He surveys the inpact of CND on British politics. 'Unilateral nuclear disarmament is the biggest issue in politics'. He denies that it is an emotional movement but observes, 'It certainly is a movement of morality' (p 1). 'Nuclear weapons are wicked' (p 8). He argues that they do not deter, criticises the idea of Britain joining with others to produce 'a NATO deterrent', and denounces the idea of Britain sheltering under an

American nuclear umbrella (pp 2–6). He urges that Britain should try to become like Finland and Yugoslavia, the invasion of which would be too much trouble for the Russians (p 6). He deplores the idea of using nuclear weapons on Russian cities in any circumstances and doubts if the Russians have any intentions to conquer the world (p 7)

Instead of owning nuclear weapons Britain should concentrate on ground-forces and take the lead in setting-up a non-nuclear zone from the Soviet frontier to the Atlantic. 'Europe would then possess greater security than it has known in modern times' (p 8)

C7. *Politics in the First World War* (*see* D26), repr. as a pamphlet for the British Academy, London, Oxford U.P., 1959, repr. 1975, 29 p

This was the Raleigh lecture on History, given at the British Academy on 4 Feb. 1959

Repr. in A13, pp 11–44, and A21, pp 218–254

C8. *Lloyd George: Rise and Fall*, London, Cambridge U.P., 1961, 38 p

This was the Leslie Stephen lecture for 1961, given in the Senate House of Cambridge University on 21 Apr. 1961

A sparkling study of Lloyd George, 'the great 'rogue' of British political life', which attempts to answer the questions-how did such an outsider attain supreme power and how did he lose it. A perceptive analysis of Lloyd George's character and his effectiveness as a politician.

Repr. in A13, pp 123–149, and A21, pp 254–282. Part of it, pp 11–14 and pp 33–7, repr. as 'His Balance Sheet of Success', pp 169–174, in *Lloyd George* (Great Lives Observed Series, ed. G.E. Stearn), ed. M. Gilbert, Englewood Cliffe, New Jersey, Prentice-Hall, 1968

C9. *World War*, London, Rediffusion Television Limited, n.d. (in fact 1966), 24 p

It consists of four television lectures out of a series of ten transmitted late on Wednesday evenings during the summer of 1966. The four published are: (1) Great

Britain's War, pp 2–7; (2) Russia's War, pp 8–13; (3) America's War, pp 14–19; (4) The Cold War Spreads, pp 20–4. The series of ten half hour lectures were: 1. The World at Peace 1919–1933 (2317 hours, 29 Jun.); 2. The Disturbers 1933–1938 (2315 hours, 6 Jul.); 3. Germany's War (2327 hours, 27 Jul.); 4. Great Britain's War (2312 hours, 3 Aug.); 5. Italy's War (2307 hours, 10 Aug.); 6. Russia's War (2312 hours, 17 Aug.); 7. Japan's War (2341 hours, 24 Aug.); 8. America's War (2312 hours, 31 Aug.); 9. The Cold War Starts (2329 hours, 7 Sept.); 10. The Cold War Spreads (2327 hours, 14 Sept.)

The lectures in the pamphlet provide a popular account of some aspects of the Second World War and its aftermath. In the first he makes characteristic judgments on German war production (still slack in 1941), bombing (harmful to Britain, not Germany) and the Mediterranean (the British 'bothered about the Mediterranean . . . simply because they were there.') (p 5) He concludes, 'I think you can say that the British were more responsible than anyone for the destruction of Nazism and Fascism in Europe.' (p 7) The second deals with Russia's 'great patriotic war'. In it he stresses the toughness of the Russian army, the 'intense ruthlessness of the high command' and the barbaric behaviour of the Germans in the east. He argues that 'security was the soviet theme'. (p 12) He ends by observing, ' . . . whether the restoration of dictatorship in Russia was due to Stalin's own will or to pressure from outside dangers, it is, I think, still too early to say'. (p 13) In the third, amongst other observations, he argues that Roosevelt moved away from Britain as the war went on because he 'was always a man who turned to the successful and as Russia came up in the world, it was Russia that Roosevelt co-operated with and was ready to support'. (p 16) In the fourth he argues that the Cold War ended in 1956 with the Hungarian rising; this showed 'that the two sides had accepted a division of Europe, a division which they tended to talk about as though it was a division of the world, assuming that Europe was all the world'. (p 21) He also praises the division of Germany – 'When Germany doesn't exist as a great power, there is really nobody to cause world wars.' (p 22) He also discusses developments in Yugoslavia, China and Korea. He draws the moral that 'the greatest power cannot afford to be intolerant, cannot afford to insist upon its own way. Because if it does, it will get either cold war or ultimately war.' (p 24)

C10. *Film and the Historian*, (pub. by the British Universities' Film Council, in conjunction with the Univ. Historians' Film Committee), London, British Universities Film Council, 1968, 50 p

It is a nearly verbatim report of a conference held on 18 and 19 Apr. 1968 at University College, London. A.J.P.T. was the chairman of the conference. The pamphlet has a brief introduction by Mrs. L.A. Bawden. In this she explains that the Slade Film Department and the History Department of University College arranged programmes of films in 1966 and 1967 'designed as far as possible to co-ordinate with lectures delivered to the University by Mr. A.J.P. Taylor'.

In his contributions he warns that film is a very dangerous source for the historian. He cites film on the Second World War where 'the same shots would be used for propaganda by the opposing sides. (p 1) He argues that film can be used 'to illustrate what people felt, and thought at the time' or itself be used as historical evidence. The latter is dangerous. British inter-war newsreel had 'to be very short and express conventional right-wing views'. (p 10)

C11. *Bismarck and Germany*, (HE6), London, Sussex Tapes, 1971, 8p

Booklet which contains a very brief summary of a taped discussion between A.J.P.T. and Professor Geoffrey Barraclough. The discussion is in two parts: (1) Bismarck and Unification; (2) Bismarck in Power.

C12. *The Path to World War II*, (HB4), London, Sussex Tapes, 1971, 8 p

Booklet which contains a very brief summary of a taped discussion between A.J.P.T. and Christopher Thorne. The discussion is in two parts: (1) The Appeasers; (2) Hitler and World War II

C13. *The Second World War*, London, Athlone Press, 1974, 15 p

This was the Creighton Lecture for 1973, given in Senate House, University of London, and was the basis of Chap. 1 of A20

D: HISTORICAL ESSAYS IN BOOKS, ENCYCLOPEDIAS, LEARNED JOURNALS AND OTHERS

(This section includes appropriate pieces published in the *Saturday Review of Books*, *Times Literary Supplement*, *History Today* and *Encounter*).

D1. European Mediation and the Agreement of Villa franca, 1859, *EHR*. 51, 201. Jan. 1936. pp 52–78

A detailed diplomatic study.

D2. Prelude to Fashoda: The Question of the Upper Nile 1894–5, *EHR*. 65, 254. Jan. 1950. pp 52–80

A detailed diplomatic study.

Repr. in A6, pp 81–113, and A21, pp 129–69. In introducing it in the latter book he comments that it 'was stimulated by the publication of the relevant volume of French diplomatic documents and the opening of the Foreign Office papers to the end of 1902. The essay contains my only discovery of something previously unknown: the Anglo-Congolese agreement of 12 April 1894 . . .'

D3. Les Premieres Années De L'Alliance Russe (1892–1895) (D'Apres Les Documents Diplomatiques Francais), *Rev. His.* 74, 204. Jul-Sept. 1950. pp 62–76

A detailed diplomatic study, largely based on *Documents diplomatiques francais 1871–1914*, 1st Series, Vols. 10 and 11, 1945 and 1947.

D4. History in England, *TLS*. 2534. 25 Aug. 1950. Supplement 'A Critical and Descriptive Survey of Contemporary British Writing for Readers Overseas,' iv–v

This survey repr. in A6, pp 1–8, omitting a brief mention of his books, A4 and A5, which was made to maintain his anonymity. In the original he mentioned his books along with several books by other authors and commented 'all of these contribute something to the history of the country concerned which might have escaped a native historian'.

D5. Crimea: The War That Would Not Boil, *Hist. Today*. 1, 2. Feb. 1951. pp 23–31

Repr. in A6, pp 30–40, A15, pp 60–70 and A17, pp 67–77

D6. British Policy in Morocco 1886–1902, *EHR*. 66, 260. Jul. 1951. pp 342–74

A detailed diplomatic study, based on British Foreign Office papers and the published French and German documents.

Repr. in A6, pp 114–52

D7. Lord Palmerston, *Hist. Today*. 1, 7. Jul. 1951. pp 35–41

Repr. in *British Prime Ministers : A Portrait Gallery*, introduced by Duff Cooper, London, Allan Wingate, 1953, pp 80–9 and also in A9, pp 36–44, and A21, pp 104–115

D8. La Conférence d'Algeciras, *Rev His*. 76, 208. Oct-Dec. 1952. pp 236–54

A detailed diplomatic study based on the published French, German, British and Russian documents.

Repr. as 'The Conference at Algéciras', A9, pp 88–107, and A15, pp 135–54

D9. Contributions to the *Encyclopedia Britannica*, 1952

(a) Austria, History, Vol. 2, pp 746–9. This section covers the period 1918–1949. In it he lays particular stress on the attempts to unite with Germany. The piece concludes with the observation that the second republic (after the Second World War) 'resembled the first in that *anschluss* with Germany was the only real question in Austrian politics'.

Repr. in the 1954 and 1955 edns. (pp 746–9 in both). Repr., with an extension to 1957, in the 1957 and 1962 edns. (pp 746–9)

(b) The Austrian Empire, Vol. 2, pp 763–8. This section surveys the period 1804–1867.

Repr., pp 763–8, in the 1954, 1955, 1957 and 1962 edns.

(c) Austria-Hungary, Vol. 2, pp 768–73 and bibliography, pp 773–4. This section surveys the period 1867–1918.

Repr. (pp 768–73, pp 773–4) in the 1954, 1955, 1957, 1962 and (pp 835–46) 1970 edns.

(d) Bethlen, Stephen, Vol. 3, pp 482–3. Portrays him as the champion of the great landowners against the remnants of Karolyi's supporters and also of Hungarian 'grievances' against the Treaty of Trianon.

Repr. (pp 482–3) in the 1954, 1957 and (pp 484–5) 1962 edns.

D10. The Namier View of History, *TLS*. 2691. 28 Aug. 1953. Supplement 'Thoughts And Second Thoughts upon some Outstanding Books of the Half Century 1900–1950', pp xxii–xxiii

In it he naturally concentrates on Namier's *The Structure of Politics at the Accession of George III*, of which he comments that it 'remains fresh and stimulating, many of the ideas still not worked out even by the author himself'. He feels Namier's great flaw was to ignore principles: 'He has ignored the liberal spirit.' 'A political structure without principles does not even work; it runs inevitably to ossification.'

D11. Contribution to *Oxford Junior Encyclopedia*, Oxford University Press, London, Cumberlege, 1953

Bismarck, Vol. 5, *Great Lives*, pp 43–5. A simple outline life of Bismarck.

D12. French History in Dispute, *TLS*. 2721. 26 Mar. 1954. Supplement 'French Writing Today', p iii

In it he discusses the work of the major French historians. He regrets that in England in history 'there is not enough bitterness and dispute. There is no battle of interpretations, not even a battle of facts'. In contrast: 'To be a historian in France is to be a combatant, to be also a politician, and even (in the old fashioned sense of the term) a prophet, a moral teacher.'

D13. John Bright and the Crimean War, *Bulletin of the John Rylands Library*. 36, 2. Mar. 1954. pp 501–22

Also published as a pamphlet (*see* C3).

Repr. in A9, pp 45–64, and A21, pp 79–104

D14. The Judgement of the Diplomat, *Saturday Review of Literature*. 37. 11 Dec. 1954. pp 9, 10, 54–6

A polemical survey of diplomats in history. Among the morals drawn are 'democratic opinion is usually right', 'the people temper their idealism with common sense' and 'the professional diplomats must have ideals, and the idealists must have common sense'. Overall the piece is urging no crusades against communism.

D15. Contributions to the *Encyclopedia Britannica*, 1954

(a) Bismarck, Otto, Vol. 3, pp 659–68. A biographical sketch plus bibliography. 'Bismarck was a political genius of the highest rank, but he lacked one essential quality of the constructive statesman: he had no faith in the future.'

Repr. (pp 659–68) in the 1955, 1957, 1962 and (pp 714–22) 1970 edns.; and also in *The New Encyclopedia Britannica, Macropaedia*, 1974, Vol. 2. pp 1077–85

See also A8

(b) Germany, The German Empire, Vol. 10, pp 269–78. A survey of German history 1866–1919.

Repr. (pp 269–78) in the 1955, 1957, 1962 and (pp 322–334) 1970 edns.

D16. The Seizure of Power, *The Third Reich*, Chap. 15, pp 523–36, International Council for Philosophy and Humanistic Studies, London, Weidenfeld and Nicolson, 1955, xv, 910 p

Repr. as 'Hitler's Seizure of Power' in A9, pp 139–53, and A17, pp 204–19

D17. Contribution to *The Encyclopedia Britannica*, 1955

Prussia, History, Vol. 18, pp 652–5. A survey from the time of the Teutonic knights to 1933 (the period after 1864 is very brief, with cross references to other sections of the encyclopedia for the events of 1864–71).

Repr. in the 1957 edn. The 1962 edn. has just the part from 1815, Vol. 18, pp 654–5. The 1970 edn. has 'The Kingdom from 1815' and 'The End of Prussia' (the latter surveys the period 1918–47), Vol. 18, pp 700–3

D18. The Rise and Fall of "Pure" Diplomatic History, *TLS*. 2810. 6 Jan. 1956. Supplement 'Historical

Writing', pp xxviii and xxx

Repr. as 'The Rise and Fall of Diplomatic History' in A9, pp 81–87, and A17, pp 167–73

D19. Manchester, *En.* 8, 3. Mar. 1957. pp 3–13

An historical and personal sketch of Manchester. It was the first of a series on The World's Cities in the journal.

Repr. in A21, pp 307–25. In introducing it for this volume A.J.P.T. briefly describes how Manchester has changed since he wrote it.

D20. Fascism, *The Saturday Review of Literature*. 40, 23. 8 Jun. 1957. pp 9–10

One of seven articles on 'The Isms in 1957' by various contributors. In it he discusses various aspects of Fascism and concludes, 'Fascism is the irrational made vocal; and therefore any attempt to reduce it to rational terms defeats itself.'

D21. The Thing, *The Twentieth Century*. 162, 968. Oct. 1957. pp 293–7

The first article in a section entitled 'Is There A Power Elite?' in an issue devoted to the theme 'Who Governs Britain?'

A witty irreverent essay on the British Establishment. 'The THING is on the surface a system of public morals. Underneath it is a system of public plunder.'

D22. Contributions to the *Encyclopedia Britannica*, 1957

(a) Leopold II, Vol. 13, pp 941–2. A biographical sketch plus bibliography.

Repr. in the 1962 edn.

(b) Radowitz, Joseph Maria von, Vol. 18, pp 921–2. A biographical sketch plus bibliography. 'Radowitz combined romantic conservatism with a strong will for military efficiency.'

Repr. in the 1962 edn.

D23. A Look Back at British Socialism 1922–37, *En.* 10, 3. Mar. 1958. pp 27–33

The first article in a series in the journal entitled 'Once Upon A Time . . . '

A survey of the British Labour Movement in the

period. He concludes that the Left had two credits in the period, the General Strike and support of the Spanish Republic, and one major debit, Ramsay MacDonald.

Repr. as 'Confusion On The Left', pp 66–79, of *The Baldwin Age*, ed. John Raymond London, Eyre and Spottiswoode, 1960, 248 p

D24. Pieter Geyl: Historian, Patriot, European, *Delta.* 1, 3. Autumn 1958. pp 7–10

Praises Geyl very warmly – a man 'unflinching in his historical honesty'. 'The outstanding quality of Geyl's work, to my mind, is his judgement.'

See also E88.

D25. Keeping It Dark: Half Century Secrets, *En.* 13, 2. Aug. 1959. pp 40–5

He vigorously criticises the then fifty year restriction on access to Government records, and reviews the record of the official historians and the Cabinet Office.

D26. Politics in the First World War. The Raleigh Lecture on History for 1959, *The Proceedings of The British Academy*, 1959. pp 67–95

Also published as a pamphlet (*see* C7).

Repr. in A13, pp 11–44, and A21, pp 218–54

D27. Who Burnt the Reichstag? The Story of A Legend, *Hist. Today*. 10, 8. Aug. 1960. pp 515–22

A.J.P.T. believed that Nazis started the Reichstag fire until Fritz Tobias reviewed the evidence and published his results in *Der Spiegel*. A.J.P.T. retells the story, using this source. He draws the moral 'The affair should change our estimate of Hitler's methods. He was far from being the far-sighted planner that he is usually made to appear. He had a genius for improvision; and his behaviour over the Reichstag fire was a wonderful example of it.' He draws the larger moral from this case of Hitler's luck: 'That is the way of history. Events happen by chance; and men then mould them into a pattern.'

Repr. in A13, pp 179–89

See also B6 and Appendix

D28. International Relations, *The New Cambridge Modern History*, Vol. 11: *Material Progress and World Wide Problems 1870–1898*, ed. F.H. Hinsley, chap. 20, pp 542–66, Cambridge University Press, 1962

D29. How To Quote: Exercises For Beginners, *En.* 19, 3. Sept. 1961. pp 72–3

His reply to H. Trevor Roper's review of All in *En.* 19, 1. Jul. 1961. pp 88–96

Repr. pp 100–2, *The Origins of the Second World War*, ed. by Esmonde M. Robertson, London, Macmillan, 1971, 312 p

D30. Gli Storia E Le Origini Della Seconda Guerra Mondiale, *Storia E Politica.* 4, 1. Jan-Mar. 1965. pp 1–21

A lecture given in the University of Rome.

D31. War Origins Again, P. & P. 30 Apr. 1965. pp 110–13

A reply to the essay on A.J.P.T.'s book All, by T.W. Mason in P. & P. 29 Dec. 1964. pp 67–87

Repr. pp 136–41, *The Origins of the Second World War*, ed. Esmonde M. Robertson (*see above* D29)

D32. Neville Chamberlain E Il Cedimento Delle Democrazie, *L'Europa fra le due Guerre*, ed. Guieseppe Rossini, chap. pp 63–74, Torino, Edizioni Rai Radiotelevisione italiana, 1966

This chap., Neville Chamberlain and the Surrender of the Democracies, was the text of the talk he gave in a cycle of radio transmissions on Italian radio.

D33. Michael Karolyi in Exile, *New Hungarian Quarterly.* 9, 31. Autumn 1968. pp 18–22

It is based on personal recollections by A.J.P.T., who first met Karolyi in Oxford in 1940.

D34. Fiction in History, *TLS.* 3707. 23 Mar. 1973. pp 327–8

In the same issue there was a piece, 'History in Fiction', pp 315–6, by Mary Renault.

Repr. in A21, pp 9–17

D35. Introductory note, p 547, to Lord Beaverbrook's Two War Leaders: Lloyd George and Churchill, *Hist. Today.* 23, 8. Aug. 1973. pp 546–553

In his note he sketches Beaverbrook's relationship with Lloyd George and Churchill and explains that the essay probably was intended to be the introduction to Beaverbrook's projected book *Churchill's Victory*.

D36. Birthpangs of Commonwealth, *The History of the British Empire*, ed. John Man, Issue 68, pp 1877–1904 London, Time-Life International (Nederland) B.V. in co-operation with the British Broadcasting Corporation, 1973–5, iss. in magazine form in 98 parts.

A survey of the history of the five Dominions 1830–1930.

D37. Conquerors and Profiteers, *The History of the British Empire* (*see above* D36), Issue 97, pp 2689–2718

A.J.P.T.'s contribution to the conclusion in the last section of text, The Balance Sheet of Empire.

Repr. in A21, pp 26–45

D38. The Beaverbrook Library, *Hist.* 59. Feb. 1974. pp 47–54

Number 11 in the journal's 'Libraries and Archives' series.

A survey of the manuscript holdings, books and visual material which were held by the Library, and mention of the research seminars which used to be held on Thursday evenings during university vacations.

Most of the manuscript collections were transferred to the House of Lords Record Office when the Beaverbrook Library closed in March 1975. A.J.P.T. began holding research seminars again, in association with Martin Ceadel and John Ramsden, on Wednesday nights in term time from the Autumn of 1977 in the Institute of Historical Research, London University.

D39. Le Illusioni Di Yalta, *Storia Illustrata.* 210. May 1975. pp 20–7

'Yalta was a false dawn.' Instead of a lasting peace, it marked the start of thirty years of cold war.

D40. Comment, *JMH.* 47, 4. Dec. 1975. pp 622–3

A.J.P.T. defends his comments on using 'England' not 'Britain' in his preface to A14. The comment is on 'British History: A Plea For A New Subject' by J.G.A. Pocock, *Ibid.* pp 601–21

D41. Accident Prone, or What Happened Next, *JMH*. 49, ,1. Mar. 1977. pp 1–18

This account of his development and career as a historian was the first piece in an issue of the journal devoted to him.

Repr. in *En*. 69, 4. Oct. 1977. pp 52–61, in that journal's series 'Men and Ideas'. In a note at the end, p 61, A.J.P.T. describes the essay as 'a sort of intellectual biography'.

D42. The Monarchy, Past and Present, *Punch and the Monarchy*, ed. William Davis, essay, pp 11, 13–15, 18, London, Hutchinson, 1977

The book was the journal *Punch*'s offering in Queen Elizabeth II's Jubilee Year.

In the essay he surveys the Monarchy's constitutional and social role from the time of the Hanoverians; and makes some comments on the Crown today.

D43. Contributions to *Enciclopedia Europea*, ed. Aldo Garzanti, Milan, Garzanti, 1977

(a) Churchill, Winston Leonard Spencer. A brief outline of his career.

(b) Gran Bretagna e Irlanda del Nord: storia, Vol. 5, pp 678–91. It was written in 1971 and expanded in Spring 1977. It is an outline of British history from prehistoric times to the present, written in about 15,000 words. It has characteristic emphases – such as Charles I, 'the man of blood', 1688 and the importance of the French Revolution.

D44. 1932–1945, *Coalitions In British Politics*, ed. David Butler, chap. 4, pp 74–94, Macmillan, 1978

The first part focusses on the rise of Churchill and the fall of Chamberlain. The essay then surveys the political fortunes of Churchill's Coalition Government.

D45. The Second World War: (A) The Battle of Britain; (B) The Naval War in the Mediterranean; (C) The War In North Africa; (D) The War In The Middle East, *La Historia Mundial Contemporanea 1900–1975*, Barcelona, Salvat, (?1978)

The Battle of Britain is divided into six sections: (1) Churchill at the head of the Government; (2) Sea Lion: the projected German invasion of England; (3) The Battle of Britain; (4) The Blitz; (5) The Commonwealth; (6) Britain's Economic Mobilisation. (About 4,500 words in all)

The Naval War in the Mediterranean is divided into four sections: (1) The Mediterranean: a secondary sea; (2) Mers-el-Kebir; (3) Naval Battles in the Mediterranean; (4) The Battle for Malta. (About 1,500 words in all)

The War In North Africa is divided into six sections: (1) The Desert War: Background and First Encounters; (2) Compass: O'Connor's Victories; (3) The coming of Rommel; (4) Crusader: the second British offensive; (5) The Battle of Gazala: Bir Hacheim and Tobruk; (6) The German advance to El Alamein. (About 5,000 words in all)

The War In The Middle East is divided into three sections: (1) The Rising in Irak; (2) The Campaign in Syria; (3) The Occupation of Persia. (About 1,500 words in all)

There are brief bibliographies for the four pieces.

E: HISTORICAL ESSAYS IN NEWSPAPERS, PERIODICALS AND OTHERS

(This includes appropriate pieces published in *The Manchester Guardian*, *Observer*, *New Statesman*, and *Listener*).

E1. The Case of Mr. Eden: An Historical View, *MG*. 23 Feb. 1938. p 11

Discusses possible historical parallels, finding the case of Delcassé to be the closest. Also discusses Derby in 1878, Palmerston 1851, Rosebery and Gladstone 1892–4 and the campaign against Grey 1909–12.

Concludes with the observation '... we are now to see, with some variants, what would have happened if Grey had resigned after the Haldane Mission of 1912 and his place had been taken by one of his more sentimental critics who was determined to get an agreement with Germany at any cost'.

E2. The Revision of Treaties: 1830 and 1938, *MG*. 23 Sept. 1938. pp 9–10

'The factor which gave Belgium not one but three generations of undisturbed neutrality was not a diplomatic agreement but the totally unforeseen shifting of the European balance consequent upon the economic and political growth of Prussia-Germany and the relative decline of France. Similarly the only thing which can preserve the independence of Czecho-Slovakia will be the decline of German strength relative to that of her neighbours.'

E3. The French in Morocco, *MG*. 15 May 1939. pp 11, 12

'The French in Morocco have accomplished, with the minimum of violence, one of the greatest works of civilisation in our time.'

Repr. *MGW*. 40, 20. 19 May 1939. p 396

E4. France in Indo-China, *MG*. 29 Jul. 1941. p 4

A survey from the time of Napoleon III, with the theme 'Indo-China is the greatest and most successful part of the French Empire'.

Repr. *MGW*. 45, 5. 1 Aug. 1941. p 75

E5. French North Africa, Creation of a Century, *MG*. 13 Nov. 1942. pp 4, 6

Reviews its history, observing that 'this great achievement is as much evidence of the decline of France's European position as of the development of her imperial power'.

Repr. in A5, pp 89–92

E6. Czechoslovakia's 25 Years: Her Place In Europe, *MG*. 27 Oct. 1943. p 4

A shortened version of his lecture of 29 April 1943, which was published as a pamphlet (C1).

Repr. as '25 Years of Czechoslovakia', *MGW*. 49, 19. 5 Nov. 1943. p 260

E7. German Unity, The Background of the Reich, *MG*. 29 Mar. 1944. pp 4, 8

An historical survey with the theme, 'What is wrong with Germany is that there is too much of it. There are too many Germans, and Germany is too strong, too well organised, too well equipped with industrial resources.'

Repr. *MGW*. 50, 14. 6 Apr. 1944. p 189, A5, pp 83–5 and A17, pp 121–3

E8. German Unity: The Reich of Bismarck and Hitler, *MG*. 30 Mar. 1944. pp 4, 8

Argues that it is not practical to resurrect the German states. 'It is more practicable to make Germany's neighbours strong than to make Germany weak. There is no escaping the responsibility of being a Great Power, and a permanent and sincere Anglo-Soviet alliance will ensure the peace of Europe more effectively than any high-flown 'dismembering of Germany into her component parts'.'

Repr. *MGW*. 50, 16. 21 Apr. 1944. p 217, A5, pp 85–8, and A17, pp 123–6

E9. The Entente Cordiale, *MG*. 8 Apr. 1944. pp 4, 6

Repr. *MGW*. 50, 15. 14 Apr. 1944. p 205, A5, pp 97–100, A15, pp 124–7 and A17, pp 143–5

E10. East Prussia: Is It A 'Junker Stronghold'? *MG*. 18 Jul. 1944. pp 4, 8

Reviews the history of East Prussia and finds, 'Were Germany deprived of East Prussia it would injure the Junker class very little and the military class . . . not at all.'

Repr. as 'The Myth of 'Junker' East Prussia: An Old German Conquest', *MGW*. 51, 3. 21 Jul. 1944. p 33

E11. Tangier in British Diplomacy, *MG*. 10 Jul. 1945. pp 4, 6

Reviews the issue in the twentieth century and concludes by urging the Foreign Office to co-operate with the French there.

Repr. *MGW*. 53, 2. 13 Jul. 1945. p 19 and A5, pp 108–10

E12. The Last Great Whig, *Li*. 37, 947. 20 Mar. 1947. pp 419–20

A radio talk given on the BBC's Third Programme; *see* Appendix.

Repr. as 'Lord John Russell' in A5, pp 111–6, and A21, pp 67–72

E13. A Tory Statesman of Genius, *Li*. 37, 952. 24 Apr. 1947. pp 621–2

A radio talk given on the BBC's Third Programme; *see* Appendix.

Repr. as 'Lord Salisbury' in A5, pp 117–22, and A21, pp 122–8

E14. 1848: Year of Revolution, *MG*. 1 Jan. 1948. pp 4, 6

Repr. *MGW*. 58, 2. 8 Jan. 1948. p 12, A5, pp 33–6, A15, pp 26–9, and A17, pp 27–30

E15. French Revolution of 1848: Weakness of the Radical Movement, *MG*. 24 Feb. 1948. p 4

Repr. as 'The French Revolution', A5, pp 37–40, A15, pp 30–33 and A17, pp 30–33

E16. Vienna and Berlin: The German Revolutions of 1848, *MG*. 13 Mar. 1948. p 4

Repr. *MGW*. 58, 12. 18 Mar. 1948. p 12, and as 'Vienna and Berlin', A5, pp 40–3, A15, pp 33–6, and A17, pp 33–6

E17. The Springs of Soviet Diplomacy, *NS & N*. 35, 898. 22 May 1948. p 410

Discusses the Nazi-Soviet Pact, on the occasion of the Russians publishing documents on Munich.

Repr. in A5, pp 167–71, and A17, pp 270–3

E18. The Slav Congress 1848: Central Europe and the Habsburgs, *MG*. 2 Jun. 1948. p 4

Repr. as 'The Slav Congress', A5, pp43–6, A15, pp 36–9, and A17, pp 37–9

E19. Ancestry of the 'New Democracies', *Li*. 40, 1016. 15 Jul. 1948. pp 92–3

The first of two talks on totalitarianism given on the BBC's European Service; *see* Appendix. A review of democracy in history from the time of Plato. 'The French Revolution set the pattern for all later history: the more men talk about democracy, the less they respect it in practice . . . '

E20. Bismarck: Fifty Years After. The Man of German Destiny, *MG*. 30 Jul. 1948. p 4

Repr. as 'Bismarck: The Man of German Destiny', *MGW*. 59, 6. 5 Aug. 1948. p6, A5, pp71–4, and A17, pp 87–90

E21. Fashoda: A Turning Point in Diplomacy, *MG*. 18 Sept. 1948. p 4

Repr. as 'Fashoda', A5, pp 93–6

E22. Ten Years After, *NS & N*. 36, 917. 2 Oct. 1948. pp 278–9

Repr. as 'Munich Ten Years After', A5, pp 129–33, and A17, pp 284–8

E23. Francis Joseph: The Last Age of the Habsburgs, *MG*. 2 Dec. 1948. p 4

Repr. as 'Emperor Francis Joseph', *MGW*. 59, 24. 9 Dec. 1948. p 12, and under the original title, A5, pp 67–70, A15, pp 111–4, and A17, pp 78–81

E24. The Man of Blood, *NS & N*. 37, 934. 29 Jan. 1949. p 100

An essay marking the 300th anniversary of the

execution of King Charles I. 'The execution of Charles I ought, no doubt, to have been a great act of psychological liberation, long pursued, the culmination of a generation of revolt. In fact it was a surprise to every one concerned . . . ; like many great historical events, the result seemingly of casual circumstance.'

E25. Foreign Office Archives: Publishing the German Documents, *MG*. 18 Jul. 1949. p 4

He discusses the problems of publishing selections from the 400 tons of captured German Foreign Office Papers.

Repr. *MGW*. 61, 3. 21 Jul. 1949. p 5

E26. The Boer War: The Issues after Fifty Years, *MG*. 11 Oct. 1949. p 6

Repr. as 'The Boer War', A6, pp 156–8, and A21, pp 182–6

E27. Thomas Garrigue Masaryk: Humane Nationalism's Last Exponent, *MG*. 7 Mar. 1950. p 6

Repr. as 'Masaryk', *MGW*. 62, 10. 9 Mar. 1950. p 6 and as 'Thomas Garrigue Masaryk' A6, pp 72–4, A15, pp 162–4, and A17, pp 179–82

E28. Up From Utopia: How Two Generations Survived Their Wars, *New Republic*. 123, 18. 30 Oct. 1950. pp 15–18

Repr. A6, pp 255–62, and A17, pp 328–36

E29. Queen Victoria: Her Influence on the Constitution, *MG*. 20 Jan. 1951. p 4

Repr. *MGW*. 64, 4. 25 Jan. 1951. p 15, and as 'Queen Victoria and the Constitution', A6, pp 163–6, and A21, pp 62–6

E30. The Man of December, *Li*. 46, 1188. 6 Dec. 1951. pp 961–2

A radio talk broadcast on the BBC's Third Programme; *see* Appendix.

Repr. A6, pp 24–9, A15, pp 76–81, and A17, pp 60–6

E31. The Art of Writing History, *Li*. 50, 1272. 16 Jul. 1953. pp 108–9

Repr. (with additions; *see* G508), A9, pp 19–25, and A21, pp 54–62

In his introduction to it in the latter book, A.J.P.T. writes, 'A talk given on the Third Programme ... somewhat reinforced by passages from a review of an anthology of Macaulay's writings ...' (in fact of Carlyle's)

E32. Lord Salisbury: Last Tory and First Unionist, *MG*. 22 Aug. 1953. p 4 Repr. *MGW*, 69, 10. 3 Sep. 1953. p 5

A portrait of Salisbury, which finds him lacking in idealism. 'The cynic does best to comment on events, not try to make them. Once drawn into practical affairs, his distrust of idealism leaves him defenceless against baser forces.'

E33. The Crimean War: A Triumph of Muddle, *MG*. 27 Mar. 1954. p 4

It concludes: 'English Radicals ceased to regard themselves as the liberators of Europe ... The Crimean war taught Englishmen of the Left the doctrine of isolation, after which they still secretly hanker.'

Repr. *MGW*. 70, 15. 1 Apr. 1954. p 12

E34. Could the War of 1914–18 have been Averted? *Li*. 52, 1328. 12 Aug. 1954. pp 233–4

A radio talk given on the Third Programme of the BBC; *see* Appendix.

Repr. as 'The Outbreak of the First World War', A9, pp 119–25, A15, pp 155–61, and A17, pp 183–9

E35. The Crimean War, *Obs*. 12 Sept. 1954. p 6

A survey of the causes of the war and its development, and also its diplomatic repercussions.

E36. J.A. Hobson's Imperialism, *NS & N*. 49, 1255. 26 Mar. 1955. pp 441–2

An essay in a series, 'Reassessments'.

Repr. as 'Economic Imperialism', A9, pp 76–80, A21, pp 169–74 and as 'Hobson's Misapplication of Theory', pp 125–9, *The Theory of Capitalist Imperialism*, ed. D.K. Fieldhouse, London, Longman, 1967

B37. The Birth of Red Russia (published in three parts), *John Bull*. 99, 2598. 14 Apr. 1956. pp 9–11, 41, 43,

45; 2599. 21 Apr. 1956. pp 14, 15, 17, 43, 45–6, 49–50; and 2600. 28 Apr. 1956. pp 14–15, 17, 19, 49–50

A very 'popular' account of the Russian Revolution.

E38. Shaw the Court Jester, *Obs.* 22 Jul. 1956. p 6

'Shaw was a court jester who never lost his place at the high table.' 'He was the greatest arguer there has ever been.' However he finds him less important in his ideas than H.G. Wells, and gives the verdict that Posterity 'will find that he has nothing to say'.

E39. To the Commons in a Cap, *MG.* 11 Aug. 1956. p 4

Repr. as 'The Socialism of Keir Hardie', *MGW.* 75, 8. 23 Aug. 1956. p 12 and as 'The Man in the Cloth Cap', A13, pp 45–8, and A21, pp 182–6

E40. Charles James Fox, *MG.* 13 Sept. 1956. p 8

Repr. *MGW.* 75, 12. 20 Sept. 1956. p 11, A13, pp 161–4, and A21, pp 45–9

E41. Letter on A.P. Wadsworth on his retirement as editor of *The Manchester Guardian*, *MG.* 31 Oct. 1956. p 5

A.J.P.T.'s recollection of first meeting Wadsworth and his assessment of him as 'a great editor . . . His Radical spirit has never faltered even when he has stood alone . . . '

Repr. amidst other tributes pp 241–2, *The Beside Guardian 6*, ed. Ivor Brown, London, Collins, 1957

E42. Forgotten Anniversary: The Anglo-Russian Entente, *MG.* 31 Aug. 1957. p 6

Repr. as 'The Anglo-Russian Entente', A13, pp 49–52, and A21, pp 196–9

E43. The Improbable King (published in three parts), *Sun Ex.* 15, 22, 29 Sept. 1957. pp 2–3

A 'popular' account of King George VI. The most interesting section is the third, 'George VI and the Politicians'.

E44. The rebel who lost his nerve, *Ev. Stan.* 11 Feb. 1958. p 7

The second in the newspaper's series 'London

Dramas'. A 'popular' account of the Chartist demonstration of 10 April 1848, 'the day of the revolution which never happened'.

E45. Nothing Left To Reform: Political Consequences of 1945–50, *MG.* 11 Feb. 1958. p 6

Regrets that British politics lack controversy and offers consolation in a study of similar periods in the past. He discusses the period from the 1830s to 1914.

Repr. *MGW.* 78, 9. 27 Feb. 1958. p 7

E46. Historical commentary to 'I Was The Wife of Mussolini' by Rachele Mussolini (a series of articles adapted from her book *My Man Benito*), *Sun Ex.* 4, 11, 18 and 25 May, 1, 8 and 15 Jun. 1958. pp 2–3

E47. Cromwell and the Historians, *MG.* 3 Sept. 1958. p 6

Repr. A13, pp 157–60, and A21, pp 23–6

E48. Munich Twenty Years After: Appeasement – with the wrong man, *MG.* 30 Sept. 1958. p 6

Reviews Munich observing, 'The leading actors at Munich were sincere – at any rate for the time being.' Concludes: 'Appeasement was a sensible course, even though it was tried with the wrong man; and it remains the noblest word in the diplomatist's vocabulary.'

Repr. *MGW.* 79, 14. 2 Oct. 1958. p 7

E49. How A World War Began: Murder at Sarajevo, *Obs.* 16 Nov. 1958. pp 3, 5

Repr. A13, pp 65–74

E50. How A World War Began: 2 Dead Man's Battle Orders, *Obs.* 23 Nov. 1958. pp 3–4

Repr. A 13, pp 74–84

E51. How A World War Began: 3 Britain on the Brink, *Obs.* 30 Nov. 1958. pp 7–8

Repr. A13, pp 84–92

E52. The Dreadnought Programme: 'We want eight and we won't wait.', *MG.* 23 Feb. 1959. p 6

Repr. as 'We want eight, and we won't wait', A13, pp 53–6, and A21, pp 199–203

E53. Metternich and his 'System' for Europe, *Li.* 62, 1583. 30 Jul. 1959. pp 167–8

Repr. as 'Metternich and his 'System'', A13, pp 165–72

E54. Lancashire, *Vogue*. 116, 5. Mid-March, 1960. pp 89–90, 93–4, 164–5

The essay is interspaced between 24 pages about Lancashire clothes and fashion advertisements. An interesting and entertaining essay on Lancashire and Lancashire people, past and present.

E55. About Prime Ministers, *TV Times*. 20, 247. 22 Jul. 1960. p 9

He briefly discusses Walpole, Pitt, Gladstone, Disraeli, Lloyd George and Baldwin. The article was linked to a series of television lectures he gave between 2235 and 2305 hrs. on Monday nights in 1960 on British Independent Television: Walpole, 25 Jul; The Younger Pitt, 22 Aug; Gladstone, 5 Sept; and (2230–2300 hrs.) Disraeli, 19 Sept.

E56. His life was shaped the day he walked down Cowley Road, *Sun Ex*. 25 Sept. 1960. p 8

A 'popular' study of Hugh Gaitskell's earlier career. He recalls Gaitskell's role in the General Strike, 1926, and argues that the rest of his career followed on from that. He also argues that friendship with Hugh Dalton determined Gaitskell's outlook on foreign policy. 'Dalton has the fascination of a snake-charmer for those who listen to him.'

E57. A master stroke ends his clash with Bevan, *Sun Ex*. 2 Oct. 1960. p 8

Recounts the 'three strokes of fate, as though destiny had decreed that Gaitskell should rise to the top' (the 1947 fuel crisis; Dalton's resignation; and Cripps' health) and also the clashes with Bevan. A.J.P.T. observes of Gaitskell: 'He is trying to make the Labour Party think. Maybe it prefers to feel.'

E58. Agadir: The Panther's Spring, *Gdn*. 1 Jul. 1961. p 6

Repr. A13, pp 57–60

E59. 1931 was a year of crisis – but I remember the Marx brothers best, *TV Times*. 299. 21 Jul. 1961. pp 8–9

A personal and political portrait of 1931, in which

his main theme is that at the time the year did not seem to be a turning point in modern history.

E60. The Twenties, *Radio Times*. 154, 1995. 1 Feb. 1962. p 4

He introduces his series of television lectures on this period, observing that they are on political history. He also comments, 'These lectures are intended as serious history, or as serious as I can make it. They are exactly like lectures which I give at Oxford University except they are shorter and rather faster . . . The lectures are taken out of books and records as they would be on any earlier period. They are not presented as anecdotes or personal recollections.' *See* Appendix.

E61. A New World? *Li.* 67, 1715. 8 Feb. 1962. pp 247–50

The first of his BBC television lectures in the series 'The Twenties'. He surveys the legacy of the First World War and some aspects of the post-war Lloyd George Coalition Government.

E62. The Irish Troubles, *Li.* 67, 1716. 15 Feb. 1962. pp 283–6

The second of 'The Twenties' series. An account of the situation in Ireland between the Armistice and the settlement of December 1921.

E63. Peacemaking, *Li.* 67, 1717. 22 Feb. 1962. pp 331–4

The third of 'The Twenties' series. He surveys the conferences 1919–25. 'The truth is that, purely as a territorial settlement of changes of frontiers, the Treaty of Versailles was staggeringly moderate, and if there is such a thing in international affairs as justice, it was just.' He adds that the exception to this was the removal of the German colonies.

E64. The General Strike, *Li.* 67, 1719. 8 Mar. 1962. pp 409–12

The fourth of 'The Twenties' series.

E65. Voice of the Many, *Gdn.* 9 Mar. 1962. p 9

Cobbett was 'a great writer, a remarkable personality, and, beyond question, the greatest of English radicals. Cobbett was more than a man of the people. He was the people, the voice of the Many.'

Repr. *MGW*. 86, 11. 15 Mar. 1962. p 13

E66. The Baldwin Years, *Li*. 67, 1720. 15 Mar. 1962. pp 466–8

The fifth of 'The Twenties' series. A discussion of Baldwin ('Baldwin was really an intellectual in disguise') and certain characteristic features of Britain in the 1920s. The latter include the change in the position of trade union leaders ('instead of being merely instruments of resistance, (they) have accepted their responsible position in society and particularly in industrial organisation') and the activities of Dr. Marie Stopes.

E67. The Great Depression, *Li*. 67, 1721. 22 Mar. 1962. pp 505–8

The sixth of 'The Twenties' series. The story of the Labour Government's handling of the economic crisis and the British decision to abandon the Gold Standard. Of the 1931 crisis, 'the things they did were as futile as the appalling waste of infantry in the mud of Passachendaele'.

This talk was taken to task by Paul Einzig in his essay 'The Financial Crisis of 1931', pp 233–43, in *A Century of Conflict 1850–1950 : Essays for A.J.P. Taylor*, ed. Martin Gilbert, London, Hamish Hamilton, 1966. A.J.P.T. acknowledged this criticism in his review of the book; see G1135.

E68. Why do I write for this 'Awful Newspaper'? *Sun Ex*. 27 May 1962. p 16

In fact the article is a sketch of Lord Beaverbrook. 'He belongs to a party of his own, the party of Creators ... Lord Beaverbrook has always been on the side of Life.'

E69. Was he the greatest Prime Minister of all time? *Sun Ex*. 20 Jan. 1963. p 8

(Lloyd George) 'In the long retrospect of time he is likely to be seen as the greatest British statesman of the twentieth century and perhaps the greatest Prime Minister of all time.' He also commented in it, 'Only the other day an inquiry among Labour MPs revealed that more of them had drawn their inspiration from Lloyd George than ever from Keir Hardie.'

E70. The Titans of Utopia, *Punch.* 244, 6388. 13 Feb. 1963. pp 220–2

The first in the journal's series 'The Sixties Then: What men and women were thinking and doing one hundred years ago'. The article is a survey of the Western world in the 1860s, with the theme that the old liberal Utopias were achieved but 'in practice much went sour'. Praises the setting up of the Red Cross as 'the greatest international achievement of the decade'.

E71. Men of 1862, *Radio Times.* 159, 2063. 23 May 1963. p 21

See Appendix.

E72. Men of the 1860s – I: Napoleon III, *Li.* 69, 1784. 6 Jun. 1963. pp 955–7

E73. Men of the 1860s – II: Francis Joseph, Emperor of Austria, *Li.* 69, 1785. 13 Jun. 1963. pp 993–5

E74. Men of the 1860s – III: Lord Palmerston, *Li.* 69, 1786. 20 Jun. 1963. pp 1033–5

E75. Men of the 1860s – IV: Alexander II, Tsar of Russia, *Li.* 69, 1787. 27 Jun. 1963. pp 1069–71

E76. Men of the 1860s – V: Karl Marx, *Li.* 70, 1788. 4 Jul. 1963. pp 13–15

E77. Men of the 1860s – VI: Bismarck, *Li.* 70, 1789. 11 Jul. 1963. pp 47–9

'With all his faults, I feel he was an attractive and fascinating character. But he had the common German characteristic – he always blamed other people.'

E78. Are we so bad? *TV Times.* 411. 13 Sept. 1963. pp 10–11

A review of the morals of prime ministers and others in the past, written in the aftermath of the Profumo scandal.

E79. Der letze Rheinbündler, *Der Spiegel.* 17. 9 Oct. 1963. pp 64–5

One of several assessments of Adenauer on the occasion of his retirement. A.J.P.T.'s contribution argues that Adenauer was 'the last proponent of the Confederation of the Rhine'. The secret of his success as a politician was that the defeat of Germany gave him what he wanted – the division of Germany moved its centre from Berlin to the Rhine, creating a Catholic majority, reducing the socialist influence, and giving his party a more or less permanent majority.

E80. They all want to be heroes now, *Sun Ex.* 19 Jan. 1964. p 14

He uses published diaries and other sources to show that on 10 May 1940 Sinclair, the Liberal leader, wanted Chamberlain to stay in office and that the Labour leaders preferred Halifax to Churchill. Despite this, in retrospect everybody concerned has claimed that they were for Churchill.

E81. The man who deals in sunshine, *Sun Ex.* 24 May 1964. p 16

A tribute to Lord Beaverbrook, marking his 85th birthday.

E82. 1914: Events in Britain, *Li.* 72, 1842. 16 Jul. 1964. pp 79–82

A radio talk given on the BBC's Third Programme, in a series 'Moving towards war'.; *see* Appendix.

E83. The Big Rows, *TV Times*. 471. 5 Nov. 1964. p 11

Introduces a series of television lectures: 'Each lecture will tell the story of some great topic – parliamentary reform or home rule – and will relate it to a general election which revolved round it.' The programmes were broadcast on Monday night 2230–2300 hrs. (except the first, 2235–2305 hrs.) in 1964: (1) The Great Reform Bill, 9 Nov; (2) The Bulgarian Horrors, 16 Nov; (3) The Irish Home Rule Controversy, 23 Nov; (4) The Boer War, 30 Nov; (5) The Battle with the Lords, 7 Dec; (6) The Man Who Won The War, 14 Dec.

E84. The man who gave us our finest hour, *Sun Ex.* 29 Nov. 1964. pp 8–9

A tribute to Sir Winston Churchill, marking his 90th birthday. 'He was the saviour of his country and the saviour of freedom throughout the world.'

E85. When The Saints March In . . . , *TV Times*. 548. 28 Apr. 1966. p 5

He discusses pacifism in Britain in the First World War, prefacing his remarks with a brief survey of pacifism from the time of the English Civil War.

'Were pacifists against wrongful war, capitalist war, or all war? The question still racks their conscience, as it must rack the conscience of all others.'

E86. The man who tried to work miracles, *Li.* 76, 1947. 21 Jul. 1966. pp 81–4

A radio talk given on the BBC's Third Programme to mark the 100th anniversary of H.G. Wells' birth. An entertaining discussion of Wells as a novelist and as a prophet. *See* Appendix.

E87. Six Angles on One War, *TV Times*. 560. 21 Jul. 1966 p 13

In it he discusses the Second World War, arguing that the war started at different times for different countries and that it had a different character for each of them. *See* C9 for details of the series.

E88. Pieter Geyl: a great historian, *Obs.* 8 Jan. 1967. p 25

A tribute to Geyl. In it he names Geyl as 'the historian whom I have most venerated in my lifetime'. He also comments, 'What distinguishes the truly great historian is integrity, a single minded devotion to the past and its problems.'

E89. Did The P.M. Lie To Save His Skin? *Sun Ex.* 16 Apr. 1967. p 10

In it he discusses Lloyd George and the Maurice debate of 9 May 1918. A.J.P.T. suggests that Lloyd George may have known that figures he gave in the House of Commons had been corrected – but suppressed the correction for his own political advantage. Anyway Milner told him six days later of this correction and Lloyd George did not confess to the Commons that his information was inaccurate. A.J.P.T. suggests that Lloyd George's estrangement from Milner stems from this.

See also Note E to Chap. 3, pp 117–8, of A14

E90. 1917. . . . The Year That Changed The World, *TV Times*. 620. 14 Sept. 1967. p 8

He discusses 1917 as a turning point in history, and devotes most of his remarks to the events in Russia. He regrets that 'latterday Communists will not allow these legends (about Russia in 1917) to be dispelled'.

The article preceded a set of five lectures he gave on television, entitled 'Revolution 1917'. These were twenty five minutes long, transmitted at 1808 hours, Monday to Friday, 18–22 Sept. on commercial television. The lectures were: (1) Old Russia; (2) February: Revolution Old Style; (3) Free Russia; (4) October: Revolution New Style; (5) New Russia and the World.

E91. Lord Attlee, *Li.* 78, 2011. 12 Oct. 1967. pp 470–1

A tribute to Lord Attlee broadcast on the BBC's radio programme 'The World This Weekend'; *see* Appendix.

E92. Alamein, *TV Times.* 625. 19 Oct. 1967. p 2

He gives a brief assessment of the significance of the battle of El Alamein.

E93. Daddy, What Was Winston Churchill? *New York Times.* 28 Apr. 1974. Magazine, p 30, 80, 82, 84, 92

A review of Churchill's record in the Second World War, on the 100th anniversary of his birth.

Repr. A21, pp 295–307

E94. Class War: 1926, *NS.* 91, 2354. 30 Apr. 1976. pp 572–3

He gives his reminiscences of his part in the General Strike. 'My experiences in the General Strike cured me of communism.'

E95. The war lords – 1. Mussolini, *Li.* 96, 2469. 5 Aug. 1976. pp 132–4

The first of a series of television lectures given on BBC 1; *see* Appendix.

Repr. A22

E96. The war lords – 2. Hitler, *Li.* 96, 1470. 12 Aug. 1976. pp 165–8

Repr. A22

E97. The war lords – 3. Churchill, *Li.* 96, 2471. 19 Aug. 1976. pp 196–8

Repr. A22

E98. The war lords – 4. Stalin, *Li.* 96, 2472. 26 Aug. 1976. pp 233–5

Repr. A22

E99. The war lords – 5. Roosevelt, *Li.* 96, 2473. 2 Sept. 1976. pp 265–7

Repr. A22

E100. 6. War lords anonymous, *Li.* 96, 2474. 9 Sept. 1976. pp 301–3

Repr. A22

E101. Made in Manchester, *Li.* 96, 2475. 16 Sept. 1976. pp 334–4

Extracts from a television programme on Manchester presented by A.J.P.T., broadcast on BBC 2; *see* Appendix. A survey of Manchester's history from the eighteenth century; most of it is on the nineteenth century. It concludes with comments on Manchester when A.J.P.T. was a lecturer there, and how it has changed since then.

E102. War: the revolutionary model, *Li.* 98, 2517. 14 Jul. 1977. pp 44–6

The first in a series of television lectures entitled 'How Wars Begin', broadcast on BBC 1; *see* Appendix. In it he discusses the French Revolutionary and Napoleonic wars.

Repr. A23

E103. Two contrasting wars, *Li.* 98, 2518. 21 Jul. 1977. pp 72–4

The second in the 'How Wars Begin' series. In it he discusses the Crimean war and the war of Italian unification. In the latter part Garibaldi is described as 'the most wholly admirable man in modern history'.

E104. Bismarck's wars, *Li.* 98, 2519. 28 Jul. 1977. pp 106–8

The third in the 'How Wars Begin' series.

E105. In defence of small nations, *Li.* 98, 2520. 4 Aug. 1977. pp 138–40

The fourth in the 'How Wars Begin' series. In it he discusses the outbreak of the First World War.

E106. Empires v. powers, *Li.* 98, 2521. 11 Aug. 1977. pp 175–7

The fifth in the 'How Wars Begin' series. In it he discusses just when the Second World War began. He refers to the final paragraph of A11, in which he recognised that he was writing only about a European war.

E107. First frosts and cold war, *Li.* 98, 2522. 18 Aug. 1977. pp 200–2

The sixth in the 'How Wars Begin' series. In it he discusses relations between Russia and the West from the time of Napoleon. He ends, '. . . I think . . . that there will be a third world war. One day, the deterrent will fail to deter'.

E108. Days of revolution, *Radio Times.* 220, 2852. 6 Jul. 1978. p 14

He introduces his series of television lectures 'Revolution'. In it he discusses the word 'revolution'. He observes, 'The essence of revolution was movement.' He finds three principal ideas underlying modern revolutions – democracy, socialism and nationalism.

E109. The first modern revolution, *Li.* 100, 2568. 13 Jul. 1978. pp 40–2

The first in the series of television lectures entitled 'Revolution', broadcast on BBC 1; *see* Appendix. He discusses the French Revolution, 1789–1794.

E110. The revolution that never was, *Li.* 100, 2569. 20 Jul. 1978. pp 78–80

The second in the 'Revolution' series. He discusses the Chartists.

E111. The year of social revolution, *Li.* 100, 2570. 27 Jul. 1978. pp 106–8

The third in the 'Revolution' series. He discusses the 1848 revolution in France, and observes, 'this was the last time that France gave the revolutionary signal to Europe'.

E112. The year of national revolutions, *Li.* 100, 2571. 3 Aug. 1978. pp 142–4

The fourth in the 'Revolution' series. He discusses the 1848 revolution in Germany, Central Europe and Italy. He pays much attention to German attitudes. 'There was already an equivocation which was to continue very strongly throughout later German history: a belief that liberalism could be imposed from above.' In particular he discusses German attitudes to the other peoples of the Habsburg lands.

E113. Wanted: a revolution, *Li.* 100, 2572. 10 Aug. 1978. pp 177–9

The fifth in the 'Revolution' series. In it he discusses revolutionary episodes in the second half of the nineteenth century, notably the Commune, and the attitude of peasants. He then discusses revolutionaries Marx, Engels and Bakunin.

E114. The first red revolution, *Li.* 100, 2573. 17 Aug 1978. pp 204–6

The sixth in the 'Revolution' series. He discusses the two Russian revolutions of 1917. He concludes, '... for all practical purposes, in Europe, though not perhaps in the rest of the world, the old revolutionary inspiration flagged and died away when the revolution failed to become international after the Bolshevik revolution of 1917'.

E115. The man who never stood still. *Daily Express*, 25 May 1979, p. 8

An appreciation of Lord Beaverbrook, on the hundredth anniversary of his birth. Now the Empire has perished, Beaverbrook's newspapers have changed their character in accordance with the needs of the time. Only his works of history endure.

F: ARTICLES ETC. ON CURRENT AFFAIRS

(Letters to newspapers and journals are not listed).

1942

F1. Notes on the Way, *T & T*. 23, 27. 4 Jul. p 537
'The way out is not to bring Germany down but to raise others up . . . ' 'Unfortunately the Nazi's have by now carried through their schemes of economic conquest so thoroughly that if private capitalism survives in Europe, German hegemony will survive with it; public ownership of industry is the only way of avoiding the ownership of Europe by the Germans and their agents'.

1944

F2. A Feudal Society, *MG*. 23 Mar. p 4
A leader in which he warns that the Allies should not be taken in by Hungary's constitutional facade – 'it is a Constitution for the aristocracy and gentry'. He also argues that 'if the Allies help to preserve the great estates and the political power of the traditional governing class they will preserve allies for Germany in a future war'.

F3. What is the future of the Baltic States? *Picture Post*. 23, 1. 1 Apr. pp 7–11
He argues that the lesson of Baltic history is that Latvia, Lithuania and Esthonia can 'enjoy a secure national existence only within the framework of the Soviet Union'.

F4. Quatorze Juillet, *MG*. 14 Jul. p 4
A leader in which he eulogises the French Revolution and France. He calls on the Allies to recognise De Gaulle wholeheartedly. 'Western Europe can know no security and Western civilisation cannot

flourish without a deep and lasting partnership between England and France.'

Repr. pp 214–6, *Faith in France: A Selection of Leading Articles in the Manchester Guardian between June 1940 and September 1944*, Preface by D.W. Brogan, Manchester, Sherratt, 1946

F5. Britain and Russia, *MG.* 11 Oct. p 4

A leader in which he urges wholehearted co-operation with Russia by Britain. He reviews various contentious issues, such as Franco and Spain, Hungary, and Turkey and finds the Russian position to be the more noble.

F6. Persia, *MG.* 11 Nov. p 4

A leader in which he urges 'Anglo-Soviet co-operation is the key to European peace and Persia is the key to Anglo-Soviet co-operation. He compares the significance of the issue of Persia to that of the Straits in the nineteenth century; Anglo-Russian estrangement over the latter 'gave Bismarck his chance to lay the foundations for German domination of Europe'.

F7. Trieste or Trst? *NS & N.* 28, 720. 9 Dec. pp 386–7

He argues that Isria and Trieste naturally belong to the South Slavs not to Italy. 'Here the Slav world and the world of Western democracy can overlap and combine. In short we can be more confident of the future of the Anglo-Soviet alliance when we have learnt to think of Trieste as Trst.'

1945

F8. Austria, *MG.* 3 Feb. p 4

A leader in which he argues that Austria must not be allowed to fall into German hands again. 'Independence may have to be imposed from without by the Great Powers until an independent Austrian national idea grows up . . .'

F9. Death of an Empire, *MG.* 16 Apr. p 4

A leader which argues that no one wishes to destroy the German people and their sense of a common nationhood but the Reich, the Army and the Nazi party must be destroyed.He also argues that soon the problem will not be 'of how to keep a powerful, aggressive nation subdued, but rather how to start among the Germans the practice of initiative and self-help'.

F10. Berlin, *MG.* 24 Apr. p 4

A leader in which he discusses Berlin's history. 'Berlin has contributed nothing to civilisation . . . it represents nothing but the idea of conquest. . . . '

F11. Hitler's Germany, *MG.* 5 May. p 4

A leader in which he comments on the destruction left behind by Hitler. 'Now that he has perished the Germans may try to load their responsibility on to him, but they will make no moral condemnation. In German eyes the only crime of Hitler, as of Germany, is to have failed. And no German would have condemned Hitler if he had won.'

F12. British Policy, *MG.* 4 Jun. p 4

A leader in which he urges that Britain should take on the leadership of Europe. 'We have become part of Europe. In an age of rockets and amphibious operations we must lead in Europe or ourselves be led; we cannot stand aside . . . '

F13. The Straits, *MG.* 9 Jul. p 4

A leader in which he urges that the Russian's wishes on the Straits should be met providing that they do not endanger Turkish independence. 'We who hold strategic bases all over the world cannot grudge the Russians the right to protect the seaway to their greatest industrial and agricultural area, the Ukraine.'

F14. The Mediterranean, *MG.* 23 Jul. p 4

A leader in which he urges that Britain should cede her spheres of influence to the common good. 'The Mediterranean should be the first care of the World Security Council, its strategy controlled by the four Great Powers.' This should be 'the first demonstration of Allied co-operation in time of peace'.

F15. Russia's Return as a Great Power, *Li.* 34, 872.

27 Sept. pp 341–2, 355

A radio talk broadcast on the BBC's Home Service; *see* Appendix. He argues that the Russians must be treated as equals in the post-war settlement and that the Russians have the right to ask for concessions, even in the Mediterranean.

F16. National Independence and the 'Austrian Idea', *Political Quarterly*. 16, 3. Autumn. pp 234–46

'In Central Europe the Old Adam of reality is the desire for national independence . . . ' He also argues that 'in regard to Europe the Soviet Union is at bottom 'isolationist'. It desires security, not domination; and therefore desires to see on its frontiers stable states, states which are viable particularly among the Slav 'brothers', so that it may cease to trouble about them.'

F17. The European Revolution, *Li*. 34, 880. 22 Nov. pp 575–6

In it he argues that 'all over Europe the Right has ceased to exist as an organised political force' and private enterprise is finished there. However, he argues, people do not want Communism. 'They want the state to do things for the good of individual human beings; they do not want individuals to have to do things for the good of the state. In other words, they want Socialism, but they also want the Rights of Man.'

F18. Russian Policy *MG*. 20 Dec. p 4

A leader in which he urges Ernest Bevin to maintain the alliance with Russia. 'Ever since the wars of intervention ended the Bolshevists have expected their renewal; and that is the key to all Soviet foreign policy. Its sole aim is to prevent a united front of capitalist States.'

1946

F19. Problems of the Peace Makers, *Li*. 35, 887. 10 Jan. pp 35–6

A radio talk given on the BBC's Home Service; *see* Appendix. In it he argues that Britain must be independent and co-operate equally with like-minded people in the USA and Russia. He discusses whether Britain is still a Great Power – and suggests the key to this is British coal production, until atomic energy is harnessed for cheap power. '... knowledge of the past is the first condition for shaping the future'.

F20. What is Russia's Policy? *Li.* 35, 895. 7 Mar. pp 294–5

A radio talk given on the BBC's Home Service; *see* Appendix. 'The whole aim of their policy is to secure a long period of peace in order to carry through reconstruction.'

F21. To Fight or to Share: Alternative policies in the Middle East, *Li.* 35, 898. 28 Mar. pp 389–90

A radio talk given on the BBC's Home Service; *see* Appendix. In it he argues that Britain must either fight Russia in the Middle East or co-operate with her. 'The modern form of sharing is not partition, but to put the responsibility on to the United Nations.' The Three Great Powers 'but principally Great Britain and Russia, must assume joint responsibility for it, politically and economically'.

F22. The Way to Agreement? *Li.* 35, 905. 16 May. pp 633–4

A radio talk given on the BBC's Home Service; *see* Appendix. He discusses the disagreements of the Great Powers and foresees a crisis of capitalism after the post-war boom. Urges 'an Anglo-Soviet trade agreement on the widest scale'.

F23. The Problem of Germany, *Li.* 35, 910. 20 Jun. pp 799–800

A radio talk given on the BBC's Home Service; *see* Appendix. He praises the Potsdam proposals for Germany – the extraction of reparations for Poland and Russia and the reduction of Germany's level of industrialisation. 'Germany has to be dis-industrialised as consciously, as deliberately, as Russia was industrialised by the five year plans'; but he does add 'it is more important and decisive to raise the industrial resources of the rest of Europe than to de-industrialise Germany'.

F24. Czechoslovakia Today: 1 – The Situation in the Czech Lands, *MG*. 24 Jul. pp 4, 6

He discusses the political situation, observing that how long it lasts will depend on the Communists remaining democratic and 'on the resolution with which the non-Communist parties defend their liberal morality and philosophy without slipping into a defence of capitalism' (as well as external factors). The three pieces are marked 'Prague, July'.

Repr. *MGW*. 55, 5. 2 Aug. p 59

F25. Czechoslovakia Today: II – The Position of the Slovaks, *MG*. 25 Jul. pp 4, 6

He discusses the political situation.

Repr. *MGW*. 55, 6. 9 Aug. p 71

F26. Czechoslovakia Today: III – Questions of Foreign Policy and Trade, *MG*. 29 Jul. pp 4, 6

He argues that after the years of German terror the Czechs are terrified by a revival of German power and are firmly aligned to the Russians, just as the Dominions are to Britain.

Repr. *MGW*. 55, 7. 16 Aug. p 87

F27. The Need for Controversy, *Li*. 36, 935. 12 Dec. pp 834–5

The first of four radio talks on British Foreign Policy given on the BBC's Third Programme; *see* Appendix. In it he discusses the forces which mould foreign policy. He argues that the Second World War has removed the old assumptions; the British navy is no longer supreme and the Balance of Power has gone on the mainland of Europe, leaving only Russia as a Great Power there.

F28. Britain's relations with the United States, *Li*. 36, 936. 19 Dec. pp 873, 889

The second of the series on British Foreign Policy. He deplores Britain's policy of pretending to be the equal of the US yet timidly agreeing to all that America requires. In particular he condemns American strategy: 'they are only concerned to use this island (like Japan on the other side of the world) as an aircraft carrier from which to discharge atomic bombs . . . ' He praises Sweden's trading agreement with Russia. In contrast he condemns America's attempt to restore pre-war conditions – 'it does not occur to them that if you restore the circumstances that existed before Hitler you restore the circumstances that created Hitler'.

F29. British Policy towards Russia, *Li.* 36, 937. 26 Dec. pp 918–9

The third of the series on British Foreign Policy. He argues that 'Russia has neither the power nor the will to follow an aggressive policy' and regrets that Britain and Russia have been drifting apart since Potsdam. He concludes that 'the only possible policy . . . by which this country can remain prosperous and a Great Power, is the policy of the Anglo-Russian alliance'.

1947

F30. Great Britain and Europe, *Li.* 37, 938. 2 Jan. pp 8–9

The fourth of the series on British foreign policy. He urges the policy of 'not of cutting Germany down but of raising the rest of Europe as the solution of the German problem. He calls for 'a socialist reconstruction of Europe'. He suggests that a Socialist Europe should develop the resources of Africa, 'not seeking to exploit the Africans, but to bring them into Socialist partnership'.

F31. Le Problème de Notre Temps, *Le Monde Illustré.* 91, 4406. 12 Apr. p 409

In the journal's series 'Reflexions du Monde Vivant'. He looks glumly on the line up on one side of the USA, representing nineteenth-century individualism, and on the other, of the USSR, representing nineteenth-century socialism, in the age of the atomic bomb. He argues that the Anglo-French alliance should provide the hope for mankind.

F32. Impressions of Yugoslavia – 1. A Regime of Youth, *MG.* 8 May. p 4

The articles give his impressions after spending

three weeks travelling in Yugoslavia. He is impressed by the energy and enthusiasm in the country. He finds the leading men to be former school teachers. 'The effect is as though the Left Book Club suddenly took over both the central and local government of this country'.

Repr. *MGW*. 56, 18. 15 May. p 9

F33. Impressions of Yugoslavia – 2. Economics and Politics, *MG*. 9 May. p 4

He discusses their plans for economic development and urges the West to be generous with economic help.

Repr. *MGW*. 56, 19. 22 May. p 13

1948

F34. The Europe of 1848: A Congress of Historians in Paris, *MG*. 17 Apr. p 4

An account of the conference arranged to mark the revolutions of 1848.

Repr. *MGW*. 58, 17. 22 Apr. p 13 and as 'The Paris Congress of the History of 1848', A5, pp 218–21

F35. Intellectuals at Wroclaw: A Strange Congress, *MG*. 2 Sept. p 4

His account of the 'treason of intellectuals' at the conference organised at Wroclaw which was intended 'to lessen international tension by bringing men of culture together'.

Repr. *MGW*. 59, 11. 9 Sept. p 12 (also letter by A.J.P.T. and others, p 7); also as 'Intellectuals Betrayed Liberty At Wroclaw', *Sydney Morning Herald*. 9 Sept. p 2; and as 'The Wroclaw Congress of Intellectuals', A5, p 221–4

F36. Vagaries of British Diplomacy, *NS & N*. 36, 928. 18 Dec. p 542

In it he discusses the failures of policy towards Germany both at that time and in 1938–9. He regrets that Britain and America did not take seriously Russia's proposals at the Warsaw Conference, June

1948. He warns that 'if the Ruhr is rebuilt, the second German war will have been fought in vain'.

1949

F37. Tito and Stalin: The Revolt from Within, *Li.* 41, 1043. 20 Jan. pp 86–8

A radio talk given on the BBC's Third Programme; *see* Appendix. In it he discusses the significance of the published correspondence between Tito and Stalin.

Repr. A5, pp 209–17. Extracts from the talk were published in advance under the heading 'The New Henry VIII', *News Chronicle.* 13 Jan. p 2

F38. German Mastery Unless ..., *Oxford Mail.* 17 Jul. p 4

The second in a series "The Future of Europe"; the other contributors being Bertrand Russell and Sir Arthur Salter. In it he deplores the restoration of the Ruhr's industrial capacity.

F39. The Free Territory of Trieste, *NS & N.* 38, 973. 29 Oct. pp 478–9

He still wishes that Trieste had been given to Yugoslavia. As that is impossible at present he urges that it be made a Free Territory run jointly by Yugoslavia and Italy.

1950

F40. How Should We Choose Our Allies? *Picture Post.* 48, 10. 2 Sept. pp 34–6

It is in the form of a discussion between A.J.P.T. and Fitzroy Maclean MP. In it he argues that 'the greatest Bolshevik asset is still in the world of ideas' and that 'somehow we have got to combine a policy of guns and butter, and that the guns have got to defend something more than a comfortable way of life'. He condemns the idea of rearming the Germans.

F41. The Turn of the Half Century: Western Man's Future, *MG.* 30 Dec. p 4

Repr. A6, pp 252–4, and A17, pp 372–5

1951

F42. UNO has Failed! *Sun Pic.* 28 Jan. p 5

Observes that the League of Nations failed to stop Mussolini in Abyssinia and argues, 'Our present troubles in the Far East are due to the attempt by one Great Power – the greatest of them all – to steal the United Nations and use the organisation for its own policy.' Generally condemns collective security.

F43. Should We Get Out of Asia? *Public Opinion.* 4655. 9 Feb. pp 9–10

Urges a withdrawal from Asia. 'As in our domestic affairs the ultimate solution is to be found in a policy of equality, of fair shares, and not in the maintenance of privileges which have lost all moral justification.'

F44. Fear of Russia, *Sun Pic.* 11 Feb. p 5

Points out that fear of Russia is nothing new in British foreign policy. He compares the economic strength of America and her allies with that of Russia and hers and observes that 'the world balance, far from moving in Russia's favour, is moving against her'.

F45. Agreement with Russia? *New York Times.* 4 Mar. Magazine, p 7, pp 52–5

He argues that 'the overriding Russian motive is still fear and not aggression or desire to dominate the world'. He also calls for a truce, as time will show that democracy is more fertile and constructive than communism.

Repr. as 'Can We Agree With the Russians?', A6, pp 232–9, and A17, pp 346–53

F46. We Are Slaves of Science; *Sun Pic.* 4 Mar. p 5

He accepts and welcomes science's benefits but argues that 'the more we complain about the triumphs of science the more chance there is that the scientists will look for the answers to the new problems which they are creating'.

F47. Case for a Return to the Old Diplomacy, *New York Times.* 18 Mar. Magazine, pp 9, 30–31, 33, 35

In it he urges that secret diplomacy is the way to settle the Cold War; he argues that open diplomacy merely fosters propaganda not accord.

Repr. as 'Old Diplomacy – and New', A6, pp 173–80, and A17, pp 364–71

F48. So the Churches are empty again today! *Sun Pic.* 1 Apr. p 7

In it he argues, 'For the first time in human history, the bulk of mankind is living without revealed religion, without belief in another world;' and he deems this 'the biggest thing that has happened in the twentieth century'.

He was vigorously denounced for this in the letters column, *Sun Pic.* 8 Apr. p 6

F49. Should We Celebrate? *Sun Pic.* 13 May. p 5

He contrasts the spirit of the Great Exhibition of 1851 with that of 1951. In 1951, 'We are celebrating what we have done; not what we are going to do.' He finds the most exciting thing in 1951 is that in China, India and Africa 'they are shaking themselves free from slavery to nature and from slavery to their white exploiters'.

F50. Blunt Words About Korea, *Sun Pic.* 10 Jun. p 6

He denounces the blockade. 'Men and women are more important than any principle in the world, and what matters in Korea is the Koreans.'

F51. We must not silence our "Reds"! *Sun Pic.* 24 Jun. p 7

He observes that while the defection of the diplomats Burgess and McLean to Russia may do the country harm, it is not as harmful as a witch-hunt would be. That would start against communists and end up silencing all who disagree. Witch-hunts 'will catch the people whom the communists most hate: the people of independent judgement who try to make up their own minds, without fear of communists or of anyone else'.

F52. I back America! *Sun.Pic.* 1 Jul. p 5

He praises America for many actions (such as the Marshall Plan) and condemns some aspects of American society (notably race relations); but overall he feels that America reveres freedom and 'has stuck to the principles of the Declaration of Indpendence'.

F53. Stuffed shirts at the BBC, *Sun Pic.* 22 Jul. p 7

He feels that the BBC's claims to be discharging a great social function to be impertinent. He wishes programmes were intended to be fun not to do the public good.

F54. It Looks Like Peace – So Be Warned! *Sun. Pic.* 5 Aug. p 5

He feels that war with Russia is becoming less and less likely; warns against German and Japanese rearmament; and condemns France's colonial war in Indo-China. He urges the West to turn its resources to a war against povery all over the world and to prove that 'democratic socialism is a better cause than communism'.

F55. Scrap These Stupid Drink Laws! *Sun. Pic.* 19 Aug. p 5

He condemns British licencing laws, which restrict opening times and prevent parents taking their children with them into pubs.

F56. A date we dare not forget: September 3, *Sun. Pic.* 2 Sept. p 5

He discusses the Second World War and argues that it could have been avoided. He regrets that Britain is no longer on good terms with Russia, and attributes Britain's problems to this fact.

F57. The Battle Bill, *The Nation.* 173, 10. 8 Sept. pp 186–7

He condemns Representative Battle's Bill against trading with Communist countries as an American attempt to put up an Iron Curtain and generally adopt Stalin's style. He gives his interpretation of what British people think.

F58. Secret Police? Britain has them too, *Sun. Pic.* 16 Sept. p 6

'Freedom is in more danger from attacks from within than from attacks from without.'

He condemns the anti-communist campaign in the US; and, in Britain, the police surveillance of the Left and also the attacks on Bevan within the Labour Party.

F59. Revolution Without Blood, *Sun. Pic.* 30 Sept. p 6

He commends E.H. Carr's *New Society* (London, Macmillan) and urges that we have to decide 'how to get Equality without losing Freedom, how to make people well off without destroying their spirit'.

F60. The Big Truth, *Sun. Pic.* 14 Oct. p 5

He argues that foreign policy is the most important issue in the General Election. He urges Fair Shares For All in the world and complains that the Conservatives 'would like to treat Persia and Egypt just as the Russians have treated Czechoslovakia and Poland'. He calls for independence for the Empire countries.

F61. Common Sense About Peace, *Sun. Pic.* 11 Nov. p 5

He argues that disarmament will only follow trust. He suggests a three point peace programme: (1) a cease fire in Korea; (2) Germany should be unified but kept disarmed; (3) the US should recognise the Communist Government in China and allow China to take her rightful place at the UN.

F62. Stalin as Statesman: A Look at the Record, *New York Times*. 18 Nov. Magazine, p 9, 59–60

He reviews Russian policies and argues that they are 'without flexibility or imagination, incapable of sudden change'. He urges as the answer to Stalin, 'Be strong; be united, and then be friendly.'

Repr. as 'Is Stalin a Statesman?', A6, pp 240–8, and A17, pp 337–45

F63. What Sort of Friend Can This Man Be? *Sun. Pic.* 9 Dec. p 5

He denounces Adenauer's plans for German rearmament and a new German army, and also the West German attitude to the frontier between East Germany and Poland. He urges the West to negotiate a settlement with the Russians rather than treat them as enemies.

1952

F64. The *simple* facts on why we are broke, *Sun. Pic.* 3 Feb. p 5

He argues that the Conservatives will try to solve

Britain's problems by cutting real wages in order to make Britain's goods more competitive abroad. He urges as the alternative 'the policy of planning our national resources'.

1953

F65. 1952: Right Turn, *Picture Post*. 58, 1. 3 Jan. pp 4–6

In it he discusses the political situation in Britain and the world. He warns against German rearmament. He observes, 'Korea showed a real war could be as much a stalemate as a cold one . . . The cold war is here to stay.' Against communism 'Democracy will only win if it believes in the superiority of its ideas for all men, whether White, Black, Brown or Yellow', and concludes, 'We must hold on until Communism destroys itself.'

F66. My Religion, *D Her*. 10 Jan. p 5

He attacks Christianity for its dogmas and for being used as an instrument of social control in the past. 'Human reason is the only saviour we have . . . We need more education, not less; more science, not less; more hope for the future, and more confidence in it.'

F67. TV's no menace – and no fun! *D Her*. 17 Jan. p 3

He praises television as 'one of the few inventions of modern times that do nothing but good'; but he condemns the BBC as a monopoly and regrets that those who run it wish to educate not entertain people.

F68. Forgive but don't Forget, *D Her*. 24 Jan. p 3

He comments on the current French trial of those responsible for the massacre at Oradour. He argues that the Germans have not changed since the days of Hitler and warns, 'Our country is within sight of committing a great international crime. That crime would be the rearmament of Germany.' 'The massacre of Oradour will happen again if Germany is rearmed.'

F69. Don't Be Fooled By An Ox-Roast, *D Her*. 31 Jan. p 3

He discusses the Coronation celebrations. He

argues that people should enjoy them but remember to 'treat the coronation as a great demonstration of privilege'. 'A constitutional King is better than the politburo.'

F70. Don't cut out charity, *D Her.* 7 Feb. p 3

After the floods he comments that the State must provide relief; but he argues that 'There will still be need for charity even when we think that we are secure from the cradle to the grave.'

F71. Public schools? Away With Them, *D Her.* 14 Feb. p 3

He calls for the abolition of public schools and the use of their buildings for adult education.

F72. We're Fools over Pools, *D Her.* 21 Feb. p 3

He discusses gambling and concludes that the only thing wrong with the football pools is that they are not run by the State.

F73. We're the hypocrites about this! *D Her.* 28 Feb. p 3

He discusses nationalism in Europe and in Wales and Scotland. 'National freedom is as important as economic freedom or the freedom of the individual.'

F74. It's we who are the aristocrats, *D Her.* 7 Mar. p 3

He discusses conditions in the undeveloped areas of the world and comments that these areas expect better economic as well as political conditions. He urges Britain to help these people. 'The world can know peace and security only if privilege is brought to an end everywhere.'

F75. Save us from these new Elizabethans, *D Her.* 14 Mar. p 3

He denounces the Elizabethan age as 'an age of oppression and suffering for the poor'. He argues that 'there is only one path which will lead to a great future. That is the path of international Socialism.' At home, 'All the resources of the community must be planned to serve the community and for no other purpose.'

F76. With Stalin Gone, Is War Less Likely? *Picture Post.* 58, 11. 14 Mar. Special Supplement 'Is It Peace?', pp ii–iv

He argues, 'Stalin had many evil qualities. But he was a real ruler, a master of men, and maintained autocratic control of Soviet Russia until the moment of his death. Now Soviet Russia is out of control . . . We must look out for collisions.' He suggests that the leadership of world communism might go to China.

F77. Women Prefer To Be Slaves! *D Her.* 21 Mar. p 3

'I am against inequality of the sexes, as much as I am against class privilege or colour prejudice.' He comments that he prepares the family breakfast each day – and urges that husbands and wives should share the household income equally.

F78. You can buy a licence to kill, *D Her.* 28 Mar. p 4

He condemns the numbers of deaths on Britain's raods and calls for the building of motor-ways and banning people using cars for journeys of less than five miles.

F79. For a change be yourself! *D Her.* 4 Apr. p 3

He urges people to enjoy themselves and suggests that money should be spent making towns bright and cheerful.

F80. We're too hard on our MPs, *D Her.* 11 Apr. p 3

He urges the provision of better pay and conditions for Members of Parliament. But he also calls for a reorganisation of the way business is conducted in Parliament. He urges that MPs should have other work as well, to make them better representatives.

F81. Let them hunt! *D Her.* 18 Apr. p 3

He looks forward to the day when high taxation makes hunting impossible. He feels that there is too much sentimentality about wild animals, and observes that fishing is just as cruel as fox hunting.

F82. Don't tell us: show us! *D Her.* 25 Apr. p 3

He regrets the craving for publicity which is a major feature of the age.

F83. How to run a war! *D Her.* 2 May. p 3

He condemns the American attempts to bribe Chinese pilots to desert with a Russian jet fighter. 'Our answer to Communism should be to show that we stand for something better, not that we have more money.'

F84. Let's get rid of the Lords, *D Her.* 9 May. p 3

He quotes the words of a French democrat with approval: 'If the Second Chamber agrees with the first, it is unnecessary. If it disagrees, it is undesirable.' He calls for the abolition of the House of Lords.

F85. MPs and their privilege, *D Her.* 16 May. p 3

He suggests that the House of Commons is too sensitive about its privileges. However despite its antiquated procedures and other faults, '... the House of Commons is the greatest institution in the world ... It represents freedom.'

F86. Stop this sham! *D Her.* 23 May. p 3

He wishes foreigners coming to Britain to see the Coronation pageantry would see Britain as it really is – slag heaps and all. He concludes, 'We shall have more to show our visitors at the next Coronation, if we think less of economics and more of William Morris.'

F87. Let's be rude! *D Her.* 30 May. p 4

A.J.P.T. comes to the support of Gilbert Harding, who had been the subject of many complaints about remarks he had made on television. He calls for more plain speaking and less running away from reality. 'I have faith in democracy. People will find out what is best for them without having to rely on the good taste of the BBC.'

F88. We can still be great, *D Her.* 6 Jun. p 5

With the Coronation over, he feels Britain must face up to the future. 'The world does not owe us a living – let alone a better living than anyone else.' In order to earn it he urges socialist measures. 'Socialism means planning. It can succeed where the old system of private profit has failed.'

F89. Equality? Women hate it! *D Her.* 13 Jun. p 3

On the 25th anniversary of all women getting the vote. He observes that it has not made much difference in politics, other than strengthening support for the Tories.

F90. We need these 'bad' citizens, *D Her.* 20 Jun. p 4

He regrets that spending on the arts is the first thing to be cut in an economic crisis. 'Books and paintings aren't a luxury. They are an essential part of a civilised life.'

F91. Sport? Bah! *D Her.* 27 Jun. p 3

He feels that watching sport does not do people any good.

F92. Does today mean *nothing* to you? *D Her.* 4 Jul. p 4

He comments on the Declaration of Independence and also on the activities of Senator McCarthy. After discussing the bad side of American life he concludes that, nevertheless, 'the United States remains a country where there is trial by jury and more freedom of expression of every sort of opinion than anywhere else in the world – including England'.

F93. We've got a lot to learn – and the French can teach us, *D Her.* 11 Jul. p 3

On his return from spending a week in France, he praises French civilisation.

F94. Leave us alone! *D Her.* 18 Jul. p 3

'I detest the idea that other people know how to run my life. I detest just as much the idea that I know how to run other people's lives.' In discussing this he condemns such bodies as the BBC and such restrictions on people's liberty as the divorce laws.

F95. Thank the Crank, *D Her.* 25 Jul. p 3

After the deportation of Garry Davis, the self-styled World Citizen No. 1, A.J.P.T. praises cranks. 'It is more important to stick to your principles than to succeed.'

F96. You lucky wives! *D Her.* 1 Aug. p 3

In it he remarks that women have less children and now have labour-saving devices to help with housework yet still expect their husbands to keep them as in Victorian times.

F97. First, women must be sensible! *D Her.* 8 Aug. p 3

After a deluge of criticism for writing the previous article, he returns to the role of women in modern society. 'Women should be the equals of men', but he wishes that they would 'behave in a reasonable and sensible way'. He comments on women's fashions, hand-bags, smoking and the habit of keeping front rooms of houses for show.

F98. Who's afraid of the big bad bomb? *D Her.* 15 Aug. p 3

He discusses the dangers to ordinary people of the atom bomb, and suggests that the 'way of giving the world peace, security and prosperity' is 'the way of International Socialism'.

F99. Then there were seven, *D Her.* 22 Aug. p 3

He discusses the survival of hereditary monarchs and emperors and observes that in Europe they survive in the most stable of democracies.

F100. I hate the average man, *D Her.* 29 Aug. p 4

He denounces the idea of there being an average man or woman. 'Everyone is different from everyone else. So long live the individual and down with the average man.'

F101. Why not a 7 year marriage? *D Her.* 5 Sept. p 4

He suggests that most people get married by chance and do not really know the other person then. He suggests that marriages should be dissolved automatically after seven years.

F102. Stick to religion, *D. Her.* 12 Sept. p 3

He calls on clergymen to devote their energies to preaching religion. Those who are not Christians 'have to find a way of life that fits in with the modern world of science and knowledge'.

F103. Let's all worry about Arsenal, *D Her.* 19 Sept. p 3

He discusses whether or not it is a good thing for millions of English people to have the success of a football team as the main issue on their minds on Saturday mornings.

F104. Time to wake up! *D Her.* 26 Sept. p 3

After riding on the last train from Freshwater on the Isle of Wight he reflects on the passing of the old foundations of Britain's strength and asks what Britain is going to put in their place. He concludes by observing, 'we can make England alive and progressive if each one of us keeps lively and fears no man'.

F105. We're A Nation of Wastrels! *D Her.* 3 Oct. p 5

He argues that Britain wastes its resources. He urges, 'No more electric power-stations. No houses outside the existing towns. No private motor-cars. And no rich people.'

F106. Make a fuss, *D Her.* 10 Oct. p 3

He wishes people were more willing to protest over such issues as atomic bombs – and comments on how nonconformists refused to pay taxes rather than have their money spent on Church schools. 'I'd have only one golden rule . . . Make a fuss. It doesn't matter about what. But make a fuss.'

F107. Laughter please! *D Her.* 17 Oct. p 3

He praises Stan Laurel and Oliver Hardy. ' To make people laugh is the greatest service anyone can do for humanity . . . laughter is the common bond of humanity.'

F108. TV forgives me! *D Her.* 24 Oct. p 3

He comments on his return to a television discussion programme after nearly a year's absence. He discusses the merits of television.

F109. We're beating ourselves, *D Her.* 31 Oct. p 3

He complains about various man made ills, such as smog, motor cars and processed food.

F110. When our grandchildren judge us. . . . They'll get us wrong! *D Her.* 7 Nov. p 4

He was shocked by a historian who portrayed Guy Fawkes and his associates as kindly innocent men and he observes, 'In history, though not in real life, I am a conservative. For me the old explanations are the best ones.' He wonders what legends will exist about the present – about Churchill, the Second World War, and the atom bomb.

F111. Pay Us All Alike! *D. Her.* 14 Nov. p 4

He discusses the high salaries paid to the heads of nationalised industries. He argues that 'the only Socialist solution for the problem of wages and salaries is Equal Pay for All'.

F112. We're Animal Crackers, *D Her.* 21 Nov. p 4

He criticises the British for being so sentimental about animals. He denounces dogs ('that detestable animal') but praises cats.

F113. The Church Is Wrong About Sex, *D Her.* 28 Nov. p 3

After the Archbishop of Canterbury had denounced sex, he discusses sex in the arts and urges no censorship.

F114. We're Silly About Marriage! *D Her.* 5 Dec. p 3

He denounces all restrictions on marriage – especially parental prejudices about partners who are foreign, of a different colour or of a different age group. He urges the automatic termination of marriages after 5 or 7 years, after which people can remarry if they wish to.

F115. The Santa Claus conspiracy, *D Her.* 12 Dec. p 3

He argues that the myth of Father Christmas is an unnecessary and futile deception of children.

F116. We Fear Leisure! *D Her.* 19 Dec. p 3

He argues that people are afraid of leisure and, above all, of spending time on their own.

1954

F117. Don't be so soft! – in 1954, *D Her.* 2 Jan. p 3

He discusses New Year resolutions – and hopes that 'everyone will kick against something in 1954'.

F118. Move Over, Old 'Uns, *D Her.* 7 Jan. p 4

He argues that the worst tyranny in the world is that of the old over the young. In particular he condemns the restriction on marrying before 21. He suggests that the two reasonable conditions before marriage are 'a certificate of good health ... And, of course, a certificate that they have lived together for three months or so before the marriage, so as to know the worst.'

F119. Hurrah For The Little Man! *D Her.* 14 Jan. p 4

He condemns the British love of the amateur and distrust of the clever and professional.

F120. So if you want to be happy, *D Her.* 21 Jan. p 4

He urges people to develop hobbies. He praises

astronomers for having so great an interest in something. 'How much better for everybody concerned than fighting wars or thinking you can be happy by falling in love with someone else.'

F121. Give Wives A Day Off, *D Her.* 28 Jan. p 4

He praises Sweden for giving wives a day off whilst the men did the housework.

F122. They'll Ban All Walking Next! *D Her.* 4 Feb. p 4

He condemns Ministry of Transport talk that pedestrains may have to cross the road at fixed points or be fined. He denounces the motor car.

F123. Oh, Nudists Next Door! *D Her.* 11 Feb. p 4

He discusses the shock of an Essex village at the establishment of a nudist camp nearby, and observes that the British are very intolerant of anything which is unconventional.

F124. Gather round, smokers! *D Her.* 18 Feb. p 4

He argues that nearly everything in life has a risk in it. 'I shall be sorry if we start fussing over our health just when we have stopped fussing over our conscience.'

F125. Don't do it yourself, *D Her.* 25 Feb. p 4

He discusses 'Do it yourself' and concludes that it is better for people to stick to their own specialisation.

F126. All right, call me an idealist, *D Her.* 5 Mar. p 4

He regrets that the Labour Party has lost its early idealism. 'In my opinion, socialism is a way of life, not a programme of social reform. It has to do with men's motives, not with rewards.'

F127. He's dead – but they can't lie down, *D Her.* 11 Mar. p 4

He discusses Will H. Hays and film censorship. He advocates no censorship of sex in films but instead of violence and war.

F128. Service? Put An End To This Slavery! *D Her.* 18 Mar. p 4

He calls for a complete ending of National Service in Britain.

F129. Many Happy Returns To. . . . *D Her.* 25 Mar. p 4

On the occasion of his birthday he reflects on the past thirty years. He comments on the loss of faith he has had in seeing a Socialist Britain in his lifetime and on disillusionment with Soviet Russia.

F130. Vienna – City of No Dreams, *D Her.* 1 Apr. p 4

He writes from Austria of Austria. He urges that the solution to the problem of Austria is the setting up of a neutral state.

F131. It's a deadly place, *D Her.* 8 Apr. p 4

He regrets that the British Museum is short of money. He denounces the rule that a subject cannot be discussed on the BBC within a fortnight of a Parliamentary debate. He comments that Germany is back again as an independent power and warns that she will not be on the side of either Russia or the West – 'She'll be on the side of Germany.'

F132. Down With Days Out! *D Her.* 15 Apr. p 4

He writes from the Isle of Wight. He complains of bank holiday crowds. 'It is the worst condemnation of our civilisation that holidays are more important for us than the work we do ... If there is a future life, Hell will be a perpetual holiday. And there will be no holidays in heaven.'

F133. Marriage is a soft option, *D Her.* 22 Apr. p 4

He argues that women get married in order to get 'a man who will keep them in idleness for the rest of their lives'. He denounces the special treatment given to VIPs at airports and elsewhere.

F134. There's no dodging the H-bomb, *D Her.* 29 Apr. p 4

He urges that renunciation of the H-bomb 'is a question of morals'. The British should renounce it and say, 'Even if this makes it certain that London or all England will be destroyed, we will not plan to blow up a million people in Moscow or Warsaw.'

F135. I'm GLAD to see the end of my ration book, *D Her.* 6 May. p 4

He welcomes the end of rationing of food, even though in the 1950 and 1951 general elections he had argued that 'Fair Shares for All and the Ration Book ... went together.' He admits that he was wrong –

'you can't have freedom of ideas without freedom in the grocer's shop'. He urges socialists, 'to remember that human beings come first' and that 'Every sort of trade and industry exists to serve that almost forgotten character, the consumer.'

F136. Let's raise a few objections, *D Her*. 13 May. p 4

He denounces the possibility of National Servicemen fighting in Korea who do not even know what the war is about. He calls on the older generation to protest. He regrets that Labour Party meetings rarely have young people at them.

F137. Law and order? I want freedom, *D Her*. 20 May. p 4

He calls for a distinctive socialist foreign policy. He urges 'freedom and equality' not 'law and order'; support for the Viet Minh not for the French.

F138. Stop the Sulks. Someone has to lose, *D Her*. 27 May. p 4

He deplores the view that Britain should not send football teams abroad if they are likely to be beaten.

F139. What *is* Europe? *D Her*. 3 Jun. p 4

He discusses whether 'Europe' means anything.

F140. I May Be Odd – They're Not, *D Her*. 17 Jun. p 4

He discusses university students. He refuses to generalise, observing that they are 'individual human beings, each with his own problems'. He deems them 'extremely normal' whereas he has 'grave doubts about the sanity of some of my colleagues'.

F141. Why The Russians Have Their Little Joke, *D Her*. 24 Jun. p 4

He discusses the Russians' habit of claiming all inventions to be the work of Russians.

F142. *This* Is History, *D Her*. 1 Jul. p 4

He argues that the meeting of Nehru and Chou En-Lai at Delhi is the most historic event of 1954.

F143. You CAN'T get rid of exams, *D Her*. 8 Jul. p 4

He feels that exams are a necessary evil, but comments that 'there are many important things in life that can't be tested by examination'. He denounces the fact that 'more than a third of the boys at Oxford and Cambridge are there simply because their parents can pay for them'.

F144. It's not worth being great, *D Her.* 15 Jul. p 4

He argues that Britain should give up trying to be a great power. He points to Switzerland and Sweden as examples of prosperous and democratic states which are not Great Powers.

F145. Tolerance? I call it Indifference, *D Her.* 22 Jul. p 4

He argues that 'co-existence' between communism and the West is a sham. 'Communism and freedom can't live together, sooner or later one will destroy the other'.

F146. 10 doctors, 50 cars, or 10 houses = a bomber pilot, *D Her.* 29 Jul. p 4

He is shocked by the information that it costs £25,000 to train a bomber pilot.

F147. I Read Anything (even other people's letters), *D. Her.* 5 Aug. p 4

He urges people to read more for pleasure. He feels that the only contemporary novelist who writes for everybody is J.B. Priestley. He recommends reading out loud Carlyle's *French Revolution.*

F148. We Are All The Working Classes, *D Her.* 26 Aug. p 4

'The real difference in our society is the difference between all those who are doing a useful job in the world and those who live in idleness, simply because they own something.'

F149. I asked my children – they didn't know, *D Her.* 16 Sept. p 4

He wonders what children learn at school. They could not give a reasoned reply to the question why we oppose Communism.

F150. I Don't Want Do-Gooders, *D Her.* 23 Sept. p 4

He denounces the BBC for trying to do the viewers good instead of entertaining them.

F151. Fill It In! *D Her.* 30 Sept. p 4

He discusses what should be done with the remains of the temple of Mithras in the City of London – and suggests that a fortune should not be spent preserving it. He welcomes the Tory Party organising its own Brains Trusts.

F152. This is Lunacy, *D Her.* 7 Oct. p 4.

He regrets that there is little passion in current politics. He feels that it is lunatic to make an ally of Germany yet forbid her to build up a big army. He suggests Britain should either be entirely for Germany or alternatively make an alliance with Russia.

F153. I'm ashamed of my sex, *D Her.* 14 Oct. p 4

He denounces Oxford and Cambridge colleges for not sharing their resources with women students. He calls for equality for women throughout society.

F154. Has a book EVER corrupted anyone? *D Her.* 21 Oct. p 4

He discusses censorship and condemns it; with the exception of children's comics which are 'full of violence, brutality and race hatred'.

F155. I Walked in A Dead City. . . . , *D Her.* 28 Oct. p 4

He regrets that the City of London is dead on a Sunday – even the churches were locked. He calls for a return of living accommodation in city centres.

F156. But who is this Guy? *D Her.* 4 Nov. p 2

He is glad that sectarian bitterness has gone in England.

F157. It Isn't Enough To Learn To Earn, *D Her.* 11 Nov. p 4

He condemns the fact that only a small proportion of university students are of working class origin. He regrets that working class parents don't encourage their children to go to university. 'The object of making money is to enjoy things that only a university education can give.'

F158. Let's all be dumb And Happier, *D Her.* 18 Nov. p 4

He praises ordinary people all over the world for turning their backs on politicians. 'It isn't apathy at all. It is common-sense anarchism – the best of political creeds.'

F159. A Bishop took my breath away (and that's no mean feat), *D Her.* 25 Nov. p 4

He denounces a bishop for saying that working

for a football pools firm is worse than for an armaments firm. He calls for an end to caning in schools.

F160. Can we win this war? *D Her.* 2 Dec. p 4

He discusses the current flooding in Britain and whether Man will ever control nature. He condemns people who make a fuss in restaurants or over late trains.

F161. No eye-for-an-eye or H-bomb for H-bomb, *D Her.* 9 Dec. p 6

He is horrified at Churchill's comment 'In future we must rely on deterrence, not defence.' He urges that Britain should not use H-bombs in any circumstance and should not allow America to use them from this country. 'Perhaps we shall shame the rulers of Russia into following our example.'

F162. The Judgement of the Diplomat, *Saturday Review of Literature*. 37. 11 Dec. pp 9–10, 54–6

'The professional diplomats must have ideals; and the idealists must have some common sense.'

Repr. as 'Democracy and Diplomacy', A9, pp 184–92, and A17, pp 354–63

F163. The *B*ig *B*rother *C*orporation. TV is already turning us into 1984 types, *D Her.* 15 Dec. p 4

He praises the BBC for repeating the play of George Orwell's *1984* and regrets that only the inoffensive is shown on television. He condemns the BBC for killing off the political discussion programme 'In The News'.

F164. Who's saying Merry Christmas? *D Her.* 22 Dec. p 4

He discusses the origins of Christmas celebrations.

F165. Look! No war, *D Her.* 29 Dec. p 2

He observes that the surprising thing of 1954 has been that there has been no war. This was due to the balance of power – 'But there is no guarantee that this balance will last.'

1955

F166. Old generals can't fight new battles, *D Her.* 19 Jan. p 4

He urges that the best and cheapest defence policy is to give up being a great power.

F167. I'll stay my old sweet self, *D Her.* 26 Jan. p 4

He criticises Professor J.B.S. Haldane for wanting to be an Indian citizen as running away from responsibility. He is critical of such indulgences by intellectuals.

F168. Repeal the Old Pals' Act! *D Her.* 2 Feb. p 4

He regrets the lack of passion in politics.

F169. We're next door to destruction, *D Her.* 16 Feb. p 4

He denounces politicians of both the West and Russia for their attitude to the H-bomb. Also he urges everyone to buy a book a week – 'The individual buying books according to his own personal taste is the only sure guardian for freedom of expression.'

F170. And I Said I Wouldn't Laugh At The BBC. . . . , *D Her.* 23 Feb. p 4

He jeers at the BBC – and comments that they are adopting a new enthusiasm for free speech because of the coming of commercial television.

E171. A Gourmet's Europe, *NS & N.* 49, 1251. 26 Feb. pp 286–7

He suggests that good food 'goes with a settled, peaceful civilisation and a prosperous middle class'. He discusses food in France and suggests that 'a safe rule is that the food is best where there is the best wine'. Overall he observes, 'There is not much to provoke gastronomic travel beyond Italy and France.'

F172. The fact is: We're scared of strangers, *D Her.* 2 Mar. p 4

He condemns colour prejudice – and says that there is no justification for hostility to newcomers be they Welsh, Irish or West Indian. Also he condemns Franco and observes that he shall die happy if democracy is restored in Spain.

F173. Babies are still being born (And That's News!), *D Her.* 9 Mar. p 4

He feels that it is extraordinary that people are not panic-stricken about the H-bomb. That they are not is 'wonderful evidence of the sanity of human beings'.

F174. Scrap those wedding bells, *D Her.* 16 Mar. p 4

He discusses marriage and argues that the traditional basis for marriage has ceased to exist. He condemns women claiming alimony – though he agrees that fathers must pay for the upkeep of children while they are small.

F175. Publish – and be damned, *D Her.* 23 Mar. p 4

He comments on the row over the publication of records of Yalta by America. He is against bargaining in public but in favour of quick publication of important records.

F176. Pick 'em out of a hat, *D Her.* 27 Apr. p 6

He discusses the electoral system – and suggests that as 'We want Parliament to represent ordinary folk' 600 names should be drawn from a hat.

F177. I'd rather look at a lovely view than march on May Day, *D Her.* 4 May. p 4

He comments that the enthusiasm has gone from those celebrating May Day. 'The things that really matter have nothing to do with politics. Love between friends. Good books. The beauties of nature.' Also he condemns the banning of horror comics.

F178. Must this scandalous farce go on for ever? *D Her.* 11 May. p 6

He calls for the abolition of the House of Lords. Also he argues that the great statesmen 'don't care what is happening so long as it keeps them in the limelight. If there was ever real peace they would all be out of a job.'

F179. What a hole! ... That's My Verdict On Those Northern Towns The Locals Are So Proud Of, *D Her.* 25 May. p 6

He condemns the towns for ugliness. He urges socialists, 'Let us make our towns as beautiful as our countryside.' Also he condemns the holding of Empire Day.

F180. Dear old pals, But I Don't Believe A Word They Say, *D Her.* 8 Jun. p 2

He criticises political leaders both in Eastern Europe and in the West for vigorously praising other leaders at one time and vigorously condemning them at another, as it suits them.

F181. Nosey Parkers, who are wasting the time of us all, *D Her.* 15 Jun. p 4

He condemns investigators who are asking children questions about the effects of television on their family life. Also he distrusts 'the doctrine that men are played out when they are 65 or 70'.

F182. It isn't all holiday for us, *D Her.* 22 Jun. p 6

He comments that university lecturers spend much of the summer marking examination papers and carrying out research. He feels that university teachers 'worry too much about research and not enough about *communication* . . . We ought to be explaining our work in popular books, in newspapers, on the radio.'

F183. A Living Mother Or The Honoured Dead? They should have given Mrs. Sispera the roses, *D Her.* 29 Jun. p 4

He welcomes the British friends of Czechoslovakia sending roses in remembrance of the dead of Lidice but condemns the imprisonment in that country of a woman for trying to leave the country 'illegally'. Also he praises Indian statesmen for their frank comments in Russia and the USA.

F184. Do Bridegrooms Need Dutch Courage? No sober man would face this, *D Her.* 6 Jul. p 4

He comments on numerous things including education.

F185. I Say What I Please, *D Her.* 13 Jul. p 4

He blames scientists for the H-bomb. 'We shall never get rid of war until men stop being *proud* of having been soldiers.'

F186. I Say What I Please, *D Her.* 20 Jul. p 4

Amongst other points, he condemns snobbery on BBC television and praises a woman who has educated her own children. He condemns magistrates for dealing lightly with rugby hooligans yet sending teddy boys to Borstal.

F187. I Say What I Please, *D Her.* 27 Jul. p 4

Amongst other points, he condemns assaults on beauty spots, such as Donald Campbell's record breaking motor-boat speed trial on Lake Ullswater.

F188. I Say What I Please, *D Her.* 3 Aug. p 4

He argues that the miners have learnt the tricks of the capitalists in using monopoly and scarcity to raise their living standards – 'The miners are just as entitled to demand this ransom as anyone else.' His other comments include the view that breach of promise suits degrade women.

F189. I Say What I Please, *D Her.* 10 Aug. p 4

'The man who wants freedom to change his job or to go on strike won't get it unless he stands up for *my* freedom to say what I like on TV.' He also regrets the waste of money on the space programme and urges that divorce should be made easier.

F190. I Say What I Please, *D Her.* 17 Aug. p 4

Amongst other things he praises the recent Geneva Conference – 'The conference of atomic scientists has done more for the good of mankind than all the high pressure international meetings since the peace treaty of Versailles.'

F191. I Say What I Please, *D Her.* 24 Aug. p 4

He applauds Nehru's efforts to free Goa. 'In my opinion he is the wisest and best statesman in the world today.' Amongst other points, he urges the Press to leave the Royal Family alone when on holiday – 'and give us a holiday from the Royal Family'.

F192. I Say What I Please, *D Her.* 31 Aug. p 4

He condemns Eden for preaching 'the only idea the Tories have had for the last 150 years . . . (that) we must all work harder and spend less'. Amongst other points, he condemns the British habit of throwing litter everywhere.

F193. I Say What I Please, *D Her.* 7 Sept. p 4

Amongst other points he calls on English rugby teams not to play in South Africa.

F194. I Say What I Please, *D Her.* 14 Sept. p 4

He welcomes Kruschev's bad temper over Adenauer's complaints about the behaviour of Russian troops in Germany. He praises the National Trust. He defends holiday makers who walk round barefoot.

F195. I Say What I Please – This is a Monstrous Dodge! *D Her.* 21 Sept. p 4

He urges a complete ending of national service – and not it being phased out. He condemns the Foreign Office for not telling the public of the defection of Burgess and Maclean. He feels that the view that equal pay for women leads to more marriage break-ups is correct – but is happy if that is so.

F196. I Say What I Please – and Now I Can Say It On TV! *D Her.* 28 Sept. p 4

He praises commercial television – 'ITV wants us to be exciting. The BBC wanted us to be harmless.' He urges self-determination for the Cypriots. He suggests the great majority would vote to join Greece; he calls for the protection of the Turkish minority.

F197. I Say What I Please, *D Her.* 5 Oct. p 4

He condemns the British betting laws – 'Our Puritanical laws against betting play into the hands of the race-gangs.' He sees the end of prohibition in Sweden as 'a great victory for freedom', and observes: 'Take away the restrictions. Let people do what they like. And they'll behave sensibly. That's my creed.' Amongst other points, he condemns great sums of money being spent on bishop's palaces when country clergy are so poor.

F198. I Say What I Please, *D Her.* 12 Oct. p 4

He calls on British politicians to follow Molotov's example and to confess their faults. In discussing television he observes that there is the problem of freedom depending on rich men or the search for profits – 'this is the biggest problem for the Labour Party to solve in the near future'. He comments that the real marriage guidance advice is, 'Tolerance, tolerance, tolerance'.

F199. I Say What I Please. I Blame The Church For All The Fuss, *D Her.* 19 Oct. p 4

He condemns the leaders of the Church of England for the fuss over Princess Margaret. He vigorously attacks the bishops and argues that 'this affair is not a crisis of Royalty. It is a crisis of the Established Church.'

F200. I Say What I Please. Quit guessing and give us the facts, *D Her.* 26 Oct. p 4

He argues that 'accurate and detailed facts about our present economic system are the most revolutionary demand that the Labour Party could make', for if these were available 'we could really start PLANNING our economic life'. He feels that the vote by the people of the Saar ends the story of European unity. He praises subsidies for Covent Garden. He calls for a ban on cars in cities.

F201. I Say What I Please. This Tradition Is Poppycock! *D Her.* 2 Nov. p 2

He praises the opening of new universities and urges the closing down of Oxford and Cambridge, as they 'are the most effective way ever invented of taming the rebellious and discontented'. Amongst other points, he argues that Britain should pull out of the Middle East.

F202. I Say What I Please. The Bishops are after bigger game, *D Her.* 9 Nov. p 4

He comments on the Prime Minister's power to appoint bishops. He wishes people remembered on Remembrance Sunday that we fought the Germans in the two world wars. He urges, 'we can't turn this world into a heaven on earth. But if this generation sees the end of capital punishment in Britain, it will have done something to justify itself at the Day of Judgement.' He condemns the expulsion of school girls for not conforming in their attire: 'Every one should be different in character, in ideas, and even in dress. At least that is what I think education is for.'

F203. I Say What I Please. Pity The Man Who Retires, *D Her.* 16 Nov. p 4

He argues that the retired man ends up 'as unpaid domestic servant to his wife'. He denounces the Church of England: 'An Established Church is an established hypocrisy. It does not exist to preach a divine revelation. It exists to prop up the existing social order.' Also he denounces the House of Lords.

F204. I say what I please. We've made these silly young men into martyrs, *D Her*. 23 Nov. p 4

He condemns the savage sentences passed on the IRA youths who raided Arborfield Camp. Amongst other points, he urges a campaign against smog in cities.

F205. I say what I please. What a comedy act! *D Her*. 30 Nov. p 4

He condemns the remarks made by Kruschev whilst touring in India.

F206. I say what I please. Make the little beggars walk! *D Her*. 7 Dec. p 4

He supports bus conductors who expect good manners from school children. He says how much he enjoyed watching 'Free Speech' on television. He condemns the way journalists treat press conferences on television as 'a sort of verbal boxing match'.

F207. I say what I please. Let the teachers TEACH, *D Her*. 14 Dec. p 4

He supports the teachers in objecting to having to collect savings or run school meals. He sends no Christmas cards. He is pleased with the growing competition for viewers between the BBC and the ITA (Independent Television Authority).

F208. I say what I please. Nehru is the Good Fairy, *D Her*. 21 Dec. p 4

He praises Nehru for his efforts on behalf of the UN and world peace. He condemns those who damage public property. He welcomes the suggestion of long hours in summer and short hours in winter.

F209. London Diary, *NS & N*. 50, 1294. 24 Dec. p 849

In it he denounces the House of Lords and deplores the running down of canals. He praises Trollope's political novels and names Lord Acton as the King of Bores.

F210. I say what I please. Youth doen't believe (in anything), *D Her*. 28 Dec. p 4

He regrets that the young lack enthusiasm for politics.

F211. London Diary, *NS & N.* 50, 1295. 31 Dec. p 875

He denounces National Service and the hydrogen bomb. He deplores the likely increase in the numbers of students going to university. He applauds the arrival of commercial television – and especially the political discussion programme 'Free Speech'. The BBC ended their programme as it received 'too positive a response'.

1956

F212. I say what I please. You can't apply rules to love, *D Her.* 4 Jan. p 4

He argues that the legal bargain of marriage should be reserved for couples with a family. Amongst other points he discusses the effect of H-bombs being dropped on Britain.

F213. London Diary, *NS & N.* 51, 1296. 7 Jan. p 6

He applauds Kruschev's speeches in India and Burma and observes that they were 'fine, old fashioned radicalism'. He argues that far from keeping the capitalist system going, the colonies have nearly ruined it financially. 'I am against colonies becausc I think colonies morally wrong and imperialists wicked.' He suggests, 'If Kruschev and his associates really want to ruin capitalism, they would disarm tomorrow . . . '; but he observes that both systems buttress each other up by the armaments race. He deplores the way homosexuality is treated. He praises the Historical Association, on the occasion of its 50th anniversary.

F214. I say what I please. What a princely farce, *D Her.* 11 Jan. p 4

He comments on the marriage of Grace Kelly to the Prince of Monaco. Also he discusses the time alotted to religious programmes on television.

F215. I say what I please. Dog-collars, white-collars, no collars, let's mix 'em, *D Her.* 18 Jan. p 4

He condemns the sacking of a poorly paid minister for taking a second job as a shop assistant. He condemns the Tories for wanting an incomes policy on its own; he advocates socialist planning. He urges a more enlightened approach to crime: 'We must treat crime as a social disease, not as something we want to take vengeance for.'

F216. I Say What I Please. What A Bargain That Was, *D Her.* 25 Jan. p 4

He comments on a woman who had offered herself as a wife for £100 – and observes that the shocking thing was that the price was too low. Amongst other points, he suggests that the Anglo-American alliance will only gain the support of the peoples of Asia and Africa 'by treating them as brothers – and meaning it'.

F217. I say what I please, *D Her.* 1 Feb. p 4

Amongst other points, he jeers at the annual speeches of chairmen of banks who always urge others to work harder and spend less.

F218. I Say What I Please. Royalty have no cause to complain, *D Her.* 8 Feb. p 4

He comments that the Royal Family have to expect endless press attention as the price of their privileges. He regrets that the Archbishop of Canterbury has not campaigned against the hydrogen bomb and the colour bar, not that he has failed to condemn fox-hunting. He predicts that the Churches will keep the Dead Sea scrolls quiet as long as possible.

F219. I Say What I Please. Tito was right after all, *D Her.* 22 Feb. p 4

He welcomes signs that the Russian Communist leaders are coming to their senses. He praises the House of Commons for voting against the death penalty. He condemns the banning of a jazz club at a public school.

F220. I Say I Please. Let parents be the censors. . . . , *D Her.* 29 Feb. p 4

He urges that it should be left to the parents to shield their children from the less pleasant aspects of life – and writers and television producers should not take it on themselves to do this. He denounces a vicar who condemned trains running late.

F221. I say what I please. I'd let the girl marry, *D Her.* 7 Mar. p 4

He criticises some parents who refuse to let their seventeen-year old daughter marry a coloured man. 'I'm not only glad to call a coloured man brother. I shall be proud if a coloured man is ever ready to call me father-in-law.' He is not at all sorry to see manuscripts of Tennyson's poems being bought by Harvard university.

F222. I Say What I Please. I'd Cane Them For Talking Such Rot, *D Her.* 14 Mar. p 4

He denounces Essex Education Committee for making rules for the sake of it. He comments on the unveiling of a monument to Karl Marx in Highgate cemetary. He sees Marx's achievement as being 'to give the working classes of Europe confidence in themselves'.

F223. I Say What I Please. Ban cars – and go by BIKE! *D Her.* 21 Mar. p 6

He urges the banning of cars during the summer months and the provision of cycle tracks everywhere. Amongst other points, he praises the architecture of the Victorian great railway stations.

F224. I Say What I Please. Let's be fair to the rich, *D Her.* 28 Mar. p 4

He is against the starting point for surtax being raised. However he is against a Means Test in university education preventing middle class children going to university. Amongst other points, he deems Bernard Shaw's will to be silly.

F225. I say what I please, *D Her.* 4 Apr. p 4

Amongst other points, he condemns those Soviet leaders who were involved in Stalin's mass murders.

F226. I Say What I Please, *D Her.* 11 Apr. p 4

He urges the cutting of commitments in Germany and the Empire as ways to help Britain get out of her economic problems. He is disgusted by 'the sight of Stalin's creatures in Russia turning against him and loading all their crimes on his dead body' – but finds even worse the conduct of the communist rulers in the satellite countries.

F227. I Say What I Please, *D. Her.* 25 Apr. p 4

He regrets that people in Britain treat the Russian leaders as jokes. 'They are two men of sinister power who have fought their way to the top by the most unscrupulous means and now control the fiercest dictatorship in existence.' He feels that after his Budget Macmillan has joined the list of future Tory Prime Ministers who failed to make it. He praises J.B. Priestley for refusing to autograph copies of his books.

F228. I Say What I Please, *D Her.* 2 May. p 6

He praises the Archbishop of Canterbury for attacking the Government over Cyprus. He comments on the meaning of May Day. Also he advises young people with problems to turn to others of their own age group for advice.

F229. I Say What I Please, *D Her.* 9 May. p 4

He reflects on the General Strike and comments that was the only time in his life when he was really excited about politics. He is pleased that the German problem has gone – at least while Germany is divided. He is unsympathetic to Kilburn council tenants' disapproval of naked stone figures outside their homes.

F230. I Say What I Please, *D Her.* 16 May. p 6

He condemns the British Government's policy in Cyprus. Amongst other points, he comments on Harry Pollitt; he feels Pollitt's has been a wasted life – he 'should have been a great working-class leader'.

F231. I Say What I Please, *D Her.* 23 May. p 4

He calls for 'a new policy to meet the rising tide of national independence', observing that the Government's policy towards the Empire is bankrupt. After a visit to the Moscow Circus when it was in London, he observes, 'it is my guess that one day soon the 200 million gay Russians will clear the poker-faced

Communists out and have the circus all day long.'

F232. I Say What I Please, *D Her*. 30 May. p 4

He criticizes Macmillan for urging wage restraint. He advocates defence cuts. Also he comments on the latest German foreign policy documents – pointing to the evidence of leading figures in English society telling Hitler that they really wanted an alliance with him. He urges that prostitution and homosexuality are sins not crime – and the legal penalties for them should be taken off the statute book.

F233. I Say What I Please. Don't shout too soon, *D Her*. 6 Jun. p 6

He is wary of coming too quickly to the conclusion that Russia is moving nearer to freedom. He calls for someone to find a way to keep prices static. As a boy he felt the time he spent playing football or cricket to be 'hours of uninterrupted misery'. He feels that boxing should be banned.

F234. I Say What I Please. I approve that £20, *D Her*. 13 Jun. p 4

He supports the ETU in sending money to the Cyprus Emergency Fund and urges all in the Labour Movement to do likewise – 'as long as they are oppressed, WE are not free'. He comments on Kruschev's speech on Stalin. He comments on the dangers of white bread.

F235. I Say What I Please. AT last – a spot of fun, *D Her*. 20 Jun. p 6

He jeers at the apparent surprise expressed by communist leaders round the world at Stalin's crimes. He discusses freedom. He also discusses the results of the 1951 census.

F236. I Say What I Please, *D Her*. 27 Jun. p 4

He discusses the forthcoming Commonwealth Prime Ministers' conference and observes that the Commonwealth's duty is: 'To defend freedom everywhere – and particularly against our own government.' He comments on Cyprus – and states that he has no sympathy with the argument that we must protect the Turkish minority. Also he regrets the state of disrepair of old churches, but he feels that when they lose their congregations 'they must make room for new buildings with a more modern purpose.'

F237. If You Are Under 25. . . . Report on the Rising Generation Part 1, *Reynolds News*. 21 Oct. p 3

He comments that university students take the Welfare State for granted. They have no faith in the UN and are not attracted to Communism or religion.

F238. Report on the Rising Generation. Part 2: Those Two Wasted Years, *Reynolds News*. 28 Oct. p 3

He denounces National Service. 'They are taught to conform, where they should be discovering how to rebel. They are made to keep in step when they should be striking out for themselves.' He argues that Oxford and Cambridge provide a social life which is harmful. He also regrets that in Britain there is a scorn for anything that is intellectual – in the House of Commons 'You only have to call a man a professor, and all the members rock with laughter.'

F239. Report on the Rising Generation. Part 3: The gloves are off today, *Reynolds News*. 4 Nov. p 3

He bemoans the respectability of the Labour Party, especially its line at the start of the Suez crisis. He argues that it can win over the young – 'There must be no hesitation, no moderation, no half-heartedness.' He concludes, 'We are back with the old Radical ideals. Freedom for all men. Equality between nations. And the building up of the International Co-operative Commonwealth that we call Socialism.'

1957

F240. London Diary, *NS*. 54, 1373. 6 Jul. p 6

He denounces telephone tapping. He compares the current state of politics to that of the eighteenth century. He praises Hugh Trevor-Roper's essay in *Encounter*, which attacks Toynbee's *Study of History*. He discusses the views of the British Left and of the Government on foreign affairs in the 1930s: 'The hard truth about the situation before 1939 is that whatever we did was wrong. There was no right course. The choice was not between the wise and unwise, but between the honourable and dishonourable. The men in power chose the second. And little good it did them.'

F241. London Diary, *NS*. 54, 1376. 27 Jul. p 106

He praises commercial television, and expresses a wish to see the BBC ended before he dies – 'This will be the biggest knock at THE THING since the Abdication.' He eulogises G.D.H. Cole. Also he comments on inflation, foreign travel and the selection of MPs.

F242. London Diary, *NS*. 54, 1377. 3 Aug. p 138

He feels that world war is unlikely in the near future, but little wars are likely. He predicts trouble from Germany by about 1960. He praises seaside comic postcards and denounces sexual intolerance. He comments on the preservation of terraced houses in Regent's Park and on the French August holiday. He observes that leisure has become the greatest problem of the time, 'a more pressing affair than the hydrogen bomb'.

F243. Let's wind up the Empire, *News Chronicle*. 7 Oct. p 4

An article in the newspaper's 'Argument' series. He urges Britain to give independence to the rest of her African colonies. 'Let us mind our own business and not go where we are no longer wanted.'

F244. I'm a little Englander – but my England must be modern, *News Chronicle*. 21 Oct. p 4

An article in the newspaper's 'Argument' series. He is glad to see Britain's power over others diminishing. 'One day – not far off either – inequalities between nations and classes will disappear.'

F245. Why Must We Soft Soap the Germans? *Sun Ex*. 27 Oct. p 12

He denounces the US for cutting off aid to Tito in order to appease Adenauer. He hopes that the partition of Germany will remain and observes that 'whoever supports the reunification of Germany commits himself to the Munich settlement and to the demands which Hitler made on Poland in August 1939'.

F246. Our Destiny, *Sunday Graphic.* 10 Nov. p 13

His piece is one of twelve contributions under this heading, written after the Russians had launched a sattelite into space. 'The only way to beat the Russians is for us to *do* seriously what they *promise* to do. That is to give people a fair deal all over the world. By that I mean racial equality and better economic conditions.' He also calls on nations to renounce the hydrogen bomb.

F247. Our party leaders are not worth a vote, *News Chronicle.* 29 Nov. p 4

An article in the newspaper's 'Argument' series. He regrets that party leaders no longer have the fire in them that such leaders as Cobden and Keir Hardie had in the past. He calls for a real choice in policies: 'more social equality or less social equality . . . hydrogen bombs or no hydrogen bombs . . . holding the colonies down or setting them free'.

F248. What's so wrong about talking with Kruschev? *Sun Ex.* 22 Dec. p 8

He urges that there should be an end to the threat of nuclear war and calls for a summit meeting as soon as possible. 'Kruschev is the most sensible, most enlightened leader Russia has had since the death of Lenin.'

1958

F249. What would you like me to talk about? *TV Times.* 10, 119. 7 Feb. p 15

In it he discusses the freedom of choice of subject he has on independent television, in contrast to the restrictions on BBC.

F250. I Say Scrap The Lords, *Sun Ex.* 16 Feb. p 10

He comments that the Labour Party has no policy towards the House of Lords, and he suggests that 'the only improvement it needs is that it should vanish, leaving a record of emptiness and folly'.

F251. These Men Imperil Freedom, *Sun. Ex.* 2 Mar. p 12

He attacks the critics of the Press, and in particular the British Establishment. 'Our liberties depend on all sorts of things: trades unions and churches, the law courts and the Constitution, politicians and newspapers. But if I had to plump for one, I would plump for the Press. Its freedom is the guarantee for all other freedoms.'

F252. Why This Picture Alarms Me (Photograph of the Queen with Adenauer), *Sun Ex.* 20 Apr. p 12

He comments that Adenauer 'has made Germany the leading Power in Europe'. He calls for closer ties with France and negotiations with Kruschev to avert the nuclear peril.

F253. Campaign Report, *NS.* 55, 1423. 21 Jun. pp 799–800

He gives a report on the progress of the Campaign for Nuclear Disarmament (CND), on the basis of his own experience of addressing meetings all over Britain. He calls on CND to avoid all equivocation and 'to insist that unilateral abandonment is the only solution'. He comments that young supporters have a distaste for the moral argument. He urges that the moral case must be made. 'The Campaign will never succeed if we are in it merely to save our own miserable skins'; and adds, 'sooner or later we shall have to win the younger generation back to morality'. As for the Labour Party, CND's aim is not to disrupt it but to win it over – 'We offer it the moral leadership of the world.'

F254. We must not turn our backs on Kruschev, *Sun Ex.* 22 Jun. p 10

He argues that despite the murder of Imre Nagy and his associates 'Kruschev has not shown himself the suspicious, blood-stained tyrant that Stalin was'. He urges that there should be no return to the Cold War, and comments that that would merely strengthen Kruschev's hard line opponents. He calls for an immediate summit conference.

F255. Well, could YOU name the Minister of Power? *Sun Ex.* 6 Jul. p 7

He argues that Cabinet ministers are little more than cyphers – with the exception of Ernest Marples. He urges that each Minister should tell the House of Commons annually 'what difference he has made by existing'.

F256. Is this the way to get better TV? *Sun Ex.* 13 Jul. p 10

He complains that the BBC, having collected the viewers' licence fees, 'puts on not what the viewer wants, but what high officials of the BBC . . . think is good for him', whereas the ITV, dependent on advertisers, 'must always put on what a *great many* viewers want . . . Despite this, I thought commercial television an improvement on the previous BBC monopoly.' He advocates 'Pay As You View' for extra programmes catering for minority tastes.

F257. Let's Scrap This Farce At U.N.O.! *Sun Ex.* 10 Aug. p 8

He wishes world leaders would meet at summit conferences not at the United Nations' Assembly, where they will only make propaganda speeches. He calls the UNO a pretence and wishes that Britain would withdraw from it.

F258. Why not hand over Chiang to U.N.O.? *Sun Ex.* 31 Aug. p 10

He argues that the greatest threat of war comes from the Far East, and that there the main problem is 'the refusal of American leaders to face reality'. 'If Chiang Kai-shek is still President of China, then the United States are still British colonies, and Elizabeth II is their Queen.' He urges America to recognise Mao, and suggests that the least humiliating procedure for her would be to refer the question of the islands and Formosa to the UN Assembly.

F259. Should the Queen go to Germany? *Sun Ex.* 19 Oct. p 12

'We cannot be friendly with all Germans until the generation which served Hitler has passed away.'

F260. I hate these women who are all clatter and clank!

Woman's Mirror. 31 Oct. p 11

An article in the newspaper's series 'Top Names Talking'. He argues that giving women the vote has been a regressive move as women vote for safety – or for a handsome candidate. 'Men argue. Women *feel*.' However men have followed women's lead in recent years in having contempt for public affairs. Also he denounces society women and condemns women novelists.

F261. London Diary, *NS*. 56, 1443. 8 Nov. p 622

He denounces scientists as being men without moral concern, and appeals for more funds for CND. He also condemns the British banks other than Barclays for not allowing trade unions. He supports Boothby's bid for the Rectorship of St Andrews.

F262. London Diary, *NS*. 56, 1444. 15 Nov. p 663

Discussing Remembrance Sunday, he observes that the Second World War was the one war that was right – it was 'a war of the people'. He suggests, 'Anyone who wishes to understand the origins of the Second World War should study the psychology of Armistice Day. It explains everything – pacifism, appeasement, the failure to distinguish the real evil of Hitler's Germany from the lesser evils of 'the Hun' and Kaiser Bill.'

He also comments on the Wolfenden Report. He would take all penalties off homosexuality immediately – but he would not relax penalties at all for those attacking young girls. He finds the proposals to move prostitutes off the streets objectionable as they are purely aimed at 'keeping up appearances'.

F263. A free Berlin? Why Not! *Sun Ex*. 30 Nov. p 12

'To desert the West Berliners would be an act of shame.' He comments on the experience of Austria, and urges, 'A free city of Berlin increases the chances of freedom. It lessens the chances of war.'

F264. Thoughts on Television, *Television Annual 1959*, London, Odhams Press, 1958. pp 99–102

In it he discusses 'how thoughts, ideas, information,

can be conveyed on television; how television can be used as an instrument of education and still more of intellectual stimulus'. He feels that argument – such as the 'Free Speech' programmes – is more stimulating than lectures on television.

1959

F265. Can we ever make a friend of Russia? *Sun Ex.* 18 Jan. p 12

In it he argues that 'the spectre of Communism, like every other ghost, is a creation of our imagination'. He observes, 'The key to Soviet policy is this: THEY ARE AFRAID' – and adds that the West is 'rearming the very Germans who nearly destroyed Russia not so long ago'.

F266. The Westminster Show on TV? Oh No! *Sun Ex.* 8 Feb. p 12

He suggests that the best way to halt the decline of Parliament is to 'take the Whips off . . . Let the Members stand up as independent individuals with something vital to stay.'

F267. Is this why Mr. K. froze up? *Sun Ex.* 1 Mar. p 12

He calls for the settling of the German question – and suggests that 'the only sensible way' is to establish 'a free Germany, peaceful and united, but without arms'.

F268. Has the time come for Ike to step down? *Sun Ex.* 19 Apr. p 12

He urges that the Anglo-American alliance should be made to work. He argues that it lacks leadership, comments that Roosevelt 'threw away at Yalta the fruits of victory', and calls on Eisenhower to resign as President.

F269. Is it SAFE to send this man to Moscow? *Sun Ex.* 3 May. p 12

He argues that Sir David Eccles is too favourable to the Germans and should not be sent to Moscow to promote British trade. He also comments that 'the European Common Market is working out in practice as a device for bringing all Continental resources under German control'.

F270. Why can't Selwyn be more like de Gaulle? *Sun Ex.* 14 Jun. p 12

He regrets that Selwyn Lloyd does not show signs of independence from the Americans. He asserts, 'The fact is that very little divides the British people from the Russians.'

F271. Must our tourists stay in chains? *Sun Ex.* 28 Jun. p 12

He denounces all limitations on foreign travel as pointless bureaucracy.

F272. The Faceless Ones will be happy – the day the newspapers stop, *Sun Ex.* 5 Jul. p 6

He regrets the threatened newspaper strike and argues that those who will gain from it will be high-handed bureaucrats, magistrates and politicians who will not be kept in check.

F273. What would happen if Kruschev died? *Sun Ex.* 26 Jul. p 8

'Kruschev, with all his faults, is the best Soviet leader we are likely to get . . . He is a man, not a machine.' He feels that Eisenhower wishes to arm Germany with nuclear weapons, whereas Nixon is a man who can do business with Kruschev.

F274. Will Ike stand up to Adenauer? *Sun Ex.* 23 Aug. p 12

He discusses the prospects for Eisenhower's European visit. 'We want to see Eastern Germany freed from the Communist yoke. That will happen as soon as the Russians get real and lasting security against a new German danger.'

F275. How Near Is World War III? Dangers of a power balance, *Gdn.* 28 Aug. p 6

He argues that preparations for war in the past have nearly always led to war – and that currently 'preparations for war are being made on a more gigantic scale than ever before'. He predicts that 'If men continue to behave as they have behaved, we should reach World War III within the next six or eight years, unless, of course, one Power manages . . . to dominate the world'.

Repr. *MGW*. 81, 10. 3 Sept. p 5

For correspondence on this, see *MGW*. 81, 11. 10 Sept. p 12

F276. Is this the way to run our railways? *Sun Ex*. 23 Oct. p 8

He calls for the modernisation of Britain's railways. He argues that the expectation that the railways should be run at a profit 'seems to me about as silly as expecting the National Health Service to pay its way or our educational system to show a profit'.

F277. How big a threat is Mao? *Sun Ex*. 8 Nov. p 12

He argues that China will only be a danger to world peace if she is driven into a common isolation with Russia. He suggests that 'we should get Russia to join with us and the other advanced nations in helping to develop China, India and the other centres of world poverty'.

F278. What should Ike tell Nehru? *Sun Ex*. 6 Dec. p 12

A.J.P.T. does not presume that China has provoked the border troubles – 'the Chinese case has never been heard'. He hopes that Eisenhower will resist attempts to get him to promise support against China.

1960

F279. Backwards to Utopia, *NS*. 59, 1503. 2 Jan. pp 5–6

Part of a survey 'Look Back at the Fifties'. He sees the 1950s as a decade when 'we have become contemporary, facing the problems of today instead of trying to recreate those of yesterday'. For him 'the best things in it . . . were the opposition to Suez; Aldermaston; and independent television. But they are only types of a general pattern.'

Kingsley Martin's front page editorial, 'Jack's Ten Years', took a very different line: 'Cynical, materialistic, selfish, the decade made the rich richer, the poor poorer . . . Despite A.J.P. Taylor's sanguine appreciation . . . it was a decade without a hero and without a message.'

F280. Why not ask Mao to London? *Sun Ex*. 3 Jan. p 12

He argues that summit diplomacy will fail to settle world problems as long as China is excluded.

F281. Don't give him a title, *Sun Ex.* 28 Feb. p 12

He is delighted at Princess Margaret's engagement. He comments that Anthony Armstrong-Jones should be proud to be a commoner and should stay one and continue to practise his profession.

F282. Why not end this humbug on divorce, *Sun Ex.* 13 Mar. p 12

He denounces the Church's tough line on divorce as hypocrisy.

F283. Must the faceless men of America rule us too? *Sun Ex.* 27 Mar. p 12

He urges that nuclear tests must be ended and 'then an agreement over disarmament can follow'.

F284. Let us slap down these holiday dictators, *Sun Ex.* 10 Apr. p 12

He calls for shorter school holidays at Christmas and Easter and for three months in the summer. Then industry could stagger its holidays between mid-June to mid-September.

F285. Too Good to be True? *NS.* 59, 1520. 30 Apr. p 613–4

An article giving his impressions of Hungary on his return from a ten day trip to that country, where he had been entertained by the Hungarian Academy of Sciences. He comments that 'the Communists have heeded the warning of 1956 and now . . . are anxious to do everying for the masses except get off their backs'.

F286. Does Russia *really* want to do a Deal? *Sun Ex.* 15 May. p 12

He urges both sides at summit meetings to reassure the other that they have nothing to fear – and to start better relations by banning nuclear tests.

F287. Should the Princess now withdraw from public life? *Sun Ex.* 12 Jun. p 12

He praises Princess Margaret for deciding to marry a commoner – and urges her, for the sake of her happiness, to withdraw into private life.

F288. Kennedy or Nixon: Does it matter to us in Britain?

Sun Ex. 26 Jun. p 12

He feels that Nixon is not insincere in politics – 'Perhaps I'm a bit handicapped because Nixon is the only really prominent figure in any country I have every talked to privately.' He feels that Nixon has the 'courage and capacity' to overcome the defects of the Eisenhower administration. He concludes that 'either of them will put some life into the free world', they both have the 'big bouncing virtues of zest and creative endeavour'.

F289. This is Mr. K's chance to make amends, *Sun Ex.* 7 Aug. p 8

He feels that Kruschev has overplayed his hand in his handling of the U2 incident – 'it is really a bit too much when he talks as though Soviet Russia never employed spies at all'.

F290. Are our public men too squeamish? *Sun Ex.* 30 Oct. p 12

Randolph Churchill had successfully sued Sir Gerald Nabarro for calling him (R.C.) a coward. A.J.P.T. regrets that public figures are now too prone to take people to court.

F291. Is it right to kick these men upstairs? *Sun Ex.* 20 Nov. p 12

He regrets that the political careers of such men as Anthony Wedgwood Benn and Quintin Hogg will be shattered through them being forced to go into the House of Lords.

F292. What does the future hold for Mr. Anthony Armstrong-Jones? *Sun Ex.* 18 Dec. p 12

He hopes that those who are connected with the Royal Family will be allowed to carry out rewarding and independent activities.

1961

F293. Can Kennedy Make Sure of Peace in 1961? *Sun Ex.* 1 Jan. p 12

He argues, 'The cause of war is suspicion, Get rid of suspicion and the danger of war will vanish of itself.' He urges Kennedy to give the lead to mankind.

F294. Surely Prince Philip is the Man to Go to Moscow, *Sun Ex.* 8 Jan. p 12

He urges that Prince Philip should open the British Trade Fair in Moscow.

F295. I Say – Let Him Quit, *Sun Ex.* 19 Feb. p 12

He denounces the UN for the failures in the Congo. He wishes to be rid of both Hammarskjold and the UN. He argues that if that happened then 'We should see the relations of the Great Powers improving almost at once.'

F296. Are you wrong to enjoy your newspaper? *Sun Ex.* 5 Mar. p 12

He comments on the Royal Commission on the Press. He champions the investigations by the press into the affairs of public figures and praises successful newspapers. Freedom of the press 'does not mean conformity to some arbitrary standard of good taste or to the whims of political parties.'

F297. Why can a man lay down a crown – but not a peerage? *Sun Ex.* 2 Apr. p 12

He contrasts the treatment of King Edward VIII and that of Wedgwood Benn – and calls for the latter's release from the House of Lords.

F298. Will they talk sense about Berlin at last? *Sun Ex.* 21 May. p 12

He urges the Americans to recognise that a united Germany close to Russia threatens Russia as much as America claims Cuba threatens her. He calls for the recognition of East Germany and for West Berlin to be made a free city.

F299. Would you pay an office boy £40,000 a year? *Sun Ex.* 4 Jun. p 12

He observes that ambassador's reports are worthless – and calls for the ending of the diplomatic service as it is an enormous waste of money.

F300. Could Berlin be Macmillan's chance to regain prestige? *Sun Ex.* 30 Jul. p 14

He argues that there is no crisis over West Berlin but one over the failure to recognise East Germany. 'German revisionism is the only threat to world peace.' He advocates security for West Berlin and recognition of East Germany.

F301. Why don't our politicians tell the truth? *Sun Ex.* 17 Sept. p 16

He complains that the British Government conceals facts from the people. He instances its attitude to West Germany's eastern claims, the Common Market and nuclear weapons, and also its silence on the activities of Blake, Burgess and Maclean.

F302. How many of these men can you name? (Pictures of Lord John Hope, Lord Carrington, Reginald Bevins and John Boyd Carpenter), *Sun Ex.* 8 Oct. p 16

He complains, 'The politicians have created a vested interest in dullness and orthodoxy.' He calls for the business of the House of Commons to be fitted into two nights a week and then the Commons could become 'the real forum of the nation'.

F303. Does this mean Mr. K is on his way out? *Sun Ex.* 29 Oct. p 12

He comments on recent events in Russia and feels that they suggest that Kruschev 'is fighting for his life politically and, perhaps, in the most literal sense'. He praises Kruschev for believing in peaceful co-existence – 'For what it is worth, I am on Kruschev's side.'

F304. Are we really being fair to the Russians? *Sun Ex.* 19 Nov. p 16

He feels that the Russians are blamed unfairly for all the ills of the world; in fact they have been more cautious and moderate than the West in recent months.

F305. Why do we stir up trouble in the family? *Sun Ex.* 3 Dec. p 16

He praises the Commonwealth and prefers it to the Common Market. 'The fact remains that the nations of the Commonwealth are our brothers and sisters and that foreign countries are not.'

F306. Must we always take orders from America? *Sun Ex.* 31 Dec. p 12

'The more we take our own line the more anxious the Americans will be to co-operate with us.'

1962

F307. What Mr. K's Battle Is All About, *Sun Ex.* 21 Jan. p 8

He comments that the top men in Russia 'are locked in fierce debate over future policy' and suggests that all the enlightened leaders of Communist states are for Kruschev, whereas the hated ones are against him.

F308. Must de Gaulle's enemies drag us down too? *Sun Ex.* 11 Feb. p 16

He denounces the activities of the extreme Right in France – and urges that Britain should not become involved in France's problems by joining the Common Market.

F309. I Believe in Toleration, *TV Times.* 329. 16 Feb. p 15

He discusses religious persecution in the past and, more recently, persecution of communists in Western countries. He concludes by commenting on toleration: 'I cannot think of anything else worth believing in.'

F310. Kennedy – The 1962 Baldwin, *Sun Ex.* 4 Mar. p 12

He compares Kennedy with Baldwin. He argues that Kennedy is leading the American people away from catastrophe. He feels that Kennedy is 'imperceptibly . . . lowering the level of suspicion in America against Russia'.

F311. Will we EVER be able to trust Kruschev? *Sun Ex.* 1 Apr. p 16

He comments that in the past he has praised Kruschev but he feels that Kruschev is now wrong in not being more helpful on disarmament – 'inspection is the solid rock on which alone disarmament can be built'.

F312. Is Marples really the Man for the Job? *Sun Ex.* 22 Apr. p 16

He feels that the Government has no real transport policy. He urges Ernest Marples to behave as Beaverbrook did at the Ministry of Aircraft Production. 'We need a traffic dictator imposing uniform rules throughout the country, building roads to the limit of physical capacity, riding roughshod over local and sectional interests.'

F313. I Say Ormsby-Gore should be recalled, *Sun Ex.* 13 May. p 8

He argues that the ambassador in Washington is the key figure in Anglo-American relations and that Ormsby-Gore is not an adequate figure for the job. He suggests the appointment of a Canadian, Australian or New Zealander, then the British case will be put 'with more resolution and independence'.

F314. Macmillan has not found the answer yet, *Sun Ex.* 15 Jul. p 12

He feels that the sacking of ministers wholesale is not the answer to Macmillan's problems. He suggests that there has been a 'failure to define what the Government stands for'. In particular he is critical of its attitude to the Common Market.

F315. Will Menzies speak for Britain? *Sun Ex.* 9 Sept. p 14

He urges the leading Commonwealth prime ministers to 'speak for Britain' and not endorse Britain's entry into the Common Market.

F316. Is this £90 million being spent the right way? *Sun Ex.* 7 Oct. p 16

He wonders if it is right to set up the six new universities at Brighton, Canterbury, Colchester, Lancaster, Norwich and York. He regrets that only Norwich will teach science subjects.

F317. Why don't these 'Top People' think for themselves? *Sun Ex.* 21 Oct. p 16

He regrets that it is fashionable to be in favour of the Common Market. 'Politically we are not Europeans and never have been.'

F318. Now let Mr. Kennedy settle Berlin, *Sun Ex.* 11 Nov. p 16

He urges Kennedy to solve the problem of Berlin

before he becomes involved in the 1964 presidential election campaign. He argues that the West should take their troops out of Berlin – and the people of West Berlin can choose whether to stay or to move into West Germany.

F319. The bitter truth about Britain's unemployed, *Sun Ex.* 2 Dec. p 16

He blames the Government for the rising unemployment, and claims that it is due to uncertainty over whether Britain will join the Common Market.

F320. Going into Europe, *En.* 19. Dec. p 62

One of several contributions by well-known people. He dislikes the Common Market – 'the Europe now offered to me is not my Europe'. He does not like excluding Eastern Europe – 'If any people have put themselves outside by their behaviour, it is the Germans . . . ' He speaks up for the Commonwealth and observes, 'Europe of the Common Market is a colour-bar community in economics, if not in politics.'

F321. Must this man stay in prison for ever? *Sun Ex.* 23 Dec. p 10

He calls for mercy for Rudolf Hess – and asks for his immediate release from Spandau prison.

1963

F322. We must not share the guilt for U.N.O.'s crimes, *Sun Ex.* 6 Jan. p 16

He denounces the shooting of people in Katanga by UN troops. He urges Britain to make no further contributions to UNO.

F323. Why don't we have an election now? *Sun Ex.* 27 Jan. p 16

He calls for the Government to settle the Common Market issue and to call a general election, thereby ending the current political uncertainty.

F324. Is Mr. Brooke the right man to hold this office? *Sun Ex.* 17 Mar. p 16

He complains of the Home Secretary's handling of the cases of Chief Enaharo, Soblen, two journalists imprisoned for refusing to name their source, and a murderer. 'If he does not defend freedom, then he shall not remain in office.'

F325. Is Mr. Wilson's journey really necessary? *Sun Ex.* 31 Mar. p 16

He regrets that Harold Wilson feels it necessary to go to see Kennedy so soon after becoming Leader of the Opposition, as if Kennedy's approval of him was necessary. He calls for better Anglo-Soviet relations.

F326. After Vassall – there's one big question left. . . , *Sun Ex.* 28 Apr. p 16

He praises the press, observing that nine-tenths of their allegations were true. He agrees that homosexuals are a security risk because of possible blackmail. He calls for the release of the two jailed journalists.

F327. Must we put up with this holiday madness? *Sun Ex.* 19 May. p 16

He finds it to be absurd that most of the population have to take their holidays in August to fit in with school holidays and examinations. He calls for examinations to take place in November and December and for educational institutions to run their year from 1 January.

F328. Why must *you* pay for the culture snobs? *Sun Ex.* 26 May. p 16

He denounces public subsidies for minority culture – and in particular cites the cases of opera and BBC radio's Third Programme.

F329. On Satan's Side, *NS.* 65, 1681. 31 May. p 826

He writes about universities and being a university lecturer, on the occasion of his last lecture at Oxford.

F330. Why is it so hard to get rid of a premier? *Sun Ex.* 23 Jun. p 16

An historical review of the difficulty of displacing premiers – and of the fate of junior ministers such as Hore Belisha and Nigel Birch who revolt.

F331. The Great Secrecy Plot – Against the British people,

Sun Ex. 7 Jul. p 12

He denounces the secrecy over such scandals as Burgess and Maclean, Philby and Profumo. 'The proudest duty of a Minister is to be the watchdog for the public. At present Ministers behave as though they wish democracy had not been invented.'

F332. Why the police are losing the war against crime, *Sun. Ex.* 11 Aug. p 10

He praises the British police and regrets that so much of their time is taken up by trivial traffic offences. He calls for higher pay and more graduates for the police in order to cope with such crimes as the great train robbery of August 1963.

F333. Has Heath given the show away? *Sun Ex.* 15 Sept. p 16

He denounces the Government's equivocations over the Common Market. He warns Edward Heath that the opponents of the EEC are happy to fight on the issues ('We shall kill it again as we did before') and that this will finish his political career.

F334. A hazard the Queen must never face again, *Sun Ex.* 20 Oct. p 16

He refers to Lord Home as 'a good amateur Foreign Secretary' who has displayed 'independence and judgement', but deems him to have been the weakest of the main contenders for the premiership. He calls for a better selection procedure for the Tory leadership.

F335. Dangerous! That's what I call this foolish document, *Sun Ex.* 27 Oct. p 14

He deems the Robbins Report on the future of universities to be 'feeble in its arguments, mistaken in its conclusions, and dangerous in the consequences which follow from them'. 'Every increase of students means a lowering of standards' and he agrees with Kingsley Amis in feeling that 'More means worse.'

F336. The man who runs away from Christmas, *Sun Ex.* 15 Dec. p 16

He calls on Ernest Marples to restrict the use of

private cars in city centres.

1964

F337. Will 1964 sce Kruschev fall from power? *Sun Ex.* 5 Jan. p 12

He speculates on what will happen if Kruschev goes – and he urges the West to take speedy and constructive action before this occurs. He sees Leonid Brezhnev as his likeliest successor.

F338. Why should Princess Anne have to step down at all? *Sun Ex.* 15 Mar. p 16

He calls for equality for women in the order of the succession to the throne, and so Princess Anne should be second in line.

F339. Let Winston Stay! *Sun Ex.* 5 Apr. p 16

He praises Sir Winston Churchill and urges the House of Commons to resolve that Churchill should be able to stay in it without being the representative of a constituency.

F340. Let us ask Kruschev to come to London, *Sun Ex.* 19 Apr. p 14

'So long as Kruschev is alive and active, we had a chance of making a secure and permanent peace, a peace that may last for generations.'

F341. I Say These Polls Are A Farce, *Sun Ex.* 17 May. p 16

He denounces election opinion polls as absurd.

F342. Why not ban these dawdling drivers? *Sun Ex.* 2 Aug. p 12

He calls for minimum speed limits to remove the hazard of motorists who drive slowly and obstruct the roads.

F343. The Great Election Puzzle – Where Is The Battle? *Sun Ex.* 20 Sept. p 16

He regrets that the general election is dominated by the cry from all sides of 'Me Too' and not by real argument.

F344. The nerve of the BBC do-gooders, *Sun Ex.* 22 Nov. p 16

He urges that there should be no increase in

television licence fees. The BBC should earn its money first by attracting more viewers than commercial television.

F345. Why pick on the private motorist? *Sun Ex.* 6 Dec. p 16

Whilst condemning drunken drivers, he feels that the breathalyser campaign smacks of a moral campaign against drink. He suggests that the commercial lorry is a greater danger to road safety.

1965

F346. Let Britain put an end to this bad dream, *Sun Ex.* 10 Jan. p 16

He denounces President Johnson's intention of reuniting Germany. He argues that this would be followed by demands for reunification with Austria and with parts of Poland and Czechoslovakia.

F347. It's time the BBC's viewers went on strike, *Sun Ex.* 28 Feb. p 16

'Minorities can cater for themselves ... The BBC should give the people what they want.'

F348. Stop playing politics with the Queen, *Sun Ex.* 14 Mar. p 16

He calls for the cancellation of the Queen's visit to Berlin, and condemns the idea of reuniting Germany.

F349. Let's scrap these out of date Bank Holidays, *Sun Ex.* 18 Apr. p 16

He calls for an ending of the Bank Holiday chaos, and in place of them giving everybody four long weekends in addition to their usual holidays.

F350. Why should these people get tax perks? *Sun Ex.* 25 Apr. p 8

He calls for an end to the current practice whereby when barristers cease to practise, any fees they receive are tax free.

F351. Let's have a law to wake up the dawdlers, *Sun Ex.* 6 Jun. p 16

He calls for a minimum speed of 40 mph on all main roads and 50 mph on motorways.

F352. Here's one bill we *could* cut out, *Sun Ex.* 22 Aug. p 10

He urges the Government not to pay contributions to the UNO, which is notable for '20 years of talk and futility'.

F353. Let Mr. Brown dream – its time We woke up! *Sun Ex.* 19 Sept. p 8

He derides George Brown's National Plan. He notes the cuts in education and road building and the high mortgage rates, and calls for the withdrawal of the army from the Rhine and the cutting of foreign aid.

F354. This is Mr. Fraser's biggest blunder yet, *Sun Ex.* 28 Nov. p 16

He deems Tom Fraser to be the worst Minister of Transport for many years and condemns his proposed 70 mph speed limit.

1966

F355. Q. Should the pollsters be banned? A. My answer is YES, YES, YES at election time, *Sun Ex.* 27 Mar. p 9

'It will be a good day for democracy when we try to decide the better policy instead of trying to spot the winner.'

F356. This scandal of the lawyers' closed shop, *Sun Ex.* 1 May. p 16

He observes that for the ordinary man going to court can spell ruin because of the high legal fees. 'Justice is an essential social service, just as much as health or education, and it should be available for all.'

F357. Peace Comes of Age, *New York Times.* 14 Aug. Magazine, pp 14–15, 64, 66, 68, 72

He sees the US-USSR power balance to be the principal factor behind the 21 year period without a major war, and he concludes: 'The peace of the world depends on American strength and, still more, on American restraint.'

F358. Should we hail Cousins as a hero? *Sun Ex.* 11 Sept. p 16

He praises Frank Cousins for bringing common sense into economic discussions. 'Economic planning from above can be carried out in peacetime only by the aid of fines, prisons, and ultimately concentration camps.' He argues that Britain's economic difficulties 'have one cause and one cause only. And that is unbridled foreign spending by the Government on which we obtain no return.'

F359. The great foreign holiday fraud, *Sun Ex.* 25 Sept. p 16

He denounces the £50 limit on holiday spending abroad. He praises the widespread taking of foreign holidays as a way of helping to improve international relations.

F360. Is this Churchill warning coming true? ('Gestapo in Britain if the Socialists win'), *Sun Ex.* 16 Oct. p 16

He complains of the Government interfering with firms paying higher wages and dividends yet giving preferential treatment to nationalised industries. In particular he objects to this being done by 'secret influence instead of legal process'. He argues that the Government should spend less, not more, in order to improve Britain's economic position.

F361. Why not let MPs share the misery? *Sun Ex.* 6 Nov. p 16

He comments on the fact that the House of Commons' deficit on catering is met by the tax payer – and urges generally that MPs should not be shielded from a period of hardship and economy.

F362. How to get paid without actually earning, *Sun Ex.* 27 Nov. p 16

He calls for the abolition of the House of Lords.

1967

F363. Why should *they* tell *you* what to read, *Sun Ex.* 8 Jan. p 16

He condemns the idea that newspapers should be subsidised by the Government. 'It is the job of newspapers to give readers what they want. The papers which do succeed.'

F364. Bravo Mr. Shinwell – now do it again, *Sun Ex.* 29 Jan. p 16

He praises Emmanuel Shinwell for creating uproar – and he hopes he will do it again over Harold Wilson's change of attitude to the Common Market.

F365. Scrap this absurd £50 rule *now*, *Sun Ex.* 26 Mar. p 16

He calls for the abolition of the £50 limit to holiday spending abroad.

F366. The question Wilson dare not ask. . . . , *Sun Ex.* 30 Apr. p 14

He denounces Harold Wilson for breaking his electoral promises on the Common Market. He calls for a referendum on the question, 'Do you wish to become European instead of British?'

F367. The awkward truth that no one wants to face, *Sun Ex.* 14 May. p 14

He argues that the Common Market 'is a political device for creating a European alliance by a back door' and that joining it 'will saddle us with associates, many of whom are in a shaky political state'. He concludes of Britain's leaders, 'From feebleness, folly or sheer blindness, they are betraying all that has made us great over the centuries.'

F368. Should They Have The Right To Spy On *You? Sun Ex.* 18 Jun. p 12

He wants the system of security tightened up, but not in the way Harold Wilson intends. He argues that 'the system of D-notices is designed far more against the British public than against spies or potential criminals'.

F369. The menace of de Gaulle to *us*, *Sun Ex.* 30 Jul. p 10

He deems de Gaulle's comments in Canada to be 'the most extraordinary act of his career' and warns that if Britain joins the Common Market then she will be involved in his folly. He praises the British system of government – 'at least we are safe from a Stalin or a de Gaulle'.

F370. This nonsense of making us all go slow, *Sun Ex.* 27 Aug. p 10

He argues that a general speed limit on the roads will not reduce the numbers killed or injured. He comments that such a proposal 'panders to the intolerance which is the worst feature of our age'.

F371. October 9 Could Be A Day of Danger, *Sun Ex.* 1 Oct. p 16

With the introduction of the breathalyser he feels that 'British citizens will cease to be treated as human beings and will become slaves of the machine.' He denounces drunken drivers – but feels that Puritanism lies behind the measure as much as concern for road safety.

F372. Labour's First Year: A Review Of The Government's Record. Radicals Comment on the Anniversary, NS. 70, 1805. 15 Oct. p 557

A.J.P.T. deems the Capital Gains Tax to be its best achievement. However he condemns support for America in Viet Nam and the Immigration Bill. 'CARD (Campaign Against Racial Discrimination) should be by now a bigger movement than CND at its biggest. It isn't. We have all turned cowards.'

F373. The strange silence of the 'freedom' brigade, *Sun Ex.* 22 Oct. p 16

He calls for those who campaign for freedom for the oppressed in various parts of the world to consider the cases of Rudolf Hess and Tshombe.

F374. DO YOU want to go to work in the dark? *Sun Ex.* 29 Oct. p 12

He condemns the decision to give up Greenwich Mean Time in favour of adopting Summer Time all year round, thereby making mornings darker in winter.

F375. What is the future for the man in the background? *Sun Ex.* 19 Nov. p 7

On the occasion of the Queen's twentieth wedding anniversary he praises Prince Philip and calls for him to be allowed to apply his energy and abilities to wider uses.

F376. How much more must we take from de Gaulle? *Sun Ex.* 26 Nov. p 16

He comments that de Gaulle 'has done all he could to injure this country and its financial position', and calls for Britain to turn away from the Common Market. He urges that 'we should stand on our own feet and turn back to our own kith and kin in the Commonwealth.'

F377. Will Christmas presents be illegal next? *Sun Ex.* 24 Dec. p 14

He condemns Kenneth Robinson's (the Minister of Health) campaign against gift tokens in packets of cigarettes. He observes that more people die of heart ailments than cancer yet butter and milk are not banned.

1968

F378. Why not put the embassies up to auction? *Sun Ex.* 10 Mar. p 16

He praises the choices of John Freeman and Christopher Soames as ambassadors, but he wishes that the diplomatic service was abolished so as to save vast sums of money.

F379. This Sordid Plot to Exploit Prince Charles, *Sun Ex.* 12 May. p 16

He regrets that Prince Charles' studies at Cambridge will be interrupted for him to spend a year at Aberystwyth, as this is purely for publicity reasons to suit the Government's political purposes.

F380. Will Germany be the next to explode? *Sun Ex.* 2 Jun. p 14

He argues that national character is reasserting itself – barricades in France and Grand Coalition in Germany. He warns that 'what spells Order for the Germans spells Danger for everyone else'. He draws the moral that Britain should keep out of the Common Market: 'We too should be true to our tradition. That tradition is one of national independence and Splendid Isolation.'

F381. Why not some *Fun* from the BBC? *Sun Ex.* 11 Aug. p 12

He feels that too many people regard the BBC 'as a sort of a secular church, a branch of the Establishment rather like the public schools or the West End clubs'. He calls for 'less bureaucracy and more fun'.

F382. What a way to end a holiday, *Sun Ex.* 15 Sept. p 16

He calls for the abolition of customs barriers for holiday makers on their return from the continent.

F383. Who says the Tax-man has no favourites? *Sun Ex.* 27 Oct. p 16

He contrasts the amount of money he has accumulated (even having written one best seller) with that of Nureyev, the Beatles, Mick Jagger and Vanessa Redgrave. He wishes the tax rules were made to apply equally to all.

F384. Callaghan's Dark Age, *Sun Ex.* 1 Dec. p 7

He denounces the keeping of Summer Time all the year round. He comments that it may favour business contacts with the rest of Europe but it endangers the lives of the children who have to go to school in the dark.

1969

F385. What will history say about the Queen? *Sun Ex.* 2 Feb. p 16

He feels that the historians of the future 'will judge her personally to have been a successful Monarch, as her father and grandfather were before her'. He regrets that the Commonwealth has declined during her reign.

F386. Wilson's Blunder Over Berlin, *Sun Ex.* 16 Feb. p 16

He condemns Wilson for supporting the West German Government over Berlin. 'A divided Germany means peace. A united Germany means war.'

F387. The forgotten man has one last hope. . . . , *Sun Ex.* 9 Mar. p 16

He calls for the release of Tshombe – and hopes that Israeli commandos will carry this out. He condemns the Great Powers for ignoring Tshombe's fate.

F388. Why is the motorist always to blame? *Sun Ex.* 6 Apr. p 16

He condemns Richard Marsh's verbal attacks on the motorist. He comments that 'instead of scientific inquiry, there is emotion' on the subject of road accidents.

F389. Why can't Wilson speak out for this lonely man? *Sun Ex.* 27 Apr. p 12

He calls on Harold Wilson to 'appeal to the conscience of mankind' and get Rudolf Hess released.

F390. Why not tell us where you stand, Mr. Heath? *Sun Ex.* 25 May. p 16

He demands that the Common Market issue 'should be presented clearly and honestly to the British people'. He asks if Edward Heath is favourable to Franz-Josef Strauss' proposals for a West European Federation.

F391. Would you risk going to Russia now? *Sun Ex.* 27 Jul. p 14

He comments that after what has happened to Gerald Brooke 'nothing would induce me to go' to Moscow 'to provide material as an exchange for the next Soviet spy who happens to be caught'. As one who has always argued for friendship with Russia he deeply regrets the Russians' actions. He calls for an end to the KGB.

F392. You pay the bills for our new aristocrats, *Sun Ex.* 12 Oct. p 16

He comments on the salaries and other benefits given to the chairmen of the nationalised industries. 'The patronage wielded by Sir Robert Walpole is trivial to that wielded by Mr. Harold Wilson or any other contemporary Prime Minister.'

F393. Is it a crime to sack an M.P.? *Sun Ex.* 2 Nov. p 16

He comments on the controversy aroused by the attempt to replace Nigel Fisher as Conservative candidate for Surbiton. He argues that MPs should be liable to replacement by constituency parties. He regrets that the party system will make it hard to vote against entry into the Common Market.

F394. Has the time come to ban all drink for drivers? *Sun Ex*. 28 Dec. p 16

He doubts the value of the breathalyser and feels that 'banning even the single drink is the only way of getting rid of the drunken driver'.

F395. How much for talking? *The Author*. 80, 4. Winter. pp 155–7

He welcomes the exchange of information on fees for lecturing. 'I have operated a minimum of £50 and expenses for some years.' He deplores the fact that Government departments, libraries and universities still offer only nominal fees. 'Authors are not dispensers of charity just because they are fools enough to write books.' He suggests the only justification for free lectures are promotional exercises and 'lecturing to a specialist audience of fellow enthusiasts' (hence his Historical Association lectures).

1970

F396. Is this the Great Retreat from Europe? *Sun Ex*. 15 Feb. p 16

He feels that the Government's White Paper on the Common Market is so damning to the case for Britain joining that it must signify that Harold Wilson is changing his position on the issue.

F397. How much do *you* want to pay for culture? *Sun Ex*. 22 Feb. p 16

He suggests that the lovers of culture should go to private enterprise for it, 'then we shall see how highly the lovers of culture value culture'. He argues that the BBC should provide programmes 'designed to give the listeners what they want to hear'.

F398. What are we voting for – A Party or a Poll? *Sun Ex*. 17 May. p 16

He argues of election opinion polls, 'These polls

no longer present public opinion. They make it. The result of one poll helps to dominate the next.' He suggests that the fault is with the politicians who treat them so seriously.

F399. Why I won't be voting Labour this time, *Sun Ex.* 7 Jun. p 25

He condemns Harold Wilson for going to the country a year before he needs to do so simply because of favourable opinion polls. 'There are some moral principles more important to me than economics. I am against racial discrimination. I am against privilege. I am for the sovereign independence of this country and for the unity of the Commonwealth. Labour does not help me on any of these.'

F400. Would you like a bonus holiday? *Sun Ex.* 5 Jul. p 14

'I think all the world has gone mad for work.' He calls for 'More Leisure. Shorter Hours, Longer Holidays. And better conditions for taking them.'

F401. Surprise Party, *NYRB*. 15, 3. 13 Aug. pp 33–4

He discusses the 1970 General Election result and the subsequent embarrassment of the pollsters. He observes that Harold Wilson 'was the victim of the polls, lured by them to disaster as often happens with those who consult an oracle'. He comments, 'Labour men do not believe in Socialism. Instead of politics there are expedients, and these expedients wait upon events.' He regrets the lack of real radical leaders: 'In this century we have only had Lloyd George and Aneurin Bevan, and I am not sure about Bevan.'

F402. This Metric Madness, *Sun Ex.* 23 Aug. p 12

He urges everyone to write to their MPs to denounce the move to metrication.

F403. Never Again. An Airline Ticket to Terror, *Sun Ex.* 13 Sept. p 16

He urges 'all civilised Powers to combine against the hijacking of aircraft'. He urges that all hijacked aircraft and hijackers must be returned to the country where the offence took place, even if this means returning those from Eastern Europe to behind the

Iron Curtain.

F404. The Gift Mr. Heath Could Give The World, *Sun Ex.* 20 Dec. p 14

He urges Edward Heath to go to Peking. He argues that China must be allowed to take her place amongst the Great Powers and be given her rightful place at the UN Security Council.

1971

F405. When doctors become dictators, *Sun Ex.* 10 Jan. p 16

He argues that the link between cigarettes and lung cancer is not proved and doctors should not terrify the populace about this. He suggests the best philosophy for a pleasant life is 'Nothing too much, and nothing too little either.'

F406. Ask the People, Mr. Heath, *Sun Ex.* 31 Jan. p 16

He urges the Government to hold a referendum on the issue of the Common Market.

F407. The Folly of Tomorrow, *Sun Ex.* 14 Feb. p 14

He denounces the coming of decimal currency, pointing out that 'there was no public demand for decimal coinage. The British people were never consulted.'

F408. Don't be fooled by the wily Mr. Sadat, *Sun Ex.* 21 Mar. p 16

Of Egypt's peace plans, he comments, 'She merely wants to be in a position to strangle Israel again.' He calls on President Sadat to renounce for ever all desire to destroy Israel and to be willing to negotiate immediately.

F409. Must the motor be our master? *Sun Ex.* 11 Apr. p 16

He condemns the private car and the spread of motorways. 'I am ready and eager to abandon my car the moment that everyonc else does the same.'

F410. Are You A Man . . . or Are You A Number? *Sun Ex.* 13 Jun. p 16

He denounces the British Post Office's use of postal (zip) codes, the removal of letters from telephone dials, and also the spread of computerised accounts.

F411. The Path to Ruin, *Sun Ex.* 11 Jul. p 16

He denounces the possibility of Britain joining the Common Market, and especially the idea that it would make Britain part of a super-power. He regrets the turning away from 'our own kith and kin' in the Commonwealth.

F412. I Say Down With August! *Sun Ex.* 1 Aug. p 14

He criticises the habit of everyone going on holiday in August. He praises Britain as a place to take holidays between June and September.

F413. What a way to end a holiday, *Sun Ex.* 29 Aug. p 14

He calls for an end to the customs checks on holiday makers returning from the continent.

F414. Just how much pay and perks is your M.P. worth? *Sun Ex.* 31 Oct. p 16

He condemns the pay rises given to Ministers and MPs, observing that they are safeguarded against the dramatic rises in the cost of living which everyone else suffers.

F415. Would you move for more money? *Sun Ex.* 4 Dec. p 12

He regrets that most of the population lives in the south-east of England. He urges that living in the north of the United Kingdom should be made more attractive by cutting taxes progressively the further north that people live.

1972

F416. Fifty Eggs for a shilling . . . and Beer a Penny a Pint!. . . . But would you want to live in 1872? *Sun Ex.* 2 Jan. p 7

He compares the situation in 1872 with that at the start of 1972 and points to the great social advances of the past century.

F417. Man with the olive branch, *Sun Ex.* 30 Jan. p 16

He praises Kissinger's and Nixon's secret diplomacy which has led to Nixon going to Peking and may end the Viet Nam war. He praises Nixon as a man who has 'always had the gift, as he showed in the Hiss affair, of seeing the simple truth where others saw only complications. And he has always been ready to learn from experience.'

1973

F418. But – Has Justice Really Been Done? *Sun Ex.* 7 Jan. p 16

He feels that the Distillers Company have been unduly pilloried for their tragic mistake over the drug thalidomide. He suggests that the Government is also culpable and it should match the company's compensation money to set up a fund for 'the benefit of all handicapped children throughout the land'.

F419. Who wants the Channel Tunnel? *Sun Ex.* 25 Mar. p 7

He feels that the planned Channel Tunnel excels other public follies, such as the proposed Maplin airport. He objects to the cost of it and to the likelihood of it making the south-east of England even more overcrowded.

F420. What's so new about a call girl? *Sun Ex.* 27 May. p 16

He feels that the enforced resignations of Lord Lambton and Lord Jellicoe over visits to call girls are unnecessary. 'In my opinion, and that of everyone I have talked to, the Prime Minister, Mr. Wilson, and most members of the House of Commons have taken leave of their senses.' He reviews the sex lives of famous Englishmen of the past.

F421. Ban The Motor Car! *Sun Ex.* 24 Jun. p 7

He urges the banning of the private motor car, before it brings all traffic in cities to a halt.

F422. You want the best scandals? We have them! *Sun Ex.* 22 Jul. p 16

He is bored by the Watergate scandal and feels that it is a fuss about nothing. 'The U.S. have a damned good President or had until recently . . . Nixon has done things that were beyond the much praised John Kennedy and certainly beyond the late Lyndon B. Johnson. Nixon has ended the Cold War.'

He comments, 'The Cold War was a false alarm from start to finish.'

F423. Now we have a second chance to make a better life for everyone, *Sun Ex.* 2 Dec. p 25

He suggests that 1973 is the beginning of the end of the Oil Age. He denounces Juggernaut lorries and motor cars. He feels that the running out of oil could be the best news for many years.

1974

F424. This lonely prisoner shames the world, *Sun Ex.* 7 Apr. p 7

He calls for the release of Rudolf Hess, and observes that 'it is a scandal and a disgrace that successive British Governments have co-operated in his imprisonment'.

F425. Let's get rid of opinion polls at election time, *Sun Ex.* 8 Sept. p 16

He argues that 'far from helping to shape public opinion they pervert it and destroy it'. He calls for a ban on them from seven days before polling.

F426. The headline I would like to see . . . PM Gives Up Car, And Walks, *Sun Ex.* 8 Dec. p 14

He urges Ministers to start making sacrifices themselves to help the country to get out of its economic difficulties. Good leadership is needed when the people 'are offered a choice between hardships coming chaotically and getting even worse and hardships consciously planned, equally shared, and leading to recovery'.

1975

F427. The Little Nation I Salute This Morning, *Sun Ex.* 9 Mar. p 16

He denounces the kidnappings and hijackings – and praises Israel's courage in dealing with terrorism. 'The Arabs have justified grievances in the Middle East. The Palestinians should weigh heavy on the conscience of the Great Powers.' But terrorism is not the way to achieve redress of grievances.

F428. The Referendum Choice, *NS*. 89, 2306. 30 May. p 719

One of sixteen authors who give their view. He observes that he dislikes anything 'that cuts us off from the peoples of Eastern Europe who share our European heritage'. He does not care for the leading advocates of Britain joining the Common Market. He is not convinced one way or the other about the economics of the matter. 'But if I vote at all in the referendum I shall vote 'No'. Like Clemenceau I am always *contre*.'

F429. How The Bureaucrats Have Conned Us On Speed Limits, *Sun Ex*. 17 Aug. p 7

He argues that the speed restrictions brought in to cut oil consumption were 'a typical bureaucratic attempt to give the appearance of doing something dramatic when in fact no real result was being achieved'. He suggests that the Government should show the public the case for such restrictions or scrap them.

F430. We Pay Them Highly. . . . Must We Knight Them Too? *Sun Ex*. 28 Dec. p 7

He argues that Civil Servants should not be in the New Year's Honours Lists, and comments that they serve the community no more than school teachers and many others.

1976

F431. What a load of Metric Nonsense! *Sun Ex*. 15 Feb. p 7

He condemns the moves to metric measurements. 'Metrication is yet another product of those superior people who claim to know what is good for us and that they can run our lives better than we can ourselves.'

F432. London Diary, *NS*. 91, 2358. 28 May. p 711

He discusses the giving of honours – and regrets that Evelyn Waugh was not given an honour as he wanted one. He condemns the House of Lords.

He calls for a fee of 5p to go to the author each time a book is borrowed from a library; 'authors have a right to be paid for their work like anyone else'. He suggests that a siege economy is the only sensible course if Britain's economy deteriorates rapidly. He condemns the EEC rules which endanger British beer and have hit Italy's Toscanas (cigars). He comments that CND was 'the best cause I ever championed'.

F433. London Diary, *NS*. 91, 2359. 4 Jun. p 742

He regrets that education always comes off worst in an economic crisis; there is 'an obstinate conviction that education is a luxury . . . '. He suggests that the best economy would be to withdraw the British army from Germany and to leave the Germans (whom he no longer believes to be militaristic) to spend their own money on their defence. He discusses devolution, making some comparisons with the Austrian Empire. He wonders if foreign works of art acquired in the days of imperialism will have to be returned. He comments on his success against a case of petty bureaucracy.

Tom Baistow replied to A.J.P.T.'s insistence on using 'Scotch' on the Scots in an article 'U Too, A.J.P.?', *NS*. 91, 2360. 11 Jun. p 772. See also the letter by David Daiches, *NS*. 91, 2361. 18 Jun. p 814

F434. London Diary, *NS*. 92, 2368. 6 Aug. p 173

He discusses the drought – and compares responses to it to the responses to Britain's economic problems. He comments pessimistically on the likelihood of scientists bringing an end to civilisation. He complains of dogs fouling public places. He comments on myths about his lectures at Oxford.

F435. London Diary, *NS*. 92, 2369. 13 Aug. p 205

He comments on John Stonehouse's trial. He contrasts Lord Thomson with Northcliffe and Beaverbrook. He complains of how pedestrians' interests are always put second to the motorists'. He condemns the obsession in Government circles with the preservation of official records from the public for as long as possible. He comments on the television discussion programmes in which he took part with Robert Boothby, W.J. Brown and Michael Foot. He complains of the design of the National Theatre.

F436. London Diary, *NS*. 92, 2370. 20 Aug. p 238

He reminiscences about Tom Driberg, one of his oldest friends, and about his opposition to Suez. He calls for 'Troops Out Now' to be the policy for Northern Ireland. He comments on male attire. He writes of his recent visit to Essex churches – 'such churches are our greatest national treasure'.

F437. Let's All Travel Free On Trains, *Sun Ex*. 22 Aug. p 14

He comments that the number of deaths on the roads is unacceptable and urges that the interests of pedestrians should come first. He argues that the running of the railways is not simply an economic matter: 'it is a profound social question, one of the most important . . . of our time'. He calls for the railways to be paid for by the community in the same ways as are other essential services.

F438. London Diary, *NS*. 92, 2371. 27 Aug. p 268

He discusses South Africa, observing that the situation there resembles Europe before the revolutions of 1848. He wishes that the libel laws were abolished – and offers the advice 'keep out of court at all costs'. He comments on his love for chamber music. He praises London Transport's *Country Walks*. He feels that he cannot write a history of Britain between 1901 and 1976 as it would be too depressing. He complains of James Callaghan's soporific speeches.

F439. Why sweat your guts out if a man can be £4 a week better off than you without doing a stroke of work? *Sun Ex*. 3 Oct. p 7

He argues that Britain's problems stem from our assuming that we are a rich country. 'Our basic conviction is that the world owes us a living.' He points to social security anomalies. 'We need new and ruthless leadership. We need an economic order where the creative leaders receive greater rewards and the administrators receive less.'

F440. London Diary, *NS*. 92, 2385. 3 Dec. p 791

He denounces Lord Chalfont and social democratic witch-hunts in the Labour Party. He condemns outdated Parliamentary procedures. He compares the present economic troubles with those of 1931. 'Soon all the money in the world will be in the hands of four Arab oil-states' – and then all the world's financial institutions will collapse. He praises Hampstead Heath. He mentions the centenary of the Bulgarian Horrors and observes that their scale was small compared with those of this century.

F441. London Diary, *NS*. 92, 2386. 10 Dec. p 836

He feels that children should be left alone and not be subject to such things as 'a television course in smut' to liberate them from their inhibitions. He comments on his choice of Winifred Gerin's *Mrs. Gaskell* for a Whitbread literary prize – and observes that Mrs. Gaskell was a more interesting person than most politicians or kings. He advocates, 'Authors should be paid by those who borrow books from the public libraries and not by the taxpayer.' He comments on his trips to Bristol as Joseph Meaker Visiting Professor. He observes that with the deaths of Goronwy Edwards and Vivian Galbraith 'an epoch has ended in English history' – a tradition, stretching from Stubbs and Tout, of worshipping documents. He discusses Gatton as a place characteristic of Old England.

F442. London Diary, *NS*. 92, 2387. 17 Dec. p 868

He condemns all nuclear power as a danger to humanity. He condemns the building of more roads and the scrapping of more railways. He complains of the effects on food prices of Britain's entry into the Common Market. He feels that the 'last 30 years, surveyed in detachment, have been a wonderful period'. He comments on his visit to the Museum of London. He gives his views on Mrs Mary Whitehouse's action in raising again the old charge of blasphemy.

F443. London Diary, *NS.* 92, 2388. 24 and 31 Dec. p 902

He hopes that the next economic crisis will be dealt with effectively. He calls for 'harnessing the power of the winds' to provide power. He comments, 'I recognise the usefulness of motor cars, much as I deplore them. But television is pure luxury.' He condemns single sex colleges at Oxford and Cambridge. If he could recall three people from the dead, they would be Gerald Berners, Max Beaverbrook and Michael Karolyi – 'What the three had in common was an enormous sense of fun.'

1977

F444. 25 years on . . . It's Still Great To Be British, *Sun Ex.* 6 Feb. p 16

He is critical of the present, but in contrasting it with the time of Queen Elizabeth I he comments: 'Instead of grieving over parallels with an imaginary past we should be counting our blessings.' He concludes that the British people 'are still the sanest, most tolerant and most agreeable people in the world and Great Britain, or even diminished England, is still the finest country in the world to live in'.

F445. Who *Was* The Fourth Man, *Sun Ex.* 19 Jun. p 25

He discusses whether there was a fourth man involved in the defection of Burgess and Maclean. He calls for 'the end to this system of security which operates not against Foreign Powers, but against the British people'.

F446. London Diary, *NS.* 94, 2420. 5 Aug. p 176

He comments on how he gives his lectures on television and elsewhere. He discusses the Isle of Wight and politics. He comments on the House of Commons' debate on the MPs who had been under suspicion of corruption. He discusses the possibility of CND's views becoming the new orthodoxy. He complains of old churches being allowed to fall into ruin – and calls for their preservation.

F447. London Diary, *NS.* 94, 2421. 12 Aug. p 209

He comments on his enjoyment of chamber music and on the art exhibition on the theme of the Thames at Somerset House. He discusses causes he has supported – and not supported. He comments on the dangers of nuclear power. He remarks on the enjoyment he has derived from reading the complete Pepys *Diary* at bed-time. He praises cats.

F448. London Diary, *NS.* 94, 2422. 19 Aug. p 240

He deems the constant diplomatic travelling of Cyrus Vance and David Owen to be futile. He comments on summer schools held in Oxford – and feels that English students are wise in preferring to spend their summers on archaeological excavations. He praises London Transport's new edition of *Country Walks*. He comments on his visit to Hawksmoor's churches in London. He complains of the number of huge books being published.

F449. London Diary, *NS.* 94, 2423. 26 Aug. p 270

He doubts if demonstrations achieve practical political results. He condemns the Common Market for failing to provide cheaper fruit and vegetables. He writes with pleasure of skateboarding. He comments on how 'monetarism has triumphed . . . whatever Callaghan and others may say Enoch Powell, it seems, has been right all along . . . Jim Callaghan becomes more like Baldwin every day'.

F450. The Sad Case of Mr. Clean, *Sun Ex.* 23 Oct. p 16

He argues that President Carter has 'enunciated many fine principles' but has achieved very little. He compares him with Woodrow Wilson and deems him to be 'a cruder version of the same sort'. He compares him unfavourably to Nixon – 'he accepted the realities of the world and would have gone down as a great President if it had not been for the trivial scandal of the Watergate'. He has little optimism that Carter will become 'more realistic and sensible' – 'I fear that do gooding is an incurable disease.'

F451. The Old Man Who Will Again Spend Christmas Alone, *Sun Ex.* 18 Dec. p 14

He protests at the continued incarceration of

Rudolf Hess – 'His continuing imprisonment is a crime against humanity, quite as grave as the crimes against humanity which were condemned by the International Tribunal.' He urges that he should be released the next time that Britain provides the guard at Spandau.

1978

F452. London Diary, *NS*. 95, 2446. 3 Feb. p 149

He remarks on the failure of the House of Commons to change its procedures with the passing of time. He comments on nationalists in the past and the Scottish Nationalist Party of the present. He discusses an exhibition of paintings of 1935, held at the Tate Gallery.

F453. London Diary, *NS*. 95, 2447. 10 Feb. p 182

He wishes that the British Government would take positive steps to settle the Northern Ireland problem. A.J.P.T. advocates withdrawal of British troops either immediately or at a set date in the near future. He discusses the growing links between the Anglican and Roman Catholic churches. He believes that British museums have brought financial problems on themselves by resisting the imposition of admission charges. Commenting on opinions that Mrs. Thatcher is an electoral liability for the Conservative Party, A.J.P.T. observes that the biggest electoral victories in Britain in the twentieth century have come under leaders who have been far from striking personalities.

F454. London Diary, *NS*. 95, 2448. 17 Feb. p 216

He discusses the 1981 census and the attempts to discover the colour of citizens. He condemns 'decimal folly'. He regrets that the Chinese Embassy is heavily shuttered. He wishes students were more active, protesting as in the past. He comments on the closing down of Victorian churches.

F455. London Diary, *NS*. 95, 2449. 24 Feb. p 249

He comments on CND: 'It was . . . a last exercise in British chauvinism. We thought that if Great Britain renounced nuclear weapons everyone else would be impressed by this moral example and follow suit.' He ascribes many of the world ills to 'no stable money'. He comments that economics, politics and history 'are exercises of the imagination like writing poetry or painting pictures'. He praises *The Oxford Literary Guide to the British Isles*, ed. Dorothy Eagle and Hilary Carnell, Oxford U.P., 1977.

F456. London Diary, *NS*. 95, 2450. 3 Mar. p 284

On banning National Front marches he observes that 'It is foolish to use a sledge hammer to crack a few nuts. Argument is the best weapon against violence and unreason. . . . ' He regrets that Edinburgh has not shown the Prince of Wales courtesy and respect. He praises Schubert.

F457. The best of British, *Ev Stan*. 2 Jun. p 17

He reviews changes in Britain during Queen Elizabeth II's reign, commenting favourably on most features other than membership of the Common Market and the state of Northern Ireland. 'Our future is likely to be less glorious than our past and more agreeable.'

F458. Is It Fear That Grips The Kremlin? *Sun Ex*. 16 Jul. p 7

He argues that the trials of the dissidents in Russia are 'a symptom of fear and the sign of a political order in decay' rather than 'a symbol of ruthless power'. He concludes, 'Perhaps the days of a new freedom for Russia are nearer than we think.'

F459. To think we call THIS a holiday! *Sun Ex*. 27 Aug. p 14

He condemns Bank Holidays in their present form and calls for staggered holidays.

G: BOOK REVIEWS

Item (1) under a review is intended to give an impression of A.J.P.T.'s view of the book; item (2) to give an impression of his attitude to the topic.

Throughout the list the place of publication is London, unless otherwise stated or issued by a university press. The publisher is given by surname only (e.g. Jonathan Cape as Cape). Subtitles of books under review are not given unless they help clarify which topic A.J.P.T. is discussing.

1928

G1. Forster's Dickens, *The Life of Dickens*, 2 Vols. John Forster, London, Palmer (new edn.), *The Saturday Review*. 145, 3790. 16 Jun. p 774

(1) 'An extraordinarily interesting biography' but not as great a work as Boswell's Johnson. 'Boswell shows us a grown man; the picture of Dickens is always (and quite truthfully) that of a precocious child.'

(2) Argues that before the Idea of Progress men 'full of the classical tradition, were perpetually chastened by the knowledge that there had been better men than they were' whereas the Victorians 'believed that, automatically, they were better than their fathers'.

1934

G2. Robespierre, *Maximillian Robespierre*, Reginald S. Ward, Macmillan, *MG*. 21 Nov. p 5

(1) 'A sound account of his career', spoilt by 'some rather elementary moralising'.

(2) 'His tragedy was not that of a good man succumbing to the lust for power; it was that he expressed the Revolution without ever dominating it.

Robespierre had intelligence, courage and honesty, but he lacked personality . . . '

1935

G3. A Study in 19th Century Diplomacy, *Disraeli, Gladstone and the Eastern Question*, R.W. Seton-Watson, Macmillan, *MG*. 19 Mar. p 7

(1) One of the 'finest achievements of contemporary historical writing'.

(2) Agrees with the author that Disraeli's foreign policy was incompetent and bellicose, but is not so sure that Gladstone deserves a panegyric. 'Only Bismarck and Salisbury emerged with credit.'

Repr. *MGW*. 32, 12. 22 Mar. p 235

G4. *Marat*, Piers Compton, Muller, *MG*. 18 Apr. p 5

(1) Dislikes the style, but deems it 'an adequate and unpretentious account' of his career.

(2) Marat was 'the first man to owe his political importance solely to his journalistic activities . . . the prototype of the demagogue journalist . . .

G5. Dollfuss and Austria, *Dollfuss and His Times*, J.D. Gregory, Hutchinson, *MG*. 8 Jul. p 5

(1) Unfavourable

(2) Observes that the author 'does not realise that the Austrian idea – that German Austria can be the centre for the co-operation of the peoples of the Danube Valley – could only have been achieved by the liberalism and tolerance which he so despises; it can never be achieved by clericalism, dictatorship, and a Habsburg restoration'.

Repr. *MGW*. 33, 2. 12 Jul. p 35

G6. Charlotte Corday, *The Angel of Assassination*, Joseph Shearing, Heinemann, *MG*. 8 Jul. p 5

(1) Guardedly favourable. He observes that the latter part 'lacks the sense of emergency without which the Revolution is uncomprehensible'.

(2) Her action was pointless as Marat was dying anyway, and 'the murder of Marat increased the fear and therefore the Terror in France'.

G7. Washington, *George Washington*, Michael de la Bedoyere, Harrap. *MG.* 10 Jul. p 5

(1) 'An interesting and valuable book'.

(2) He was one of 'the three great revolutionary generals of modern times'. 'His work, unlike Cromwell's, was permanent, and his victories, unlike Napoleon's, were final.'

G8. Metternich, *Metternich*, H. du Coudray, Cape, *MG.* 6 Nov. p 7

(1) Mildly favourable – 'one of the better' of popular biographies.

G9. The Naval Race, *Great Britain and the German Navy*, E.L. Woodward, Oxford U.P., *MG.* 6 Nov. p 7

(1) Favourable.

(2) Observes that England was in favour of France and Russia 'so long as Germany appeared to threaten the balance of power'. Feels that the naval race was not an essential cause of Anglo-German hostility and that it 'had little influence on the general trend of British policy'.

G10. A Romantic Comedy, *The Turbulent Duchess*, Baroness Orczy, Hodder and Stoughton, *MG.* 19 Nov. p 7

(1) 'A model of its kind'; there are no serious historical mistakes 'for it contains little serious history'.

G11. The Police, *The English Policeman 1871–1935*, Alwyn Solmes, Allen & Unwin, *MG.* 27 Nov. p 7

(1) Good on the Metropolitan Police, but inadequate on other areas.

G12. The Dreyfus Case, *The Dreyfus Case*, Armand Charpentier, Bles, *MG.* 21 Dec. p 7

(1) Very favourable on the treatment of legal questions – but the trial is not put sufficiently into the context of French politics.

G13. Louis XVII, *The Son of Marie Antoinette*, Meade Minnigerode, Jarrolds, *MG.* 9 Dec. p 5

(1) Very unfavourable – the conspiracy theory of history run riot.

1936

G14. Nelson's Emma, *Patriotic Lady*, Marjorie Bowen, Lane, *MG*. 3 Jan. p 5

(1) 'Accurate and brilliant' on the love story but underrates Nelson's achievements at sea.

(2) Condemns Nelson for his part in the atrocious White Terror of the restored Bourbon monarchy in Naples.

G15. Robespierre, *Robespierre*, 2 Vols. J.M. Thompson, Oxford, Blackwell, *MG*. 14 Jan. p 5

(1) 'The best work on the French Revolution written by an Englishman in our generation and the best life of Robespierre in any language.' The author 'understands that a revolution cannot be judged by the ordinary standards of academic morality'.

(2) The French Revolution 'comprised the greatest events, though not the greatest men, in modern history'.

G16. Law Reform, *Sir Samuel Romilly*, C.C. Oakes, Allen & Unwin, 1935, *MG*. 21 Jan. p 5

(1) Good on Romilly's legal work but inadequate on the politics of the period.

G17. Danton, *Danton*, Herman Wendel, Constable, *MG*. 25 Feb. p 7

(1) 'Not a work of scholarship', but the story is told clearly and well.

(2) 'Danton was the first and greatest of modern demagogues', and he suggests there are parallels with Gambetta, Clemenceau, Trotsky and Lloyd George.

'No one man can control a revolution; he must work with a party, like Robespierre and Lenin, or with the army, like Napoleon. Individual genius is not enough.'

G18. History, (a) *England and the Near East: The Crimea*, Harold Temperley, Longmans; (b) *Elizabeth, Empress of Austria*, Count Corti, Thornton Butterworth; (c) *The Bastille Falls and Other Studies of the French Revolution*, J.B. Morton, Longmans, *MG*. 27 Mar. p 6

(a1) Praises it warmly. 'For the first time the Eastern Question is surveyed from the angle of Constantinople and becomes a living thing.'

(b1) It uses original material but the portrait of Elizabeth is 'sandwiched between indigestible and often innacurate lumps of Austrian history'.

(c1) Suggests these dramatic sketches should have been entitled 'Thrilling Episodes from the French Revolution for Boys of All Ages'.

G19. Ali of Jannina, *Ali The Lion*, William Plomer, Cape, *MG*. 3 Apr. p 7

(1) A biography written with force and brilliance.

(2) The effort needed to overthrow Ali left the Turkish Empire too weak to cope with the Greek revolt later that year.

G20. Regency Lady, *The Fortunes of Harriette*, Angela Thirkell, Hamilton, *MG*. 1 May. p 7

(1) The book is essentially an anthology of the best of Harriette Wilson's stories from her Memoirs.

G21. The Last Habsburg, *Death of an Empire*, Imre Balassa, Hutchinson, *MG*. 22 May. p 7

(1) Unreliable on the politics and history of the period but good on Charles.

(2) Dismisses the author's call for a restoration of the Habsburg Monarchy.

Repr. *MGW*.34, 22. 29 May. p 437

G22. Two Rebels: Lafeyette and Riel, (a) *Lafayette*, Andreas Latzko, Methuen; (b) *The Birth of Western Canada*, George F.G. Stanley, Longmans, *MG*. 26 Jun. p 7

(a1) 'The author rightly depicts Lafayette as a Don Quixote, not as a hero. A hero must have a sense of reality, and Lafayette had none.'

(b1) 'A striking demonstration that the scholar not only writes better history than the 'popular historian but can also provide better entertainment.'

Repr. *MGW*. 35, 3. 17 Jul. p 55

G23. Unofficial History, *Characters of the Reformation*,

Hilaire Belloc, Sheed and Ward, *MG*. 25 Sept. p 7

(1) A.J.P.T. is unimpressed by Belloc's interpretation of the Reformation, his extreme Catholic loyalties, and his general methodology.

G24. Three Essays in History, (a) *Sophia of Hanover and Her Times*, F.E. Baily, Hutchinson; (b) *Regency Pageant*, Paul H. Emden, Hodder and Stoughton; (c) *The Kaiser and English Relations*, E.F. Benson, Longmans, *MG*. 23 Oct. p 6

(a and b1) Merely light reading.

(c1) Amusing but not important, as the author does not question whether 'the incredible German policy of the pre-war years' was 'merely due to William's unbalanced psychology or a norm of German statesmen'.

G25. Trouble in the Balkans, *A Diplomatic History of the Balkan Crisis of 1875–8: The First Year*, David Harris, Milford, *MG*. 6 Nov. p 6

(1) 'Scholarly and exhaustive' but difficult to read.

(2) Confirms the view that Disraeli's policy 'was based neither on knowledge nor on principle, but solely on the desire to achieve a striking foreign policy at whatever cost'.

G26. Popular Biography, (a) *Baron Stein*, Constantin de Grunwald, Cape; (b) *Maria Theresa of Austria*, Margaret Goldsmith, Barker, *MG*. 10 Nov. p 7

(a1) A model of popular biography.

(a2) Stein is the most important figure in modern German history 'for he can claim to be the founder both of modern Prussia and of German nationalism'.

(b1) Unimpressive – it is based on well known sources and it fails 'to understand the complexity of the Habsburg lands'.

G27. Two Biographies, (a) *Louis XVI and Marie Antoinette*, Vol. 1, Nesta H. Webster, Constable; (b) *Madame Roland*, M.P. Willcocks, Hutchinson, *MG*. 13 Nov. p 7

(a1) Deplores her view that the French Revolution was the work of Freemasons, but praises her for clearing Marie Antoinette of the libels that were circulated about her at the time.

(b1) Unfavourable to the book – and to Madame Roland ('At any ordinary time she would have been a provincial snob').

G28. *The Diplomacy of Imperialism 1890–1902*, William L. Langer, 2 Vols. New York and London, Knopf, 1935, *Int. Affairs*. 15, 6. Nov-Dec. pp 926–7

(1) 'An exhaustive and painstaking account'; but observes that it has its limitations, most of which stem from it being restricted to printed sources.

(2) 'Great Britain's position appears precarious only if attention is concentrated on extra-European affairs . . . In the last resort none of Great Britain's rivals would have been willing to see the British Empire destroyed.'

G29. Seventeenth Century Letters, *Postman's Horn*, Arthur Bryant, Longmans, *MG*. 4 Dec. p 7

(1) 'A delightful anthology of domestic letters.'

G30. History and Biography. A survey of the year's books in *MG* Gift Books Supplement, 4 Dec. p xii

He selects H.A.L. Fisher's one volume *History of Europe*, Arnold, for the general reader; J. Wheeler Bennett's *Hindenburg*, Macmillan ('a really remarkable work'); Thompson's *Robespierre* (see G15); Temperley on the Crimea (see G18); and R. Pares *War and Trade in the West Indies*, Oxford U.P. ('a brilliant book').

Amongst other books he singles out are: R.C.K. Ensor's *England 1870–1914*, Oxford U.P., (it 'cannot give a final verdict on subjects which are still controversial'); D. Lloyd Geroge's *War Memoirs*, Vols. 5 and 6, Nicholson and Watson, ('with unabated zest he continues to show that he won the war and that the soldiers and sailors nearly lost it'); and W.S. Churchill's *Marlborough*, Vol. 3, Harrap.

Repr. *MGW*. 35, 23. 4 Dec. p xii

G31. Historic Marriages, *The Spanish Marriages 1841–1846*, E. Jones Parry, Macmillan, *MG*. 15 Dec. p 7

(1) A 'scholarly and interesting book'.

(2) Comments wittily on 'the preposterous nature' of the issue: 'two elderly statesmen wrangling for years, puffing and blowing about the honour and prestige of their respective countries, over the question which degenerate and diseased Bourbon should marry a precociously depraved girl?'

1937

G32. Two Followers of Napoleon, (a) *The Adventurour Life of Count Lavellette*, by Himself, Dickinson, 1936; (b) *Bernadotte*, Friedrich Wencker-Wildberg, Jarrolds, 1936, *MG*. 1 Jan. p 5

(a1) Dull memoirs until Napoleon appears, then 'a fascinating source of great value'.

(b1) 'The author has not made up his mind whether to take Bernadotte at his own valuation as an unselfish statesman and a great general or whether to expose him as a posturing braggart'.

G33. A Life of Kossuth, *Kossuth*, Otto Zarek, Selwyn and Blount, *MG*. 23 Feb. p 7

(1) More a romance than a history.

(2) 'The real Kossuth was about as liberal as Mussolini, whom he closely resembled ... Kossuth taught the Magyars that they were the only representatives of civilisation in Hungary ... '

Repr. as 'Kossuth', *MGW*. 36, 9. 26 Feb. p 174

G34. Rogues' Gallery, (a) *Adventures in the Eighteenth Century*, Peter Wilding, Cresset; (b) *Secret Diplomacy*, J.W. Thompson and S.K. Padover, Jarrolds, *MG*. 9 Mar. p 7

(a1) Not a serious book, but 'well written and very amusing'.

(b1) Unfavourable: the authors are not concerned with accuracy, but do retell some amusing anecdotes.

G35. Guns, not Butter, *Armaments: the Race and the Crisis*, Francis W. Hirst, Cobden-Sanderson, *MG*. 12 Mar. p 9

(1) Unfavourable. He outlines the author's inter-

pretation of modern history: 'He misses no opportunity of approving of German grievances.'

(2) 'Great armaments are abhorrent, but they are not themselves the cause of war; they are the symptoms of international conflicts; and war can be prevented only by removing the causes of conflict, not by denouncing the symptoms.'

G36. The Amberley Papers, *The Amberley Papers*, 2 Vols. ed. Bertrand and Patricia Russell, Hogarth Press, *MG*. 16 Mar. p 7

(1) 'An invaluable picture of political and literary society in the mid-nineteenth century as seen by two able and detached minds.' He praises Bertrand Russell's 'witty and illuminating comments'.

G37. M. Maurois on England, *A History of England*, André Maurois, Cape, *MG*. 19 Mar. p 9

(1) Presented with 'wit and penetration', but not based on modern research.

Repr. *MGW*. 36, 13. 25 Mar. p 254

G38. The Commune, *The Paris Commune of 1871*, Frank Jellinck, Gollancz, *MG*. 30 Mar. p 5

(1) 'Free from contemporary passions' but 'shaky' on general history and neglects the less dramatic political developments.

(2) The Commune sprang from the traditions of 1789. It 'drew its inspiration quite as much from patriotic indignation at a shameful peace as from enthusiasm for the International ...'

G39. Talleyrand, *Talleyrand*, Comte de Saint-Aulaire, Macmillan, *MG*. 6 Apr. p 7

(1) Dislikes the author's conservative interpretation of the period.

(2) Talleyrand 'made the common mistake of conservatives: he thought he could prevent change by proving that change would involve a lot of trouble'.

Repr. *MGW*. 36, 14. 9 Apr. p 294

G40. Studies in Hero Worship, (a) *Louis XVI and Marie Antoinette* Vol. 2, Nesta H. Webster, Constable; (b) *Robespierre*, Ralph Korngold, Macmillan; (c) *The*

Adventurous Life of Count Lavellette by Himself, Dickinson, *MG*. 16 Apr. p 7

a1) It does clear away some old stories, but is spoilt by conspiracy theories.

(b1) Like Mathiez, he makes the mistake of trying to make Robespierre great in himself.

(c1) Good on 'the curious romantic interlude' of Napoleon's 100 Days. Lavellette's devotion is 'striking testimony to Napoleon's personal greatness'.

G41. Dreyfus, *Dreyfus*, Pierre Dreyfus, Hutchinson, *MG*. 7 May. p 7

(1) The main interest of the book is as a 'study of Dreyfus the man'.

(2) 'The Dreyfus case, at its outset was a disgrace for France; but because of the struggles of a small minority it ended by bringing France more glory than the campaigns of Napoleon.'

G42. *When Victoria Began to Reign*, Margaret Lambert, Faber, *MG*. 11 May. p 7

(1) Enjoyable miscellaneous gossip.

G43. Baron Stockmar, *Victoria's Guardian Angel*, Pierre Crabites, Routledge, *MG*. 14 May. p 7

(1) 'A very amusing book'; the author is too credulous of his sources.

G44. Napoleon, *Bonaparte*, Eugene Tarlé, Secker and Warburg, *MG*. 18 May. p 5

(1) The author has the sense to recognise Napoleon as a genius.

(2) Napoleon was 'a man of stupendous, unapproachable genius'. However he was not 'well meaning or morally admirable; to apply ethical standards to Napoleon is like praising a county cricketer for his marital fidelity'.

G45. Napoleon: First and Last Phases, (a) *Bonaparte: Governor of Egypt*, F. Charles-Roux, Methuen; (b) *St. Helena*, Octave Aubry, Gollancz, *MG*. 11 Jun. p 7

(a1) 'A most valuable book'.

(a2) 'The Egyptian campaign presents Napoleon at his most attractive ... resourceful, daring, irrepressible.' In Egypt Napoleon 'worked out the principle, which he applied throughout the Empire and on which French colonies are run to this day – development of the national character, combined with the benefits of the Revolution'.

(b1) 'Hagiography rather than history'.

G46. A German Exile, *Rebel in Crinoline: Memoirs of Malwida von Meysenbug*, ed. Mildred Ahams, Allen and Unwin, *MG*. 18 Jun. p 7

(1) 'She was too kind to be able to write great memoirs, but she met many interesting people, and her spirit reflected perfectly the ineffectual idealism of the German Liberals of '48.'

G47. Napoleon and Talleyrand, (a) *Napoleon and Talleyrand*, Emile Dard, Allan; (b) *Courtesan Princess*, Annette Joelson, Bles, *MG*. 29 Jun. p 7

(a1) Important and interesting.

(a2) Prefers Napoleon to Talleyrand or Metternich. 'Talleyrand advocated a policy of peace and moderation; but peace and good sense can never prosper in Europe if they be attained only by Talleyrand's method of treachery, cynicism and intrigue.'

(b1) 'A dramatically written life' of Talleyrand's mistress.

Repr. *MGW*. 37, 2. 9 Jul. p 35

G48. One Way to Peace, *Ordeal in England*, Philip Gibbs, Heinemann, *MG*. 2 Jul. p 7

(1) Very critical of the author's arguments for an alliance with Hitler and Germany and of his idea of leaving Russia and Czechoslovakia to fend for themselves.

Repr. *MGW*. 37, 3. 16 Jul. p 55

G49. Balkan History, *Russia and the Balkans 1870–1880*, B.H. Sumner, Oxford U.P., *MG*. 24 Aug. p 5

(1) 'A brilliant book', which will not be quickly superseded. Provides pleasure for 'all those who enjoy the story of incompetence and folly in high places'.

(2) Writes of Pan-Slavism as 'that strange mixture of mysticism and unscientific racialism (very similar to the Nordic doctrine of the present day) which

reached the height of its influence in the years 1876–8'.

G50. Legend of Europe, (a) *The Dauphin*, J.B. Morton, Longmans; (b) *Marshal Ney*, Legette Blythe, Jarrolds, *MG.* 19 Oct. p 7

(a1) Praises the author for deploring the fate of Louis XVI's son, whilst still recognising 'that the French Revolution was the greatest event in modern history'.

(a2) 'All human suffering is horrible; but that human beings should suffer because of the labels they bear – Trotskyite, Jew, Nigger or what not – is peculiarly horrible.'

(b1) Dismisses as nonsense the idea that Marshal Ney escaped to America.

G51. Life at Three Courts, (a) *The Letters of Tsar Nicholas and Empress Marie*, ed. Edward J. Bing, Nicholson and Watson; (b) *The Private Letters of Princess Lieven to Prince Metternich 1820–1826*, ed. Peter Quennell, Murray; (c) *I Was To Be Empress*, Princess Stephanie of Belgium, Nicholson and Watson, *MG.* 26 Nov. p 7

(a1) Praises the book but observes that 'history will be hard put to it to make Nicholas II a hero'.

(b1) Observes that the Princess carefully edited her misjudgments out of the letters. Nevertheless, 'This is Court gossip of an inspired order.'

(c1) Little of interest in them.

G52. History and Biography. A survey of the year's books in *MG.* Gift Books Supplement, 3 Dec. p xvii

He selects E.H. Carr's *Michael Bakunin*, Macmillan, as his book of the year – praising its scholarship, judgment and entertainment value. 'The balance is evenly held between the greatness and futility of Bakunin, which is also the greatness and futility of anarchism.'

Amongst others, he praises W.S. Churchill's *Great Contemporaries*, Butterworth, 'the epigrammatic brilliance of which leaves the reader dazzled and almost stunned'.

Repr. *MGW*. 37, 23. 3 Dec. p xvii

G53. Revolution Incarnate, *Michael Bakunin*, E.H. Carr (*see above* G52), *MG*. 10 Dec. p 6

(1) One of 'the great biographies in our language', 'a masterpiece of scholarship and wit'.

Repr. as 'A Born Rebel', *MGW*. 37, 25. 17 Dec. p 494

G54. A Whig House, *Chronicles of Holland House 1820–1900*, the Earl of Ilchester, Murray, *MG*. 21 Dec. p 7

(1) 'no better picture of a great salon has ever been painted'.

Repr. *MGW*. 37, 26. 24 Dec. p 515

G55. The Maker of the Suez Canal, *Ferdinand de Lesseps*, Hugh J. Schonfield, Joseph, *MG*. 24 Dec. p 7

(1) 'Written with great clarity and force; he is rather lost in some of the political detail, but so was De Lesseps.'

G56. A German on War's Effects, *The War and German Society : The Testament of a Liberal*, A. Mendelssohn Bartholdy, Milford, *MG*. 28 Dec. p 7

(1) Praises it and its author's career. Outlines the author's thesis that the damage done to German society was done by the subordination of everything to the Schlieffen Plan.

Repr. *MGW*. 37, 27. 31 Dec. p 534

G57. A Life of Philip Egalité, *Prince of the Blood*, Evarts S. Scudder, Collins, *MG*. 31 Dec. p 5

(1) A popular biography, written in 'an easy, readable style'.

G58. *Hungary and Her Successors*, C.A. Macartney, Oxford U.P. (unidentified journal, probably late 1937)

(1) The book is invaluable. The author 'knows more of the problems of the Danube basin in 1937 than any other living man'.

1938

G59. Modern Europe, *European Civilisation*, Vol. 6,

ed. Edward Eyre, Oxford U.P., *MG*. 14 Jan. p 7

(1) 'It is almost as uncritical and as ill-proportioned as the most primitive medieval chronicle.'

G60. A History of Denmark, *Denmark in History*, J.H.S. Birch, Murray, *MG*. 21 Jan. p 7

(1) A reliable survey – but 'few will turn to the book for entertainment'.

G61. Consular Adventures, *British Consul*, Ernest Hamblock, Harrap, *MG*. 1 Feb. p 5

(1) Well written memoirs of a consul with a sense of humour.

G62. The Last of John Byng, *The Torrington Diaries*, Vol. 4, ed. C. Bruyn Andrews, Eyre and Spottiswoode, *MG*. 8 Feb. p 5

(1) 'The three tours are Byng at his best.'

Repr. as 'John Byng', *MGW*. 38, 6. 11 Feb. p 115

G63. *British History in the Nineteenth Century and After*, G.M. Trevelyan, Longmans, 2nd edn. 1937, *MG*. 15 Feb. p 7

(1) The spirit of the book is still 'urbane, enlightened Whiggism', but now the author is a National Liberal, A.J.P.T. feels the author is unsympathetic to Lloyd George and unduly favourable to Grey.

Repr. as 'Prof. Trevelyan's History', *MGW*. 38, 7. 18 Feb. p 134

G64. High Jinks, *Memoirs of H.R.H. Prince Christopher of Greece*, Hurst and Blackett, *MG*. 1 Mar. p 7

(1) Amusing anecdotes about European courts.

Repr. *MGW*. 38, 9. 4 Mar. p 175

G65. Lively History, (a) *England's Year of Danger*, Paul Frischauer, Cassel; (b) *Strafford*, Lord Birkenhead, Hutchinson, *MG*. 22 Mar. p 7

(a1) 'Books should be books and not radio scripts.'

(b1) It rests on rhetoric – 'to be wholly successful this sort of thing needs the genius of a Macaulay'.

G66. *Irish Historical Studies*, *MG*. 29 Mar. p 7

(1) Welcomes the journal and observes, 'In the near future Ireland may once again, as in the

Dark Ages, be called upon to preserve the last remnants of civilisation in Europe.'

G67. An Optimist on Europe, *Across the Frontiers*, Sir Philip Gibbs, Joseph, *MG*. 8 Apr. p 7

(1) Denounces his 'fairy tales'.

G68. Two Diplomats, (a) *Ambassador to Bismarck: Lord Odo Russell*, Winifred Taffs, Muller; (b) *Heritage of Yesterday*, Richard von Kühlman, Hodge, *MG*. 6 May. p 7

(a1) Confined too much to Russell's official reports of which she gives 'an exhaustive precis'.

(a2) Russell was 'one of the last of the political diplomatists . . . he was always a Whig in spirit'. 'His distrust of Disraeli added to the difficulties of the Eastern crisis.'

(b) Full of 'ponderous platitudes'.

G69. History At First Hand, (a) *English Witnesses of the French Revolution*, J.M. Thompson, Oxford, Blackwell; (b) *The Kaiser on Trial*, George Sylvester Viereck, Duckworth, *MG*. 10 Jun. p 7

(a1) 'A fascinating anthology'.

(b1) 'Wild speculations' and 'absurdities' by the author and equally wild assertions by G. Bernard Shaw in a preface to the book.

G70. A Group of Noble Dames, (a) *The Ladies of Alderley*, ed. Nancy Mitford, Chapman and Hall; (b) *Princess Lieven*, H. Montgomery Hyde, Harrap, *MG*. 17 Jun. p 7

(a1) A delightful book of family correspondence.

(b1) 'A humdrum narrative supplies a useful background for Princess Lieven's own writings.'

G71. St. Helena, *St. Helena 1502–1938*, Philip Gosse, Cassell, *MG*. 12 Jul. p 7

(1) 'A valuable contribution to Imperial history'.

Repr. *MGW*. 39, 3. 15 Jul. p 55

G72. A Revolutionary Saint, *My Life as a Rebel*, Angelica Balabanoff, Hamilton, *MG*. 19 Jul. p 7

(1) 'These fascinating memoirs recall the far off days when international socialism had the char-

acter of an inspired religion and when to join the movement was to experience all the ecstasies of conversion'.

G73. Britain and South America, *Britain and the Independence of Latin America 1812–1830: Select Documents*, 2 Vols. ed. C.K. Webster, Oxford U.P., *MG*. 22 Jul. p 7

(1) Praises 'the masterly introduction' and the choice of documents.

(2) 'At no time and on no topic has British policy been more moderate and more successful.'

G74. Wellbeck Abbey, *A History of Wellbeck Abbey and Its Owners*, Vol. 1, A.S. Turberville, Faber, *MG*. 26 Jul. p 7

(1) 'A dazzling panorama of English life'. Praises the author for 'so painstaking, so readable, and so authoritative' an account.

G75. (a) *Deutsche Gesandtschaftsberichte zum Kriegsausbruch* 1914, Berlin, Quaderverlag, 1937; (b) *Europa Und Die Deutsche Frage*, Friedrich Wilhelm Foerster, Luzern, Vita Nova, 1937, *Int. Affairs*. 17, 4. Jul-Aug. pp 556–7

(a1) Very unfavourable to the editor's introduction which blames the Entente Powers for the First World War. The documents confirm one's general impressions of the attitudes of the German Government and General Staff.

(b1) 'A book to be read for its ideas rather than its accuracy.'

G76. *Germany and Morocco Before 1905*, Francis Torrance Williamson, Baltimore, John Hopkins Press, 1937, *Ibid*. p 557

(1) A useful background to the 1905 crisis.

(2) 'German policy in 1905 was not concerned with economic needs, nor indeed with Morocco, but was a policy of prestige, designed to frighten France into accepting German patronage. Morocco was the excuse. . . . '

G77. The Historian, *The Modern Historian*, C.H. Williams, Nelson, *MG*. 5 Aug. p 5

(1) A stimulating book.

(2) 'The only danger to history today is that historians are sometimes too modest and try to find excuses for their task. It is safer as well as sounder to be confident. Men write history for the same reason that they write poetry, study the properties of numbers, or play football – for the joy of creation; men read history for the same reason that they listen to music or watch cricket – for the joy of appreciation. Once abandon that firm ground, once plead that history has a 'message' or that history has a 'social responsibility' (to produce good Marxists or good Imperialists or good citizens) and there is no logical excape from the censor and the Index, the O.G.P.U. and the Gestapo.'

G78. *Lichtenberg's Visits to England*, trans. Margaret L. Mare and W.H. Quarrell, Oxford U.P., *MG*. 9 Aug. p 5

(1) Lichtenberg was 'an acute observer and a brilliant writer' – his letters give a valuable picture of 'Wilkes' London and Whig England before its confidence was shaken by the American War or its tolerance destroyed by the French Revolution'.

G79. Marxist Thriller, *Nine Days That Shook England*, H. Fagan, Gollancz, *MG*. 23 Aug. p 5

(1) The Peasants Revolt of 1381 dealt with in 'that bellicose atmosphere of the intellectual barricades which characterises all Mr. Gollancz's Left Books'.

(2) Denounces the passage in which the Austrian workers are criticized for not conducting the struggle of 1934 as 'downright offensive to anyone who knows that many of the same workers escaped to the Socialist paradise and are now suffering in Russian prisons for their Socialist beliefs'.

G80. History for Various Tastes, (a) *Aspects of History*, E.E. Kellet, Cape; (b) *The Police Idea*, Charles Reith, Oxford U.P.; (c) *Letters from Benjamin Disraeli to Frances Anne, Marchioness of Londonderry 1837–1861*, ed. Marchioness of Londonderry, Macmillan; (d) *The Life Story of H.R.H. the Duke of Cambridge*, Ethel M. Duff, Paul, *MG.* 16 Sept. p 5

(a1) 'So sane and so charming'.

(b1) Valuable – best when describing the problems of crime and violence.

(c1) Entertaining. 'Like everything Disraeli wrote, they are witty and brilliant, presenting the day-to-day events of politics with unexcelled clarity.'

(d1) 'The only memorable thing about the Duke of Cambridge . . . is that he married an actress.'

G81. Three Books on History, (a) *Six Contemporaneous Revolutions*, Roger Bigelow Merriman, Oxford, Clarendon Press; (b) *Elizabeth Woodville*, David MacGibbon, Barker; (c) *Rococo: The Life and Times of Prince Henry of Prussia*, A.B. Grantham, Lane, *MG.* 7 Oct. p 7

(a1) Praises this study of seventeenth – century European revolutions.

(b1) The narrative is 'both clear and sensible'.

(c1) He was of little importance.

G82. Private Lives of Public Men, (a) *A Vanished Victorian*, George Villiers, Eyre and Spottiswoode; (b) *Prince Metternich in Love and War*, Frederick de Reichenberg, Secker, *MG.* 14 Oct. p 7

(a1) 'A thoroughly readable and entertaining book', which paints an interesting picture of Whig society.

(b1) 'What can be more dreary or insignificant than someone else's dead love affairs?'

G83. Madame de Staël, *Madame de Staël*, Margaret Goldsmith, Longmans, *MG.* 28 Oct. p 7

(1) A well written and constructed study.

(2) 'Madame de Staël believed that she was persecuted by Napoleon, but anyone who reads her life or looks at her portrait will feel that in sending her to exile Napoleon was for once behaving in a wholly admirable way.'

G84. Royal Comedy, (a) *Ludwig I of Bavaria*, Count Corti, Thornton Butterworth; (b) *Baron Ward and the Dukes of Parma*, Jesse Myers, Longmans,

MG. 18 Nov. p 6

(a1) The book is 'ponderous, plodding and humourless, the superbly comic material buried beneath slabs of dullness.'

(b1) Too closely confined to Thomas Ward's papers.

G85. The Common People, *The Common People*, G.D.H. Cole and Raymond Postgate, Methuen, *Ibid.* p 7

(1) Praises Coles' clear and persuasive economic history. Observes of Postgate's political chapters, 'these . . . are based on the common but quite mistaken belief that the common people and the political Left are synonymous, and are further disfigured by certain whimsies peculiar to Mr. Postgate, as that the aristocratic rake Wilkes had some connection with the common people or that it was the Battle of Culloden which made England safe for capitalism.'

G86. (a) *Spanien Und Das Französisch – Englische Mittelmeer*, Hans Hallman, Stuttgart, Kohlhammer, 1937; (b) *Europas Diplomatie Am Vorabend Des Weltkrieges*, Ernest Anrich, Berlin, Quaderverlag, 1937, *Int. Affairs.* 17, 6. Nov-Dec. pp 835–6

(a1) Very unfavourable – an uninspired precis from British and French documents.

(b1) Unfavourable – 'a competent expression of what is now presumably the official German view'.

G87. *The Annexation of Bosnia 1908–1909*, Bernadotte E. Schmitt, Cambridge U.P., 1937, *Ibid.* p 836

(1) 'Within its limits the book is impeccable' – but criticises the author for not going beyond the available diplomatic documents to discuss the underlying causes of the crisis or the pressures on the policy makers which affected their decisions.

G88. *Mon Ambassade En Russie*, Maurice Bompard, Paris, Plon, 1937. *Ibid.* p 837

(1) Well written but, apart from throwing some additional light on Deleassé's fall, very few revelations.

G89. *The International Anarchy 1904–1914*, 2nd edn.

G. Lowes Dickinson, Allen and Unwin, 1937, *Ibid.* pp 837–8

(1) A book full of errors and misconceptions.

(2) The book 'is a curious memorial of a time when well-meaning men thought that peace could be secured by being sympathetic to Germany; that the Concert of Europe could be made real by calling it the League of Nations; and that the League of Nations could then over-awe the law-breaker without the backing of superior force'.

G90. History and Biography. A survey of the year's books in *MG*. Gift Books Supplement, 2 Dec. p xvii

He selects J.H. Clapham's Economic History of *Great Britain*, Vol. 3, – 'no greater work of scholarship has been produced in our time'. He deems 'second only in importance' W.S. Churchill's *Marlborough*, Vol. 4, Harrap. He finds J.L. Hammond's *Gladstone and the Irish Nation*, Longmans, 'the most important study in recent political history' – 'it is rare to find original research and fine style so happily wedded'.

Amongst other books he praises E.L. Woodward's *The Age of Reform 1815–1970*, Oxford U.P., – 'at once a textbook and a work of original scholarship' which is 'enlivened . . . with many stimulating judgments and illuminating asides'.

Repr. *MGW*. 39, 24. 9 Dec. p xvii

G91. The Real Lord North, *Lord North*, W. Baring Pemberton, Longmans, *MG*. 27 Dec. p 5

(1) 'Eminently readable and . . . sensible.'

(2) The author has grasped 'that the initiative still lay with the King'. North 'was no more a royal puppet than Walpole fifty years before or Melbourne fifty years after'.

Repr. *MGW*. 39, 27. 30 Dec. p 534

1939

G92. *Mitre and Musket*, B. Dew Roberts, Oxford U.P., 1938, *MG*. 3 Jan. p 5

(1) 'Both learned and delightfully easy to read.'

G93. Contemporary History, *Europe in the Nineteenth and Twentieth Centuries 1789–1938*, 5th ed., A.J. Grant and Harold Temperley, Longmans, *MG*. 31 Jan. p 7

(1) A most valuable textbook – but the interwar chapters are inadequate and are an apologia for the appeasers.

G94. The Whigs: Myth and Reality, (a) *The Young Melbourne*, Lord David Cecil, Constable; (b) *The Whig Party 1807–1812*, Michael Roberts, Macmillan, *MG*. 24 Feb. p 7

(a1) 'The story of the marriage of incompatibles is told . . . with great charm in a Lytton Strachey style, purified from the worst vices of the master.' However A.J.P.T. criticises the historical judgments.

(a2) Until William Lamb was over 50, the main interest in him is as 'an ornament of society'.

(b1) 'A contribution to scholarship of the first importance.'

Repr. *MGW*. 40, 9. 3 Mar. p 174

G95. *Robespierre*, J.M. Thompson, Oxford, Blackwell, *MG*. 28 Feb. p 7

(1) Welcomes the cheap one volume edition.

G96. *Germans in the Cameroons 1884–1914*, Harry R. Rudin, Cape, 1938, *Int. Affairs*. 18, 2. Mar-Apr. p 270

(1) Praises the detailed account of German administration but is critical of the account of the acquisition of the territory, and condemns the author's comments in favour of restoring former colonies to Germany.

(2) 'Mr. Rudin likes the German system for the conspicuous absence of slogans about the high moral purposes in forming colonies. But these slogans count for something; and one looks in vain for a German Lugard.'

G97. Constitutions, *Modern Constitutions since 1787*, John A. Hawgood, Macmillan, *MG*. 9 May. p 7

(1) Tends to be superficial, but there are 'many illuminating judgements'.

(2) 'The last hundred and fifty years have been the age of the middle class – that is the class which possesses property and yet does not want (either from timidity or because it prefers to make money) to run the State itself. Those who run the State had therefore to be tied down, for a constitution is nothing but a device for putting obstacles in the way of government.'

Repr. *MGW*. 40, 19. 12 May. p 375

G98. *Marlborough*, Maurice Ashley, Ducksworth, *MG*. 19 May. p 7

(1) 'Worthy treatment', written with a pleasant style.

(2) 'The greatest of British soldiers ... a great Englishman who was, despite all his faults, in the widest sense admirable'.

G99. Diplomatic History, (a) *The Great Powers and the Balkans 1875–1878*, Mihailo D. Stojanovic, Cambridge U.P.; (b) *Italy and the Vatican at War*, S. William Halperin, Cambridge U.P., *MG*. 23 May. p 7

(a1) Painstaking and reliable but pedestrian. The best part is on Austrian policy, 'for, while not pro-Austrian, he is not determined, as Dr. Seton-Watson was, to prove that Austria was completely unreliable and Disraeli therefore completely wrong'.

(b1) Painstaking and reliable but stays too closely to diplomatic detail.

(2) 'The details of diplomatic history do indeed seem of irremediable triviality; but in fact, diplomatic history deals with the greatest of themes – with the relations of States, with peace and war, with the existence and destruction of communities and civilisations.'

Repr. *MGW*. 40, 21. 26 May. p 415

G100. *The Zollverein*, W.O. Henderson, Cambridge U.P., *OM*. 57, 22. 1 Jun. pp 691–2

(1) A 'most competent account ... His book is an accurate précis of the history of the Zollverein. Accurate précis writing is no doubt the basis of

history; but history is something more than accurate précis writing.'

G101. *A Century of Diplomatic Blue Books 1814–1914*, ed. Harold Temperley and Lillian M. Penson, Cambridge U.P., 1938, *Int. Affairs*. 18, 3. May-Jun. p 422

(1) Praises both the lists, as 'one of the most valuable aids to English historical research', and the introductions.

G102. *Le Drang Nach Osten Du Congrès De Berlin Aux Guerres Balkaniques*, Jean Francois Dainville de la Tournelle, Paris, Pedone, 1938, *Ibid.* p 422

(1) 'Adds little of value to the subject'.

G103. *Foundations of British Foreign Policy*, ed. Harold Temperley and Lillian M. Penson, Cambridge U.P., 1938, *Ibid.* pp 423–4

(1) Welcomes such a large volume of documents but would have preferred a more limited aspect to have been covered thoroughly.

G104. *European Civilisations*, Vol. 7, ed. Edward Eyre, Oxford U.P., *MG*. 6 Jun. p 7

(1) Includes one or two interesting articles, but these 'are embedded in a ponderous edifice of Roman Catholic propaganda'.

G105. The French Revolution, *A Diary of the French Revolution 1789–1793*, 2 Vols. Governeur Morris, ed. Beatrix Cary Davenport, Harrap, *MG*. 13 Jun. p 7

(1) In this diary 'that delightful, well-meaning but incompetent and bankrupt society lives again'.

Repr. *MGW*. 40, 24. 16 Jun. p 475

G106. English Life, High and Low, (a) *A History of Welbeck Abbey and its Owners*, Vol. 2, A.S. Turbeville, Faber; (b) *Journey to England in Victoria's Early Days 1844–1859*, T. Fontane, Massie, *MG*. 16 Sept. p 7

(a1) 'Well written and conscientiously documented'.

(b1) Entertaining – 'presents the England of Dickens without the Dickens vivacity and exaggeration; everything is very bourgeois and very John Bull'.

G107. Europe in Peace and War, (a) *The War Behind the War 1914–1918*, Frank Chambers, Faber; (b) *The Keystone of Europe*, Emile Cammaerts, Davies, *MG*. 4 Jul. p 7

(a1) 'Despite shortcomings ... a useful contribution to the study of communities in war time.'

b1) Excellent in itself, but it is also 'very skilful special pleading for the latest form of Belgian neutrality and for appeasement'.

Repr. *MGW*. 41, 1. 7 Jul. p 15

G108. Historical Diversions, (a) *Crimea*, C.E. Vulliamy, Cape; (b) *Hell-Fire Francis*, Ronald Fuller, Chatto and Windus, *MG*. 18 Jul. p 7

(a1) Praises the author for conveying 'the confusion and futility' of the war but criticises the account of the diplomacy.

(a2) 'Everything about the war surpassed the ordinary limits of incompetence.'

(b1) Praises the account, but Dashwood's life was 'sheer futility from beginning to end'. He observes, 'rich young men will always be silly and rich men who are idle all their lives will remain silly all their lives'.

Repr. *MGW*. 41, 3. 21 Jul. p 55

G109. *Le Racisme Allemand*, Edmond Vermeil, Paris, Sorlot, *Int. Affairs*. 18, 4. Jul-Aug. p 571

(1) The pamphlet is 'a useful answer to the activities of the 'Fifth column' in France'.

G110. Hanoverian England, (a) *The Whig Supremecy 1714–1760*, Basil Williams, Oxford U.P.; (b) *England Under George I*, Vol. 2, Wolfgang Michael, Macmillan; (c) *Caroline of Ansbach*, R.L. Arkell, Oxford U.P., *MG*. 11 Aug. p 5

(a1) Criticises it for taking little notice of Namier and because 'for the most part the account is laudatory and even complacent'. 'All the actors and all the institutions are in their best clothes and on their best behaviour.'

(b1) A work of enduring merit.

(c1) An honest and unpretensious book on an unimportant subject.

Repr. *MGW*. 41, 7. 18 Aug. p 135

G111. Studies of Austria, (a) *The Imperial Crown*, Paul Frischauer, Cassell; (b) *Austria 1918–1938*, Captain Malcolm Bullock, M.P., Macmillan, *MG*. 17 Oct. p 3

(a1) 'Good Vienna coffee-house talk rather than serious history'.

(b1) Too detached and impersonal, and not analytic.

(2) 'Socialism, like democracy, is lost when it stands on the defensive; and the real decision had been made in 1919 when the Socialists shrank back from revolution and made a compromise with the old order.'

G112. Revolutionary Hero, *Saint Just*, J.B. Morton, Longmans, *MG*. 3 Nov. p 3

(1) Praises it, observing that the author has written 'with a new seriousness added to his accustomed brilliance'.

G113. *The American War of Independence in Perspective*, Lieutenant General Sir George MacMunn, Bell, *MG*. 21 Nov. p 3

(1) 'A very stalwart and soldierly account', which reveals reactionary political views.

Repr. *MGW*. 41, 21. 24 Nov. p 414

G114. *Deutschtum Im Völkerraum*, Vol. 1, Rudolf Craemer, Stuttgart, Kohlhammer, 1938, *Int. Affairs*. 18, 6. Nov-Dec. p 856

(1) 'Style apart, it is scholarly, informative and reasonably fair'.

(2) 'The German penetration into eastern Europe and the conflict of nationalities which this created is one of the most fundamental processes of modern European history, and cannot be too often studied.'

G115. History and Politics, A survey of the year's books in *MG*. Gift Books Supplement, 1 Dec. p vii

Praises E.H. Carr's *The Twenty Year's Crisis*,

London, Macmillan – 'the most important book on world politics published this year, learned, witty and free from hollow phrases, but I cannot follow Carr in believing that the problem of peaceful territorial change is the most urgent which we must solve'.

He observes of *In the Margin of History*, Lewis Namier, Macmillan, 'No reader of these hard gems of wisdom will ever ask again what is the use of history – or of historians.' Of Toynbee's *A Study of History*, Oxford U.P., he comments that 'one reader must confess that the pontifical determination to force every event into a rigid scheme has made it increasingly difficult for him to accept the main argument'. On Stalin (*Stalin*, B. Souvarine, Secker and Warburg) – 'deliberate villainy plays less a part in world affairs than is sometimes supposed'. On the Balkan crisis 1875–8 (*see* G99) – 'to understand that crisis is to possess the key to international relations from that time to this'.

Repr. *MGW*. 41, 22. 1 Dec. p vii

G116. Whig Ladies, (a) *Caroline of England*, Peter Quennell, Collins; (b) *A Regency Chapter*, Ethel Colborn Mayne, Macmillan, *MG*. 5 Dec. p 3

(a1) 'In (his) book everything is brilliant except the main figure.'

(b1) The author does not possess sufficient literary gifts to maintain interest in Lady Bessborough.

Repr. *MGW*. 41, 23. 8 Dec. p 455

G117. *My Royal Past*, 'Baroness von Bulop', Batsford, *MG*. 22 Dec. p 3

(1) 'This very funny book is an epitome of all the court reminiscences ever written.' The photographs resemble Cecil Beaton's work and the people in them his friends.

1940

G118. *Searchlight on German Africa*, F.W. Pick, Allen and Unwin, 1939, *MG*. 5 Jan. p 3

(1) Contains valuable material on German economic imperialism in Morocco before 1914 and after.

G119. Passage of Old Regimes, (a) *The Last Rally : A Study of Charles II*, Hilaire Belloc, Cassell; (b) *Imperial Twilight*, Bertita Harding, Harrap; (c) *History of the German Army Since the Armistice*, Vol. 1, J. Benoist-Méchin Zwich, Scientia AG., *MG*. 6 Feb. p 3

(a1) An odd thesis, typical of Belloc; presented with his usual vigour and clarity.

(b1) Treated 'as a romantic, not too tragic, novel'.

(c1) A story told before but "never been told better".

(c2) 'The real tragedy of this book is the failure of the German revolution . . . for that failure made the persistence of German militarism inevitable . . . But the Allies must share responsibility, for in their fear of 'Bolshevism' they tolerated the suppression of free Germany, the Germany of small liberal states which are the true inheritance of German history. A united Germany must be militarist . . . '

Repr. as 'Old Regimes', *MGW*. 42, 6. 9 Feb. p 114

G120. A Nazi Apologist, *Unfinished Victory*, Arthur Bryant, Macmillan, *MG*. 9 Feb. p 3

(1) Condemns it as 'an argument for the peace of appeasement'. 'It is the duty of an historian to weigh evidence, not to write emotional political tracts.'

Repr. *MGW*. 42, 7. 16 Feb. p 134

G121. *The Locks of Norbury*, Duchess of Sermoneta, Murray, *MG*. 13 Feb. p 3

(1) 'An interesting miscellany of eighteenth and nineteenth century life'.

Repr. *MGW*. 42, 7. 16 Feb. p 135

G122. The Real George III, *Letters from George III to Lord Bute*, ed. Romney Sedgwick, Macmillan, *MG*. 20 Feb. p 3

(1) 'The brilliant and unanswerable introduction' gives the deathblow to the myth that George III

attempted to recover the powers of the throne.

Repr. *MGW*. 42, 8. 23 Feb. p 154

G123. *Europe in the Nineteenth Century*, D.G. Ayerst, Cambridge U.P., *MG*. 29 Mar. p 3

(1) A book by a headmaster which has 'a little of something very well done for every type of schoolmaster'.

G124. Thiers and Stresemann, (a) *The Beginnings of the Third Republic in France*, the Rev. Canon F.H. Brabant, Macmillan; (b) *Gustav Stresemann: His Diaries, Letters and Papers*, Vol. 3, ed. Eric Sutton, Macmillan, *MG*. 5 Apr. p 3

(a1) 'A learned book . . . brilliant and witty, every page a delight to read'.

(a2) Thiers saved France from 'infantile reversions' to former forms of government – he was 'the man of reality'.

(b1) Contains few new items.

(b2) Stresemann was the nearest German equivalent of Thiers. However he looked backwards to better times for liberalism. 'But liberalism, with its confidence in humanity, must look with hope to the future; a liberalism that wishes to recall the past has lost contact with reality and must dismiss reality as 'of no importance'.'

Repr. *MGW*. 42, 15. 12 Apr. p 294

G125. Masaryk, *Masaryk*, Paul Selver, Joseph, *MG*. 29 Apr. p 7

(1) A competent book. 'But how can one expect a perfect biography of the greatest man of his age, a man who honoured us by being our contemporary?'

Repr. *MGW*. 42, 18. 3 May. p 348

G126. Richelieu, *Richelieu: His Rise to Power*, Carl J. Burckhardt, Allen and Unwin, *MG*. 6 May. p 7

(1) Poor on the intrigues which brought him to power, better on him as a statesman.

(2) 'It is impossible to be interested in Richelieu as an individual; he was not a man, but a method, not a person, but a plan – the method of monarchical absolutism for order at home and the plan of the

balance of power for French security abroad.'

G127. *The Making of a Queen: Victoria at Kensington Palace*, Eleanor Graham, Cape, *MG*. 20 May. p 6

(1) Not much more than a romantic novel.

G128. *Horace Walpole*, R.W. Ketton-Cremer, Duckworth, *MG*. 3 Jun. p 7

(1) Very enjoyable – 'the most scholarly and most interesting life of Horace Walpole ever written'.

G129. An Obituary of Free France, *The Development of Modern France 1870–1939*, D.W. Brogan, Hamilton, *MG*. 5 Jul. p 7

(1) Brilliant narrative 'but the reader may complain that he cannot see the wood for the trees'. 'Dominating all French life, but absent from (this) ... book, is an ever-present consciousness of the great revolution.'

Repr. as 'Modern France', *MGW*. 43, 2. 12. Jul. p 26

G130. *The Mongol Empire*, Michael Prawdin, Allen and Unwin, *MG*. 16 Jul. p 7

(1) 'A finely written, dramatic story'.

G131. Turkey of Today, *Modern Turkey*, John Parker M.P. and Charles Smith, Routledge, *MG*. 23 Aug. p 7

(1) 'Like the Turks, this is sensible and without nonsense'.

G132. Rehabilitations, (a) *Spanish Tudor: The Life of Bloody Mary*, H.F.M. Prescott, Constable; (b) *Judge Jeffreys*, H. Montgomery Hyde, Harrap, *MG*. 15 Oct. p 7

(a1) 'A biography of first-class quality' – it 'gives the reader the rare experience not merely of reading words but of meeting living people and of moving in a century past but here not dead'.

(b1) 'A competent, uninspired chronicle of an unattractive lawyer'.

Repr. *MGW*. 43, 16. 18 Oct. p 287

G133. Violent Lives, (a) *The Life of John Knox*, George

R. Preedy, Jenkins; (b) *Queen of Tears: the Story of Henrietta Maria*, Jane Oliver, Collins; (c) *Some English Dictators*, Milton Waldman, Blackie, *MG.* 19 Nov. p 7

(abc1) They make 'no pretence of being serious history' but are competent, well written and reasonably interesting.

(2) 'In the days, already distant, when the European storm was plainly rising people asked from history what they also asked from statesmen – an escape – and taste was all for the uneventful domesticity of eighteenth century lives. Now that the storm is here the desire to escape seems less and we are anxious to read about the stormy lives of others, so fashion returns to the fierce age of the Reformation and to the turmoil of the English civil wars.'

Repr. *MGW.* 43, 21. 22 Nov. p 390

G134. The Gold Rushes, *The Gold Rushes*, W.P. Morrell, Black, *MG.* 20 Dec. p 7

(1) He has chosen the right approach – 'writing in the same grave and prosaic tone which a medieval chronicler uses to record the madness and romance of the crusades'.

G135. Tory Socialism, *English Saga (1840–1940)*, Arthur Bryant, Collins and Eyre and Spottiswoode, *MG.* 27 Dec. p 8

(1) Very critical of such Tory history – and comments on the author's rapid change from defending the appeasers to becoming the historian of collectivist democracy.

Repr. *MGW.* 44, 2. 10 Jan. p 26

1941

G136. Science and Social History, *The Century of Science*, F. Sherwood Taylor, Heinemann, *MG.* 28 Feb. p 7

(1) A useful social history but one which exaggerates the part played by science in bringing about social change.

Repr. *MGW*. 44, 17. 25 Apr. p 309

G137. Feeling about the War, (a) *England's Hour*, Vera Brittain, Macmillan; (b) *A Faith to Fight For*, John Strachey, Gollancz, *MG*. 7 Mar. p 7

(a1) 'This trite and lachrymose account of 'What Hitler Did to Vera Brittain' . . . '

(b1) Praises it as 'an impassioned statement of the democratic socialist faith' but observes that he feels the author 'is wrong in asserting that it is the only faith worth fighting for or that unless we all adopt it we shall lose'; in fact many are fighting 'not . . . for a better England but for the England they know'.

'Without democracy socialism would be worth nothing, but democracy is worth a great deal even when it is not socialist.'

Repr. *MGW*. 44, 22. 30 May. p 389

G138. Old Turkey and New, *Britain and Turkey*, Philip P. Graves, Hutchinson, *MG*. 22 Apr. p 3

(1) Interesting when based on the author's personal experiences, dull and conventional otherwise.

Repr. *MGW*. 44, 22. 30 May. p 387

G139. Masaryk, *The Life and Times of Masaryk*, Victor Cohen, Murray, *Sp*. 5905. 29 Aug. p 212

(1) Unfavourable – its background history is vague and inaccurate.

(2) A.J.P.T. calls for no more lives of Masaryk 'but a serious discussion of his work, of his failures as well as of his successes'.

G140. Marx and Others, *To the Finland Station*, Edmund Wilson, Secker and Warburg, *MG*. 2 Sept. p 3

(1) Judges the author's attempts to apply his methods of literary criticism to the writing and acting of history to be 'sometimes stimulating, but often disappointing'. The best is on Marx and Engels 'because they had little existence outside their writings'.

Repr. *MGW*. 45, 13. 26 Sept. p 203

G141. South Africa, *A History of South Africa*, C.W.

de Kiewiet, Oxford U.P., *MG.* 5 Sept. p 3

(1) 'The scholarship and penetration give the reader that exhilarating intellectual pleasure which one gets only once or twice in a decade.'

(2) 'Whatever the efforts at 'segregation', the fortunes of black and white in South Africa are inextricably mingled and one cannot prosper while the other is degraded.'

Repr. *MGW.* 45, 11. 12 Sept. p 172

G142. A History of Poland, *The Cambridge History of Poland 1697–1935*, ed. W.F. Reddaway, J.H. Penson, O. Halecki, R. Dyboski, Cambridge U.P., *MG.* 9 Sept. p 3

(1) 'A competent narrative of political history'. Criticises it for not explaining that Poland, like Hungary, is 'a political nation', where 'nationality and landowning were synonymous and where the awakening of the masses has brought new nations into life in the former 'Greater Poland''.

Repr. *MGW.* 45, 11. 12 Sept. p 172

G143. The Collapse of France, (a) *The Scum of the Earth*, Arthur Koestler, Cape; (b) *The Fall of the French Republic*, D.N. Pritt, Muller, *MG.* 7 Oct. p 3

(a1) 'A book in a thousand'.

(a2) The failure of France 'was the failure of a nation's will not the wickedness of a few men'. Does not share Koestler's belief in European union: 'why should European union – even if it ended wars – end man's inhumanity to man?'

(b1) 'Written in his deceptively simple style, Communism Told to the Children, his book presents the orthodox Communist case. . . . All fundamental questions are avoided'.

Repr. *MGW.* 45, 15. 10 Oct. p 236

G144. Which Poland? *The Cambridge History of Poland* (*see above* G142), *Sp.* 5911. 10 Oct. p 360

(1) Tougher on it – deeming it nationalist history, not an impartial and accurate assessment.

(2) 'Poland has two neighbours: one is, and always has been, bent on her destruction; the

other is, and often has been, ready to recognise and support ethnic Poland, but will always oppose Polish rule over Lithuanians, Little Russians or White Russians.'

G145. Dickens as Historian, *The Dickens World*, Humphry House, Oxford U.P., *MG*. 14 Oct. p 3

(1) 'A most fascinating account of the world as Dickens saw it'.

Repr. *MGW*. 45, 18. 31 Oct. p 282

G146. Left Illusions, *Is Innocence Enough*? D.W. Brogan, Hamilton, *MG*. 16 Dec. p 3

(1) At bottom the author has 'nothing to advocate except the accumulation of knowledge'.

Repr. *MGW*. 45, 25. 19 Dec. p 396

1942

G147. The Shakers, *The Shaker Adventure*, Marguerite Fellows Melcher, Milford, *MG*. 10 Feb. p 3

(1) 'A well-written, sympathetic account of the sect, taking it perhaps too seriously'.

(2) 'Shakerism was at once a parody of revivalism, of communism, and of monasticism'.

Repr. *MGW*. 46, 14. 2 Apr. p 212

G148. Great Astrologer, *Nostradamus, Or the Future Foretold*, James Laver, Collins, *MG*. 17 Feb. p 3

(1) Exercises his wit on it, and observes the reader will get 'a good deal of entertainment' from the book.

Repr. *MGW*. 46, 8. 20 Feb. p 124

G149. *Black Lamb and Grey Falcon*, 2 Vols. Rebecca West, Macmillan, *T & T*. 23, 10. 7 Mar. pp 195–6

(1) Very favourable. He acknowledges inaccuracies of detail but observes that 'her profound purpose' is 'to depict the soul of a people as a novelist draws the character of an individual'.

(2) 'The existence and compelling reality of national communities is the fundamental, inescapable fact of European politics both past and present.'

A letter to supplement the review by Wickham Steed, *Ibid*. 9. 28 Feb. pp 178–9

G150. Peace Settlements, (a) *Versailles Twenty Years After*, Paul Birdsall, Allen and Unwin; (b) *Report on France*, Thomas Kernan, Bodley Head; (c) *Federation in Central Europe*, Milan Hodža, Jarrolds, *T & T*. 23, 15. 11 Apr. p 314

(a1) Favourable – but the book is really about 'the influence of Wilson's personality and doctrines on the settlement of Versailles'.

(a2) Draws two conclusions. 'Versailles did not settle Europe; Europe settled itself, either by preliminary secret treaties or by simultaneous popular action, and negotiations only tidied up the edges.' 'No peace settlement, however sensible (and Versailles was pretty sensible) can ensure that people will behave with foresight or commonsense twenty years later.'

(b1) A vivid account of the Germans organising French economic life for their own purposes.

(c1) A disappointing book, which explains nothing – 'all arranged to show that Dr. Hodza has been advocating a federation of central Europe for forty years'.

G151. Federation, *Federation in Central Europe* (*see above* G150), *MG*. 15 Apr. p 3

(1) Only interesting when the author abandons theory for recollections.

Repr. *MGW*. 46, 25. 19 Jun. p 364

G152. Period Pieces, (a) *The Mother of Victoria*, Dorothy Margaret Stuart, Macmillan; (b) *Victoria's Heir*, George Dangerfield, Constable, *MG*. 17 Apr. p 3

(a1) A delightful book – but nothing new or important in it.

(b1) The author writes about anything 'which interests and amuses him' in Victoria's reign.

G153. Borgia Pope, *The Borgia Pope, Alexander VI*, O. Ferrara, Sheed and Ward, *MG*. 24 Apr. p 3

(1) A fine book which 'destroys a myth dear to the hearts of each succeeding generation'.

Repr. *MGW*. 46, 18. 1 May. p 268

G154. Paris of the 70's, *Letters from Paris 1870–1875*,

ed. Robert Henrey, Dent, *MG*. 29 Apr. p 3

(1) Good reading. Observes that the author of the letters 'was a Vichyite of the seventies'.

G155. Europe As It Was, (a) *Epitaph for Europe*, Paul Tabori, Hodder and Stoughton; (b) *Berlin Embassy*, William Russell, Joseph; (c) *A German Protectorate: the Czechs under Nazi Rule*, Sheila Grant Duff, Macmillan, *T & T*. 23, 18. 2 May. p 372

(a1) Very unfavourable – a collection of received ideas.

(b1) Contains little of importance, but is extremely well written.

(c1) 'The best book yet written on the workings of the Nazi Empire'.

(c2) 'To remake Czechoslovakia will demand as much ruthlessness, foresight and energy as the Germans brought to its destruction; it will involve as much suffering, though not by the same people. But unless Czechoslovakia is remade with complete political and economic independence Germany will have won the war . . . '

G156. *Problems of the Danube Basin*, C.A. Macartney, Cambridge U.P., *OM*. 60, 18. 7 May. pp 283–4

(1) Too much packed into too little space. 'After such a display of impeccable learning . . . (his) ideas for the future are disappointingly platitudinous.'

G157. Prince Starhemberg, *Between Hitler and Mussolini*, Prince Starhemberg, Hodder and Stoughton, *MG*. 13 May. p 3

(1) A brilliant writer trying to exculpate himself.

Repr. *MGW*. 46, 21. 22 May. p 309

G158. Balkan Affairs, (a) *The Revolt of the Serbs Against the Turks 1804–13*, W.A. Morison, Cambridge U.P.; (b) *Turkey*, Barbara Ward, Oxford U.P.; (c) *The Greek White Book*, Hutchinson, *T & T*. 23, 21. 23 May. pp 436, 438

(a1) Ballads inspired by the 'spirit of national independence'.

(b1) A good book.

(c1) Shows the innocence of Greece.

(c2) Praises the resistance of the Serbs and deplores Turkish neutrality and that of Greece in the past. 'The documents . . . prove that Greek policy (and that of every small power in Europe) was utterly wrong. The object of policy is not to prove one's moral worth, but to succeed; Greek policy failed, and it is no consolation to learn that the Italian Government is unscrupulous. In the modern world neutrality is not a virtue, but a folly; and a folly which the Greeks, along with others, are now atoning for in suffering and struggle.'

G159. Intourism, (a) *Mission to Moscow*, Joseph E. Davies, Gollancz; (b) *The Kremlin and the People*, Walter Duranty, Hamilton; (c) *In Russia Now*, Sir Walter Citrine, Hale; (d) *Russian Newsreel*, Charlotte Haldane, Secker and Warburg, *T & T*. 23, 23. 6 Jun. p 470

(a1) A sensible and valuable book.

(b1) Unfavourable – the author has not penetrated to reality and is too favourable to Stalin.

(c1) Not much of interest, beyond observing that working conditions had improved since 1935.

(d1) Too enthusiastic and uncritical – she never mentions Freedom.

G160. German Empire, (a) *The Spoil of Europe*, Thomas Reveille, Allen and Unwin; (b) *A Combine of Aggression*, Karl Otten, Allen and Unwin, *MG*. 17 Jun. p 3

(a1) 'A most important and interesting book'.

(a2) 'German economic control, established by legal means, is now so complete throughout Europe that if private capitalism survives German domination will survive with it.'

(b1) An unreadable psycho-sociological study.

G161. Commentary, *Conflicts*, L.B. Namier, Macmillan, *MG*. 24 Jul. p 3

(1) Welcomes the essays – they 'should be compulsory reading for every student of history and of international affairs'.

Repr. *MGW*. 47, 9. 28 Aug. p 121

G162. The Namier Way, *Conflicts* (*see above* G161), *T & T*. 23, 30. 25 Jul. p 604

(1) Eulogistic of his style and clarity – but criticises him for being too much the social psychologist and being 'inclined to overlook the merely economic'. 'Will, not coal, is to Namier the basis of greatness; I should have thought will and coal together were nearer the historic reality.'

G163. Two Peoples, (a) *The History of Poland*, Oscar Halecki, Dent; (b) *The Germans*, Emil Ludwig, Hamilton, *MG*. 28 Aug. p 3

(a1) A 'straightforward political narrative'. It fails to 'distinguish clearly between earlier Poland, when the Polish nation was exclusively the landed class, and contemporary Poland, where people and nation have become synonymous. Hence its failure to penetrate to the heart of the Russo-Polish conflict, which sprang in a large part from the determination of Russian Governments, past and present, to free Russian peoples from their Polish lords.'

(b1) Not a profound book.

Repr. *MGW*. 47, 10. 4 Sept. p 136

G164. *Kurt Von Schuschnigg*, R.K. Sheridon, English Universities Press, *MG*. 4 Sept. p 3

(1) 'Hagiography, but quite good hagiography'.

Repr. *MGW*. 47, 13. 25 Sept. p 178

G165. Paris in 1940, *Death and Tomorrow*, Peter de Polnay, Secker and Warburg, *MG*. 23 Sept. p 3

(1) Too much on de Polnay, but nevertheless a valuable book which 'adds a great deal to our understanding of France after defeat'.

G166. An Epic Year, *Twelve Who Ruled*, R.R. Palmer, Princeton U.P.; Milford, *MG*. 25 Sept. p 3

(1) 'An admirable book' (on the Committee of Public Safety 1793–4).

G167. Disgrace at Danzig, *The Nazi Conquest of Danzig*, Hans L. Leonhardt, Chicago U.P., *MG*. 14 Oct. p 3

(1) 'A detailed account of the betrayal of Danzig

by the forces of order'.

(2) 'The story of Danzig is appeasement at its worst, as sorry a story as that of the Spanish non-intervention committee.'

Repr. *MGW*. 47, 21. 20 Nov. p 289

G168. *Studies in Diplomacy and Statecraft*, G.P. Gooch, Longmans, *OM*. 61, 1. 15 Oct. pp 12–13

(1) Comments that 'informed opinion in England on these topics has been more influenced by Dr. Gooch than by any other writer' and asserts, 'The new generation of historians has now the obligation to make a new analysis of the underlying forces in Europe which will be closer to reality and so to prepare a British policy which will suffer from fewer illusions and make fewer mistakes.'

G169. A Europe of Beautiful Wishes, *The New Europe*, Bernard Newman, Hale, *T & T*. 23, 44. 31 Oct. p 873

(1) 'A blue-print for cloud-cuckoo land'.

(2) 'Russian policy has a single object, security, and she regards the frontiers of 1941 as essential to this object.'

'The peoples of Europe can enjoy freedom only under the joint protection of England and Russia; and just as we postulate a group of friendly states in Western Europe with similar social and political systems to our own, so does Russia in Eastern Europe.'

(There was a furore over his views as to the lot of Poland and the Baltic States; *see* letters, *Ibid*. 45. 7 Nov. p 888; A.J.P.T.'s reply and editorial, *Ibid*. 46. 14 Nov. p 907. This led to the end of his reviews for the journal.)

G170. French Camp, *The Devil in France*, L. Feuchtwanger, Hutchinson, *MG*. 4 Nov. p 3

(1) A well written account of his time in a French internment camp. A.J.P.T. feels that there are thousands receiving worse treatment elsewhere in Europe.

G171. Historic Parallel, *The Years of Endurance 1793–1802*, Arthur Bryant, Collins, *MG*. 18 Nov. p 3

(1) The best of the recent books on the French Wars. 'Tory England defending itself is a theme congenial to his pen . . .'

Repr. *MGW*. 48, 17. 22 Apr. 1943. p 230

G172. Pre-War, (a) *Documents on International Affairs, 1938*, Vol. 1, ed. Monica Curtis, Oxford U.P.; (b) *The Agadir Crisis*, Ima Christina Barlow, North Carolina U.P.; Milford, *T & T*. 23, 48. 28 Nov. pp 955–6

(a1) Finds a collection of the appeaser's excuses and the dictators' lies unedifying.

(b1) A painstaking book but its conclusion is wrong. The crisis was not 'something to do with Germany's desire for colonies' but stemmed from 'Germany's aim . . . to disrupt the Anglo-French entente'.

G173. A Traveller, *Memoirs of the Life of Philip Mazzei*, trans. Howard R. Marraro, Columbia U.P.; Milford, *MG*. 23 Dec. p 3

(1) An interesting story. The author 'was a prig as well as a bore, but obviously a most worthy person'.

G174. *War as a Social Institution : the Historian's Perspective*, ed. Jesse D. Clarkson and Thomas C. Cochran, Columbia U.P.; Oxford U.P., 1941, *Int. Affairs*. 19, 10. Dec. pp 536–7

(1) It has the lack of unity common to published conference papers, but 'it is a remarkable testimony to the social duty of American historians'.

1943

G175. British Institutions, *Britain and the British People*, Ernest Barker, Oxford U.P., 1942, *MG*. 13 Jan. p 3

(1) 'A delight to read' – but 'this is the England you see from a Cambridge college window'.

G176. *Palmyra of the North*, Christopher Marsden, Faber, 1942, *MG*. 22 Jan. p 3

(1) 'A brilliant book' (on St. Petersburg).

Repr. *MGW*. 48, 5. 29 Jan. p 60

G177. *A Wavering Friendship: Russia and Austria 1876–1878*, George Hoover Rupp, Harvard U.P., 1941, *EHR*. 58, 229. Jan. pp 112–3

(1) 'The subject, when finally arrived at, is treated with penetration.' Criticises the style and the inadequate account of Austria-Hungary's domestic politics. 'Austro-Hungarian policy, like Russian policy, was largely determined by internal considerations.'

G178. *Bismark*, Vol. 1, Erich Eyck, Erlenbach-Zurich, Rentsch, 1941. *Ibid.* pp 113–5

(1) Praises the author for going deeply into all the controversial issues and for mastering the vast literature. Critical of the length of the book and of the author assuming that Bismarck always intended creating a united Germany.

(2) 'Bismarck always claimed as most deliberate the events least welcome to him.' 'The psychological key to Bismarck is his parentage ... His non-Junker brain told him the old order was doomed; his Junker prejudices determined him to preserve it. He went with the current of events in order to achieve the exact reverse of this current; and in some ways he achieved it.'

G179. Masaryk in England, *Masaryk in England*, R.W. Seton-Watson, Cambridge U.P., *MG*. 3 Mar. p 3

(1) The author 'has fulfilled his duty to Masaryk and to Czechoslovakia with a perfect modesty and accomplishment'.

(2) 'Masaryk was the greatest democratic politician of this century; every word of his is precious.' Praises his attitude to Russia.

Repr. *MGW*. 48, 11. 12 Mar. p 148

G180. The Liberator, *Masaryk in England* (*see above* G179), *T & T*. 24, 11. 13 Mar. p 216

(2) 'Masaryk was the greatest man whom the Four Years' War brought on the world stage; Lenin,

his only equal, had a more limited influence in his lifetime, and all others were pygmies in comparison . . . the creation of Czechoslovakia was a political performance without parallel.'

G181. American Angle, *A Time for Greatness*, Herbert Agar, Eyre and Spottiswoode, *MG*. 26 Mar. p 3

(1) 'A vigorous statement of the case for liberal reformed capitalism'. A.J.P.T. sees most of this as wishful thinking – and observes 'that we have as much to learn from Russia as Russia from us'.

Repr. *MGW*. 48, 14. 2 Apr. p 188

G182. World's End, (a) *The Great O'Neil*, Sean O'Faolain, Longmans; (b) *The Land of the Great Image*, Maurice Collis, Faber, *MG*. 31 Mar. p 3

(a1) 'A most able book, written with style and a sharply critical intelligence'.

(b1) This book on Golden Goa and the land of Arakan is written 'by the hand of a master . . . everything in his book is perfect, an evocation of far places and distant ages which is at once convincing'. However he doubts some of the speculations.

Repr. *MGW*. 48, 15. 9 Apr. p 204

G183. The Defeated, *The Two Marshals*, Philip Guedella, Hodder and Stoughton, *MG*. 21 Apr. p 3

(1) The part on Bazaine is 'as a biography, brilliant; as a defence, not altogether convincing'. Wishes he 'had resisted the temptation to drag Petain in'.

Repr. *MGW*. 48, 18. 30 Apr. p 244

G184. Rumania, *Athene Palace, Bucharest*, Countess Waldeck, Constable, *MG*. 28 Apr. p 3

(1) 'A very clever book, indeed brilliant, full of vivid portraits' but superficial in its judgment of international affairs.

G185. Colour Problem, *Hell in the Sunshine*, Cedric Dover, Secker and Warburg, *MG*. 28 May. p 3

(1) Praises the author for urging that the war against Japan should not be one for white supremacy and for showing 'with much detail and some exaggeration how little the coloured peoples of the world

have benefitted from the spread of white civilisation'.

Repr. *MGW*. 48, 24. 11 Jun. p 328

G186. The Other Germany, *Need Germany Survive?* Julius Braunthal, Gollancz, *MG*. 25 Jun. p 3

(1) Finds its arguments unimpressive.

(2) 'Socialism will succeed if it offers to Germany ... 'a full larder and empty arsenals'; if, in the name of equality, it either gives Germany full arsenals or empties the arsenals of others, then the German State will have its third, and successful, opportunity.'

Repr. *MGW*. 49, 5. 30 Jul. p 59

G187. Thomas Mann, *Order of the Day*, Thomas Mann, Secker and Warburg, *MG*. 25 Aug. p 3

(1) Praises him as 'the outstanding intellect amongst the German opponents of Nazism' but asks if this is the best they can do. 'Every essay is ponderous, abstract'.

(2) 'Hitler is the logical outcome of the Reich; and the Liberal Nationalists of seventy years ago were his begetters. A Thomas Mann regime in Germany would save the Reich, as the Weimar Republic did; and would produce another Stresemann, the St. John the Baptist of the Nazis. For if they save the Reich they will save the future for the Nazis; the Reich has no other meaning except as an instrument of domination.'

Repr. *MGW*. 49, 13. 24 Sept. p 172

G188. Those Twenty Years, (a) *World in Trance*, Leopold Schwarzschild, Hamilton; (b) *The Twenty Years' Truce*, R.M. Rayner, Longmans, *MG*. 3 Sept. p 3

(a1) 'Contemporary history in the style of Voltaire, one of the most exciting – as well as the most entertaining – books published for years'. 'His only omission is to ignore Anglo-Russian estrangement, the most profound cause of the present war.'

(b1) 'A summary of newspaper headlines, not contemporary history'.

Repr. *MGW*. 49, 12. 17 Sep. p 160

G189. French Revolution, *The French Revolution*, J.M. Thompson, Oxford, Blackwell, *MG*. 15 Sept. p 3

(1) 'Every generation must, no doubt, write the history of the French Revolution anew, but Mr. Thompson has certainly written it for our generation.'

Repr. *MGW*. 49, 13. 24 Sept. p 174

G190. Ancient and Modern, (a) *The Age of Catherine de Medici*, J.E. Neale, Cape; (b) *Van Loon's Lives*, Hendrick van Loon, Harrap, *MG*. 3 Nov. p 3

(a1) 'Four modest lectures'.

(b1) 'The whole is done with such naive gusto and such resolutely enlightened principles that one almost forgets to be repelled by the ghastly bad taste of the whole affair.'

Repr. *MGW*. 49, 20. 12 Nov. p 272

G191. *The Spirit of English History*, A.L. Rowse, Cape, *MG*. 10 Dec. p 3

(1) 'Fascinatingly readable, a triumph of restraint and artistry. . . . If it errs it is in not attempting to modify traditional views according to the evidence of more recent historians.'

Repr. *MGW*. 49, 25. 17 Nov. p 342

G192. *Great Britain, France and the German Problem 1918–1939*, W.M. Jordan, Royal Institute of International Affairs, *OM*. 62, 7. 25 Nov. p 97

(1) Praises the first part which deals with the problem of French security at the Paris Peace Conference; after 1919 'it is good précis writing from the official sources of the sort which Professor Webster (who contributes an introduction) so often mistakes for diplomatic history'.

G193. *Wings of Destiny*, Marquess of Londonderry, Macmillan, *OM*. 62, 8. 2 Dec. p 108a

(1) 'Here, interspersed with rambling personal reminiscences, is his defence and explanation . . . posterity will marvel that the writer of this book could be a Cabinet minister even in the age of MacDonald, Baldwin and 'National' government.'

G194. Eminent Georgians, *Cartaret and Newcastle*, Basil

Williams, Cambridge U.P., *MG.* 15 Dec. p 3

(1) Written with charm but 'sticks to the personal . . . it does not go very deep'. Calls for a serious discussion of 'Newcastle's significance in politics'.

Repr. *MGW.* 49, 26. 24 Dec. p 356

G195. Portugal, *Salazar*, F.C.C. Egerton, Hodder and Stoughton, *MG.* 17 Dec. p 3

(1) It has some merits, 'but like most eulogies of Fascist States . . . it avoids the concrete'.

Repr. *MGW.* 50, 12. 12 Mar. 1944. p 161

1944

G196. Between Two Wars, *Eastern Europe*, Josef Hanc, Museum Press, 1943, *MG.* 14 Jan. p 3

(1) A competent survey.

(2) 'The disruption and collapse of the 1919 settlement was not due to the faults of the small powers but to the selfishness and negligence of the Great Powers – above all, of England and the United States.'

Repr. *MGW.* 50, 3. 21 Jan. p 36

G197. *Aberoni, or the Spanish Conspiracy*, Simon Harcourt-Smith, Faber, 1943, *MG.* 19 Jan. p 3

(1) 'A piece of baroque history in the style of Sacheverell Sitwell, but with a harder foundation of fact and a more successful effect'.

G198. Czechoslovaks, *A History of the Czechs and Slovaks*, R.W. Seton-Watson, Hutchinson, 1943, *MG.* 26 Jan. p 3

(1) It fills a gap but is not entirely satisfactory – it is too uncritical of these peoples and 'there is none of the rigorous examination of economic factors which would alone make the story comprehensible.'

Repr. *MGW.* 50, 8. 25 Feb. p 105

G199. *Bismarck*, Ian F.D. Morrow, Duckworth, 1943, *OM.* 62, 10. 27 Jan. p 135

(1) 'A fine narrative, vividly written', but it is

'the Bismarck of legend, Bismarck as he would appear to a decent conservative nationalist of about 1910'.

G200. (a) *Redbrick University*, Bruce Truscott, Faber, 1943; (b) *A Student's View of the Universities*, Brian Simon, Longmans, *OM*. 62, 12. 10 Feb. pp 157–8

(a1) He 'writes only of modern universities, and writes of them well; though, unintentionally, he makes them sound less attractive than they are'.

(b1) It is 'more naive, a dogmatic expression of the Marxist views of some leaders of the N.U.S. Of course everyone under twenty-five should be a Marxist; but equally of course, no one under twenty-five should publish a book about universities (or indeed about anything else).'

G201. Vivid Portrait, *The Young Lincoln*, Esther Maynell, Chapman and Hall, *MG*. 15 Mar. p 3

(1) 'Intimate biography of the highest quality'.

Repr. *MGW*. 50, 12. 24 Mar. p 161

G202. *Anglo-Russian Relations 1689–1943*, Sir John Marriott, Methuen, *MG*. 19 Apr. p 3

(1) Fills a gap, but is 'by no means a good book'. 'The underlying assumption . . . is that England has usually been right and Russia wrong.'

Repr. *MGW*. 50, 17. 28 Apr. p 229

G203. German Contrasts, (a) *The Rise and Fall of the House of Ullstein*, Herman Ullstein, Nicholson and Watson; (b) *The Turning Point*, Klaus Mann, Gollancz, *MG*. 26 Apr. p 3

(a1) Much interest in the story 'but publishers do not usually write good books, and this one is no exception'.

(b1) 'The best picture yet painted of the cultured middle class of the nineteen-twenties, striving almost too conscientiously to be good Europeans.'

Repr. *MGW*. 50, 18. 5 May. p 244

G204. Russian Relations, *Maisky*, George Bilainkin, Allen

and Unwin, *MG*. 3 May. p 3

(1) It consists mostly of press cuttings written about the Soviet Union. Deplores the failure to achieve an Anglo-Soviet alliance before the War.

Repr. *MGW*. 50, 21. 26 May. p 285

G205. Heroes, (a) *The Poisoned Crown*, Hugh Kingsmill, Eyre and Spottiswoode; (b) *William the Silent*, C.V. Wedgwood, Cape, *MG*. 24 May. p 3

(a1) 'Kingsmill at his best'. 'Nothing better and more penetrating than his discussion of the intellectual geneology of Hitler has been written for many years'.

(b1) A well written, well constructed book. She 'has now joined Mr. Rowse in the practice of eulogistic history'.

Repr. *MGW*. 50, 25. 23 Jun. p 339

G206. Distorting Mirror, *The Mirror of the Past*, K. Zilliacus, Gollancz, *MG*. 14 Jan. p 3

(1) Outmoded views, which exculpate Germany of the blame for the First World War.

Repr. *MGW*. 51, 1. 7 Jul. p 6

G207. Bulgaria Emerges, *The Establishment of Constitutional Government in Bulgaria*, C.E. Black, Milford, *MG*. 21 Jul. p 3

(1) 'A credit to American scholarship'.

Repr. *MGW*. 51, 8. 25 Aug. p 105

G208. Memoirs, *Courts and Cabinets*, G.P. Gooch, Longmans, *MG*. 2 Aug. p 3

(1) 'A sort of glorified gossiping about gossip writers'.

Repr. *MGW*. 51, 10. 8 Sept. p 130

G209. Poland and Beck, *Colonel Beck and His Policy*, Stanislaw Mackiewicz, Eyre and Spottiswoode, *MG*. 9 Aug. p 3

(1) Finds it curious that in 1944 a book should be published 'arguing that Polish policy should be as much anti-Russian as anti-German'.

Repr. *MGW*. 51, 8. 25 Aug. p 105

G210. Dutch Unity, *The Dutch Nation*, G.J. Renier, Allen and Unwin, *MG*. 13 Sept. p 3

(1) Praises the analysis, but it is heavy going and was written in haste.

Repr. *MGW*. 51, 12. 22 Sept. p 162

G211. U.S.A. and Russia, *The Road to Tehran*, Foster Rea Dulles, Princeton U.P.; Milford, *MG*. 15 Sept. p 3

(1) 'Historical journalism of a very high order ... a first rate book, written with great ability, containing both scholarship and common sense'.

Repr. as 'The Americans and the Russians', *MGW*. 51, 13. 29 Sept. p 174

G212. Rights of Man, *Clemenceau*, Geoffrey Braun, Harvard U.P.; Milford, *MG*. 29 Sept. p 3

(1) Unfavourable – he 'does not understand Jacobinism and so thinks Clemenceau old fashioned and out of date'.

Repr. *MGW*. 51, 14. 6 Oct. p 186

G213. *A History of the Czechs and Slovaks* (*see above* G198), *EHR*. 59, 235. Sept. pp 431–2

(1) 'To write a history of the national movement without a class analysis is to be reduced to a series of anecdotes and literary pictures'.

G214. German History, (a) *A Short History of Germany*, S.H. Steinberg, Cambridge U.P.; (b) *Max Weber and German Politics*, J.P. Mayer, Faber, *MG*. 18 Oct. p 3

(a1) 'His point of view is German – liberal, and of all observers it is the well-meaning liberals who have understood least.'

(a2) 'A painstaking exercise in the mistaken view that it is the task of the historian to accumulate facts. Of course the real task of the historian is to throw overboard all facts but the essential.'

(b1) A 'rather scrappy, rambling book'.

(b2) Weber was typical of German liberals whose insecurity led them to reject 'the common heritage of Western European civilisation'.

Repr. *MGW*. 51, 20. 17 Nov. p 273

G215. Two Nations, (a) *Czechoslovakia in European History*, S. Harrison Thomson, Princeton U.P.; Milford;

(b) *The Evolution of Modern Italy 1715–1920*, A.J. Whyte, Oxford, Blackwell, *MG*. 1 Nov. p 3

(a1) 'A remarkable and distinguished book'.

(a2) 'There is probably no other people in Europe where national sentiment has passed so successfully from the intellectual minority to the broad masses of the nation.'

(b1) Within conventional limits, a good book.

Repr. *MGW*. 51, 19. 10 Nov. p 258

G216. *The Evolution of Modern Italy*, (*see* G215), *OM*. 63, 3. 2 Nov. p 38–9

(1) 'The best single-volume history of modern Italy in English.' However it is weak on economic history and foreign policy. Observes that the author 'cannot rid himself of the prepossession that unification was the spontaneous movement of a united people'.

G217. *A Short History of Germany*, S.H. Steinberg, Cambridge U.P., *OM*. 63, 7. 30 Nov. pp 85–6

(1) 'Like most German liberals he understands neither German liberalism or German conservatism.'

G218. Norfolk Portraits, *Norfolk Portraits*, R.W. Ketton-Cremer, Faber, *MG*. 24 Nov. p 3

(1) The portraits are drawn 'with wit and distinction'. The most valuable essay is on the decline of the Paston family.

Repr. *MGW*. 51, 22. 1 Dec. p 301

G219. German Legends, *Germany Between Two Wars*, Lindley Fraser, Oxford U.P., *MG*. 29 Dec. p 3

(1) Suffers from being published radio broadcasts. Praises it for exploding 'the myths and complaints on which Hitler built up his appeal to the German people'.

(2) 'Its weakness is its assumption that the Germans had to be argued into supporting Hitler (and therefore can be argued out of supporting him). In reality Hitler did not argue with the German people, but expressed, in somewhat violent form, their outlook and wishes. It is therefore not enough to demolish Hitler's case; there must be a positive alternative to put in its place.'

Repr. *MGW*. 52, 1. 5 Jan. 1945. p 8

1945

G220. A Real Policy, *Primer of the Coming World*, Leopold Schwarzchild, Hamilton, 1944, *MG*. 3 Jan. p 3

(1) 'An indispensable book . . . a primer of wisdom'.

(2) 'The total disarmament of Germany is the key to peace and it must be enforced by permanent Allied garrisons on German soils . . . no nonsense about re-educating Germany or compelling the Germans to be democratic – that is something the Germans must do for themselves.'

Repr. *MGW*. 52, 4. 26 Jan. p 54

G221. German Problem, *The United States of Europe*, K.K. Doberer, Drummond, 1944, *MG*. 10 Jan. p 3

(1) 'A clear and well argued statement of the historical and political case for German federalism'.

(2) 'The Germans will have to be made, and kept, free – that is divided by Allied arms.'

Repr. *MGW*. 52, 4. 26 Jan. p 54

G222. War Years 1802–12, *Years of Victory 1802–12*, Arthur Bryant, Collins, 1944, *MG*. 17 Jan. p 3

(1) A very good book.

Repr. *MGW*. 52, 4. 26 Jan. p 52

G223. The Hitler Cult, *Der Fuehrer*, Konrad Heiden, Gollancz, *MG*. 14 Feb. p 3

(1) 'The best book on its subject'.

Repr. *MGW*. 52, 8. 23 Feb. p 109

G224. Franco's Spain, *An Interlude in Spain*, Charles d'Ydewalle, Macmillan, *MG*. 23 Feb. p 3

(1) A devastating indictment of Franco's Spain by a bewildered admirer who spent eight months in Spanish political prisons.

Repr. *MGW*. 52, 9. 2 Mar. p 122

G225. *Germany's Three Reichs*, Edmond Vermeil, Dakers, *OM*. 63, 13. 1 Mar. pp 183–4

(1) 'A remarkable book, constantly stimulating, but by no means an easy book to read'.

G226. War Against Britain, *Thrice Against England*, Kurt Stechert, Cape, *MG*. 20 Apr. p 3

(1) It has 'real value in its revelations of both the merits and defects of German military science'.

Repr. *MGW*. 52, 17. 27 Apr. p 234

G227. *Czechoslovakia in European History* (*see above* G215), *EHR*. 60, 237. May. pp 261–4

(1) Praises it warmly but suggests that the author exaggerates the coherence of the Czech national movement and underestimates the strength of the 'Austrian idea'.

G228. *The Establishment of Constitutional Government in Bulgaria* (*see above* G207), *Ibid.* p 284

G229. *Intervention in Archangel*, Leonid I. Strakhovsky, Princeton U.P.; Milford, *Ibid.* pp 286–7

(1) A narrow theme, well done. The internal politics of Archangel were not important. 'The only reality was the allied force; and when this departed, the other reality of Bolshevik rule took its place.'

G230. *Stalin 1879–1944*, J.T. Murphy, Lane, *MG*. 1 Jun. p 3

(1) 'Devotional literature for the edification of the faithful'.

Repr. *MGW*. 52, 23. 8 Jun. p 314

G231. *Citizen Toussaint*, Ralph Korngold, Gollancz, *MG*. 8 Jun. p 3

(1) 'A fine book'.

(2) 'One of the most astonishing products of the astonishing age of the French Revolution'. 'Everything about him was noble . . . probably the greatest man the Negro race has produced'.

Repr. *MGW*. 53, 3. 20 Jul. p 33

G232. Eastern Europe, *Eastern Europe Between the Wars 1918–1941*, Hugh Seton-Watson, Cambridge U.P., *MG*. 3 Aug. p 3

(1) 'The most comprehensive' and 'most level-headed' book on the subject.

Repr. *MGW*. 53, 12. 21 Sept. p 152

G233. Lyons Mail, *The Lyons Mail*, Sir Charles Oman, Methuen, *MG*. 19 Sept. p 3

(1) Admirably written – very good both as history and a detective story.

G234. *The German Mind and Outlook*, Institute of Sociology, Chapman and Hall, *MG*. 3 Oct. p 3

(1) Most of these 1942 lectures 'fail to break new ground'; but praises one by Professor Butler which demonstrates 'the decisive part which German idealist writers played in producing all that is most repellent in the modern German people'.

(2) 'Not Frederick the Great but Fichte, not Bismarck but his liberal opponents, were the spiritual forerunners of Hitler'.

G235. Napoleon in Private, *In Search of Two Characters*, Dormer Creston, Macmillan, *MG*. 19 Oct. p 3

(1) 'Light reading, not history'.

Repr. *MGW*. 53, 23. 7 Dec. p 297

G236. *Eastern Europe Between The Wars 1918–1941* (*see above* G232), *OM*. 64, 5. 15 Nov. p 79

(1) 'This is certainly the most considerable and, in some ways, the best book that has been written on Eastern Europe between the wars.' 'It has the Seton-Watson virtues: sincerity, impeccable honesty, great labour' – but it also has the defects, which make it dull and encyclopedic.

(2) '... the Communists, with all their dogmatism and violence and intolerance, will be an improvement on the old police states'.

1946

G237. Europe's Trend, *European Balance*, Peter Matthews, Chatto and Windus, *MG*. 30 Jan. p 3

(1) Events have overtaken the German part, and that on Russia is not profound.

G238. (a) *Germany, Russia and the Future*, J.T. McCurdy, Cambridge U.P., 1944; (b) *Russo-Polish Relations*, ed. S. Konovalov, Cresset, 1945, *OM*. 64, 10. 31 Jan. pp 154–5

(a1) 'Psychology seems to be another name for guessing'.

(b1) 'Too short and too scrappy to do justice to its subject'.

G239. *Bismarck*, Vol. 2, Eric Eyck, Erlenbach-Zwich, Rentsch, 1943, *EHR*. 61, 239. Jan. pp 109–12

(1) Supersedes all previous accounts, but 'it stands nearer to the Life and Letters of one just dead than to the review of a historian'.

G240. *The Junker in the Prussian Administration under William II 1888–1914*, Lysbeth Walker Muncy, Brown U.P., 1944, *Ibid.* pp 125–6

(1) 'Her methods are laborious and her presentation sometimes pedestrian; but the results are fascinating.'

G241. *The German Record*, William Ebenstein, New York, Farrar and Rinehard, 1945, *Int. Affairs*. 22, 1. Jan. p 136

(1) Praises the arguments and opinions of the book but criticises the presentation.

G242. The "Good" Germans, *Germany: From Defeat to Conquest 1913–33*, W.M. Knight-Patterson, Allen and Unwin, *Sun. Times*. 17 Mar. p 3

(1) Favourable to its theme, 'a formidable indictment' of the Germans, but otherwise critical.

(2) The moral of German history 'is the overriding duty laid on the victorious Powers to maintain their unity in peace'.

G243. Vintage 1848, *1848: The Revolution of the Intellectuals*, L.B. Namier, Cumberlege, *MG*. 5 Apr. p 3

(1) 'A contribution to nineteenth century European history of the first importance'.

(2) 'The revolution of the intellectuals foreshadowed the treason of the intellectuals which has determined the character of Europe in our own time.'

Repr. *MGW*. 54, 17. 26 Apr. p 218

G244. German Tangle, *Confusion of Faces*, Eric Meissner, Faber, *MG*. 24 Apr. p 3

(1) 'A hotch-potch of brilliant ideas about German history and German politics'.

Repr. *MGW*. 54, 21. 24 May. p 269

G245. Phantom Emperor, *Mexican Empire*, H. Montgomery Hyde, Macmillan, *MG*. 1 May. p 3

(1) 'A book without faults, though also without outstanding virtues', on a trivial subject.

Repr. *MGW*. 55, 7. 16 Aug. p 86

G246. Foreign Policy, *Diplomatic History 1713–1933*, Sir Charles Petrie, Hollis and Carter, *MG*. 28 Jun. p 3

(1) A competent but drab narrative.

Repr. *MGW*. 55, 3. 19 Jul. p 34

G247. Reorganising Europe: The Odour of Vienna, *The Congress of Vienna*, Harold Nicolson, Constable, *TLS*. 2317. 29 Jun. pp 301–2

(1) Diplomacy presented 'as it would appear to a well-intentioned British diplomat, with sympathy but not much understanding for the attitude of others'.

(2) 'Had the Concert of Europe been as negative as Castlereagh wished, or had broken down as Canning intended, France would have had her revenge in 1830, if not earlier.'

G248. *European Balance (see above* G237), *Int. Affairs*. 22, 3. July. pp 443–4

G249. Lassalle, *The Primrose Path*, David Footman, Cresset, *MG*. 15 Oct. p 3

(1) 'A pleasure to read, makes full and skilful use of all the sources, and – most important – it comes off as a biography'.

(2) 'Lassalle was a great showman, rather a rogue, but courageous and quick-witted.'

Repr. *MGW*. 55, 21. 22 Nov. p 287

G250. *The Evolution of Prussia*, Sir J.A.R. Marriot and Sir Charles Grant Robertson, Oxford, Clarendon Press, *Int. Affairs*. 22, 4. Oct. p 581

(1) Deems the never ending additions to the first edition (1915) to be quite inadequate.

G251. *German Kultur*, Otto Zarek, Hutchinson, *Ibid.* 581

(1) An expansion of Thomas Mann's idea 'of the conflict between Kultur and civilisation'. This,

A.J.P.T. feels, is a 'far-fetched idea'.

G252. *The Germans and Ourselves*, Karl Barth, Nisbet, 1945, *Ibid.* 590

(1) 'A work of the greatest power, but in parts out-of-date'. Praises the author for seeing 'that German aggression and brutality are not the creation of Hitler, but inherent in modern German political development'.

G253. Canning, *George Canning*, 2nd edn. Sir Charles Petrie, Eyre and Spottiswoode, *MG.* 19 Nov. p 3

(1) A sensible unassuming work without any obvious virtues.

(2) 'Canning was probably the most striking personality in British public life between Chatham and Churchill.'

Repr. *MGW.* 55, 22. 29 Nov. p 304

G254. Louis Quatorze, *Louis XIV and the Greatness of France*, Maurice Ashley, English Universities Press, *MG.* 19 Nov. p 3

(1) 'An accomplished writer of short lives'; like the rest of the 'Teach Yourself History' series it is pleasant though not important.

G255. A German View, *The Germans in History*, Prince Hubertus Zu Loewenstein, Columbia U.P.; Cumberlege, *MG.* 22 Nov. p 3

(1) A rambling and somewhat eccentric book.

Repr. *MGW.* 56, 1. 2 Jan. 1947. p 10

G256. The Diplomacy of Munich: M. Bonnet's Defence, *Défense de la Paix : De Washington au Quai d'Orsay*, Georges Bonnet, Geneva, Bourquin, review article in *MG.* 23 Nov. pp 4, 6

Repr. *MGW.* 55, 22. 29 Nov. p 298 and as 'The Diplomacy of Mr. Bonnet' in A5, pp 134–8 and A17, pp 249–52

G257. Autobiography, *Memories of Four Score Years*, Sir John Marriott, Blackie, *MG.* 10 Dec. p 3

(1) Like his historical books it has 'a simple style, skilful marshalling of a vast assemblage of facts, and a healthy old-Conservative partiality, disarming

because never concealed'.

G258. Trustees of Europe, (a) *Histoire du Consulat et de l'Empire*, Vol. 10, Louis Madelin, Paris, Librairie Hachette; (b) *Secretary of Europe*, Golo Mann, Yale U.P.; Cumberlege; (c) *Friedrich von Gentz*, Paul R. Sweet, Wisconsin U.P., *TLS*. 2343. 28 Dec. pp 637–8

(a1) Written in a pleasant style, but not based on his own research; 'a book to lie on the drawing room table, not to stand permanently in the library'.

(b1) An attempt to write a work of art with Gentz as hero.

(c1) Drab and erudite.

Repr. as 'Napoleon and Gentz' in A5, pp 24–32 and A15, pp 12–20

G259. *Armistice 1918*, Harry R. Rudin, Oxford U.P., (unidentified journal, probably late 1946 or early 1947)

(1) A competent account of the negotiations from the German side, written in 'a clumsy style'.

1947

G260. Trade with China, *Foreign Mud*, Maurice Collis, Faber, 1946, *MG*. 3 Jan. p 3

(1) 'The best book of a most admirable writer'.

Repr. *MGW*. 56, 3. 16 Jan. p 8

G261. *The Growth of Modern Germany*, Roy Pascal, Cobbett Press, 1946, *Int. Affairs*. 23, 1. Jan. pp 110–11

(1) Much of value – but many old myths about the Germans in it.

G262. A Great Austrian, *Prince Felix zu Schwarzenberg*, Adolph Schwarzenberg, Columbia U.P.; Cumberlege, *TLS*. 2349. 8 Feb. p 75

(1) Favourable – contains no new material but is competently done.

(2) Schwarzenberg 'was the most forceful and perhaps the most successful Austrian statesman of the nineteenth century. . . . Though a counter-revolutionary he was not a reactionary nor even a

conservative. . . . He believed solely in authority, and that authority his own.'

G263. German Unity, *The Origins of Modern Germany*, G. Barraclough, Oxford, Blackwell, *Sp.* 6193. 7 Mar. pp 248, 250

(1) Favourable to his treatment of medieval Germany but is critical of the 'exhausted metaphors' and the author exaggerating 'the elements of purpose in human affairs'. Dislikes the moral of the book that 'the harmless, pacific Germans should be given the national unity for which they have always wished'.

G264. The Degradation of Germany, (a) *The History of Liberty in Germany*, Rudolf Olden, Gollancz; (b) *Die Deutsche Katastrophe*, Friedrich Meinecke, Zwich, Aero; (c) *Irrweg und Umkehr*, 'Constantin Silens', Basel, Birkhäuser; (d) *Psychologist in Germany*, Saul K. Padover, Phoenix House, *TLS.* 2355. 22 Mar. pp 121–2

(a1) Not an easy book to read, or a successful one.

(a2) The 'German disease . . . is not tyranny, but the willingness to obey tyrants, even with joy'. The men of 1848 and 1918 wished to preserve the armed forces 'as the agents of German expansion in the East'.

(b1) 'Slight and cryptic', but 'remarkable evidence on the German mind'. The author expects freedom of thought, but always 'expected it . . . within the framework of an authoritarian State'.

(c1) A book by a thorough going Conservative who regrets the previous 150 years of German history.

(d1) The author interviewed thousands of Germans, and found that the leaders of German society repudiated Hitler for failure not for moral reasons.

G265. French Diplomacy in the 1930's: The Testimony of General Gamelin, *Servir*, Vol. 2, General Gamelin, Paris, Plon, *MG.* 29 Mar. p 4

(1) 'More orderly and of more value to the historian' than the first volume.

Repr. as 'Pre-War French Diplomacy: The Testimony of General Gamelin', *MGW*. 56, 13. 10 Apr. p 11

G266. Comment L'On Court A Sa Perte, (a) *Servir* (*see above* G265); (b) *Les Fossoyeurs*, Pertinax, Paris, Sagittaire, 1946; (c) *Défense de la Paix* (*see above* G256), *Crit*. 2, 10. Mar. pp 240–51

(a1) Memoirs damaging to his reputation – his 'wisest course would have been to remain silent'.

The review centres on Gamelin. This part is repr. as 'General Gamelin: Or How To Lose' in A5, pp 144–7, and A17, pp 289–92

G267. The Secrets of Diplomacy, *BD*, 2nd Ser., 1, *1919*, *TLS*. 2358. 12 Apr. pp 165–6

(1) Deplores the sorting of the documents into topics rather than keeping them in chronological order and the fact that the volume is limited to official despatches and telegrams (with no private letters or minutes), unlike the Gooch and Temperley volumes. The volume appears 'to have the deliberate purpose of vindicating the British foreign service'.

(2) Discusses the publication of diplomatic records by various Governments from the time of Canning onwards. Observes that *The Foreign Policy of the European Cabinets 1871–1914* was 'as good as a military victory for Germany, for it was a decisive weapon in shaking the moral foundations of Versailles'.

'The conflict between secrecy and publicity is the trickiest question in foreign policy . . . Negotiations can only be flexible if they are secret; they will be barren unless they secure popular consent.'

G268. *Europe and Italy's acquisition of Libya 1911–12*, William C. Askew, Duke U.P., 1942, *EHR*. 62, 243. Apr. p 286.

(1) Competent but dull. Criticises detailed studies of diplomatic questions: 'they are all precis writing, not history'. On the author's study of the European

press: 'It is a misconception common in studies of this period that 'public opinion' on international questions of secondary importance can be discovered by assiduous reading of leading articles'.

G269. Winnowed Frederick, *Frederick the Great*, G.P. Gooch, Longmans, *MG*. 2 May. p 3

(1) In the author's usual style – 'a kind of historical anthology with running comments'. 'It contains all one needs to know about a repulsive figure.'

Repr. *MGW*. 56, 17. 8 May. p 10

G270. World of the Past, *Carlota Joaquina Queen of Portugal*, Marcus Cheke, Sidgwick and Jackson, *MG*. 16 May. p 3

(1) An admirable book which portrays old fashioned monarchy 'at once more regal and more plebeian than anything that can now be imagined'.

Repr. *MGW*. 56, 22. 12 Jun. p 11

G271. Witchcraft and Policy, *Four Centuries of Witch Beliefs*, R. Trevor Davies, Methuen, *MG*. 23 May. p 3

(1) 'Pugnacious, learned, plausible', but it becomes wrong headed when he claims that Puritan opposition to Charles I was in part due to horror at Charles' lenient treatment of witches.

Repr. *MGW*. 56, 22. 12 Jun. p 11

G272. Changing Power in China, *La Question D'Extrême-Orient 1840–1940*, Pierre Renouvin, Paris and London, Hachette, *TLS*. 2364. 24 May. p 247

(1) 'A remarkable and valuable book', the best in its field.

G273. Political Sailor, *Lord Cochrane*, Christopher Lloyd, Longmans, *MG*. 17 Jun. p 3

(1) 'Written with elegance and good sense'.

Repr. *MGW*. 57, 5. 31 Jul. p 10

G274. *The Babeuf Plot*, David Thomson, Kegan Paul, *TLS*. 2368. 21 Jul. p 304

(1) An unaffected account of Babeuf's career and legend.

(2) Babeuf is the equivalent of Winstanley and the Diggers to English Marxists for French social

revolutionaries. But there was no real tradition of Babouvism – 'a legendary figure whose legend even is legendary'.

G275. *Bismarck*, Vol. 3, Eric Eyck, Erlenbach-Zwich, Rentsch, 1944, *EHR*. 62, 244. Jul. pp 390–3

(1) The best of the volumes. With the earlier volumes 'it was impossible to escape the feeling that Mr. Eyck had been mastered by his material, instead of mastering it'.

(2) Draws the moral that Bismarck's life and German history 'cannot be comprehended without as full a grasp of Russia's place in Europe as western historians have shown for that of England and France'.

G276. The Third Republic's End, The Narrative of M. Reynaud, *La France a Sauvé l'Europe*, 2 Vols. Paul Reynaud, Paris, Flamarrion, *MG*. 19 Aug. p 4

(1) A book in which old battles are fought again. He 'wages against his critics a more successful war than he waged against the Germans'.

Repr. *MGW*. 57, 10. 4 Sept. p 11 and as 'The End of the Third Republic' in A5, pp 150–2

G277. Europe in 1939, The Negotiations with Russia, *Derniers Jours de l'Europe*, Gregoire Gafencu, Paris, LUF., *MG*. 2 Sept. p 4

(1) Valuable on the attitudes prevailing in Paris and London in 1939.

Repr. as 'European Diplomacy in 1939', *MGW*. 57, 11. 11 Sept. p 11

1948

G278. How The War Began, *Diplomatic Prelude 1938–9*, L.B. Namier, Macmillan, *MG*. 10 Jan. p 4

(1) 'A show piece of the historian's art ... Meticulous scholarship and deep insight go together, and a sentence often says as much as many pages by another writer.'

Repr. *MGW*. 58, 3. 14 Jan. p 12

G279. Karl Marx, *The Red Prussian*, L. Schwarzchild, Hamilton, *MG*. 16 Jan. p 3

(1) Entertaining and interesting but it lacks 'understanding of the reasons for Marx's posthumous success'.

(2) 'Marx would rank as the most unattractive character in nineteenth-century history were it not for Bismarck, who had the same repellent qualities even more intensely.'

Repr. *MGW*. 58, 4. 22 Jan. p 10

G280. M. Flandin and French Policy, The Reoccupation of the Rhineland, *Politique Francaise, 1919–1940*, Pierre-Etienne Flandin, Paris, Les Editions Nouvelles, *MG*. 24 Jan. p 4

(1) Confirms other accounts of the events of 1936 and that France was lacking in leadership.

Repr. *MGW*. 58, 6. 5 Feb. p 12 and in A5, pp125–8, and A17, pp 229–32

G281. *The Awakening of Modern Egypt*, Rifaat Bey, Longmans, *MG*. 27 Jan. p 3

(1) 'Well written, not oversimplified, nationalistic without being querulous or challenging'. Observes that the title is mistaken for the nineteenth century – 'the people of Egypt remained sullenly asleep'.

Repr. *MGW*. 58, 8. 19 Feb. p 10

G282. *Les Derniers Jours de Hitler*, H.R. Trevor Roper, Paris, Calman-Levy, 1947, *Crit*. 3, 4. 20 Jan. pp 90–2

(1) Praises it very highly: a book which is both instructive and well written, and which develops its story with all the brilliance of a symphony conducted by a great master.

(2) Warns that if Germany ever recovers her power then she will speak again in the tone and manner of Hitler.

G283. Gamelin and the 'Phoney War', *Servir*, Vol. 3, General Gamelin, Paris, Plon, *MG*. 13 Feb. p 4

(1) Its value lies in its discussion of diplomacy and politics not war. 'Germelin was more suited to be a negotiator than a fighter.'

Repr. *MGW*. 58, 10. 4 Mar. p 12

G284. *Mes Memoirs*, 3 Vols. Joseph Caillaux, Paris, Plon, 1942–7, *Crit*. 3, 4, 21. Feb. pp 154–60

(1) His justification – 'a subtly delayed revenge' against his political opponents.

(2) 'If France had followed Caillaux in 1911, in 1914, or in 1917, she would have been cut off from England and Russia and would have given Germany the mastery of Europe without a struggle. It needed two German wars to repudiate the policy of Agadir. . . .'

Repr. as 'The Secret of the Third Republic' in A5, pp 101–7, A15, pp 128–34 and A17, pp 146–52

G285. The failure of the German Universities, *The Abuse of Learning*, Frederick Lilge, Macmillan, *NS & N*. 35, 887. 6 Mar. pp 198–9

(1) It gives an account of German thinking about the purpose of universities but it does not explain 'why the German universities fell down before Hitler'.

(2) 'Universities, like any other institution, can only be explained by Marxist analysis.' Deplores the work for the military done by British and American scientists. 'The scientists have been the Trojan Horse of conformity; and the academic world in this country, too, will pay a bitter penalty for ever having admitted them within its walls.'

G286. The Supreme Council, 1919, *BD*, 1st Ser., 1, *1919*, *TLS*. 2405. 6 Mar. p 131

(1) The proceedings of the Supreme Council after the great men had gone. Regrets that Foreign Office minutes and all records of the Cabinet are excluded.

G287. The Great Revolution, *The Coming of the French Revolution*, Georges Lefebvre, Princeton U.P.; London, Cumberlege, *MG*. 6 Apr. p 3

(1) 'This is that rare thing a learned work in which a scholar of the first rank transcends scholarship and writes a book of general significance.'

Repr. *MGW*. 58, 17. 22 Apr. p 11

G288. *48 : The Year of Revolution*, Paul Tabori and James Eastwood, Meridian, *MG*. 9 Apr. p 3

(1) Praises it as good historical journalism, but regrets that it 'lacks . . . any attempt to penetrate to the deeper significance of the revolutions'.

Repr. *MGW*. 58, 17. 22 Apr. p 11

G289. Munich Examined, Mr. Wheeler-Bennett's History, *Munich: Prologue to Tragedy*, J.W. Wheeler-Bennett, Macmillan, *MG*. 15 May. p 4

(1) 'A work of scholarship and of controversy, a reconstruction of the diplomatic details, and an advocacy of collective security'.

(2) 'If after 1936 there ever was a chance of stopping Hitler without war Munich was the moment; but perhaps there was no such moment.' The failure to bring Russia 'back into the system of European order' was 'the ineffaceable sin, before their own people and before posterity, of the men of Munich'.

G290. French Diplomacy in 1939, 1 – Between Poland and Russia; 2 – M. Bonnet and the Crisis, *Fin d'une Europe*, Georges Bonnet, Geneva, Bibliothéque du Cheval Ailé, 1 – *MG*. 19 Jun. p 4; 2 – *MG*. 23 Jun. p 4

(1) Provides 'the most valuable evidence on French policy so far published'. It will not change the views of those who saw him as 'a sinister figure, deliberately promoting appeasement'.

Repr. 1 – *MGW*. 58, 26. 24 Jun. p 13; 2 – *MGW*. 59, 1. 1 Jul. p 12 and in A5, pp 138–43 and A17, pp 252–8

G291. *BD*, 2nd Ser., 2, *1931*, *TLS*. 2420. 19 Jun. p 339

(1) It does not add much to knowledge of the period.

(2) On the basis of these documents 'it would not be possible . . . to credit the British Government with a policy. It exuded good will and hoped that every one would behave sensibly if it displayed enough belief in their so doing.'

G292. A German Prince, *The Great Elector*, Ferdinand

Schevill, Cambridge U.P., *TLS*. 2429. 21 Aug. p 473

(1) Much solid research – but tainted with the Whig interpretation of history.

(2) Observes that 'Frederick William can claim to be the originator of the Prussian army, with all its historical consequences'.

G293. The Groundwork of History, *BD*, 2nd Ser., 2, *1919*, *TLS*. 2431. 4 Sept. p 495

(1) Praises the editorial work but doubts if the series is meeting its objectives. The reader 'has frequent cause to suspect that he is getting all the crumbs from the cake, and hardly any of the plums'.

(2) In discussing Lloyd George and Clemenceau and Fiume he comments on 'the British liberal with his inherent belief that all that is required for the solution of difficulty is to bring men of good will together to discuss it, and the hard-headed French radical who understands revolutions by experience and knows that in the end it is the guns that talk'.

G294. *Napoleon's Memoirs*, ed. Somerset de Chair, Faber, *NS & N*. 37, 916. 25 Sept. p 263

(1) Dull and boring. They were written for effect – 'to launch a legend'.

The review was criticised by G. Bernard Shaw in a lengthy letter, *ibid*. 918. 9 Oct. p 304, in which he accused him, like H.G. Wells in his *Outline of History*, of failing to understand Napoleon. 'People who believe that a nobody such as Mr. Taylor has described could have achieved Napoleon's fame can believe anything.'

A.J.P.T. replied, *ibid*. 919. 16 Oct. p 326. 'The real catastrophe was for the French people to have fallen into the hands of a genius. Without Napoleon there would have been no Napoleonic Empire; all the same, without Napoleon, France would probably have kept her natural frontiers and remained the greatest Power in Europe. As it was, Napoleon started France on her way downhill. For my part, I find the historic truth in the Emperor of Turania rather than in the Man of Destiny.'

Repr. as 'Napoleon on Himself' in A5, pp 13–18, A15, pp 1–6 and A17, pp 11–16

G295. Talleyrand, *Talleyrand*, Louis Madelin, Rolls, *MG*. 1 Oct. p 3

(1) Easy to read, but 'as a work of history this volume has little to recommend it'.

Repr. *MGW*. 59, 15. 7 Oct. p 11

G296. The Beginnings of Vichy, *The Private Diaries of Paul Baudouin :*, trans. Sir Charles Petrie, Eyre and Spottiswoode, *MG*. 5 Oct. p 3

(1) Useful but not very interesting, 'a story of muddle and feebleness'.

Repr. *MGW*. 59, 17. 21 Oct. p 11

G297. 'Forty-Eight, *A Hundred Years of Revolution*, ed. George Woodcock, Porcupine Press, *MG*. 19 Oct. p 3

(1) Part essays, part anthology, the volume lacks direction and explanation.

Repr. *MGW*. 59, 18. 28 Oct. p 10

G298. The Austrian Illusion, *The Tragedy of Austria*, Julius Braunthal, Gollancz, *NS & N*. 36, 920. 23 Oct. p 352

(1) Unfavourable. Observes of Michael Foot, who wrote the introduction, 'Though he commends the book he does not seem to have read it and has certainly not understood it.'

(2) Observes that between the Wars British Socialists had a romantic attachment to 'Red Vienna'. 'In fact democratic Austria was the demonstration piece that neither democracy nor Socialism can succeed in a country mainly inhabited by peasants.' Denounces 'the myth' of Austrian particularism.

See also A5, pp 176–8

G299. La Fin de la IIIe Republique, (a) *Servir*, Vol. 3 (*see above* G283); (b) *La France a sauvé l'Europe*, (*see above* G276); (c) *Montoire : Verdun diplomatique*, Louis-Dominique Girard, Paris, Bonne; (d) *Laval Parle*, ed. Pierre Laval, Geneve, A l'Enseigne du

Cheval Ailé, 1947, *Crit.* 3, 4. 29 Oct. pp 920–30

(a1) His autobiography does not explain the events in which he was involved, but it does reveal his character – 'precise, honourable, conciliatory, and above all, zeal in editing reports'.

(b1) The volumes lack plan or proportion; they are the work of an intelligent man who has not understood the realities of political life or how to write well.

(c1) A defence of Petain's role, in which the author condemns England for betraying France and attempts to argue that Petain always worked for the defeat of Germany. A.J.P.T. finds the arguments absurd, indeed offensive, in view of the millions of British and Russian dead.

(d1) In comparison the defence of Laval is more honest and convincing.

(d2) Laval was the Talleyrand of our time, a cynical politician who faced up to reality and made the best of the situation.

G300. Vanished Worlds, Memoirs of Cordell Hull, *The Memoirs of Cordell Hull*, 2 Vols. Hodder and Stoughton, *MG.* 8 Nov. p 4

(1) Complacent, assertive and verbose.

Repr. *MGW.* 59, 21. 18 Nov. p 12 and A5, pp 172–5

G301. Hitler at Sea, *Hitler and His Admirals*, Anthony Martienssen, Secker and Warburg, *NS & N.* 36, 923. 13 Nov. pp 424–5

(1) Favourable – it 'exploits fully the German sources'.

(2) 'Germany lost both German wars by failing to devote everything to U-boat construction. Hitler, being a strategist of genius, arrived at this conclusion in 1943; by then, it was too late.'

G302. Espionage, *The Silent Company*, Remy (pseud. G.L.E.T. Renault-Roulier), Barker, *MG.* 26 Nov. p 3

(1) 'The work of an extremely intelligent man, quick-witted, observant, and with a sense of

humour . . . ' Reminds one that 'until the mass deportations to Germany, the great majority of Frenchmen supported Petain and were indifferent to De Gaulle'.

Repr. *MGW*. 59, 25. 16 Dec. p 11

G303. *Recollections*, Alexis de Tocqueville, ed. J.P. Mayer, Harvill, *NS & N*. 36, 925. 27 Nov. p 465

(1) 'The best book about a revolution ever written by a contemporary'.

(2) 'He who loves liberty must have faith in the people. Otherwise he will . . . withdraw from public life and despair of the future.'

Repr. as 'De Tocqueville in 1848' in A5, pp 61–6, A 15, pp 54–9 and A17, pp 40–5

G304. The Ruler in Berlin, *Das Persönliche Regiment Wilhelms II*, Erich Eyck, Erlenbach-Zwich, Rentsch, *TLS*. 2445. 11 Dec. pp 689–90

(1) The book is through and accurate, but it is out of proportion for it devotes too much space to foreign policy at the expense of domestic history' which should have dominated the book'.

(2) 'The fault of William was his failure to rule, not that he ruled wrongly.'

Repr. in A5, pp 75–82, A15, pp 103–10, A 17, pp 159–66 and *Majority 1931–1952: An Anthology of 21 Years of Publishing*, Hamish Hamilton, 1952, pp 479–86

G305. Jackal Diplomacy, Ciano and Italian Foreign Policy, *Ciano's Diplomatic Papers*, ed. Malcolm Muggeridge, Odhams, *MG*. 16 Dec. p 4

(1) More formal and less entertaining than his diaries; particularly valuable on the pre-war period.

Repr. *MGW*. 59, 26. 23 Dec. p 11 and A5, pp 157–60

1949

G306. Variegated Biography, (a) *Four English Portraits 1800–1851*, Richard Aldington, Evans Brothers, 1948; (b) *Four Favourites*, D.B. Wyndham Lewis, Evans Brothers, 1948; (c) *Lady Anne Barnard*,

Madeleine Mason, Allen and Unwin, 1948, *MG.* 4 Jan. p 3

(a1) Delightful essays on figure of rich colour and pronounced character.

(b1) Enjoyable essays on royal figures.

(c1) Well written – but it is too serious, 'always a mistake except in the greatest of the biographies. After all human life is a preposterous affair'.

Repr. *MGW.* 60, 3. 20 Jan. p 11

G307. Dr. Schacht's Defence, The Defects of Cleverness, *Abrechnung mit Hitler*, Dr. Hjalmar Schacht, Hamburg, Rowohlt, 1948, *MG.* 7 Jan. p 4

(1) A defence but not an apology.

Repr. *MGW.* 60, 2. 13 Jan. p 11 and in A5, pp 153–6

G308. Bismarck, *Bismarck and the Creation of the Second Reich*, F. Darmstaedtler, Methuen, 1948, *MG.* 14 Jan. p 3

(1) Sound in its scholarship and sensible in its judgments but almost unreadable as it is a word-for-word transcription from the German.

G309. Mirabeau, *Mirabeau*, Antonia Vallentin, Hamilton, 1948, *MG.* 21 Jan. p 3

(1) A thorough and imaginative biography – but it leaves many questions unanswered.

(2) 'No figure expressed more completely the confusion and decay of the old order.'

G310. *The Volunteer Earl*, Maurice J. Craig, Cresset, 1948, *MG.* 28 Jan. p 3

(1) An admirable life of the Earl of Charlemont.

G311. Problèms De Quarante-Huit, (a) *Le Livre du Centenaire*, ed. Charles Moulin, Paris, Atlas, 1947; (b) *1848 dans le Monde*, 2 Vols. ed. Francois Fejto, Paris, Ed. de Minuit, 1948, *Crit.* 4, 5, 32. Jan. pp 40–46

(a1) Its excessive concentration on France gives a false picture of even French events as these were bound up with foreign developments.

(b1) Praises many of the essays. Very critical of the three Marxist essays which he sees as propaganda, displacing honesty and scientific enquiry for automatic phrases recited in the manner of the medieval church.

G312. *Das Persönliche Regiment Wilhelms II* (*see above* p304), *EHR*. 64, 250. Jan. pp 115–7

(1) Praises it, but observes that 'the proportions of the book are determined by the printed material, not the historical needs . . . He has produced a very useful narrative, and there are many who think that this exhausts the historian's duty. To my mind the historian must also analyse, interpret and explain. In doing this he runs the risk (indeed the certainty) of making mistakes . . .'

G313. Historians of Napoleon, *Napoleon For and Against*, Pieter Geyl, Cape, *MG*. 1 Feb. p 3

(1) 'An original contribution to historical understanding and . . . a discussion of profound moral questions.' The very varied attitudes to Napoleon 'is a warning against believing that 'history', as distinct from any individual historian offers any verdict or conclusion'.

Repr. *MGW*. 60, 6. 10 Feb. p 12

G314. Jewish History, *The House of Nasi*, Cecil Roth, Philadelphia, Jewish Historical Society of America, 1948, *MG*. 11 Feb. p 3

(1) A fascinating piece of Jewish history.

Repr. *MGW*. 60, 7. 17 Feb. p 12

G315. Vox Et . . . ? *Mirabeau* (*see above* G309), *NS & N*. 37, 936. 12 Feb. pp 161–2

(1) Less favourable than in the earlier review!

G316. On the Munich Road, British Foreign Policy 1938, *BD*, 3rd Ser., 1, *1938*, *MG*. 16 Feb. p 4

(1) As full an account of the background to Munich as can be given without the Cabinet or Chamberlain's Papers.

(2) It explodes the myth that Munich was 'an unexpected accident'. It 'represented the victory of the policy which the British Government had pursued consciously and persistently since the

German annexation of Austria in March'.

Repr. *MGW*. 60, 8. 24 Feb. p 11

G317. *Napoleon For and Against* (*see above* G313), *NS & N*. 37, 938. 26 Feb. p 207

(1) 'It is rare to find a work of history which is interesting, let alone exciting. This book is vastly more, an infinite consolation to the professional historian: it shows that history is a subject which can provoke thought . . . (It) enables the historian to look the philosopher in the face without cringing for quite a week.'

Repr. as 'Napoleon: The Verdict of History' in A5, pp 18–23, A15, pp 6–11 and A17, pp 16–21

G318. Soviet Foreign Policy, *The Foreign Policy of Soviet Russia*, Vol. 2, Max Beloff, Oxford U.P., *NS & N*. 37943. 2 Apr. pp 330–1

(1) Criticises the Chatham House formula, which involves 'an impartial approach, a colourless tone and a factual account . . . The tedious productions of Chatham House rest on the assumption that the public utterances of governments are valuable historical material.'

(2) 'The Soviet rulers have an unrivalled legal ingenuity, with which they put others in the wrong; but they have also an unrivalled capacity for arousing distrust in others . . . The public record of Soviet diplomacy reveals little except these two characteristics.'

G319. *Studies in German History*, G.P. Gooch, Longmans, *MG*. 12 Apr. p 3

(1) The author 'has a method all his own of summarising the writings of others and linking his quotations with a colourless narrative'. Suggests he exaggerates the importance of Holstein.

G320. Foreign Policy, *The Management of British Foreign Policy before the First World War*, F. Gosses, Leiden, A.W. Uitgeversmaatschappij, *MG*. 14 Apr. p 3

(1) An able and stimulating essay.

Repr. *MGW*. 60, 16. 21 Apr. p 11

G321. The Earnest Age, *Ideas and Beliefs of the Victorians*, (BBC), Sylvan, *NS & N*. 37, 945. 16 Apr. p 383

(1) Very critical of these brief essays. Suggests that those included qualify because 'they were prigs, earnest about everything and especially about themselves'.

G322. The Spirit of Vichy, (a) *Le Temps Des Illusions*, H. Du Moulin De Labarthête, Paris, La Diffusion Du Livre; (b) *Montoire: Verdun Diplomatique* (*see above* G299), *TLS*. 2464. 23 Apr. p 269

(a1) An attempt to recapture the spirit of Vichy – 'a work of great truth and also of the greatest literary charm'.

(a2) 'In retrospect Laval appears to have been no more than the most pro-German of the *attentistes*. Moreover, he alone, in the twilight world of Vichy, was without illusions, and did not waste his time in futile plans of 'national regeneration'. He was the man of practical expedients, shrinking from nothing if it would lessen, however slightly, the burden of occupation . . . '

(b1) 'A pugnacious defence of Petain, ludicrous in its claims and nonsensical in its assertions'.

(b2) 'Vichy and Gaullism both lived on echoes . . . Both had little relevance to the present'.

G323. The Axis, *The Rome-Berlin Axis*, Elizabeth Wiskemann, Oxford U.P., *MG*. 3 May. p 4

(1) 'A book of painstaking scholarship'. Though he feels that she exculpates the Italians too readily for their role in the Axis.

Repr. *MGW*. 60, 19. 12 May. p 10

G324. Liberalism, *Liberalism and the Challenge of Fascism*, J. Salwyn Schapiro, McGraw Hill, *MG*. 13 May. p 4

(1) It has many acute observations – but is inconclusive and generally disappointing.

G325. *The Rome-Berlin Axis* (*see above* G323), *NS & N*. 37, 949. 14 May. p 504

(1) Praises it but suggests that she does not

sufficiently recognise that Mussolini was limited in his actions by Italy's economic weakness. 'Coal is the most important index of power.'

Repr. as 'The Supermen: Hitler and Mussolini' in A5, pp 161–6, A17, pp 220–4 and *Majority 1931–1952: An Anthology of 21 Years of Publishing*, Hamish Hamilton, 1952, pp 487–90

G326. *Napoleon at St. Helena*, Frederic Masson, Oxford, Pen-in-Hand, *MG*. 24 May. p 4

(1) 'A work of great energy and scholarship, inspired by the wildest hero-worship for Napoleon'.

G327. Feudal Rights and Public Freedom, *Magna Carta: Its Role in the Making of the English Constitution 1300–1629*, Faith Thompson, Minnesota U.P., *NR*. 120, 22. 30 May. pp 16–17

(1) Praises her approach to history.

(2) Calls for Britain and America 'to maintain their standards of impartial justice and not pervert their inheritance of liberty into the defense of conservatism and privilege'.

G328. Political Manager, *The Jenkinson Papers 1760–1766*, ed. Ninetta Jucker, Macmillan, *MG*. 14 Jun. p 4

(1) An indispensable book for understanding the political system of the early part of the reign of George III.

Repr. *MGW*. 60, 25. 23 Jun. p 11

G329. *Contemporary History*, F.W. Pick, Oxford, Pen-in-Hand, *MG*. 15 Jun. p 3

(1) Written with much learning but little sparkle.

G330. *Black Liberator*, Stephen Alexis, Benn, *MG*. 17 Jun. p 4

(1) 'An admirable biography of Toussaint Louverture'.

G331. The Intellectual, *Benjamin Constant*, Harold Nicolson, Constable, *MG*. 21 Jun. p 4

(1) An admirable biography – 'the true portrait of a man in which every intellectual will catch a reflection of himself'.

See also Appendix

Repr. *MGW*. 60, 26. 30 Jun. p 11

G332. A Revision of History, *The Coming of the First World War 1878–1914*, Nicholas Mansergh, Longmans, *MG.* 24 Jun. p 4

(1) A book redeemed by the novelty of approach. Praises the author for revolting against 'the old picture of a meaningless drift of events, in which nothing can be found to be condemned except the sovereignty of States'.

Repr. *MGW.* 61, 2. 14 Jul. p 11

G333. Unreality Between the Wars, *Documentary Background of World War II 1931–1941*, ed. J.W. Gantenbein, Columbia U.P.; Cumberlege, *TLS.* 2473. 24 Jun. p 415

(1) The documents display 'the absence of all thought, the repetition of empty phrases, the endless vanity of those in public places'.

(2) 'The inter-war period had an unreality all of its own . . . Between the wars men spoke for the record, not to persuade.'

G334. The Balance of Power, *The Coming of the First World War 1878–1914* (*see above* G332), *NS & N.* 38, 958. 16 Jul. pp 74–5

(2) 'The real theme of the generation before 1914 is the loss of the Balance of Power and the attempt to recover it.' Compares the world position of the USA to that of Germany before 1914 and implies that Britain should switch her allegiance to the second most powerful nation to maintain the Balance of Power.

G335. *Studies in German History* (*see above* G319), *EHR.* 64, 252. pp 404–5

G336. *The Concept of Empire in German Romanticism and its Influence on the National Assembly at Frankfurt 1848–1849*, Ulrich Stephen Allers, Washington, Catholic University of America, 1948, *Ibid.* pp 410–11

(1) Useful, but criticises the author's style.

(2) 'The Reich . . . had a universalist, almost mystical element and gave a special, arrogant character to the claims of German nationalism.'

G337. Singing History, *The Spirit of Revolution in 1789*, Cornwell B. Rogers, Princeton U.P.; Cumberlege, *NS & N*. 38, 961. 6 Aug. p 151

(1) Critical of the author's style and approach, but finds some interesting points in this study of French popular songs of 1789.

(2) 'My taste in history is old fashioned and orthodox. I like narrative based on documents: no guesses, no psychological jargon, no attempt to turn history into anthropology.'

G338. German Policy 1937–1938, *GD*, Ser. D., 1, *1937–1938*, Part 1: The Last Days of Neurath, *MG*. 19 Aug. p 4; Part II Austria and After, *MG*. 22 Aug. p 4

(1) Criticises the way the editors have organised the documents.

Part 1 (2) 'The German Foreign Office under Hitler was a subordinate department, performing technical duties rather than deciding policy ... Hitler hardly appears ... he provides the noises off, as in a Greek tragedy.'

'German policy ... aimed to undo the settlement of Versailles without a general war.'

Part II (2) 'The Austrian affair was a striking illustration of violence brought on by muddle.' 'Before the Austrian affair and the appointment of Ribbentrop appeasement had some plausibility. ... After March 1938, it had no chance of success.'

Repr. Part 1: *MGW*. 61, 8. 25 Aug. p 10; Part II: *MGW*. 61, 9. 1 Sept. p 10

G339. *Les Iles Britanniques et la Révolution francaise 1789–1803*, Jules Dechamps, Brussels, La Renaissance du Livre, *MG*. 30. Aug. p 3

(1) Criticises it for seeing no more than anti-Jacobinism in British opposition to Napoleon, and points to the issue of the liberties of small nations.

G340. Historians of the Revolution, (a) *Actes du Congrès Historique du Centenairé de la Revolution de 1848*, Paris, Presses Universitaires de France; (b) *Soziale und Politische Geschichte der Revolution von 1848*,

Rudolf Stadelmann, Munich, Münchner, *TLS*. 2483. 2 Sept. p 566

(a1) Praises the 'dazzling performances by M. Morazé and Professor Labrousse' and observes of other contributions, 'Good Marxist historians are stimulating; bad Marxist historians are funny.'

(b1) 'An admirable little book', a genuinely liberal account, which understands the social question but fails 'when it approaches the question of power and of foreign policy'.

G341. A History of France, *France 1814–1940*, J.P.T. Bury, Methuen, *MG*. 6 Sept. p 4

(1) 'A sound text-book chronicle'.

(2) 'History is a great art, not merely something for school children; and, to adapt a phrase, accuracy is not enough.'

G342. How Germany Lost the War, A German General on Hitler, *Hitler als Feldherr*, Franz Halder, Munich, Münchner, *Ibid*. p 6

(1) The pamphlet ought to end the legend of Hitler as the great war leader, but 'in condemning Hitler, Halder condemns himself still more'.

Repr. as 'Halder on Hitler', *MGW*. 61, 11. 15 Sept. p 11

G343. He's A Born Traveller, *Eastern Approaches*, Fitzroy MacLean, Cape, *News Chronicle*. 10 Sept. p 2

(1) The author 'is very good reading when he is on his travels; less interesting when he arrives'.

(2) Praises Churchill for supporting in Yugoslavia whoever would be most effective in fighting the Germans; but regrets the failure to remain on good terms with Yugoslavia after the war.

G344. British Foreign Policy 1938, *BD*, 3rd Ser., 2, *1938*, Part 1: The Runciman Mission, *MG*. 13 Sept. 6, 8; Part 2: Berchtesgaden to Godesberg, *MG*. 14 Sept. p 6; Part 3: The Week Before Munich, *MG*. 15 Sept. p 4

Repr. Part 1: *MGW*. 61, 12. 22 Sept. p 11; Part 2: *MGW*. 61, 13. 29 Sept. p 11; Part 3: *MGW*. 61, 14. 6 Oct. p 11 and the three repr. as 'Full Speed to Munich' in A6, pp 184–93 and A17, pp 239–48

G345. Bee in Bonnet, *Alexander I of Russia*, Leonid I. Strakhovsky, Williams and Norgate, *NS & N*. 38, 968. 24 Sept. p 339

(1) Suggests it should have the subtitle 'The man who did not die at Taganrog', as it deals with Alexander's supposed existence from 1825–64 as a holy man.

(2) 'Alexander I is the most interesting, though not the greatest of Tsars ... He was the only liberal at the Congress of Vienna, but also the most ruthless and unscrupulous diplomat.'

G346. The Liberal Creed, *Liberalism and the Challenge of Fascism* (*see above* G324), *TLS*. 2489. 14 Oct. p 660

(1) An admirable analysis of liberalism in Britain and France 1815–70 but very weak on fascism.

G347. More Light on Munich *BD*, 3rd Ser., 2, *1938* (*see above* G344), *NS & N*. 38, 971. 15 Oct. p 428

(1) These documents 'give us some, though not all, the truth about British policy at the time of Munich'.

(2) They show 'that thc humdrum explanations were on the whole right and the melodramatic explanations on the whole wrong'. The British ministers 'were the survivors of a generation which had been brought up to believe that all the troubles of Europe would be ended if the frontiers were redrawn on national lines'.

G348. Ambassador, *The Fateful Years*, A. Francois-Poncet, Gollancz, *MG*. 21 Oct. p 4

(1) 'Nothing of value to the student of history'.

G349. *Soziale und Politische Geschichte der Revolution von 1848* (*see above* G340), *EHR*. 64, 253. Oct. pp 528–30

(1) Praises it highly – and prefers the author's view, to Namier's, on the importance of the desire for a strong national authority.

G350. *Noble Landowners and Agriculture in Austria 1815–48*, Jerome Blum, John Hopkins U.P.; Cumberlege, *Ibid.* pp 559–60

(1) 'A useful contribution to the background of the revolutions of 1848' but suggests he exaggerates the capitalist mentality of landowners.

G351. *La Rivoluzione Europea 1848–9*, Luigi Salvatorelli, Milan, Rizzoli, Ibid. p 561

(1) With reservations, finds it a useful introduction to the subject.

G352. *Aus Österreichs Vergangenheit*, Heinrich von Srbik, Salzburg, Muller, *Ibid.* p 563

(1) Praises some of the essays but observes that the author 'displays his usual failing of making many bricks with a very small allowance of straw'.

G353. *Deutschland und Westeuropa*, Rudolf Stadelman, Württemberg, Steiner, 1948, *Ibid.* pp 566–7

(1) Praises the essay on Tirpitz which shows that in Tirpitz's view 'the German navy was never an instrument of policy, but was policy itself'.

G354. Quelques Livres sur Vichy et la Résistance, (a) *Private Diary*, Paul Baudouin, Eyre and Spottiswoode, 1948; (b) *The Role of General Weygand*, Eyre and Spottiswoode, 1948; (c) *Laval parle*, Paris, La Diffusion du livre (*see above* G299); (d) *La Délégation francaise auprès de la Commission allemande de l'Armistice*, Paris, Imprimerie nationale; (e) *Le jeu american á Vichy*, W.L. Langer, Paris, Plon, 1948; (f) *The Republic of Silence*, A.J. Liebling, New York, Harcourt and Brace, 1947; (g) *Suite francaise*, Chamine, Albin Michel, 1946; (h) *Souvenirs*, 2 Vols. Colonel Passy, Paris, Raoul Solar, 1947, *Rev. His.* 73, 202. Oct-Dec. pp 232–7

(a1) An interesting and useful book, but it needs to be used with caution.

(b1) A defence of Weygand, which is neither satisfactory nor of value to the historian.

(c1) It is unsatisfactory because the author did not understand the problems which faced him.

(d1) The most useful source on the early days of Vichy.

(e1) Though based on the American archives it is a work of propaganda not history.

(f1) A sentimental collection of material on the resistance, which contains nothing of interest for the historian.

(g1) Written in an extravagant style; it gives the impression of being a work of fiction rather than a contribution to history.

(h1) Without doubt the most important account of the Gaullist movement in London during the war.

G355. A Revolution That Failed, *George III, Lord North and the People 1779–1780*, H. Butterfield, Bell, *NS & N.* 38, 975. 12 Nov. pp 556, 558

(1) 'An admirable piece of research', but spoilt by repetition and vagueness as to the meaning of 'party' and 'people' in this period.

G356. 1938, A German Version, *GD*, Ser. D., 2, *1937–8*, Part 1: The German Appeasers, *MG.* 15 Nov. pp 6, 8; Part II: The Triumph of Hitler, *MG.* 16 Nov. p 4

(1) It deals with German relations with Czechoslovakia – but only insofar as these were known to the German Foreign Office, which 'was often remote from the point of decision'.

Repr. Part 1: *MGW.* 61, 21. 24 Nov. p 13; Part II: *MGW.* 61, 23. 8 Dec. p 13

G357. Appeasement: German Version, *GD*, Ser. D., 1, *1937–8* (*see above* G356), *NS & N.* 38, 980. 17 Dec. p 730

(1) The editors are more impartial than Thimme was on pre – 1914 German policy.

(2) The Hossbach memorandum does not provide evidence that Hitler 'had any concrete projects'. The volume 'does not provide the evidence that there was a German, or even a Nazi conspiracy against peace, if by conspiracy it meant a coherent objective plan. It provides the evidence that the Germans, and especially the German governing class allowed a criminal lunatic to establish himself in supreme power; and that they were abetted by those in England and France who, from feebleness

or fear of Communism, treated the lunatic as a sane man.'

G358. The Stick and the Carrot, *Memoirs 1942–1943*, Benito Mussolini Weidenfeld and Nicolson, *NS & N.* 38, 982. 31 Dec. pp 784–5

(1) Comments that they are really newspaper articles written in 1944; and observes, having compared them with Napoleon's writings, 'Obviously it is easier to be a dictator than a good writer.'

1950

G359. Dragons' teeth, *BD*, 1st Ser., 3, *1919*, *NS & N.* 39, 984. 14 Jan. pp 42–3

(1) Welcomes the addition of Foreign Secretary's minutes to the material included in these volumes. The theme of the volume is the failure to find a policy for Russia.

G360. The End of Czech Freedom, (a) *Czechoslovakia Enslaved*, Hubert Ripka, Gollancz; (b) *East Wind Over Prague*, Jan Stransky, Hillis and Carter, *MG.* 27 Jan. p 4

(a1) His book shows that co-operation with the Communists is impossible – but it does not show that the *coup* was premeditated by the Communists.

(a2) '... the course of Benes was determined by his resolve that if a people was to be sent to destruction in order to save the world from Hitler or the Communists it should not be the Czechs'.

Repr. as 'The Czech Communist Coup', *MGW.* 62, 5. 2 Feb. p 12

G361. *The Emancipation of the Austrian Peasant 1740–1798*, Edith Murr Link, Columbia U.P.; Cumberlege, 1949, *EHR.* 65, 254. Jan. p 139

(1) Adds nothing of value to earlier books.

G362. *Les Politiques d'Expansion Impérialiste*, ed. P. Renouvin, Paris, Presses Universitaires de France, 1949, *Ibid.* p 141

(1) Praises the five sketches of imperialist statesmen but feels that the one on Joseph Chamberlain lacks caution.

G363. *Austria from Habsburg to Hitler*, 2 Vols. Charles A. Gulick, California U.P., 1948, *Ibid.* p 143

(1) Useful information in it but it is too long and often presents issues in black and white terms.

G364. The Innocent Banker, *Account Settled*, Hjamar Schacht, Weidenfeld and Nicolson (*see above* G307), *NS & N.* 39, 987. 4 Feb. p 135

(1) 'His writing is banal and his thought even more so.'

(2) 'The ruling classes of Germany – military, legal, financial, clerical – accepted Hitler and the Nazis in a way that would have been impossible in any other civilised country.'

G365. After Algeciras, *FD*, 2nd Ser., 10, *1906–7*, *TLS.* 2506. 10 Feb. p 83

(1) Praises the French editors' system of presenting the documents.

(2) 'The Anglo-Russian *entente*, far from being directed against Germany, aimed solely at stablising European relations on a peaceful basis.' 'Far from encircling Germany, French policy was fully strained merely to keep a balance in Europe; and the object of French policy was security, not *revanche*.'

G366. Peter the Great, *Peter the Great and the Ottoman Empire*, B.H. Sumner, Oxford, Blackwell, *MG.* 14 Feb. p 4

(1) Invaluable for the student, but too dry and technical for the general reader.

G367. The Spirit of Switzerland, *Switzerland*, André Siegfried, Cape, *TLS.* 2509. 3 Mar. p 139

(1) 'A model of exposition'.

(2) Switzerland is a 'practical realisation of everything radicals dreamed of in 1848 . . . a civilised world in which we could all live if only we were more sensible'.

G368. Diplomatic Supplement, *Europe in Decay*, L.B. Namier, Macmillan, *MG.* 7 Mar. p 4

(1) A collection of reviews and essays which update his *Diplomatic Prelude*. Wishes he concentrated his energies on at last publishing his Ford

lectures.

Repr. *MGW*. 62, 11. 16 Mar. p 12

G369. Eighty Years of Europe, *The European World 1870–1945*, T. K. Derry and T.L. Jarman, Bell, *TLS*. 2510. 10 Mar. p 151

(1) A textbook 'slightly above the usual level', though it is relatively weak on the internal history of the countries.

G370. Panic Refurbished, *Conservatism Revisited*, Peter Viereck, Lehmann, *NS & N*. 39, 992. 11 Mar. pp 278, 280.

(1) An able but implausible defence of conservatisms of Metternich and Burke.

(2) The conservatives of the past and present 'believe in the incantation of civilised values to keep the masses quiet; and if that does not work, they believe – as Metternich's career shows – in repression'.

G371. A Tory History of England, *A History of England*, Keith Feiling, Macmillan, *MG*. 11 Apr. p 4

(1) 'The most formidable and successful since Dr. Trevelyan.' 'Though probably not a great book, this is a very honest one.' It is 'Tory history, a history . . . for squires and imperial administrators.'

Repr. as 'A Tory History of England', *MGW*. 62, 16. 20 Apr. p 12

G372. Munich Once More, *GD*, Ser. D., 2, *1937–8* (*see above* G356), *NS & N*. 39, 997. 15 Apr. p 434, 436

(2) The old style diplomatists 'meant to establish Germany as the dominant power of Europe; and they would have done it except for Hitler's pursuit of theatrical violence. We should therefore be very grateful that Hitler broke loose in 1938.'

G373. France in Defeat, More Vichy Memoirs, (a) *Le Drame de Vichy*, Vol. 1, Yves Bouthillier, Paris, Plon; (b) *Mémoires*, General Weygand, Paris, Flammarion, *MG*. 19 Apr. p 6

(1) 'The great blunder of Vichy was to fail to understand when it had outlived its usefulness.'

Repr. *MGW*. 62, 17. 27 Apr. p 11 and in A6, pp 220–2 and A17, pp 295–8

G374. The German Problem, *Germany: What Now?* Basil Davidson, Muller, *NS & N*. 39, 999. 29 Apr. pp 489–90

(1) Superficial in its judgements.

(2) 'If we could solve the German problem, we should have no worries in Europe . . . does anyone really think that the Germans are any more willing to fit in with the rest of Europe than they were in 1933 or 1940?'

G375. *Francis the Good*, Walter C. Langsam, New York, Macmillan, 1949, *EHR*. 65, 255. Apr. pp 283–4

(1) 'Solidly based on original authorities, sober and unpretentious in style'.

G376. *La Confederazione Danubana nel Pennero degli Italiani ed Ungheresi nel Risorgimento*, Lajos Pasztor, Rome, the author, 1949, *Ibid.* p 285

(1) The author has 'made the most of the subject'.

G377. *The Ideology of French Imperialism 1871–1881*, Agnes Murphy, Washington, Catholic University of America Press, 1949, *Ibid.* pp 286–7

(1) 'A useful contribution', though 'rather pedestrian'.

G378. *A History of England* (*see above* G371), *NS & N*. 39, 1000. 6 May. pp 517–8

Repr. as 'Tory History' in A6, pp 14–18 and A21, pp 17–22

G379. The Dedicated Historian: Leopold Von Ranke's Correspondence. On the occasion of the publication of (a) *Das Briefwerk*, ed. Walther Peter Fuchs, Hamburg, Hoffman and Campe; (b) *Neue Briefe*, ed. Hans Herzfeld, Hamburg, Hoffman und Campe, *TLS*. 2519. 12 May. pp 285–6

(1) The essay concludes with an assertion of the historian or scientist's duty to take a moral role in public affairs. Of Ranke's attitude: 'The State

could never sin; and if it did, this was not his affair. This was the spirit of the learned classes in Germany which brought Hitler to power.'

The essay set off controversy in the *TLS*, with Noel Annan asserting that Ranke 'was not a positivist but a moderate Hegelian' (*Ibid.* 2521. 26 May. p 325) and A.J.P.T. replying, restating his views, as above (*Ibid.* 2522. 2 Jun. p 341). There were also letters by G.P. Gooch (*Ibid.*), Pieter Geyl and Howard Brogan (*Ibid.* 2525. 23 Jun. p 389). Geyl also discussed part of this essay in his article 'Ranke in the Light of Catastrophe', repr. in his *Debates With Historians*, Fontana/Collins, 1962 (*see* 21ff).

Repr. as 'Ranke' in A9, pp 12–18 and A17, pp 113–20

G380. Political Dynasties, *Pitt v. Fox: Father and Son*, Erich Eyck, Bell, *NS & N.* 1005. 10 Jun. p 661

(1) Praises Eyck's 'high ability to reduce an enormous subject to manageable proportions'.

(2) 'Was lasting peace any more possible with Napoleon than with Hitler?'

G381. Rational Marxism, *Studies in Revolution*, E.H. Carr, Macmillan, *MG.* 13 Jun. p 4

(1) The collection of essays 'demonstrates afresh the advantages and the defects, of Mr. Carr's philosophic approach'. 'There is no moral condemnation of communism; and no suggestion that the failure of communism may be due to the moral revolt of mankind, not to the blunders in tactics.'

(2) 'To write about evil with detachment is to be on the side of evil.'

Repr. *MGW.* 62, 25. 22 Jun. p 12

G382. America's War, The Record of Admiral Leahy, *I Was There*, W.D. Leahy, Gollancz, *MG.* 22 Jun. p 6

(1) Tedious, but provides 'a striking impression' of America's emergence from Isolation in the Second World War.

Repr. *MGW.* 62, 26. 29 Jun. p 11 and in A6, pp 229–31 and A17, pp 316–9

G383. Reflections on Germany, *The German Catastrophe*,

Friedrich Meinecke, Harvard U.P.; Cumberlege, *MG.* 27 Jun. p 4

(1) 'The most revealing book to come out of Germany since the war', a condemnation of the governing classes in Germany; yet it argues Hitler owed his success to chance.

Repr. as 'Germany', *MGW.* 63, 1. 6 Jul. p 12

G384. The Bunker Revisited, *The Last Days of Hitler*, 2nd edn. H.R. Trevor Roper, Macmillan, *NS & N.* 40, 1009. 8 Jul. p 44

(1) Praises the new introduction which explains the methods of research. 'This is an incomparable book, by far the best book written on any aspect of the second German war; a book sound in its scholarship, brilliant in its presentation, a delight for history and layman alike. No words of praise are too strong for it.'

G385. Augustan Figures, *Pitt v. Fox* (*see above* G380) *MG.* 11 Jul. p 4

(1) Praises it as reliable in its facts and stimulating in its judgments but observes that 'the conflict of families can be overdone'.

G386. Documents, *BD*, 2nd Ser., 4, *1932–3*, *MG.* 14 Jul. p 4

(1) Includes interesting reports from Berlin. It shows that at Geneva 'MacDonald to have been an extremely competent negotiator – certainly an improvement on his Foreign Secretary'.

G387. Before the Storm, *BD*, 2nd Ser., 4, *1932–3* (*see above* G386), *NS & N.* 40, 1010. 15 Jul. p 73

(1) Regrets that the Foreign Secretaries' minutes and correspondence are not included; nor the minutes of Foreign Office officials.

G388. Bismarck, *Bismarck and the German Empire*, Eric Eyck, Allen and Unwin, *MG.* 25 Jul. p 4

(1) Praises it as an accurate outline of Bismarck's whole life, but regrets that 'the standpoint is old-fashioned German Liberal – praising Bismarck's work while condemning his standards of political morality'.

Repr. *MGW.* 63, 11. 14 Sept. p 11

G389. M. Bouthillier's Memoirs, *Le Drame de Vichy* (*see above* G373), *TLS*. 2530. 28 Jul. p 471

(1) As is appropriate for 'an administrator without politics', the author aims to be impersonal. He places the blame on Reynaud before the armistice, and Laval after it.

G390. *Bismarck and the German Empire* (*see above* G388), *NS & N*. 40, 1015. 19 Aug. pp 204–5

Repr. as 'Bismarck's Morality' in A6, pp 41–5, A15, pp 82–6 and A17, pp 90–5

G391. Tale of Woe, *The English Middle Classes*, Roy Lewis and Angus Maude, New York, Knopf, *NR*. 123, 9. 28 Aug. pp 20–1

(1) 'A rambling series of reflections on the English middle classes, some with merit, some without'.

(2) Denounces the British class education system ('one system for the masters, another for the slaves'). Observes that 'the Welfare State makes the middle classes more important than ever'. Regrets 'that the possession of superior ability, still more the using of the ability to acquire superior rewards is widely regarded in England as wicked, even by those who possess the ability'.

G392. Mayerling, *Rudolf*, Count Carl Lonjay, Hamilton, *MG*. 5 Sept. p 4

(1) He 'has disposed of an historical legend' in a book which exaggerates the defects of the Habsburg Court.

G393. Napoleonic Propaganda, *Napoleonic Propaganda*, Robert B. Holtman, Louisiana State U.P., *MG*. 22 Sept. p 4

(1) 'A competent, rather plodding account of this fascinating topic'.

Repr. as 'Propaganda', *MGW*. 63, 18. 2 Nov. p 12

G394. Germany and the West, *Germany's Drive to the West*, Hans W. Gatzke, John Hopkins U.P.; Camberlege, *MG*. 29 Sept. p 4

(1) 'Thorough and conscientious in its research, convincing in its conclusions'.

G395. *Men in Crisis*, Arnold Whitridge, Scribners, *TLS*. 2540. 6 Oct. p 634

(1) 'Written with sense and judgment' but 'nothing novel in the treatment or conclusions'.

G396. Wicked or Stupid? *The Russo-German Alliance 1939–1941*, A. Rossi, Chapman and Hall, *NS & N*. 40, 1022. 7 Oct. p 343

(1) Criticises the underlying assumption that the Russians preferred a German alliance to other alternatives, and observes 'it really seems more likely that in the spring of 1939 . . . the Soviet leaders knew no better than anyone else what to do'.

G397. Essays on Burke, *Edmund Burke*, Thomas W. Copeland, Cape, *MG*. 13 Oct. p 4

(1) A book of literary scholarship 'written with distinction and sometimes even with charm'.

Repr. *MGW*. 63, 19. 9 Nov. p 12

G398. Anti-Bolshevik Primer, *Verdict of Three Decades*, Julian Steinberg, New York, Duell, Sloan and Pearce, *NR*. 123, 16. 16 Oct. pp 20–21

(1) 'This book is . . . a case for the prosecution, not a verdict. . . . Communist rule is detestable, and Communist principles even more so; all the same it is better to try to understand them.'

This review aroused some criticism as to the importance of the February 1917 Revolution. A.J.P.T. replied to defend his view that Russia was not already a socialist country in Feb-Oct. 1917, *Ibid*. 23. 4 Dec. p 4

G399. "Old Nick", *The Discourses of Niccolo Machiavelli*, 2 Vols. ed. Leslie J. Walker, Routledge and Kegan Paul, *MG*. 17 Oct. p 4

(1) Deems this a better book than *The Prince*, but feels that his speculations are futile.

Repr. *MGW*. 63, 17. 26 Nov. p 12

G400. Textbook of Anti-Communism, *The Coming Defeat of Communism*, James Burnham, Cape, *NS & N*. 40, 1024. 21 Oct. pp 373–4

(1) Unfavourable, though he observes that the author is the only anti-communist who 'writes

with some sense, judgment and consistency'.

(2) Dismisses the view that 'every Communist move is a matter of rational calculation, long worked out and part of a long-term plan which never varies' and argues that 'in reality political behaviour is the result of a conflict of forces, not of reason'.

G401. The Soviet Satellites, *The East European Revolution*, Hugh Seton-Watson, Methuen, *MG.* 24 Oct. p 4

(1) An admirable account written from an 'enlightened Left Wing' view point.

Repr. as 'Revolution', *MGW*. 63, 18. 2 Nov. p 12

G402. Another "Good German", *Erinnerungen*, Ernst von Weizsäcker, Munich, List, *MG.* 28 Oct. p 6

(1) His memoirs 'are inevitably a case for the defence, not a contribution to impartial history'.

Repr. *MGW*. 63, 20. 16 Nov. p 10 and in A6, pp 216–9

G403. *The Evolution of the Zollverein*, Arnold H. Price, Michigan U.P.; Cumberlege, 1949, *EHR*. 65, 257. Oct. pp 555–6

(1) 'An excellent account, ... approached ... from a new angle'.

G404. *The Austrian Electoral Reform of 1907*, W.A. Jenks, Columbia U.P.; Cumberlege, *Ibid.* p 558

(1) A competent account of the debates but 'little discussion, of the fundamental issues at stake'.

G405. *The German Social Democratic Party 1914–1921*, A. Joseph Berlau, Columbia U.P.; Cumberlege, 1949, *Ibid.* p 559

(1) A competent narrative but a 'not very rewarding book'.

(2) 'In 1918 the German Social Democratic party held the destinies of Germany in its hands, it made nothing of the opportunity. This failure presents a theme of prime importance for the history of Germany and for that of Socialist parties.'

G406. *Nationalism and Internationalism*, ed. Edward Mead Earle, Columbia U.P.; Cumberlege, *Ibid.* p 563

(1) The choice of area covered suggests that 'nationalism is very much an affair of Western Europe'.

G407. Triumph of a Legend, *Envers et Contre Tous*, 2 Vols. Jacques Soustelle, Paris, Laffont, 1947, *TLS*. 2544. 3 Nov. p 695

(i) 'Personal reminiscence ... mixed with general narrative'.

Repr. as 'De Gaulle: Triumph of a Legend' in A6, pp 223–8, and A17, pp 299–305

G408. Heroes of '48, *Men in Crisis* (*see above* G395), *NS & N*. 40, 1026. 4 Nov. p 404

G409. Two Views of Eastern Europe, (a) *The Eastern European Revolution* (*see above* G401); (b) *Revolution in Eastern Europe*, Doreen Warriner, Turnstile, *NS & N*. 1028. 18 Nov. pp 478, 480

(a1) Critical of its failure to discuss economic policy since 1945 at any length.

(b1) Dismisses it for being uncritical of the Communists – she is 'ready to lower the flag of freedom and, still worse, to besmirch it'.

(2) 'Eastern Europe cannot have real independence until it is industrialised and its agriculture modernised ... unless the peoples of eastern Europe use their new strength to turn against their Communist and Russian oppressors, they will never gain the freedom which they have always wanted and for which they have so often fought.'

G410. Failure of the Munich Policy, *BD*, 3rd Ser., 3, *1938–9*, *MG*. 22 Nov. p 4

Repr. *MGW*. 64, 1. 4 Jan. p 11 and as part of 'From Munich to Prague: British Version' in A6, pp 194–7 and A17, pp 274–7

G411. The Bad Years, *The Age of Elegance 1812–22*, Arthur Bryant, Collins, *MG*. 24 Nov. p 4

(1) It lacks a theme and the title is not appropriate for the period of post-war social unrest.

G412. The Morning After, *BD*, 3rd Ser., 3, *1938–9* (*see above* G410), *NS & N*. 40, 1029. 25 Nov. p 514

(1) It mostly deals with trivial matters. The

theme is how to win over Italy without estranging France.

(2) '. . . the time is approaching when the polite silence concerning Lord Halifax's conduct of foreign policy will have to be broken'. Suggests a serious study will lead to surprises and 'might even by comparison enhance the reputation of Sir John Simon'.

G413. Penguin Histories, (a) *England in the Eighteenth Century*, J.H. Plumb, Penguin; (b) *England in the Nineteenth Century*, David Thomson, Penguin, *MG*. 8 Dec. p 4

(a1) It 'tries to carry further the socio-political analysis devised by Namier'. He feels that 'there is something out of focus in an approach to the eighteenth century which ranks politicians after machines and landowners, scientists and preachers'.

(b1) 'Breezier and more slapdash in its approach'.

Repr. *MGW*. 64, 1. 4 Jan. 1951. p 11

G414. Stalin and the West, Origins of the Nazi Soviet Pact, *De Staline à Hitler*, Robert Coulondre, Paris, Hachette, *MG*. 8 Dec. p 6

(1) Particularly interesting on his time in Moscow. The book shows that 'the real decisions were taken in 1938'.

Repr. as 'France, Germany and the Soviet Union', *MGW*. 64, 2. 11 Jan. 1951. p 11 and under the original title in A6, pp 204–6

G415. Beyond Good and Evil, *A History of Soviet Russia: The Bolshevik Revolution 1917–1923*, Vol. 1, E.H. Carr, Macmillan, *NS & N*. 40, 1032. 16 Dec. p 628

(1) 'Very good indeed' within the author's limits – he 'has written a history with the events left out'. Argues that the author's criteria is success in achieving power, and as the Bolsheviks succeeded he is uncritical of them and the characterisations have no life in them.

1951

G416. The Decade Behind Us, (a) *Classics and Commercials*,

Edmund Wilson, New York, Farrar, Strauss, 1950; (b) *The Forties*, Alan Ross, Weidenfeld and Nicolson, 1950, *TLS*. 2553. 5 Jan. p 6

(a1) Finds his frankness refreshing.

(b1) A survey in which 'photography abets the vivid images of a coloured and evocative prose'.

(2) Discusses why the 1940s was a culturally barren decade. He suggests that in Britain and America writers have been too involved in public affairs. Also that 'the everyday experience of modern war . . . was never complete enough . . . Even in the context of war they suffered from that sense of privilege which has been one of the main inhibiting forces of the last 30 years.'

G417. The World Made Easy, *Policy for the West*, Barbara Ward, Harmondsworth, Penguin Books, *NS & N.* 41, 1038. 27 Jan. p 112

(1) Very unfavourable – 'a collection of political commonplaces'. 'Penguin Books are reprints of books that have been tried and proved successful; Penguin Specials are rearrangements of ideas that have been tried and proved successful.'

G418. *L'alleanza di Crimea*, Franco Valsecchi, Milan, Arnoldo Mondadori 1948, *EHR*. 66, 258. Jan. pp 121–3

(1) 'A sound attempt to see Italy from the side of Europe'; but it deals inadequately with Russia and Britain.

G419. Diplomacy: Plain and Coloured, (a) *Hitler's Interpreter*, Paul Schmidt, Heinemann; (b) *Soviet Documents on Foreign Policy, Vol. 1, 1917–1924*, ed. Jane Degras, Oxford U.P., *NS & N.* 41, 1044. 10 Mar. p 278

(a1) Finds nothing new in these memoirs.

(a2) 'Though international relations are certainly exciting . . . they are exciting from the clash of policy and ideas, not from personalities.'

(b1) Fascinating reading. It shows the development of Bolshevik policy, including the way they learned 'the method of turning western idealism against its inventors'.

G420. Mirabeau Again, *Mirabeau*, Oliver J.G. Welch, Cape, *NS & N.* 41, 1048. 7 Apr. pp 401–2

(1) A story told well, but it has been told too often.

(2) 'Mirabeau is of little interest as a political thinker.' His importance is as 'the first of the Tribunes' of French history.

G421. Franco's Friends, *GD*, Ser. D., 3, *The Spanish Civil War*, *NS & N.* 41, 1049. 14 Apr. p 427

(1) Doubts if it is worth publishing these records so fully as they will not be widely read: 'there is so little evidence and so much verbiage'.

(2) 'It seems to be forgotten that history – not only contemporary history, but all history – is not a game for scholars; it has a great social purpose, and it achieves this purpose only when it reaches a wide body of readers.'

G422. Spain and the Axis: Evidence From the German Foreign Office, *GD*, Ser. D., 3 (*see above* G421), *MG.* 18 Apr. p 4

(1) 'The main concern of German policy was not directly with Spain: it was to keep Italy estranged from England and France, a purpose admirably served by the Italian intervention in Spain.'

Repr. *MGW.* 64, 18. 3 May. p 11 and in A6, pp 181–3 and A17, pp 225–8

G423. Hitler Speaks Again, *Hitler Directs His War*, ed. Felix Gilbert, Oxford U.P., *MG.* 24 Apr. p 3

(1) Fascinating records of Hitler's conversations, which were 'all in the nature of showpieces – talking to impress foreign statesmen or even his own followers'.

Repr. as 'Hitler's Military Conferences', *MGW.* 64, 18. 3 May. p 12

G424. The Failure of the Habsburg Monarchy, *The Multinational Empire*, 2 Vols. Robert A. Kann, Columbia U.P.; Cumberlege, *TLS.* 2569. 27 Apr. p 265

(1) Provides much information but it is rather uncritical. 'Altogether his book illustrates the modern

delusion that if only we know enough facts we shall arrive at the answer.'

(2) 'In the last resort the Habsburg Monarchy . . . was an attempt to find a 'third way' in central Europe which should be neither German nor Russian. Once the Habsburgs became Germany's satellites in war they had failed in their mission. Their doom was of their own making.'

Repr. in A6, pp 67–71, A15, pp 115–19 and A17, p 127–32

G425. *La Consulta Straordinaria della Lombardia*, ed. Frederico Curato, Verona, Arnoldo Mondadori, 1950, *EHR*. 66, 259. Apr. pp 314–5

(1) The author 'has presented the story well'.

G426. *Holsteins Geheimpolitik in der Era Bismarck 1886–1890*, Helmut Krausnick, Hamburg, Hanseatische Verlagsaanstalt, 1942, *Ibid.* pp 317–8

(1) 'A useful addition to our knowledge and helps to explain the later development of German policy under Holstein's influence'.

G427. For Reference, *The Columbia Encyclopedia*, 2nd edn. ed. W. Bridgwater and Elizabeth J. Sherwood, Columbia U.P.; Cumberlege, *TLS*. 2571. 11 May. p 297

(1) 'A most useful book . . . this work of reference is of an exceptional order'.

G428. More Good Germans, (a) *We Defended Normandy*, Lieut. General Hans Speidel, Jenkins; (b) *Chief of Intelligence*, Ian Colvin, Gollancz, *NS & N*. 41, 1054. 19 May. pp 572–3

(a1) 'Despite the hero worship, this is an honest book'.

(b1) 'Ingenious fantasy'. On Canaris; written in the manner of *The Quest for Corvo*.

G429. Jan Masaryk, *Jan Masaryk: A Personal Memoir*, R.H. Bruce-Lockhart, Dropmore Press, *NS & N*. 41, 1056. 2 Jun. p 630

(1) 'A tribute of affection and regret'.

(2) 'A very good man, though not a great one'. His failure as a politician was due to the fact 'he

had no organised party and interest behind him'. 'The moral of his life and death is distressingly simple: against Communists decency is not enough.'

G430. Joe at his Zenith: From South Africa to Tariff Reform, *The Life of Joseph Chamberlain*, Vol. 4, Julian Amery, Macmillan, *MG*. 8 Jun. p 6

Repr. as 'Chamberlain's Imperial Preference', *MGW*. 64, 25. 21 Jun. p 11 and under original title in A 16, pp 159–62 and A21, pp 186–90

G431. *Memoirs of Ernst von Weizsäcker*, Gollancz (*see above* G402), *MG*. 12 Jun. p 4

G432. Yet Another, *Memoirs of Ernst von Weizsäcker* (*see above* G431), *NS & N*. 41, 1058. 16 Jun. p 686

(1) Ironically observes that if all the German memoirs are to be believed Hitler was an even greater genius than one suspected – as every German was against him.

G433. Statistics and History, *The Incidence of the Emigration During the French Revolution*, Donald Greer, Harvard U.P.; Cumberlege, *MG*. 29 Jun. p 4

(1) 'Everyone who is interested in the French Revolution will benefit from this book.'

(2) 'Statistics open a new and most exciting door to history . . . Though statistical history lacks literary grace, it brings increased knowledge and understanding in a different way; and ultimately the elegant writer can work its conclusions into a new synthesis.'

Repr. *MGW*. 65, 2. 12 Jul. p 11

G434. The Paradox of France, *Modern France*, ed. Edward Meade Earle, Princeton U.P.; Cumberlege, *TLS*. 2578. 29 Jun. p 408

(1) Interesting conference papers; regrets that the style is generally poor.

(2) 'The history of the last 150 years might be summarised in a phrase: the decline of France.'

G435. Nietzsche and the Germans, *Nietzsche*, Walter A. Kaufmann, Princeton U.P.; Cumberlege, *NS & N*. 41, 1060. 30 Jun. pp 749–50

(1) 'The most sensible exposition of Nietzsche's

philosophy ever made; if it fails to reveal the full secret it is because it forgets that Nietzsche, as well as being a philosopher, was something more important – a writer of the highest genius.'

Repr. in A6, pp 46–50 and A17, pp 194–8

G436. Jos Wedgwood, *The Last of the Radicals*, C.V. Wedgwood, Cape, *NS & N*. 42, 1062. 14 Jul. pp 46, 48

(1) 'A model of art and charm'.

(2) Wedgwood 'was wrong to call himself the last of the radicals. Radicalism has to learn new techniques; but it will keep alive so long as the spirit of rebellion lives in anyone.'

G437. French Parliament, *The Parliament of France*, D.W.S. Lidderdale, Hansard Society, *TLS*. 2582. 27 Jul. p 463

(1) 'It is full of fascinating points' and contains valuable information even for the expert.

G438. Munich Again, *Survey of International Affairs 1938, Vol. 2*, R.G.D. Laffan, Oxford U.P., *MG*. 3 Aug. p 4

(1) 'The standpoint is what might be called 'British respectable'. . . . The author clings firmly to the principle of writing nothing which might give offence to any member of Chatham House or to anyone likely to dine at the high table of any Cambridge or Oxford college.'

G439. The End of Appeasement. British Foreign Policy January-April 1939, *BD*, 3rd Ser., 4, *1939*, *MG*. 16 Aug. pp 4, 5

Repr. *MGW*. 65, 9. 30 Aug. p 11 and as part of 'From Munich to Prague: British Version' in A6, pp 197–200 and A17, pp 277–80

G440. Historical Scrap Book, *Huskisson and His Age*, C.R. Fay, Longmans, *NS & N*. 42, 1067. 18 Aug. p 186

(1) 'It is a rag-bag, a historical scrap-book, into which ideas, topics, original letters and diaries have been miscellaneously crammed'.

G441. The Irish at Westminster, *The Irish Parliamentary Party 1890–1910*, F.S. Lyons, Faber, *NS & N*.

42, 1068. 25 Aug. pp 210–1

(1) 'One of those rare books which will give equal pleasure to the professional historian and the general reader'.

G442. Symptom of Discontent, *Anti-Semitism in Modern France*, Vol. 1, Robert F. Byrnes, Rutgers U.P.; Cambridge U.P., *TLS*. 2587. 31 Aug. p 553

(1) 'Both scholarly and eminently readable'.

(2) 'Victor Adler called anti-semitism 'the socialism of fools'; it would be truer to say that it is the form in which the discontent of fools most easily finds expression.'

G443. *Democracy in America*, Alexis de Tocqueville, (a) Paris, Libraire de Medicis; London, Anglo-French Literary Services; (b) Introduction by Harold Laski, Paris, Gallimard, *NS*. 42, 1070. 8 Sept. pp 257–8

(1) Observes of (a), 'garnished with an excess of notes'. Praises the introduction to (b) as 'a fine piece of scholarship' which has 'greater clarity and force than much of Laski's later writing'.

Repr. A6, pp 19–23

G444. No Illusions: And No Ideas, *In Defence of the National Interest*, Hans J. Morgenthau. New York, Knopf, *The Nation*. 173, 10. 8 Sept. pp 196–7

(1) Unimpressed by the author's call for realism not idealism to be the guiding light of American foreign policy.

(2) 'It is the best form of realism to have superior ideals'. A.J.P.T. argues that the real problem in world affairs is not the Soviet Union but the overwhelming power of the USA and its inability to know what to do with it.

G445. The Making of Latin America, (a) *British Policy and the Independence of Latin America 1804–1828*, William W. Kaufmann, Yale U.O.; Cumberlege; (b) *Castlereagh*, Ione Leigh, Collins, *MG*. 11 Sept. p 4

(a1) 'An admirable work of synthesis'; but his

style 'is almost too spritely and often too summary as to be cryptic'.

(b1) 'With few obvious faults, this book has also few virtues'.

(2) Canning was not a great liberal statesman; in reality he 'was a thorough going isolationist, with all the attractiveness and all the illusions of that school'.

Repr. *MGW*. 65, 11. 13 Sept. p 11

G446. The Moment of Decision, *BD*, 3rd Ser., 4, *1939* (*see above* G439), *NS & N*. 42, 1071. 15 Sept. p 286

(1) 'An admirable volume, excellently arranged'; regrets the omission of the military advice given to the British Government.

(2) 'British and Soviet policy alike took Poland seriously as a Great Power. If the Russians had realised that Poland would collapse within a month, they would probably not have made a Nazi-Soviet pact; if the British had realised it, they would not have given their guarantee. In that case Hitler would have overrun the whole of Europe without a war. He was defeated by the blunders of his opponents, not by their foresight.'

G447. A Diplomatic History, *Austria-Hungary and Great Britain 1908–1914*, A.F. Pribram, Oxford U.P., *MG*. 25 Sept. p 4

(1) Dry diplomatic history based almost entirely entirely on the published documents; welcomes a new examination by a historian of his distinction.

G448. A Life of Disraeli, *Dizzy*, Hesketh Pearson, Methuen, *MG*. 12 Oct. p 4

(1) Good on his early life, weaker on his career and does not penetrate 'the nature' of Disraeli.

(2) 'When you have nothing to say the best course is to appear enigmatical and mysterious; perhaps this was Disraeli's secret.'

Repr. *MGW*. 65, 17. 25 Oct. p 13

G449. Lost: A Prime Minister, *Dizzy* (*see above* G448), *NS & N*. 42, 1075. 13 Oct. p 412

G450. Town Versus Country, *Marx Against the Peasants*, David Mitranz, Weidenfeld and Nicolson, *NS & N.* 42, 1076. 20 Oct. p 439

(1) 'A book of the first importance'; though he disagrees with some of its implications.

(2) 'Marxism postulated workers' revolutions in advanced industrial countries; in fact it has won power only in backward countries as the by-product of peasant revolution.'

G451. Palmerston's Foreign Policy, *The Foreign Policy of Palmerston 1830–1841*, 2 Vols. Sir Charles Webster, Bell, *MG.* 26 Oct. p 3

(1) A 'painstaking and accurate chronicle'.

Repr. *MGW.* 65, 18. 1 Nov. p 11

G452. The Best of Palmerston, *The Foreign Policy of Palmerston 1830–1841*, 2 Vols. (*see above* G451), *NS & N.* 42, 1078. 3 Nov. p 498

(1) He 'has established Palmerson's greatness beyond dispute'; but finds the style dull.

(2) In this period Palmerston 'achieved success without parallel in time of peace. Moreover he achieved them single-handed'. His achievements were accomplished 'by great industry, a mastery of diplomatic technique, and confidence in himself'.

G453. Lady Hester, *The Nun of Lebanon*, ed. Ian Bruce, Collins, *MG.* 13 Nov. p 4

(1) 'An extraordinary story, told with extraordinary materials'.

G454. Mr. Carr Backs A Winner, *The New Society*, E.H. Carr, Macmillan, *The Twentieth Century.* 150. 15 Nov. pp 407–15

(1) A review article in which he criticises Carr's past and present views. 'Like Hegel, he tries to discover where history is going, in order to go with it; like Bismarck, he wants the governing classes to save themselves by leading the revolution and so keeping it within bounds.'

G455. *Maria Theresa and Other Studies*, G.P. Gooch, Longmans, *MG.* 16 Nov. p 4

(1) The author 'has perfected a literary form of

his own – a sort of anthology with running comments'.

G456. *History and Human Relations*, Herbert Butterfield, Collins, *NS & N*. 42, 1081. 24 Nov. pp 594, 596

(1) His best book. Critical of his advocacy of 'technical history' and of his attitude to Germany.

(2) He rebels at the idea 'We must judge men according to their standards, not ours', arguing that the Nazi treatment of the Jews must be condemned.

Repr. as 'History Without Morality' in A6, pp 9–13

G457. The Heyday of Appeasement: German Policy from Munich to Prague, *GD*, Ser. D., 4, *The Aftermath of Munich*, *MG*. 20 Dec. p 4

Repr. *MGW*. 66, 3. 17 Jan. 1952. p 11 and as 'From Munich to Prague: German Version' in A6, pp 200–3, and A17, pp 280–3

1952

G458. Thus Spake Hitler, (a) *Hitler's Strategy*, F.H. Hinsley, Cambridge U.P., 1951; (b) *Hitlers Tischgespräche in Führerhauptquartier 1941–42*, Henry Picker, Bonn, Atheneaum, 1951, *TLS*. 2605. 4 Jan. pp 1–2

(a1) Feels that in putting the emphasis on the sea this inevitably 'gives the impression that Hitler made nothing but mistakes'.

(b1) 'The interminable meal-time harangues ... can be paralleled only by Coleridge table-talking ...'

Repr. A6, pp 211–5 and A17, pp 199–203

G459. Fellow-Traveller, *Sven Hedin's German Diary 1935–1942*, trans. Joan Bulman, Euphorion, 1951, *MG*. 8 Jan. p 4

(1) His conversations with leading Nazis are not very revealing.

G460. The Jameson Raid of 1895: New Light on Chamberlain's Part, *The Jameson Raid*, Jean van der Poel, Oxford U.P., 1951, *MG*. 24 Jan. p 6

Repr. *MGW*. 66, 5. 31 Jan. p 11 and A6, pp 153–5 and A21, pp 175–7

G461. British Historians, *Some Modern Historians of Britain*, New York, Dryden Press, *MG*. 25 Jan. p 4

(1) Praises the essays warmly.

Repr. *MGW*. 66, 6. 7 Feb. p 12

G462. *FD*, 2nd Ser., 9–11 (Jan. 1906-Feb. 1909). 1946, 1948, 1950. *EHR*. 67, 262. Jan. pp 97–102

(1) The issue of Morocco dominates the volumes.

(2) 'Algeciras was strictly a defensive victory. It kept the Germans out of Morocco and it kept the door open to the French; but it did not let them in.'

'The Bosnian crisis was to show that France could win German friendship only by abandoning Russia; and the Agadir crisis that she would win it only by abandoning Great Britain.'

G463. *The Multinational Empire* (*see above* G424), *Ibid.* p 134

(1) Based on secondary sources; 'it is a catalogue rather than a history'.

G464. Burke Up to Date, (a) *The Making of France*, Marie-Madeleine Martin, Eyre and Spottiswoode; (b) *The Origins of Totalitarian Democracy*, J.L. Talmon, Secker and Warburg, *MG*. 6 Feb. p 4

(a1) Essentially it is 'a hymn of praise to the ancien regime and the old monarchy and an attack on everything the French Revolution advocated or achieved'.

(b1) 'His discussion is rather abstract and academic' but it is a 'valid theme, admirably worked out'.

Repr. *MGW*. 66, 6. 7 Feb. p 11

G465. Mr. "X" Rides Again, *American Diplomacy 1900–50*, George Kennan, Secker and Warburg, *MG*. 8 Feb. p 6

Repr. as 'Speculations of Mr.X', *MGW*. 66, 8. 21 Feb. p 11 and under the original title in A6, pp 249–51

G466. Germany at High Tide, G.D., Ser. D., 4 (*see above* G457), *NS & N*. 43, 1094. 23 Feb. pp 222–3

(1) 'It was expected that a full publication of German diplomatic documents would establish

Germany's war-guilt; but since the foreign ministry was remote from Hitler and his policy, the volumes have only displayed the impotence and ignorance of the professional diplomats.'

G467. European Diplomacy After Sedan, (a) *European Alliances and Alignments 1871–1890*, 2nd edn. (b) *The Diplomacy of Imperialism 1890–1902*, 2nd edn., William L. Langer, New York, Knopf, *TLS*. 2615. 14 Mar. p 183

(a1) When it was first published, 'A new wind blew. This was international history without moral preconceptions' – it got away from the obsessions with war guilt. This is 'more effective in arrangement and with a greater unity of theme' than (b).

(b1) Its real theme is 'the disintegration of the Bismarckian system'. The treatment of imperialism is 'no more than a sustained attack on British jingoism'. Criticises his treatment of British policy towards France and Russia and his inability to 'understand the motives of those who resisted German hegemony'.

G468. The Liberal Idea, (a) *Liberalism, Nationalism, and the German Intellectuals 1822–1847*, Hinton Thomas, Cambridge, Heffer; (b) *The Liberal Anglican Idea of History*, Duncan Forbes, Cambridge U.P., *MG*. 21 Mar. p 4

(a1) 'A rewarding study, which confirms the generalisation that German thinkers sacrificed liberal principle for the sake of national power'.

(b1) A gallant attempt 'to sustain interest in a group of historians none of whose books will ever be opened again'.

G469. Revolution in Practice, *The Bolshevik Revolution 1917–1923*, Vol. 2, E.H. Carr, Macmillan, *NS & N*. 43, 1098. 22 Mar. p 350

(1) Critical of his treatment of ideas. 'But regarded in detachment as a study of the development in Bolshevik economic policy, this is a work of the highest excellence'.

(2) 'For, detestable as is their political tyranny,

the Bolsheviks found out how to make Socialism work.' They found a solution for industrial but not agrarian society.

G470. Germany and Russia, *German-Soviet Relations Between The Two World Wars 1919–1939*, E.H. Carr, Oxford U.P., *MG*. 28 Mar. p 4

(1) A very good preliminary survey of the topic.

(2) The Treaty of Rapallo: 'The Russian anxiety was, as always, defensive; German policy aimed at recovery for another bid at the domination of Europe.'

Repr. as 'Germany and the Soviet Union', *MGW*. 66, 14. 3 Apr. p 10

G471. American Foreign Policy, *The Challenge to Isolation, 1937–1940*, W.F. Langer and S.E. Gleason, Royal Institute of International Affairs, *MG*. 8 Apr. p 4

(1) 'Incomparably the best account of international affairs at the opening of the Second World War'. Apart from the treatment of Vichy it is 'a brilliant analysis of the development of foreign policy in a democracy'. Reveals that Roosevelt 'was a great man'.

Repr. *MGW*. 66, 16. 17 Apr. p 10

G472. Ciano Once More, *Ciano's Diary 1937–1938*, trans. Andreas Mayor, Methuen, *MG*. 25 Apr. p 4

(1) Though of less historical importance than the later diaries, it is more entertaining. It is 'an incomparable picture of Fascism in the days of its glory'.

(2) 'Mussolini was a sham-Napoleon, a Bonaparte gone sour. Ciano was more valet than Foreign Minister and tried to make a hero of him.'

Repr. *MGW*. 66, 18. 1 May. p 10

G473. *The History of the Times*, Vol. 4, *The 150th Anniversary And Beyond 1912–1948*, *NS & N*. 43, 1103. 26 Apr. pp 499–500

(1) 'Much of this History . . . is delayed revenge of the old Toryism against the new.'

(2) 'There was nothing wrong with the British people in the interwar years except its leaders.

The traditional governing class turned timid, failed to lead.'

Repr. as 'Northcliffe and Dawson' in A6, pp 167–72

G474. *The Habsburg Monarchy 1867–1914*, Arthur J. May, Cambridge, Harvard U.P., 1951, *Am.Hist.R.* 57, 3. Apr. pp 669–70

(1) 'Good old-fashioned literary history, with agreeable phrases instead of statistics'.

G475. *F.D.*, 1st Ser., 10–12 (Aug. 1892-May 1895). 1945, 1947, 1951, *EHR*. 67, 263. Apr. pp 276–8

(1) The dominating theme is Egypt – the issue which had to be cleared up before an entente could be completed.

G476. *German Agrarian Politics After Bismarck's Fall*, Sarah Rebecca Tirrell, Columbia U.P. ; Cumberlege, 1951, *Ibid.* p 310

(1) Too long – but a useful book.

G477. The Years of Illusion, *A History of the League of Nations*, 2 Vols. F.P. Walters, Oxford U.P., *Hist. Today*. 2, 4. Apr. pp 287, 289

(1) 'A work of piety', written by the League's Deputy Secretary General.

(2) He suggests that 'readers . . . may ponder the point that, if it had not been for the illusions and outlook engendered by the League of Nations, the war of 1939 might not have occurred'.

G478. The General as Politician, (a) *Lafayette*, David Loth, Cassell; (b) *Recalled to Service*, General Maxime Weygand, Heinemann, *NS & N.* 43, 1104. 3 May. pp 529–30

(a1) A good popular biography.

(b1) Memoirs which attempt to shift the blame of French defeat on to others.

G479. Namier At His Best, *Avenues of History*, L.B. Namier, Hamilton, *MG*. 20 May. p 4

(1) His volumes of essays 'contain pieces which can stand comparison with the essays of Macaulay, Ranke and Sorel'.

(2) 'He is a Jacobin with a taste for the society of dukes.'

Repr. *MGW*. 66, 23. 4 Jun. p 10

G480. The Powers On The Eve: Guesses And Facts About 1939, *Survey of International Affairs 1939–1946. The World in March 1939*, ed. Arnold Toynbee and Frank T. Ashton-Gwatkin, Oxford U.P., *MG*. 22 May. p 6

Repr. *MGW*. 66, 22. 29 May. p 11 and as 'On the Eve' in A6, pp 207–10

G481. Bonaparte, *Napoleon Bonaparte*, J.M. Thompson, Blackwell, *Hist. Today*. 2, 5. May. pp 366–7

(1) 'A remarkable biography of a great man ... Its learning is beyond challenge; it covers every disputed point, great and small; and it is also extremely entertaining to read.'

(2) Napoleon: 'a great man – one of the greatest, though also one of the nastiest, men in history'.

G482. End of Isolation, *Some Aspects of Britain's Splendid Isolation 1898–1904*, J.M. Goudswaard, Rotterdam, Brusse's Uitgeversmij, *MG*. 20 Jun. p 4

(1) 'He adds little in the way of new understanding'.

G483. Von Papen Explains: How Mistakes Make History, *Memoirs*, Franz von Papen, Deutsch, *MG*. 14 Jul. p 6

(1) 'His defence can be summarised in a sentence: 'It was all a mistake'.'

Repr. as 'Making History By Mistake', *MGW*. 67, 6. 7 Aug. p 11

G484. *Imperialismus vor 1914*, 2 Vols. George W.F. Hallgarten, Munich, Beckische Verlags buchhandlung, 1951, *EHR*. 67, 264. Jul. pp 423–5

(1) Observes that it was ready for publication in 1933 and it is now 'dated'. 'It does not deal with diplomacy; but 'given that it presents a one-sided picture, it is well done and, in its way, important'.

G485. *The Nazi Elite*, Daniel Lerner, Stanford U.P.; Cumberlege, 1951, *Ibid*. pp 461–2

(1) 'A remarkable example of the statistical method'. Of value to those 'interested in historical

method as well as by those concerned with German history'.

G486. The Use of Monarchy, *King George V*, Harold Nicolson, Constable, *Tribune*. 765. 22 Aug-4 Sept. pp 5–6

Repr. in A9, pp 70–5, and A21, pp 204–10

G487. Wicked Uncle, *The Life and Death of Stalin*, Louis Fischer, New York, Harper, *The Nation*. 175, 9. 30 Aug. p 175

(1) 'Anyone who wishes to be convinced that Stalin is a wicked man with no redeeming features will read this book with pleasure.'

G488. "Hero-Tito! Hero-Tito!" *Tito of Yugoslavia*, K. Zilliacus, Joseph, *NS & N*. 44, 1123. 13 Sept. p 294

(1) 'An excellent book as a picture of an individual' but the author is 'slap-dash and shaky in his facts' as a historian. Doubts some of his judgements: 'The movement to political freedom is . . . mythical . . . (Tito) keeps in prison politicians of impeccable democratic convictions.'

(2) 'Tito is as good a hero as our age can produce. Charm, courage, resolution, simplicity – Tito has them all.'

G489. The Alliance That Failed: Britain and Russia in 1939, *BD*, 3 Ser., 4, *1939*, *MG*. 29 Sept. p 4

(2) 'The failure to make an alliance with the Soviet Union in 1939 was the greatest setback for British diplomacy in the twentieth century.'

Repr. as 'British diplomacy towards Russia in 1939', *MGW*. 67, 16. 16 Oct. p 11 and as part of 'The Alliance That Failed' in A9, pp 157–9 and A17, pp 259–61

G490. *A History of Europe*, 2 Vols. H.A.L. Fisher, Eyre and Spottiswoode, New Edition, *NS & N*. 44, 1127. 11 Oct. pp 424–5

(1) 'A useful text book for schoolboys'. He attacks it as the work of a middle class humanist, for whom the classical era was Europe's greatest. 'Two things were missing in Fisher's Europe . . .

the Slavs and the class struggle . . . His understanding faltered when the masses broke into politics. There is nothing weaker in his book than the account of the revolutions of 1848, when politics escaped from the middle-class control and middle-class virtues.'

G491. A Devil's Advocate: Roosevelt and the War, *Back Door to War*, Charles Callan Tansill, Chicago, Regnery, *MG*. 24 Oct. p 6

(1) Warmly praises the Americans for opening their archives to all on equal terms, with no special privileges for 'official' historians. He finds the author's arguments completely unconvincing – but, nevertheless, he welcomes such attempts at revisionism. 'A democratic foreign policy is possible only if its background and assumptions are constantly discussed.' He wonders whether Russia really is 'incurably hostile in 1952', as all in authority assume.

Repr. *MGW*. 67, 18. 30 Oct. 11

G492. Hitler's accomplices, *In The Nazi Era*, Sir Lewis Namier, Macmillan, *NS & N*. 44, 1129. 25 Oct. pp 486, 8

(1) 'Meticulous scholarship, deep understanding, and an easy style leavened with wit, put this new book high in the canon of his works.'

(2) 'British statesmen, in their longing for peace and quiet, threw policies and allies overboard helter-skelter without thought of the morrow.'

G493. The Great Dictator, *Hitler: A Study in Tyranny*, Alan Bullock, Odhams, *MG*. 28 Oct. p 4

(1) On Hitler, he has 'filled the gap triumphantly'. 'With this book he puts himself in the front rank of contemporary historians.'

(2) 'Hitler loved power, or rather the struggle for power. Once he had attained it he put it to no use except to struggle for more. He was the will to power run mad . . . '

Repr. *MGW*. 67, 21. 20 Nov. p 10

G494. Milner Again, *The Forsaken Idea*, Edward Crankshaw, Longmans, *MG*. 8 Nov. p 4

(1) It is 'a tract for the times rather than a contribution to history'. 'A skilful statement of Toryism at its most enlightened'.

G495. The Last Tsars, *The Decline of Imperial Russia*, Hugh Seton-Watson, Methuen, *NS & N*. 44, 1133. 22 Nov. p 610

(1) 'A badly needed' book, which gives 'a competent analysis of the old Empire'. He finds the foreign policy sections least satisfactory.

(2) 'The Russian people are sensible and civilised; their economic system admirable. All is made barren by the disease of despotism, chronic in Russian history; and until the Russians discover the secret of political liberty they will be a great nuisance to the rest of us.'

1953

G496. *Harold Laski*, Kingsley Martin, Gollancz, *NS & N*. 45, 1141. 17 Jan. pp 68–9

(1) 'A serious contribution to our political history', which 'presents his dead friend without fear or favour'. Though he observes that the history is weak in places and too much space is given to his last ten years.

(2) Laski 'was the most important influence in remaking English Social Democracy and giving it its present form'. 'Though he often talked in terms of class war, he really assumed that the English governing class could be cajoled and argued into abdicating. He did not understand their skill, their tenacity or, above all, their ruthlessness; and he was hurt and surprised when they bit the hand that stroked them.'

G497. Diplomacy in the Sudan, *British Policy in the Sudan 1882–1902*, Mekki Shibeika, Oxford U.P., 1952, *MG*. 20 Jan. p 4

(1) 'An admirable book . . . We have here the last word on Gordon's failure and death.'

G498. George III: New Version, *King George III and the*

Politicians, Richard Pares, Oxford, Clarendon, *NS & N.* 45, 1142. 24 Jan. p 98

(1) 'A book of the highest quality . . . full of wit and gaiety, enlivened with anecdote and a delight to read.' It shows that 'the full Namier gospel' can be preached at Oxford.

(2) 'I sometimes wonder whether the new version has not swung a little too far in the opposite direction from Macaulay and Charles James Fox.' He suggests that 'Whig' and 'Tory' did mean something to men such as Fox and Dr. Johnson.

G499. Historians, *From Ranke to Toynbee*, Pieter Geyl, Northampton, Mass., Smith College Studies in History, 1952, *MG.* 30 Jan. p 4

(1) Geyl 'is among the nicest and most penetrating of living historians . . . His essays cannot be too highly recommended.'

Repr. *MGW.* 68, 8. 19 Feb. p 10

G500. Comparing Revolutions, *The Anatomy of Revolutions*, 2nd edn., Crane Brinton, Cape, *TLS.* 2661. 30 Jan. p 70

(1) Feels that 'the comparisons amount to very little'. His 'anatomy is nothing more than a summary of the French Revolution imposed upon his other cases'. Compares his approach to Toynbee's study of civilisations.

G501. *Storia della Politica Estera Italiana del 1870 al 1896*, Vol. 1, Frederico Chabod, Bari, Gius, Laterza and Figli, 1951, *EHR.* 68, 266. Jan. pp 104–6

(1) 'It is a contribution to the history of ideas rather than to diplomatic history strictly interpreted; and the spirit of Meinecke broods over it.'

(2) The Franco-Prussian war 'challenged, if it did not destroy, the validity of French ideas; and many Italian politicians, particularly of the Left, turned from idealism to Realpolitik'.

G502. *The Origins of the War of 1914*, Vol. 1, Luigi Albertini, Oxford U.P., 1952, *Ibid.* pp 113–5

(1) Praises him as the first writer to use all the

diplomatic documents but observes that it is really centred on Austro-Hungarian and Italian policy. 'Like all journalists he studied the past in order to discover how it led to the present.'

G503. Conversion, *The Communist Technique in Britain*, Bob Darke, Collins, *NS & N.* 45, 1145. 14 Feb. pp 185–6

(1) 'Slightly rambling' but it 'should be read by everyone who believes that Communists can ever be trusted or that it is possible to work with them'.

(2) 'The Communist Party is not concerned with peace or with better conditions; it is only concerned with power. It exploits everyone, including its own members, for this purpose.'

G504. The Radical Rat, *A Political Memoir 1880–1892*, Joseph Chamberlain, ed. C.D.H. Howard, Batchworth, *NS & N.* 45, 1148. 7 Mar. pp 267–8

(1) Suggests the title should be 'a record of grievances'.

(2) 'Freedom cannot be preserved in an island pocket. A radical of Chamberlains day had to be on the side of the Irish and a radical of ours has to be on the side of the Kikuyu and the Egyptians.'

G505. The Worst German, *Himmler*, Willi Frischauer, Odhams, *MG.* 10 Mar. p 4

(1) Praises the book, 'It is a loathsome story, without equal in history, bestiality turned into a system . . . the story of this very ordinary German should be compulsory reading for all those who think that the Germans are civilised beings, much like ourselves.'

G506. Fathers of the Movement, *History of Socialist Thought*, Vol. 1, G.D.H. Cole, Macmillan, *Tribune.* 13 Mar. p 6

(1) Favourable, but critical of his interpretation on many points.

(2) 'The truth is, we like to think that socialism has always been democratic, a movement of the people. But in reality, it has often been a device for

keeping the people quiet; and it needs constant injections of the radical spirit to bring it back on the right lines.'

G507. Miniature Portrait, *Macaulay*, Giles St. Aubyn, Falcon, *TLS*. 2672. 17 Apr. p 255

(1) Praises it warmly as a good introduction to Macaulay.

G508. *Carlyle : An Anthology*, ed. G.M. Trevelyan, Longmans, *NS & N*. 45, 1154. 18 Apr. pp 459–60

(2) 'Carlyle senses the masses, as no other writer has ever done; he expressed their outlook against his own conscious convictions . . . In the *French Revolution* there is no fault or weakness at all; it is a book without a peer . . .'

G509. American Diplomacy: From Isolation to World Power, *Turbulent Era*, 2 Vols. Joseph C. Grew, Hammond, *MG*. 15 Apr. p 6

(1) 'A mound of undigested raw material' – but it illustrates 'uniquely the breakneck speed at which the United States has passed from isolation to being the centre of the world'.

Repr. as 'America's Rise to World Power', *MGW*. 68, 17. 23 Apr. p 11 and as 'From Isolation to World Power' in A9, pp 168–70

G510. Eatanswill, *Politics in the Age of Peel*, Norman Gash, Longmans, *NS & N*. 45, 1155. 25 Apr. p 490

(1) Praises its scholarship and its style. However as 'the evidence is drawn largely from the parliamentary enquiries into corrupt elections' the details are not typical.

G511. Profitable Idealism, *Cecil Rhodes*, André Maurois, Collins, *Obs*. 26 Apr. p 9

(1) A clearly written, urbane life.

G512. *Revolutions of 1848*, Priscilla Robertson, Princeton U.P.; Cumberlege, 1952, *EHR*. 68, 267. Apr. p 329

(1) Finds it a very uneven book and disagrees with her dismal view of the 1848 revolutions.

G513. *La Lotta Sociale nel Risorgimento*, Guido Quazza, Turin, Typografia Coggiola, 1951, *Ibid*. pp. 329–30

G514. Napoleon's Last Days, *Napoleon at St. Helena*, General Bertrand, Cassell, *MG*. 1 May. p 4

(1) Those 'who find Napoleon rather less than divine will find principally the pathetic record of a very ordinary sick-bed'.

Repr. in *The Bedside Guardian: 2*, ed. Ivor Brown, Collins, pp 158–9

G514a Bolshevik Realism, *The Bolshevik Revolution*, Vol. 3, E.H. Carr, Macmillan, *NS & N*, 45, 1157, 9 May, p 555

(1) 'No more important work of contemporary history has been written in our time.'

G514b King Carson, *Carson*, H. Montgomery Hyde, Heinemann, Obs. 10 May, p 10

G514c Tory Fabian, *My Political Life*, Vol. 1, L.S. Amery, Hutchinson, *NS & N*, 45, 1159, 23 May, p 618

(1) Though 'exciting and well written, it lacks historical perspective'.

G515. Hitler's Table Talk, *Hitler's Table Talk 1941–44*, intro. H.R. Trevor-Roper, Weidenfeld and Nicolson (*see also* G458), *MGW*. 68, 26. 25 Jun. p 11

(1) The introduction 'is beyond dispute the most penetrating study of Hitler yet made . . . Its inevitable fault is to be too rational. It tries to pin Hitler down within the confines of systematic thought.'

G516. Before Hitler, (a) *Modern German History*, Ralph Flenley, Dent; (b) *Deutsche Geschichte im Zeitalter der Massen*, Carl Misch, Stuttgart, Kohlhammer, *TLS*. 2682. 26 Jun. p 410

(a1) An indifferent account – the reader 'will not be disturbed by novel ideas nor by the discarding of legends'.

(b1) A good university text book; but it 'remains a history of rulers and political leaders'.

G517. Stuck in the Mud, *French Politics : The First Years of the Fourth Republic*, Dorothy Pickles, Royal Institute of International Affairs, *NS & N*. 46, 1165. 4 Jul. p 21

(1) 'Scholarly, accurate, well-balanced', but lacking in character. 'Chatham House is not much more than a glorified press-cutting establishment.'

G518. Red Cross, *Man Born to Live*, Ellen Hart, Gollancz, *MG*. 10 Jul. p 4

(1) 'A first class life of (Henri) Dunant: scholarly, critical, and with a sound grasp of history.'

Repr. *MGW*. 69, 3. 16 Jul. p 10

G519. A Christian Cynic, *Christianity*, *Diplomacy and War*, Herbert Butterfield, Epworth, *MG*. 21 Jul. p 4

(1) Scathing in his comments – he indicts the author for advocating 'worldly wisdom', not pacifism.

Repr. *MGW*. 69, 7. 13 Aug. p 10

G520. The Appeasement Years: Germany and Her Neighbours, *GD*, Ser. D., 5, *MG*. 28 Jul. p 4

(1) 'Hitler hardly appears; and we can therefore judge how Germany would have behaved as a Great Power if her old ruling class had gone its way without his interference.' He finds, 'They had the same aims as Hitler; only more caution.'

Repr. *MGW*. 69, 6. 6 Aug. p 11 and A9, pp 154–6

G521. *Scharnhorst*, Rudolf Stadelmann, Wiesbaden, Limes, 1952, *EHR*. 68, 268. Jul. p 491

(1) The two completed chapters contain many bricks made from little straw.

G522. *Die politischen Wahlen in Niedersachen 1867–1949*, Gunther Franz, Bremen-Horn, Dorn, 1951, Ibid. p 492

(1) A good mixed area to choose for a statistical study of German electoral behaviour.

G523. The Other Dictator, *Mussolini*, Paola Monelli, Thames and Hudson, *Obs*. 23 Aug. p 7

(1) Unfavourable – it is more concerned with his love life than in appraising his importance. He suggests that the Italians depict him as a clown and plead 'It was all a joke' in much the same way as the Germans plead 'Hitler deceived us'.

G524. William Cobbett, *A Bibliography of William Cobbett's Writings*, M.L. Pearl, Oxford U.P., *NS & N*. 46, 1173. 29 Aug. pp 236–7

(2) The book is merely the occasion for a piece which praises Bunyan and Cobbett and denounces

the Establishment – the THING.

In his introduction to the essay in A21 he writes, 'The essay contains, I think, the first use of the term, The Establishment, an invention usually attributed to Henry Fairlie.'

Repr. A9, pp 7–11 and A21, pp 49–54

G525. The Secret of Communism, *The Pattern of Communist Revolution*, Hugh Seton-Watson, Methuen, *Obs.* 6 Sept. p 8

(1) The author 'makes more sense of Communism than anyone has made before', though in places he 'gets submerged by his facts'.

G526. The Abyssinian War, *Prelude to World War II*, Gaetano Salvemini, Gollancz, *MG.* 25 Sept. p 4

(1) Feels it is more of a polemical tract than detached history.

G527. Family History, *The Onslow Family*, C.E. Vulliamy, Chapman and Hall, *MG.* 29 Sept. p 4

(1) The author is more interested in 'historical colour' than in the aristocracy as a social and political institution.

G528. War Guilt, *The Origins of the War of 1914*, Vol. 2, Luigi Albertini, Oxford U.P., *MG.* 6 Oct. p 4

(1) 'More worth while' than volume one. 'The strength of the book lies in its intense examination of these well known details.'

(2) 'No Great Power wanted a general war ... the responsibility for starting the crisis lay with Vienna; the responsibility for letting it turn into a general war lay with Berlin.'

Repr. *MGW.* 69, 16. 15 Oct. p 10

G529. A New Voice for Culture, *Encounter* (monthly journal, ed. Stephen Spender and Irving Kristol), Secker and Warburg, *Li.* 50, 1284. 8 Oct. pp 596, 599

(1) Comments that the articles are 'by the elderly and established ... Perhaps future numbers will finds for us writers who cannot remember the first world war and were unknown before the second'. 'It is difficult to resist the suspicion that the practical

impulse which brought them together was anti-communism.'

G530. Revolution, *The French Revolution*, A. Goodwin, Hutchinson, *MG*. 16 Oct. p 4

(1) 'A useful little summary of what the French think about the revolution at the moment ... Life and passion are lacking.'

G531. Our Rude Forefathers, (a) *The Age of Paradox*, John W. Dodds, Gollancz; (b) *English Radicalism*, S. Maccoby, Allen and Unwin, *NS & N*. 46, 1180. 17 Oct. p 462

(a1) A collection of articles which are 'at first exciting and stimulating', then irritating.

(b1) There is no analysis of 'who the Radicals were or where they found support, no analysis of the ideas, no estimate of their backing'; a book written on the 'rag-bag principle'.

G532. Moscow Mission 1939, *BD*. 3rd Ser., 6, *1939*, Part 1: The Setting, *MG*. 20 Oct. p 6; Part 2: The Details, *MG*. 21 Oct. p 4

Repr. Part 1: *MGW*. 69, 19. 5 Nov. p 11; Part 2: *MGW*. 69; 20. 5 Nov. p 12 and as part of 'The Alliance That Failed', A9, pp 159–62 and A17, pp 261–4

G533. Boomtime, *The Great Frontier*, Walter Prescott Webb, Secker and Warburg, *MG*. 23 Oct. p 4

(1) Sceptical about his interpretation of modern history.

G534. Bloomsbury Lost, *Principia Politica*, Leonard Woolf, Hogarth, *Obs*. 25 Oct. p 10

(1) Criticises the book as 'an hysterical denunciation of Soviet totalitarianism'.

G535. Problem Child, *The Rebirth of Austria*, Richard Hiscocks, Oxford U.P., *NS & N*. 46, 1182. 31 Oct. pp 528, 530

(1) The account is marred by 'its cautious official tone' and its belief in 'an imaginary opposition against Hitler'.

G536. *La Diplomazia del Regno di Sardegna durante la prima Guerra d'Independenza*, Vol. 3, ed. Guido

Quazza, Turin, Museo Nazionale del Risorgimento, 1952, *EHR*. 68, 269. Oct. p 659

(1) 'The project of an alliance (between Sardinia and the Two Sicilies) was always illusory. As with Austria and Prussia in Germany, there was no room for two serious Italian kingdoms once the national idea had been launched.'

G537. *ID*, 3rd Ser., 1 (Mar. 1896-Apr. 1897), ed. Carlo Morandi. *Ibid.* pp 660–1

(1) 'The volume contains no surprises'. It is overshadowed by the defeat at Adowa.

G538. *Vanguard of Nazism*, Robert G.L. Waite, Harvard U.P., 1952, *Ibid.* p 666

(1) 'A book of high scholarship'. It deals with the Free Corps, who 'had only the violence of National Socialism, not its ideas'.

G539. Diplomacy Between The Wars, *The Diplomats 1919–1939*, ed. Gordon Craig and Felix Gilbert, Princeton U.P.; Cumberlege, *MG*. 3 Nov. p 4

(1) 'A collection of brilliant essays, each one well written and with solid learning behind it.'

G540. The German Generals in Politics, *The Nemesis of Power*, J.W. Wheeler-Bennett, Macmillan, *NS & N*. 46, 1184. 14 Nov. pp 604, 606

(1) Feels that 'it seems hard to blame the generals for not saving the German people from themselves'. The book is too long and covers ground covered in the author's other books.

G541. France, *A History of France*, Lucien Romier, Macmillan, *MG*. 17 Nov. p 4

(1) A history of the French monarchy, not of the French people. Critical of his interpretation.

G542. More of Mr. Amery, *My Political Life*, Vol. 2, L.S. Amery, Hutchinson, *NS & N*. 46, 1185. 21 Nov. p 642

(1) 'His political autobiography is designed to advocate an imperial tariff union as much as to contribute to the historical record.'

G543. Stumbling Into War: American Policy 1940–1, *The Undeclared War 1940–41*, William L. Langer and S. Everett Gleason, Royal Institute of International Affairs, *MG*. 25 Nov. p 6

(1) 'Their book establishes itself at once as the leading authority for the period.'

Repr. as 'America's Entry', *MGW*. 69, 23. 3 Dec. p 11 and under the original title in A9, pp 171–3 and A17, pp 306–9

G544. A Monopolist Explains, *The BBC From Within*, Lord Simon of Wythenshawe, Gollancz, *The National and English Review*. 141. Nov. pp 303–5

(1) This, like all such descriptions of bureaucracies, does 'nothing to suggest the reality'. He denounces the BBC as being run by and for the Establishment.

(2) BBC controllers: 'Their task is to stop things going out, or rather to see that everything which goes out is innocuous. Their attention is focussed on possible complaints, not on pleasing the public.'

G545. Thoughts on Tolstoy, *The Hedgehog and the Fox*, Isaiah Berlin, Weidenfeld and Nicolson, *NS & N*. 46, 1188. 12 Dec. p 768

(1) Very favourable – 'one sometimes feels that he has more ideas than all the historical authors he sets out to illuminate'. The book is 'something in the nature of an intellectual firework display'.

G546. The Grand Alliance, *America, Britain and Russia*, William Hardy McNeill, Oxford, *NS & N*. 46, 1189. 19 Dec. p 800

(1) 'He has the true historian's detachment' and 'writes a clear and effective prose' but it 'tells us at great length what we knew already'. 'Chatham House seems to have lost interest in the problem of communication.'

1954

G547. Lord Ripon, *The Viceroyalty of Lord Ripon 1880–1884*, S. Gopal, Oxford U.P., 1953, *MG*. 8 Jan. p 4

(1) Praises the book as being 'full of interest as well as being oddly moving. But there are some dreary pages.'

G548. Metternich, *Metternich*, Constantin De Grunwald, Falcon, 1953, *NS & N*. 47, 1192. 9 Jan. pp 43–4

(2) A.J.P.T.'s essay deflates Metternich, who, at the time the essay was written, was finding favour amongst conservatives.

Repr. in A9, pp 26–30 A15, pp 21–5 and A17, pp 22–6

G549. A Soldier Without Politics, *The Memoirs of Field Marshal Kesselring* Kimber, 1953, *NS & N*. 47, 1193. 16 Jan. p 76

(1) 'Even duller than most' military memoirs.

G550. Nobility, *The European Nobility in the Eighteenth Century*, ed. A. Goodwin, Black, 1953, *MG*. 20 Jan. p 4

(1) 'A volume which can occupy a profitable half hour but without much addition to our understanding.'

Repr. *MGW*. 70, 5. 28 Jan. p 10

G551. *The Origins of the War of 1914*, Vol. 2 (*see above* G528), *EHR*. 69, 270. Jan. pp 122–5

(1) Feels that it supersedes previous accounts. However, 'It is a final contribution to the controversy over 'war guilt', rather than the beginning of detached study; the work, in fact, of a contemporary, not of a historian.'

(2) 'German policy cannot be understood on a purely diplomatic basis; and, though the military material is scantier than the diplomatic, enough is known to make it clear that in Germany alone strategy dictated policy. This is surely the essential reason why the crisis of July 1914 ended in war.'

G552. The Devil on the Wall, *How Russia Makes War*, Raymond L. Garthoff, Allen and Unwin, *NS & N*. 47, 1197. 13 Feb. pp 198, 200

(1) It has serious defects such as a weak historical background and a tendency to draw political conclusions from the military writings.

G553. *The Prophet Armed*, Isaac Deutscher, Oxford, *NS & N*. 47, 1198. 20 Feb. pp 226, 228

(1) 'A striking work of rehabilitation' – but warns

that the author 'like all Marxists . . . wants always to discover profound historical forces when there was only the will of men'.

Repr. as 'Trotsky' in A9, pp 131–5, A15, pp 170–4 and A17, pp 174–8

G554. Private Life of a Nazi, *The Bormann Letters*, ed. H.R. Trevor-Roper, Weidenfeld and Nicolson, *MG*. 26 Feb. p 4

(1) 'If any private soldier was chosen at random from the British (or German) Army and his letters home published, they would be more entertaining and of more historical value than these.'

G555. Interplay, *Russia and the Weimar Republic*, Lionel Kochan, Cambridge, Bowes and Bowes, *MG*. 5 Mar. p 4

(1) 'It deals with a vital subject of recent history more effectively than it has ever been dealt with before. It also merits high praise technically as an attempt to write diplomatic history without dullness.'

G556. High and Low Politics, (a) *The Origins of the Labour Party*, Henry Pelling, Macmillan; (b) *Mr. Balfour's Poodle*, Roy Jenkins, Heinemann, *NS & N*. 47, 1200. 6 Mar. p 292

(a1) 'His book has rare distinction as a work of scholarship, told simply, without display and final in its results.'

(a2) Keir Hardie 'gave the Labour Movement the dual character that it has always retained: concerned both with the practical improvement of day-to-day conditions and with the achievement of a Socialist Utopia. It is a betrayal of the Labour Party to think that it should aim exclusively at either.'

(b1) 'A brilliant and instructive book', though 'the story is told in strictly parliamentary terms'.

G557. Popes and Progress, (a) *Politics of Belief in Nineteenth Century France*, Philip Spencer, Faber; (b) *Pio Nono*, E.E.Y. Hales, Eyre and Spottiswoode, *Obs*. 7 Mar. p 9

(a1) 'A brilliant book . . . at once sympathetic,

learned and dispassionate.'

(b1) 'A good book, though a more controversial one.'

G558. All in Fun, *Madame de Pompadour*, Nancy Mitford, Hamilton, *MG.* 12 Mar. p 6

(1) 'All who admired *The Pursuit of Love* will be delighted to hear that its characters have appeared again, this time in fancy dress. They now claim to be leading figures in French history.'

Repr. as 'Versailles Was All Such Fun', *MGW.* 70, 12. 18 Mar. p 10

G559. The Red Light Again, (a) *Russia: A History*, Sydney Harcave, Cleaver-Hume; (b) *The Dynamics of Soviet Society*, W.W. Rostow, Secker and Warburg, *NS & N.* 47, 1202. 20 Mar. pp 376–7

(a1) A useful text book, but thin on interpretation.

(b1) 'It is written in a sort of sociological gibberish'. It 'starts from the assumption that the American outlook is the only one that is morally valid'.

G560. Beating the Idol, *German History*, ed. Hans Kohn, Allen and Unwin, *NS & N.* 47, 1203. 27 Mar. pp 416–7

(1) 'None of the writers attempt to increase our understanding of the past; they merely moralise about it in the light of the present.' 'Now German power is in ruins; and thc historians have rounded on their old idol.'

G561. Historical Essays, *Catherine the Great and Other Studies*, G.P. Gooch, Longmans, *MG.* 30 Mar. p 4

(1) Agreeable to read – but really anthologies of letters.

G562. *Cavour and Garibaldi 1860*, D. Mack Smith, Cambridge U.P., *NS & N.* 47, 1207. pp 535–6

Repr. as 'Cavour and Garibaldi' in A9, pp 31–35, A15, pp 71–5, and A17, pp 82–6

G563. Down to Earth, *The Secret People*, E.W. Martin, Phoenix House, *Obs.* 9 May. p 9

(1) A good book, but contradictory in its views

on rural change. Written by a man 'soaked in rural experience'.

G564. Engaged Historians, *The European Inheritance*, 3 Vols. ed. Sir Ernest Barker, Sir George Clark and P. Vaucher, Oxford, *NS & N*. 47, 1210. 15 May. pp 636, 638

(1) Criticises the volumes for the unevenness of treatment and for most of the essays being on Western Europe. However he warmly praises Sir George Clark's essay on the sixteenth and seventeenth centuries: 'This is a work of rare mastery, which challenges comparison with that of the greatest historians . . . Sir George Clark is the Voltaire of our times, though a Voltaire rather ashamed of his wit.'

G565. Prophets of Humanism, *French Liberal Thought in the Eighteenth Century*, 2nd edn. Kingsley Martin, Turnstile Press, *TLS*. 2729. 21 May. p 328

(1) Feels that his criticisms of the philosophers 'now strike us as unduly timid'.

Repr. as 'Prophets of Man' in A9, pp 1–6

G566. Ding-Dong, *The Decisive Battles of the Western World*, Vol. 1, Major General J.F.C. Fuller, Eyre and Spottiswoode, *Obs*. 23 May. p 8

(1) 'An exciting book . . . but rather indigestible when taken in longer doses'.

(2) 'War must come into the record of history, whatever else is left out. It has been the greatest single factor in the shaping of human history.' Suggests. that historians do not like to admit this, 'We prefer to regard them as delivering verdicts that have already been determined by more profound causes.'

G567. *German Marxism and Russian Communism*, John Plamenatz, Longmans, *NS & N*. 47, 1212. 29 May. pp 702, 704

Repr. as 'Marx and Lenin' in A9, pp 126–30, A15, pp 165–9, and A17, pp 133–7

G568. Historical Wisdom, *The Historian's Craft*, Marc

Bloch, Manchester U.P., *NS & N.* 47, 1213. 5 Jun. p 736

(1) 'There could be no better introduction than this book to work on history. But in the last resort the best introduction is work itself; and it cannot be conveyed by any manual.'

(2) 'There are those who regard social history as merely 'history with the politics left out'. Bloch taught that it was rather history with everything put in – a hard doctrine, but the only one worth applying.'

G569. Hard Facts, *Poland: White Eagle on a Red Field*, Samuel L. Sharp, Harvard U.P.; Cumberlege, *MG.* 15 Jun. p 4

(1) 'An historical and political analysis written with strict scientific detachment'.

G570. World's-Eye View, *World History from 1914–1950*, David Thomson, Oxford U.P., *TLS.* 2734. 25 Jun. p 403

(1) 'His enterprise merits the warmest praise, even though the task is sometimes beyond him.' His angle is very much European, indeed English.

G571. Thinkers and Thoughts, (a) *European Thought in the Eighteenth Century*, Paul Hazard, Hollis and Carter; (b) *Politics and Opinion in the Nineteenth Century*, John Bowle, Cape, *NS & N.* 47, 1216. 26 Jun. pp 838–9

(a1) 'A brilliant failure, despite its scholarship and exuberance'. He finds the treatment of European thought as a unity to be unconvincing.

(b1) Unfavourable – feels that the author 'pats on the back' any thinker who anticipated the way the author thinks that the world should be going.

G572. Soft Words, *The Evolution of Diplomatic Method*, Harold Nicolson, Constable, *Obs.* 4 Jul. p 10

(1) Suggests that 'he has confused two different things – diplomatic method and the principles of international relations'.

(2) 'Diplomacy is not only the art of peace.

It is also the art of getting your way by evoking the shadow of war.' Points to Palmerston in 1840 and Bismarck 1871–90.

G573. Napolcon In His Letters, *Napoleon's Letters*, ed. J.M. Thompson, Everyman Edition, Dent, *MG*. 6 Jul. p 6

(1) An admirable anthology.

Repr. *MGW*. 71, 2. 8 Jul. p 11

G574. Hitler's Empire, (a) *Hitler's Europe: Survey of International Affairs 1939–1946*, ed. Arnold Toynbee and Veronica Toynbee, Oxford; (b) *Documents on International Affairs 1939–1946*, Vol. 2, ed. Margaret Carlyle, Oxford, *NS & N*. 48, 1218. 10 Jul. p 47

(a1) 'A survey, based solely on printed sources, to a rather idiosyncratic design by Professor Toynbee'.

(a and b1) Chatham House's books lead 'people to think that contemporary history can be based only on intelligent use of newspapers'.

(2) '... they did little to mobilise the economic resources of Europe even at the height of the war. Germany itself was no better case; the war effort itself was trivial until after Stalingrad.'

G575. French Democracy, *Politics in Post-War France*, Philip Williams, Longmans, *NS & N*. 48, 1220. 24 Jul. p 108

(2) 'What France suffers from is *incivisme*, not a faulty constitution; and the politicians do their best to operate democracy in a country where the will of the people is mainly negative.'

G576. Bobs Bahadur, *The Life of Lord Roberts*, David James, Hollis and Carter, *Obs*. 25 Jul. p 9

(1) 'A sensible book' – and the section on Roberts part in military reforms is 'an important addition to our political history'.

(2) 'If he failed to catch the Boer guerrillas, the Germans – with infinitely superior equipment – did no better against the Yugoslav partisans in the last war. Indeed these achievements (Afghanistan and South Africa) of the old British Army seem miraculous ... '

G577. Diplomatic Episode, *Ambassadors and Secret Agents*, Alfred Cobban, Cape, *MG*. 27 Jul. p 4

(1) 'Accuracy and scholarship are here in plenty' – but 'the reader finds it hard to discover what was at stake'.

G578. *ID*, 1st Ser., 1, (1861) and 8th Ser., 7 and 8 (May-Nov. 1939), *EHR*. 69, 272. Jul. pp 460–2

(1) Praises the editors for arranging the volumes in chronological order, but regrets that the summaries have not been organised by topic.

G579. *Les Socialismes francais et allemand et le problème de la Guerre 1870–1914*, M.M. Drachkovitch, Geneva, Droz, *Ibid.* pp 504–5

(1) 'A most penetrating account'.

(2) 'The Germans . . . had the strongest of all Socialist parties and they boasted a theoretical superiority which they had inherited from Marx. But they also inherited from him a belief in German primacy and a contempt for the Slav peoples.'

G580. The Twilight of the God, *The Last Days of Hitler* (*see above* G282 and G384), *TLS*. 2740. 6 Aug. Special Supplement, 'Personal Preference Appreciations', p xxv

Repr. in A9, pp 179–83, and A17, pp 320–4

G581. The Uneasy Alliance, *Dictators Face to Face*, Dino Alfieri, Elek, *MG*. 13 Aug. p 4

(1) He is 'a good and serious writer', but 'there is little that is startlingly new'. Better than most ambassador's memoirs.

Repr. as 'Dictators', *MGW*. 71, 9. 26 Aug. p 10

G582. Don't Forget The Literature! *The Challenge of Socialism*, ed. Henry Pelling, Black, *NS & N*. 48, 1223. 14 Aug. pp 187–8

(1) Argues that the approach of the series, of evolving doctrines, is 'irresistible to the children of the Darwinian age'.

(2) 'British Socialism did not 'evolve'. It appeared fully fledged in the eighteen-eighties. The so-called forerunners appeal only to historical curiosity . . . British Socialism had a certain international background, but no British background even

unconsciously.'

G583. Blue No Longer, *Russia's Danubian Empire*, Gordon Shepherd, Heinemann, *NS & N*. 48, 1225. 28 Aug. p 240

(1) 'A sensible, well-balanced survey'.

G584. The Last Twenty Days: A Warning Disregarded? *BD*, 3rd Ser., 7, (Aug-Sept. 1939), *MG*. 1 Sept. p 4

Repr. *MGW*. 71, 11. 9 Sept. p 11 and as part of 'The Alliance That Failed', A9, pp 165–7 and A17, pp 267–9

G585. *Louis Napoleon and the Second Empire*, J.M. Thompson, Oxford, Blackwell, *NS & N*. 48, 1228. 18 Sept. pp 327–8

(1) A good book but weak on the diplomacy and the system of government of the Second Empire. 'Less clever and sparkling than Guedella's'.

(2) A.J.P.T. vigorously denounces Louis Napoleon. 'By his negligence, he let France slither down from her great position in Europe. Only after his fall did men discover the easy excuse that the decline was inevitable.'

G586. The End of the Affair, *BD*, 3rd Ser., 7 (*see above* G584), *NS & N*. 48, 1229. 25 Sept. p 364

(1) Criticises the printing of only selected minutes by the permanent officials of the Foreign Office. The documents show that 'whoever conducted British foreign policy, it was not the Foreign Office'.

G587. The End of the Russian Revolution, *A History of Soviet Russia*, Vol. 4, E.H. Carr, Macmillan, *NS & N*. 48, 1230. 2 Oct. p 396

(1) 'The best of the series. Events and policies, measures and men, are merged into a coherent whole.' However, 'His work tells the story of Russia's rulers, not of Russia's people.'

G588. The G.O.M. *Gladstone*, Philip Magnus, Murray, *NS & N*. 48, 1231. 9 Oct. p 446

(1) 'A model of unassuming scholarship and understanding'; very good on his personality, less satisfactory on his politics.

(2) 'He was a human volcano; but what made

him so terrifying and impressive . . . was that the volcano was always under control.' 'It is difficult to resist the feeling that Gladstone was on God's side because God had so arranged things as always to be on Gladstone's.'

G589. Philosopher Kings, *The Men Who Ruled India: The Guardians*, Philip Woodruff, Cape, *Obs*. 10 Oct. p 8

(1) 'Moving and brilliant'.

(2) Observes of British administration in India: 'It is the nearest thing there ever has been to Plato's ideal state. The Indian civilians saw themselves as Plato's Guardians, ruling in complete detachment, secure in their position and with a modest pension to look forward to, but otherwise without any motive of material reward.' However the merchants and businessmen were less altruistic.

G590. "Much Learning. . . ." *A Study of History*, Vols. 7–10, Arnold Toynbee, Oxford, *NS & N*. 48, 1232. 16 Oct. pp 478–80

(1) Argues that Toynbee's scheme is 'a generalisation from the history of the Ancient World', indeed it 'applied only to one part of the Roman world'.

(2) 'These monstrous volumes with their parade of learning are a repudiation of Rationalism. The worst sin is to believe that Man made himself . . . Faith, or to put it more bluntly, Superstition, is the only thing that will save us from the Wrath to Come.'

G591. A Cracked Hero, (a) *General Gordon*, Lord Elton, Collins; (b) *His Country Was The World*, Charles Beatty, Chatto and Windus, *MG*. 29 Oct. p 4

(1) Beatty comes nearer to understanding Gordon.

(2) 'We can all agree that the failure to relieve Gordon was the most discreditable episode in Gladstone's career.'

Repr. *MGW*. 71, 22. 25 Nov. p 10

G592. *FD*, 1st Ser., 13 (Oct 1896-Dec. 1897), 1953, *EHR*. 69, 273. Oct. pp 637–9

(1) It tells the story of Hanotaux's disappoint-

ments with the Russian alliance after Nicholas II had returned to St Petersburg.

G593. *ID*, 7th Ser., 1 (Oct 1922-Apr 1923), ed. R. Moscati, 1953, *Ibid.* pp 639–41

(1) Adds to our knowledge of German reparations and peace with Turkey. 'In neither did Italian policy show a specifically Fascist character'.

G594. *Erzherzog Franz Ferdinand von Österreich-Este*, Rudolf Kiszling, Graz-Köln, Böhlaus, 1953, *Ibid.* pp 687–8

(1) 'A work of monarchist piety', which is accurately compiled and which makes use of the arch-duke's archives.

G595. *Geschichte der Weimarer Republik*, Vol. 1, Eric Eyck, Erlenbach-Zwich, Rentsch, *Ibid.* pp 689–90

(1) Lucid, but its judgements are those of a participant not of an historian.

G596. A Satellite, *Hungarian Premier*, Nicholas Kallay, Oxford U.P., *MG.* 9 Nov. p 4

(1) 'An important contribution to recent history . . . It shows all the civilisation of old Hungary, but also its arrogance.'

G597. Appeaser's Apology, *Nine Troubled Years*, Viscount Templewood, Collins, *NS & N.* 48, 1236. 13 Nov. pp 620–1

(1) Observes that it is a clever book, but it 'revives the half-forgotten impression that Sir Samuel Hoare was the most complacent and fatuous, even the most detestable, of the four Appeasers'.

(2) 'Quakerism has always been in danger of smugness, and is redeemed from it only by obstinate radicalism.'

G598. The Dear Old Dialectic, (a) *Marxism Past and Present*, R.N. Carew Hunt, Bles; (b) *Dialectical Materialism*, Vol. 3, Maurice Cornforth, Lawrence and Wishart, *NS & N.* 48, 1238. 27 Nov. p 700

(a1) 'A conscientious anti-Marxist'.

(b1) 'A believer gifted with an admirably clear style of exposition'.

(2) Suggests that Marxism has all the qualities

of a religion. 'It will make wonderful material for a Gibbon one day – as farcical a chapter of human history as any devised.'

G599. Benes the Optimist, *Memoirs of Dr. Edward Benes*, Allen and Unwin, *MG*. 30 Nov. p 4

(1) 'A dull formal book. The reader will recognise the precise Benes whom we knew during the war.'

Repr. as 'The Optimist', *MGW*. 72, 3. 20 Jan. 1955. p 11

G600. Acton, *Acton on History*, Lionel Kochan, Deutsch, *MG*. 3 Dec. p 6

(1) 'A brief, subtle essay' – the author 'has analysed Acton's doctrines and contradictions with fascinating clarity'.

(2) 'Lord Acton is probably the greatest historian whose books were never written.'

G601. The Death of an Illusion, *Assignment to Catastrophe*, Vol. 2, Major-General Sir Edward Spears, Heinemann, *Obs*. 12 Dec. p 9

(1) 'Churchill and Sir Edward Spears are the only two men who have written books of superlative excellence about both wars.'

G602. The Policeman of Europe, (a) *Tsar Nicholas I*, Constantin De Grunwald, MacGibbon and Kee; (b) *A Diary of the Crimea*, George Palmer Evelyn, Duckworth; (c) *Roger Fenton: Photographer of the Crimean War*, Helmut and Alison Gernsheim, Secker and Warburg, *NS & N*. 48, 1241. 18 Dec. p 832

(a1) 'An effective, compact biography, well written, sensible in judgment, and buttressed with some original research'.

(b1) Not a great contribution to history, but 'it does recapture the atmosphere of that odd, gentlemanly war'.

(c1) Praises the photographs, Fenton's letters and 'the valuable introduction'.

G603. "I Was France": General de Gaulle's War Memoirs, *Mémoirs de Guerre*, Vol. 1, General de Gaulle, Paris, Plon, *MG*. 22 Dec. p 4

(1) 'They are impersonal, dispassionate, with no attempt to interpret his past actions for the sake of the present'.

(2) 'De Gaulle was uncompromising, impatient, tactless, yet with it all the most unselfish among all the leaders of the Second World War.'

Repr. *MGW*. 71, 27. 30 Dec. p 11

G604. Politics in a Vacuum, *Histoire de Vichy 1940–1944*, Robert Aron, Paris, Artheme Fayard, *TLS*. 2761. 31 Dec. p 847

(1) 'Deserves warm praise for attempting to write with a scholar's detachment. He has got somewhere near what will probably be the verdict of the future.'

(2) Laval: 'He remained to the end a sordid intriguer; yet he was redeemed by the nobility which always accompanies those who devote themselves to a cause.'

1955

G605. The Phoney War, *GD*, Ser. D., 8, *4 Sep 1939–18 Mar. 1940*, 1954, *NS & N*. 49, 1243. 1 Jan. p 21

(1) Of such volumes: 'Their bulk, their jargon, their insistence on forgotten issues combine to make them unreadable'.

(2) 'Hitler could really judge a situation as it existed at the moment without worrying about systems of geopolitics or what he said the day before. ... He was a man without aims – the greatest asset for success (or failure) ... perhaps he was always mad. If he was ever sane, he certainly became mad in the six months covered by these documents.'

G606. *Tradition and Change: Nine Oxford Lectures*, Conservative Central Office, 1954, *NS & N*. 49, 1246. 22 Jan. pp 108–9

(2) '... his secret was the absence of moral earnestness ... Gladstone was the Victorian conscience; Disraeli the release from it'.

Repr. as 'Dizzy' in A9, pp 65–9, and A21, pp 116–21

G607. Soviet Fables, (a) *Soviet Russia*, Jacob Miller, Hutchinson; (b) *In The Workshop of the Revolution*, I.N. Steinberg, Gollancz, *NS & N.* 49, 1248. 5 Feb. p 188

(a1) It lacks reality – it accepts the Stalinist arguments.

(b1) Not a great contribution to history – but it is a reminder of 'the way Lenin swept aside legal and moral scruples'.

G608. Sad Satellite, *Alexander von Battenberg*, 2nd edn. Egan Cesar Conte Corti, Cassell, *MG.* 8 Feb. p 4

(1) 'Honest and reliable though a little drab' – 'the historian will find some useful information'.

G609. Satan's Offspring, *The Old Cause*, John Carswell, Cresset, *NS & N.* 49, 1250. 19 Feb. p 252

(1) 'It is easier to commend his enterprise than his achievement'. 'If Whiggism had lost all meaning, why did men attach so much importance to being Whigs?'

G610. Liberals and South Africa, *Imperial Policy and South Africa 1902–10*, G.B. Pyrah, Oxford, Clarendon, *MG.* 25 Feb. p 6

(1) 'An interesting account . . . the story has never been told with such care and detail before'.

G611. Tupper on the Air, *Britain and the Tide of World Affairs*, Oliver S. Franks, Oxford, *NS & N.* 49, 1253. 12 Mar. p 366

(1) He denounces these Reith lectures – 'No writer has assembled so many platitudes in so few pages since Martin Tupper was in his prime'.

G612. Good Germans, (a) *Stresemann and the Rearmament of Germany*, Hans W. Gatzke, John Hopkins; Cumberlege; (b) *The Wilhelmstrasse*, Paul Seabury, California U.P.; Cambridge U.P., *MG.* 18 Mar. p 6

(a1) 'Rather slight and leaves some problems unsolved; but it presents a more convincing picture of Stresemann than was current in the days when he received the Nobel Prize'.

(b1) 'A book which, though specialised, can be

read with pleasure by the general reader. It is written with nerve as well as scholarship . . .'

Repr. as 'The Problem of German Diplomacy', *MGW*. 72, 12. 24 Mar. p 11

G613. Humility, *The Letters of Jacob Burckhardt*, ed. Alexander Dru, Routledge, *MG*. 25 Mar. p 9

(1) Praises the selection and the 'first rate sketch of Burckhardt's life' in the introduction.

Repr. as 'Burckhardt's Life and Letters', *MGW*. 72, 14. 7 Apr. p 11

G614. King For a Week, *A King's Heritage*, King Peter II of Yugoslavia, Cassell, *MG*. 1 Apr. p 4

(1) 'Sad and drab'. 'Of serious historical information there is little . . . though enough to show that, whatever King Peter's virtues, his Ministers would have ruined any cause.'

G615. How Power Corrupts, *The Origins of the Communist Autocracy*, Leonard Schapiro, Bell, *NS & N*. 49, 1257. 9 Apr. pp 510, 512

(1) 'Almost incredible that a book of such impartiality could be written in . . . the cold war'; though he regrets the pedestrian style.

(2) 'There was a time when capitalism seemed the greatest of evils and its overthrow the greatest of goods. Now power – political power, scientific power, any sort of power – has taken first place among human ills.'

G616. The Affair, *The Dreyfus Case*, Guy Chapman, Hart-Davis, *NS & N*. 49, 1259. 23 Apr. pp 584, 586

(1) Praises it, but observes that the author is Establishment minded.

(2) 'Once hitch yourself to the Establishment and you must become the supporter of injustice sooner or later.'

G617. Socialists, *The Second International 1889–1914*, James Joll, Weidenfeld and Nicolson, *MG*. 29 Apr. p 8

(1) 'Admirable as far as it goes'. Regrets that the author does not analyse its discussions adequately.

G618. Straws Without Brick, *Heretics and Renegades*,

Isaac Deutscher, Hamilton, *NS & N.* 49, 1260. 30 Apr. pp 622–3

(1) Very critical of the author's views, which he sees as special pleading in order to portray Stalinism as an aberration in Soviet Communism. He observes that 'the hard brick of Power is missing' from the analysis.

G619. *ID*, 5th Ser., 1, (Aug-Oct 1914), ed. Augusto Torre, 1954, *EHR*. 70, 275. Apr. pp 302–5

(1) Particularly valuable, as the only set of documents after the outbreak of war, other than the Russian.

G620. *Der Krimkrieg und die Entstehung der modernen Flotten*, Wilhelm Treue, Göttingen, Musterschmidt, 1954, *Ibid.* p 343

(1) As the Crimean War was not naval, this is 'a thin book – a record of failures and futility'.

G621. A Wasted Life, *James Maxton*, John McNair, Allen and Unwin, *Obs.* 15 May. p 16

(1) 'His admirable book is a straight essay in hero-worship . . . The triumphs of the platform are accepted as sufficient in themselves.'

(2) 'Maxton's failure was more than the failure of a man. It was the failure of a movement – the movement of romantic revolutionary socialism. Keir Hardie, Maxton's predecessor, could combine romance and reality . . . Revolutionary Socialism turned into the Bolshevik dictatorship; parliamentary Socialism achieved the practical gains of the Welfare State. There was no third way between Lenin and Arthur Henderson.'

G622. How It All Began, *The Russian Revolution 1917*, N.N. Sukhanov, Oxford U.P., *NS & N.* 49, 1263. 21 May. p 724

(1) 'Incomparably the best and most important account of those tremendous events'. Regrets that this is an abridged version.

G623. God's Eye View, *A Train of Powder*, Rebecca West, Macmillan, *MG*. 3 Jun. p 2

(1) He has serious reservations about her

approach; but feels, 'When this method comes off it is tremendous' – and praises her essays on the Nuremburg trials as being 'above anything that has been written about Germany since the war'.

Repr. *MGW*. 72, 24. 16 Jun. p 10

G624. No Button A, *Failure of a Revolution*, Rudolf Coper, Cambridge U.P., *NS & N*. 49, 1265. 4 Jun. p 791

(1) Unfavourable, both to its style and content. 'Reading this book is like a conversation on the telephone with someone who has failed to press Button A.' (This refers to the former public telephones in Britain, where the caller pressed a button marked A on hearing the call answered, and a connection was effected.)

G625. William Morris: Marxist, *William Morris : Romantic to Revolutionary*, E.P. Thompson, Lawrence and Wishart, *Obs*. 10 Jul. p 12

(1) 'Of the greatest value and interest'; but marred by being too long and dominated by the Communist Party line.

G626. Much as Before, *Liberated France*, Catherine Gavin, Cape, *NS & N*.50, 1271. 16 Jul. pp 78–9

(1) A familiar story, told with 'an admirable gift for simplification' and the combination of 'love of France with an extreme dislike of de Gaulle'.

(2) Observes that de Gaulle's outlook in retrospect appears 'impractical, romantic, rather absurd ... But, in so far as France still counts in the world, she owes it to de Gaulle and to him alone. Moreover, de Gaulle was the only European politician to co-operate with the Communists and to outwit them. Without de Gaulle, there would have been civil war in France, and perhaps Communist dictatorship.'

G627. Evil Genius of the Wilhelmstrasse? *Holstein Papers*, Vol. 1, *Memoirs*, ed. Norman Rich and M.H. Fisher, Cambridge U.P., *Li*. 54, 1377. 21 Jul. pp 102–4

Repr. as 'Holstein: The Mystery Man' in A9, pp 108–13, and A17, pp 153–8

G628. National History, *Biography of a Nation*, Angus Maude and Enoch Powell, Phoenix House, *MG*. 26 Jul. p 4

(1) 'A very satisfactory and very comforting history for the company directors who now determine the character of the Conservative party'.

Repr. as 'Without Tears' *MGW*. 73, 5. 4 Aug. p 10

G629. Litvinov Speaks – Or Does He? *Notes for a Journal*, Maxim Litvinov, Deutsch, *NS & N*. 50, 1273. 30 Jul. p 138

(1) Impossible to be sure if it is genuine. He feels that the gossip is convincing but is more doubtful about the political passages.

G630. The Innocent Banker, *My First Seventy Six Years*, Hjalmar Schacht, Wingate, *Obs*. 31 Jul. p 6

(1) Very long, dull and complacent.

G631. *The Wilhelmstrasse* (*see above* G612), *Am.Hist.R*. 60, 4. Jul. pp 893–4

G632. *l'Europe des Nationalités et l'Eveil de nouveaux Mondes*, Pierre Renouvin, Paris, Hachette, 1954, *EHR*. 70, 276. Jul. pp 503–4

(1) 'Distinguished by a sobriety of style and a mastery of sources' but feels that 'the strict diplomatic history comes off very badly'.

G633. *Alexander von Battenberg* (*see above* G608), *Ibid*. pp 505–6

(1) The author exaggerates the importance of Bulgaria in Russian policy.

G634. *Les Relations Germano-Sovietiques de 1933 à 1939*, ed. J.B. Duroselle, Paris, Colin, 1954, *Ibid*. pp 507–8

(1) 'All four essays combine scholarly impartiality with clear stimulating judgments.' Praises very highly the essay by G. Castellan.

G635. Raw Meat, (a) *Les Déliberations du Conseil des Quatre*, 2 Vols. Paul Mantoux, Paris, Centre national de la récherche scientifique; (b) *BD*, 3rd Ser., 8 (1938–9); (c) *Survey of International Affairs 1939–1946*, Vol. 2, ed. Arnold Toynbee and Veronica Toynbee, Oxford U.P., *NS & N*. 50, 1274. 6 Aug. p 166 (a1) Valuable and 'very good reading'. It is a different story to Keynes' 'ignorant evil men'; it tells of 'high minded statesmen, overwhelmed by their tasks but trying above all to be fair'.

(b1) 'Not much more than a tidying up operation' for Vols. 1–7.

(c1) 'Something between raw material and digested narrative', redeemed by Toynbee's brilliant introduction.

G636. Historical Essays, *Debates With Historians*, Pieter Geyl, Batsford, *MG*. 9 Aug. p 4

(1) 'The most important survey of general historical problems that has appeared for many years'.

Repr. *MGW*. 73, 8. 25 Aug. p 10

G637. Churchill and Myself, *My Political Life*, Vol. 3, L.S. Amery, Hutchinson, *NS & N*. 50, 1275. 13 Aug. pp 190–1

(1) Points to Amery's vanity; but observes that the man who made the speech that brought Neville Chamberlain down and so thereby 'ended a disgraceful era in British politics', 'does right to be vain'.

G638. Czech Statesmen, *Czech Tragedy*, Glorney Bolton, Watts, *MG*. 19 Aug. p 4

(1) 'moving and surprisingly frank . . . an admirable book full of interest'.

Repr. *MGW*. 73, 8. 25 Aug. p 10

G639. Masaryk on Russia, *The Spirit of Russia*, 2 Vols. T.G. Masaryk, Allen and Unwin, *NS & N*. 50, 1276. 20 Aug. p 222

(1) 'His greatest book' – 'the only man who mastered every aspect of the subject'. 'There is no nonsense here about Russia being alien to Europe, still less about Russian backwardness or barbarity . . . It is not the difference from Europe, but the fact of being different and similar at the same time which made Russia unique – the most attractive and tantalising of subjects.'

G640. A State Within A State: The German Army in Politics, *The Politics of the Prussian Army 1640–1945*,

Gordon A. Craig, Oxford, Clarendon, *MG*. 1 Sept. p 6

(1) 'A fascinating book'. 'Most of it is based on well-known printed sources, though it is none the worse for that. Narrative is the lifeblood of history; and scholars err grievously if they think they have discharged the historian's task by writing articles or books of learned detail.'

Repr. as 'German Generals in Politics', *MGW*. 73, 10. 8 Sept. p 11 and as 'German Army in Politics' in A9, pp 136–8, and A17, pp 190–3

G641. Socialism for Us, *Socialism and the Individual*, W.A. Sinclair, Hale, *MG*. 2 Sept. p 4

(1) 'There is a fine intellectual honesty, a readiness to think things through from the beginning that Socialist literature has lost for a long time'.

(2) 'Experience so far shows that the Labour party will tolerate capitalist anarchy so long as it can exact tribute in the form of the Welfare State.'

Repr. as 'Socialism for Unbelievers', *MGW*. 73, 10. 8 Sept. p 10

G642. Lord Chatham, *Lord Chatham*, Vol. 2, O.A. Sherrard, Bodley Head, *MG*. 9 Sept. p 4

(1) It ignores Namier's work. 'There can rarely have been a biography inspired by a more unalloyed hero-worship.'

G643. M. Reynaud Remembers, *In The Thick of the Fight*, Paul Reynaud, Cassell, *Obs*. 25 Sept. p 13

(1) A further volume exculpating himself from blame – but there is very little which is new or about Reynaud.

G644. The Last Week, *War Premeditated*, Walther Hofer, Thames and Hudson, *NS & N*. 50, 1282. 1 Oct. p 407

(1) A sound book, but overshadowed by Namier's *Diplomatic Prelude*.

G645. Cassandra, *The Trail of the Dinosaur and Other Essays*, Arthur Koestler, Collins, *MG*. 7 Oct. p 10

(1) 'A writer of infinite resource but obsessed with a single message'.

(2) The warning against communism was valuable in 'the now forgotten days of the Left Book Club'. Now 'one is almost tempted to say that there are too few Communists in the Western World, or at any rate too few who appreciate the ideals for which communism once stood'.

Repr. *MGW*. 73, 15. 13 Oct. p 11

G646. History as Parable, *The Eastern Schism*, Steven Runciman, Oxford, *NS & N*. 50, 1283. 8 Oct. pp 438–9

(1) 'Lectures should entertain as well as instruct; and these lectures are entertainment of a high kind. They are dry, detached, lacking the sparkle which Gibbon brought to the same subject; yet full of telling judgments as apposite to our day as to the time with which they deal.'

G647. Iron Merchant, *The Unknown Prime Minister*, Robert Blake, Eyre and Spottiswoode, *Obs*. 9 Oct. p 10

(1) It 'is as sober as its subject; but like its subject, extremely competent ...'

(2) Bonar Law 'lacked the fuel of enthusiasm, of passion, of belief'. 'No harder man has risen to the top in British political life.'

G648. A Slice of the Past, *Story of A Year : 1848*, Raymond Postgate, Cape, *NS & N*. 50, 1285. 22 Oct. p 517

(1) 'A book of admirable entertainment' but not a work of serious scholarship.

G649. Man of An Idea, *War Memoirs*, Vol. 1, General de Gaulle (*see above* G603), *NS & N*. 50, 1286. 29 Oct. pp 545–6

Repr. in A9, pp 174–8, and A 17, pp 310–5

G650. *ID*, 9th Ser., 1, (Sep-Oct 1939), ed. Mario Toscano, 1954, *EHR*. 70, 277. Oct. pp 653–5

(1) 'The editing is impeccable, a model of conscientious efficiency' – but 'It would be simpler and cheaper for everyone to stop these publications and to open all archives without restriction.'

G651. *FD*, 2nd Ser., 12, (Feb 1909-Oct 1910), 1954, *Ibid.* p 648

(1) 'No great questions were raised' in this period. 'The most complicated question in the volume is the N'Goko Sangha affair – a model case of economic imperialism.'

G652. Lenin's Rehearsal, *Lenin And His Rivals*, Donald W. Treadgold, Methuen, *NS & N.* 50, 1287. 5 Nov. pp 585–6

(1) Sceptical as to whether Lenin really had clear-cut long term plans before and during the Revolution.

G653. Letters to Grandmama, *The Capel Letters 1814–1817*, ed. Marquess of Anglesey, Cape, *Obs.* 6 Nov. p 11

(1) Enjoyable reading. The Capels 'would have done well in what is still called Society at the present day – barbarians with refined accents'.

G654. Kippers and Champagne, *Horatio Bottomley*, Julian Symons, Cresset, *Obs.* 13 Nov. p 10

(1) 'Tells the story admirably – though, perhaps, he makes Bottomley too much a figure of fun'.

G655. The Mystery of the Indispensable Man, *Lord Crewe*, James Pope-Hennessy, Constable, *Ev. Stan.* 21 Nov. p 18

(1) The biography resembles Crewe – 'it reveals little beyond the good taste of both subject and author'.

(2) Observes that whilst his colleagues praised Crewe's wisdom, it is hard for the historian to find evidence of it. Denounces Crewe for being against Lloyd George: 'Lloyd George was the man who won the war and, as the years recede, he stands out ever more clearly as the greatest political genius that the twentieth century produced in this country.'

G656. Their Times, *Geoffrey Dawson and Our Times*, John Evelyn Wrench, Hutchinson, *Obs.* 27 Nov. p 10

(1) A dull book without revelations, but in itself

revealing about the interwar period.

(2) 'Dawson was extremely hard working and by no means ill informed . . . he was a courageous man'. His real weakness 'was a growing complacency, a conviction ever stronger that 'We alone had the secret of righteousness', a conviction that was in the last resort inhuman . . . Between the wars England surrendered to its Civil Servants; and Dawson was their mouthpiece.'

G657. Napoleon, *The Mind of Napoleon*, ed. J. Christopher Herold, Columbia U.P.; Cumberlege, *MG*. 16 Dec. p 6

(1) An admirable anthology – but 'sayings without personality pall'; biographies are more valuable.

1956

G658. Heartland, *Mitteleuropa in German Thought and Action 1815–1945*, Henry Cord Meyer, The Hague, Nijhoff; Batsford, 1955, *MG*. 13 Jan. p 4

(1) 'A first rate contribution to historical understanding, one of the most original and valuable books on international affairs published for many years'. He proves that 'mitteleuropa' did not count for much in practice.

Repr. *MGW*. 74, 3. 19 Jan. p 10

G659. Hero of Two Worlds, *The Apostle of Liberty*, M. del la Fuye and E.A. Babeau, Thames and Hudson, *Obs*. 22 Jan. p 9

(1) 'A lively narrative, admirably translated and a pleasure to read'; marred, however, because 'Freemasonry shows it cloven hoof at every turn' of Lafayette's career.

(2) 'The interest in his career was in what he did, not what he said or thought . . . there are few men who remain as fervent for liberty at eighty as they were in adolescence.'

G660. A Failure, *The Shirt of Nessus*, Constantine Fitzgibbon, Cassell, *MG*. 27 Jan. p 6

(1) He 'has nothing to add to our knowledge'. Rebuts the idea that the German generals' attempt

to assassinate Hitler on 20 July, 1944 should be taken more seriously.

G661. Uncrowned King, *Czartoryski and European Unity 1770–1861*, M. Kukiel, Princeton U.P.; Oxford, 1955, *NS & N*. 51, 1299. 28 Jan. pp 104–5

(1) 'A most scholarly book' – though it 'naturally judges Europe from the angle of Poland'.

(2) 'Czartoryski was the noblest of the liberal revolutionaries'. 'The fascination of Czartoryski's career is that he tried to achieve the freedom of Poland both ways round – first by co-operation with Russia and later by action against her.'

G662. Sound and Fury, *Beaverbrook*, Tom Driberg, Weidenfeld and Nicolson, *Obs*. 26 Feb. p 10

(1) 'Like the *Daily Express* itself the book is wonderfully entertaining', but afterwards 'the reader rubs his eyes and wonders whether he is any wiser'.

(2) 'What Lord Beaverbrook demands from life is excitement . . . When life fails to provide this excitement, his newspapers do it instead . . . He ranks with C.P. Scott, not with Northcliffe: a crusader, not a Press Lord.'

G663. Punctured Balloon, *Mussolini in Twilight and Fall*, Roman Dombrowski, Heinemann, *Obs*. 11 Mar. p 16

(1) 'Unenterprising for a journalist'.

(2) 'Mussolini was a nasty man and as wicked as he knew how – cruel, unscrupulous, selfish. But he was also trivial, a gigantic Nothing.'

G664. Sales Talk, *History in a Changing World*, Geoffrey Barraclough, Oxford, Blackwell, *NS & N*. 51, 1305. 17 Mar. p 252

(1) 'Many of his ideas are brilliantly exciting', but argues that the author is mistaken to judge what was important in the past on the basis of what is important now.

(2) 'History needs no justification other than itself . . . It satisfies some basic human need . . . The only thing we learn from history is that nothing is as white or as black as it is painted. Despite this

men go on painting, historians included.'

G665. Sagacity, *Use and Abuse of History*, Pieter Geyl, Yale U.P.; Cumberlege, *MG*. 6 Apr. p 4

(1) Warmly praises him – 'In true historical spirit . . . (he) does not dogmatise what history should do. He reviews what historians have done.'

(2) 'We should study the past not for moral or immoral lessons but to appreciate the complexity of human existence.' 'The historian can be happy if he does no harm.'

Repr. as 'Approaches to History', *MGW*. 74, 16. 19 Apr. p 10

G666. Hope No More, *The Second International*, 2 Vols. G.D.H. Cole, Macmillan, *NS & N*. 51, 1309. 14 Apr. pp 391–2

Repr. as 'The Second International' in A9, pp 114–8, and A17, pp 138–42

G667. From Passfield to Moscow, *Beatrice Webb's Diaries 1924–1932*, ed. Margaret Cole, Longmans, *Obs*. 15 Apr. p 16

(1) 'Frankness is tempered by discretion to produce an incomparable historical record . . . It is a book in a thousand for the individual portraits alone'

(2) 'Beatrice Webb was the ablest woman this country has known in the last hundred years, perhaps the ablest Englishwoman there has ever been. She combined a first-rate intellect with deep feminine intuition.'

G668. Statecraft in Lilliput, *Sir Robert Walpole: The Making of a Statesman*, J.H. Plumb, Cresset, *NS & N*. 51, 1310. 21 Apr. pp 424–5

(1) The book has 'great merits' but Walpole's career was 'unredeemably dull'.

(2) Walpole 'did nothing to further the great Whig principles of freedom and toleration; and his negligence left the Dissenters in a political half-life for another century'.

G669. *The Politics of the Prussian Army 1640–1945* (*see above* G640), *EHR*. 71, 279. Apr. pp 289–91

(1) Regrets that he has not defined 'Prussian militarism' and complains that it is uneven in its treatment because of its different source material.

(2) 'If Germany was peculiarly 'militaristic', this was not the work of the generals. It rested on the general belief of Germans that an overwhelmingly powerful army was essential to their security; and in view of Germany's geographical position, this is not surprising. Substitute 'British admirals' for 'German generals' and is the story very different?'

G670. *Histoire générale des civilisations*, Vol. 6, Robert Schnerb, Paris, Presses Universitaires de France, 1955, *Ibid.* pp 315–7

(1) Observes that to the author 'civilisation means production', and that when political history is left out the 1815–1914 boundaries are not that significant.

G671. *The Catholics and German Unity 1866–1871*, George G. Windell, Minnesota U.P.; Cumberlege, 1955, *Ibid.* pp344–5

(1) 'A most useful study'.

(2) 'It is quite clear from this account that Bismarck was in no hurry to absorb south Germany and that he was pushed into activity in 1870 largely because the clerical victory in Bavaria had upset the *status quo*.'

G672. *Histoire des Relations Internationales, Le XIXe siècle*, Vol. 2, Pierre Renouvin, Hachette, 1955, *EHR*. 71, 279. Apr. pp 345–6

(1) 'The style is sober, the scholarship is profound'. 'The volume asserts again and again that political forces – prestige and power – were decisive. Economic and imperialist conflicts, far from making war, were subordinated to the European tensions and often lessened them. No more effective, though gentle, blow has ever been struck against the economic interpretation of history.'

G673. *ID*, 7th Ser., 2, (Apr 1923-Feb 1924), ed. R. Moscati, 1955, *Ibid.* pp 348–9

(1) 'The general impression of the volume is

one of unreal Machiavellianism – dramatic actions which ended in nothing, unscrupulous strokes made against phantoms . . . Mussolini already showed all his qualities – unstable, violent, touchy, changing his course over-night yet furious when others did the same.'

G674. French Roundabout, *France 1940–1955*, Alexander Werth, Hale, *NS & N*. 51, 1313. 12 May. p 534

(1) 'His best and most ambitious book', but he has the fault of including the irrelevant as well as the essential.

(2) 'Every sensible man would choose to be a Frenchman, if he could be born again.'

G675. What Bit Them? *Mutiny at the Curragh*, A.P. Ryan, Macmillan, *Obs*. 13 May. p 13

(1) Told with 'elegant detachment'.

(2) 'The Parliament Act sprang from slovenly thinking – from the belief that delay is always healing; whereas sometimes a radical operation is the most gentle, as well as the most certain cure.'

G676. The Religion of Communism, (a) *Three Who Made A Revolution*, Bertram Wolfe, Thames and Hudson; (b) *Soviet Attitudes Towards Authority*, Margaret Mead, Tavistock, *NS & N*. 51, 1314. 19 May. p 572

(a1) Feels that it suffers from a delay in publication in Britain of eight years after US; it also suffers from ending in 1914 and lacking unity.

(b1) An unsuccessful attempt to apply the methods of anthropology to a civilised people.

G677. Russia's Past, *A Short History of Russia*, Richard Charques, Phoenix House, *NS &* N. 51, 1316. 2 Jun. p 636

(1) 'A model of brevity and arrangement', but has reservations about the way some themes are handled.

(2) Russia is 'unmistakeably European . . . The great cleavage between Russia and the western world is an affair only of the last hundred years, starting perhaps when Russia escaped the revolutions of

1848. . . . By the beginning of the twentieth century Russia was becoming 'Europeanised' once more; and even the Bolshevik revolution was rather a conquest of Russia by Europe than the other way round.'

G678. The Dying Peace, *GD*, Ser. D., 6, (Mar-Aug 1939), *NS & N.* 51, 1317. 9 Jun. pp 661–2

(1) Praises the editors – 'they have surpassed themselves in the present volume'.

(2) The volume rebuts the idea that Hitler planned in April 1939 the attack on Poland. 'This is not a record of planning for an inevitable war, but a study of passive drift, waiting for something to turn up.' Hitler, 'meant some time to pull off a great stroke, but he had no clear idea when, or what it would be'. 'Decision lay in Moscow and London, not with the fumbling manoeuvres of Berlin.'

G679. War's Alarms, *The Decisive Battles of the Western World*, Vol. 3, Major General J.F.C. Fuller, Eyre and Spottiswoode, *Obs.* 1 Jul. p 11

(1) 'At once very good and very bad'. 'He has a wonderful gift for analysing battles' – but criticises his selection, his failure to deal adequately with the Russians in the Second World War, and his dislike of democracy.

G680. Voice of the People, *Pierre-Joseph Proudhon*, George Woodcock, Routledge, *NS & N.* 52, 1321. 7 Jul. pp 22–3

(1) 'A most competent biography'.

(2) His ideas deserve to be taken seriously. He was 'a saintly figure', but 'it is impossible not to find Proudhon rather ridiculous'.

G681. Resistance, *Conspiracy Among Generals*, Wilhelm von Schramm, Allen and Unwin, *MG.* 20 Jul. p 4

(1) 'To call the chatter of German generals 'resistance' is a libel on the noble men in France, Italy and elsewhere who actually did something against Hitler's tyranny.'

Repr. *MGW.* 75, 4. 26 Jul. p 10

G682. *The Prussian Election Statistics 1862 and 1863*, ed. Eugene N. Anderson, Lincoln, Nebraska U.P., 1954, *EHR*. 71, 280. Jul. p 503

(1) A useful source as the original was destroyed in the Second World War.

G683. *Das Nationale als europäisches Problem*, Reinhard Wittram, Göttingen, Vandenhoeck and Ruprecht, 1955, *Ibid.* p 509

(1) 'Sensible and stimulating'. 'These essays reinforce what English readers have learnt from the writings of Sir Lewis Namier – particularly the emphasis on the changing quality of nationalism.'

G684. The Canalist, *Ferdinand de Lesseps*, Charles Beatty, Eyre and Spottiswoode, *NS & N*. 52, 1325. 4 Aug. pp 138–9

(1) 'A steady conscientious work' with no claim to originality.

(2) 'The Suez Canal turned the Eastern question upside down and created the problem of Egypt into the bargain.'

G685. A Sad Tale, *The Empress Frederick*, Richard Barkeley, Macmillan, *Obs*. 5 Aug. p 7

(1) Not a well written biography.

G686. Martyred Nation, *A History of Poland* (*see also*, G162) new ed. O. Halecki, Dent, *NS & N*. 52, 1329. 1 Sept. p 258

(1) 'The story is told competently, but it is rather dull'.

G687. The Way We Live Now, *Life in Britain*, J.D. Scott, Eyre and Spottiswoode, *NS & N*. 52, 1330. 8 Sept. pp 288–9

(1) The survey is done well, but the author has not been clear if he was writing for foreigners or the home audience.

G688. Curtain Raiser, *Russia Without Stalin*, Edward Crankshaw, Joseph, *Obs*. 23 Sept. p 13

(1) 'The Russians are a wonderful people; and this is a wonderful book about them.'

G689. German Riddles, *The German Scene*, Edmond Vermeil, Harrap, *NS & N*. 52, 1334. 6 Oct. p 427

(1) 'Enlightening, though very tough going'. Praises the author's attempt 'to treat German problems as a unity – not economic or social or political or literary, but the single 'crisis' of a civilisation'.

(2) A.J.P.T. sees part of the German problem being due to Romanticism. One day – 'They may shake off the terrible legacy of Romantic ideas and come to their senses.'

G690. Two Diplomatists, (a) *Home and Abroad*, Lord Strang, Deutsch; (b) *The Moffat Papers*, ed. Nancy Harvison Hooker, Harvard U.P.; Cumberlege, *MG*. 9 Oct. p 4

(a1) 'The reader, instead of becoming wiser, actually feels at the end that he knows less than before.'

(b1) 'The extracts from his diary recall the vanished days of American isolation.'

Repr. *MGW*. 75, 15. 11 Oct. p 11

G691. Foreign Policy, *British Foreign Policy since 1898*, M.R.D. Foot, Hutchinson, *MG*. 12 Oct. p 6

(1) The author 'seems to lack a point of view . . . As a result we are soon submerged in a drab chronicle . . . '

G692. The Golden West, *America and the British Left*, Henry Pelling, Black, *NS & N*. 52, 1337. 27 Oct. pp 523–4

(1) It is 'fascinating, full of new information and new angles', but it is too short. Observes that the author writes of the Labour Party 'much as a Roman senator might have done about the early Christians'.

G693. Lord Beaverbrook as Historian, *Men and Power 1917–1918*, Lord Beaverbrook, Hutchinson, *Obs*. 28 Oct. p 16

(1) 'The present book is equally exciting and equally entertaining (as *Politicians and the War*). It is less systematic. Instead of ordered narrative, it leaps from one crisis to the next.' 'He may sometimes exaggerate the part that he has played in events.

No one could exaggerate his gifts in chronicling them.'

In 1964 Beaverbrook named this review as the rccollection which gave him most pleasure. *See* A19, pp 629–30

G694. *Die schriftlichen Nachlässe in den zentralen deutschen und preussischen Archiven*, Wolfgang Mommsen, Koblenz, Bundesarchiv, 1955, *EHR*. 71, 281. Oct. p 693

(1) A valuable list of German archives.

G695. After Versailles, *BD*, 1st Ser., 6, *1919*, *NS & N*. 52, 1341. 24 Nov. pp 676–7

(1) Questions the wisdom of publishing documents on such a gigantic scale.

G696. Concert or Conflict? *Bismarck, Gladstone and the Concert of Europe*, W.N. Medlicott, Athlone Press, *MG*. 9 Nov. p 6

(1) Warmly praises the introduction and conclusion, but regrets that 'sandwiched in between are 300 pages of drab diplomatic detail which illustrate nothing except that most diplomacy is trivial and unimportant'.

Repr. *MGW*. 75, 22. 29 Nov. p 11

G697. The Schlieffen Plan, *Der Schlieffenplan*, Gerhard Ritter, Munich, Oldenbourg, *MG*. 13 Nov. p 6

Repr. *MGW*. 75, 21. 22 Nov. p 11 and A13, pp 61–4

G698. The School of Namier, *The Chatham Administration 1766–1768*, John Brooke, Macmillan, *MG*. 16 Nov. p 8

(1) He 'does not merely use the Namier method: he writes in the Namier style, and even makes the Namier jokes. The book is first rate scholarship of its kind'. But he is very critical of this approach to politics.

G699. Burgess—Fall Guy of His Age? *Guy Burgess*, Tom Driberg, Weidenfeld and Nicolson, *Reynolds News*. 2 Dec. p 8

(1) A.J.P.T. finds Burgess' explanation of his defection unconvincing.

(2) 'You can't oppose the British ruling class

by going to Moscow: you will merely find the same men dressed up in different clothes.' Recommends opposing both establishments.

G700. The Cold Shoulder, *Russia Leaves The War*, George Kennan, Faber, *NS & N.* 52, 1343. 8 Dec. pp 762–3

(1) 'Mr. Kennan has developed a true scholar's integrity; and he writes too with delightful elegance'; though he reveals many of the professional diplomat's prejudices and is against the Bolsheviks.

G701. Collapse of Versailles: The Moment of Crisis, *BD*, 2nd Ser., 5, *1933*, *MG*. 10 Dec. p 6

(2) October 1933 was a turning point. 'The settlement of Versailles was in ruins. Post-war history ended; and pre-war history began.'

G702. A Great Man? *Fear God and Dread Nought*, Vol. 2, ed. Arthur J. Marder, Cape, *NS & N.* 52, 1345. 22 Dec. p 824

(1) 'Every letter is a peach . . . Reading them straight through is almost as shattering as a broadside from one of Fisher's beloved Dreadnoughts.'

G703. Books of the Year, *Men and Power 1917–1918* (*see above* G693); *Russia Leaves the War* (G700); and *Der Schlieffenplan* (G697), *Obs.* 23 Dec. p 6

G704. Mighty Originals, *English Historical Documents*, Vol. 12, (1) *1833–1974*, ed. G.M. Young and W.D. Handcock, Eyre and Spottiswoode, *Obs.* 23 Dec. p 25

(1) Feels that this approach is more appropriate for the medieval period and deplores it for modern history. Criticises the selection of subjects – and then the treatment of such subjects as Chartism (where there is 'not a word by a Chartist'). 'It is a version of English history by those who admire Civil Servants and conventional politicians, for those who hope to become Civil Servants and conventional politicians.'

1957

G705. When Hitler was Winning, *GD*, Ser. D., 9, (Mar-Jun 1940), 1956, *NS & N.* 53, 1347. 5 Jan. pp 19–20

(1) The most valuable items are the correspondence between Mussolini and Hitler.

G706. A Ghost Goes West, *The Ghost of Versailles*, Lucille Iremonger, Faber, *Obs*. 6 Jan. p 8

(1) Praises this book which undermines the book *An Adventure;* it is 'the more devastating from its moderation, charm and reserve'.

G707. Light on Hungary, *La Tragédie Hongroise*, Francois Fejto, Paris, Horay, 1956, *NS & N*. 53, 1349. 19 Jan. pp 75–6

(1) Valuable on the period before 1956. From the Hungarian Communist Press he draws 'a devastating picture of failure, tyranny and corruption'.

G708. The Outsiders, *Survey of International Affairs 1939–46 : The War and the Neutrals*, ed. Arnold Toynbee and Veronica M. Toynbee, Oxford U.P., *MG*. 25 Jan. p 6

(1) 'A ponderous volume' which does not throw light on the key questions.

Repr. *MGW*. 76, 5. 31 Jan. p 11

G709. The Rogue Elephant, (a) *The Life of Hilaire Belloc*, Robert Speaight, Hollis and Carter; (b) *Testimony to Hilaire Belloc*, Eleanor and Reginald Jebb, Methuen, 1956, *Obs*. 27 Jan. p 12

(a1) 'Admirably full and surprisingly critical' for an official biography; but the author is too kind to the upper classes and non-committal about the Marconi Scandal.

(b1) This memoir explains the fuss over Marconi.

(c1) 'I find myself almost alone in the opinion that he (Belloc) and Wells are the writers of their generation safe for immortality. And this though I dislike most of his opinions – on history, on religion, sometimes on politics.

G710. A Brilliant Crank, *Laurence Oliphant*, Philip Henderson, Hale, 1956, *MG*. 29 Jan. p 4

(1) His extraordinary tale told 'with scholarly detachment and even distaste'.

Repr. *MGW*. 76, 6. 7 Feb. p 10

G711. *The Failure of the Prussian Reform Movement*

1807–1819, Walter M. Simon, Cornell U.P.; Cumberlege, 1956, *EHR*. 72, 282. Jan. pp 189–90

(1) 'A lively, intelligent book, widely based on the printed sources'.

G712. *FD*, 2 Ser., 13, (Oct 1910-Jun 1911), 1955, *Ibid.* pp 195–6

(1) Apart from new information about Kiderlen and Mogador the volume 'is rather dull'.

G713. How Hitler Went to War: The German Record, *GD*, Ser. D., 7, (Aug-Sep 1939), *MG*. 19 Feb. p 6

(2) 'The Nazi-Soviet pact gave the final push to war, but it was not as decisive as some writers have made out. Russia would have remained neutral, pact or no pact, and Hitler would have gone to war even without a firm promise of Russian neutrality.'

Repr. *MGW*. 76, 9. 28 Feb. p 11

G714. The Riddle of the Reds, (a) *The Two Revolutions*, R.H. Bruce-Lockhart, Phoenix House; (b) *British Labour and the Russian Revolution*, S.R. Graubard, Harvard U.P.; Oxford, *NS & N*. 53, 1357. 16 Mar. p 349

(a1) 'A brief sketch' of slight importance.

(b1) 'An academic thesis at its drabbest ... plenty of materials for a tasty dish, but no cooking'.

G715. Letters of Majesty, *The English Empress*, Egon Caesar Conte Corti, Cassell, *Obs*. 24 Mar. p 14

(1) Like his other biographies it is packed with original material, but it is ill digested and ill organised.

G716. Parnell in Prose, *Parnell and His Party 1880–1890*, Conor Cruise O'Brien, Oxford, *Obs*. 31 Mar. p 15

(1) 'Admirable for its scholarship, its style and its wisdom ... It is long since a book taught me so much or which I read with such unalloyed enjoyment.'

(2) Parnell was 'a king among men. He was the equal of the greatest English statesmen; and he knew it'.

G717. Horthy-Culture, *October Fifteenth: A History of Modern Hungary 1929–1945*, 2 Vols. C.A. Macartney, Edinburgh U.P., *NS & N.* 53, 1360. 6 Apr. p 449

(1) 'A monument of misplaced learning'. It is a political tract, which is 'a defence of the Hungarian collaborators'.

G718. The King-Maker, *The Fateful Years: Memoirs 1931–1945*, Hugh Dalton, Muller, *Obs.* 7 Apr. p 16

(1) 'Mr. Dalton reveals his secrets – so far as he has any'.

(2) 'What Mr. Dalton has really provided in politics is neither leadership nor ideas but energy.'

G719. On the Move, *Progress in the Age of Reason*, R.V. Sampson, Heinemann, *NS & N.* 53, 1362. 20 Apr. p 518

(1) Enjoyable. It is the book of a philosopher not a historian.

(2) '. . . Marx was the contemporary of Darwin. Marxism was really an attempt to turn capitalists into monkeys and then to show that Socialists would be their improved descendants.'

G720. Hesitation Waltz, *A World Restored*, Henry Kissinger, Weidenfeld and Nicolson, *TLS.* 2878. 26 Apr. p 252

(1) 'His book is a work of interpretation, not a contribution to original scholarship.' A.J.P.T. suggests that the author hero-worships Metternich. 'There are long passages which could be safely attributed to Metternich himself if put in quotations.'

G721. Reason and Reform, (a) *Scotch Reviewers: The Edinburgh Review 1802–1815*, John Clive, Faber and Faber; (b) *Henry Brougham*, Frances Hawes, Cape, *Obs.* 5 May. p 17

(a1) Praises it, especially the political side of it.

(a2) 'The *Edinburgh Review* is one of the few periodicals which have changed society . . . Jeffrey, Sydney Smith and Brougham . . . did for Great Britain what it needed a host of *philosophes* to do in France.'

(b1) 'A competent piece of work, though rarely

exciting and occasionally tinsel'.

(b2) 'He suffered from an excess of brains. He ran after ideas like a fox-terrier out for a walk. You can be as stupid as you like and yet succeed in politics so long as you love Power. The fatal defect is to be well equipped intellectually and to be honest at the same time.'

G722. Background To Peterloo, *Waterloo to Peterloo*, R.J. White, Heinemann, *TLS.* 2881. 17 May. p 302

(1) Feels that the author suffers from too many ideas, none of which are adequately explored. He criticises the author for rejecting the Hammonds' view of the period.

G723. War for the Union, *This Hallowed Ground*, Bruce Catton, Gollancz, *Obs.* 19 May. p 16

(1) 'A book in Carlyle's spirit . . . a great sprawling torrent of a book, seemingly as thick and confused as the war itself.'

G724. How To Win Without Trying, *Fulness of Days*, Earl of Halifax, Collins, *NS & N.* 53, 1367. 25 May. p 676

(1) Condemns the author's 'display of patrician insolence' when writing on the Foreign Office and his time as Foreign Secretary. He finds the description of his aristocratic society to be the most agreeable part of the book.

G725. Feebler and Feebler, *BD*, 2nd Ser., 6, *1933–4*, *MG.* 31 May. p 6

(1) 'It covers one of the saddest periods in British policy.'

Repr. *MGW.* 76, 23. 6 Jun. p 11

G726. Hit and Miss, *Democracy in England*, Diana Spearman, Rockliff, *NS & N.* 53, 1368. 1 Jun. p 714

(1) 'Her enthusiasm for the classical constitution has only been outdone by the late Sir William Holdsworth.'

(2) 'Democracy is the homage which men with power pay to those without it; and that is better than no homage at all.'

G727. *Holstein's Diaries*, ed. Norman Rich and M.H. Fisher, Cambridge U.P., *Obs.* 9 Jun. p 13

(1) They contain nothing startling. There are some good anecdotes, but 'there is also a thick undergrowth of political detail, unreliable for the historian and uninteresting for anyone else'.

G728. Divided Nation, (a) *The French Nation from Napoleon to Petain*, D.W. Brogan, Hamilton; (b) *The Trial of Marshal Ney*, Harold Kurtz, Hamilton, *NS & N.* 53, 1372. 29 Jun. pp 847–8

(a1) An excellent brief history.

(b1) Praises the book, but observes that Ney was not as important as the author thinks.

G729. Road to Nowhere, *Road to Revolution*, Avrahm Yarmolinsky, Cassell, *Obs.* 30 Jun. p 13

(1) 'An admirable narrative of the revolutionary movements in Russia' from 1790 to the late nineteenth century. However he criticises the author for trying 'to discover evolution in the revolutionary programme. In fact no such evolution took place, nor could take place. All programmes boiled down to pushing the Tsar off his autocratic throne.'

G730. Dr. Adenauer shoots an arrow at the H-bomb, *Adenauer*, Paul Weymar, Deutsch, *Ev. Stan.* 2 Jul. p 12

(1) 'The most unreadable biography of recent years'.

G731. On the Boulevards, *The Life and Times of Baron Hausmann*, J.M. and Brian Chapman, Weidenfeld and Nicolson, *NS.* 54, 1375. 20 Jul. pp 89–90

(1) Presented in a rather disjointed fashion.

(2) Hausmann's projects 'were conducted exactly as the military campaigns of Napoleon I had been: a bold design, and then daring improvisation until victory was achieved'.

G732. The thousand million dollar match trick, *The Incredible Ivar Kreuger*, Allen Churchill, Weidenfeld and Nicolson, *Ev. Stan.* 23 Jul. p 10

(1) 'A glossy, fast moving biography'.

G733. The New Deal Redealt, *The Age of Roosevelt*,

Vol. 1, Arthur M. Schlesinger Jr., Heinemann, *Obs.* 28 Jul. p 11

(1) 'A great book, passionately exciting and, for the most part, eminently convincing ... On the scale of Macaulay, and like his works arranges the evidence to point a conclusion ... He is out to vindicate the New Deal as the most beneficient revolution of the twentieth century.'

(2) 'If we had found a dynamic leader to apply his (Keynes') ideas, we could have escaped the frustration of the thirties, escaped unemployment and depression, set an example to the world. It was our tragedy that Socialists and Conservatives alike lived in the past and that Lloyd George, the English Roosevelt, had used up his prestige in the First World War.'

G734. *Gesichte der Weimarer Republik*, Vol. 2, Eric Eyck, Erlenbach-Zurich, Rentsch, 1956, *EHR*. 72, 284. Jul. pp 517–9

(1) 'This is a splendid achievement – a wide sweep of narrative, firmly based on the evidence available.'

G735. *l'Impresa di Massawa*, Carlo Giglio, Rome, Instituto Italino per l'Africa, 1955, *Ibid.* p 564

(1) 'He clings to diplomatic detail', but does make some important points.

G736. *ID*, 6th Ser., 1. (Nov 1918-Jan 1919), ed. R. Mosca, 1956, *Ibid.* pp 566–7

(1) 'The documents ... provide an indispensable introduction to Italy's difficulties at the peace conference.'

G737. *The S.S.: Alibi of a Nation 1922–1945*, Gerald Reitlinger, Heinemann, 1956, *Ibid.* pp 567–8

(1) Specialists will learn from the book, even though they may well disagree with it. A.J.P.T. feels that the author is too sceptical of the German revolution: 'there was a moral – or if one prefers an immoral – revolution under National Socialism' and the S.S. incorporated 'the ideology of the new order'.

G738. When Germany Ruled Europe, *GD*, Ser. D., 9, (Jun-Aug 1940), *MG*. 9 Aug. p 4

(1) 'This volume has caused a sensation by its documents relating to the Duke of Windsor. Good popular stuff, but nothing in it for the serious historian.'

Repr. *MGW*. 77, 7. 15 Aug. p 10

G739. The Great Engineer, *Isambard Kingdom Brunel*, L.T.C. Rolt, Longmans, *NS*. 54, 1379. 17 Aug. p 204

(1) A biography which is 'very near perfect, a first rate contribution to history as well as a pleasure to read'.

G740. The bluest stocking that ever lived, *The Little Deaf Woman From Norwich*, Vera Wheatley, Secker and Warburg, *Ev. Stan.* 20 Aug. p 10

G741. A Sceptic at Large, *The Opium of the Intellectuals*, Raymond Aron, Secker and Warburg, *NS*. 54, 1381. 31 Aug. pp 252–3

(1) Regrets that French intellectuals see things only in black and white. 'This book confirms my suspicion that sociology is history with the history left out.'

G742. Lord Protector, *The Greatness of Oliver Cromwell*, Maurice Ashley, Hodder and Stoughton, *Obs*. 1 Sept. p 13

(1) Praises his knowledge but observes, 'He lacks the imaginative insight which is essential for inspired biography. His book is more a *Times* obituary than the re-creation of a tumultous human being.'

(2) ' . . . toleration only springs from indifference. If religious beliefs and observances are important, toleration is a sin. For Cromwell they were very important indeed . . . His contemporaries did not dispute that he wrestled with the Lord. They took it rather hard that he always won.'

G743. Not Trying, (a) *Accusés Hors Série*, Henry Torres, Paris, Gallimard; (b) *Histoire de la Justice sous la IIIe Republique*, 2 Vols. Maurice Garcon, Paris,

Fayard, *NS*. 54, 1382. 7 Sept. pp 293–4

(1) Pedestrian volumes.

(2) 'The French have no middle-brow writers and readers – only refined culture on the highest level or a cheap nineteenth-century sensationalism . . .'

G744. Petain thought Hitler was bound to win, *Petain*, Glorney Bolton, Allen and Unwin, *Ev. Stan.* 17 Sept. p 12

(1) An unconvincing attempt to make a case out for Petain.

G745. Russian Vista, *Russia in the Making*, John Lawrence, Allen and Unwin, *NS*. 54, 1384. 21 Sept. p 363

(1) 'An admirable survey of Russian history'; 'much may be forgiven Mr. Lawrence for his deep love for the Russian people and his understanding of the Russian Church.'

G746. Forgotten Imperialist, *Sir Harry Johnston and the Scramble for Africa*, Roland Oliver, Chatto and Windus, *Obs*. 22 Sept. p 15

(1) Overloaded with documentation.

(2) 'I would rank Johnston above Lugard. Both wanted to protect the native inhabitants. But while Lugard wanted to preserve, Johnston wanted to improve them.'

G747. The Butcher, (a) *The Tichborne Claimant*, Douglas Woodruff, Hollis and Carter; (b) *The Claimant*, Michael Gilbert, Constable, *En*. 9, 3. Sept. pp 79–80

(a1) It contains new material, is good on atmosphere but 'it loses grip in the courts'.

(b1) It is 'shorter, clearer and more effective'.

(2) 'A mass electorate chooses odd heroes; and the butcher of Wapping was the first of them, a sort of John the Baptist for Horatio Bottomley.'

G748. Did Mr. Five-per-cent stop war in the Middle East? *Mr. Five Per Cent*, Ralph Hewins, Hutchinson, *Ev. Stan.* 1 Oct. p 14

(2) 'The life of Gulbenkian is a cautionary tale against riches.'

G749. Battles Long Ago, *A History of the English Speaking People*, Vol. 3, Winston S. Churchill, Cassell, *Obs*. 13 Oct. p 14

(1) 'Every page can be read with relaxed pleasure' but 'the puckish asides, which made the first volume a delight, are missing . . . Sir Winston's true gift is to clothe ordinary views in extraordinary language. So it is here. The book is a palimpsest of received ideas. Its foundation, shaping the whole, is the version of English history taught at Harrow School nearly seventy years ago.'

G750. The Press Officer is bursting with old news, *Less Than Kin*, William Clark, Hamilton, *Ev. Stan.* 15 Oct. p 14

(1) 'You will find a lot in this book which you knew already.'

G751. A Corner in Rationality, *Historical Essays*, Hugh Trevor-Roper, Macmillan, *NS*. 54, 1388. 19 Oct. pp 502–4

(1) 'Professor Trevor-Roper writes like an angel . . . Each piece has a zest and perfection of a Mozart symphony.' Though he observes that the book will enable him 'to conceal for some time the fact that he has not yet produced a sustained book of mature historical scholarship'. A.J.P.T. feels that the decline of the gentry is '*an* explanation, but not *the* explanation, of the Great Rebellion', and protests, 'I jib when it comes to jettisoning religion' as an explanation.

G752. The Prime Minister was not at home, *No. 10 Downing Street*, Hector Bolitho, Hutchinson, *Ev. Stan.* 22 Oct. p 14

(1) 'A subject which sounds attractive, but does not fulfil its promise when worked out.'

G753. The Entertainers, *The Sugar Pill*, T.S. Matthews, Gollancz, *MG*. 22 Oct. p 4

(1) A 'debunking' book on the Press, which studies *The Daily Mirror* and *The Manchester Guardian*. A.J.P.T. feels he underestimates the

influence of the latter: 'Certainly it cannot dictate to Governments; but in the long run its weight is irresistable when it cares to use it.'

Repr. as 'Two Daily Pills', *MGW*. 77, 18. 31 Oct. p 11

G754. A True Believer, *Child of the Revolution*, Wolfgang Leonhard, Collins, *Obs*. 27 Oct. p 18

(1) 'An invaluable document of Communist education'. The author took Tito's side against Moscow, 'He bolted to Yugoslavia, not because he had lost his faith, but because he had retained it.'

G755. 7000 birds in two days was King Edward's target, *Edwardian Portraits*, W.S. Adams, Secker and Warburg, *Ev. Stan*. 29 Oct. p 12

(1) 'A splendidly enlightened book even when occasionally wrongheaded.'

G756. Hitler the valet fooled the reds, *Hitler: The Missing Years*, Putzi Hanfstaengl, Eyre and Spottiswoode, *Ev. Stan*. 5 Nov. p 12

(1) 'An enchanting book, instructive for the serious historian, but equally entertaining for the general reader.' The author is 'among the great raconteurs of our age'.

G757. Class War: British Style, (a) *The General Strike*, Julian Symonds, Cresset; (b) *The First Labour* Government *1924*, Richard W. Lyman, Chapman and Hall, *Obs*. 10 Nov. p 16

(a1) 'A book of high excellence', though he regrets that there was not more attention paid to 'the preliminaries in the mining industry'.

(a2) 'Here was the clearest example of the class struggle in modern history, fought by men for whom the doctrine of the class war was repugnant.'

(b1) 'No drama, no depth'.

G758. Failed Dictator, *Peron*, Frank Owen, Cresset, *MG*. 15 Nov. p 4

(1) Not a good book – though it is good on Evita.

(2) 'Peron was no Napoleon. But his policy was a sort of Bonapartism translated into South American

terms.' In addition 'he claimed to 'liberate' his country from capitalist exploitation'. Evita – 'It is difficult not to admire her; and difficult not to believe that she was the cause of her husband's success.'

Repr. as 'Fallen Idol', *MGW*. 77, 21. 21 Nov. p 11

G759. Good King George, (a) *The Structure of Politics at the Accession of George III*, 2nd Edn. Sir Lewis Namier, Macmillan; (b) *George III and the Historians*, Herbert Butterfield, Collins; (c) *King and Commons 1660–1832*, Betty Kemp, Macmillan, *Obs*. 17 Nov. p 18

(a1) His best book – 'irresistable for its meticulous learning, magical for its literary charm'. A.J.P.T. suggests, 'A Gallup Poll of the period would probably have produced fewer 'Don't Knows' than at the present day', and complains that the Namierites 'have never analysed a great popular constituency such as Westminster where real political feeling was likely to show itself'. 'It is hard to resist the feeling that Sir Lewis not merely wished to find an absence of principle in the eighteenth century, but welcomed this as a lesson for the present day.'

(b1) 'An invigorating controversy'.

(c1) She 'explains in modest but telling terms' her theme.

G760. Another Version of the Same, *The Pen and the Sword*, Michael Foot, MacGibbon and Kee, *NS*. 54, 1394. 30 Nov. p 743

(1) Although professional historians will find faults in it, his version 'has excitement and truth'.

(2) The unintended moral is, 'Fine arguments and high principles are all very well. But when something decisive has to be done, you need the block vote . . . and an adroit, daring leader, a Henry St. John or . . . a David Lloyd George.'

G760a The Infernal Machinist, *The Bombs of Orsini*, Michael Packe, Secker and Warburg, *Obs*. 1 Dec. p 18

(1) 'Admirably written' but 'rather light weight.'

G761. The Grand Illusion, *Churchill, Roosevelt, Stalin*, Henry Feis, Princeton U.P.; Oxford U.P., *Obs.* 15 Dec. p 12

(1) 'The book is a précis on the highest level of all the available documents, not a literary recreation of the past. The personalities do not come alive.'

(2) The greatest fault of the West was to hesitate over recognising the Curzon line as the Polish frontier. The second fault was America's failure to give the Russians the money they asked for in January 1945.

G762. Books of the Year, *Obs.* 22 Dec. p 10

Names *The Age of Roosevelt*, Vol. 1 (*see above* G733), *Parnell and His Party* (G716) and Anthony Powell's *At Lady Molly's*, Heinemann. 'All that is wrong with Mr. Powell's books is that there are not enough of them and they are too short.'

1958

G763. Taylor's Law Confirmed, *Bismarck and the Hohenzollern Candidature for the Spanish Throne*, ed. Georges Bonnin, Chatto and Windus, 1957, *Obs.* 19 Jan. p 16

(1) The truth was revealed in 1913, and the German archives add little. It confirms his 'law' that Foreign Offices know no secrets.

G764. *FD*, 2nd Ser., 14, (Jul-Nov 1911), 1955, *EHR.* 73, 286. Jan. pp 123–5

(1) The theme is Agadir. Comments that the innacuracies in the *Life of Cambon* are revealed by this collection.

G765. *Krupp und die Hohenzollern*, ed. Willi Boelcke, Berlin, Rutten Loening, 1956, *Ibid.* p 182

(1) 'This is Marxist scholarship at its most assertive.'

(2) 'The odd thing . . . is how little Krupps meddled in politics, apart from trying to keep the workers free from the taint of Social Democracy. They were tradesmen supplying a demand; and there is no evidence from these papers that the

demand needed or received any stimulus from them.'

G766. *Hochschulschriften zur neueren Geschichte*, Bonn, Kommission für Geschichte des Parlamentarismus, 1956, *Ibid.* p 192

(1) A list of theses on recent German history – copious on German, many American but a derisory listing of British theses.

G767. Dead End, *The Channel Tunnel*, Humphrey Slater and Corelli Barnett, Wingate, *NS.* 55, 1404. 8 Feb. p 173

(1) 'Entertaining and instructive'; marred only by 'a daubed backcloth of general history'.

G768. Out of the Diplomatic Bag, (a) *GD*, Ser. C. 1, (Jan-Oct 1933); (b) *BD*, 1st Ser., 12, *1920*, *MG.* 14 Feb. p 6

(a1) Welcomes the decision to publish less of the German records than originally planned. This volume covers the period when Hitler was 'parading his respectability and learning how the machine of government worked'.

(b1) It gives the full record of the Conference of London.

Repr. *MGW.* 78, 9. 27 Feb. p 11

G769. Appearance and Reality, (a) *Titoism: Pattern for International Communism*, C.P. McVicker, Macmillan; (b) *The Triumphant Heretic*, Ernest Halperin, Heinemann, *NS.* 55, 1405. 15 Feb. p 207

(a1) Compares it with the Webbs' *Soviet Russia* for gullibility. Observes that the reality is 'a poverty stricken people and an efficient secret police'.

(b1) The 'best and most ingenious' book on Yugoslavia.

G770. Old Namier, *Vanished Supremacies*, Sir Lewis Namier, Hamilton, *MG.* 21 Feb. p 6

(1) Welcomes the reprinting of the more substantial items – 'it is a pleasure to read again their familiar phrases'.

Repr. *MGW.* 78, 13. 27 Mar. p 10

G771. Letters from high altitudes, *Stalin's Correspondence with Churchill, Attlee, Roosevelt and Truman 1941–*

45, Lawrence and Wishart, *MG*. 28 Feb. p 8

(1) Many of the letters are not important, but they are valuable 'for their general impression'. 'Only one of the writers appears as a human being' – Churchill. 'On the evidence of these letters, Roosevelt was the hardest man of the three.'

Repr. *MGW*. 78, 10. 6 Mar. p 10

G772. An English Massacre, *Peterloo*, Donald Read, Manchester U.P., *Obs*. 2 Mar. p 16

(1) 'A neat professional job'.

(2) 'The massacre of Peterloo shook the moral prestige of the old order as nothing else had done; and English democracy owes a lasting debt to the eleven martyrs of St. Peter's Fields.'

G773. Chatham, *Lord Chatham* Vol. 3, O.A. Sherrard, Bodley Head, *MG*. 14 Mar. p 9

(1) 'An essay in rehabilitation'; but this is not very convincing for Chatham's last years.

G774. As Winterhalter Saw It, *A History of the English Speaking Peoples*, Vol. 4, Winston S. Churchill, Cassell, *Obs*. 16 Mar. p 17

(1) 'Clearly the teaching of history at Harrow stopped at 1815 . . . Many passages show a wonderful freedom from prejudice or tradition.' 'Sir Winston does not grasp the significance of democracy . . . What . . . (he) admires is not democracy, but constitutional monarchy and ordered freedom broadening down from precedent to precedent . . . this admirable version of what history looks like to the English governing class.'

G775. Lights going out over Europe, *Survey of International Affairs 1939–46 : The Eve of War 1939*, ed. Arnold Toynbee and Veronica M Toynbee, Oxford U.P., *MG*. 25 Mar. p 6

(1) Critical of the whole project; and in particular that 'the plan is shaped by the material instead of mastering it'.

Repr. *MGW*. 78, 13. 27 Mar. p 11

G776. Foreign Relations, *BD*, 2nd Ser., 7, *1929–34*, *MG*. 3 Apr. p 4

(1) It deal with Anglo-Soviet relations – 'The conversations might have taken place yesterday ... Studying Anglo-Soviet relations is a life-sentence on the treadmill: an endless round of incomprehension.'

Repr. as 'Anglo-Soviet Complications', *MGW*. 78, 15. 10 Apr. p 11

G777. Forgotten Rebel, *The Chartist Challenge*, A.R. Schoyen, Heinemann, *Obs*. 6 Apr. p 14

(1) 'First rate: a delight to read and, at the same time, a work of scholarship. There has not been a book for a long time which added so decisively to our knowledge of nineteenth century England.'

(2) George Harney 'was the first 'class conscious proletarian'; and far from learning this from Marx, it was Marx who learnt it from him – and then abused him'.

G778. A Very Nasty Man, *Napoleon In His Time*, Jean Savant, Putnam, *Obs*. 20 Apr. p 17

(1) A good anthology of contemporary views of Napoleon.

(2) 'All this bragging and strutting ... now seem to be poor stuff ... Our rejection of Napoleon is a harbinger of the time when we shall reject all the great and the glorious and when we shall come to think that the only thing that matters in life is love for one's fellows.'

G779. Sealed train to Russia, *Germany and the Revolution in Russia 1915–1918*, ed. Z.A.B. Zeman, Oxford, *MG*. 29 Apr. p 4

(1) 'He has edited, with admirable scholarship, all the material on the subject.'

Repr. *MGW*. 78, 20. 15 May. p 11

G780. *The Origins of the War of 1914*, Vol. 3, Luigi Albertini, Oxford U.P., 1957, *EHR*. 73, 287. Apr. pp 321–4

(1) This volume is really an epilogue. On the origins, A.J.P.T. still feels that Bernadotte Schmitt's book is the best single work.

G781. S-Day Minus, (a) *Operation Sea Lion*, Ronald Wheatley, Oxford; (b) *The Silent Victory*, Duncan

Grinnell-Milne, Bodley Head, *NS*. 55, 1418. 17 May. pp 642–3

(a1) An offshoot of the Official History. It contains much invaluable information but it is 'almost unreadable in its method of presentation'.

(b1) It argues in a spirited, convincing fashion that sea power not air power checked Hitler's invasion plans.

G782. Bad Old Cause, *Georgian Oxford*, W.R. Ward, Oxford, *Obs*. 18 May. p 16

(1) A careful study of Oxford politics in the eighteenth century.

G783. Death of a Legend, *The Schlieffen Plan*, Gerhard Ritter, Wolff, (*see above* G697), *Obs*. 25 May. p 17

(1) The publication of the text 'is devastating. The legends go crashing down one after another'.

G784. Historians in conference, *Historical Studies I*, (Irish Conference of Historians), Cambridge, Bowes and Bowes, *MG*. 30 May. p 8

G785. Lil' Old Schicklgruber, *Hitler's Youth*, Franz Jetzinger, Hutchinson, *NS*. 55, 1421. 7 Jun. p 739

(1) The author establishes that the early autobiographical part of *Mein Kampf* is a pack of lies and absurdities. On the author's speculation that Hitler's grandfather was a Jew, A.J.P.T. asks, 'Why deny the Germans the credit for Hitler?'

G786. Pride and Prejudice, *The House of Lords in the Age of Reform 1784–1837*, A.S. Turberville, Faber, *MG*. 3 Jun. p 6

(1) A not very satisfactory posthumous compilation. A.J.P.T. argues of House of Lords that 'when we seek to draw its character we have only to determine whether stupidity or selfishness predominated'.

G787. *The Day Before Yesterday*. (a) *The Boer War*, Edgar Holt, Putnam; (b) *The Advent of the Labour Party*, Philip P. Poirier, Allen and Unwin, *Obs*. 8 Jun. p 16

(a1) 'Straight story telling' – clear on the military side, weak on politics.

(b1) 'An admirable study in political history' –

'important for the new material that it contains, not for its brilliant phrases'.

G788. Hitler's Victories, *Survey of International Affairs 1939–49: The Initial Triumph of the Axis*, ed. Arnold Toynbee and Veronica Toynbee, Oxford U.P., *MG*. 17 Jun. p 4

(1) 'It would be difficult to think of any more useless collection than these eleven ponderous volumes; and the reader groans as he goes through stories which have been better told elsewhere.'

Repr. as 'From Poland to Pearl Harbour', *MGW*. 79. 1. 3 Jul. p 10

G789. The Strong Persuaders, *The Anti-Corn Law League 1838–1846*, Norman McCord, Allen and Unwin, *MG*. 4 Jul. p 5

(1) Praises the book, but regrets that it 'skates over the process of argument'. 'Cobden argued the Corn Laws out of existence.'

G790. Thank God for Him, *Nineteen Thirty One: Political Crisis*, R. Bassett, Macmillan, *Obs*. 6 Jul. p 17

(1) His strong point is 'pedantic accuracy' but he fails to put events into perspective. 'Mr. Bassett was a partisan for MacDonald in 1931; and such he has remained.'

G791. Philosophic Traveller, *Journeys to England and Ireland*, Alexis de Tocqueville, Faber, *NS*. 56, 1426. 12 Jul. pp 51–2

(1) 'He observed, to his own satisfaction, what he had previously worked out theoretically ... A country is far better understood by studying its history and its institutions than by visiting it.'

G792. The Abyss Opens, *The Decision to Intervene*, George Kennan, Faber, *Obs*. 13 Jul. p 17

(1) 'A literary artist with dazzling gifts'; but his work is not history but 'a tract on behalf of diplomatists against statesmen'.

G793. *The Viennese Revolution of 1848*, R. John Rath, Austin, Texas, U.P., 1957, *EHR*. 73, 288. July. pp 505–7

(1) 'A substantial affair', accurate and detailed,

but with little new to say. He puts too much weight on radical broadsheets.

G794. *The Young Turks*, Ernest Edmondson Ramsaur Jr., Princeton U.P.; Oxford U.P., 1957, *Ibid.* p 544

(1) A thorough examination of a topic never before dealt with properly.

G795. *ID*, 9th Ser., 2, (Oct-Dec 1939), ed. Mario Toscano, *Ibid.* p 548

(1) More interesting than Vol. 1, but there are too many documents which merely summarise newspaper opinions. Praises the editing.

G796. The First Years of Labour: From pressure-group to party, *Labour and Politics 1900–1906*, Frank Bealey and Henry Pelling, Macmillan, *MG.* 14 Aug. p 6

(1) A 'most admirable volume'.

Repr. as 'Beginnings of the Labour Party', *MGW.* 79, 8. 21 Aug. p 11

G797. The Man of No Luck, *Alfred Lord Milner*, John Evelyn Wrench, Eyre and Spottiswoode, *Obs.* 24 Aug. p 12

(1) Not 'a particularly telling defence or even an effective biography. But it is full of valuable information, much of it new.'

(2) Milner 'was at once too honest, too narrow and too able to succeed in British politics. Like all the Milner kindergarten . . . he wanted to run things without paying the democratic price.'

G798. End of the Line, *Stalingrad*, Heinz Schroter, Joseph, *Obs.* 31 Aug. p 14

(1) 'A clear picture of Stalingrad's significance from the German side'; not very well written.

G799. Writ in Water, *The Vichy Regime 1940–44*, Raymond Aron, Putnam, *NS.* 56, 1436. 20 Sept. p 388

(1) It 'tells the squalid story in a lively enough fashion. The result recalls the intrigues in an Oxford common-room, or some episode in the last days of Byzantium.'

G800. Serious Circumnavigation, *East to West*, Arnold J.

Toynbee, Oxford U.P., *MG.* 3 Oct. p 10

(1) 'Dr. Toynbee is a fine product of the traditional English education which studied only dead civilisations and disliked contact with life.'

Repr. as 'Dr. Toynbee's round trip', *MGW.* 79, 15. 9 Oct. p 10

G801. Ancient Lights, *The Munich Conspiracy*, Andrew Rothstein, Lawrence and Wishart, *NS.* 56, 1438. 4 Oct. pp 456–7

(1) Dismisses the idea that the men of Munich were Machiavellian plotters; they were 'puzzle-headed men'. Dismisses 'the legend that the Czech crisis was deliberately engineered by Hitler, as the next stage in a carefully conceived plan of world conquest. On the contrary each crisis took Hitler by surprise.' Observes that the Hossbach memorandum contains a plan for war – but for 1942 not 1938.

G802. Conjurer's Pattern, *The Russian Revolution*, Alan Moorehead, Collins and Hamilton, *Obs.* 12 Oct. p 21

(1) 'Highly readable in a superficial way' – and A.J.P.T. points out a number of factual blemishes.

(2) 'The truth asserts itself. The Russian Revolution was not 'made' by anyone, not even by the Bolsheviks. It was 'made' by the Russian people.'

G803. The Red Nuisance, *The British Communist Party*, Henry Pelling, Black, *MG.* 17 Oct. p 6

(1) 'Henry Pelling has done a good job on its history . . . There is no flicker of fine writing, no attempt to make the characters come alive; simply a precise, neat narrative' – but this is not surprising in view of the topic.

Repr. *MGW.* 79, 17. 23 Oct. p 11

G804. Spam on a Gold Plate, *King George VI*, John Wheeler-Bennett, Macmillan, *NS.* 56, 1440. 18 Oct. pp 533–4

Repr. in A13, pp 202–7 and A21, pp 282–8

G805. A Failed Prime Minister? *Sir Charles Dilke*, Roy Jenkins, Collins, *Obs.* 26 Oct. p 20

(1) Dilke's 'life makes an excellent story . . .

and . . . it has been told by a writer of the highest quality'.

G806. A Man of Wood and Iron, *Kitchener*, Philip Magnus, Murray, *Obs.* 2 Nov. p 20

(1) The author 'is that rare thing – an honest biographer. In unassuming style he tells the truth without either hero-worship or mud-slinging. His life of Gladstone was good; this . . . is even better.'

G807. On the Rocks, *Socialism in One Country 1924–1926*, Vol. 1, E.H. Carr, Macmillan, *NS.* 56, 1443. 8 Nov. pp 645–6

(1) The first volume to do justice to the subject of how the Bolsheviks changed their country. Carr 'shows more than scholarship. He shows understanding. No more important book has been published in our time.'

G808. A Cobweb at Windsor, *Love and the Princess*, Lucille Iremonger, Faber, *NS.* 56, 1444. 15 Nov. pp 702–3

(1) A delightful book in which 'we learn a great deal about Hanoverian royalty and about human nature in general'.

G809. Finance Imperialism in Nineteenth Century Egypt, *Bankers and Pashas*, David Landes, Heinemann, *Obs.* 16 Nov. p 20

(1) 'A model of how history should be written: rich in detail but never losing sight of the general picture.'

(2) 'The exploitation of Egypt is the classic case of 'finance capitalism'. Great economic advances were made. All the world benefitted; and the Egyptians paid for it.'

G810. Bewitched by Power, *The Charm of Politics*, R.H.S. Crossman, Hamilton, *MG.* 21 Nov. p 6

(1) The essays are 'splendid reading indeed, but not the great book that he ought to have written'. 'Mr. Crossman is the Burke of our day.'

(2) 'The true art of politics is to have ideals and to believe in them, but not too much.'

Repr. as 'Bewitched by Politics', *MGW.* 79,

22. 27 Nov. p 10, also repr. in *The Bedside Guardian 8*, intro. Alistair Cooke, 1959

G811. The Great Rebellion, *The King's War 1641–1647*, C.V. Wedgwood, Collins, *Obs.* 23 Nov. Christmas Books Supplement. p 3

(1) The book is 'good, fair, discriminating, sympathetic'. Her prose 'though clear and orderly, is rather pedestrian'. 'The 'professional' historian approaches history from inside; and his literary accomplishments, often great, grow out of his history, not the other way round. Miss Wedgwood approaches history as a writer . . .'

G812. Non-resisters, *The German Resistance*, Gerhard Ritter, Allen and Unwin, *MG.* 28 Nov. p 6

(1) Pours scorn on the idea that there was in any real sense a German Resistance.

Repr. as 'Somewhat passive 'resistance'', *MGW.* 79, 23. 4 Dec. p 11

G813. Money Troubles, *Puritanism and Revolution*, Christopher Hill, Secker and Warburg, *Obs.* 7 Dec. p 16

(1) Not very impressed with either the treatment of Puritan preachers or the author's claim that those who are revolutionaries have a special insight into this period. 'I would suggest that only a Radical, who hates all people in authority, is qualified to deal with the Independents.'

G814. Books of the Year, *Obs.* 28 Dec. p 11

'The book I most enjoyed was *Crossing the Line* by Claud Cockburn (McKibbon and Kee). The book I most admired was the first volume of *Socialism in One Country* (*see above* G807) . . . The book I bought was *Collins' Guide to English Parish Churches*, edited somewhat whimsically by John Betjeman.'

1959

G815. Munich: The Absent Friend, Soviet policy and Czechoslovakia, *New Documents on the history of Munich*, Orbis-Prague, 1958, *MG.* 5 Jan. p 6

(1) It provides some solid evidence on Russia's

role. 'The record suggests that they were willing to act and that the weakness of France bewildered them as it ruined the Czechs.'

G816. The State in business, *The State and the Industrial Revolution in Prussia 1740–1870*, W.O. Henderson, Liverpool U.P., *MG.* 16 Jan. p 6

(1) 'A series of careful essays'.

G817. Peeling the Onion, *George Washington*, Marcus Cunliffe, Collins, *Obs.* 18 Jan. p 21

(1) An entertaining discussion of Washington and of the legends about him.

(2) 'Washington was tedious and worthy – very much the impeccable prig whom Parson Weems described'; he was also 'abnormally grasping in money matters'.

G818. Powers behind the P.M. *The Powers Behind the Prime Ministers*, Sir Charles Petrie, MacGibbon and Kee, *MG.* 30 Jan. p 6

(1) 'At the end the reader is no wiser'.

Repr. as 'Men behind the great men', *MGW.* 80, 6. 5 Feb. p 10

G819. *Histoire des Revolutions Internationales*, Vol. 7, Pierre Renouvin, Paris, Hachette, 1957, *EHR.* 74, 290. Jan. pp 141–3

(1) It suffers from poor organisation and sometimes inadequate source material but has many substantial and stimulating judgments. He feels that the author 'does not treat adequately the idealism which was bound to become a factor in international relations once the masses were drawn in'.

G820. *Briefe*, Schlieffen, ed. Eberhard Kessel, Gottingen, Vandenhoeck and Ruprecht, 1958, *Ibid.* p 181

(1) Unimportant letters to his family.

G821. Carpenter Tsar, *Peter the Great*, Vasili Klyuchevsky, Macmillan, *Obs.* 1 Feb. p 18

(1) The book is in fact the fourth volume of the author's *History of Russia*, published in 1910. The author's outspokenness then 'is a curious reminder that ramshackle Tsardom was a very

different sort of tyranny from the one that took its place'.

G822. Getting Up Steam, *The Age of Improvement*, Asa Briggs, Longmans, *Obs.* 8 Feb. p 20

(1) Praises the economic and social history; but regrets the omission of India and Ireland, the lack of attention given to great men, and that the political narrative is divided into subjects, thus breaking up the chronological order of great events.

G823. The battle in the mud, *In Flanders Field*, Leon Wolff, Longmans, *MG.* 27 Feb. p 6

(1) Weak on the politics but good on the front line. 'This is fine, vivid narrative, strategy and individual experience firmly welded together.'

(2) Passchendaele: 'Posterity will be baffled that Haig was allowed to keep his command, rather than that he was not impeached or dismissed with ignominy as responsible for the most pointless disaster in British military history.'

Repr. *MGW.* 80, 10. 5 Mar. p 11

G824. A Good German, *The Prince Consort*, Frank Eyck, Chatto and Windus, *Obs.* 1 Mar. p 18

(1) Not very successful – 'it would need a more experienced hand to reduce the voluminous material to order'.

G825. "How On Earth". . . ." (a) *A Short History of Germany 1815–1945*, E.J. Passant, Cambridge; (b) *German History 1933–1945*, H. Mau and H. Kraunick, Wolff; (c) *Germany and World Politics in the Twentieth Century*, Ludwig Delio, Chatto and Windus, *NS.* 57, 1460. 7 Mar. p 341

(a1) A competent summary, but colourless.

(b1) 'A courageous book within certain limits . . . There is no attempt to make out that Hitler seized power by accident or against the will of the German people.'

(c1) Praises his abilities, but rejects his systems making.

(2) 'The honest historian has to confess that the German record is beyond his grasp. Hell broke

loose. How on earth did it happen?'

G826. Heirs of Bismarck, *Germany after Bismarck*, J. Alden, Nichols, Harvard U.P.; Cambridge U.P., *TLS*. 58, 2976. 13 Mar. p 143

(1) 'It contains no mistakes and no surprises'.

G827. The Other Randolph, *Lord Randolph Churchill*, Robert Rhodes James, Weidenfeld and Nicolson, *Obs*. 22 Mar. p 25

(1) 'Lord Randolph returns to life with all his charm, wit and irresponsibility.'

G828. Why Did He Do It? *The Strange Death of Lord Castlereagh*, H. Montgomery Hyde, Heinemann, *Obs*. 29 Mar. p 14

(1) Agreeable light reading.

(2) 'But who cares why he committed suicide? Better to rejoice at it along with Shelley, Byron and Cobbett and every right-minded radical.'

G829. Lloyd George in action, *BD*, 1st Ser., 8, *1920*, *MG*. 3 Apr. p 4

(1) Regrets that the documents were not published twenty years before, when they 'would still have had relevance to political issues'. 'They present a wonderful picture of Lloyd George in action, the statesman of infinite resource . . . '

G830. Big-Gun Man, *Fear God and Dread Nought*, Vol. 3, ed. Arthur J. Marder, Cape, *Obs*. 26 Apr. p 22

(1) 'A book of great historical importance', but 'as a letter writer . . . (Fisher) . . . survives only as a figure of fun'.

G831. *FD*, 1st Ser., 14, (1898), 1957, *EHR*. 74, 291. Apr. pp 318–20

(1) The French Government did not foresee Fashoda, though they did receive warnings.

(2) 'The British had the power, and they meant to use it. . . . The French used the resources of diplomacy; the British rejected diplomacy until Marchand was withdrawn.'

G832. A Most Impossible Person, *Mistress to an Age*, J. Christopher Herold, Hamilton, *Obs*. 10 May. p 5

(1) He 'has come as near as anyone can to achieving the impossible and making Germaine de Staël creditable within the compass of a single book'.

(2) 'The conflict between Madame de Staël and Napoleon was the first engagement between liberalism and a totalitarian dictator.'

G833. Woodrow Wilson and the British, *Peace Without Victory*, Lawrence M. Martin, Yale U.P.; Oxford U.P., *MG*. 29 May. p 6

(1) 'Not a very satisfactory book' – the link between Wilson and English advocates of peace is never established.

Repr. *MGW*. 80, 24. 11 Jun. p 10

G834. Caged Lion, *Trotsky's Diary in Exile*, Faber, *NS*. 57, 1475. 20 Jun. pp 868–70

(1) 'Any scrap of Trotsky's writing is worth having. He can always provide the biting comment, the brilliant pen-portrait.'

(2) 'Trotsky was the last revolutionary of the old school'.

G835. Acton Eclipsed, *Judgments on History*, Jacob Burckhardt, Allen and Unwin, *Obs*. 21 Jun. p 19

(1) The author 'now takes first place as the most powerful Bore in Christendom'.

(2) 'Burckhardt surveyed the human record with gloomy detachment and yet gloomier foreboding. Progress was, for him, a meaningless concept; the pursuit of happiness a delusion . . . I dislike prophets of woe even more than enthusiasts for Progress.'

G836. The Chief, *Northcliffe*, Reginald Pound and Geoffrey Harmsworth, Cassell, *NS*. 57, 1476. 27 Jun. pp 896–7

In his introduction to the essay in A21, at the start of his introduction to A19, and elsewhere, he recounts Beaverbrook's comment, 'It weighs too much' before Beaverbrook sent it unread to the University of New Brunswick.

Repr. in A13, pp 150–4, and A21, pp 190–5

G837. Black Record, *The Black and Tans*, Richard Bennett,

Hulton, *NS*. 58, 1479. 18 Jul. pp 84–5

(1) A journalistic account of many of the famous events in the Irish Civil War – not a sociological analysis, such as Reitlinger's study of the S.S.

(2) 'The most shameful episode in the history of the British Empire is that of the Black and Tans.'

G838. Sins of Omission, *English Historical Documents*, Vol. 11, ed. A. Aspinall and E. Anthony Smith, Eyre and Spottiswoode, *Obs*. 9 Aug. p 10

(1) 'With dazzling ingenuity the editors have managed to give us nearly a thousand pages without telling us anything of what really happened in England between 1783 and 1832.'

G839. The Latin Sisters, (a) *France*, Albert Guerrard, Mayflower; (b) *Italy*, Denis Mack Smith, Mayflower, *Obs*. 23 Aug. p 14

(a1) Quite a competent general history, though very weak on recent history.

(b1) 'One of the most adventurous and successful historical works in recent years'; a book that is likely to stand the test of time.

G840. Betwixt And Between, *England: Weg der Mitte*, Hans-Oskar Wilde, Stuttgart, Deutsche Verlags-Anstalt, *TLS*. 58, 3002. 11 Sept. p 515

(1) 'Even its moderation and earnestness fail to conceal how dangerous it is to generalise about the national character.'

G841. Trotsky Without Lenin, *The Prophet Unarmed: Trotsky 1921–1929*, Issac Deutscher, Oxford, *NS*. 58, 1489. 26 Sept. p 398

(1) The most accurate and detailed account, though it has its faults.

(2) 'Trotsky carried to excess the weakness of the intellectual in politics. He was ruthless in stating principles; he was soft and indifferent in questions of personality.'

G842. France in the First Person, *War Memoirs*, Vol. 2, General de Gaulle, Weidenfeld and Nicolson, *Obs*. 27 Sept. p 23

(1) A strange volume. He is generous to all, except to Frenchmen who attempted to set up a

rival authority to his own and to General Eisenhower.

G843. Game Without Object? *On The Game of Politics in France*, Nathan Leites, Stanford U.P., *Commentary*. 28, 3. Sept. pp 270–2

(1) Entertaining – but if fails to explain the politican's objectives.

(2) 'The French system guarantees that nothing will ever happen . . . The Communists are a built in safety valve, a guarantee that discontent – even when it exists – will achieve nothing.'

G844. End of an Era, *1914*, James Cameron, Cassell, *Obs*. 4 Oct. p 25

(1) 'Compelling readability', but flawed by mistakes of detail.

G845. British Trade Unionism, *The Growth of British Industrial Relations*, E.H. Phelps Brown, Macmillan, *Gdn*. 16 Oct. p 10

(1) 'A splendid achievement, a remarkable combination of history and social science . . . Every trade union leader, and for that matter every public man, ought to read it and consider its lessons.'

G846. Master of None, *The Spare Chancellor*, Alastair Buchan, Chatto and Windus, *Obs*. 18 Oct. p 22

(1) 'A model for every would-be biographer'.

(2) Bagehot 'was an intellectual Jack-of-all-trades, and master of none . . . All his writings are admirably clear' but they lack 'the indefinable touch of genius'.

G847. Babe in the Wood, *Communism and British Intellectuals*, Neal Wood, Gollancz, *NS*. 58, 1494. 31 Oct. pp 590, 592

(1) 'A silly, trivial book on an important subject'– the author does not separate 'communism' as a system of ideas from the Party.

(2) 'In my experience, Communism is intellectual alcohol – nasty and harmful if taken neat, but an essential ingredient of every stimulating drink.'

G848. *Österreich und der Vatikan*, Vol. 1, Friedrich Engel-Janosi, Graz, Styria, 1958, *EHR*. 74, 293. Oct. pp 706–7

(1) 'A model of how such a story should be told'.

G849. *The Works of Moses Hess*, Edmund Silberner, Leiden, Brill, 1958, *Ibid.* p 745

(1) A list of 1,063 printed works, 241 manuscripts plus miscellaneous correspondence. Hess' output was 'a staggering achievement'.

G850. *Staat und Gesellschaft im Wandel unserer Zeit*, Theodor Schieder, Munich, Oldenbourg, 1958, *Ibid.* p 754

(1) It 'offers some of the intellectual stimulus which we received from Max Weber . . . a rewarding little volume . . . each of the essays deserves a book to itself'.

G851. Behind the Scenes in War: Last chapters of the Brooke diary, *Triumph in the West*, ed. Sir Arthur Bryant, Collins, *Gdn.* 2 Nov. p 6

(1) 'The book does not add much to our knowledge' though it does give 'atmosphere: the hasty muddles with which elderly, weary men confronted the problems of a great war'. The hero of the book is Churchill, 'who emerges from the record greater than ever – impossibly difficult to deal with in private, but always rising to the challenge of events when it came to the point'.

Repr. *MGW.* 81, 20. 12 Nov. p 10

G852. A Wicked War, *Goodbye Dolly Gray*, Rayne Kruger, Cassell, *Obs.* 8 Nov. p 23

(1) 'Competent, careful military history: the best coherent account of the Boer War within a reasonable compass'; but weak on political history.

G853. Hitler's Secret, *GD*, Ser. C., 3, (Jun 1934-Mar 1935), *NS.* 58, 1496. 14 Nov. pp 682–3

(1) 'Thin stuff' – such interest as there is in it lies in what it reveals about Hitler.

(2) Hitler 'had only to sit up on the Berghof, eating cream buns, and the artificial system of European security fell to pieces before his eyes. Hitler did not plan his victory. It was presented to him by the statesmen of Great Britain, France and Soviet Russia. Such are the advantages of being in the centre of Europe and having strong nerves.

The lesson has not been lost on Dr. Adenauer.'

G854. Diplomat of the Inner Circle: Sir Ivone Kirpatrick's Memoirs, *The Inner Circle*, Sir Ivone Kirkpatrick, Macmillan, *Gdn.* 19 Nov. p 10

(1) 'A book of anecdote and entertainment'.

Repr. as 'Inner Circle Diplomacy', *MGW.* 81, 22. 26 Nov. p 10

G855. The British Revolution, *Chartist Studies*, ed. Asa Briggs, Macmillan, *Obs.* 22 Nov. p 23

(1) An excellent volume.

(2) 'Chartism sprang from the masses and was dependent on them for its strength. But its ideas came from middle class minds; and its leadership revealed middle class hesitations. What should have been the British revolution turned out to be depressingly like the Labour Party.'

G856. Expediency as a political system, *British Conservatism 1832–1914*, R.B. McDowell, Faber, *Gdn.* 27 Nov. p 13

(1) Entirely on ideas, not on organisation. It is 'a most valuable contribution to our understanding of Victorian times; and it makes good reading as well'.

G857. Birkenhead Revisited, *F.E.*, the second Earl of Birkenhead, Eyre and Spottiswoode, *Obs.* 6 Dec. p 23

(1) The original version was 'competent, well informed but rather dull'; the revised version is 'an admirable biography, recapturing something of F.E.'s personality'.

(2) Every utterance of F.E.'s, and every story about him, confirms Beaverbrook's judgment that he was the cleverest man in the kingdom.

G858. Opening Fire, *The First Russian Radical*, David Marshall Lang, Allen and Unwin, *Obs.* 27 Dec. p 8

(1) A useful book on Alexander Radishchev, which 'will satisfy both scholars and the general reader'.

G859. Books of the Year, *Obs.* 27 Dec. p 8

'The outstanding book' on the First World War – *In Flanders Fields* (*see above* G823); the 'most original and exciting biography' – *Northcliffe* (G836); 'high scholarship' – *Socialism in One Country*, Vol. 2, E.H. Carr, Macmillan.

1960

G860. Jolly Jack Tars, *A Social History of the Navy 1793–1815*, Michael Lewis, Allen and Unwin, *Obs*. 24 Jan. p 22

(1) 'Rather complacent about the Navy and the spirit of the men', but the author is 'a steady historian, who has collected information of great value'.

G861. Who Knew What? *Jameson's Raid*, Elizabeth Pakenham, Weidenfeld and Nicolson, *Obs*. 31 Jan. p 21

(1) The book 'has almost every merit'; lively, well organised and with a scholarly grasp of sources.

(2) Commenting on the failure to expose Chamberlain: 'The Liberals simply could not believe that a Minister had acted according to the standards of a financial adventurer like Rhodes.'

G862. *Histoire des relations internationales*, Vol. 8, Part 2, Pierre Renouvin, Paris, Hachette, 1958, *EHR*. 75, 294. Jan. pp 139–41

(1) 'Hints for the study of history rather than historical narrative'.

G863. De Gaulle: Dictator Without A Cause, *War Memoirs*, Vol. 3, General de Gaulle, Weidenfeld and Nicolson, *Obs*. 7 Feb. p 10

(1) 'He has never admitted doubt'.

(2) 'De Gaulle seems like some prehistoric monster, a dinosaur who has survived into the clear light of modern day by mistake ... De Gaulle has always been greatest in refusal; and, alone among dictators, he knows how to refuse power.'

G864. Socialist Labour of Love, *Essays in Labour History*, ed. Asa Briggs and John Saville, Macmillan, *Gdn*. 12 Feb. p 8

(1) 'A good, solid volume', containing 'well-written essays on useful subjects'.

G865. Some Awkward Questions, *BD*, 2nd Ser., 8, *Chinese Questions 1929–31*, *Gdn.* 19 Feb. p 7

(1) It is the heaviest going to read of the series, but is of value.

G866. The Second Munich, *The Communist Subversion of Czechoslovakia 1938–1948*, Josef Korbel, Princeton U.P.; Oxford U.P., *NS.* 59, 1510. 20 Feb. pp 260–1

(1) The author 'has accumulated valuable material, and presents it with clarity'. The book shows yet again 'that Communists have no principle or belief except the seizure of power by their party'.

G867. Hero or Madman? *The Fall of Parnell 1890–91*, F.S. Lyons, Routledge, *Obs.* 6 Mar. p 21

(1) 'A splendid achievement, finely written and firmly based on a thorough examination of the sources'.

(2) Parnell was 'beaten by the Irish people; beaten by their reluctance to stake all, as Parnell did, on the cause of independence'.

G868. Germany in Russia, *The House Built on Sand*, Gerald Reitlinger, Weidenfeld and Nicolson, *Obs.* 13 Mar. p 20

(1) A careful exposition based on the German records.

G869. Grand Old Earl of Derby, *Lord Derby*, Randolph S. Churchill, Heinemann, *Obs.* 10 Apr. p 21

(1) 'Much of the book is heavy going'.

G870. Battles Long Ago, *The First World War*, Cyril Falls, Longmans, *Obs.* 17 Apr. p 20

(1) 'A careful, competent book', giving the Westerner outlook. German casualty figures are increased 'just enough to discredit Lloyd George, but not enough to excite incredulity'.

See also Footnote 1, A14, p 87

G871. The Generals' Revenge, *The Private Papers of Hore-Belisha*, R.J. Minney, Collins, *Obs.* 24 Apr. p 23

(1) The discreditable dismissal of Hore-Belisha, 'though worth telling, is a bit thin to sustain a book'.

G872. *Maximilian Harden*, Harry F. Young, The Hague, Nijhoff, 1959, *EHR*. 75, 295. Apr. p 370

(1) A survey of the changing views of a brilliant political writer.

(2) 'Harden's spirit was essentially critical and destructive'. His main achievement was to hound Eulenberg from public life – 'not really much to be proud of'.

G873. *ID*, 3rd Ser., 2, (May 1897-Jun. 1898), ed. G. Perticone, 1958, *Ibid*. p 371

(1) Not much of importance in the volume.

G874. Conflict at Versailles – and after, *BD*, 1st Ser., 9, (early 1920), *Gdn*. 6 May. p 8

(1) 'Though there are no startling revelations, the documents give a clear picture of the conflicting trends.'

Repr. as 'Versailles and after', *MGW*. 82, 19. 12 May. p 11

G875. The World Surveyed, *Neither War nor Peace*, Hugh Seton-Watson, Methuen, *NS*. 59, 1521. 7 May. pp 687–8

(1) Praises his learning but finds the book too encyclopaedic on world affairs and dissents from his fears of communism.

G876. Men at Work, *The Age of Roosevelt*, Vol. 2, Arthur M. Schlesinger Jr., Heinemann, *Obs*. 8 May. p 23

(1) A 'dynamic and compelling' book – 'every ounce of drama has been squeezed out of this highly dramatic story'.

(2) 'The New Deal was the nearest thing to a revolution ever carried out in a democracy . . . the Roosevelt of the New Deal (was) a more democratic and . . . a greater figure than the Roosevelt of the Second World War.'

G877. Unlucky Dip, *The New Cambridge Modern History*, Vol. 12, ed. David Thomson, Cambridge U.P., *Obs*. 22 May. p 21

(1) Very critical of the random organisation. The only part of the world to get a chapter to itself is Latin America, and this 'confirms that the mission

of Latin America is to prove that even history can be uninteresting'. 'It is history with the history left out.'

G878. Three Fish Out of Water, *Intellectuals in Politics*, James Joll, Weidenfeld and Nicolson, *Obs*. 26 Jun. p 28

(1) 'A display of great gifts, which ought now to be turned to a more formidable task.'

G879. After Parnell, *The Shaping of Modern Ireland*, ed. Conor Cruise O'Brien, Routledge, *Obs*. 10 Jul. p 28

(1) Fifteen radio talks which are 'fresh, readable, enlightening'.

G880. Testament of a Socialist, *A History of Socialist Thought*, Vol. 5, G.D.H. Cole, Macmillan, *Gdn*. 22 Jul. p 6

(1) 'It has all the qualities which distinguish Cole's work – clarity, precision, economy. It has also his defects – a drabness of tone, a refusal to distinguish great things from small, a reluctance to advance original ideas.'

Repr. *MGW*. 83, 4. 28 Jul. p 10

G881. Europe on Top, *The New Cambridge Modern History*, Vol. 10, ed. J.P.T. Bury, Cambridge U.P., *Obs*. 24 Jul. p 26

(1) 'A sound volume ... admirably planned and admirably executed'.

G882. *ID*, 7th Ser., 3, (Feb. 1924 – May 1925), 1959, *EHR*. 75, 296. Jul. pp 506–8

(1) Valuable material. It shows 'Italy's European policy and her Mediterranean policy did not correspond'.

G883. How to Seize Power, *Politicians and the War 1914–1916*, Lord Beaverbrook, Oldbourne, *Obs*. 21 Aug. p 26

(1) Welcomes the one volume edition, praises it warmly, and observes that 'it is likely to endure as a historical work of the first importance'. Comments that whilst the book deals with the struggle at the top the attitude of the Conservative and

Liberal backbenchers was equally decisive.

G884. Thin White Line, *Victorian England*, G.M. Young, Oxford U.P., *Obs.* 18 Sept. p 28

(1) 'One of the very few successful attempts at unified history, fusing events and ideas, laws and opinions, into a coherent pattern'. Regrets that he writes 'as though Oxford counted more than Manchester' and that the book exalts 'the Civil Servant above the political leader, and the administrator above the creator'.

G885. Poor Old Muse, *History the Betrayer*, E.H. Dance, Hutchinson, *NS.* 60, 1541. 24 Sept. pp 440–1

(1) Dismisses the author's plea for 'agreed' history to be compiled and then taught internationally.

(2) 'History is the great propagator of Doubt. It is sceptical of the authorities; of historians; of our own views and of those of others ... What we need is more chaos, more disagreement, not less ...'

G886. Accounts Settled, *The Reign of George III*, J. Steven Watson, Oxford U.P., *Obs.* 2 Oct. p 28

(1) 'A dispassionate survey, giving the new orthodoxy for this period. The main failure is the treatment of Fox.'

G887. Capital Gains, (a) *The South Sea Bubble*, John Carswell, Cresset; (b) *The Great Swindle*, Virginia Cowles, Collins, *Obs.* 16 Oct. p 25

(a1) Thorough, but not very entertaining to read.

(b1) 'An attractive, rather superficial account', 'she has caught out Walpole and his latest biographer'.

G888. A Terrible Beauty, *Portrait in Arms*, Edgar Holt, Putnam, *Obs.* 30 Oct. p 23

(1) A chronicle of the Irish troubles, written with dispassionate accuracy.

(2) The Irish Question: 'Why did men otherwise so sensible, lose all moderation when they came to deal with this problem? Why did Lloyd George,

the master of compromise, make himself responsible for crimes as dreadful as those which brought men to the scaffold at Nuremberg.'

G889. Nobody's Uncle, *The Life and Times of Ernest Bevin*, Vol. 1, Alan Bullock, Heinemann, *En.* 15, 4. Oct. pp 76–8, 80

(1) The author 'is a biographer in the Victorian manner: solid, accurate, exhaustive'.

(2) Bevin was not a typical union leader. 'In fact he was unique for good and ill, a strange solitary character, self made in career and, still more, in ideas . . . There was something lacking in a Labour leader who knew little of industry and nothing of the north of England . . . He lacked the comradeship, the unconscious solidarity which the Labour movement represented.'

G890. The Bureaucracy of War, *Defence By Committee*, Franklyn Arthur Johnson, Oxford, *NS.* 60, 1551. 3 Dec. pp 898–9

(1) A valuable addition to recent British history.

(2) 'The C.I.D. deserves a footnote in the history of the two world wars; Lloyd George and Churchill provide the text.'

G891. Yesterday and the day before, (a) *Modern Britain 1885–1955*, Henry Pelling, Nelson; (b) *The Economic History of England 1870–1939*, W.A. Ashworth, Methuen, *Gdn.* 2 Dec. p 6

(a1) A long period in a brief space – 'The general effect is rather helter-skelter'.

(b1) 'A remarkable intellectual achievement . . . an essay of interpretation, not an encyclopaedia'.

Repr. *MGW.* 83, 23. 8 Dec. p 10

G892. What A Scamp! *The Young Disraeli*, B.R. Jerman, Princeton U.P.; Oxford U.P., *Obs.* 11 Dec. p 29

(1) A book 'full of revelations', but not very exciting otherwise. The author 'has green fingers as a researcher'.

G893. Diplomatic essays, *The Diplomacy of the Great Powers*, Sir William Hayter, Hamilton, *Gdn.* 16 Dec. p 7

(1) 'Perhaps the most slender, though not the least perceptive study ever devoted to the subject'.

Repr. *MGW*. 83, 25. 22 Dec. p 11

G894. Books of the Year, *Obs*. 18 Dec. p 22

'More fun and probably more sex is to be derived from Kingsley Amis', *Take A Girl Like You*, than *Lady Chatterley's Lover*'. His book of the Year – *Jameson's Raid* (*see above* G861). He also praises *The Age of Roosevelt*, Vol. 2, (G876).

1961

G895. Criminal Crimea, *Crimean War Reader*, Kellow Chesney, Muller, 1960, *Obs*. 1 Jan. p 16

(1) 'A fascinating anthology' – though he regrets that there are no quotations from Bright's speeches. 'These were the most telling oratory; they contain some of the best passages in the English language; and they were Bright's greatest performance, an example for ages to come.'

G896. Potsdam: The Seeds of Cold War, *Between War and Peace*, Herbert Feis, Princeton U.P.; Oxford U.P., *Gdn*. 12 Jan. p 8

(1) Based closely on Western documents – 'His style is drab and aloof, leaving the story to speak for itself.' However 'it is a State Department brief, translated into terms of historical scholarship'. A.J.P.T. regrets that, 'In the cold war, apparently, even the world of scholarship knows no detachment.'

Repr. *MGW*. 84, 3. 19 Jan. p 11

G897. Do-It-Yourself History, (a) *The French Revolution*, George Pernoud and Saline Flaissier, Secker and Warburg; (b) *They Saw It Happen* (1897–1940), ed. Asa Briggs, Oxford, Blackwell, *NS*. 61, 1557. 13 Jan. pp 52–3

(a1) 'A collection . . . with the revolution left out'.

(b1) A more skilful anthology – but one still needs the historian's judgment. 'In the end, history at its best is narrative . . . '

G898. Lilliput to the Life, *Sir Robert Walpole: The King's*

Minister, J.H. Plumb, Cresset, *Obs.* 15 Jan. p 28

(1) A useful biography which does throw new light on how the eighteenth-century system of influence worked and on how Walpole managed Parliament.

G899. Man of No Nonsense, *Man of Reason*, Alfred Owen Aldridge, Cresset, *Obs.* 29 Jan. p 28

(1) 'An effective picture of one of the greatest of Englishmen'.

(2) 'No one reads his books now because everyone agrees with them'. 'There was a tiresome side' to Tom Paine; 'despite all his heroic acts, it is impossible to make a hero out of him'.

G900. Old Ferrovian, *Wellington at War 1794–1815*, ed. Anthony Brett-James, Macmillan, *Obs.* 19 Mar. p 30

(1) 'A wise improvement on conventional biography, fun to read, and useful history into the bargain'.

(2) 'A lesser general . . . than Marlborough, his only rival, but a more attractive man'.

G901. Lindemann and Tizard: More Luck Than Judgement? *Science and Government*, C.P. Snow, Oxford U.P., *Obs.* 9 Apr. p 21

(1) The book 'is as fascinating as one of his best novels, with the added advantage of being a true story'. A.J.P.T. disagrees with the portraits of the two men and gives his own impressions of them (both of whom he had met).

G902. Keeping The Minutes, *The Supreme Command 1914–1978*, 2 Vols. Lord Hankey, Allen and Unwin, *Obs.* 16 Apr. p 28

(1) They contain little that is new or sensational; they are 'a wonderful exercise in tact'.

(2) 'Hankey's achievement was to bring order and system into the previous chaos of British Government at its highest level . . . Hankey created the entire system of British Government as we know it today.'

G903. Grand Old Marxist, *H.M. Hyndman and British*

Socialism, Chusichi Tsuzuki, Oxford, *NS*. 61, 1572. 28 Apr. pp 674–5

(1) 'A sound piece of scholarship, laboriously based on the sources and persistently dull'.

(2) 'The truth is that Hyndman was a romantic Radical, who grabbed at Marxism just as he ran after wild-cat schemes in his private finance.'

G904. *FD*, 1st Ser., Vols. 15 (Jan-Nov 1899) and 16 (Nov 1899-Dec 1900), 1959, *EHR*. 76, 299. Apr. pp 339–41

(1) The last of the 41 volumes, which comprise the largest and most valuable collection on the period 1871–1914. However there is little of importance in these two volumes.

(2) Surveying the series, A.J.P.T. observes that 'what stands out most clearly is the key significance in French policy of the Russian alliance'. The Anglo-French Entente 'was a supplement . . . not an alternative'. 'What the French wanted from the Russian alliance was independence, not revenge; and there was no moment throughout the period when they contemplated a war against Germany with any cheerfulness.'

G905. Orange Peel, *Mr. Secretary Peel*, Norman Gash, Longmans, *Obs*. 7 May. p 31

(1) A standard work of nineteenth-century British history, which is scholarly and written clearly; but, nevertheless, it is 'a crushing monument of dullness'.

(2) 'By inclination he was simply a first-rate administrator with a tidy mind, the sort of man who in a slightly later period would have gone into the Civil Service. He had no desire to change things, nor any belief that change would do good . . . '

G906. New Deal Redealt, *The Age of Roosevelt*, Vol. 3, Arthur M. Schlesinger, Jr., Heinemann, *Obs*. 21 May. p 25

(1) As good as the other volumes but 'the excitement has been sustained too long'.

(2) The New Deal: 'Far from being a coherent policy which developed consistently in the same

direction, it was rather a series of improvised responses to varying difficulties.'

G907. Napoleon: a master of words? *Letters and Documents of Napoleon*, Vol, 1, ed. John Eldred Howard, Cresset, *Obs.* 11 Jun. p 27

(1) 'An admirable production'.

(2) A.J.P.T. observes that men such as Cromwell, Bismarck and Lenin wrote interesting letters; but 'Napoleon's letters seem to me plumb boring ... His letters are full of lies ... His emotions are all sham.'

G908. Freeborn John, *The Levellers and the English Revolution*, H.N. Brailsford, Cresset, *Obs.* 9 Jul. p 24

(1) 'Literature rather than history' – it contains no new research and is written to 'extol men whom he admired'.

G909. Sequel to Gretna Green, *Edward Gibbon Wakefield*, Paul Bloomfield, Longmans, *Gdn.* 14 Jul. p 5

(1) 'A delightful biography ... just right for the subject; careful, scholarly and discursive at the same time'. Though he observes that the author at times overstates his achievements.

(2) 'No man has left a deeper or more enduring mark on the Commonwealth of Nations'.

Repr. *MGW*. 85, 3. 20 Jul. p 10

G910. The Sad Career of Little Willie, *Life of Crown Prince William*, Klaus Jonas, Routledge, *Obs.* 16 Jul. p 24

(1) The story is 'told honestly, concealing nothing, but in respectful and slightly awed tones'.

G911. The Television Wars, *Pressure Group*, H.H. Wilson, Secker and Warburg, *NS*. 62, 1584. 21 Jul. pp 85–7

(1) 'In my opinion this book is wrong from start to finish' – commercial television in Britain was not set up as a result of the activities of a pressure group.

(2) A.J.P.T. suggests that commercial television was a victory for common sense, just as the changes in the licensing laws and the arrival of betting shops at that time were.

The New Statesman printed next to A.J.P.T.'s review another review 'Socialist Answer', *Ibid.* pp 85–7 hostile to A.J.P.T. by Stuart Hampshire. In the issue of 28 July (*Ibid.* 1585. p 119) A.J.P.T. protested in a letter of this, and advocated Pay As You View television.

G912. Diaries Bring Doom, (a) *The Donkeys.* Alan Clark, Hutchinson; (b) *Brasshat*, Basil Collier, Secker and Warburg, *Obs.* 23 Jul. p 19

(a1) 'Debunking is always fun' – but, on the whole, the book is valueless as a serious contribution to history.

(b1) 'An essay in rehabilitation', on General Wilson, which is not a success.

G913. Under the Shadow of Blenheim, *The Age of Churchill*, Vol. 1, Peter de Mendelssohn, Thames and Hudson, *Obs.* 27 Aug. p 19

(1) Regrets that the author does not explain why Churchill failed so often.

(2) 'Though often presented as a typical English figure, a John Bull, Churchill lacked one characteristic of almost all English political figures: he was never a trimmer. He has been strenuous on the right side, and equally strenuous . . . on the wrong side.'

G914. The Workers' Friend, *Social Thought and Action*, Asa Briggs, Longmans, *Obs.* 3 Sept. p 25

(1) The biography suits Seebohm Rowntree well – 'it is a sound utility product, plodding steadily forward without literary adornment and built to last'.

G915. All Big Guns, *From The Dreadnought To Scapa Flow*, Vol. 1, Arthur J. Marder, Oxford, *NS.* 62, 1591. 8 Sept. p 314

(1) 'A unique account of British naval policy'.

(2) 'The Liberal Government accepted policy from the service chiefs instead of devising one. Asquith, as usual, drifted with events; and his colleagues drifted with him.'

G916. Who is to be master? *The Franco-Prussian War*, Michael Howard, Hart-Davis, *Obs*. 17 Sept. p 31

(1) A most valuable military history.

G917. Cloud of Words, *Hitler's Zweites Buch*, ed. Gerhard L. Weinberg, Deutsche-Verlags Anstalt, *NS*. 62, 1594. 29 Sept. pp 430, 432

(1) 'Nearly all of it can be found in Hitler's contemporary speeches and in *Mein Kampf*'. A.J.P.T. feels that the lesson of the book (written in 1928) is that an English alliance was the keystone of Hitler's foreign policy; and so it again casts doubt on Hitler 'as the most calculating statesman of all time'.

G918. Bombing Germany, *The Strategic Air Offensive Against Germany 1939–1945*, 4 Vols. Sir Charles Webster and Nobel Frankland, H.M.S.O., *NS*. 62, 1595. 6 Oct. pp 482–3

(1) 'A model of scholarly accuracy and impartiality . . . a great achievement'.

(2) ' . . . the bomber offensive did not knock Germany out in 1943. Nevertheless it prevented the Germans from putting a far greater air strength on the Eastern front, and so helped the Soviet victories.'

G919. Moving With the Times, *What is History?* E.H. Carr, Macmillan, *Obs*. 22 Oct. p 30

(1) 'I sympathise with so much that Mr. Carr says . . . But I cannot understand how knowledge of the past provides us with morality, let alone with knowledge of the future.'

(2) 'The task of the historian is to explain the past; neither to justify nor to condemn it. Study of history enables us to understand the past: no more and no less. Perhaps even that is too high a claim. In most European languages 'history' and 'story' are the same word.'

G920. Universal Darkness, (a) *The Unmentionable Nechaev*, Michael Prawdin, Allen and Unwin; (b) *Civil War in Russia*, David Footman, Faber, *NS*. 62, 1598. 27 Oct. pp 607–8 (a1) A serious study of Nechaev, followed by a discussion of the ridiculous idea that Lenin was a Nechaevist.

(b1) A simple narrative of some episodes, lacking a unifying theme.

G921. The steam intellect man, *The Life of Henry Brougham to 1830*, Chester W. New, Oxford U.P., *Obs.* 29 Oct. p 31

(1) 'The most important political biography ... for a long time'.

(2) 'No man did so much for so many great causes ... the supreme example of the reformer who won the day by argument and rhetoric ... The Bad Old Cause was argued out of existence; and Brougham was the greatest arguer.'

G922. *ID*, 1st Ser., 2, (Jan-Aug 1862), ed. W. Maturi, 1959, *EHR*. 76, 301. Oct. p 750

(1) Too much detail for such a short time span.

G923. *The Observer and J.L. Garvin*, Alfred M. Gollin, Oxford U.P., 1960, *Ibid.* pp 754–5

(1) 'A vivid and dramatic study', which 'makes good reading'.

(2) Garvin 'carried weight in the political world only so long as he was regarded as Northcliffe's mouthpiece'.

G924. The Triumph of Masaryk, *The Break-up of the Habsburg Empire 1914–1918*, Z.A.B. Zeman, Oxford U.P., *Obs.* 12 Nov. p 29

(1) A valuable addition to our knowledge.

G925. In the Snob Section, *The Story of Fabian Socialism*, M. Cole, Heinemann, *Obs.* 19 Nov. p 29

(1) 'Though she fought in many controversies, she is remarkably fair to old opponents and by no means blind to Fabian faults'.

(2) The Fabians 'were the extreme victims of the modern delusion that, if enough information is collected, the answer will emerge of itself'. Their answer all along 'was that other peoples' lives should be organised as the Fabians thought good'.

G926. St. Helena: German Style, (a) *The Kaiser and His*

Court, ed. Walter Görlitz, MacDonald; (b) *Dollfuss*, Gordon Brook-Shephered, Macmillan, *NS*. 62, 1602. 24 Nov. pp 802–3

(a1) 'There is nothing startling' in von Muller's diaries.

(b1) A book 'spoilt ... by turning Dollfuss into a hero'.

G927. Unlucky Find, *Neville Chamberlain*, Iain Macleod, Muller, *NS*. 62, 1603. 1 Dec. pp 833–4

(1) 'Feiling's book is superior on nearly every point'.

Repr. in A13, pp 190–5, and A21, pp 289–95

G928. History in Paperbacks, (a) *The England of Elizabeth*, A.L. Rowse, Macmillan; (b) *The Congress of Vienna*, Harold Nicolson, University Paperback (*see also above* G247); (c) *Stalin*, Isaac Deutscher, Harmondsworth, Pelican; (d) *The British Constitution*, Sir Ivor Jennings, Cambridge U.P.; (e) *The Acquisitive Society*, R.H. Tawney, Fontana; (f) *The Idea of History*, R.G. Collingwood, Oxford U.P., *Obs*. 10 Dec. p 28

(a1) 'A work of literature ... No more attractive book has been written in our time. It tingles with infectious zest ... It brings the age back to life.'

(b1) 'Strong on the dissection of character and unrivalled in simplifying great issues'. However it was written in 1946 and 'the book now appears rather as an early, though urbane, shot in the cold war'.

(c1) The most valuable book on Stalin – but the author 'romanticises the Bolshevik revolution' and 'idealises the Russian working class'.

(d1) 'An admirably clear account of how the British Constitution works' but it does not explain 'what it works for'.

(d2) 'The British Constitution is an extremely effective way of stifling real dissent. It preserves complacency and lives on it.'

(e1) 'If the members of the Labour Party studied this book more they would not now be wandering around in search of a programme or even of a majority.'

(f1) 'Too abstract for me'.

G929. Books of the Year, *Obs.* 17 Dec. p 22

Praises *The Franco-Prussian War* (*see above* G916) and *Mr. Secretary Peel* (G905). His nomination for the best book is *Unconditional Surrender*, Evelyn Waugh, 'best not only as a novel but as a document for future historians. If they read it carefully they will get their understanding of the Second World War right.'

1962

G930 The City of York, *The City of York*, ed. P.M. Tillott, Oxford U.P., for the Institute of Historical Research, 1961, *Gdn.* 12 Jan. p 7

(1) 'This is not a book for the casual visitor in either size or treatment. To appreciate it properly, the reader must know York well or be prepared to settle there for a month or so; he will reap a rich reward.'

G931. Dictator Without A Cause, (a) *Mussolini*, Laura Fermi, Chicago U.P., 1961; (b) *Benito Mussolini*, Christopher Hibbert, Longmans, *NS.* 63, 1609. 12 Jan. pp 53–4

(a1) 'The early part is admirable', on the years before he seized power.

(b1) More dramatic, more exciting but also more superficial.

Repr. A13, pp 196–201

G932. *ID*, 9th Ser., 3, (Jan-Apr 1940), ed. Mario Toscano, *EHR.* 77, 302. Jan. pp 205–6

G933. A Monument to the Revolution, *Ten Days That Shook the World*, John Reed, Lawrence and Wishart, *Obs.* 4 Feb. p 30

(1) The book deserved Lenin's commendation – it is 'one of the most exciting and important ever written'. A.J.P.T. gives the publishers credit for bringing it out again with the original text intact.

He comments on several points missed by Reed.

See also B24

G934. The Beginnings of Modern Radicalism, *Wilkes and Liberty*, George Rudé, Oxford U.P., *Gdn.* 9 Feb. p 6

(1) 'Immense research, clarity of expression, firm grasp of the essential questions, combine to produce a book of creative originality . . . He has put mind back into history and restored the dignity of man.' He 'produces an innocent stick of dynamite which levels the Namier view to the ground'.

Repr. *MGW.* 86, 7. 15 Feb. p 10

G935. Fairly Happy Nation, *Scotland from 1603 to the Present Day*, George Pryde, Nelson, *NS.* 63, 1614. 16 Feb. p 236

(1) 'A scholarly study . . . a good work'.

(2) 'There would not be much Scottish history to record if the seventeenth century Episcopalian order had survived triumphant.'

G936. The Fall of the Curtain, *Intervention and the War*, Vol. 1, R.H. Ullman, Princeton U.P.; Oxford U.P., *Obs.* 18 Feb. p 31

(1) A scholarly book – but without 'fine narration or glow of personalities'.

G937. Old Foreign Office Tie, *British Foreign Policy in the Second World War*, Sir Llewellyn Woodward, H.M.S.O., *NS.* 63, 1618. 16 Mar. p 372

(1) A précis of Foreign Office documents – an unsatisfactory approach as bodies other than it determined policy during the Second World War.

G938. The matter with Shaw, *The Matter with Ireland*, Bernard Shaw, ed. David H. Greene and Dan H. Lawrence, Hart-Davis, *Obs.* 25 Mar. p 26

(1) It contains much of 'the old magic' but there are also 'some very silly things . . . too'.

(2) 'Shaw, telling the Irish to be sensible, was the last of the stage-Irishmen who performed for the delight of the British public.'

G939. Boom and Bombs, *Trenchard*, Andrew Boyle,

Collins, *NS*. 63, 1620. 30 Mar. pp 457–8

(1) An excellent biography.

(2) In the inter-war period, 'The bomber aeroplane was the stragegical equivalent of a fist banged on the table.'

G940. Marxism and its Heretics, (a) *The First Russian Revisionists*, Richard Kindersley, Oxford U.P.; (b) *Revisionism*, ed. Leopold Labedz, Allen and Unwin, *Obs*. 15 Apr. p 24

(a1) An admirable book, with Peter Struve as its hero.

(b1) 'A rambling miscellany'; apart from an essay on Otto Bauer, 'most of this book seems to me gibberish'.

G941. *Sozialistenfrage und Revolutionsfurcht in ihren Zusammenhang mit den angeblichen Staatsstreichplänen Bismarcks*, Werner Pöls, Lübeck and Hamburg, Mathieson, 1960, *EHR*. 77, 303. Apr. p 408

(1) Observes that the author has overemphasised Bismarck as statesman at the expense of Bismarck the political tactician, making him more innocent and high minded than he was.

G942. The man who came too soon, *Rudolf Hess*, James Leasor, Allen and Unwin, *Obs*. 6 May. p 28

(1) 'A lively story, replete with anecdotes', but too ingenious in places.

G943. All good clean fun, *Regina v. Palmerston*, Brian Connell, Evans, *Obs*. 20 May. p 24

(1) 'Good reading' – but of no political importance. 'Victoria wrote forcefully though not well. Palmerston was a master of insidious and impertinent argument. His letters have that combination of obstinacy and guile which made him one of the greatest diplomats of all time.'

G944. When Everyone Was Wrong, *August 1914*, Barbara Tuchman, Constable, *Obs*. 3 Jun. p 23

(1) The work of 'a narrator, not a historian'. Highly readable, but she uses the sources without discrimination and often does not see the significance of events.

G945. Frigate Re-fitted, *The Age of Reform 1815–1870*, 2nd edn. Sir. Llewellyn Woodward, Oxford, *NS*. 63, 1630. 8 Jun. pp 832–3

(1) Onc of the few books which seem better as time passes – 'a quiet book without epigrams or startling discoveries'. However it is 'governing class history'.

G946. The Victorians: revised version, *The Making of Victorian England*, G. Kitson Clark, Methuen, *Obs*. 17 Jun. p 25

(1) Rather than revising accepted views the author has defined the views which have become agreed in recent years. The book 'can be read with much profit and some pleasure'.

G947. Socialist Snobs, *Fabian Essays*, new edn. intro. Asa Briggs, Allen and Unwin, *NS*. 63, 1632. 22 Jun. pp 907–8

(1) 'Much of the essays seem commonplace; much seems wrong; most seem irrelevant'. A.J.P.T. judges Sidney Webb's introduction and essay to be the best.

(2) 'Fabianism as the socialism of snobs will always be with us. Fabianism, as a system of ideas and policies, was really Sidney Webb, and nothing much else.'

G948. God Still Failing, *Conversations with Stalin*, Milovan Djilas, Hart Davis, *NS*. 63, 1633. 29 Jun. p 942

(1) 'Simple, effective, moving' – but it does not reveal much new about communism.

G949. What happened to the Whigs? *The Passing of the Whigs 1832–1886*, Donald Southgate, Macmillan, *Obs*. 22 Jul. p 19

(1) 'A book of considerable learning', written in a lively style; but 'at the end we are little wiser than we were at the beginning'.

(2) 'The Tories kept the name. The Whigs took over the party.' A.J.P.T. suggests Harold Macmillan and Bertrand Russell are the last Whigs.

G950. Not So Black, (a) *The Development of the British Economy 1914–1950*, Sidney Pollard, Arnold;

(b) *Britain's Locust Years 1918–1940*, William McElwee, Faber, *NS*. 64, 1637. 27 Jul. p 116

(a1) 'An almost encyclopedic work' not easy to read, 'though essential as a work of reference'.

(b1) Feels that the author goes too far in rescuing the reputations of Baldwin and Ramsay MacDonald.

G951. *European Socialism*, 2 Vols. Carl A. Landauer, California U.P.; Cambridge U.P., 1959, *EHR*. 77, 304. Jul. pp 570–1

(1) Highly critical of its size, its organisation and the author's propensity to use ten words where one would do; but it does have useful information in it.

(2) 'Marx called himself a scientist; but he lacked the solid groundwork of facts on which to operate a scientific method. His theories are dogma, true only because he said so; and any study of them is nearer to theology than to science.'

G952. *ID*, 2nd Ser., 1, (Sep-Dec 1870), ed. Frederico Chabod, 1960, *Ibid*. pp 579–80

(1) Praises the editing. The material does not change existing interpretations.

G953. *Osterreich und der Vatican*, Vol. 2, Friedrich Engel-Janosi, Graz, Styria, 1960, *Ibid*. p 585

(1) The author 'writes with grace' and 'provides as full and accurate an account as we can have until the Vatican archives are opened'.

G954. Granite or cardboard? *Metternich and His Times*, G. de Bertier de Sauvigny, Darton, Longman and Todd, *Obs*. 5 Aug. p 14

(1) 'A sort of anthology of Metternich', which is quite entertaining.

(2) Metternich 'was a stage figure, elegantly got up; the original stuffed shirt, starch outside and sawdust within'.

G955. Mountain or Molehill, *The Marconi Scandal*, Frances Donaldson, Hart-Davis, *Obs*. 26 Aug. p 16

(1) 'Very good indeed, one of the most entertaining and enlightening books that I have read for a long time. It analyses the technical and financial

issues clearly; it is extremely well written; it is impeccably impartial.'

G956. Friends of Every Country, *Great Britain and Austria-Hungary During The First World War*, Harry Hanak, Oxford, *NS*. 64, 1646. 28 Sept. pp 412–3

(1) It deals with public opinion, and in doing this by analysing articles in periodicals, it raises the usual questions as to whether such pieces shape opinion, express it, or are 'merely written by a small group for other members of the same group'.

G957. Battles Long Ago, (a) *The First Battle of the Marne*, Robert B. Asprey, Weidenfeld and Nicolson; (b) *1916: Year of Decisions*, James Cameron, Oldbourne; (c) *Mutiny, 1917*, John Williams, Heinemann; (d) *1918: The Last Act*, Barrie Pitt, Cassell, *Obs*. 30 Sept. p 28

(a1) A clear, precise narrative; 'a 'bunking' book, seeking to restore reputations which have been tarnished'.

(b1) Very well written, but in basing his book on Lloyd George's papers his book is out of balance.

(c1) A good popular account of the mutinies from the military point of view but it lacks a political dimension.

(d1) The best of the books; it explains why there was deadlock in the trenches and how it was broken.

G958. Last of the Romans, *John Anderson*, Sir John Wheeler Bennett, Macmillan, *Gdn*. 5 Oct. p 13

(1) It 'is in tune with its subject. It even has a touch of the same agreeable pomposity . . . The book is like an eighteenth-century memorial monument.'

Repr. *MGW*. 87, 15. 11 Oct. p 11

G959. Nazi Germany's reluctant ally, *The Brutal Friendship*, F.W. Deakin, Weidenfeld and Nicolson, *Obs*. 21 Oct. p 26

(1) 'A ponderous tome of 800 pages', but a book which will be read for a very long time.

G960. City of Destruction, (a) *On the Prevention of War*,

John Strachey, Macmillan; (b) *The Spread of Nuclear Weapons*, Leonard Beaton and John Maddox, Chatto and Windus; (c) *Negotiation From Strength*, Coral Bell, Chatto and Windus; (d) *Studies of War*, P.M.S. Blackett, Oliver and Boyd. *NS*. 64, 1650. 26 Oct. p 578

(1) Denounces, or rather ridicules, Strachey's views. He uses the other books to support his attack.

G961. Hunting Slim Jannie, *Smuts*, Vol. 1, W.K. Hancock, Cambridge U.P., *Obs*. 28 Oct. p 25

(1) Written by 'an historian of faultless grasp', who is 'a beautiful writer'. 'A model of political biography, clear, perceptive, judicious'.

G962. *Gegen Bajonett und Dividende*, Kurt Stenkewitz, Berlin, Rütten and Loening, 1960, *EHR*. 77, 305. Oct. p 812

(1) 'The author would clearly have liked to show that 'militarists' deliberately embarked on war (in 1914) in order to escape from their difficulties at home; but evidence for this is lacking.'

G963. War for war's sake, *The Price of Glory: Verdun 1916*, Alistair Horne, Macmillan, *Obs*. 4 Nov. p 27

(1) The best First World War book since Leon Woolf's. This 'has almost every merit'.

G964. Sidelights on the phoney war, *The Ironside Diaries 1937–1940*, ed. Roderick MacLeod and Denis Kelly, Constable, *Obs*. 11 Nov. p 25

(1) 'His diaries present him as a bull in a china shop, smashing all the crockery, including his own.' Valuable for the atmosphere, but not much solid information in them.

G965. Eden in the Thirties, *The Eden Memoirs*, Vol. 2, the Earl of Avon, Cassell, *Obs*. 18 Nov. p 24

(1) 'An important contribution to historical knowledge'. A.J.P.T. finds the author's attempt 'to show that he was not tarred with the appeasement brush' unconvincing.

G966. Genocide, *The Great Hunger*, Cecil Woodham-Smith, Hamilton, *NS*. 64, 1654. 23 Nov. pp 741–2

(1) A 'most admirable and thorough book'.
Repr. in A13, pp 173–8 and A21, pp 73–9

G967. Umbrella Man, or The Two Revolutions, *The Age of Revolution*, E.J. Hobsbawm, Weidenfeld and Nicolson, *NS*. 64, 1655..30 Nov. p 780

(1) 'A brilliant account of Europe in its revolutionary age . . . New Hobsbawm is old Marx writ large. His book is the *Communist Manifesto* transformed with great skill and knowledge into a work of history.' 'This book is very often right; often, I think, wrong; always stimulating. No one could ask for more.'

G968. A famous British victory, *Victory in the West*, Vol. 1, Major L.F. Ellis, H.M.S.O., *Obs*. 16 Dec. p 22

(1) Warmly praises the official history series on the Second World War, and this volume in particular.

G969. Books of the Year, *Obs*. 23 Dec. p 7

The Marconi Scandal (*see above* G955) 'combined a high measure of enlightenment and entertainment'. *The Age of Revolution*, (G967) – 'the most remarkable achievement of historical scholarship . . . though its approach often seemed to me perverse. It makes good reading as well as exciting history.' *John Anderson* (G958) and *The Eden Memoirs*, Vol. 2, (G965) 'tied for first place as the dullest book of the year'.

G970. Germany's breakthrough, *GD*, Ser. C., 4, 1935–6, *Obs*. 30 Dec. p 16

(1) 'A mountain of dreary stuff', mostly routine business.

(2) 'Others provided the opportunity for Hitler; he duly took advantage of it. The fate of Europe was shaped by Mussolini's absurd desire to build an empire in Africa, and by the equally absurd attempt of others to stop him.'

1963

G971. Travelling with Churchill, *The War and Colonel Warden*, Gerald Pawle, Harrap, *Obs*. 20 Jan. p 22

(1) A good anecdotal biography of Churchill during the Second World War.

G972. Telling the Tale, (a) *Bonaparte in Egypt*, J. Christopher Herold, Hamilton; (b) *Eighteen Fifteen*, John Fisher, Cassell; (c) *The Peace of Christmas Eve*, Fred Engelman, Hart-Davis, *NS*. 65, 1664. 1 Feb. p 160

(a1) The author is 'a superb story teller'.

(b1) An enjoyable diary of events in 1815. 'Next time he must settle on a theme. Time is essential in history, but it is not the only thing.'

(c1) A well researched book but 'the theme is lost in detail'.

G973. The Great Days of Europe, *L'Europe du XIXe et du XXe Siecle*, (1870–1914), 2 Vols. Milan, Marsorati; Oxford, Parker, *TLS*. 3179. 1 Feb. p 75

(1) He regrets that 'the history of eastern Europe is passed over almost entirely except for Russia . . . ' and that the smaller countries are ignored. He also finds that 'most of the writers are content with a pedestrian narrative'. He is very critical of the treatment of international relations.

G974. Old Tunes, *The Appeasers*, Martin Gilbert and Richard Gott, Weidenfeld and Nicolson, *NS*. 65, 1666. 15 Feb. pp 238, 240

(1) 'It depresses me that two young historians . . . should be content to play old tunes.' 'Accurate and honest within its limits. These limits are narrow.'

G975. Comedy in High Places, *Rosebery*, Robert Rhodes James, Weidenfeld and Nicolson, *Obs*. 17 Feb. p 22

(1) The book 'is the richest comedy to be produced for years. I cannot remember when I have enjoyed a book more.'

G976. How not to do it, *The Yankee Marlborough*, R.W. Thompson, Allen and Unwin, *Obs*. 24 Feb. p 22

(1) Churchill is unrecognisable. The author 'repeats every discreditable story known, and adds some more of his own'.

G977. Big Beast at Bay, *The Decline and Fall of Lloyd George*, Lord Beaverbrook, Collins, *NS*. 65, 1669. 8 Mar. pp 341–2

(1) Like the author's other history books 'it is a unique combination of political history and personal recollection. There is the same sparkling style, an equally rich stock of anecdotes, and the same endearing frankness of Lord Beaverbrook about himself.'

G978. Odd Man In, *Arthur James Balfour*, Kenneth Young, Bell, *NS*. 65, 1670. 15 Mar. pp 390–1

(1) An 'excellent though occasionally sententious new biography . . . His book will take a permanent place among political biographies.'

(2) 'Intellectual foolery was Balfour's incurable weakness. Intellectual policy was intermittently his strength.'

G979. Murder or Suicide? *Anschluss*, Gordon Brook-Shepherd, Macmillan, *Obs*. 17 Mar. p 26

(1) A.J.P.T. observes that it bears out his view that Hitler was a great improviser, rather than a man with a time-table for aggression.

G980. A statesman who was guilty of one sin, *Guizot*, Douglas Johnson, Routledge, *Obs*. 24 Mar. p 22

(1) A collection of essays written with detached judgment.

(2) Guizot 'was a bourgeois Metternich: equally sententious; equally distrustful of movement; equally confident in his own judgement'.

G981. Voice from the Dead, *The Soviet Revolution*, Raphael Abramovitch, Allen and Unwin, *NS*. 65, 1673. 5 Apr. pp 492, 494

(1) 'The book is a mixture of detached history, political criticism and general complaint. It is designed to show that the Mensheviks were right, or at any rate the Bolsheviks were wrong.'

G982. Hitler's Third Book, *Diary of a German Soldier*, Wilhelm Prüller, Faber, *NS*. 65, 1675. 19 Apr. pp 595–6

(1) 'His diary is a little demonstration that Hitler

far from misleading the Germans or tyrannising over them, gave them exactly what they wanted.'

G983. Giving Haig Fair Treatment, *Douglas Haig*, John Terraine, Hutchinson, *Obs.* 21 Apr. p 24

(1) A.J.P.T. feels that, after the blows to his reputation given by Lloyd George's *War Memoirs* and the publication of his own diaries, Haig at last gets fair treatment. He wishes the author had been equally fair to Lloyd George.

(2) Haig 'represented finely the British Army of the time: dogged, courageous and antiquated'.

G984. Old Bill Goes Into Politics, *The Politics of Influence*, Graham Wooton, Routledge, *Obs.* 5 May. p 27

(1) One of the most sensible studies of a pressure group.

G985. Stage Effects, (a) *Alliance against Hitler*, William Evans Scott, Duke U.P.; (b) *Laval*, Hubert Cole, Heinemann; (c) *The Liberation of Paris*, Willis Thornton, Hart-Davis, *NS.* 65, 1678. 10 May. p 714

(a1) The author takes the Franco-Soviet Pact too seriously. The French Radicals behind it 'were the greatest masters of pretence in an age of pretence'.

(b1) 'A lively biography . . . His book is sympathetic without being an apology.'

(b2) 'Explanations can be found for Laval, and excuses. It remains true that no honest man would wish to have acted as he did.' 'His was the patriotism of survival.'

(c1) The story of the French Resistance written in romantic terms.

G986. No Golden Age, *Prophets of Yesterday*, Gerhard Masar, Weidenfeld and Nicolson, *Obs.* 19 May. p 24

(1) Quite a useful cultural history but often 'the judgements suggest that Mr. Charles Pooter holds the pen'.

G987. An unbalanced pattern, *The Precarious Balance*, Ludwig Dehio, Chatto and Windus, *Obs.* 9 Jun. p 26

(1) Despite its careful scholarship, 'it is a terrifying example of how a historian can be bewitched by his

own phrases'. 'The balance of power, like other patterns is a construction by the historian for most of the time; and even those conscious of the balance did not pursue it as rigorously as Professor Dehio makes out.'

(2) 'The First World War was as near perhaps as Europe got to a pure war for the balance.'

G988. Imperial Ring o'Roses, *The Fall of Dynasties*, Edmund Taylor, Weidenfeld and Nicolson, *Obs.* 23 Jun. p 24

(1) 'The presentation is relentlessly dramatic', and it is marked by minor errors.

G989. Guardians of Morality, *Tribal Feelings*, Michael Astor, Murray, *NS.* 65, 1685. 28 Jun. p 973

(1) The story of the Astor family is of great interest, but the book is not a profound family study.

G990. Boer War Blunderer, *Buller's Campaign*, Julian Symons, Cresset, *Obs.* 30 Jun. p 21

(1) An admirable book.

G991. Flickering Figures, (a) *Mr. Wilson's War*, John Dos Passos, Hamilton; (b) *Munich*, Keith Eubank, Oklahoma U.P., *NS.* 66, 1687. 12 Jul. p 49

(a1) Deems his method to be that of putting 'the cinema newsreel into words . . . (The historical figures) are not even cardboard, merely shadows on a screen . . . The method makes for compulsive reading.' However as history it lacks depth, and the author does not use new material.

(b1) The author 'firmly presents the accepted version of Munich. He cannot demonstrate that it is the right one.'

G992. World Cabinet secretary, *The Supreme Control at the Paris Peace Conference 1919*, Lord Hankey, Allen and Unwin, *Obs.* 14 Jul. p 24

(1) A dull book – 'useful for the budding bureaucrat. It is a model text book of how to get to the top without anyone noticing or minding.'

(2) 'The Treaty of Versailles had many good qualities and far fewer defects than is commonly

supposed. It is hard to see how it could have been done better in the circumstances of the time.'

G993. Discreditable Episodes, (a) *The Fate of Admiral Kolchak*, Peter Fleming, Hart-Davis; (b) *The Transcaspian Episode*, C.H. Ellis, Hutchinson; (c) *World War I*, Hanson Baldwin, Hutchinson; (d) *From Metternich to Hitler*, ed. W.N. Medlicott, Routledge, *NS*. 66, 1689. 26 Jul. p 118

(a1) 'A fascinating account of this sad tale'.

(b1) 'A careful, scholarly account, with few personal touches, but vivid and important all the same'.

(c1) A competent and clear brief outline, marred by minor mistakes.

(d1) The best of the essays, which first appeared as Historical Association pamphlets, is that by Bernadotte Schmitt.

G994. Literature in a Vacuum, *Eight Modern Writers: The Oxford History of English Literature*, Vol. 12, J.I.M. Stewart, Oxford U.P., *Obs*. 28 Jul. p 20

(1) Denounces it for dealing with writers' books in a vacuum without dealing with the society in which the books were written; as a result the book is 'the most flagrant manifesto of unbridled individualism ever penned'.

G995. War Plans or Improvisations? *Hitler's Pre-War Policy and Military Plans 1933–39*, E.M. Robertson, Longmans, *Obs*. 1 Sept. p 19

(1) The book is narrower in scope than its title would suggest.

G996. The bull of Assyria, *Layard of Nineveh*, Gordon Waterfield, Murray, *Obs*. 8 Sept. p 24

(1) The author 'excels on every count . . . Layard deserves immortality and Mr. Waterfield has given it to him.'

G997. Lament for Imperial Vienna, *The Fall of the House of Habsburg*, Edward Crankshaw, Longmans, *Obs*. 15 Sept. p 22

(1) Praises the author for his analysis of the problems of the Habsburg Monarchy and for his

character sketches, but dislikes his nostalgia for Imperial Vienna.

G998. Mean Cities, *Victorian Cities*, Asa Briggs, Odhams, *Gdn.* 20 Sept. p 9

(1) The author 'handles his fascinating theme with a Victorian fertility. Statistics and quotations tumble from his typewriter. He is quick with anecdotes and penetrating comments ... This is a delightful and entertaining book ... (but) There is not much intensity or bite.'

Repr. as 'Cities of the Industrial Revolution', *MGW*. 89, 13. 26 Sept. p 10

G999. Cliveden in Reverse, *Focus*, Eugen Spier, Wolff, *NS*. 86, 1698. 27 Sept. p 400

(1) It provides 'a good deal of useful information' on this group which campaigned on the dangers of Nazi Germany.

G1000. Escapades of a Modern Historian, *Encounters in History*, Pieter Geyl, Collins, *Obs.* 6 Oct. p 24

(1) A book of 'incomparable understanding ... in some ways the most rewarding ... ' of his books. Regrets that the author 'fails to appreciate the deeply European character even of present-day Russia'.

G1001. Fighting Men, (a) *Gallipoli to the Somme*, Alexander Aitken, Oxford; (b) *Years of Combat*, Sholto Douglas, Collins; (c) *Evans of the Broke*, Reginald Pound, Oxford; (d) *Soldier True*, Victor Bonham-Carter, Muller; (e) *The Royal George*, Giles St. Aubyn, Constable, *NS*. 86, 1700. 11 Oct. pp 490–1

(a1) 'In a class by itself ... a literary classic'.

(b1) 'A good book with its own atmosphere'.

(c1) 'Evans was a schoolboy's hero ... The book has the fine old-fashioned glamour of an adventure story.'

(d1) The author 'adds some details from Robertson's private papers which strengthen what we know already. Robertson's conduct cannot be defended.'

(e1) 'A most delightful book about an unusual, though wooden-headed character'.

G1002. Pirate King, *The King Incorporated*, Neal Ascherson, Allen and Unwin, *NS*. 86, 1702. 25 Oct. p 576

(1) 'A brilliant composition. It is lively, clear, good both as biography and as history.'

G1003. Trotsky, the Old Pretender, *The Prophet Outcast*, Isaac Deutscher, Oxford U.P., *Obs*. 27 Oct. p 24

(1) 'As a personal portrait of a great man this is a very good and moving book.'

(2) Trotsky's activities in exile 'were an honour to the human race' – they 'were the noblest period of his life'.

G1004. The Reason Why, *Winston Churchill and the Dardanelles*, Trumbull Higgins, Macmillan, *NYRB*. 1, 5. 31 Oct. pp 9–10

(1) The author 'has written a first-rate political study of the Gallipoli affair. The results are not as novel as he makes out.' He criticises the author for his thesis that there was a clear choice between total and limited war.

G1005. *ID*, 9th Ser., 4, (Apr-Jun 1940), ed. Mario Toscano, 1960, *EHR*. 78, 309. Oct. p 820

(1) 'There is no exciting information, though much interesting detail particularly on Balkan politics.'

G1006. How to play the war game, *The Swordbearers*, Corelli Barnett, Eyre and Spottiswoode, *Obs*. 3 Nov. p 25

(1) 'An excellent and provocative book'; free from mistakes of fact, though A.J.P.T. disagrees with some of his judgments.

G1007. Speak for England! *The Age of Illusion*, Ronald Blythe, Hamilton, *NS*. 86, 1705. 15 Nov. p 709

(1) In surveying the interwar period the author 'does quite well, but not well enough'. 'He who comes to equity must come with clean hands, and he who comes to history must come with accuracy.'

G1008. Armies and Navies, (a) *The Two-Ocean War*, S.E. Morison, Oxford; (b) *The March on Delhi*,

A.J. Barker, Faber; (c) *Neither Fear Nor Hope*, F. von Senger und Etterlin, MacDonald; (d) *Rescue in Denmark*, Harold Flender, Allen, *NS*. 86, 1707. 29 Nov. p 786

(a1) The author 'has no peer. He is a distinguished scholar, a brilliant and, what is even more unusual, a productive writer . . . This is a miraculous book, which wastes none of its 500 pages.'

(b1) The author 'tells exceedingly well the story of a single campaign'.

(c1) 'He presents a clear strategical narrative and makes some useful comments . . . His general speculations are less rewarding.'

(d1) The author does full justice to the story of the rescue of the Jews. 'What happened in Denmark is an invaluable reminder that it was a struggle between right and wrong.'

G1009. What Went Wrong, *The Road to Dictatorship*, trans. Lawrence Wilson, Wolff, *NS*. 86, 1709. 13 Dec. pp 881–2

(1) These essays by ten German professors omit discussion of anti-semitism in Germany and why there was widespread German support for Hitler. A.J.P.T. suggests the explanation for the latter is their national character; an explanation, 'No doubt very shocking, prejudiced and old-fashioned'.

G1010. Books of the Year, *Obs*. 22 Dec. p 15

Names *Rosebery* (*see above* G975) and *Layard of Nineveh* (G996) as the best biographies. The best book of the year was *Gallipoli to the Somme* (G1001), which 'eclipsed all others as a book both true and moving'. 'A special award goes to *Fanny Hill*, the most overrated book of the year.'

1964

G1011. My Uncle Arly, *James Anthony Froude*, Vol. 2, Waldo Hilary Dunn, Oxford U.P., *Obs*. 12 Jan. p 25

(1) A detailed study, which tends to obscure Froude's personality.

(2) 'He had a wonderful gift for getting himself into a tangle without apparently intending to do so. Everything he wrote stirred up controversy.'

G1012. After the Feast, *The Age of Equipoise*, W.L. Burn, Allen and Unwin, *NS*. 67, 1715. 24 Jan. pp 129–30

(1) Observes that authors of impressionistic history tend to shape it in their own likeness. 'Mr. Burn is a justice of the peace and a landowner on a modest scale, as well as being a university professor of, I should guess, Conservative inclination.' Writes warmly of it, but feels that 'the age was redeemed only by those who kicked against it'.

G1013. The army that went on strike, *Dare Call It Treason*, Richard M. Watt, Chatto and Windus, *Obs*. 26 Jan. p 26

(1) The author has pieced together thc details of the French army mutinies of 1917 'with scholarly ingenuity'; it is 'faultless' on these, but weaker on general history.

G1014. Elephants in India, *Peace in Their Time*, Emery Kelen, Gollancz, *NS*. 67, 1716. 31 Jan. pp 170, 172

(1) 'This is an anthology of delusions as well as old stories.'

G1015. Man who stayed out in the cold, *Proconsul In Politics*, Alfred Gollin, Blond, *Obs*. 2 Feb. p 27

(1) The author 'is perhaps the most formidable researcher now at work on recent British history'. 'The Right was a real danger to British democracy, the Left never. This is the dynamic lesson of Mr. Gollin's exhaustive and splendid book ... (It is) a historical contribution second to none.'

G1016. Bag and Baggage, (a) *Gladstone and the Bulgarian Agitation, 1876*, R.T. Shannon, Nelson; (b) *Coercion and Conciliation in Ireland 1880–1892*, L.P. Curtis Jr., Princeton U.P.; (c) *Lord Salisbury and Foreign Policy*, J.A.S. Grenville, Athlone; (d) *The End of Isolation*, G.W. Monger, Nelson; (e) *Land and Power*, Harold Nelson, Routledge, *NS*. 67, 1719.

21 Feb. pp 296, 298

(a1) 'Essential reading for anyone interested either in Gladstone or in the intellectual history of nineteenth century England'.

(b1) The author 'deserves a cheer for seeking to explain what Balfour and Salisbury tried to do in Ireland'.

(c1) Praises it, but observes that the author's 'central argument seems to conflict with the new evidence which he has produced ... The detailed narrative shows Salisbury as a rather helpless muddler over everything except Egypt, repeatedly overruled by his own Cabinet because he had nothing serious to propose.'

(d1) 'A very good book of its kind'.

(e1) 'His detailed and dispassionate narrative confirms the merit of one peacemaker' – Lloyd George. 'In vision he had no equal among the statesmen of his time.'

G1017. When the Cold War Began, *Socialism in One Country*, Vol. 3, E.H. Carr, Macmillan, *Obs.* 23 Feb. p 27

(1) 'A formidable contribution to historical knowledge', by a 'very great scholar and historian'.

G1018. Great Britain's War, (a) *The Battle for the Mediterranean*, Donald MacIntyre, Batsford; (b) *Monte Cassino*, Rudolf Böhmer, Cassell, *NS.* 67, 1721. 6 Mar. pp 367–8

(a1) 'Adds little new information', but he 'has done well in describing how the British won the wrong war in the wrong way'.

(b1) He 'gives a good account of the campaign from the German point of view, though he has little to say'.

G1019. Somebody Blundered, *The Curragh Incident*, James Fergusson, Faber, *NS.* 67, 1722. 13 Mar. p 405

(1) He 'is a distinguished historian, and this book adds new distinction to his name. It is exciting, a rare pleasure to read, and displays exact scholarship on every page.'

G1020. The last of the peacocks, (a) *The Kaiser and His*

Times, Michael Balfour, Cresset; (b) *King Edward The Seventh*, Philip Magnus, Murray, *Obs.* 15 Mar. p 26

(a1) 'A solid political study' – and praises in particular the chapter on William II's character.

(b1) 'A masterly biography'.

G1021. Black Spot, (a) *Stillborn Revolution*, Werner Angress, Princeton U.P.; (b) *A Mirror of Nazism*, Brigitte Grazow, Gollancz, *NS.* 67, 1727. 17 Apr. pp 608–9

(a1) 'This is a long book, quite pointless, and full of entertainment.'

(b1) Her 'conclusions give a one-sided, misleading picture'.

G1022. Twin Set, (a) *A History of the U.S.A. from Wilson to Kennedy*, André Maurois, Weidenfeld and Nicolson; (b) *A History of the U.S.S.R. from Lenin to Kruschev*, Louis Aragon, Weidenfeld and Nicolson, *Obs.* 26 Apr. p 28

(a1) 'His judgments are shrewd' – a competent but not profound or original book.

(b1) A very bad book.

G1023. *ID*, 7th Ser., 4. (1925–7), ed. R. Moscati and G. Carocci, 1962, *EHR.* 79, 311. Apr. pp 443–4

(1) The principal interest of the volume is what it reveals of Mussolini gaining confidence as foreign minister.

G1024. *Bergen-Belsen*, Eberhard Kolb, Hanover, Verlag für Literatur und Zeitgeschen, 1962, *Ibid.* p 446

(1) 'A remarkable achievement of thorough and dispassionate scholarship, though almost too horrible to read'.

G1025. A Handful, *The Easter Rebellion*, Max Caulfield, Muller, *NS.* 87, 1729. 1 May. p 685

(1) 'This is an exciting book and tells very much what happened, even if the details are drawn too confidently.' A.J.P.T. has grave doubts about the excessive weight given to later recollections of the combatants.

G1026. Westminster white elephant, *A History of Parliament*, 3 Vols. Sir Lewis Namier and John Brooke,

H.M.S.O., *Obs.* 3 May. p 26

(1) Condemns the project, in particular its approach of simply analysing the constituencies and cataloguing the MPs. He asks, 'What does all this tell us about the part played by the House of Commons in political history?'

(2) 'History, to my mind, is the record of what was significant in the past.'

G1027. Good Old Wars, (a) *Memoirs of the Bobotes*, Joyce Cary, Joseph; (b) *Armageddon 1918*, Cyril Falls, Weidenfeld and Nicolson, *NS.* 67, 1731. 15 May. p 766

(a1) 'Cary's book, as well as its subject, is a period piece . . . Cary knew that he was expected to feel certain sensations and obliged.'

(b1) 'I hope we may have many such books, with the author explaining that the battle, though brilliantly conducted, served no useful purpose.' The author 'wastes no affection on T.E. Lawrence – a neat and justified piece of dagger-work, which leaves little over of the absurd legend'.

G1028. Pen and Sword, *Generals At War*, Sir Frederick de Guingand, Hodder and Stoughton, *Obs.* 24 May. p 28

(1) Interesting on Wavell and Auchinleck but otherwise 'the book provides much material for an anthology of unfunny stories'.

G1029. Another Lost Leader, *J.H. Thomas: A Life For Unity*, Gregory Blaxland, Muller, *Gdn.* 29 May. p 8

(1) 'A sound biography', but 'virtually nothing new in it'.

(2) 'He was anchored to no firm bottom of principle and charges of treachery always pursued him.'

G1030. Our Only General, (a) *All Sir Garnett: A Life of Field Marshal Lord Wolseley*, John Lehmann, Cape; (b) *The Drums of Kumasi*, Alan Lloyd, Longmans, *Obs.* 7 Jun. p 26

(a1) 'A pedestrian book, competent and uninspiring'.

(b1) 'Lively, entertaining, and develops much understanding'.

G1031. First of the Rockers, *Mussolini*, Sir Ivone Kirkpatrick, Odhams, *Obs.* 14 Jun. p 26

(1) Critical of his style, his use of sources and the balance of the book.

G1032. The great cart-horse, *A History of British Trade Unions Since 1889*, Vol. 1, *1889–1910*, H.A. Clegg, Alan Fox and A.F. Thompson, Oxford U.P., *Obs.* 21 Jun. p 28

(1) 'There is a great deal in this book, and it will stand unchallenged for a long time as the leading authority on its subject.' 'The political part of this book is exceptionally well done and adds much to our knowledge, even though the ground has been already worked by others.' However he regrets that little attention is paid to the views of the working men.

G1033. Old Bill, *The Western Front 1914–1918*, John Terraine, Hutchinson, *NS.* 67, 1737. 26 Jun. pp 995–6

(1) The author's views have changed and he now believes 'whole-heartedly in the Western Front and Haig. Indeed he has become the original Old Bill, ready to hold the trenches until Doomsday.' He 'makes allowances for Haig and none for Lloyd George'.

G1034. Irish Problems, (a) *The Irish Administration*, R.B. McDowell, Routledge; (b) *The Catholic Question in English Politics*, G.I.T. Machin, Oxford; (c) *Gladstone and the Irish Nation*, J.L. Hammond, intro. M.R.D. Foot, Cass, *NS.* 68, 1740. 17 Jul. p 90

(a1) 'His book is gay as well as informative and competent.'

(b1) 'An admirable work of close political analysis, carefully illuminating the politics and the spirit of the 1820's.'

(c1) 'His profound book was a monument of liberal scholarship and understanding, a book without a peer . . . (It) demonstrates anew the general rule that English politicians took leave of their senses, and also of their principles, whenever they touched Ireland.'

G1035. *La Premier Internationale*, 2 Vols. ed. Jacques Freymond, Geneva, Droz, 1962, *EHR*. 79, 312. Jul. pp 571–3

(1) 'They are a contribution to historical information of high value.'

(2) 'The International was invented for industrial workers by craftsmen; it did not spring from capitalist theory.'

G1036. Sad Failure, *Charles Townshend*, L.B. Namier and John Brooke, Macmillan, *Obs*. 6 Sept. p 24

(1) Regrets that Namier spent his last years assembling 'trivialities about this trivial man's career'. The book has 'hardly a flash of Namier's old wit or insight'.

G1037. A very human Queen, *Victoria R.I.*, Elizabeth Longford, Weidenfeld and Nicolson, *Obs*. 13 Sept. p 25

(1) She draws on new material to provide 'a richer, deeper portrait, suffused with sympathy and understanding'.

G1038. Cloak over wartime mistakes, *Grand Strategy*, Vol. 3, J.M.A. Gwyner and J.R.M. Butler, H.M.S.O., *Obs*. 20 Sept. p 24

(1) It tried to cover up the mistakes that were made. Regrets that it is too dependent on non British sources.

G1039. A Patriotic War, (a) *Men, Years-Life*, Vol. 5, Ilya Ehrenburg, MacGibbon and Kee; (b) *Russia at War*, Alexander Werth, Barrie and Rockliff; (c) *Inside Hitler's Headquarters*, Walter Warlimont, Weidenfeld and Nicolson, *NS*. 68, 1752. 9 Oct. pp 543–4

(a1) The author 'has written a very good book' – though it 'has not much value as a precise historical record'.

(b1) It is too long and the author 'has brought to history the techniques of a journalist, not a historian'. 'He does not penetrate far into the spirit of the Russian people.'

(c1) Finds his personal explanations unconvincing.

G1040. By-ways of history, *Essays in British History*, ed. H.R. Trevor Roper, Macmillan, *Obs.* 18 Oct. p 26

(1) Praises the essays in this *festschrift* to Sir Keith Feiling, and in particular the editor's 'brilliant piece'.

G1041. The wild ones, *The Anarchists*, James Joll, Eyre and Spottiswoode, *Obs.* 25 Oct. p 26

(1) 'A careful scholarly book, in which grace and learning sit easily together'.

G1042. More Germans, (a) *The History of the Gestapo*, Jacques Delarue, MacDonald; (b) *While Berlin Burns*, Hans-Georg von Studnitz, Weidenfeld and Nicolson; (c) *Terror und Widerstand*, Landeszentrale für politische Bildungsarbeit, Berlin, *NS.* 68, 1755. 30 Oct. pp 656–7

(a1) An unimpressive book.

(b1) His diary gives trivial but interesting details of how German officials and society enjoyed themselves during the last two years of the Second World War.

G1043. A toga somewhat tattered, *Asquith*, Roy Jenkins, Collins, *Obs.* 1 Nov. p 26

(1) Not as revealing about Asquith as it might have been. A.J.P.T. disagrees with the author's interpretation of Asquith's fall from office.

(2) 'Asquith sought worldly success. He took on, and even exaggerated, the attitudes of the society which he aspired to enter.'

G1044. Dark Corridors, *Corridors of Power*, C.P. Snow, Macmillan, *NS.* 68, 1756. 6 Nov. p 698

(1) Feels that it is as unrealistic about politics as *The Masters* was about dons. 'It is a Victorian melodrama, told in stodgy twentieth century prose.'

G1045. Churchill versus Wavell, *Wavell*, John Connell, Collins, *Obs.* 8 Nov. p 28

(1) An admirable biography, which provides

a fascinating account of relations between Churchill and Wavell.

(2) Wavell was 'the most distinguished British general of the interwar years' but 'his fine character had one flaw: he could not get on with Churchill'.

G1046. Bismarck variations, *Bismarck*, Werner Richter, MacDonald, *Obs.* 15 Nov. p 27

(1) 'Lively and interesting', but it does not contain much new information.

G1047. British-made, *Lord Haw-Haw – and William Joyce*, J.A. Cole, Faber, *NS.* 68, 1758. 20 Nov. pp 793–4

(1) 'A most balanced, sensible book, perhaps a little too sympathetic towards Joyce'.

(2) 'he was Mr. Polly gone sour, a little man resenting the world and doing his utmost to spite it'.

G1048. Men of Labours, *Labouring Men*, E.J. Hobsbawm, Weidenfeld and Nicolson, *NS.* 68, 1559. 27 Nov. p 832

(1) Warmly praises the essays.

G1049. Books of the Year, *Obs.* 20 Dec. p 7

Praises *The Anarchists* (*see above* G1041) and *Proconsul in Politics*, 'dynamically written and rich in relevations' (G1015). *Gladstone and the Bulgarian Agitation* (G1016) 'gave me the greatest intellectual delight – a delight no doubt enhanced by discovering a canon of St. Paul's and an eminent historian among the agitators'.

1965

G1050. First shots in World War II, *BD*, 2nd Ser., 9, *1931–2*, *Obs.* 10 Jan. p 26

(2) On the Far East: 'The only British choice, in terms of action, was the moment when they should lose Singapore.'

G1051. The man who split the world, *The Life of Lenin*, Louis Fischer, Weidenfeld and Nicolson, *Obs.* 17 Jan. p 26

(1) It succeeds in bringing 'Lenin to life both as a man and as a political leader'.

(2) 'Greatness was thrust on him by events'.

G1052. 1793 And All That, *Paris In The Terror*, Stanley Loomis, Cape, *Obs.* 24 Jan. p 27

(1) Romantic history – the author 'is a pop-singer of history'.

G1053. Big Deal, *Fifty Ships That Saved The World*, Philip Goodhart, Heinemann, *Obs.* 24 Jan. p 27

(1) A valuable, detailed account of Roosevelt's gift of 50 destroyers in 1940.

G1054. Peaceful class – warriors, *Before the Socialists*, Royden Harrison, Routledge, *Obs.* 7 Feb. p 27

(1) 'A most admirable book, which is at once scholarly, delightful to read, and highly enlightening'.

G1055. Breaking the Suez silence, *Crisis*, Terence Robertson, Hutchinson, *Obs.* 21 Feb. p 27

(1) Based on non-British sources; written in an overdramatic style.

G1056. Keep the home fires burning, (a) *The Deluge*, Arthur Marwick, Bodley Head; (b) *Soldiers From the Wars Returning*, Charles Carrington, Hutchinson, *Obs.* 7 Mar. p 26

(a1) A book with many merits. Suggests the author 'exaggerates the hysteria among supporters of the war' and is too ready 'to accept the corresponding exaggerations of those who opposed the war'.

(b1) Very good on trench warfare; written by the author (pseud. 'Charles Edmonds') of *A Subaltern's War*.

G1057. Disregarded, *Vansittart in Office*, Ian Colvin, Gollancz, *NS.* 69, 1775. 19 Mar. pp 450–1

(1) 'The book does not tell much about Vansittart which we did not know already.' The most important new information is about the author's advice to the Government before it guaranteed Poland in March 1939.

G1058. The crown prince, *The Eden Memoirs*, Vol. 2, the Earl of Avon, Cassell, *Obs.* 21 Mar. p 26

(1) 'Curiously disappointing and, in general effect,

elusive . . . the great events seem remote, and there is a querulous tone.'

G1059. Snakes in Iceland, (a) *One Europe*, René Albercht-Carrié, New York, Doubleday; *Decline and Rise of Europe*, John Lukacs, New York, Doubleday, *NYRB*. 4, 4. 25 Mar. pp 8, 10

(1) Not favourable to a search for the roots of European unity: '. . . if ever history has a lesson, European disunity is surely it'.

G1060. Officers and Writers, (a) *The Education of An Army*, Jay Luvass, Cassell; (b) *The German Officer Corps in Society and State*, Karl Demeter, Weidenfeld and Nicolson, *NS*. 69, 1777. 2 Apr. pp 536–7

(a1) 'The essays are excellent as biographical studies' of writers about war, but they do not bring out so clearly the influence of the writers.

(b1) A standard work which has been brought up to date.

G1061. Scientists At War, *Tizard*, Ronald W. Clark, Methuen, *Obs*. 11 Apr. p 30

(1) A careful biography, which is extremely readable.

(2) A.J.P.T. recalls Tizard at Magdalen College, where 'Tizard's weakness was a failure to judge between great matters and small. With this went an impatience or lack of persistence which often led him to drop an affair halfway.'

G1062. Anecdotage, *From My Level*, George Mallaby, Hutchinson, *NS*. 69, 1780. 23 Apr. p 653

(1) A collection of trivial anecdotes.

G1063. Last word on Gallipoli, *Gallipoli*, Robert Rhodes James, Batsford, *Obs*. 25 Apr. p 26

(1) 'The best of his own books, and the best also, despite formidable competition, of the many books written about Gallipoli'.

G1064. *Diplomat Under Stress*, S. William Halperin, Chicago U.P., 1963, *EHR*. 80, 315. Apr. pp 432–3

(1) 'A beautiful exercise in diplomatic history'.

G1065. *Pagine di storia diplomatica contemporanea*, 2 Vols. Mario Toscano, Milan, Guiffré, 1963, *Ibid*. pp 443–4

(1) 'The detailed essays provide excellent examples of diplomatic history at its best, and the general essays provoke thought.'

G1066. The man who was always right, *Macaulay's Essays*, ed. Hugh Trevor Roper, Fontana paperback, *Obs.* 16 May. p 26

(1) Critical of the selection. Having praised Macaulay's style highly but deemed him to have been a very unoriginal mind, he gives the ambiguous verdict on the editor's introduction that 'it might have been written by Macaulay himself'.

(2) 'Macaulay had one great quality which is essential for the historian. He was excited by the past.' However he had 'no real sympathy for the past', nor did he suspend his judgment and carry out his researches impartially.

G1067. History Committee Style, *L'Europe du XIXe et du XXe siècle. Problèmes et Interprétations*, 2 Vols. Milan, Marzorati; Oxford, Parker, *TLS.* 64, 3299. 20 May. p 387

(1) Praises some of the contributions, notably Professor Renouvin on the First World War; but generally is very critical of the series.

G1068. Bedside Battles, (a) *The Battle of Konnigratz*, Gordon A. Craig, Weidenfeld and Nicolson; (b) *Caporetto*, Ronald Seth, MacDonald; (c) *The Battle of El Alamein*, Fred Majdalany, Weidenfeld and Nicolson; (d) *The Battle of D-Day*, William McElwee, Faber, *Obs.* 23 May. p 26

(a1) Brisker and shorter than Friedjung's account.

(b1) It deals with Italy's efforts in the war, not just that battle.

(c1) Less detailed than Carver's careful study but it has 'a wide grasp and understanding'.

(d1) 'A clear, effective account of the essential points', but it exaggerates Churchill's role.

G1069. Soldier out of step, *Memoirs*, Vol. 1, B.H. Liddell Hart, Cassell, *Obs.* 30 May. p 26

(1) The book is mostly about his ideas and the resistance which they encountered; with a few

personal touches of interest on Lloyd George, Churchill and T.E. Lawrence.

G1070. Churchill, *Winston Churchill : An Intimate Portrait*, Violet Bonham Carter, New York, Harcourt, Brace and World, *NYRB*. 4, 9. 3 Jun. pp 7–8

(1) Observes that most of the stories come from other books – 'Indeed it is difficult to think of anyone who could not have written this book – and most of them have.' Sees the book as being 'in part a rescue operation or take-over bid, designed to separate Churchill from Lloyd George. While both men are presented as erratic and difficult, Churchill's eccentricities are made endearing, Lloyd George's discreditable.'

G1071. Westerners versus Easterners, *British Strategy and Politics 1914–1918*, Paul Guinn, Oxford, *NS*. 69, 1786. 4 Jun. pp 884–5

(1) 'A foray into thick jungle'. The author 'has been overwhelmed by his material. The historian must first discover evidence and then throw three-quarters of it away.'

G1072. Bogeyman, *Friedrich von Holstein*, 2 Vols. Norman Rich, Cambridge U.P., *NS*. 69, 1788. 18 Jun. pp 960–1

(1) 'There is nothing of the slightest importance, only a few minor curiosities'. 'It demonstrates again 'that the legends about Holstein and the charges made against him had no foundation'.

G1073. Duty Called, *Edith Cavell*, A.E. Clark-Kennedy, Faber, *NS*. 70, 1790. 2 Jul. p 17

(1) A 'careful and scholarly work'.

G1074. Chunks of history, *The New Cambridge Modern History*, Vol. 8, ed. A. Goodwin, and Vol. 9, ed. C.W. Crawley, Cambridge U.P., *Obs*. 4 Jul. p 22

(1) Regrets that the series is in the form of compilations of essays by different authors and that it is so centred on Europe. 'Altogether the two volumes are a depressing experience for anyone who finds history exciting or even fun. There is not a laugh in 1,000 pages. This is history as stodge,

an undiluted diet of rice pudding.'

G1075. The reluctant statesman, *Halifax*, the Earl of Birkenhead, Hamilton, *Obs.* 25 Jul. p 22

(1) 'A biography of a very high order, though it is rather old fashioned in style and treatment'.

(2) 'Halifax incorporated the Establishment at its best and worst . . . Halifax was the Jeeves of the British Empire. Though he often opened the door on ill-tidings, he remained himself unruffled.'

G1076. What Else, Indeed? (a) *The Long Fuse*, Lawrence Lafore, New York, Lippincott; (b) *The Great Departure*, Daniel M. Smith, New York, Wiley; (c) *The Great War 1914–18 : A Pictorial History*, John Terraine, Macmillan, *NYRB*. 5, 1. 5 Aug. pp 9–10

(a1) Critical of the author's explanation of the causes – especially his going back to Bismarck's system.

(b1) US involvement in the First World War is handled 'with judicious detachment'.

(c1) The author 'describes the fighting well' but is less effective on the policy and direction of the war.

G1077. Bubbly and Bolshevism, *The Merchant of Revolution*, Z.A.B. Zeman and W.B. Scharlau, Oxford U.P., *Obs.* 15 Aug. p 18

(1) A good story, presented successfully.

(2) Alexander Helphard 'thought of the permanent revolution before Trotsky. Indeed he could claim to have invented the entire theoretical basis for the Bolshevik revolution.'

G1078. The Oath Man, *The Bradlaugh Case*, Walter Arnstein, Oxford U.P., *NS.* 70, 1798. 27 Aug. p 288

(1) 'A model of precise history. It is beautifully written and unfailingly accurate. It brings Bradlaugh to life. It illuminates Gladstone's intellectual complications. It further discredits that overrated figure, Lord Randolph Churchill.'

G1079. Last Crusade, (a) *The International Brigades*, Vincent

Brome, Heinemann; (b) *The Spanish Republic and the Civil War*, Gabriel Jackson, Princeton U.P., *NS*. 70, 1799. 3 Sept. pp 328–9

(a1) The author 'has done justice to them'.

(b1) He 'has mastered the sourccs. He has talked to many leading survivors and has weighed their accounts. His conclusions are clear and decisive.'

G1080. Monsters of the Deep, (a) *From The Dreadnought to Scapa Flow*, Vol. 2, Arthur J. Marder, Oxford U.P.; (b) *Dreadnought*, Richard Hough, Joseph, *Obs*. 19 Sept. p 27

(a1) 'One of the most perfect works ever published on naval strategy at a high level', written by 'a master of research and a master of narrative'.

(b1) A well written illustrated history of the modern battleship.

G1081. Stand by the Czechs, (a) *Munich*, Henri Noguères, Weidenfeld and Nicolson; (b) *The Murder of Admiral Darlan*, Peter Tompkins, Weidenfeld and Nicolson, *NS*. 70, 1802. 24 Sept. pp 442–3

(a1) 'A good example of how history should not be written. It is a hotch-potch of hackneyed quotations from the documents and miscellaneous gossip.'

(b1) The author 'offers sensation from start to finish'.

G1082. Forgotten Army, *The Gardeners of Salonika*, Alan Palmer, Deutsch, *Obs*. 3 Oct. p 28

(1) A very well written and interesting book.

G1083. A Curious Place, (a) *Victorian Oxford*, W.R. Ward, Cass; (b) *Oxford*, James Morris, Faber, *NS*. 70, 1805. 15 Oct. pp 566–7

(a1) 'A very curious book'. The author 'is a devoted pedant, who catalogues every utterance of the most obscure don as though it came from a great statesman'.

(b1) 'A mixture of rhapsody and anecdote, recorded in an over-sweet style'.

G1084. The last hero, *Garibaldi and His Enemies*, Christopher Hibbert, Longmans, *Obs*. 17 Oct. p 27

(1) A 'stirring and scholarly book'.

(2) 'All in all, there is no great figure of modern times so wholly admirable.'

G1085. No News, *Editorial*, Colin Coote, Eyre and Spottiswoode, *NS*. 70, 1807. 29 Oct. p 661

(1) It 'contains nothing of the slightest interest or importance'.

G1086. A prophet vindicated, (a) *Memoirs of Liddell Hart*, Vol. 2, Cassell; (b) *The Theory and Practice of War*, ed. Michael Howard, Cassell, *Obs*. 31 Oct. p 27

(a1) Even more revealing than the first volume.

(b1) This *festschrift* shows that Liddell Hart has been vindicated.

G1087. *ID*, 1st Ser., 13, (Jul-Sep 1870), ed. Walter Maturi, 1963, *EHR*. 80, 317. Oct. p 872

(1) An 'excellent volume'. 'It shows fully how Italy escaped from alliance with France into neutrality and also traces the preparations for the Italian occupation of Rome.'

G1088. Martyrdom of Paris, *The Fall of Paris*, Alistair Horne, Macmillan, *Obs*. 7 Nov. p 26

(1) A fine narrative writer – but the book lacks a broad perspective.

(2) 'The Commune was . . . heroic, with its strange mixture of patriotism and working class idealism, a mixture which no historian will ever clearly resolve.'

G1089. Missing the steamer, *England's Pride*, Julian Symons, Hamilton, *Obs*. 14 Nov. p 27

(1) The story of the expedition sent to relieve General Gordon, written with 'zest and brilliance'.

G1090. Trickery as a fine art, *Balfour's Burden*, Alfred Gollin, Blond, *Obs*. 21 Nov. p 28

(1) Praises the author as a writer and researcher but disagrees with his view that Balfour was a marvellous political tactician.

G1091. Better Luck Next Time, (a) *Decisive Battles of World War II*, ed. H.A. Jacobsen and J. Rohwer, Deutsch; (b) *The Memoirs of Field-Marshal Keitel*, ed. Walter Gorlitz, Kimber, *NS*. 70, 1811. 26 Nov. p 835 (a1) An unimpressive set of essays.

(b1) 'A melancholy volume'.

G1092. Keep the red flag flying, *The Clydesiders*, Robert Keith Middlemas, Hutchinson, *Obs.* 28 Nov. p 27

(1) The structure of the book is weak, but it does contain useful information, effective portraits of individuals and reliable judgments.

G1093. Books of the Year, *Obs.* 19 Dec. p 22

Praises *Gallipoli* (*see above* G1063) and *Halifax* (G1075). 'My greatest delight came from *The Bradlaugh Case* (G1078) . . . , dry and sparkling as champagne.'

1966

G1094. Laughter at No. 10, *The Most English Minister*, Donald Southgate, Macmillan, *Obs.* 9 Jan. p 24

(1) An improvement on previous lives of Palmerston, but unduly dependent on the printed sources and rather dull.

(2) 'It is difficult to think of a Foreign Secretary with a more successful record.'

G1095. The Road to Great Turnstile, *Father Figures*, Kingsley Martin, Hutchinson, *NS.* 71, 1818. 14 Jan. p 54

(1) Warmly praises the volume and observes: 'Kingsley Martin has had fun. He provided fun for the readers of his paper. He now provides it for the readers of his autobiography.'

G1096. Impatient Prophet, *H.G. Wells*, ed. W. Warren Wagar, Bodley Head, *Obs.* 30 Jan. p 26

(1) A good selection of his ephemeral and prophetic writings.

(2) Wells 'had great gifts as a novelist, gifts which made him at his best second only to Dickens. Wells despised these gifts and came near to being ashamed of them.'

G1097. All Dressed Up, (a) *The Troubled Partnership*, Henry Kissinger, McGraw-Hill; (b) *Alternative to Partition*, Zbigniew Brezinski, McGraw-Hill, *NS.* 71, 1822. 11 Feb. pp 195–6

(1) On American foreign policy neither author really examines the crucial question, 'What are we trying to do?' They just assume there is a Russian danger and must be a crusade.

G1098. Patchwork History, *The Proud Tower*, Barbara W. Tuchman, Hamilton, *Obs.* 27 Feb. p 27

(1) Very well written but 'it has no merit as a work of history'.

G1099. Sinister Story, *The Left in Europe since 1789*, David Caute, Weidenfeld and Nicolson, *NS.* 71, 1825. 4 Mar. pp 300, 302

(1) Disagrees with the author's verdict that the Left is distinguished by belief in the sovereignty of the people. A.J.P.T. cites with approval Victor Hugo's 'Je suis *contre*'.

G1100. Heroine of the Revolution, *Rosa Luxemburg*, 2 Vols. J.P. Nettl, Oxford, *Obs.* 6 Mar. p 27

(1) 'A book of the highest distinction, even though it is very long and occasionally presented in crabbed Marxist phraseology'.

G1101. The Habsburgs' fault? *The Long Fuse*, Lawrence Lafore, Weidenfeld and Nicolson, *Obs.* 13 Mar. p 26

(1) Perhaps the last book 'in the old style' on the cause of the First World War. Disagrees with putting the blame on Austria.

(2) 'Both world wars were for and against German supremacy'.

G1102. It Happened There, *The Nazi Seizure of Power*, William Sheridan Allen, Eyre and Spottiswoode, *NS.* 71, 1827. 18 Mar. p 380

(1) 'Though rather dull in presentation, (it) is the most illuminating account of Nazi victory which I have ever read.'

G1103. Athanassius in King Street, *The British Communist Party*, L.J. Macfarlane, MacGibbon and Kee, *Obs.* 27 Mar. p 26

(1) A drab book which records the C.P.'s public discussions, 'comparable to Gibbon's account of the theological wranglings among early Christians'.

G1104. Who were the Liberals? *The Formation of the Liberal Party 1857–1868*, John Vincent, Constable, *Obs.* 17 Apr. p 26

(1) The author challenges old views 'as effectively as Namier once upset similar legends about the eighteenth century'. A 'clever original book'.

G1105. Barren victory, *Caporetto 1917*, Cyril Falls, Weidenfeld and Nicolson, *Obs.* 17 Apr. p 26

(1) 'Describes the battle effectively in an old-style technical way'.

G1106. *ID*, 4th Ser., 12, (28 Jun-2 Aug 1914), ed. A. Torre, 1964, *EHR*. 81, 319. Apr. pp 429–30

(1) 'Most of the documents deal with Albania, a boring subject'.

G1107. Here's to You, Men I Never Met, (a) *The Irish Struggle 1916–1926*, ed. Desmond Williams, Routledge; (b) *Ireland Since the Rising*, Timothy Patrick Coogan, Pall Mall; (c) *Dublin 1916*, ed. Roger McHugh, Arlington; (d) *Limerick's Fighting Story*, ed. J.M. MacCarthy, Anvil, *NS*. 71, 1834. 6 May. pp 655–6

(a1) 'We learn in sharp clear sentences how a movement which set out for a united republic ended with partition and dominion status.'

(b1) 'The later history of Ireland, as presented by Mr. Coogan, is more prosaic still.'

(c1) 'The old magic is there in all its force.'

(d1) The fire of nationalism 'still blazes in these artless pages'.

(2) After observing that Ireland is an indelible blot on Lloyd George's reputation: 'Asquith's part, though often ignored, was also discreditable. Muddled and lethargic as usual, he bore the final responsibility for the killings after the Easter rising, just as he bore the main responsibility for the failure of Home Rule – one of the most disastrous prime ministers in British history.'

G1108. Some Like It Hot, *The Last Battle*, Cornelius Ryan, Collins, *Obs.* 8 May. p 27

(1) Dislikes the author's style of writing history –

it is a 'tingling narrative', which comes off best when it is dealing with ordinary people.

G1109. Fabulous Monster, (a) *An Explanation of De Gaulle*, R. Aron, New York, Harper and Row; (b) *De Gaulle*, F. Mauriac, New York, Doubleday; (c) *The French*, Jean-Francois Revel, New York, Braziller; (d) *De Gaulle's Implacable Ally*, ed. Roy C. Macridis, New York, Harper and Row, *NYRB*. 6, 8. 12 May. pp 16–18

(1) Unfavourable to all – except, perhaps, Macridis's foreword to De Gaulle's speeches.

(2) 'De Gaulle is a secular Pope . . . He is in fact the main pillar of European peace and has given to the French the blessings of a quiet life.'

G1110. What the Doctor Saw, *Churchill. The Struggle For Survival*, Lord Moran, Constable, *NS*. 71, 1837. 27 May. p 782

(1) Sees no objection to Moran writing about Churchill, but observes that it is 'inevitably one-sided. Lord Moran saw Churchill only when he was ill or needed a medical attendant on his foreign journeys.'

(2) 'Anyone can run up an account of Churchill and find plenty of faults. They weigh not a feather in the balance. There has never been anyone like him, and that is all there is to it. He was the saviour of his country at the most critical moment in its history . . . '

G1111. Last word on Jutland, (a) *From The Dreadnought to Scapa Flow*, Vol. 3, Arthur J. Marder, Oxford; (b) *The Smoke Screen of Jutland*, Commander John Irving, Kimber, *Obs*. 29 May. p 23

(a1) The book displays 'a wonderful level of accuracy, clarity, and scholarship'.

(b1) 'A vivid account', 'an admirable and exciting book'.

G1112. The great equivocator, *Selections from the Smuts Papers*, Vols. 1–4, ed. W.K. Hancock and Jean van der Poel, Cambridge U.P., *Obs*. 12 Jun. p 26

(1) They are interesting as Smuts was a good

writer and had many interesting friends.

(2) 'They confirm . . . that Smuts was a Holy Willie – the symbol of all that was weak and flatulent in twentieth century enlightenment.' He had a foot in both Vanity Fair and Heaven.

G1113. The Cold War, (a) *Three Days to Catastrophe*, Douglas Clark, Hammond; (b) *Victim of Duty*, Arnold Rogow, Hart-Davis; (c) *Oppenheimer*, Haakon Chevalier, Deutsch; (d) *Beginnings of the Cold War*, Martin Herz, Indiana U.P.; (e) *Atomic Diplomacy : Hiroshima and Potsdam*, Gar Alperovitz, Secker and Warburg, *NS*. 71, 1841. 24 Jun. pp 930–1

(a1) The planned Anglo-French expedition to Finland is dissected by a gifted amateur historian.

(b2) Suggests that it was 'the Red Spectre' which pushed James Forrestal to suicide.

(c1) The author 'now covers up for himself by presenting the episode (a communist approach to Oppenheimer) as a good deal more harmless than it was'.

(d1) It 'is presumably intended to explain the Cold War, though it reads more like another shot in it'.

(e1) The records of Potsdam 'show, perhaps almost too emphatically, that the Cold War was deliberately started by Truman and his advisers. (The author) . . . is the first in the field to make this clear'. A.J.P.T. disagrees with the author's interpretation of the use of the atomic bombs.

(2) 'The Cold War has been the greatest obstacle to rational thinking in my lifetime . . . On the Cold War attitudes have remained everywhere rigid and irrational.'

G1114. Spanish Quadrille, *Spain 1808–1939*, Raymond Carr, *Obs*. 3 Jul. p 23

(1) 'An immensely learned book, top heavy with detail'.

G1115. The Unlucky Commander, *Years of Command*, Lord Douglas of Kirtleside, Collins, *Obs*. 10 Jul. p 22

(1) Agreeably written – but no striking new information.

G1116. A political mystery story, *The Downfall of the Liberal Party 1914–1935*, Trevor Wilson, Collins, *Obs.* 24 Jul. p 23

(1) Politics at the top covered 'in a fine dramatic style'; though he regrets that the author has not covered what happened to Liberal support in the constituencies.

(2) Lloyd George: 'For the Liberals he proved the cuckoo in the nest.'

G1117. A Very Special Case, (a) *The Making of Modern Ireland 1603–1923*, J.C. Beckett, New York, Knopf; (b) *The Irish Question 1840–1921*, Nicholas Mansergh, Toronto U.P.; *Ireland Since the Rising*, Timothy Patrick Coogan, New York, Praeger (*see above* G1187), *NYRB*. 7, 1. 28 Jul. pp 8, 10

(a1) 'The best general history of modern Ireland. It is uniformly fair to every party from the Fenians to the Ulster covenanters.'

(b1) Favourable – 'the most historical of the three'.

(c1) The author deals with the current state of Ireland in a dispassionate manner, and is especially good on religious issues.

G1118. *La Relazione diplomatiche fra il Regno di Sardegna e la Gran Bretagna*, 3rd Ser., 3 and 4, (1850–2), ed. Federico Curato, Rome, Institute storico italiano, 1964, *EHR*. 81, 320. Jul. p 621

(1) The only theme of importance is their appeals to Britain for support. It contains interesting reports on British politics and politicians.

G1119. *The Red Kingdom of Saxony*, Donald Warren Jr., The Hague, Nijhoff, 1964, *Ibid.* p 631

(1) It shows how Stresemann built up a moderate Liberal group based on the little men of Saxony.

G1120. Silly Soldier Men, (a) *The Reichswehr and Politics 1918–33*, F.L. Carsten, Oxford; (b) *The German Army and the Nazi Party 1933–39*, Robert O'Neill, Cassell, *NS*. 72, 1847. 5 Aug. p 202 (a1) Criticises it for being unrealistic in condemning the German generals for co-operation with Soviet Russia.

(b1) Criticises it for drawing too sharp a distinction between Hitler and the generals – 'Hitler also had no defined plan'.

(2) Suggests that the German generals were no more sinister politically than British generals over the Ulster crisis or French ones over Algeria. 'Their great obsession was to keep the army out of trouble.'

G1121. Too Good for this World, *Left in the Centre*, Robert E. Dowse, Longmans, *Obs.* 14 Aug. p 19

(1) The author goes 'competently and devoutly over the subject' but the book is rather dull.

(2) The I.L.P. was 'a political group that had everything right with it except the ability to win support'.

G1122. An Old Friend, *A History of Income Tax*, B.E.V. Sabine, Allen and Unwin, *NS.* 72, 1849. 19 Aug. p 264

(1) Praises it – the author is 'both a good historian and a serving member of the Inland Revenue Department'.

G1123. The Finest Hour, *1940*, Lawrence Thompson, Collins, *Obs.* 28 Aug. p 17

(1) Good reading – but too ingenious in places.

G1124. Overrated general, *Ludendorff*, D.J. Goodspeed, Hart-Davis, *Obs.* 18 Sept. p 26

(1) 'An excellent biography from a technical angle'.

G1125. Europe on top of the world, *The Triumph of the Middle Classes*, Charles Morazé, Weidenfeld and Nicolson, *Obs*, 2 Oct. p 27

(1) 'Altogether the book is very exciting, though often on the speculative side'; written by an outstanding disciple of Febvre.

G1126. Before the Black-out, *Harold Nicolson: Diaries and Letters 1930–39*, ed. Nigel Nicolson, Collins, *NS.* 72, 1856. 7 Oct. pp 520–1

(1) His diary has lived up to promise 'in its delights and its limitations. Nicolson was a supremely honest recorder; he was also incurably literary.' His gifts 'were those of a journalist, the quick comment, the telling anecdote'.

G1127. Gentleman at Arms, *With Prejudice*, Lord Tedder, Cassell, *Obs*. 9 Oct. p 26

(1) Rather dull and heavy going.

G1128. Made in Birmingham, (a) *Joseph Chamberlain*, Peter Fraser, Cassell; (b) *The Chamberlains*, D.H. Elletson, Murray, *Obs*. 16 Oct. p 26

(a1) Political, with little biographical framework.

(b1) 'Not much new . . . though it is excellently composed'.

G1129. The Great Assassination, *The Road to Sarajevo*, Valdimir Dedijer, New York, Simon and Schuster, *NYRB*. 7, 6. 20 Oct. pp 8, 10, 12

(1) 'Written . . . with such competence, such mastery of sources and such profound detachment . . . likely to be the last word on the subject'.

G1130. Pushing with the best, *Winston S. Churchill*, Vol. 1, Randolph S. Churchill, Heinemann, *Obs*. 23 Oct. p 26

(1) 'It hardly could be done better . . . There is much admiration, sometimes extravagantly expressed. But there is also courageous frankness . . . '

G1131. *Der Dreibund nach dem Sturze Bismarcks*, Vol. 2, Helge Granfelt, Lund, Gleerupska, 1964, *EHR*. 81, 231. Oct. p 872

(1) An orthodox diplomatic account.

G1132. *DNVP: Right-Wing Opposition in the Weimar Republic 1918–1924*, Lewis Hertzmann, Nebraska U.P., 1963, *Ibid*. p 873

(1) 'A valuable, though rather narrow, contribution to political history'.

G1133. Peace in their time, *The Roots of Appeasement*, Martin Gilbert, Weidenfeld and Nicolson, *Obs*. 6 Nov. p 26

(1) The author is now more charitable to the appeasers, perhaps too much so.

G1134. The end of the affair, *The Parnell Tragedy*, Jules Abels, Bodley Head, *Obs.* 13 Nov. p 27

(1) Not much new information but 'a good deal in the way of new interpretation'.

G1135. Received with thanks, *A Century of Conflict 1850–1950*, ed. Martin Gilbert, Hamilton, *Obs.* 20 Nov. p 26

(1) Praises the essays as 'good reading . . . All have something new to say'. Comments that Paul Einzig's essay is 'the most slashing attack I have ever read on an historian's accuracy, and the maddening thing is that most, though not all of it is justified'. (For the essay under attack *see* E67)

G1136. Flat Earth Man, *Ironies of History*, Isaac Deutscher, Oxford, *Obs.* 4 Dec. p 26

(1) The author writes 'with wisdom and clarity'. But 'remains an unrepentant Marxist, adjusting events to his theories, instead of adjusting his theories to events'.

G1137. Books of the Year, *Obs.* 18 Dec. p 23

Praises *Rosa Luxemburg* (*see above* G1100), 'a most remarkable account of a most remarkable woman'; *From The Dreadnought to Scapa Flow*, Vol. 3 (G1111); and *Disraeli*, Robert Blake, Eyre and Spottiswoode, which 'had almost all the virtues; scholarly, instructive, well balanced, highly readable though not gay'.

1967

G1138. A Most Worthy Man, *Sir Francis Dashwood*, Betty Kemp, Macmillan, *NS.* 73, 1870, 13 Jan. p 52

(1) 'Both fascinating to read and rigorous in its scholarship'.

G1139. *Revolution in Bavaria 1918–1919*, Allan Mitchell, Princeton U.P., 1965, *EHR.* 82, 322. Jan. p 201

(1) 'A scholarly and sympathetic study'.

(2) 'The November revolution in Munich was more separated than socialist, and hardly even republican.' 'Among the revolutionary idealists

of the time, Eisner was well ahead of Kerensky and quite on the level of Karolyi.'

G1140. *The Deutschtum of Nazi Germany and the United States*, Arthur L. Smith Jr., The Hague, Nijhoff, 1965, *Ibid.* p 205

(2) 'There was much boastful talk. But in the United States as elsewhere the Fifth Column never amounted to much.'

G1141. The hidden hand, *Russia 1917: The February Revolution*, George Katkov, Longmans, *Obs.* 12 Feb. p 27

(1) Written by a gifted scholar, who is 'master of all the sources and able to draw a brilliant picture of a nation in the throes of war and revolution'; yet he manages to produce a conspiracy theory for one of the most spontaneous events in history.

G1142. Crimes beyond punishment, (a) *The Trial of the Germans*, Eugene Davidson, Macmillan; (b) *Auschwitz*, Bernard Naumann, intr. Hannah Arendt, New York, Praeger; (c) *Death in Rome*, Robert Katz, Macmillan, *NYRB*. 8, 3. 23 Feb. pp 11–13

(a1) Very unfavourable – 'pretty sketchy, slapdash stuff'.

(b1) An admirable introduction – 'the book itself is unreadable. The deeds recounted in it are loathsome beyond belief.'

(c1) Unfavourable – A.J.P.T. can see no reason why non-Catholics should expect a higher standard of behaviour and morality from the Pope than anyone else.

(2) 'There are few episodes of modern history more nauseating than the proceedings at Nuremburg, where the victors solemnly wrestled with the problem of 'aggressive war'; that is any war or even political action against the settlement established by the victors of the First World War.'

G1143. A little knowledge ... (a) *The Framework of Economic Activity*, Anthony Harrison, Macmillan; (b) *The Approach of War 1938–9*, Christopher Thorne, Macmillan; (c) *The Age of Containment*, David

Rees, Macmillan, *Obs.* 26 Feb. p 27

(a1) The author assumes that the 'Faceless Men' exist and that no-one else does.

(b1) It does not contribute much in the way of of recent scholarship.

(c1) 'Anti-communist outlook at its most extreme'.

G1144. Telling the tale *The Evolution of British Historiography*, ed. J.R. Hale, Macmillan, *Obs.* 5 Mar. p 26

(1) 'A fascinating anthology'. Praises the introduction as 'both wise and instructive'.

G1145. The Devil's Decade, *Economic Recovery in Britain 1932–39*, H.W. Richardson, Weidenfeld and Nicolson, *Obs.* 2 Apr. p 26

(1) A.J.P.T. observes that, though it is not easy to read, it 'is truly manna to me. I reached much the same conclusions . . . (*see* A14) . . . but I got there by feel not by figures – relying on my green fingers. It is delightful to find my guesses confirmed.'

G1146. The tiger who walked alone, *The Life and Times of Ernest Bevin*, Vol. 2, Alan Bullock, Heinemann, *Obs.* 16 Apr. p 27

(1) The book is too long as it is based largely on published sources; however 'the analysis of Bevin's policy and achievement is . . . competently done'.

(2) 'Bevin was a tiger who walked alone, and woe betide any who came near him. He was an elemental force, invaluable in wartime . . . Bevin often bullied for a good cause; he was a bully all the same.'

G1147. Tory butchers, Liberal grocers, *Pollbooks: How Victorians Voted*, J.R. Vincent, Cambridge U.P., *Obs.* 23 Apr. p 30

(1) 'This book is a stern warning against generalisations, especially of a Marxist character.' 'Mr. Vincent has the most brilliantly original mind among those now working on modern British history.'

G1148. *ID*, 1st Ser., 3, (1862–3), ed. R. Moscati and E. Sestan, 1965, *EHR*. 82, 323. Apr. p 426

(1) The volume is dominated by the issue of

Rome. 'As usual, Italian diplomacy appears more perceptive and subtle than any other, and also less effective.'

G1149. Against the Thing, *The Radical Tradition*, John W. Derry, Macmillan, *Obs.* 7 May. p 26

(1) The author writes 'competently, though rather superficially' about ten men. A.J.P.T. feels that Robert Owen and Lord Randolph Churchill should not be included.

G1150. Silliness in Excelsis, *Thomas Woodrow Wilson: A Psychological Study*, Sigmud Freud and William C. Bullitt, Weidenfeld and Nicolson, *NS.* 73, 1887. 12 May. pp 653–4

(1) 'Preposterous' – 'a disgrace as a scientific exercise'. Both the authors saw the Treaty of Versailles as 'wholly evil'. Deems the book to be outdated history and tawdry psychology.

G1151. The well-meaning Whigs, (a) *Samuel Whitbread*, Roger Fulford, Macmillan; (b) *Victorian Duke*, Gervas Huxley, Oxford, *Obs.* 14 May. p 26

(a1) The author has made good use of his subject's papers 'but somehow Whitbread does not add up'.

(b1) 'Much of interest in a book for anyone interested in that esoteric subject'.

G1152. Lone eagle over Britain, *The Breaking Wave*, Telford Taylor, Weidenfeld and Nicolson, *Obs.* 11 Jun. p 27

(1) 'An indispensable account of the Battle of Britain, as conducted by the Germans', but less sound on the British side.

G1153. Bedside Reading? *Winston S. Churchill, Vol. 1 Companion*, 2 Vols. Randolph S. Churchill, Heinemann, *Obs.* 18 Jun. p 23

(1) The 'sources in the raw' – expresses apprehensions as to the volume of material to be printed if this scale of printing continues for Churchill's later career.

G1154. Big fleas and little fleas, *The Enlightenment* Peter Gay, Weidenfeld and Nicolson, *Obs.* 25 Jun. p 26

(1) The book will be much to the taste of people who like books about books.

(2) 'The Enlightenment is interesting only to those who are still worried about Christianity. Otherwise it appears a rather rococo adventure, amusing enough in a trivial way, and full of absurd twiddles.'

G1155. History plods along, (a) *Europe and the World Since 1914*, E.J. Knapton and T.K. Derry, Murray; (b) *A Short History of the Second World War*, Basil Collier, Collins; (c) *A History of War and Peace 1939–1965*, Wilfred Knapp, Oxford, *Obs.* 9 Jul. p 21

(a1) The best of these books – 'written with spirit and shows a skilful balance'.

(b1) A sound narrative – but it exaggerates the importance of the Mediterranean.

(c1) Observes that like all those who are published by Chatham House, 'this embrace bestows a 100 year sleep on whoever receives it'. The book assumes that international affairs since 1945 'have been shaped almost exclusively by Soviet aggression'.

G1156. Before the Revolution, *The Russian Empire 1801–1917*, Hugh Seton-Watson, Oxford, *Obs.* 16 Jul. p 21

(1) 'A very good book' – but regrets that there is not more about relations between Russia and West European thought.

G1157. Chapter of Accidents, *1867: Disraeli, Gladstone and Revolution*, Maurice Cowling, Cambridge U.P., *Obs.* 23 Jul. p 20

(1) The author provides the attractive explanation that it all came about by accident; fascinating reading but rather long winded.

(2) 'There is much to be said for the accidental view of history. The details usually happen by accident, and the historian who sticks to detail is inclined to believe that everything happens that way. In fact, tendencies cannot be wholly accidental,

even if they are composed of accidental details.'

G1158. *United States Policy and the Partition of Turkey 1914–1924*, Lawrence Evans, Baltimore, Johns Hopkins Press, 1965, *EHR*. 82, 324. Jul. p 638

(1) 'Its length is more than the subject can carry'.

G1159. *Actes et documents du Saint Siège relatifs à la seconde guerre mondiale*, Vol. 1, ed. Pierre Blet, Angelo Martini and Burkhart Schneider, Vatican City, Libreria Editrice Vaticana, 1965, *Ibid*. pp 642–3

(1) It is of 'great interest, not least for the light it sheds on Pope Pius XII'. 'Papal policy was for peace, at almost any price.'

G1160. *La Resistenza italiana*, Guido Quazza, Turin, Giappichelli, 1966, *Ibid*. pp 643–4

(1) The first part examines the Resistance 'with almost too much scientific detachment'. The second part prints his diary, which is 'a very human document . . . illuminating about the life of a partisan'.

G1161. Old Men Remember, (a) *Acquaintances*, Arnold J. Toynbee, Oxford; (b) *Variety of Men*, C.P. Snow, New York, Scribners, *NYRB*. 9, 2. 3 Aug. pp 14–17

(a1) Dislikes Toynbee and the book – 'Toynbee is a historian, or to be more precise, he has made generalisations dressed up as history.'

(b1) Snow presents people 'as human beings . . . But somehow they slip into place as characters in one of Snow's novels.'

G1162. No secrets from Mr. Maisky, *Memoirs of a Soviet Ambassador*, Ivan Maisky, Hutchinson, *Obs*. 13 Aug. p 17

(1) 'Well written and brilliantly translated' – but it is of little value.

G1163. Undertones of war, *Harold Nicolson: Diaries and Letters 1939–45*, ed. Nigel Nicolson, Collins, *Obs*. 24 Sept. p 26

(1) It has 'the grace and charm' of the earlier volume, but 'though Nicolson lived among great events, he did not participate in them'.

G1164. Mr. Tidy Mind, (a) *Essays in Reform 1867*, ed.

Bernard Crick, Oxford; (b) *100 Years of Freethought*, David Tribe, Elek, *NS*. 74, 1907. 29 Sept. pp 404, 406

(a1) The 1867 essays are unrealistic – admirable in themselves, but no grasp of political realities. Attacks the idea of reform by experts – it should come about through the clash of rival interests.

(b2) Admires the attitude of the National Secular Society which has often raised an uproar, even if it did have its quirks. 'They wanted people to be freer, freer to think as they liked and to do what they liked.'

G1165. Inquest on a non-event, *Accident*, David Irving, Kimber, *Obs*. 8 Oct. p 27

(1) 'General Sikorski died by accident'.

G1166. Churchill the Radical, *Winston S. Churchill*, Vol. 2, Randolph S. Churchill, Heinemann, *Obs*. 22 Oct. p 30

(1) 'Five volumes of biography are a heavy prospect even for the most devoted admirer of Churchill, and in this volume there are times when the interest flags.'

G1167. Muted Love Story, *The Years That Are Past*, Frances Lloyd-George, Hutchinson, *NS*. 74, 1911. 27 Oct. pp 550, 552

(1) 'A remarkable story', told 'with restrained simplicity'. Regrets that she is reticent about her own part in it – and that her diaries were sold to Beaverbrook and closed even to her until 1971.

G1168. *Actes et documents* . . . (*see above* G1159), Vol. 2, 1966, *EHR*. 82, 325. Oct. p 875

(1) The letters of the Pope to the German bishops show that he wanted a peace of reconciliation, national independence and no racialism in the Catholic Church.

(2) 'A Protestant might have wished first to clear his individual conscience. The Pope was concerned to preserve the Church.'

G1169. *The History of Treaties and International Politics*, Mario Toscano, John Hopkins Press; Oxford U.P.,

1966, *Hist.* 52, 3. Oct. pp 370–1

(1) Praises it as a wide ranging bibliography – but comments on the lack of official military histories for the world wars and also of books on international organisations.

G1170. New Light on Aunt Beatrice, *Beatrice Webb*, Kitty Muggeridge and Ruth Adam, Secker and Warburg, *Obs.* 5 Nov. p 27

(1) A delightful biography – it 'adds a more personal note' than previous books. 'Beatrice Webb is made plain in this book. Sidney remains an enigma.'

(2) 'All the achievements of the Webbs stemmed from Sidney . . . Without him, she would have been only an interesting personality.'

G1171. The Survivor, *The Post-War Years 1945–54*, Ilya Ehrenburg, New York, World, *NYRB.* 9, 8. 9 Nov. pp 6, 8

(1) Ehrenburg's efforts for peace achieved nothing. He was 'a writer by profession instead of by accomplishment'; but A.J.P.T. feels that Western commentators have been too tough on him in expecting him to be a hero against Stalin.

G1172. Lord Norman and Prof. Skinner, *Montagu Norman*, Andrew Boyle, Cassell, *Obs.* 12 Nov. p 26

(1) 'Admirably written and psychologically penetrating' – but A.J.P.T. feels that Norman was no more eccentric than many other outstanding men.

(2) 'Norman carried old-style banking to its highest point, much as Haig was the most accomplished of old-style generals.'

G1173. Labour's first devaluation, *Politicians and the Slump*, Robert Skidelsky, Macmillan, *Obs.* 26 Nov. p 26

(1) A survey of the Labour Government's record – which A.J.P.T. argues is unfair to Labour as to its lack of ideas and action.

(2) 'Essentially Labour could think only in terms of charity, not of economic construction. Labour men refused to consider any solution other than dreamy Utopian socialism which they had neither

the ability nor the power to supply.'

G1174. No good Germans after all? (a) *Germany's Aims in the First World War*, Fritz Fischer, Chatto and Windus; (b) *Europe 1880–1945*, J.M. Roberts, Longmans; (c) *Germany 1789–1919*, Agatha Ramm, Methuen, *Obs.* 3 Dec. p 27

(a1) He 'proves his case from the records beyond a shadow of a doubt – hence the spluttering anger with which his book was received'. Though 'perhaps he exaggerates the conscious aggressiveness of German policy'. The book makes one revise the conventional view of Hitler – 'Hitler pursued, by more violent means, the traditional aims of German foreign policy'.

(b1) A competent survey. The author 'excels in the economic and social surveys'.

(c1) 'Thorough in her scholarship, impartial in her judgements and effective in her arrangement of the theme'.

G1175. Bogey Men, *The Espionage Establishment*, David Wise and Thomas B. Ross, New York, Random House, *NYRB*. 9, 10. 7 Dec. pp 12, 14, 16

(1) Dislikes 'the brisk 'instant-history' style'.

(2) It 'has exactly the same aim as any other establishment: jobs for the Boys. Spying pays high salaries and gives an illusory self-esteem to its operators.'

G1176. Books of the Year, *Obs.* 10 Dec. p 9

Praises *Montagu Norman* (*see above* G1172) and *Beatrice Webb* (G1170). The year's winner was *Chips*, ed. Robert Rhodes James, Weidenfeld and Nicolson. 'There has been no diarist so richly humorous since the great days of Mr. Pooter'.

1968

G1177. Oh what a phoney war, *The Unfought Battle*, Jon Kimche, Weidenfeld and Nicolson, *Obs.* 21 Jan. p 30

(1) 'Entertaining and sometimes stimulating' –

but 'it lacks any real sense of how policies are determined in this world'.

G1178. American Metternich, *Memoirs 1925–1950*, George Kennan, Hutchinson, *Obs.* 28 Jan. p 30

(1) Of the realists in foreign policy the author 'has been outstanding both in ability and pertinacity'.

G1179. *Letters from the Paris Peace Conference*, Charles Seymour, ed. Harold B. Whiteman Jr., Yale U.P., 1966, *EHR*. 83, 326. Jan. p 220

(1) 'Agreeable reading', but it 'contains little of importance to the historian'.

G1180. The Great Schism of Our Age, *Politics and Diplomacy of Peacemaking*, Arno J. Mayer, New York, Knopf, *NYRB*. 10, 2. 1 Feb. pp 13–15

(1) 'The merit of the book is to have a thesis – but the thesis fails to work. At the peace conference Germany was the priority, not the Soviet Union.' A.J.P.T. argues that the Bolsheviks deliberately withdrew from the European system.

(2) 'Lenin wanted to be a peril, and could hardly complain when others said he was.'

G1181. Not liberal enough. *Smuts*, Vol. 2, W.K. Hancock, Cambridge U.P., *Obs.* 11 Feb. p 26

(1) The author 'manages to be a truly honest historian who does not make a parade of his honesty'.

(2) Smuts: 'His principles were noble. His method were devious and sometimes worse. Like Lloyd George he was a liberal who took the long way round.'

G1182. Muchedumbre, *The Revolution of the Dons*, Sheldon Rothblatt, Faber, *NS*. 75, 1927. 16 Feb. p 208

(1) An 'admirably learned book' – but the review suggests that A.J.P.T., finds it too serious in its approach to a 'topic . . . of little importance'.

G1183. Very much at sea, *Naval Policy Between the Wars*, Stephen Roskill, Collins, *Obs.* 10 Mar. p 29

(1) Written in a responsible tone; he observes, 'In the inter-departmental disputes he is clearly on the Admiralty's side.'

G1184. Another mare's nest, *The Mediterranean Strategy in the Second World War*, Michael Howard, Weidenfeld and Nicolson, *Obs.* 17 Mar. p 29

(1) The author says all that needs to be said on the subject 'and says it very well'.

G1185. Hitler's great mistake, (a) *The Swastika and the Eagle*, James U. Compton, Bodley Head; (b) *Prelude to Downfall*, Saul Friedlander, Chatto and Windus, *Obs.* 31 Mar. p 28

(a1) It is easier to read and has more artistic shape than (b).

(b1) The author 'sometimes formulates the more convincing explanations' of Hitler's attitude to America.

G1186. Churchill and his critics, *Vote of Censure*, George Malcolm Thomson, Secker and Warburg, *Obs.* 14 Apr. p 26

(1) Not a very serious book – many of the stories are embellished ones originating from Beaverbrook's table talk.

G1187. Blunt Weapon, *The Bomber Offensive*, Anthony Verrier, Batsford, *NS.* 75, 1937. 26 Apr. pp 553–4

(1) Feels that the official history is a superior account.

(2) 'It was the last independent campaign which Great Britain will ever undertake.'

G1188. *Frankreich zwischen Republik und Monarchie in der Bismarckzeit*, Bert Böhmer, Kallmunz, Lassleben, 1966, *EHR.* 83, 327. Apr. pp 421–2

(1) Doubts whether the project was worth doing, but it is done well.

G1189. *Hindenberg and the Weimar Republic*, Andreas Dorpalen, Princeton U.P.; Oxford U.P., *Ibid.* p 431

(1) 'Full and careful in detail' but 'a little dull and rather long'. It moderates the picture painted by Wheeler-Bennett.

G1190. *ID*, 9th Ser., 5, (Jun-Oct 1940), ed. Mario Toscano, 1965, *Ibid.* pp 432–3

(1) 'They show clearly Mussolini's dilemma when his cleverness miscarried.' The volume is

valuable for the Balkan specialist.

G1191. *Dal 25 luglio all' 8 settembre*, Mario Toscano, Florence, Le Monnier, 1966, *Ibid.* p 433

(1) An interesting and subtle study of the armistice of 1943.

G1192. Greatness and after, *Industry and Empire*, E.J. Hobsbawm, Weidenfeld and Nicolson, *Obs.* 5 May. p 26

(1) Even better than his *Age of Revolution.* Though he feels the author 'exaggerates the working class element in Chartism, which was mainly an individualist middle-class affair'.

G1193. Lovely Wars, *Britain in the Century of Total War*, Arthur Marwick, Bodley Head, *Li.* 79, 2041. 9 May. pp 589–91

(1) 'Most of what he says is enlightening and historically sound . . . Mr. Marwick rides his hobby horse a bit hard'. Of Marwick's theoretical framework: 'This is a valuable and constructive analysis which brings sense into recent British history.'

G1194. Our greatest Victorian? *The Collected Works of Walter Bagehot*, Vols. 3 and 4, ed. Norman St. John Stevas, The Economist, *Obs.* 19 May. 28

(1) 'There is no real history in these essays'. 'If you believe . . . the dispassionate civil servant was the greatest product of the Victorian age, then clearly Bagehot was the greatest Victorian.'

G1195. Dear old Munich days, (a) *Munich 1938*, Keith Robbins, Cassell; (b) *The Years of 'The Week'*, Patricia Cockburn, MacDonald, *Obs.* 26 May. p 28

(a1) He 'may have run the case for Munich too hard, but it does no harm to be reminded, even from the writings of the high-minded, that there was no simple high-minded line to follow'.

(b1) '*The Week* provided a gay element in a somewhat dingy decade.'

G1196. Far-Away Countries, (a) *Diplomat in Berlin 1933–39*, ed. Waclaw Jedrzewicz, Columbia U.P.; (b) *Stalin, Hitler and Europe 1933–39*, Vol. 1, James E. Mc-

Sherry, New York, World, *NYRB*. 10, 11. 6 Jun. pp 12–14

(a1) Lipskii's papers are valuable – he was a skilled observer.

(b1) Nothing new on Soviet policy.

(2) 'Hitler's Russian policy was a consequence of invasion not its cause'. 'Soviet policy is more straightforward than most. Its sole aim was and is the security of the Soviet Union. This was its guiding principle before the war and remains its guiding principle now'.

G1197. Silly-clever soldier, *The Lost Dictator*, Bernard Ash, Cassell, *Obs*. 16 Jun. p 25

(1) An admirable lively account of Sir Henry Wilson. Wonders why Lloyd George and Bonar Law were impressed by him.

G1198. *The Passing of the Habsburg Monarchy 1914–18*, 2 Vols. Arthur J. May, Philadelphia U.P., 1966, *JMH*. 40, 2. Jun. pp 292–4

(1) The author shows a mastery of sources but he is sometimes uncritical of them, and he is too sympathetic to the Habsburgs. 'Much excellent detail and no wider perspective'.

G1199. The sceptical imperialist, *Balfour and the British Empire*, Dennis Judd, Macmillan, *Obs*. 11 Aug. p 22

(1) Dislikes the organisation of the book but praises its use of new sources.

(2) The Committee of Imperial Defence 'signally failed before both world wars to produce strategical ideas of any value even on the specific problem of Imperial Defence'; in short, it has been overrated. Balfour 'appears a detestable man, cynical, unprincipled, and frivolous'.

G1200. Someone had blundered, (a) *The Destruction of Convoy PQ17*, David Irving, Cassell; (b) *Sink the Tirpitz*, Leonce Paillard, Cape; (c) *The Italian Campaign 1943–5*, G.A. Shepperd, Barker, *Obs*. 15 Sept. p 28

(a1) Even better than his book on Dresden;

he 'has done a good job in revealing the true story'.

(b1) Much valuable information in it – but it is 'more a film script than a historical narrative'.

(c1) It 'reads like a brief for a staff exercise' – 'there is not a breath of life in it from start to finish'.

G1201. Funeral in Berlin, *The Death of Adolf Hitler*, Lev Bezymenski, Joseph, *Obs.* 29 Sept. p 27

(1) A book of no importance – Trevor Roper provided the answers long ago.

G1202. Watching the World Go By, (a) *A Diplomat Looks Back*, Lewis Einstein, Yale U.P.; (b) *From Prague After Munich*, George Kennan, Princeton U.P., *NYRB.* 11, 6. 10 Oct. pp 18–20

(a1) A diplomatic memoir of the old type.

(b1) These diplomatic reports 'add an important footnote to recent history'. The book 'leaves the impression that Hitler was an improviser, not a deliberate planner . . . The motive force for subsequent events in Czechoslovakia came from within, not without, though Hitler may have vaguely foreseen it.'

G1203. The leader who got lost, *My Life*, Sir Oswald Mosley, Nelson, *Obs.* 20 Oct. p 29

(1) He does not explain why he failed so completely in politics but nevertheless 'his autobiography is a work of considerable distinction, far above most such books by retired politicians'.

G1204. *La Relazioni Diplomatiche fra la Gran Bretagna e il Regno di Sardegna*, 3rd ser., 3 (1850–2), ed. T. Curato, Rome, Instituto storico italiano, 1966, *EHR.* 83, 329. Oct. pp 865–6

(1) Nothing in it of great importance.

G1205. *ID*, 2nd Ser., 2 (1871), ed. Angelo Tamborra, 1966, *Ibid.* p 867

(1) Interesting details on the issue of Rome.

G1206. Former great person, (a) *Former Naval Person*, Vice-Admiral Sir Peter Gretton, Cassell; (b) *Churchill as Historian*, Maurice Ashley, Secker and Warburg; (c) *Action This Day*, ed. Sir John Wheeler-Bennett, Macmillan; (d) *Churchill in His Time*,

Brian Gardner, Methuen, *Obs.* 10 Nov. p 25

(a1) 'A scholarly and impartial study ... a fine book, extremely valuable for the historian and very enjoyablc to read as well.'

(b1) Wishes the author had viewed Churchill's writings with more detachment, but observes 'it has great merits'.

(c1) These essays 'have few novelties ... all the writers tell more about themselves than about Churchill'.

(d1) An anthology of raw material.

G1207. War of nerves, *History of the Cold War 1917–1950*, André Fontaine, Secker and Warburg, *Obs.* 17 Nov. p 27

(1) An often told story – this version 'just manages to justify itself'.

(2) 'Perhaps there was some flicker of aggressive intent in Soviet policy between 1945 and 1948, but even this is doubtful. For the most part Soviet leaders have been obsessively defensive.'

G1208. Gossip on tapped lines, *Breach of Security*, ed. David Irving, Kimber, *Obs.* 24 Nov. p 28

(1) These German intelligence reports are unimportant.

G1209. Betting on the Liberal card, *John Dillon*, F.S. Lyons, Routledge, *Obs.* 1 Dec. p 29

(1) Praises it as a sympathetic biography of a man whose career has needed resurrecting.

(2) 'The Nationalists were ruined by British Liberals not by Irish extremists. The Home Rulers, apart from Parnell, never understood that for the British Liberal leaders the alliance was a matter of tactics, not of principle.'

G1210. Britain versus the Bolsheviks, *Britain and the Russian Civil War 1918–20*, Richard H. Ullman, Princeton U.P.; Oxford U.P., *Obs.* 8 Dec. p 29

(1) The author disentangles the confusion of British policy 'with masterly scholarship and literary grace'.

(2) Lloyd George got little credit for ending the

war. 'As often happened with him, he had pursued a wise policy by methods of intrigue and evasion, and people remembered the methods but not the results.'

G1211. Books of the Year, *Obs.* 22 Dec. p 17

Praises *Industry and Empire* (*see above* G1192) and *John Dillon* (G1209). 'The funniest book for many year was *Little Nut-Brown Man* by Colin Vines (Frewin). The author is a mixture of Pooter and Boswell, the subject (Beaverbrook) a great humourist in his latter days.'

1969

G1212. Intellectual in Politics, *John Morley*, D.A. Hamer, Oxford U.P., *Obs.* 12 Jan. p 28

(1) A 'remarkable book, firmly based on Morley's published writing and private correspondence'.

G1213. That War Again, (a) *The Origins and Legacies of World War I*, D.F. Fleming, New York, Doubleday; (b) *The United States and the League 1918–1920*, D.F. Fleming, New York, Russell and Russell; (c) *The United States and World Organisation 1920–1933*, D.F. Fleming, New York, A.M.S. Press, *NYRB*. 12, 1. 16 Jan. pp 18–20

(a1) Not a book of 'much originality or distinction', written by a 'thorough going Wilsonian' who has 'dated all subsequent ills to the day when the United States refused to join it (the League of Nations)'. Compares the author's views to those of Konni Zilliacus.

G1214. Cold blooded historian, *1917 Before and After*, E.H. Carr, Macmillan, *Obs.* 26 Jan. p 28

(1) His essays are not more superficial than his books. They are 'more compact, and this serves to emphasise the power of his vision'.

(2) 'What happened in Russia in 1917 was an epilogue to the turmoils of the nineteenth century, not the beginning of a new age.'

G1215. *Tragedy and Hope*, Carroll Quigley, Collier and Macmillan, 1966, *EHR*. 84, 330. Jan. p 223

(1) 'Sometimes interesting, sometimes eccentric and far too long'.

G1216. Turkish imbroglio, *The Chanak Affair*, David Walder, Hutchinson, *Obs*. 2 Feb. p 29

(1) Enjoyable and 'very good history'; but points to mistakes in the earlier chapters.

G1217. Revolt of the secret people, *Captain Swing*, E.J. Hobsbawm and George Rudé, Lawrence and Wishart, *Obs*. 9 Feb. p 29

(1) It 'is not only well written and skilfully arranged. Its understanding makes it a book in a thousand.'

(2) 'The revolt of the agricultural labourers in 1830 was the greatest manifestation by the English people between Monmouth's rebellion and the General Strike.'

G1218. The revolution that never was, *The Revolutionary Movement in Britain 1900–1921*, Walter Kendall, Weidenfeld and Nicolson, *Obs*. 16 Mar. p 29

(1) Feels that the detailed narrative does not confirm the author's thesis that Moscow ruined the British revolution. Nevertheless the activities of the revolutionaries 'make a wonderful story'.

G1219. Blitzkrieg in France, *To Lose A Battle*, Alistair Horne, Macmillan, *Obs*. 30 Mar. p 29

(1) Very good – it 'combines good history and good reading'.

(2) 'The failure of France was a failure of leadership, not of her people ... In the last resort France was ruined by the Napoleonic tradition, which left everything to the initiative of individual generals.'

G1220. The Hero City, *The 900 Days: The Siege of Leningrad*, Harrison E. Salisbury, New York, Harper and Row, *NYRB*. 12, 7. 10 Apr. pp 10, 12–14

(1) 'The most detailed account ... and also the most moving'; though at times 'we seem to be reading a novel'. Regrets that the German side of the siege is not given.

G1221. Presiding over catastrophe, *Wavell*, John Connell, Collins, *Obs*. 13 Apr. p 27

(1) Too long for its subject – and the author is too harsh on British unpreparedness.

G1222. *Storia Diplomatica della Questione dell Alto Adige*, Mario Toscano, Bari, Laterza, 1967, *EHR*. 84, 331. Apr. pp 440–1

(1) 'Professor Toscano writes in the spirit of Metternich, while the German Tyrolese echo the words of Garibaldi and Mazzini.'

G1223. *Nazi Germany and the American Hemisphere 1933–1941*, Alton Frye, Yale U.P., 1967, *Ibid*. p 444

(2) A.J.P.T. suggests that there is little proof of Hitler intending to attack the New World. As to his plans in 1940 for seizing the Azores and Canaries, these seem 'to have grown out of the war rather than the other way round'.

G1224. Left in doubt, *Labour's International Policy*, John F. Naylor, Weidenfeld and Nicolson, *Obs*. 11 May. p 34

(1) A useful contribution to explaining the period – a change from the usual polemics.

(2) On collective security: 'Heavy armaments plus isolation would have been the most Radical, even the most Socialist, policy. But few thought so at the time.'

B1225. The man who knew everybody, *Thomas Jones: Whitehall Diaries*, Vol. 1, ed. Keith Middlemas, Oxford U.P., *Obs*. 22 Jun. p 26

(1) 'No more important source on politics and politicians in the twentieth century has been published for many years.'

G1226. Imperial miscalculations, *The Life of Joseph Chamberlain*, Vols. 5 and 6, Julian Amery, Macmillan, *Obs*. 13 Jul. p 25

(1) 'The enthusiast for political biography would not have the book a page shorter. The details have the fascination provided by the analysis of a game of chess ... Joseph Chamberlain has at last been lucky in his biographer.'

G1227. Massacre or muddle? *Peterloo*, Robert Walmsley, Manchester U.P., *Obs*. 20 Jul. p 25

(1) 'A most scholarly book, full of fascinating detail', which has William Hutton, chairman of the magistrates, as its hero. However 'despite all his evidence, the legend was fundamentally right – in spirit, if not in fact'.

G1228. *L'altra Europe* (Turin University), Turin, Giappichelli, 1967, *EHR*. 84, 332. Jul. p 638

(1) Dispassionate studies of the Resistance by historians who served in it.

G1229. *Studies in International History*, ed. K. Bourne and D.C. Watt, Longmans, 1977, *Ibid*. p 640

(1) This *festschrift* for W.N. Medlicott 'is a tribute particularly appropriate'. Apart from the introductory essays it comprises 'dissections of diplomatic history in the most rigid sense . . . The general effect is to generate gloomy thoughts about the value of diplomatic history.'

G1230. Man behind the scenes, *Memoirs of a Conservative*, ed. Robert Rhodes James, Weidenfeld and Nicolson, *Obs*. 31 Aug. p 20

(1) Warns the reader that J.C. Davidson wrote much of this thirty years after the events. 'Despite this, the book is a unique contribution to knowledge of political events.'

G1231. Oh, what a lovely war, (a) *The Politics of War*, Gabriel Kolko, Weidenfeld and Nicolson; (b) *The People's War*, Angus Calder, Cape, *Obs*. 7 Sept. p 29

(a1) 'A tremendous stroke for the new revisionism' – which blames America for the Cold War.

(b1) On the whole an effective account – but wrong in emphasis in several places.

G1232. The man who was right, *Dowding and the Battle of Britain*, Robert Wright, MacDonald, *Obs*. 14 Sept. p 29

(1) 'A book of the first importance . . . the results are devastating.' It shows that Churchill's comments on Dowding in his account of the war 'are often wrong and sometimes deliberately untrue'.

G1233. Insights and sidelights, *Winston S. Churchill*, *Com-*

panion Volume 2, Randolph S. Churchill, Heinemann, *Obs.* 28 Sept. p 29

(1) 'Our understanding of Winston Churchill would be incomplete without them'.

G1234. This way to the mausoleum, *Baldwin*, Keith Middlemas and John Barnes, Weidenfeld and Nicolson, *Obs.* 12 Oct. p 33

(1) 'It contains over half a million words, and very pedestrian words at that. There is no zest, no simplification. No detail is spared, however trivial or even irrelevant ... Baldwin the man has disappeared.'

(2) Argues that Baldwin's early hasty actions in high office were disastrous and as a result he 'resolved never to hurry again. From that moment he waited upon events.'

G1235. *Britain and Germany in Africa*, ed. Prousser Giffard and Roger Louis, Yale U.P., 1968, *EHR*. 84, 333. Oct. pp 816–7

(1) Praises many of the contributions to this *festschrift* to Harry R. Rudin, including the survey essay by Roger Louis.

G1236. *Bismarcks auswärtige Pressepolitik und die Reichsgründung*, Eberhard Naujoks, Wiesbaden, Steiner, 1968, *Ibid.* p 868

(1) A full description of the subject based on 'fine work' in the German archives. 'A curious, though probably not a very important story'.

G1237. TJ and SB and LIG, *Thomas Jones: Whitehall Diaries*, Vol. 2, ed. K. Middlemas, Oxford U.P., *Obs.* 9 Nov. p 35

(1) 'A unique picture of politics in the making'.

(2) 'Perhaps only the accident of an inflamed prostate gland saved the country from a real National Government under Lloyd George, in which Mosley and Churchill would have been the dynamic figures.'

G1238. Cold meat at dawn, *Wellington: The Years of the Sword*, Elizabeth Longford, Weidenfeld, *Obs.* 16 Nov. p 31

(1) She 'has done every well in making an attractive picture of one so aloof'. Praises her treatment of the battles.

G1239. Admiral far from silent, *First Sea Lord*, Richard Hough, Allen and Unwin, *Obs.* 23 Nov. p 30

(1) 'A substantial and valuable volume'. He manages to combine a 'solemn and serious' and a 'high comedy' treatment of Fisher – and this is the appropriate approach to the subject.

G1240. When the Navy nearly sank us, *From the Dreadnought to Scapa Flow*, Vol. 4, Arthur J. Marder, Oxford U.P., *Obs.* 7 Dec. p 31

(1) 'He is beyond praise, as he is beyond cavil. This book, like its predecessors, is a model of humane learning. It sets a standard which few other historians can approach.'

G1241. The Emperor Industry, (a) *Napoleon*, 2 Vols. Georges Lefebvre, Columbia U.P.; (b) *Napoleon in Russia*, Alan Palmer, New York, Simon and Shuster; (c) *Napoleon Recaptures Paris*, Claude Manceron, New York, Norton; (c) *Napoleon After Waterloo*, Michael John Thornton, Stanford U.P.; (e) *Napoleon's St. Helena*, Gilbert Martineau, New York, Rand McNally, *NYRB*. 13, 11. 18 Dec. pp 33–6

(a1) Little romance in his prosaic pages.

(b1) 'A solid book, firmly grounded on the latest information'.

(c1) A sensational account.

(d1) A novel subject – an account of Napoleon between Waterloo and his going to St Helena.

(e1) Some new details of his time on St Helena, admirably told.

(2) Praises Thomas Hardy's understanding of Napoleon in his *Dynasts*, 'when he presented Napoleon as being condemned by his nature to become the sport of the gods'.

G1242. Books of the Year, *Obs.* 21 Dec. p 17

Captain Swing (*see above* G1217) – 'a book which has eclipsed all others . . . It shows how the English governing classes behave when they are really frightened. And it presents a great English hero.'

G1243. Requiescat in pace, *The Death of the Past*, J.H. Plumb, Macmillan, *Obs.* 28 Dec. p 14

(1) 'Plumb's destruction of the past is admirably done. He is less effective when he tries to discover what historians ought to do now.'

(2) 'In my opinion Sir Walter Scott, not Gibbon, was the first man with a truly historical outlook, the first man who fully recognised that the past was different from the present.'

1970

G1244. *Actes et documents* . . . (*see above* G1159), Vol. 4, (1940–1), 1967, *EHR*. 85, 334. Jan. pp 211–2

(1) 'Altogether this is an honourable record of policy under strain'.

G1245. *Actes et documents* . . . (*see above* G1159), Vol. 5, (1941–2), 1968, *Ibid.* p 212

(2) 'The Pope's sole aim was peace not victory. This disturbed combatants who thought that they were fighting for a righteous cause.'

G1246. *ID*, 7th Ser., Vols. 5 and 6, (Feb-Dec 1927 and Jan-Sep 1928), ed. Giampiero Carocci, 1967, *Ibid.* pp 212–3

(1) Observes that there is 'little in the nature of grand policy' in the period but 'one can see a pattern for the future. Italy could cause little trouble while she was on her own. Once some other Power stirred things up Mussolini would find the temptation to join in irresistable.'

G1247. The old familiar faces, *The Collapse of the Third Republic*, William L. Shirer, Heinemann and Secker and Warburg, *Obs.* 1 Mar. p 33

(1) 'The narrative is brisk, attractive, and often convincing. It tells us, at excessive length, what we knew already.'

G1248. Yesterday's religion, (a) *The Insurrectionists*, W.J. Fishman, Methuen; (b) *Revolutionists in London*, James W. Hulse, Oxford, *Obs.* 8 Mar. p 29 (a1) 'An ingenious essay in misunderstanding' – as Lenin was an orthodox Marxist.

(b1) It deals with five 'soft' revolutionaries, those who believed in a long period of education before revolution. A.J.P.T. deems William Morris to have been 'the saint of the century'.

G1249. No heaven on earth, (a) *The Russian Revolution*, Marcel Liebman, Cape; (b) *1919: Red Mirage*, David Mitchell, Cape, *Obs.* 5 Apr. p 29

(a1) He 'presents the romantic myth undiluted', a mixture of John Reed and Trotsky.

(b1) Despite minor flaws it is 'very exciting and, in its way, very good'.

G1250. Scarred Monuments, (a) *The Younger Pitt*, Vol. 1, John Ehrman, New York, Dutton; (b) *The Year of Liberty: The Great Irish Rebellion of 1798*, Thomas Pakenham, New York, Prentice-Hall, *NYRB.* 14, 7. 9 Apr. pp 15–16

(a1) 'A work of high scholarship' but Pitt remains submerged under the details of government.

(b1) 'A book which will make its readers sit up, a book devoted to great causes and brutal repression'. Well written and fair in its judgments.

G1251. The perfect secretary, *Hankey: Man of Secrets*, Vol. 1, Stephen Roskill, Collins, *Obs.* 12 Apr. p 30

(1) 'A unique account of war government from the inside . . . invaluable for historians'. However 'it is also rather dull . . . Hankey, apart from being a very efficient secretary, appears only as a staid Surrey commuter – which is what he was.'

G1252. Uncle Arthur at the F.O., *MacDonald Versus Henderson*, David Carlton, Macmillan, *Obs.* 26 Apr. p 30

(1) It reads too much like a thesis – 'topics are explored even when they contribute nothing to the central theme'.

G1253. *Victory Without Peace*, David F. Trask, Wiley, 1968, *EHR.* 85, 335. Apr. p 443

(1) A 'skilfully written . . . short account'. 'Professor Trask holds that the Cold War ended

in 1953 – yet another date for the death of an imaginary condition.'

G1254. Tortuous path to glory, *Churchill : A Study In Failure 1900–1939*, Robert Rhodes James, Weidenfeld and Nicolson, *Obs.* 17 May. p 30

(1) A fascinating story told in 'a cool narrative'. Praises the author for making 'skilful raids on the official papers which have been opened recently'.

G1255. Royal Performances, *The Political Influence of the British Monarchy 1868–1952*, Frank Hardie, Batsford, *Obs.* 31 May. p 30

(1) 'Interesting, efficient and enlightening'.

G1256. Saving Lloyd George's soul, *The Political Diaries of C.P. Scott 1911–1928*, ed. Trevor Wilson, Collins, *Obs.* 14 Jun. p 16

(1) Praises the editor for doing 'a fine job'. The principal theme of the diaries is 'saving Lloyd George's soul' for Liberalism.

G1257. Grand Fleet berthed, *From The Dreadnought to Scapa Flow*, Vol. 5, Arthur J. Marder, Oxford, *Obs.* 21 Jun. p 31

(1) 'There is the same mastery of sources, the same magic of narration as in the preceding volumes.'

(2) A.J.P.T. disagrees that all countries always put their own interests first. 'Many nations have made great sacrifices for others, and none has made more than his own two countries, Great Britain and the United States.'

G1258. *Krieg Der Illusionen*, Fritz Fischer, Dusseldorf, Droste, 1969, *Hist.* 55, 2. Jun. pp 299–301

(1) Praises him as an historian who looks 'at historical problems with a fresh eye and reopens questions on which historians seemed to have reached agreement'. Finds the author's theme that in Germany 'a clear cut annexationist programme was developing before 1914' to be 'at once the most novel and most effective' part of the book. However A.J.P.T. is less impressed with the theme that these policies were applied in practice, and finds least satisfactory Fischer's claims 'that the German

statesmen were set on a great war from the beginning of the crisis'.

G1259. Diplomacy in time of war, *British Foreign Policy in the Second World War*, Vol. 1, Sir Llewellyn Woodward, H.M.S.O., *Obs*. 16 Aug. p 20

(1) The flaw in the project is that the volumes only 'record the doings of the Foreign Office, and that these were far from the whole of British foreign policy during the war'. Warmly praises the introduction – 'a beautiful example of historical composition'.

G1260. Playing the party game, *English Party Politics*, 2 Vols. ed. Alan Beattie, Weidenfeld and Nicolson, *Obs*. 23 Aug. p 23

(1) 'A fascinating anthology of the subject from the Restoration to the present day'. The book is aimed at students. A.J.P.T. comments: 'This is rash. Original documents are much too dangerous for beginners. They are often too dangerous for most historians, who do better to copy from their predecessors.

G1261. The quiet rebellion, *Mutiny At Invergordon*, David Divine, MacDonald, *Obs*. 13 Sept. p 27

(1) 'A splendid book, combining technical mastery and a superb gift of exposition'.

G1262. Advice From a Centipede, *Political History*, G.R. Elton, Allen Lane, *NS*. 80, 2061. 18 Sept. pp 339–40

(1) It 'is full of wise words and cheering doctrine'.

G1263. *The Great Slump*, Goronwy Rees, Weidenfeld and Nicolson, *Obs*. 20 Sept. p 28

(1) 'A somewhat slapdash historian ... But he understands the technicalities of financial speculation or bank failures and has a feel for the period.'

(2) 'Ironically what perished in the Great Depression was Socialism not liberal capitalism. At any rate, socialism has not been heard of since.'

G1264. Heirs of the British Raj, *India's China War*, Neville Maxwell, Cape, *Obs*. 11 Oct. p 34

(1) 'Magnificent on every count'. Other than the lack of access to Chinese sources, 'his book is complete and final, an historical achievement of the first rank'.

G1265. One part of the battlefield, *A History of the Second World War*, B.H. Liddell Hart, Cassell, *Obs*. 25 Oct. p 35

(1) 'A work of great length and great learning, illuminated by flashes of insight. It has also the defects of Liddell Hart's virtues.' It passes over the wars at sea and in the air and the politics of war, and it is too credulous of the German generals' claims.

G1266. Friends of Every Country . . . *The Napoleonists*, E. Tangye Lean, Oxford, *NS*. 80, 2067. 30 Oct. pp 568–9

(1) 'The book is highly entertaining, but the political psychology is in my opinion poppycock. Its basic error is the belief that only conformist citizens are normal'.

G1267. *Italy's Austrian Heritage 1919–1949*, Dennison I. Rusinow, Oxford U.P., *EHR*. 85, 337. Oct. pp 875–6

(1) An 'admirable book . . . a truly brilliant book, beautifully balanced, masterly in its control of sources, and a delight to read'.

G1268. *Vom Reich zum Weltreich*, Klaus Hildebrand, Munich, Fink, 1969, *Ibid*. pp 878–9

(1) 'Packed with valuable information and stimulating ideas' but too long. Regrets that 'the author is hypnotised by Hitler's 'programme''.

G1269. The last crusade, *The Victors' Dilemma*, John Silverlight, Barrie and Jenkins, *Obs*. 1 Nov. p 30

(1) 'An admirable summary of a complicated story'.

(2) 'Lloyd George was against intervention (in Russia) when it was not succeeding but he had bouts of enthusiasm for it whenever things were going well.'

G1270. The Man Who Was Right, *Eamon de Valera*, the Earl of Longford and Thomas P. O'Neil, Hutchinson, *NS*. 80, 2068. 6 Nov. pp 601–2

(1) 'It is a remarkable achievement to have brought 60 years of political activity within the compass of a single volume and to have done so without any impression of superficiality or omission.'

However he observes that 'the authors do not face the problem that, while de Valera always knew what the Irish people wanted, the people often showed clearly that they did not want what he thought they did'.

G1271. Grand old humbug, *Lord Palmerston*, Jasper Ridley, Constable, *Obs.* 8 Nov. p 30

(1) 'A lively important book about a lively interesting man . . . an excellent biography'; but regrets that the author 'does not discriminate between great affairs and small'.

G1272. Revolution and Empire, (a) *The Nineteenth Century*, ed. Asa Briggs, Thames and Hudson; (b) *A Concise History of the British Empire*, Gerald S. Graham, Thames and Hudson; (c) *The Victorian Empire*, Dennis Judd, Weidenfeld and Nicolson, *Obs.* 29 Nov. p 30

(a1) Each of the essays is 'an important contribution to historical understanding'.

(b1) 'A miracle of compression'.

(c1) 'An effective picture of the Victorian Empire in its creation and at its zenith'.

G1273. Eatanswill on the Isis, *The Other Oxford*, Charles Fenby, Lund Humphries, *Obs.* 13 Dec. p 22

(1) A book about the Gray family which is both 'high comedy' and 'a serious contribution to history, recapturing the realities of political life in a small provincial town'.

G1274. Books of the Year, *Obs.*20 Dec. p 17

Praises *From The Dreadnought to Scapa Flow*, Vol. 5 (*see above* G1257) and *India's China War* (G1264). Deems *The Other Oxford* (G1273) to be 'the fun book of the year' which is 'full of stories which are as good as anything in Dickens and also presumably true'.

1971

G1275. Brummagen statesmanship, *The Chamberlain Cabinet*, Ian Colvin, Gollancz, *Obs.* 10 Jan. p 27

(1) It 'contains the richest revelations yet made

from the British side about the origins of the Second World War ... Vindications for Chamberlain crumble into dust.' Feels that Hoare comes out of it well.

G1276. Wars to end wars? (a) *The Russo-German War 1941–45*, Albert Seaton, Barker; (b) *Hitler's Last Offensive*, Peter Elstob, Secker and Warburg, *Obs.* 17 Jan. p 26

(a1) 'The fullest account of the war to appear in English. It makes heavy going.' Highly critical of the political judgments.

(b1) 'This is really the final word on the Ardennes battle so far as certainty is possible in military affairs.'

G1277. *British-American Relations 1917–1918*, W.B. Fowler, Princeton U.P.; Oxford U.P., 1969, *EHR*. 86, 338. Jan. p 198

(1) A book of great importance.

G1278. *Deutschland und Japan im 2 Weltkrieg*, Bernd Martin, Gottingen, Musterschmidt, 1969, *Ibid.* pp 211–2

(1) A valuable book – but based almost entirely on the German records.

G1279. Always with us, *Poverty And The Industrial Revolution*, Brian Inglis, Hodder and Stoughton, *Obs.* 7 Feb. p 26

(1) Feels that the author 'recaptures the bewilderment of the time' over the issue of poverty – but argues that he takes the classical economists too seriously.

(2) 'There is more sense in a few of Cobbett's sentences than in all the portentous volumes of the political economists put together.'

G1280. The Independent Habit, (a) *Tito*, Phyllis Auty, New York, McGraw Hill; (b) *The Battle Stalin Lost: Memoirs of Yugoslavia 1948–53*, Vladimir Dedijer, New York, Viking; (c) *Contemporary Yugoslavia*, ed. Wayne S. Vucinich, California U.P., *NYRB*. 16, 4. 11 Feb. pp 26–7

(a1) 'A satisfactory biography ... detached, sympathetic and scholarly'.

G1281. Liberal swan-song, *Politicians At War*, Cameron Hazlehurst, Cape, *Obs*. 28 Feb. p 24

(1) Praises his treatment of Lloyd George but is less happy about it as political history generally. 'He is inclined to take what politicians said at its face value and often gives the impression of being an innocent at large in a far from innocent world.' Finds the book enjoyable to read. 'His enthusiasm is captivating. He is always clear. He is often plausible. He is sometimes right.'

G1282. Sane Remnant, *The Union of Democratic Control In British Politics During The First World War*, M. Swartz, Oxford U.P., *NS*. 81, 2085. 5 Mar. pp 307–8

(1) 'He has written a compelling history of the U.D.C. during the First World War, fully based on the surviving records.'

(2) Denies that the U.D.C. captured the Labour Party. 'If anything, the Labour Party captured it.'

G1283. As it really was? (a) *The Early Victorians 1832–1851*, J.F.C. Harrison, Weidenfeld and Nicolson; (b) *Mid Victorian Britain 1851–75*, Geoffrey Best, Weidenfeld and Nicolson; (c) *Britain In The Nineteen Thirties*, Noreen Branson and Margot Heinemann, Weidenfeld and Nicolson, *Obs*. 21 Mar. p 36

(a and b1) 'Very fine. I read them with uninterrupted delight, entranced that English historians could combine so dazzling scholarship and art. The most learned can benefit from these two books; the least instructed can read them with pleasure.'

(c1) 'Their book is not history. It is a Communist tract . . . This book is a lamentable production, best forgotten.'

G1284. On the wings of a dove, *Motive For A Mission*, James Douglas-Hamilton, Macmillan, *Obs*. 28 Mar. p 32

(1) A thorough study – but the Hess affair was unimportant.

G1285. The democracy game, *The Impact of Labour 1920–*

1924, Maurice Cowling, Cambridge U.P., *Obs.* 25 Apr. p 33

(1) 'It is fun to read about politics with the policies left out.' Doubts if the politicians were 'as single minded in alarm over the social peril as he makes out'.

(2) 'Ramsay MacDonald was less of a danger to society than Lloyd George had been. With MacDonald as Labour leader the old ladies of the Conservative Party could sleep quietly in their beds ...'

G1286. Local boy makes good, *Guardian: Biography of A Newspaper*, David Ayerest, Collins, *Obs.* 2 May. p 30

(1) 'An inspired historian, who has done more for it in one volume than Stanley Morison did for *The Times* in five'.

G1287. 'What Lancashire Thinks Today ...' *Lancashire And The New Liberalism*, P.F. Clarke, Cambridge U.P., *NS.* 81, 2095. 14 May. pp 672–3

(1) 'Here is a new view, powerfully argued and well documented'. Cites the author's conclusion that class politics emerged in early twentieth-century Britain but this did not 'in any simple way' explain the replacement of the Liberal by the Labour Party, and observes 'I think he has proved his case'.

G1288. Kings and queens and hangers-on, *English History*, Sir George Clark, Oxford U.P., *Obs.* 23 May. p 28

(1) 'The cautious critic has submerged the creative scholar ... If an historian chips away at ideas and generalisations too much he will be left only with assorted facts in a chronological array.'

G1288a The Big Fella, *Michael Collins*, Margery Forester, Sidgwick and Jackson, *TLS.* 70, 3613, 28 May. p 608

G1289. A shattered Utopia, (a) *The Paris Commune 1871*, Stewart Edwards, Eyre and Spottiswoode; (b) *The Paris Commune of 1871*, Frank Jellineck, Gollancz; (c) *The Terrible Year*, Alistair Horne, Macmillan, *Obs.* 30 May. p 28

(a1) 'The most thoroughly satisfactory history

of the Commune in any language'.

(b1) 'It has become a classic. In some ways it is still the best book on the Commune, if only for its vivid sympathy.'

(c1) A straightforward narrative.

(2) 'The Commune illustrates the general principle that a revolution occurs not simply as a matter of material suffering, but when a regime is discredited by incompetence and failure.' 'The Communards, though not factory workers, were proletarians in the original sense. They were the eternally oppressed, and they aspired, however clumsily, to found a society where the tyranny of the few over the many would cease for evermore.'

G1290. *Britain And The Second World War*, Henry Pelling, Collins, 1970, *HJ*. 14, 2. Jun. pp 463–4

(1) Two thirds of the book is given to a 'competent and conventional history of the war'; the concluding chapters are 'more original and stimulating'.

G1291. Seedtime of our present chaos, *The Great Illusion 1900–1914*, Oron J. Hale, Harper and Row, *TLS*. 70, 3626. 27 Aug. p 1026

(1) 'Where so much has been excellent it is a little ungrateful to conclude that a satisfactory account of the outbreak of war must wait for a less committed writer.'

G1292. Piggy in the middle, *History of the Liberal Party 1895–1970*, Roy Douglas, Sidgwick and Jackson, *Obs*. 12 Sept. p 28

(1) 'Roy Douglas has written a most interesting, most scholarly, and also most wrong headed book.'

(2) 'The Liberals might have overcome their own mistakes. What they could not overcome was the fact that both Labour and Conservatives had more money and clearer principles.'

G1293. A Bolshevik Soul in a Fabian Muzzle, *The Life of G.D.H. Cole*, Margaret Cole, Macmillan, *NS*. 82, 2115. 1 Oct. pp 441–2

(1) 'Wives rarely make good biographers of their husbands. Dame Margaret is the exception.

Occasionally she slips too much from biography into general history and sometimes she exaggerates the importance of what were really coterie affairs. Broadly speaking, she holds the balance right.' A.J.P.T. gives his views of Cole and some Oxford anecdotes.

G1294. Distressful country, *Thomas Jones: Whitehall Diaries*, Vol. 3, ed. K. Middlemas, Oxford U.P., *Obs.* 17 Oct. p 33

(1) The most sensational of the three volumes. Through it 'Lloyd George's Irish policy can be followed in more detail than any other episode in British history'.

G1295. Churchill in the shadows, *Winston S. Churchill*, Vol. 3, Martin Gilbert, Heinemann, *Obs.* 24 Oct. p 36

(1) 'A stupendous book, almost too much so . . . (It is) a general history of British politics in the first year of the war rather than a biography of Churchill'.

(2) 'In the First World War he pined in vain for 'plenary authority'. Here was the secret of his many failures and his ultimate success. He was *capax imperii* and of nothing less.'

G1296. Rational Wars, (a) *Clausewitz*, Roger Parkinson, New York, Stein and Day; (b) *Studies in War And Peace*, Michael Howard, New York, Viking, *NYRB*. 17, 7. 4 Nov. pp 36–7

(a1) The author describes Clausewitz's career excellently.

(b1) Praises his skill as a military historian in his essays on Waterloo and Wellington's later influence on the British army, and observes that the author has moved with the times from 'history to strategic studies'.

G1297. Larger than life, (a) *Napoleon*, Vincent Cronin, Collins; (b) *The Great Duke*, Arthur Bryant, Collins, *Obs.* 7 Nov. p 34

(a1) 'The attractive individual presented . . . is far removed from the Napoleon of history . . . There is nothing . . . of Napoleon the tyrant who trampled on the liberties of France or of Napoleon the conqueror who ravaged almost every country in Europe.'

(b1) 'A study of Wellington as the invincible general'.

G1298. What went wrong in the Dardanelles? *The French and the Dardanelles*, George H. Cassar, Allen and Unwin, *TLS*. 70, 3637. 12 Nov. p 1426

(1) Praises the author for making 'an entirely fresh contribution to the subject by exploring the French archives'.

G1299. Superior person, *The Diaries of Sir Alexander Cadogan*, ed. David Dilks, Cassell, *Obs*. 14 Nov. p 32

(1) Praises the editor but finds the diary entries disappointing.

G1300. Mr. High-Mind of Balliol, *A.D. Lindsay*, Drusilla Scott, Oxford, Blackwell, *Obs*. 21 Nov. p 33

(1) 'An excellent, if slightly pious, biography'.

G1301. Giant of Fleet Street, *The House of Northcliffe*, Paul Ferris, Weidenfeld and Nicolson, *Obs*. 5 Dec. p 32

(1) 'He presents the gossip and follies of Northcliffe. He fails to do justice to Northcliffe's achievements.'

G1302. Books of the Year, *Obs*. 19 Dec. p 17

Praises *Winston S. Churchill*, Vol. 3 (*see above* G1295). 'The most exciting and original book of the year was *Britain In Balance : The Myth of Failure*, W.A.P. Manser, Longman. It is political dynamite, making a nonsense of this country's economic policies over the last 40 years. The pundits greeted it with embarrassed silence.'

G1303. Victory's the thing, *British War Aims and Peace Diplomacy 1914–18*, V.H. Rothwell, Oxford U.P., *TLS*. 70, 3643. 24 Dec. p 1595

(1) 'He provides new information . . . though he rightly hesitates to reach firm conclusions.'

G1304. *The Origins of the Second World War*, ed. Esmonde M. Robertson, Macmillan, *HJ*. 14, 4. Dec. pp 863–4

(1) 'The controversy does not seem to me very rewarding. The writers, myself included, are all on different wavelengths. Their arguments run parallel and never meet.'

1972

G1305. The forgotten gencral, *Man of Valour*, J.R. Colville, Collins, *Obs*. 9 Jan. p 32

(1) 'A fine biography, as straightforward as Gort himself.'

G1306. Britain leads the way, *Grand Strategy*, Vol. 4, Michael Howard, H.M.S.O., *Obs*. 23 Jan. p 27

(1) Written 'with a graceful ease and absolute impartiality. He is a master of the problems involved and of the records which treat them.'

G1307. Retreat from glory, *Hankey: Man of Secrets*, Vol. 2, Stephen Roskill, Collins, *Obs*. 30 Jan. p 32

(1) Less remarkable then the first volume as Hankey 'ceased to be a man of secrets and became a keeper of minutes' after the fall of Lloyd George.

G1308. Through the Keyhole, (a) *Codeword "Director"*, Heinz Hohne, New York, Coward, McCann and Geoghegan; (b) *The Double Cross System*, J.C. Masterman, Yale U.P.; (c) *The Game of the Foxes*, Ladislas Farago, New York, McKay; (d) *The London Journals of General Raymond E. Lee 1940–1*, ed. James Lenze, *NYRB*. 18, 2. 10 Feb. pp 14, 16–17

(a1) The best of these books – it has the best sense of proportion, is well researched and presented, but A.J.P.T. dislikes his journalistic mode of writing and anti-Soviet Russia outlook.

(b1) 'Neat' – but is sceptical as to whether the author was as successful as he thinks he was.

(c1) 'Bulky' and 'pretentious'.

(d1) 'We are scraping the barrel'.

(2) Scorns the importance of spying and observes that it is 'a field where human ingenuity operates almost free from contact with reality'.

G1309. *The Foreign Policy of Hitler's Germany*, Gerhard L.

Weinberg, Chicago U.P., *JMH.* 441, 1. Mar. pp 140–3

(1) A book written by 'a very competent historian with probably an unrivalled control of the archival material'. Observes that 'in writing about Hitler's early policy it would be a blessing to forget about the Second World War'.

G1310. Dark gods and all that, *Movements In European History*, D.H. Lawrence, Oxford U.P., *Obs.* 2 Apr. p 29

(1) The book bears 'Lawrence's trademarks, combining dogmatic certainties and delphic mutterings'. 'The good passages, and they are very good, were written from Lawrence's inner consciousness.' But much of it is 'romantic rubbish'.

G1311. Seeds of the cold war, *British Foreign Policy In The Second World War*, Vols. 2 and 3, Sir Llewellyn Woodward, H.M.S.O., *Obs.* 23 Apr. p 32

(1) The third volume 'provides excellent material for the beginnings of the Cold War'. Regrets that the author has not used the S.O.E. documents.

G1312. *Walter Hines Page*, Ross Gregory, Kentucky U.P., 1970, *EHR.* 87, 343. Apr. p 451

(1) Competent and reliable but not much new information.

G1313. *Friendship Under Stress*, H.K. Meier, Bern, Lang, 1970, *Ibid.* p 456

(1) Valuable and interesting – a story which is creditable to the Swiss.

G1314. *Etudes d'histoire contemporaine de la Roumanie*, Bucarest, Académie des Sciences et Politiques, 1970, *Ibid.* p 457–8

(1) Four essays by Romanian historians on the reversal of Romania's allegiance in August 1914.

G1315. How the First World War was not stopped, *Socialism and the Great War*, Georges Haupt, Oxford U.P., *TLS.* 71, 3662. 5 May. p 514

(1) 'A most valuable book, stuffed with new information and new ideas'.

G1316. Everyman at war, *The Home Fronts, 1914–1918*, John Williams, Constable, *Obs.* 14 May. p 37

(1) It 'is rather gossipy and derives from obvious sources which historians know well. But the subject is presented with vivid detail . . .'

G1317. Stuffed shirt, *Metternich*, Alan Palmer, Weidenfeld and Nicolson, *Obs.* 4 Jun. p 32

(1) 'As a work of history cannot be faulted' –but it is less good on the man.

(2) 'Metternich never risked a war unless he could be sure that he would win it. Metternich was in fact the supreme example of a diplomat.'

G1318. European entanglement, *The Continental Commitment*, Michael Howard, Temple Smith, *Obs.* 18 Jun. p 32

(1) Praises these 'admirable Ford lectures' – 'he presents the broad lines of British policy with the sure grasp of a first rate military historian'.

(2) 'It is an inescapable reality that Great Britain has been strongest when she has stood alone.'

G1319. Diplomatic delusions, *Democracy of Illusion*, Keith Middlemas, Weidenfeld and Nicolson, *Obs.* 25 Jun. p 31

(1) Criticises him for assuming that Hitler was set on world conquest all along; but this apart 'he has a great deal of interest to say'.

G1320. Two wars in one, *Total War*, Peter Calvocoressi and Guy Wint, Allen Lane, *Obs.* 2 Jul. p 30

(1) 'Fascinating reading', but regrets that it is written as two distinct books on the European and Far East.

(2) Urges that the Second World War must be presented to the younger generation with care: 'somehow it must be conveyed to them that it was that rare, perhaps unique, thing: a good war'.

G1321. When the rot set in, *The Collapse of British Power*, Correlli Barnett, Eyre Methuen, *Obs.* 9 Jul. p 33

(1) The author 'is a master of denunication with a forceful, if too colourful, style and a firm control

of his material which, in this book includes original sources' However he disagrees with the author's interpretation.

(2) 'Great Britain was never a Great Power from her intrinsic strength, as say, the U.S. and Soviet Russia are today. She became great from skill and from adroitly avoiding involvement in Europe. She let others fight her battles, and was ruined in the twentieth century when she tried to become a European Power . . . '

G1322. *Deutschland und die Vereinigten Staaten 1933–1939*, Hans-Jürgen Schröder, Wiesbaden, Steiner, 1970, *EHR*. 87, 344. Jul. p 655

(1) Suggests that the author makes too much of differences between America and Germany over trade as a cause of war.

G1323. *Probleme deutscher Zeitgeschichte*, Stockholm, Laromedelsforlagen, 1970, *Ibid*. p 656

G1324. Gladstone at first hand, *The Diary of Sir Edward Hamilton 1880–1885*, 2 Vols. ed. Dudley W.R. Bahlman, Oxford U.P., *Obs*. 6 Aug. p 25

(1) 'No doubt a great man, but a very strange one, and Hamilton describing him so close at hand, leaves him stranger than ever'.

(2) Observes that his Government already was being 'eaten away' before Gordon's death 'by Gladstone's incorrigible habit of dodging the issue, whatever it might be, instead of solving it . . . Gladstone wanted to carry radical measures without hurting anyone's feelings. Instead he hurt feelings without carrying radical measures.'

G1325. Bright little island, *The Offshore Islanders*, Paul Johnson, Weidenfeld and Nicolson, *Obs*. 10 Sept. p 32

(1) 'This is a John Bull of a book, the sort of thing that Cobbett might have written.' Agrees with the author (a former pupil of his) that continental commitments have always harmed England, but observes 'my historian's conscience is startled by some of the more sweeping judgements'.

G1326. The Cotton-Spinner's Son, *Sir Robert Peel*, Vol. 2, Norman Gash, Longmans, *NS*. 84, 2165. 15 Sept. pp 358–9

(1) The author 'has matured into a beautiful biographer'.

(2) Peel's 'record as leader and prime minister was perhaps the greatest that any modern British statesman has to show'. Observes, 'Peel's aim was to create an alliance between landowners and capitalists, to make in a sense a single nation of all those with a stake in the country', and compares him in this to Bismarck.

G1327. Peace in our time, *The Semblance of Peace*, Sir John Wheeler-Bennett and Anthony Nicholls, Macmillan, *Obs*. 24 Sept. p 37

(1) Praises the account of the peace making with Germany's various allies as 'extremely clear and competent, providing many valuable exercises in the art of diplomacy'. But feels that the book is too long and condemns the authors as 'unrepentant cold war warriors, convinced that Soviet Russia was set on dominating the world'.

G1328. Domesticating the Monarchy, (a) *Queen Victoria*, Vol. 1, Cecil Woodham-Smith, Hamilton; (b) *The Life and Times of Victoria*, Dorothy Marshall, Weidenfeld and Nicolson, *Obs*. 1 Oct. p 40

(a1) It 'is as good as any of its predecessors, with virtues its own'. Good on personal matters, weaker on politics.

(b1) Welcomes it, noting that, of the two, it has 'a deeper knowledge of social conditions'.

G1329. The Chinese cracker of Cliveden, *Nancy*, Christopher Sykes, Collins, *TLS*. 3685. 20 Oct. p 1246

(1) 'A beautiful portrait of this strange, difficult woman' – Nancy Astor. 'A most winning biography, sympathetic and almost convincing'.

G1330. *Economic Appeasement*, Bernd Jürgen Wendt, Düsseldorf, Bertelsmann U.P., 1971, *EHR*. 87, 345. Oct. pp 846–9

(1) A book which 'implies considerable revision

of our views as to British policies before the Second World War'.

G1331. Silly soldier man? *Wellington: Pillar of State*, Elizabeth Longford, Weidenfeld and Nicolson, *Obs.* 5 Nov. p 38

(1) The author 'has surpassed herself. This volume is the best she has ever written and that is saying a great deal . . . the book is scholarly, well written and above all offers lavish helpings of fun.'

G1332. Wuthering Heights, *Only The Wind Will Listen*, Andrew Boyle, Hutchinson, *Obs.* 12 Nov. p 37

(1) An 'admirable biography' of Reith.

G1333. Morals and diplomacy, (a) *The Limits of Foreign Policy*, Christopher Thorne, Hamilton; (b) *The War Hitler Won*, Nicholas Bethell, Allen Lane, *Obs.* 19 Nov. p 38

(a1) 'A major exercise in diplomatic history, exploring the question (the Far Eastern crisis 1931–3) in rigorous detachment'.

(b1) Agrees with the author's verdict that the Western Powers went to war to save Chamberlain's political career.

G1334. Soviet beginnings, (a) *The Russian Revolution of February 1917*, Marc Ferro, Routledge; (b) *Year One of the Russian Revolution*, Victor Serge, Allen Lane, *Obs.* 10 Dec. p 38

(a1) 'A lively and excitingly revisionist account of the first or February revolution . . . This is first rate historical analysis.'

(b1) 'Serge saw the Bolshevik revolution through Western eyes . . . His book was a polemic despite its air of scholarship.'

G1335. Books of the Year, *Obs.* 17 Dec. p 25

Praises *Grand Strategy*, Vol. 4 (*see above* G1306) and *The Offshore Islanders*, 'For fun, and also for intellectual stimulation' (G1325). In particular he praises *Sir Robert Peel*, Vol. 2 (G1326) as a book 'which ranks with the greatest political biographies of the past, a classic work in both scholarship and presentation'.

G1336. What history is about, *The History Primer*, J.R. Hexter, Allen Lane, *Obs*. 17 Dec. p 32

(1) 'He handles this difficult subject with effortless ease. His book provides great fun and evokes great admiration.' 'He writes with inimitable pungency.'

(2) 'I favour the sort of history that answers the questions, 'What happened next?' and 'How did it happen?' The Whys will then look after themselves.'

1973

G1337. Manchester Maestro, *The Autobiography of Charles Hallé*, ed. M. Kennedy, Elek, 1972, *NS*. 85, 2181. 5 Jan. p 24

(1) 'A modest work of bewitching charm'.

G1338. The Last Proconsul, *The Killearn Diaries 1934–46*, ed. Trefor Evans, Sidgwick and Jackson, *Obs*. 14 Jan. p 34

(1) 'A fascinating document, despite its official tone'.

G1339. Churchill's war of words, *Winston S. Churchill, Companion Volumes 3*, Martin Gilbert, Heinemann, *Obs*. 21 Jan. p 34

(1) Regrets the size of the two volumes but finds them to be 'an agreeable lucky dip'. Suggests that they modify the main volume: 'Gilbert argued that Churchill was really keen on seizing the island of Borkum and took up Gallipoli when it was proposed by others. The truth seems rather that he ran after both ideas without seriously considering that one excluded the other.'

G1340. *Stalin, Hitler and Europe*, Vol. 2, James E. McSherry, Cleveland and New York, World, 1970, *EHR*. 88, 346. Jan. p 228

(1) Interesting on the Soviet-Finnish war, but weak thereafter.

G1341. *The History of the South Tyrol Question*, Antony

Alcock, Joseph, 1971, *Ibid.* pp 229–30

(1) A blow-by-blow account with little background. Dissents from the author's belief 'that economic betterment removes national grievances'.

G1342. Roasting a parson, *The Trial of Dr. Sacheverell*, Geoffrey Holmes, Eyre Methuen, *Obs.* 11 Feb. p 36

(1) 'A magnificent book'.

(2) 'His career is a dreadful warning to any Fellow of Magdalen who neglects academic pursuits for the bright lights of publicity.'

G1343. Record breaking, *Blood, Toil, Tears and Sweat*, Roger Parkinson, Hart-Davis, MacGibbon, *Obs.* 4 Mar. p 37

(1) 'A summary of War Cabinet papers, occasionally enlivened by anecdotes from less solemn sources'. Cabinet minutes 'do not provide an adequate basis on which to write the history of the Second World War'.

G1344. Faultless to a fault, *Alex*, Nigel Nicolson, Weidenfeld and Nicolson, *Obs.* 1 Apr. p 36

(1) 'A sympathetic biography, replete with all the hero-worship felt by all those who served under Alexander'.

(2) He 'was the perfect soldier: unruffled in defeat, modest in success; admired by those under him, trusted by his political chiefs'. His weakness was in not being firm with his subordinates.

G1345. The everlasting death bed, (a) *The Liberal Imperialists*, H.C.G. Matthew, Oxford U.P.; (b) *Liberals, Radicals and Social Politics 1892–1914*, H.V. Emy, Cambridge U.P., *TLS.* 3710. 13 Apr. p 416

(a2) They 'were in search of both a leader and followers and never found either . . . They regarded politics as a device for getting jobs for themselves, not as a means of satisfying popular wishes.'

(b1) 'His somewhat opaque narrative shows how Liberals of all kinds gradually fumbled towards the view that they must have a constructive social policy if they were to win working class votes.'

G1346. Recalling Mr. Fearful-for-truth, *Kingsley*, C.H. Rolph, Gollancz, *TLS*. 3710. 13 Apr. pp 419–20

(1) It 'is not a good book. It is discursive, rambling and tantalising, like its subject. It is also sometimes inaccurate ... However, Martin's extraordinary personality is strong enough to surmount these defects.'

The *TLS*. 3712. 24 Apr. p 473, carried a letter by C.H. Rolph which replied to the review and included reference to A14 as 'that delightfully discursive if occasionally inaccurate book'.

G1347. Radical Hotspur, *Fleet Street Radical*, Stephen E. Koss, Allen Lane, *Obs*. 22 Apr. p 32

(1) 'A fine life of (A.G.) Gardiner ... It is a contribution to that neglected subject, newspaper history. It illustrates particularly the relationship between editor and proprietor.'

G1348. *Da Adua a Sarajevo*, Enrico Decleva, Bari, Laterza, 1971, *EHR*. 88, 347. Apr. p 466

(1) Sophisticated diplomatic history.

G1349. A Patriot for One Ireland, *Roger Casement*, Brian Inglis, Hodder and Stoughton, *TLS*. 3714. 11 May. pp 513–4

(1) 'He understands Casement as no previous biographer has done.'

Repr. in A21, pp 210–7

G1350. From Rank to Class, *The English Ideology*, George Watson, Allen Lane, *Obs*. 20 May. p 37

(1) Doubts whether political novels 'really tell anything significant about the political world'. Nevertheless feels that the author 'provides plenty of fascinating material'.

G1351. Premature Cold Warrior, *For The President*, ed. Orrville H. Bullitt, Deutsch, *Obs*. 27 May. p 37

(1) Though Bullitt's letters 'contain little new information, they present an incomparable picture of Paris and French politicians before the outbreak of war'.

G1352. Man in a muddle, *The Time Traveller*, Norman and Jeanne MacKenzie, Weidenfeld and Nicolson,

Obs. 17 Jun. p 33

(1) An 'admirable biography . . . Here is Wells without disguise.'

G1353. Juggernaut's Progress, *The Young Lloyd George*, John Grigg, Eyre Methuen, *NS*. 85, 2205. 22 Jun. p 926

(1) Praises the book, in particular the author's clarity and fairness. 'The truth is that Lloyd George was a spoilt child and became a spoilt man.'

G1354. Son of Zachary, *Thomas Babington Macaulay: The Shaping of the Historian*, John Clive, Secker and Warburg, *Obs*. 24 Jun. p 33

(1) This book, 'which is admirably through and scholarly, supplements, though it by no means supersedes, the biography by Sir George Trevelyan which is both a more readable book and a wiser one'. Disagrees with the author's view that Macaulay was an unhappy man.

G1355. The road to war, *1914: Delusion or Design?* ed. John Röhl, Elek, *Obs*. 29 Jul. p 32

(1) Finds the introduction more interesting than the documents, but feels that the editor 'presses his case too hard' on German aggressiveness.

G1356. *England und das Dritte Reich*, Vol. 1, Oswald Hauser, Stuttgart, Seewald, 1972, *EHR*. 88, 348. Jul. p 673

(1) An excellent but brief study, in which the author 'has turned up many treasures' from British archives.

G1357. Definite articles, *The Guardian Omnibus 1821–1971*, ed. David Ayerest, Collins, *Gdn*. 6 Aug. p 10

(1) The editor's 'purpose . . . has been entertainment of an intellectual kind rather than instruction. As an historian I would have liked more leaders.'

Repr. *Guardian Weekly*. 109, 6. 11 Aug. p 15

G1358. Sitting down with the Bolsheviks, *Anglo-Soviet Relations 1917–1921*, Vol. 3, Richard H. Ullman, Oxford U.P., *Obs*. 12 Aug. p 31

(1) 'A marvellous story and a marvellous book'. The author 'is a historian of the first rank – brilliant

in description, assiduous in research. I cannot recall any historical work that I have enjoyed more or from which I have learnt so much.'

G1359. End or beginning? *Europe Since 1870*, James Joll, Weidenfeld and Nicolson, *TLS*. 72, 3729. 24 Aug. p 968

(1) Praises it, especially on the author's treatment of thought and culture.

G1360. Reaching for Russia, (a) *German Strategy Against Russia 1939–41*, Barry A. Leach, Oxford U.P.; (b) *Codeword Barbarossa*, Barton Whaley, MIT., *Obs*. 26 Aug. p 30

(a1) Praises it warmly as a good book, which carefully reassesses the role of Hitler and the generals in the invasion of Russia.

(b1) 'Right or wrong, the book makes a fascinating detective story.'

G1361. After Appeasement *1939: The Making Of The Second World War*, Sidney Aster, Deutsch, *Obs*. 2 Sept. p 35

(1) It 'presents a competent, though by no means novel, picture of British policy in the six months before the outbreak of war'.

G1362. Monty's portrait, *A Field-Marshal In The Family*, Brian Montgomery, Constable, *Obs*. 30 Sept. p 39

(1) The author 'has done well'; 'he writes with a nice mixture of admiration and amused detachment . . . It adds up to an effective portrait of a great eccentric who turned his qualities to good account.'

G1363. Brown Studies, *Hitler*, Werner Maser, Allen Lane, *NS*. 86, 2228. 26 Oct. pp 609–10

(1) 'It is an attempt to dispel some of the legends. It is not a good book. Indeed it is almost unreadable and important only for the information that it contains.'

G1364. Sly, sir, devilish sly, *Baldwin*, H. Montgomery Hyde, Hart-Davis, MacGibbon, *Obs*. 4 Nov. p 38

(1) 'At last a true biographer has appeared . . . This is Baldwin as he really was.' The book 'is

readable, historically impeccable, and does not push Baldwin's virtues too hard'.

G1365. Kissinger fireworks, *A World Restored*, new edn. Henry A. Kissinger, Gollancz, *Obs.* 11 Nov. p 36

(1) 'As a contribution to historical knowledge or even understanding the book has few merits. What it has is a ceaseless explosion of ideas, some brilliant, some as banal as Metternich's own, some relevant to the historical period, some with no other purpose than to display the author's virtuosity.'

G1366. Horace and Percy, (a) *Sir Horace Rumbold*, Martin Gilbert, Heinemann; (b) *Professional Diplomat: Sir Percy Loraine 1880–1961*, Gordon Waterfield, Murray, *Obs.* 9 Dec. p 35

(1) 'Both these books are in their way rewarding, though more for the details than for great events . . . Both authors give vivid pictures of the old diplomacy. Things are said to be different nowadays.'

G1367. Books of the Year, *Obs.* 16 Dec. p 33

Praises *The Time Traveller* (*see above* G1352) and gives a 'warm welcome' to *The Good Soldier Svejk*, Jaroslav Hasek, Heinemann, 'now complete and unexpurgated'. 'No hesitation about the book I enjoyed most: *The Trial of Dr. Sacheverell* (G1342) . . . good history and rich entertainment'.

G1368. Momentous Indecision, (a) *Hitler's Strategy 1940–1941*, Martin van Crevald, Cambridge U.P.; (b) *Enemy At The Gates*, William Craig, Hodder and Stoughton, *Obs.* 23 Dec. p 23

(a1) 'The book explodes many myths . . . a most illuminating book'.

(b1) 'An excellent book for those who want to know what it felt like to live through the battle of Stalingrad rather than to understand what it was about.' This style of history is not to his taste.

1974

G1369. Genius or crank? *Fisher of Kilverstone*, Ruddock F. Mackay, Oxford U.P., *Obs.* 3 Feb. p 31

(1) The book puts the emphasis on his earlier

career and 'enables us to answer the question: what exactly did he do?'

G1370. The ins and outs of politics, *The Governing Passion*, A.B. Cooke and John Vincent, Hassocks, Harvester Press, *Obs.* 10 Feb. p 33

(1) The first part of the book is 'a wonderful intellectual performance which leaves the more humdrum historian out of breath and even out of sight', whereas the second part is 'meticulous scholarship for its own sake' which 'should satisfy anyone mistaken enough to be curious how Cabinets go on'.

G1371. Germany in the air, *The Rise And Fall Of The Luftwaffe*, David Irving, Weidenfeld and Nicolson, *Obs.* 10 Mar. p 33

(1) A scholarly biography of Erhard Milch, slanted towards the Luftwaffe.

G1372. Vision and crankiness, *Lord William Bentinck*, John Rosselli, Chatto and Windus and Sussex U.P., *Obs.* 7 Apr. p 36

(1) Well researched but he is critical of the construction of the book – a series of essays rather than chronological biography. 'Behind the double confusion of Bentinck and Rosselli there are fascinating ideas struggling to get out.'

G1373. Stalin the Terrible, (a) *Stalin As Revolutionary 1879–1929*, Robert C. Tucker, Chatto and Windus; (b) *Joseph Stalin: Man And Legend*, Ronald Hingley, Hutchinson; (c) *Stalin*, Adam B. Ulam, Allen Lane, *Obs.* 28 Apr. p 36

(1) 'I do not think biographers will get very far with Stalin if they regard all his ideas as cock-eyed, still less if they think he was driven on by a lust for power. It makes matters worse when all three biographers are loyally, even if unconsciously fighting the Cold War . . . ' (a) is a 'Pscho-history' – A.J.P.T. is very critical of this approach to history. (b) The idea of examining myths becomes tedious before long. (c) is the best informed but it suffers from 'inner think', the author deciding what people 'must have thought'. 'This is all right for a novelist,

as Koestler has shown. In my opinion it is not a sound historical method.'

G1374. *The Smallest Slavonic Nation*, Gerald Stone, Athlone Press, 1972, *EHR*. 89, 351. Apr. p 472

(1) A detailed examination of the Serbs of Lusatia.

G1375. All honourable men, *Maundy Gregory*, Tom Cullen, Bodley Head, *Obs*. 12 May. p 37

(1) 'Gregory provided a great deal of pleasure even if it was not always innocent. Tom Cullen has done him proud.'

G1376. A great committee man, *Hankey, Man of Secrets*, Vol. 3, Stephen Roskill, Collins, *Obs*. 26 May. p 32

(1) As with the first volume, Hankey is back at the centre of the stage. Roskill is 'sympathetic towards Hankey without concealing his faults'.

G1377. Grand strategy, *A Day's March Nearer Home*, Roger Parkinson, Hart-Davis, MacGibbon, *Obs*. 9 Jun. p 35

(1) 'Reading it is like trying to eat a steak-and-kidney pie that has never been near the oven. The meat, though excellent in quality, is highly indigestible.'

G1378. Talleyrand's Cut, *Talleyrand: The Art of Survival*, Jean Orieux, New York, Knopf, *NYRB*. 21, 10. 13 Jun. pp 15–6

(1) It 'is in the worst style of French writing – rhapsodical disorderly, overblown, more a cheap romantic novel than a work of history'.

(2) 'There was little skill or originality in Talleyrand's policy: he did what he was told and pocketed his percentage.'

G1379. One man's monument, *The Buildings of England:* (a) *Oxfordshire*, Jennifer Sherwood and Nikolaus Pevsner; (b) *Staffordshire*, Nikolaus Pevsner, Harmondsworth, Penguin, *Obs*. 30 Jun. p 32

(1) 'The present volumes are unique, miracles of scholarship and presentation, and an honour to our miserable century . . . Using the volumes is a life's work in itself, and no lifetime could be better spent.'

G1380. An unsuccessful story, *A Good Innings*, ed. Alan Clark, Murray, *Obs*. 14 Jul. p 33

(1) The editor has skilfully cut down for general reading Lord Lee of Fareham's 'interminable biography'.

(2) 'He was a man doomed not to succeed ... Lee was too sharp, too assertive ... He thought politicians liked him when they only found him tiresome.'

G1381. His finest hours, (a) *Winston Churchill*, Henry Pelling, Macmillan; (b) *Churchill At War*, Vol. 1, Patrick Cosgrave, Collins, *Obs*. 28 Jul. p 27

(a1) 'His book is a considerable achievement, the first substantial biography of Churchill in a single volume ... The tone is prim.' Regrets that the author does not speculate over many puzzling issues in Churchill's career or fully expose his mistakes.

(b1) A book 'somewhat overladen with detail'. It contains interesting material but does not outdo Ronald Lewin's book as a study of Churchill as warlord.

G1382. *Deutsche Russland politik*, Barbara Vogel, Düsseldorf, Bertelsmann, 1973, *EHR*. 89, 352. Jul. p 687

(1) In the same mould as the work of Eckhart Kehr – but like him, the author 'is driven to confess ... that diplomacy was more important than economics or class' in Bulow's policy.

G1383. A socialist saint, *R.H. Tawney And His Times*, Ross Terrill, Deutsch, *Obs*. 18 Aug. p 28

(1) Commends the author's decision to write of Tawney's ideas rather than of his life, but regrets that there is not more about him as an historian.

G1384. Four sides of Robespierre, *The Life And Opinions of Maximilian Robespierre*, Norman Hampson, Duckworth, *Obs*. 1 Sept. p 26

(1) Dislikes the author's method of giving four views of Robespierre's actions. 'Despite these extraordinary passages, much of the book is great fun, and some of it contains useful information about Robespierre.'

G1385. Operation Market Garden, *A Bridge Too Far*, Cornelius Ryan, Hamilton, *Obs.* 15 Sept. p 29

(1) 'The story is presented with absolute mastery of the situation. It is dramatic and clear at the same time.'

G1386. The man in the red shirt, *Garibaldi*, Jasper Ridley, Constable, *Obs.* 20 Oct. p 32

(1) The author has provided the first full biography of him in English. It is too long and at times a little dull. 'But the general effect is overwhelming. Here is the portrait of a romantic hero who was also an intensely human practical man.'

G1387. Manchesterismus, *Engels*, *Manchester and the Working Class*, Steven Marcus, Weidenfeld and Nicolson, *TLS*. 3790. 25 Oct. p 1181

(1) 'His book is a remarkable work of literary criticism with history brought in by a side wind.' Though the author is 'less convincing when he writes of Engels as a man'.

(2) 'It is hardly an exaggeration to say that Marxism was born in the slums of Manchester . . . What he (Engels) saw provided Marx with the material that consolidated his theories.'

G1388. Edward the Abdicator, (a) *Edward VIII*, Frances Donaldson, Weidenfeld and Nicolson; (b) *The Women He Loved*, Ralph G. Martin, W.H. Allen; (c) *The Royal House of Windsor*, Elizabeth Longford, Weidenfeld and Nicolson, *Obs.* 27 Oct. p 30

(a1) 'A serious study of a complex character . . . a convincing picture of a lost soul.'

(b1) It contains conversations with the Duchess of Windsor; otherwise it 'covers only well-trodden ground'.

G1389. *ID*, 7th Ser., 8, (Sep 1929-Apr 1930), ed. Giampiero Carocci, 1972, *EHR*. 89, 353. Oct. p 931

(1) Finds Grandi's account of the London naval conferences to be very funny.

(2) 'Mussolini was not interested in building ships; he was interested in causing a sensation, and intransigence was the best means of doing so.'

G1390. *Der Krieg der 'Achsenmächte' im Mittelmeerraum*, Walter B.E. Weichold, Göttingen, Musterschmidt, 1973, *Ibid.* pp 935–6

(1) A general account of the war in the Mediterranean from the German point of view.

G1391. The man from nowhere, *Poor Dear Brendan*, Andrew Boyle, Hutchinson, *Obs.* 3 Nov. p 33

(1) 'A book of irresistible fascination', on Brendan Bracken.

G1392. Bronze Goddess, *The Ultra Secret*, F.W. Winterbotham, Weidenfeld and Nicolson, *NS.* 88, 2278. 15 Nov. pp 703–4

(1) Finds it an interesting and important account but has many reservations about its accuracy. He feels the claims for the importance of Ultra are very much exaggerated: 'Ultra certainly contributed something against the enemy. This is very different from saying that it won the war or even much affected the war's course.'

G1393. Mr. High Mind's Party, *Edwardian Radicalism*, ed. A.J.A. Morris, Routledge, *NS.* 88, 2280. 29 Nov. pp 782

(1) Observes that the volume does not deal with the radical leader, Lloyd George, after 1905, and, with disbelief, 'We have almost got to the point of believing that, had it not been for the war, Radicalism or 'Progressivism' would have eclipsed the Labour Party.'

G1394. Naval affairs, *From The Dardanelles To Oran*, Arthur J. Marder, Oxford U.P., *Obs.* 1 Dec. p 34

(1) Praises the author's past work and observes that this volume is 'modest in size though not in accomplishment'.

G1395. Delusions of Grandeur, *Independence And Deterrence*, 2 Vols. Margaret Gowing, Macmillan, *New Scientist.* 64, 926. 5 Dec. p 761

(1) 'It is impeccably honest and ruthlessly frank . . . Mrs. Gowing has every gift, presenting political decisions, scientific technicalities and bureaucratic entanglements with equal grace.'

G1396. I remember, I remember, (A.J.P.T.'s contribution to this feature on the childrens' books 'that made the deepest impression ... in childhood'), *TLS*. 3796. 6 Dec. p 1370

He names John Bunyan's *Pilgrim's Progress*: 'I had it read to me before I could read. When I could, I read it again and again. I skipped the conversations. One of the greatest books in the world and the most subversive.' He also nominates the works of G.A. Henty, picking out *A Roving Commission* (1899) as the best of them: 'very frightening and full of colour'. He also makes 'a shameful confession' – 'I adored *The Secret Garden*. Now a few sentences of it are enough to turn my stomach.' (*The Secret Garden*, Frances Eliza Hodgson Burnett, 1911)

G1397. Books of the Year, *Obs*. 15 Dec. p 19

Praises *A Bridge Too Far* (*see above* G1385), 'the best account of a battle ever written'; *Poor Dear Brendan* (G1391), 'a brilliant reconstruction of an enigmatic figure'; and *Independence And Deterrence* (G1395), 'ought to be a best seller'.

G1398. Sad soldier, *Chief of Staff: Diaries of Lieutenant-General Sir Henry Pownall*, Vol. 2, ed. Brian Bond, Cooper, *Obs*. 15 Dec. p 27

G1399. Maker of universities, *Portrait of Haldane*, Eric Ashby and Mary Anderson, Macmillan, *Obs*. 22 Dec. p 22

(1) 'Haldane inspired the modern universities and can claim to have been the Father of many of them ... This new book by two distinguished educationists does him justice for the first time.'

1975

G1400. Battles long ago, *Ireland In The War Years 1937–1945*, Joseph T. Carroll, David and Charles, *Obs*. 19 Jan. p 29

(1) An account based on British official papers.

G1401. Strangers, *East End Jewish Radicals 1875–1914*,

W.J. Fishman, Duckworth, *NS*. 89, 2289. 31 Jan. pp 149–50

(1) The author 'has brilliantly chronicled the heroes 'of the struggles of the poor East End Jews for better conditions.

G1402. *Czechoslovakia Before Munich*, J.W. Bruegel, Cambridge U.P., 1973, *EHR*. 90, 354. Jan. pp 234–5

(1) Critical of many of the interpretations in the book.

G1403. *War And Society*, ed. M.R.D. Foot, Elek, 1973, *Hist*. 60, 198. Feb. p 85

(1) 'A most interesting volume' of essays. He doubts R.A.C. Parker's interpretation of the attitudes of Chamberlain and Halifax in the run up to the outbreak of war in 1939.

G1404. *Haig As Military Commander*, Sir James Marshall-Cornwall, Batsford, 1973, *Ibid*. p 149

(1) Feels it is a 'reasonably impartial attempt' to assess Haig's qualities and is good in explaining Haig's rise in 1915; but is uncritical on other issues.

G1405. Everything stopped, *The General Strike*, Patrick Renshaw, Weidenfeld and Nicolson, *Obs*. 9 Mar. p 30

(1) A favourable review, which notes that it is 'a history going back to the beginnings of the coal industry and strongly reinforced by the Cabinet records'.

G1406. The infantry will advance, (a) *The Art Of War*, William McElwee, Weidenfeld and Nicolson; (b) *Too Serious A Business*, Donald Cameron Watt, Temple Smith, *Obs*. 16 Mar. p 29

(a1) 'I have enjoyed his book as a great intellectual pleasure.'

(b1) A study of military history during the run-up to the Second World War, 'providing incidentally the closest study yet made of British military policy and ideas in the pre-war years'.

(b2) 'In my opinion the Second World War was a struggle for mastery or survival with Fascism or anti-Fascism thrown in as top-dressing.'

G1407. Labour's Moses, *Keir Hardie*, Kenneth O. Morgan, Weidenfeld and Nicolson, *Obs.* 23 Mar. p 30

(1) It 'is deeply sympathetic, impeccably scholarly and beautifully written. It brings out the complexity of Hardie and the full range of his interests.'

(2) 'Keir Hardie created the British Labour Party and determined its character – an alliance between trade unions and political radicals, with a leaven of well-meaning careerists . . . His socialism derived more from Carlyle and Ruskin than from Marx.'

G1408. Franz Fischer and His School, *Deutschland in der Weltpolitik des 19 and 20 Jahrhunderts*, eds. Immanuel Geiss and Bernd Jurgen Wendt, Düsseldorf, Bertelsmann U.P., 1973, *JMH.* 47, 1. Mar. pp 120–4

(1) 'An interesting collection'; and observes that it is one of the rare cases 'where the contributors and the man honoured share the same outlook'.

(2) 'Broadly speaking, Fischer has won – perhaps more than he deserved to.' Calls for English speaking historians to reassess the Cold War.

G1409. Mosley's Mis-spent Talents, *Oswald Mosley*, Robert Skidelsky, Macmillan, *Obs.* 6 Apr. p 23

(1) He feels that the British Fascist leader 'is worth at least one (biography), particularly when it is as thorough and critical as Robert Skidelsky's'.

(2) 'Mosley likes to think of himself as a Modern Man. In reality he is the last of the Romantics, intoxicated like them with words. Action is for him the most beautiful of words.'

G1410. Edward the tele-star, (a) *Edward The Seventh*, Dennis Judd, Futura; (b) *Edward VII: Prince of Hearts*, David Butler, Weidenfeld and Nicolson; (c) *Edward The Rake*, John Pearson, Weidenfeld and Nicolson; (d) *The King, The Press And The People*, Kinley Roby, Barrie and Jenkins; (e) *Uncle of Europe*, Gordon Brook-Shepherd, Collins, *Obs.* 13 Apr. p 30

(a1) 'A straight picture'.

(b1) It 'puts the authentic anecdotes into dialogue and adds some imaginary ones. I do not like this mixing of fact and fiction.'

(c1) 'In its short compass it has all the good stories, succinctly told.'

(d1) His book 'comes from the popular Press of the time and especially from the satirical verse . . . '

(e1) It deals with 'Edward the International statesman and diplomatist . . . The underlying argument of the book, that Edward's doings were of real importance, is not to my mind convincing.'

G1411. Up The Greasy Pole, *The Prime Ministers*, Vol. 2, ed. Herbert Van Thal, Allen and Unwin, *NS*. 89, 2301. 25 Apr. pp 554–5

(1) Comments on the wide range of treatment and regrets that the writers of the essays do not explain how the men got there or deal with party management.

G1412. The bubble reputation, (a) *Mark Sykes*, Roger Adelson, Cape; (b) *Goughie: The Life of General Sir Hubert Gough*, Anthony Farrar-Hockley, Hart-Davis, MacGibbon, *Obs*. 4 May. p 28

G1413. Under German rule, (a) *The German Occupation of the Channel Islands*, Charles Cruickshank, Oxford U.P.; (b) *The Giant-Killers*, John Oram Thomas, Joseph, *Obs*. 11 May. p 30

(b1) 'The Danish resistance had a record second to none' and the author has told the story 'in a vivid, if somewhat anecdotal way'.

G1414. Death of a President, *FDR's Last Year*, Jim Bishop, Hart-Davis, MacGibbon, *Obs*. 18 May. p 30

(1) 'A blow-by-blow account of Roosevelt's last year'.

G1415. On the Eastern Front, *The Road To Stalingrad*, Vol. 1, John Erickson, Weidenfeld and Nicolson, *Obs*. 1 Jun. p 23

(1) He 'has written the outstanding book on the Soviet war in any language'; though he 'is less enlightened in regard to Soviet policy. I find no difficulty, as he does, in understanding Stalin's insist-

ance throughout the war that Soviet Russia intended to recover at least its 1941 frontiers.'

G1416. Churchill in World War I, *Winston S. Churchill*, Vol. 4, Martin Gilbert, Heinemann, *Obs.* 8 Jun. p 25

(1) He 'has done very well to get all the twists in this stage of Churchill's career into a single volume, even if a very long one'.

G1417. The Anglo-German Naval Agreement, *Treaty-Breakers Or 'Realpolitiker'*, Eva H. Haraszti, Budapest, Boldt, 1974, *New Hungarian Quarterly*. 16, 58. Summer. pp 160–1

(1) 'A beautiful exercise in diplomatic history, systematic research and careful thinking'. A.J.P.T. differs in interpretation on a few points.

G1418. Yours truly, Winston, *Roosevelt and Churchill*, ed. Francis L. Loewenheim, Harold D. Langley and Manfred Jones, Barrie and Jenkins, *Obs.* 13 Jul. p 23

(1) Not much new.

(2) 'This was a curious relationship of two men who never really found common ground–except in their determination to win the war.'

G1419. Party to remember, *Nonconformity In Modern British Politics*, Stephen Koss, Batsford, *Obs.* 20 Jul. p 23

(1) 'This is a fascinating story . . . He tells it brilliantly, combining understanding, wit and profound scholarship . . . Koss is an historian of the first rank, and this is his best book to date, no mean praise.'

G1420. The pursuit of power, *The Impact of Hitler*, Maurice Cowling, Cambridge U.P., *Obs.* 27 Jul. p 23

(1) Very critical of the author's approach to the study of political history. 'The results are ingenious and dazzlingly clever. They are also, I think, wrongheaded. In particular I doubt the assumption that evidence is important merely because it is written down.'

G1421. *Friedensinitiativen und Machtpolitik im Zweiten Weltkrieg 1939–1942*, Bernd Martin, Düsseldorf,

Droste, 1974, *EHR*. 90, 356. Jul. pp 620–3

(1) Contains 'information of considerable interest' and 'stimulating if wrong-headed ideas'.

G1422. *I Sudeti e l'autodeterminazione 1918–1933*, Francesco Leoncini, Padua, Ceseo-Centro Studi Europa Orientale, 1973, *Ibid*. p 683

G1423. *Winston Churchill And The German Question In British Foreign Policy 1918–1922*, Donald Graeme Boadle, The Hague, Nijhoff, 1974, *Ibid*. pp 684–5

(1) 'A penetrating and original account' of Churchill's attempts to restore the Balance of Power in Europe.

G1424. *Das Ende des Appeasement*, Julian Campbell Doherty, Berlin, Colloquium, 1973, *Ibid*. p 689

(1) Critical of the author's judgments on Chamberlain and Halifax.

G1425. Wrapping up the war, *The Second World War*, Henri Michel, Deutsch, *Obs*. 24 Aug. p 21

(1) 'It has no rival and is unlikely ever to have any.' However there is too much emphasis on France and too little attention to the Far East and to Russia's role.

G1426. Warfare to welfare, *The Road To 1945*, Paul Addison, Cape, *Obs*. 19 Oct. p 27

(1) It meets magnificently the need for a study of British politics at the top in the Second World War. 'It tells with wit, scholarship and imagination how the British people entered the Promised Land – or seemed to.'

G1427. The unknown war, *The Eastern Front 1914–1917*, Norman Stone, Hodder and Stoughton, *Obs*. 26 Oct. p 31

(1) 'Now, at last, we have a book which tells the real story, the first such book ever published in Western language . . . Its scholarship, its penetration and impartiality are beyond reproach.'

G1428. The bourgeois boom, *The Age of Capital 1848–1875*, E.J. Hobsbawm, Weidenfeld and Nicolson, *Obs*. 23 Nov. p 31

(1) A 'brilliant and wide ranging book'.

G1429. Rattling typewriter, *The First Casualty*, Philip

Knightley, Deutsch, *Obs.* 9 Nov. p 27

(1) 'Despite the evidence that Knightley has assembled so powerfully and so entertainingly, I suspect that we have to look elsewhere for those who deceived the public in war time – or in peace time for that matter.'

G1430. The elephant's child, *The Diaries Of A Cabinet Minister*, Vol. 1, Richard Crossman, Hamilton and Cape, *Obs.* 7 Dec. p 31

(1) 'He tried very hard to write an important diary but I am afraid it is not in the Pepys class.'

(2) 'He was a very clever man and a powerful writer. His very cleverness made him impatient of others, a good talker and a bad listener. He ran from one intellectual scent to another like a fox terrier out for a walk.'

G1431. Books of the Year, *Obs.* 14 Dec. p 19

Praises *The Eastern Front* (*see above* G1427), *The Road To Stalingrad*, Vol. 1 (G1415) and *The Later Cecils*, Kenneth Rose, Weidenfeld, 'a collective biography, full of delights'. 'For me the best detective story of the year was *The Treasure of Auchinleck*, David Buchanan, Heinemann, perhaps a special taste.' Also praises *Yesterday's Spy*, Len Deighton, Cape: it 'will give pleasure to all veterans of political warfare'.

G1432. Dizzy prospects, *Disraeli's Reminiscences*, ed. Helen M. Swartz and Marvin Swartz, Hamilton, *Obs.* 21 Dec. p 23

(1) 'There is rich perfume in the jottings Disraeli made in the 1860's ... A few are genuine reminiscences ... Most are casual anecdotes ... Few other Prime Ministers could have written them and none would have had the impudence to do so.'

1976

G1433. Muddling through, *The British Campaign In Ireland 1919–1921*, Charles Townshend, Oxford U.P., *Obs.* 11 Jan. p 21

(1) 'A masterpiece of historical scholarship and

understanding. I have rarely read a book that gave me greater intellectual pleasure.'

(2) 'It is tempting to say that British policy during the Anglo-Irish war created the Irish nation.'

G1434. Rebel in search of a cause, *Lloyd George*, Peter Rowland, Barrie and Jenkins, *Obs*. 25 Jan. p 30

(1) 'A substantial work of political biography . . . ' A great improvement on previous full length biographies; but he is critical of the author for being too ready to believe some of the darker stories of Lloyd George's private life and suggests that he underrates Lloyd George's achievements at the Paris Peace Conference.

G1435. Operation Muddle, (a) *Operation Menace*, Arthur Marder, Oxford U.P.; *The Guns of Dakar*, John Williams, Heinemann, *Obs*. 8 Feb. p 27

(a1) 'As usual with his books, one feels this is the last word on the subject.'

(b1) 'Slighter and less austere'.

G1436. *Essays In Honour Of E.H. Carr*, ed. Chimen Abramsky, Macmillan, 1974, *Hist*. 61, 201. Feb. p 69

(1) Observes that unlike Carr's writings the essays are hard to understand because of their professional jargon. Disagrees with D.C. Watt's views on the Nazi-Soviet Pact.

G1437. *Stalin Und Hitler*, Sven Allard, Bern, Francke, 1974, *Ibid*. p 145

(1) Unfavourable to it; observing that it is based almost exclusively on non-Soviet sources and contains neither new information or a new interpretation.

G1437a Catch – 22 in the days of Munich. '*Appeasement*' *and the English Speaking World*, Ritchie Ovendale, Wales U.P., *TLS*. 3860. 5 Mar. p 256

(1) A book of considerable value.

G1438. Supreme commander, *Stalin As Warlord*, Albert Seaton, Batsford, *Obs*. 14 Mar. p 31

(1) 'His book is rigidly technical: an essay in military history, not a personal biography. But the personality comes through as well.'

(2) 'Measured by achievement, Stalin was the greatest of all military leaders. He commanded the largest armies; his was the most decisive of victories.'

G1439. Tell It Again, *A Man Called Intrepid*, William Stevenson, Macmillan, *NS*. 91, 2349. 26 Mar. pp 407–8

(1) Most of the content 'is either exaggerated, distorted, or already known'.

G1440. Too clever by half? *Canning*, Peter Dixon, Weidenfeld and Nicolson, *Obs*. 4 Apr. p 27

(1) He 'tells the story admirably', using new sources and handling well the political complexities of the time.

(2) 'He was the greatest orator of the age after the deaths of Pitt and Fox. He was a dynamic statesman of infinite courage and resource.'

G1441. Good plain cook? *Montgomery Of Alamein*, Alun Chalfont, Weidenfeld and Nicolson, *Obs*. 11 Apr. p 33

(1) The author has done his best to find out what made Montgomery tick, but 'there is really not much to find,out'.

G1442. Marx's better half, *The Life of Friedrich Engels*, 2 Vols. W.O. Henderson, Cass, *Obs*. 25 Apr. p 27

(1) 'His biography is very much a DIY (Do It Yourself) biography. The evidence . . . is exhaustively marshalled. Few conclusions are drawn and there is none of the psychological penetration shown in the exciting book on Engels and Manchester by Stephen Marcus.'

(2) 'Though he had talent where Marx had genius – Huxley to Mark's Darwin – he often formulated Marxist concepts clearly before Marx did.'

G1442a Boyish Masters. *A Matter of Honour*. Philip Mason, New York, Holt, Rinehart and Winston. *NYRB*, 23, 7. 29 Apr. p 43

(1) 'His book is written with affection as well as with scholarship, yet he does justice to the forces that brought the empire to an end.'

G1443. *Hitler and his Generals*, Harold C. Deutsch, Minneapolis U.P., 1974, *EHR*. 91, 359. Apr. pp 463–4

(1) It contains many new details. The 1938 conspiracy against Hitler was not as important as the author claims.

G1444. *France and Belgium 1939–1940*, Brian Bond, Davis-Poynter, 1975, *Ibid*. p 467

(1) Scholarly and informative; a more accurate title would be 'The British Campaign in France and Belgium'.

G1445. *Dieci Giugno 1940*, Ugoberti Alfassio Grimaldi and Gherardo Bozzetti, Bari, Laterza, 1974, *Ibid*. p 468

(1) Good reading – 'an exercise in the Higher Journalism'.

G1446. Let's call it quits? *The General Strike*, G.A. Philips, Weidenfeld and Nicolson, *Obs*. 9 May. p 27

(1) 'A first-rate piece of history, not at all exciting or sensational, but level-headed, sanc and above all, realistic . . . As a humble combatant in the General Strike of 1926, I think that Philips has got things about right.'

G1447. Barbarians are human, *Special Envoy To Churchill And Stalin*, W. Averell Harriman and Elie Abel, Hutchinson, *Obs*. 30 May. p 25

(1) 'If the book had appeared 30 or even 20 years ago it would have created a sensation and provided invaluable material for historians.' Now 'the merit of the book lies in the personal descriptions of the great leaders'.

G1448. 1000 years of war, *War In European History*, Michael Howard, Oxford U.P., *Obs*. 27 Jun. p 22

(1) 'Written with all his usual skill and in its small compass is perhaps the most original book he has written'.

G1449. *The Mythical World of Nazi War Propaganda 1939–45*, Jay W. Baird, Oxford U.P., 1975, *Hist*. 61, 202. Jun. p 323

(1) 'This is an interesting book though Baird makes rather much of his discoveries'.

G1450. An ocean of troubles, *Naval Policy Between The Wars*, Vol. 2, Stephen Roskill, Collins, *Obs*. 4 Jul. p 23

(1) 'Much of this narrative, with its technical details . . . is inevitably heavy going. But Roskill refreshes the reader with many personal touches, usually favourable to the admirals and less so to politicians.' He has 'gone far to set the record straight'.

G1451. Churchillian chit-chat, *Churchill And Morton*, R.W. Thompson, Hodder and Stoughton, *Obs*. 25 Jul. p 21

(1) Morton's letters 'are enjoyable to read, often rambling over themes far removed from Churchill . . . They are disappointing as sources of serious information.'

G1451a The Great Pretender. *Mussolini's Roman Empire*, Denis Mack Smith, New York, Viking. *NYRB*, 23, 13, 5 Aug., pp 3–4

(1) 'His book is admirable as entertainment'. However A.J.P.T. complains of the excessive number of references given and that there is 'little attempt to set Mussolini within the framework of his time.'

(2) 'Mussolini had one considerable gift: he was a forceful genius, and all his genius went into words. Fascism itself was a work of propaganda, not a serious program.'

G1452. Defending counsels, *Grand Strategy*, Vol. 1, N.H. Gibbs, H.M.S.O., *Obs*. 8 Aug. p 22

(1) 'Maybe there is nothing strikingly novel in the book, but defence policy has never been treated before as a single story . . . The theme is rearmament, not strategy . . . '

G1453. Any good Germans? *British Labour And Hitler's War*, T.D. Burridge, Deutsch, *Obs*. 15 Aug. p 20

(1) Much information in it, but it is 'rather on the pedestrian side, enlivening the drab Cabinet records only with passages from Dalton's diary'.

G1454. Soft-nosed Torpedo, *Asquith*, Stephen Koss, Allen

Lane, *NS*. 92, 2372. 3 Sept. p 310

(1) 'The best biography of Asquith yet to be written and a book indispensable to every lover of political history'.

(2) 'He remained complacent to the end. This had always been his great fault and also his great virtue.'

G1455. Funny old chentleman, *Edward VII*, Christopher Hibbert, Allen Lane, *Obs*. 19 Sept. p 27

(1) Favourable, in that the author 'leaves the story to tell itself' and that 'there is no nonsense about Edward being a great diplomat or even a great lover'.

G1456. More snakes than ladders, *Winston S. Churchill*, Vol. 5, Martin Gilbert, Heinemann, *Obs*. 24 Oct. p 31

(1) Praises the author's thoroughness on primary material and his putting 'the record right' on many questions. But regrets that the author does not take more account of recent interpretations of key issues, that he sees 'everything from Churchill's point of view', and that the book is so long.

G1457. *British Policy Towards Wartime Resistance in Yugoslavia and Greece*, ed. Phyllis Auty and Richard Clogg, Macmillan, 1975, *EHR*. 91, 361. Oct. p 939

(1) A fascinating collection of papers from a conference held in London.

G1458. People's forum, *Trafalgar Square: Emblem of Empire*, Rodney Mace, Lawrence and Wishart, *Obs*. 7 Nov. p 26

(1) Written with 'a delightful mixture of scholarship and wit'.

G1459. The Western Question, *The Origins Of The Morocco Question 1880–1900*, F.V. Parsons, Duckworth, *TLS*. 3898. 26 Nov. p 1477

(1) 'The most scholarly and thorough work of diplomatic history I've ever read'. Though he observes that it is excessively long and on a relatively minor subject.

G1460. Nothing to declare, *Footprints In Time*, John Colville, Collins, *Obs.* 28 Nov. p 31

(1) Observes that the author has 'remained inhibited or at any rate discreet'. There are some enjoyable anecdotes, but little on important matters.

G1461. Books of the Year, *Obs.* 12 Dec. p 26

Praises *The British Campaign In Ireland 1919–1921* (*see above* G1433) and *The Eastern Front* (G1427). 'The most enchanting book of the year, or any year, was *The Autobiography Of Arthur Ransome*, Cape, a fitting conclusion to his long run of masterpieces.'

G1462. Trenchard's obsession, *British Air Policy Between The Wars 1918–1939*, H. Montgomery Hyde, Heinemann, *Obs.* 12 Dec. p 28

(1) 'His book is dedicated to the memory of Lord Trenchard. But, being a good scholar, he unwillingly demonstrates that Trenchard had every virtue except that he was wrong.' Suggests that it should have been dedicated to Sir Thomas Inskip.

G1463. The way of the world, *The Hutchinson History Of The World*, J.M. Roberts, Hutchinson, *Obs.* 19 Dec. p 22

(1) 'A stupendous achievement . . . the unrivalled World History of our day'. The author is an impeccable scholar and a wise human being'. Disagrees with the author's views on space travel – 'To my mind it is conclusive evidence that men have taken leave of sense and are hell-bent on their own destruction.'

1977

G1464. Reputations Revisited, *TLS*. 3906. 21 Jan. p 67

Nominates as overrated Arnold Toynbee's *A Study of History* 'which is neither History nor a study but a vast miscellany of information, much like Burton's *Anatomy of Melancholy* though not so funny'. Nominates as the most underrated book the Authorised Version of the *Bible*: 'If all knowledge of the A.V. is lost much of classic English literature will be incomprehensible and English prose style is doomed.'

G1465. A Crossman of the 1830s, *The Holland House Diaries 1831–1840*, ed. Abraham D. Kriegel, Routledge, *Obs.* 23 Jan. p 26

(1) 'No other political diaries contain so complete an account of politics on the inside over so long a period . . . they are a remarkable addition to the general picture of how Cabinets work.'

G1466. *The Politics of Re-Appraisal*, ed. Gillian Peele and Chris Cook, Macmillan, 1975, *EHR*. 92, 362. Jan. p 227

(1) Praises the essays, but observes that 'the ostensible theme runs a bit thin'.

G1467. *British Public Opinion and the Abyssinian War 1935–6*, Daniel Waley, Temple Smith, 1975, *Ibid.* pp 229–30

(1) An admirable study of the topic.

(2) 'The peace ballot provided, as it were, the answer to the Abyssinian problem before it was even raised: all sanctions short of war.' Recalls his own role at a protest meeting at the time.

G1468. Overture to war, (a) *The Last European War September 1939-December 1941*, John Lukacs, Routledge; (b) *The Crucial Years 1939–1941*, Hanson W. Baldwin, Weidenfeld and Nicolson, *Obs.* 6 Feb. p 31

(a1) Observes that the author presents a conventional account of military events but is more valuable on the life of the people, where he alleges that the idea of 'the People's War' is a myth.

(b1) A competent account, 'adding nothing to the history . . . by Liddell Hart'; marred by some out-of-date views.

G1469. Imperial Germany's Jewish Banker, *Gold And Iron*, Fritz Stern, New York, Knopf, *NYRB*. 24, 2. 17 Feb. pp 14–5

(1) 'A book of great interest and often of great importance'.

G1470. *The Historian And Film*, ed. Paul Smith, Cambridge

U.P., 1976, *Hist.* 62, 204. Feb. pp 74–5

(1) The essays 'give some welcome guidance' but they 'are written in a professional jargon which should be translated'.

(2) Doubts 'whether the evidence we extract from the films is worth all the labour involved' and is even more worried as to how the film evidence is used.

G1471. Labour's lost leader, *Ramsay MacDonald*, David Marquand, Cape, *Obs.* 6 Mar. p 24

(1) 'A first rate biography, the best . . . of any Prime Minister between the wars'. MacDonald receives 'full and fair treatment'.

(2) 'Far more than Gladstone he was inebriated by the exuberance of his own verbosity. Gladstone often stopped to think; MacDonald never did so. Words came easily to him; ideas were not his concern.'

G1472. Drafting the world's future, *The Historian as Diplomat*, P.A. Reynolds and E.J. Hughes, Robertson, *TLS.* 3915. 25 Mar. p 343

(1) Most of the book is made up of excerpts from C.K. Webster's diary kept during the drafting of the UN's Charter.

G1473. Rational Martyr, *The Riddle of Erskine Childers*, Andrew Boyle, Hutchinson, *NS.* 93, 2403. 8 Apr. pp 467–8

(1) He 'has at last done justice to Erskine Childers even if he has not wholly solved the riddle'.

G1474. Who Shot Aunt Sally? *The Politics Of Deference*, David Cresap Moore, New York, Barnes and Noble, *NYRB.* 24, 6. 14 Apr. pp 36–7

(1) Valuable information in it. 'But his method of exposition is deplorable'. Observes that the methods of sociology do not take sufficient account of things changing with time.

G1475. The Martyr of Irredentism, *The Hanging Of Wilhelm Oberdank*, Alfred Alexander, London Magazine Editions, *TLS.* 3918, 15 Apr. p 456

(1) A very good book – 'dispassionate, critical and accurate'.

(2) Condemns Italy's claims to the Trentino and Trieste. 'Trieste was never Italian until the twentieth century despite Mr. Alexander's statement that the nationalists wished to 'recover' it.'

G1476. Hitler in a void, *Adolf Hitler*, John Toland, New York, Doubleday, *Obs.* 24 Apr. p 25

(1) Condemns the size of the book and observes that it 'contains little new information of any significance'.

G1477. Revolution that never was, *The British Revolution*, Vol. 2, Robert Rhodes James, Hamilton, *Obs.* 1 May. p 24

(1) 'This is a staid account of British politics ... It is agreeably written ... and there are many entertaining anecdotes to refresh the reader. But it is all very much on the surface.'

G1478. What went wrong? *Radical Joe: A Life Of Joseph Chamberlain*, Dennis Judd, Hamilton, *Obs.* 15 May. p 28

(1) 'An admirable biography, wise, accurate and penetrating'.

(2) Chamberlain was 'a democrat who was also a tyrant, a champion of the poor who lived in lavish style'. Tariff reform: 'This campaign was not Radical; it was a precursor of Fascism. Chamberlain used every Fascist impulse, including anti-semitism.'

G1479. Pen pals at war, *Roosevelt And Churchill 1939–1941*, Joseph P. Lash, Deutsch, *Obs.* 22 May. p 29

(1) A very good book, 'written with high journalistic skill of narration'. Disagrees with the author's view that Roosevelt knew where he was going. 'It was not only American opinion that had to be converted; he had to be converted himself.'

G1480. The Uncrowned King, (a) *Charles Stewart Parnell*, F.S. Lyons, Collins; (b) *The English Face of Irish Nationalism*, Alan O'Day, Dublin, Gill and Macmillan, *NS.* 93, 2411. 3 Jun. pp 751–2

(a1) He 'tells Parnell's story with incomparable scholarship and literary grace. This is a classic biography which will be read as long as anyone cares about Irish history or for that matter about history at all.'

(b1) Praises its analysis of the Parnellites.

(2) Parnell 'tamed the men of violence as firmly as he dominated the Parliamentarians . . . His aim was an uncompromising independence, not a legislative adjustment of Irish administration.'

G1481. The Führer as Mohican, *Hitler's War*, David Irving, Hodder and Soughton, *Obs.* 12 Jun. p 25

(1) 'Most of the discoveries are not new . . . what is true is not new and what is new is either untrue or unimportant.' Dismisses the claim that Hitler did not know of the murder of the Jews as 'too silly to be worth arguing about'.

(2) Hitler 'was essentially a nullity, an empty man and the least interesting of all dictators the world has known . . . he was a bad man with no redeeming features'.

G1482. A one man band, (a) *The Making Of Lloyd George*, W.R.P. George, Faber; (b) *Bounder From Wales*, Don M. Cregier, Missouri U.P.; (c) *Lloyd George: The Goat In The Wilderness*, John Campbell, Cape, *Obs.* 19 Jun. p 28

(a1) An 'unassuming little book' on the family background.

(b1) It covers well trodden ground; it 'becomes more useful later on'. 'A lively book'.

(c1) 'An outstanding contribution to historical knowledge'; but the author 'has succumbed to Lloyd George's magic and blames everyone except Lloyd George' for his exclusion from office after 1922.

G1483. Still, That Is What Tom Liked, *Ruling Passions*, Tom Driberg, Cape, *NS.* 93, 2414. 24 Jun. pp 857–8

(1) 'It is, alas, incomplete'.

(2) He was 'the best newspaper diarist of his time'. 'With all his strange contradictions he was a character of almost saintly innocence.'

G1484. Reoccupational hazards, *The Rhineland Crisis*, J.T. Emmerson, Temple Smith, *TLS.* 3928. 24 Jun. p 748

(1) He 'has disentangled the diplomatic moves with great devotion to detail. He is perhaps inclined to exaggerate the qualities of Flandin . . . '

(2) 'In retrospect this seemed the turning point of inter-war history: the last occasion when Hitler could have been stopped without a general war . . . (The author) shows that this was not a case of missing the bus; there was no bus to miss.'

G1485. *In The Anglo-Arab Labyrinth*, Elie Kedourie, Cambridge U.P., 1976, *Hist.* 62, 205. Jun. p 283

(1) A 'splendid book' which carefully exposes the legend of McMahon's promise of the Arab lands of the Ottoman Empire to Husayn, Sharif of Mecca.

G1486. Very superior persons, *The First Fabians*, Norman and Jeanne MacKenzie, Weidenfeld and Nicolson, *Obs.* 3 Jul. p 24

(1) 'A delightful book', in which familiar material is brought together 'with wit and understanding'.

G1487. Baldwin's fall guy, *Sir Samuel Hoare*, J.A. Cross, Cape, *Obs.* 10 Jul. p 25

(1) 'A model of careful scholarship'. It includes the best account of the Hoare-Laval plan.

G1488. Its that man again, *The Psychopathic God*, Robert G.L. Waite, Basic Books, *Obs.* 17 Jul. p 29

(1) 'Hitler is placed firmly on the analyst's couch and pronounced a psychopath. The verdict precedes the analysis.' A.J.P.T. argues that nobody is completely 'normal' and observes that the author comes to realise that 'Hitler was a medium for German national emotion, not a lone operator'. The book 'seems to me to fly in the face of reason'.

G1489. The record of the Admiralty, *Naval Warfare in the Twentieth Century 1900–1945*, ed. Gerald Jordan, Croom Helm, *TLS*. 3933. 29 Jul. p 920

(1) The essays in this *festschrift* to Arthur Marder are 'a worthy tribute to one of the greatest historians of the age'. A.J.P.T. expresses his own 'unstinted admiration' for him.

G1490. Going Dutch, *Patriots and Liberators*, Simon Schama, Collins, *Obs.* 31 Jul. p 29

(1) A 'remarkable work' which 'is more than a revision: it is a revolution', restoring the integrity of the Patriots of the Dutch revolution of the 1780s-1813.

G1491. *Spanien im Zweiten Weltkrieg*, Klaus-Jorg Ruhl, Hamburg, Hoffman und Campe, 1975, *EHR*. 92, 364. Jul. pp 691–2

(1) It provides 'a classic example of the confusion with which Nazi Germany's foreign policy was conducted'.

G1492. An English Clausewitz, *Liddell Hart*, Brian Bond, Cassell, *Obs*. 28 Aug. p 24

(1) Praises this book by a personal friend of Liddell Hart; though he disagrees with some of the author's views.

(2) Liddell Hart: 'No man has done more to shape military thought and practice in the twentieth century.'

G1493. Hiroshima Story, *Ruin From The Air: The Atomic Mission to Hiroshima*, Gordon Thomas and Max Morgan Witts, Hamilton, *Obs*. 11 Sept. p 24

(1) '... yet another blow-by-blow account of a sensational event in the Second World War'.

G1494. The luckless general, *The Auk*, Roger Parkinson, Granada, *Obs*. 2 Oct. p 26

(1) He 'makes a strong case for Auchinleck's leadership, but he presses it too far'.

G1495. Half-way revolution, *Revolution Principles*, J.P. Kenyon, Cambridge U.P., *Obs*. 9 Oct. p 26

(1) In his entertaining Ford Lectures the author demonstrates the 'equivocations and confusions' of the statesmen who made the Revolution of 1688. 'I think he is a little hard on all concerned' – the 'Glorious Revolution' did represent important achievements.

G1496. The Gowk, *C.P. Trevelyan 1870–1958*, A.J.A. Morris, Blackstaff Press, *NS*. 94, 2431. 21 Oct. pp 548–50

(2) The UDC: 'perhaps the most formidable radical body ever to influence British foreign policy'.

G1497. Up the Republic, *The Damnable Question*, George Dangerfield, Constable, *Obs.* 23 Oct. p 23

(1) It has the same virtues as his *The Strange Death of Liberal England*, 'brilliant style, wide scholarship, clear exposition'; and the same weaknesses, 'judgments too confident and a failure to appreciate the inevitable compromises and evasions statesmen have to make'. 'It is a fascinating book all the same, essential reading for all those interested in the Irish question, and who is not?'

G1498. *British Policy in South-East Europe in the Second World War*, Elizabeth Barker, Macmillan, 1976, *EHR*. 92,365. Oct. p 934

(1) A fascinating story; the author writes it on the basis of research in the official archives.

G1499. *The Home Front*, Arthur Marwick, Thames and Hudson, 1976, *Hist.* 62, 206. Oct. pp 540–1

(1) 'It is a model of how illustrations should be used'. Agrees with the author that there was considerable social reform in Britain during the Second World War and after, though it was not of a socialist nature.

G1500. Bottom of the class, *A Prime Minister on Prime Ministers*, Harold Wilson, Weidenfeld and Nicolson, *Obs.* 6 Nov. p 30

(1) 'The prevailing tone is that of *1066 And All That* . . . Sir Harold says that anyone who aspires to be Prime Minister should have the gift of falling asleep at a moment's notice. He has clearly followed this advice and often fallen asleep while writing this book . . . If a university student submitted these essays, I should mark them NS – *non satis*.'

G1501. Rommel's betrayal, *The Trail Of The Fox*, David Irving, Weidenfeld, and Nicolson *Obs.* 20 Nov. p 28

(1) Feels that the new information in it does not change the familiar view of Rommel. The book provides 'the most complete account we have of Rommel in North Africa'. However he points to the author's sensational conjectures amidst 'the generally

acceptable narrative'.

G1502. England's greatest monument, *A History Of York Minster*, ed. G.E. Aylmer and Reginald Cant, Oxford U.P., *Gdn.* 24 Nov.

(1) A 'splendid volume which marks the approaching completion of the greatest work of restoration in the Minster's history'.

Repr. *Guardian Weekly*.

G1503. Winston out of his depth, *Churchill and the Admirals*, Stephen Roskill, Collins, *Obs.* 27 Nov. p 28

(1) 'A scholarly book as powerful as any naval broadside'.

G1504. Books of the Year, *Obs.* 18 Dec. p 21

Praises *France 1848–1945*, Vol. 2, Theodore Zeldin, Oxford U.P. – the author 'defiantly discards narrative history and provides instead an entrancing medley of miscellaneous information'; *Churchill and the Admirals* (*see above* G1503); and *Charles Stewart Parnell* (G1480), 'a work of classic dignity and proportions'.

G1505. Disenchantment, *Fulfilment Of A Mission*, Major-General Sir Edward Spears, Cooper, *Obs.* 18 Dec. p 24

(1) 'Spears was a writer of the first rank as well as a man of action.' The book has 'touches of . . . brilliance. There is in it also a brooding air of melancholy.'

G1506. The Black Book, *Salome's Last Veil*, Michael Kettle, Granada, *NS.* 94, 2440. 23 Dec. pp 905–6

(1) A full account of Maud Allan's criminal libel case against Pemberton Billing MP in 1918 – 'every word is a delight'. However A.J.P.T. deals ironically with the two plots which the author feels he has discovered.

1978

G1507. Back on their pedestals, (a) *Kitchener*, George H. Cassar, Kimber; (b) *The Road to Passchendaele*, John Terraine, Cooper, *Obs.* 1 Jan. p 33

(a1) 'An outstanding biography, rich in material

from new sources and with a grasp of the issues at stake'.

(a2) 'Kitchener was the greatest military figure produced by Great Britain during the First World War. It was his misfortune to be placed in power at a time when no one could succeed.'

(b1) 'The book is a series of quotations skilfully arranged . . . a true do-it-yourself book.' A.J.P.T. vigorously dismisses the argument that Passchendaele was inevitable.

G1508. Christ Stopped At Potsdam, *Shattered Peace: The Origins of the Cold War and the National Security State*, Daniel Yergin, New York, Houghton Mifflin, *NS*. 95, 2443. 13 Jan. pp 49–50

(1) The 'interpretation is not new, but Daniel Yergin draws on more sources than any previous writer'.

G1509. *March 1939: The British Guarantee to Poland*, Simon Newman, Oxford U.P., 1976, *EHR*. 93, 366. Jan. pp 238–9

(1) He 'has produced the best and most original book on war origins for many years'.

G1510. Stumbling to the brink, *Britain And The Origins of the First World War*, Zara Steiner, Macmillan, *Obs*. 5 Feb. p 24

(1) Warmly praises the author's abilities but doubts if the matter was as clear-cut as she concludes. 'At any rate her brilliant exposition provides many ideas to argue over and some to agree with.'

(2) 'The Balance of Power changed . . . not because the Germans planned to change it but because changes followed inevitably from the increasing economic strength of Germany and the relative decline of the French.'

G1511. Scientists at war, (a) *Most Secret War*, R.V. Jones, Hamilton; (b) *The Secret War*, Brian Johnson, BBC, *Obs*. 26 Feb. p 36

(a1) He judges it to be 'in the first rank among war books. Indeed I am inclined to say that with its combination of science and human character it is the most fascinating book on the Second World War that I have read.'

(b1) 'It is of course less personal than Professor Jones' book and also more technical'.

G1512. War of the British Succession, (a) *Allies Of A Kind*, Christopher Thorne, Hamilton; (b) *Imperialism At Bay*, William Roger Louis, Oxford U.P., *Obs.* 5 Mar. p 32

(a1) 'A staggering achievement . . . He is a master of diplomacy as well as of war and also, what is perhaps even more important for an historian, a master of personalities.'

(b1) Praises it as a magnificent book.

G1513. Strong silent man, *Portal of Hungerford*, Denis Richards, Heinemann, *Obs.* 12 Mar. p 33

(1) Portal's 'contribution to the war has to be reconstructed largely from the official records, a task that Denis Richards has performed admirably'.

G1514. When the bobbins stopped, *The Hungry Mills*, Norman Longmate, Temple Smith, *Obs.* 9 Apr. p 32

(1) 'Norman Longmate has done the people of Lancashire proud.' He praises the author's vivid account of how the cotton operatives lived during the cotton famine.

G1515. No more war, *War And The Liberal Conscience*, Michael Howard, Temple Smith, *Obs.* 23 Apr. p 29

(1) An 'admirable book'. However he observes, 'It is in my opinion pushing things too hard to suggest, as Howard does, that without the idealists wars would have been fewer and less terrible. The idealists were more practical men than Howard makes out.'

(2) 'I do not claim that the critics of war have always been wise in their diagnosis. But nine times out of ten they have been on the right side and I am glad to have been associated with them.'

G1516. *The Precarious Truce*, Gabriel Gorodetsky, Cambridge U.P., *EHR*. 93, 367. Apr. pp 471–2

(1) 'An admirable work of research . . . of considerable value to students of both British and Soviet affairs'.

G1517. Infamous last words, *The Goebbels Diaries*, ed. H.R. Trevor Roper, Secker and Warburg, *Obs.* 7 May. p 34

(1) 'These entries arc no great shakes despite the editor's enthusiasm for them . . . These records are of little historical interest . . . The best part of the book is the introduction by Trevor-Roper.'

G1518. Circular Tour, *A Guide to the London Countryway*, Keith Chesterton, Constable, *NS.* 95, 2464. 9 Jun. pp 785–6

(1) 'This delightful book is a compendium of our present enthusiasms – country-walking, sightseeing and real ale. The book is a pleasure to read, its historical facts nearly always correct.'

G1519. Foundation stones, *Anglo-Saxon Architecture*, Vol. 3, H.M. Taylor, Cambridge U.P., *Obs.* 11 Jun. p 28

(1) Praises 'his incomparable work of scholarship. His book is one that every lover of Anglo-Saxon architecture will rejoice in.'

(2) ' . . . the Normans were savage destroyers who brought ruin to a flourishing culture and stamped their brutality on the land and on its architecture. The old Radicals were not all that wrong when they attributed the evils of our society to the Norman conquest and looked back to Anglo Saxon times as a golden age.'

G1520. Hitler the opportunist, *The War Path: Hitler's Germany 1933–39*, David Irving, Joseph, *Obs.* 18 Jun. p 28

(1) 'There is more good scholarship than sensationalism in Irving's book, though there is some sensationalism as well.'

(2) 'The great merit of Irving's book is not in its novelty but in its careful repetition of the version, already accepted by sensible historians, that Hitler was an opportunist who took advantages when they offered themselves.'

G1521. Eden and Churchill, *The War Diaries Of Oliver Harvey*, ed. John Harvey, Collins, *Obs.* 30 Jul. p 26

(1) 'The new selection is even more illuminating' than the pre-war extracts. 'This is very much a view from the Foreign Office or, to be more precise, from Eden's room.'

(2) 'In retrospect Eden had a good record as Foreign Secretary, coming as near to a sensible answer on almost every question as anyone else did. Perhaps Eden's weakness was that unlike Churchill, Roosevelt and some of the other great figures he was not 'a lunatic'. Since war is itself a form of lunacy, the lunatics are best at it.'

G1522. Muddling through, (a) *Lord Aberdeen*, Lucille Iremonger, Collins; (b) *The Myth That Will Not Die*, Humphrey Berkeley, Croom Helm, *Obs.* 10 Sept. p 34

(a1) 'Her book is a reliable work of scholarship. As an essay in vindication, however, I feel that it does not come off.'

(b1) He suggests that no-one still believes the myth that the author sets out to demolish. He comments that the book 'finishes off the remnants of the myth by a day-to-day account'.

(b2) 'MacDonald now appears as totally at a loss, with no understanding of economics, no idea what to do and more bewildered than the most ignorant speculator.'

G1523. Crusading civil servant, *Vansittart*, Norman Rose, Heinemann, *Obs.* 17 Sept. p 34

(1) 'A fine biography'.

(2) A.J.P.T. gives his impressions of Vansittart, in particular remembering 'his almost irresistible charm'. However – 'it must be confessed that he was not suited to be Permanent Under Secretary for Foreign Affairs'.

G1524. A political insider, *Disraeli, Derby And The Conservative Party*, ed. J.R. Vincent, Hassocks, Harvester Press, *Obs.* 24 Sept. p 34

(1) 'The diaries of Lord Stanley, who became fifteenth earl of Derby in 1869, are a great find and John Vincent has edited them impeccably . . . Here is essential material for the historians who seek to explain how a new Conservative and a new Liberal party emerged after the second Reform Act.'

G1525. The unknown benefactors, *Two Rothschilds And The Land Of Israel*, Simon Schama, Collins, *Gdn*. 12 Oct. p 11

(1) 'It is a remarkable story, now fully told for the first time by Simon Schama with his usual brilliance.'

G1526. Bismarck to Hitler, *Germany 1866–1945*, Gordon Craig, Oxford U.P., *Obs*. 22 Oct. p 34

(1) 'A political narrative for the most part excellent; a good account of German foreign policy until it comes to Hitler; interesting chapters on German literature, culture and universities, weak however on the side of economic developments.' However he feels that it offers nothing new.

G1527. *Media Manipulation: The Press And Bismarck In Imperial Germany*, Robert H. Keyserlingk, Montreal, Renouf, 1977, *Hist*. 63, 209. Oct. p 471

(1) 'It has long been known that Bismarck manipulated the German press. This book shows how it was done.'

G1528. *Germany And Europe 1919–1939*, John Hiden, Longman, 1977, *Ibid*. p 482

(1) Praises it for surveying German foreign policy between the wars as a single theme but otherwise is unenthusiastic about the book.

G1529. L.G. at his best, *Lloyd George: The People's Champion 1902–1911*, John Grigg, Eyre Methuen, Obs. 29 Oct. p 34

(1) 'A biography of the first rank'. 'The book is a delight to read and a contribution to our political history of the greatest importance. Above all it does full justice to David Lloyd George, the greatest British statesman of our century.'

G1530. Not World Enough, *The Times Atlas of World*

History, ed. Geoffrey Barraclough, Times Books, *New Review*. 5, 2. Autumn. pp 89–91

(1) He criticises the assumptions behind the book, notably that the world is a valuable unit in which to discuss the history of the past before very recent times. 'The grandiloquent phrase, World History, is salestalk, not a practical guide to historical understanding.' He finds that 'the choice of topics for illustration is strikingly conventional'. He deems it 'a curious combination of old-fashioned historical interests and One World romanticism'.

G1531. Homely genius, *The Magic Years of Beatrix Potter*, Margaret Lane, Warne, *Obs*. 5 Nov. p 30

(1) He praises the author's previous book on Beatrix Potter as one 'which ranks high among the biographies of our century'. 'Now she has delighted us again.'

(2) He warmly praises Beatrix Potter's books. Of *The Tailor of Gloucester* he comments, 'I rank it with the masterpieces of Balzac.'

G1532. The cockpit of Europe, *The Low Countries 1780–1940*, E.H. Kossman, Oxford U.P., *Obs*. 3 Dec. p 34

(1) 'His book is a contribution to knowledge of the first importance.'

G1533. Books Of The Year, *Obs*. 17 Dec. p 33

He praises *Most Secret War* (*see above* G1511) as 'one of the most delightful war memoirs'. 'John Grigg demonstrated in *Lloyd George: The People's Champion* (G 1529) the superiority of classical biography over the Psychopathic probings of present fashion.' He comments that Graham Green ('our greatest living novelist') was 'at the height of his powers' when he wrote *The Human Factor* (Bodley Head). 'This was undoubtedly the finest novel of the year and indeed of the decade.'

G1534. Political grandmaster, *The Discipline of Popular Government: Lord Salisbury's Domestic Statecraft 1881–1902*, Peter Marsh, Hassocks, Harvester Press, *Obs*. 24 Dec. p 20

(1) 'Peter Marsh has at last vindicated Salisbury as a domestic statesman and party leader. Marsh's book is long; it spares no detail. But it will fascinate every reader who enjoys the world of political monoeuvre.'

(2) 'Being sceptical by nature, I hesitate to credit statesmen, however able, with such foresight and deliberate purpose. In my view statesmen are no more purposeful in their struggle for power than in any of their activities. They wait upon events and then act by intuitive genius – what Gladstone called 'the sense of right timing'.'

'Of the great men of the nineteenth century Salisbury is the only one whose influence on political life is still with us.' 'In a longer perspective Salisbury appears to have tamed democracy even if he could not thwart it.'

1979

G1535. From Left to Right, *Liberals and Social Democrats*, Peter Clarke, Cambridge U.P.; *A History of the Conservative Party Vol. 3: The Age of Balfour and Baldwin 1902–1940*, John Ramsden, Longman, *Obs.* 21 Jan. p 35

(1) 'Both are outstanding works of scholarship. Both have given me much intellectual pleasure ... and some cynical entertainment ... Both shed new light on British politics in the twentieth century ... '

G1536. Hero or humbug? *John Bright*, Keith Robbins, Routledge. *Obs.* 28 Jan. p 34

(1) An 'excellent biography'.

(2) 'Bright was a hero and there was something of the humbug in him as well.'

G1537. *British Rearmament In The Thirties*, Robert Paul Shay Jr., Princeton U.P., 1977, *EHR*, 370, Jan. pp 238–9

(1) A study of the financial and industrial obstacles to rearmament which makes 'ample use of the Treasury papers'.

G1538. Assault on the BBC. *The History of Broadcasting in*

the United Kingdom, Vol. 4: Sound and Vision, Asa Briggs, Oxford U.P., *Gdn.* 1 Feb. p 10

(1) Observes that 'it is a history of the British Broadcasting Corporation, not of British broadcasting . . . a partisan record, as seen from Broadcasting House . . .'

G1539. Edward the affable. *Edward VII: Prince and King*, Giles St. Aubyn, Collins. *Obs.* 25 Feb. p 36

(1) Feels that as the author has had access to the papers of Viscount Knollys another biography of Edward is justified. 'Everything the book tells us about Knollys is new and full of interest. The general narrative tells little that was not known before.'

G1540. *Tormented Warrior: Ludendorff And The Supreme Command*, Roger Parkinson, Hodder and Stoughton, 1978, *Hist.*, 64, 210. Feb. p 148

(1) 'A skilful essay in rehabilitation. His book is not easy to read and derives entirely from secondary sources. But it is undoubtedly the best book on Ludendorff in English.'

G1541. *Labour Und Weimarer Republik 1918–1924*, Wolfgang Krieger, Bonn, Neue Gessellschaft, 1978, *Ibid.* pp 126–7

(2) ' . . . he criticises me with some justification for taking Morel too seriously'.

'By the end the Labour Party had arrived at a foreign policy little different from that of enlightened Conservatives such as Austen Chamberlain'.

G1542. The eternal scapegoats. *Political Anti-Sernitism in England 1918–1939*, Gisela C. Lebzelter, Macmillan. *Obs.* 11 Mar. p 36

(2) 'England had a relatively mild attack though Ms. Lebzelter is unduly charitable about its earlier appearances.'

G1542a War in Our time, *Munich: The Price of Peace*, Telford Taylor, New York, Doubleday, *NYRB*, 26, 4. 22 Mar. p 3–4

(1) It 'is the most formidable and scholarly' on Munich.

G1543. Alarm in high places. *Ministry of Morale*, Ian McLaine, Allen and Unwin. *Obs.* 8 Apr. p 36

(2) 'The comedy extracted from the MOI files . . . surpasses even the fantasies provided by Evelyn Waugh in 'Put Out More Flags.'

G1544. Undated cheques for India. *Watershed in India 1914–1922*, Sir Algernon Rumbold, Athlone Press, *Obs*. 22 Apr. p 37

(1) 'A fascinating book about the twists and turns of British policy during and after the First World War. The theme is sternly confined to the British side of the story.'

G1545. Life in the Bunker. *The Berlin Bunker*, James O'Donnell, Dent, *Obs*. 29 Apr. p 36

(1) The interest of the book is that it is not just about Hitler but 'about the Bunker, its occupants and the life they led.'

G1546. *Guernica! Guernica!*, Herbert R. Southworth, California U.P., 1977, *EHR*. 94, 371. Apr. p 471

(1) Feels that the author takes an excessive length to explode a myth. 'This book is less a contribution to history than the monument to an obsession.'

G1547. Balfour to Begin. *The Palestine Triangle*, Nicholas Bethell, Deutsch, *Obs*. 20 May. p 37

(1) The story is told 'with admirable clarity and scholarly devotion'.

(2) 'It is a story that no Englishman can read without shame.'

G1548. Wedded to greatness. *Clementine Churchill*, Mary Soames, Cassell, *Obs*. 24 Jun. p 36

(1) 'A delightful book about her mother. The book is affectionate and also frank. The many troubles are not concealed though they are kept in proportion.'

(2) 'Clementine Churchill proved the perfect wife for Winston Churchill; no woman had a more difficult assignment.'

G1549. *Bismarck And His Times*, George O. Kent, Southern Illinois U.P., 1978, *Hist*. 64, 211. Jun. pp 324–5

(1) 'An acceptable short biography of Bismarck with few novelities.'

G1550. *To Win A War: 1918, The Year Of Victory*, John Terraine, Sidgwick and Jackson, 1978. *Ibid*. p 330

(1) 'Another essay in vindication . . . The account is admirably done.' Regrets that the author is slighting to people other than Haig.

G1551. The games generals play. *The War Plans of the Great Powers 1880–1914*, ed. Paul Kennedy, Allen and Unwin, *Obs.* 1 Jul. p 36

(1) A 'fascinating collection' of essays.

G1552. Reds under beds. *The British Connection*, Richard Deacon, Hamilton, *Obs.* 22 Jul. p 37

(1) 'No more preposterous book has ever been written.'

G1553. Leviathan of history. *Lord Macaulay : The History of England*, ed. Hugh Trevor-Roper. Harmondsworth, Penguin, *Obs.* 29 Jul. p 37

(1) Praises the editor's introduction and the intention of luring readers back to Macaulay, but observes, 'Of course the result is a series of isolated delights, not Macaulay's History'.

(2) 'Trevor-Roper is inclined to depreciate the Whig interpretation of history. I still see its merits. After all, our political forerunners stumbled on a system of government the least imperfect that has been known. We still benefit from their inheritance. We still enjoy ordered liberty. The authority of the states is still limited though not as much as it should be. Macaulay erred, I think, when he added to the Whig interpretation the great delusion of his age, which was until the other day the great delusion of ours: belief in limitless progress and in the possibility, indeed the inevitability, of limitless improvement, both moral and material'.

G1554. *Arms and the Wizard*, R.J.Q. Adams, Cassell, 1978. *EHR*. 94, 372. Jul. pp 672–3

(1) An 'admirable book – the first scholarly treatment of its subject'.

G1555. Guderian's battle. *Blitzkrieg*, Len Deighton, Cape, *Obs.* 2 Sept. p 36

(1) Praises the book – but observes that the 1940 campaign 'only lasted ten days and there are already some highly efficient books about it'.

APPENDIX: BBC RADIO AND TV BROADCASTS

*Indicates that the scripts are held at the BBC Written Archives Centre. I would like to offer my thanks to the BBC Written Archives Centre.

(a) *Radio : Home*

Transmission	*Series and Programme Title*	*Transmission Time*	*Date*
			1942
1. Forces	The World at War – Your Questions Answered	1730–1745	17 Mar.
2.	– Ditto –		31
3.	– Ditto –		21 Apr.
4.	– Ditto –		5 May.
5.	– Ditto –		19
6.	– Ditto –		26
7.	– Ditto –		23 Jun.
			1944
8. Talks	The Future of Germany (one of four speakers)* Pub. as 'What Shall We Do with Germany?', *Li.* 32, 823. 19 Oct. pp 423–4, 436	1930–2000	13 Oct.
9.	– Ditto* – Pub. as 'What Shall We Do with Germany? –2', *Li.* 32, 824. 26 Oct. pp		20

		459–60, 465		
10.		What Shall We Do with Germany? (one of four speakers)* Pub. in *Li.* 32, 830. 7 Dec. pp 619–20, 632	1925–2000	1 Dec.
				1945
11.	Home	The Brains Trust – 4th Series (one of a panel)	2015–2100	23 Jan.
12.	Talks	Do Alliances Help World Peace?* (with three other speakers)	1930–2000	20 Jul.
13.	Home	World Affairs: A Weekly Survey – Russia's Return as a Great Power Pub. in *Li.* 34, 872. 27 Sept. pp 341–2, 355	2115–2130	17 Sept.
14.		World Affairs: A Weekly Survey – San Francisco and the Atom Bomb* (Discussion with Captain Raymond Blackburn, Prof. J.D. Bernal and Rt. Hon. Richard Law) Pub. in *Li.* 34, 873. 14 Oct. pp 367–8, 381–2		24
15.		World Affairs: A Weekly Survey. Pub. as 'The European Revolution', *Li.* 34, 880.		14 Nov.

	22 Nov. pp 575–6		
			1946
16.	– Ditto* – Pub. as 'Problems of the Peace Makers', *Li.* 35, 887. 10 Jan. pp 35–6		2 Jan.
17. Light	Current Affairs*	2245–2300	3 Jan.
18. Home	World Affairs: A Weekly Survey – Russia Today* Pub. as 'What is Russia's Policy', *Li.* 35, 895. 7 Mar. pp 294–5	2115–2130	27 Feb.
19.	World Affairs: A Weekly Survey – The Middle East* Pub. as 'To Fight or To Share: Alternative policies in the Middle East', *Li.* 35, 898. 28 Mar. pp 389–90		20 Mar.
(i) Light	Current Affairs (amended version)*	2245–2300	11 Apr.
20. Home	Questions in the Air: What Is A Great Power?*	1930–2000	12
21.	World Affairs: The First Year of Victory* Pub. as 'The Way to Agreement?', *Li.* 35, 905. 16 May. pp 633–4	2115–2130	8 May.
22.	World Affairs: The Problem of Ger-		12 Jun.

		many* Pub. in *Li.* 35, 910. 20 Jun. pp 799–800		
23.	Third	The Roots of British Foreign Policy (1)* Pub. as 'The Need for Controversy', *Li.* 36, 935. 12 Dec. pp 834–5		29 Nov.
24.		– Ditto – (2)* Pub. as 'Britain's relations with the United States', *Li.* 36, 936. 19 Dec. pp 873, 889		6 Dec.
25.		– Ditto – (3)* Pub. as 'British Policy towards Russia', *Li.* 36, 937. 26 Dec. pp 918–9		13
26.		– Ditto – (4)* Pub. as 'Great Britain and Europe', *Li.* 37, 938. 2 Jan. pp 8–9	1942	20
				1947
27.		British Prime Ministers: Lord John Russell* Pub. in *Li.* 37, 947. 20 Mar. pp 419–20 and in A5 and A21	1913–1930	7 Mar.
28.		British Prime Ministers: Lord Salisbury* Pub. in *Li.* 37, 952. 24 Apr. pp 621–2 and in A5 and A21	1900–1915	?
29.		Book review: *Speaking Frankly*, by	2130–2150	27 Dec.

		James Byrne*		
				1948
30.		Book review: *Diplomatic Prelude* by L.B. Namier*	1820–1840	13 Jan.
31.	Home	The Brains Trust (one of a panel)	1630–1700	31 Oct.
	(i)	Repeat	1530–1600	3 Nov.
				1949
32.	Third	Book review: *The Stalin-Tito correspondence** Pub. as 'Tito and Stalin: The Revolt from Within', *Li.* 41, 1043. 20 Jan. pp 86–8	1905–1925	11 Jan.
33.		Benjamin Constant: The Liberal Intellectual*	1900–1920	17 Aug.
	(i)	Repeat	2215–2235	24 Oct.
				1951
34.		Book review: The Traditions of British Foreign Policy Pub. in A6, pp 75–80	2200–2220	6 Jan.
35.	Home	Taking Stock: Britain's Role in the World* (Scripted discussion with four other speakers)	2115–2300	1 Feb.
36.	Third	The Man of December	2045–2105	2 Dec.

		Pub. in *Li.* 46, 1188. 6 Dec. pp 961–2 and in A6, A16 and A17		
				1952
	(i)	Repeat	1800–1820	28 May.
				1953
37.	Home (North of England)	Fifty One Society – Is There A Pattern in History?	1930–2015	18 May.
38.	Third	Book Review: Two Historians – Carlyle and Macaulay, (i) talk, followed by (ii) readings	2158–2216 2216–2246	4 Jul.
		Pub. in *Li.* 50, 1272. 16 Jul. pp 108–9		
	(i)	Repeat	2308	8
39.	Light	Any Questions?	2015–2100	6 Nov.
	(i)	Repeat	1310–1355	10
				1963
	(ii)	Repeated in Looking Back on Any Questions	2040	5 Jul.
				1954
40.	Third	John Bright and the Crimean War*	2015–2055	31 Mar.
	(i)	Repeat	1810–1850	5 Apr.
41.		John Bright and the Crimean War: Readings from his	2107–2122	2 Apr.

		Speeches*		
	(i)	Repeat	1845–1900	6
42.		War To End War* Pub. as 'Could the War of 1914–18 have been Averted?', *Li.* 52, 1328. 12 Aug. pp 233–4	1920–1940	4 Aug.
	(i)	Repeat	2250–2340	24
				1954
43.	Light	Any Questions?	2015–2100	15 Oct.
	(i)	Repeat	1910–1955	19
				1955
44.	Home	Scrapbook for 1935	2115	4 May.
	(i)	Repeat	1500	29 Jul.
45.	Third	The Bogey-Man: Friedrich von Holstein's Private Papers* Pub. as Evil Genius of Wilhelmstrasse?', *Li.* 54, 1377. 21 Jul. pp 102–4 and in A9 and A17	2042–2100	12 Jul.
				1956
46.		The Other Foreign Policy: (1) The Radical Tradition* For these six lectures see *The Troublemakers* (A10)	2140	4 Apr.
	(i)	Repeat	1800	9
47.		(2) Dissenting Rivals*	2139	11

	(i)	Repeat	1800	16
48.		(3) The Contradictions of Morality*	2037	18
	(i)	Repeat	1800	24
49.		(4) The Radical Alternative Before 1914*	2115	25
	(i)	Repeat	1800	30
50.		(5) The Great War and the Great Peace*	2030	2 May.
	(i)	Repeat	1800	7
51.		(6) Between the Wars*	2120	9
	(i)	Repeat	1820	15
				1958
52.		The World of Books: review of *Kitchener* by P. Magnus*	(5 mins. between 1630–1700)	25 Oct.
				1959
	(i)	Repeated in 'Second Hearing, Kitchener Two Views'	2110	3 Feb.
53.		Politics in The First World War (a shortened version of his British Academy lecture; *see* D26)	1840–1920	25 Apr.
54.		Two Centenaries: Metternich and Solferino* Pub. as 'Metternich and his 'system' for Europe', *Li.* 62, 1583. 30 Jul. pp 167–8 and in A13	2045–2105	21 Jul.

				1961
55.	Home	In Our Time – Who Burnt The Reichstag? ('new evidence presented in documentary form by A.J.P. Taylor and discussed by him and Alan Bullock')	1930–2030	31 Jan.
56.	Light	Woman's Hour (Guest of the week – to discuss his *Origins of the Second World War*)* (the script only gives the banal questions asked of him)	1400–1500	12 Jul.
	(i)	Repeated in Home For The Day: Women's Hour Guests	0911	10 Sept.
57.	Home	Did Hitler Cause the War? A Discussion about the book *The Origins of the Second World War* between A.J.P.T. and Hugh Trevor Roper. (A repeat of the TV discussion of 9 Jul. 1961)	2210–2250	30 Jul.
				1962
58.	Home (North of England)	In Our Time: Geoffrey Dawson	2000	17 Jun.
				1964
59.	Light	Woman's Hour. Talk	1400–1500	25 Mar.

		of Books and Writers (on the First World War and on books by Sir James Ferguson and George Malcolm Thomson)*		
60.	Home (North of England)	Beeching: The Emerging Pattern	2105	7 Apr.
	(i)	Revised repeat	1210	3 Jul.
61.	Third	1914: Moving Towards War – (4) How War Came To Great Britain* Pub. in *Li.* 72, 1842. 16 Jul. pp 79–82	2000	3
				1965
62.	Home	This Time of Day: An Historian's view of the Queen's visit to Germany	1210	17 May.
				1966
63.		The Twentieth Century: The People – (1) The Social Scene	2210	27 Feb.
	(i)	Repeat	1400	7 Apr.
64.		The World At One. William Hardcastle interviewed A.J.P.T. on his 60th birthday	1300	25 Mar.
65.		The World at One. William Hardcastle interviewed A.J.P.T. on Beaverbrook's *The Abdication of King*	1300	21 Apr.

		Edward VIII		
66.		The World at One. Ray Davies interviewed A.J.P.T. on *The Times*	1300	2 May.
67.		The World of Books. Peter Duval Smith interviewed A.J.P.T. about Beaverbrook's *The Abdication of King Edward VIII**	2030	3
68.		Ten o'Clock Comment. The Franks Report on Oxford	2210	12 May.
69.	Third	The Man Who Tried to Work Miracles* Pub. in *Li.* 76, 1947. 21 Jul. pp 81–4	2120	7 Jul.
70.	Home	The World At One. Andrew Boyle interviewed A.J.P.T. on 'The Times'	1300	21 Dec.
71.		The World At One. Andrew Boyle interviewed A.J.P.T. on book tokens and books	1300	28 Dec.
72.		A Choice of Paperbacks. Review of *Confessions of Zeno* by Italo Svevo*	2120	31 Dec.
				1967
73.		The Eye Witness – A Reappraisal of Stanley Baldwin. A.J.P.T. interviewed by Michael Clayton	2010	16 Jul.
74.		The World This	1300	24 Sept.

		Weekend. William Hardcastle interviewed A.J.P.T. on International Relations Partly pub. in *Li.* 78, 2011. 5 Oct. p 437		
75.	Radio 4	The World This Weekend. An Appreciation of Lord Attlee. A.J.P.T. interviewed by William Hardcastle Pub. in *Li.* 78, 2011. 12 Oct. pp 470–1	1300	8 Oct.
76.		The World This Weekend. Interviewed by Andrew Boyle on Devaluation Pub. in *Li.* 78, 2017. 23 Nov. p 669	1300	19 Nov.
77.		The World At One. Interviewed by Nicholas Woolley about the economy in 1967	1300	19 Dec.
78.		The World At One. Interviewed by Nicholas Woolley on book tokens	1300	28 Dec.
				1968
79.		The World This Weekend. Interviewed by Andrew Boyle on Britain's attitude to violence Pub. in *Li.* 79,	1300	26 May.

		2044. 30 May. p 701		
80.		The World This Weekend. Interviewed by Andrew Boyle on Weekends in the Pennines	1300	30 Jun.
81.		The World This Weekend. Interviewed by David Jessell for a feature on Civil Wars	1300	11 Aug.
82.		The Time of My Life. (A discussion with Malcolm and Kitty Muggeridge) Pub. as 'Habeas Cadaver – Malcolm Muggeridge on the Russia of the Thirties', *Li.* 80, 2062. 3 Oct. pp 432–5	?	(Sept./ Oct.)
				1969
83.	Radio 1	Late Night Extra. Interviewed by Ian Ross on the *History of the English Speaking People* (*see* B11)	2200	4 Sept.
				1970
84.	Radio 4	The World At One. Interviewed by Nicholas Woolley on the effect of a newspaper strike on the General Election	1300	8 Jun.
85.		Now Read On –	2045	12 Aug.

		English History 1914–1918		
				1971
86.		Memoirs Unlimited. A discussion with Roy Jenkins and Lord Butler chaired by Robert McKenzie on political memoirs Pub. in *Li.* 85, 2188. 4 Mar. p 272	?	28 Jan.
87.		P.M. Report. Interviewed by Nicholas Woolley on *Lloyd George: Twelve Essays*	1700	23 Mar.
88.	Radio 3	From Dreadnought to Scapa Flow. A discussion with Arthur Marder about the role of the Navy in peace and war* Pub. in *Li.* 86, 2221. 21 Oct. pp 534–7	2154	17 Sept.
89.	Radio 4	The Marching Years – The Hungry Thirties. Memories and opinions from A.J.P.T. and others	2030	14 Dec.
				1972
90.		The World This Weekend. Interviewed by Nicholas Woolley on *Beaverbrook*	1300	11 Jun.

91.		Beaverbrook. A discussion on Beaverbrook's career: A.J.P.T. and Michael Foot* Pub. in *Li.* 88, 2259. 13 Jul. pp 44–7	2115	13 Jun.
92.		Pick of the Week. L'Amour and the Common Market	1930	16 Jun.
93.	Radio 3	The Roots of Irish Nationalism. A discussion with Robert Kee and Liam de Paor Pub. in *Li.* 89, 2286. 18 Jan. 1973. p 84	2156	30 Nov.
				1973
94.	Radio 4	P.M. Reports. Interviewed by Richard Cook about secret Whitehall documents and the Suez Crisis	1700	10 Jan.
95.		The World At One. Interviewed on *Off The Record*	1300	25 Jul.
96.		Candidates for Greatness: Lord Beaverbrook (repeat of World Service Programme – *see* Appendix (b), 202)	1105	22 Aug.
97.	Radio 3	The Impact of Coal: An Environmental Case Study (4) The Bread of Industry. One of the speakers	1900	7 Sept.

				1973
98.	Radio 4	P.M. Reports. Interviewed on his idea that the EEC might lead to the denationalising of history books	1700	26 Oct.
				1974
99.		Today. Interviewed in connection with books about British Prime Ministers	0750	16 Feb.
100.		The World At One. Interviewed on precedents for the current political situation	1300	2 Mar.
101.	Radio 2	Jimmy Young Show. Guest	1130	4 Mar.
102.	Radio 4	The World This Weekend. Interviewed in a feature on the appeal to finance memorials to Sir Winston Churchill	1300	31 Mar.
103.		News-desk. A discussion of D-Day, 1944 Pub. in *Li* 91, 2359. 13 Jun. p 763	?	6 Jun.
104.		P.M. Reports. Interviewed in a feature on the move of *The Times* from Printing House Square	1700	21 Jun.
105.		Pick of the Week. Repeat of part of 'Read All About It', 24 June	1930	28 Jun.

		1974. (*see* Appendix (c) 85)		
				1975
106.		Beaverbrook. A portrait of Lord Bcaverbrook by the men who worked with him (including A.J.P.T.)	2030	14 Jan.
107.		The World This Weekend. Interviewed by Roger Cook on the history of the Irish dispute and the parallels between the 1921 settlement and today	1300	19 Jan.
108.		P.M. Reports. Interviewed by Gordon Clough on *The Second World War*	1700	14 Apr.
109.		Woman's Hour. A Good War. A.J.P.T. with others	1345	8 May.
110.		The Great Debate. A discussion of the question 'Is Britain part of Europe?'; A.J.P.T., Ralf Dahrendorf and Robin Day Pub. in *Li.* 93, 2407. 22 May. p 660		May.
111.	Radio 4	The World This Weekend. Interviewed by Nicholas Woolley on the destruction by civil servants of	1300	13 Jul.

	documents because they feel them to be politically sensitive or salacious		
112.	P.M. Reports. Interviewed by William Hardcastle on *My Darling Pussy*	1700	8 Oct.
			1975
113.	Today. Interviewed by Malcolm Bellings on the history of the Spanish Monarchy	0750	22 Nov.
114.	Start the Week. A guest	0905	8 Dec.
			1976
115.	Stop The Week, with Cliff Michelmore. A guest	0615	3 Jan.
116.	P.M. Reports. Interviewed on his 70th birthday	1700	25 Mar.
117.	The World Tonight. Interviewed on the issue of British withdrawal from Northern Ireland	2200	14 Apr.
118.	Today. Interviewed on the 50th anniversary of the General Strike	0645	4 May.
119.	Today. Interviewed, in a feature, 'Who Will Advise the British People?'	0645	4 Jun.
120.	The World Tonight.	?	23 Jul.

		Interviewed on the politics of honorary degrees		
121.		Pick of the Week. The War Lords – Mussolini. (*see* Appendix (c) 96)		6 Aug.
122.		Pick of the Week. The War Lords – Stalin. (*see* Appendix (c) 99)		27 Aug. 27 Aug.
				1977
123.		My Darling Pussy. Extracts from B21 introduced by A.J.P.T.	2215–2230	30 Jan.
124.		Today. Interview	0645	11 Feb.
125.		Their Finest Hour. The first of three talks on important speeches by Churchill at turning points in the Second World War. He discusses the situation at the time of Churchill's broadcast of 19 May 1940	0845–0900	16 May.
	(i)	Repeat	1145–1200	17 May.
126.		On Hitler's invasion of Russia. The second in the series	0845–0900	20 Jun.
	(i)	Repeat	1145–1200	21 Jun.
127.	Radio Wales	Review of books on Lloyd George	?	21 Jun.
128.		On America's entry into the Second World War. The third in the series	0845–0900	11 Jul.

	(i)	Repeat	2030–2045	14 Jul.
				1977
129.	Radio London	Interview on *The War Lords*	?	30 Nov.
				1978
130.	Radio 4	Woman's Hour. 'I talk to the Camera as a Person' – A.J.P.T. in conversation with Tony Barnfield	1345–1445	8 Jun.
131.	Radio 3	Marx, Engels and Manchester. A broadcast for the Arts Faculty Foundation Course, the Open University	1910–1930	8 Aug.
	(i)	Repeat	0720–0740	12 Aug.

(b) *Radio : Overseas*

	Transmission	*Series and Programme Title*	*Transmission Time*	*Date*
				1945
1.	North American	Freedom Forum – Law and Order*	1930–2000	2 May.
2.	European	London Calling Europe – The Pattern of the News (1) The Outbreak of War (a series of about five to seven and a half minutes programmes)	1500	22 May.
3.		– Ditto –	1500	25 May.

		(2) Poland and France		
4.		– Ditto –	1500	29 May.
		(3) How Hitler was Stopped		
5.		– Ditto –	1500	1 Jun.
		(4) Europe under Hitler		
6.		– Ditto –	2030	8 Jun.
		(5) The German Attack on the Soviet Union		
7.		– Ditto –	2030	12 Jun.
		(6) How the U.S. Came into the War		
8.		– Ditto –	2030	15 Jun.
		(7) The Climax of the Axis Efforts		
9.		– Ditto –	2030	19 Jun.
		(8) Stalingrad and Alamein: The Turn of the Tide		
10.		– Ditto –	2030	22 Jun.
		(9) The Reconquest of the Mediterranean		
11.		– Ditto –	2030	26 Jun.
		(10) The Liberation of Russia 1943–4		
12.		– Ditto –	2030	29 Jun.
		(11) The End of the Fortress of Europe		
13.		– Ditto –	2030	3 Jul.
		(12) The End of the German Reich		
14.	North American	Freedom Forum (164): The Present Position and Future of Germany*	1830–1900	19 Sept.
15.		– Ditto –		10 Oct.

		(167): The Problem of Palestine		
				1946
16.		– Ditto – (180): Is World Government Possible Now?*		5 Jan.
17.		– Ditto – (182): World Government – A Mixed Blessing* (an unscripted discussion with other speakers)		23 Jan.
18.		– Ditto – (200): Is Britain A Great Power? (unscripted discussion with three other speakers)*	1930–2000	29 May.
				1947
19.		– Ditto – The Road to Peace* (with two other speakers)	1830–1900	29 Jan.
20.		– Ditto – Is an Independent Austria Possible?* (with two other speakers)	2030–2100	7 May.
21.	African	European Scene: Yugoslavia*	2015–2030	9 Jun.
22.	North American	Current Affairs*	0200–0215	7 Aug.

23.	European	London Calling Europe – Canning (British Stateman Series) (1260 words)	?	?
24.	General Overseas	British Affairs: Political scene*	1615–1630	28 Oct.
25.		– Ditto – *	1615–1630	25 Nov.
				1948
26.		– Ditto – *	1645–1700	10 Feb.
27.	Overseas Regional	London Forum – Is Britain Playing her Proper Part in the World Crisis? (with two other speakers)*	?	15 Mar.
28.		British Political Commentary	1715–1800	13 Apr.
29.		Report from Europe – The Congress of Historians in Paris*		14 Apr.
30.	North American	Sunday Commentary (five minutes)	1810	18 Apr.
31.	Overseas Regional	British Political Commentary	1715–1800	15 Jun.
32.		Sunday Commentary (four minutes)	1810	20 Jun.
33.	European English	The Western Tradition – Totalitarianism (fifteen minutes) (Also broadcast in Spanish and Portuguese on the Latin American Service). Pub. as 'Ancestry of the 'New Democracies'' in *Li.* 40, 1016. 15 Jul. pp 92–3	?	7 Jul.

34.	General Overseas	London Forum: Is the German Menace Over?* (unscripted discussion with two other speakers)	1930–2000	5 Jul.
35.	European English	Britain This Week (159): The Cultural Congress of Peace (five minutes)	between 1900 and 1930	4 Sept.
36.		Report from Europe – The Wroclaw Congress	1900–1915	7 Sept.
37.	General Overseas	London Forum – Is Democracy capable of voluntarily rising to face its crises? (with two other speakers)	1930–2000	11 Oct.
38.		London Forum	?	(rec. 17 Nov.)

1950

39.		London Forum: The Soviet Attitude Towards Art* (unscripted discussion with two other speakers)	1400–1430	31 Jan.
40.	European English	London Calling Europe: As I See It (eleven minutes)	1900	26 Apr.
41.		London Forum: 'European Letter Box' (discussion with three other speakers)	1900–1930	19 Jun.
42.		Review of *Stalin* by	?	19 Jul.

		I. Deutscher		
43.		London Calling Europe: As I See It (ten minutes)	?	26 Jul.
44.		London Calling Europe: European Letter Box	2215–2245	14 Aug.
45.	General Overseas	London Forum (unscripted general talk with three other speakers) (30 minutes)	?	(rec. 16 Aug.)
46.	European English	London Calling Europe – As I See It	1900–1910	11 Oct.
47.	General Overseas	London Forum – Is the Democratic World Organising Itself along the Right Lines?* (with two other speakers)	0200–0230	31 Oct.
48.	European English	London Calling Europe: As I See It (ten minutes)	1800–1810	20 Dec.
				1950
49.		Review of *The God That Failed*	2115–2130	(rec. 25 Jan.)
50.	North American	London Commentary (approx. $4\frac{1}{2}$ minutes each)	1930	2 Feb.
51.		– Ditto –	1930	9 Feb.
52.		– Ditto – The German Situation*	1930	16 Feb.
53.		– Ditto –:	1930	21 Feb.
		The Soviet Union and Communist China*	1930	21 Feb.

54.		– Ditto –	1930	2 Mar.
55.		– Ditto –: British Relations with France	1930	9 Mar.
56.		– Ditto –: Survey of Communism*	1936	10 Mar.
57.		– Ditto –	1930	23 Mar.
58.	General Overseas	London Forum: What are the Distinguishing Marks of Modern Revolutions? (unscripted discussion with Alan Bullock) (30 minutes)	?	(rec. 28 Mar.)
59.	North American	London Commentary: The Question of Germany*	1930	30 Mar.
60.		– Ditto – Plan For Defence*		6 Apr.
61.	European English	London Calling Europe: European Letter Box (with 3 other speakers)	2115–2145	9 Apr.
62.		London Calling Europe: Elements of the English Tradition: (1) The Rebellious Tradition (13 minutes)	1800	1 May.
63.		London Calling Europe: As I See It (10 minutes)	1900	2 May.
64.		London Calling Europe: European Letter Box (with three other speakers)	2215–2245	4 Jun.
65.		London Calling	1900	13 Jun.

		Europe: As I See It (10 minutes)		
66.	Far Eastern	Question Time (with three other speakers) (two twenty minute programmes from one recording session)	?	(rec. 10 Jul.)
67.	General Overseas	London Forum: How History Should Be Written* (with Harold Nicolson)	1745–1815	16 Jul.
68.		Mid Week Talk: The Peace Offensive (fifteen minutes)	?	(rec. 18 Jul.)
69.	Far Eastern	I Speak For Myself* (nine minutes)	1320	23 Oct.
70.	General Overseas	London Forum: The Influences which have made British Socialism what it is (unscripted discussion with Raymond Postgate) (30 minutes)	?	(rec. 10 Aug.)
71.		London Forum: Is Russian Policy based on Communism or Imperialism?* (unscripted discussion with three other speakers) (30 minutes)	?	10 Sept.
72.	Far Eastern	Question Time (with four other speakers) (one recording, two programmes)	1310–1330	30 Sept. 20 Oct.
73.	General Overseas	London Forum: General Discussion	1645–1715	12 Nov.

		(with one other speaker)		
				1951
74.	North American	London Forum: Britain Answers America (unscripted discussion) (30 minutes)		(rec. 15 Jan.)
75.	Far Eastern	Question Time (with four other speakers) (one re-recording, two programmes)	1210–1230	3, 10 Feb.
76.	European English	London Calling Europe: European Letter Box (unscripted discussion with three other speakers)	2115–2145	18 Feb.
77.	General Overseas	London Forum: General Discussion (with one other speaker) (30 minutes)		(rec. 22 May.)
78.	London Calling Asia	London Dialogues: The Conclusions of History (with Dr. Hodson)*	1425–1445	15 Jun.
79.	North American	London Commentary (all about 4 minutes)	1935	31 Aug.
80.		– Ditto –	*	14 Sept.
81.		– Ditto –	*	27 Sept.
82.		– Ditto –	*	5 Oct.
83.	European English	London Calling Europe: European Letter Box (with three other speakers)	1815–1915	7 Oct.

84.	North American	London Commentary	1935*	12 Oct.
85.		– Ditto –	*	19 Oct.
86.		– Ditto –	*	2 Nov.
87.		– Ditto –	*	12 Nov.
88.		– Ditto –	*	16 Nov.
89.		– Ditto		23 Nov.
90.		– Ditto –		30 Nov.
91.		– Ditto –		6 Dec.
92.		– Ditto –		14 Dec.
93.		– Ditto – Europe and Asia*		21 Dec.
94.		– Ditto –		28 Dec.
				1952
95.	London Calling Asia	International Affairs (unscripted discussion with one other speaker) (18 minutes)	1315	1 Jan.
96.	North American	London Commentary	1935	4 Jan.
97.		– Ditto –	1935	11 Jan.
98.	European/ English	London Calling Europe: European Letter Box (with three other speakers)	1745–1815	13 Jan.
99.	North American	London Commentary	1935	18 Jan.
100.	North American	London Commentary	1935	1 Feb.
101.		– Ditto –		18 Feb.
102.		– Ditto –		22 Feb.
103.		– Ditto –		29 Feb.
104.		– Ditto –		7 Mar.
105.		– Ditto –		14 Mar.
106.		– Ditto – : German Rearmament and the ques-		21 Mar.

		tion of the Saar*		
107.		– Ditto – : The reply of the Western Powers to the Russian Proposals about Germany*		28 Mar.
108.		– Ditto – : Germany and the European Defence Community*		18 Apr.
109.		– Ditto – : Is there a Bevanite Foreign Policy?*		24 Apr.
110.	General Overseas	London Forum: The Foreign Policy of the Soviet Union*	1715–1745	27 Apr.
111.	European	European Letter Box	1745–1815	27 Apr.
112.	North American	London Commentary: The Meaning of Recent Moves in Spanish Foreign Policy*	2035	2 May.
113.		– Ditto – : The strategic significance of the Mediterranean*		9 May.
114.		– Ditto – The strength of Communism in France and Italy*		30 May.
115.		– Ditto – : Berlin Today*		6 Jun.
116.		– Ditto – : New embarrassments in Korea*		13 Jun.
117.		– Ditto – : A London comment on developments in		9 Jul.

		France*		
118.		– Ditto – : The Labour Party and German Re-armament*		18 Jul.
119.		– Ditto – : The British Government's gesture to the Scots*		28 Jul.
120.		– Ditto – : Mr. Gromyko as Soviet Ambassador*		31 Jul.
121.		– Ditto – : The decline of British Influence in the Far East*		8 Aug.
122.	North American	London Commentary: The Perplexities of the Middle East*		15 Aug.
123.		– Ditto – Dr. Schumacker and the German Social Democrats*		22 Aug.
124.		– Ditto – : Some Constitutional issues raised in the new official life of King George VI*		25 Aug.
125.		– Ditto – : Containment and the Cold War*		29 Aug.
126.		– Ditto – : The Saar*		5 Sept.
127.	London Calling Asia	London Dialogues: The British Attitude To Communism* (scripted discussion with Lady Listowel)	1440	11 Sept.

		(17 $\frac{1}{2}$ minutes)		
128.	North American	London Commentary: Mr. Eden in Yugoslavia*	2035	19 Sept.
129.	London Calling Asia	Asian Affairs: The Peking Peace Conference* (scripted discussion with another speaker) (17 minutes)	1415	25 Sept.
130.	North American	London Commentary: A General Survey of the international Position*	2035	26 Sept.
131.	European	London Calling Europe: European Letter Box (unscripted with 3 other speakers and chairman)	1843–1915	26 Oct.
				1953
132.	North American	This I Believe ($3\frac{1}{2}$ minutes)		(rec. 14 Jan.)
133.		London Commentary	1839	15 Jan.
134.		– Ditto –		29 Jan.
135.	General Overseas	London Forum: The Present State of Western Europe* (unscripted, three other speakers)	1615–1645	1 Feb.
136.	North American	London Commentary: The Proposal of a meeting with Russia*	1839	12 Feb.
137.		– Ditto – : After Stalin*		5 Mar.
138.		– Ditto – :		19 Mar.

		Marshal Tito's Visit*		
139.		– Ditto – : Brighter Prospects for Peace*	1935	2 Apr.
140.		– Ditto –	2035	23 Apr.
141.		– Ditto – : France Today*		30 Apr.
142.	London Calling Asia	Asian Club: Why do historians Disagree?	1330–1400	3 May.
143.	North American	London Commentary	2035	7 May.
144.	General Overseas	London Forum: Recent Trends in Russian Policy*	1715–1745	10 May.
145.	North American	London Commentary: The meeting between Sir Winston Churchill, President Eisenhower and M. Mayer*	2035	21 May.
146.		– Ditto – : The Political Crisis in France*		28 May.
147.		– Ditto –		11 Jun.
148.		– Ditto – : The Riots in East Berlin*		18 Jun.
149.		– Ditto – : The Bermuda Conference*		25 Jun.
150.		– Ditto – : The Little Bermuda Conference*		9 Jul.
151.		– Ditto – : What Is Happening in Russia?*		16 Jul.
152.		– Ditto – :		23 Jul.

		The House of Commons' Debate on Foreign Affairs*		
153.		– Ditto – : The Armistice in France*		28 Jul.
154.		– Ditto – : Italy in Search of a Government*		4 Aug.
155.		– Ditto – : Malenkov's Speech*		11 Aug.
156.		– Ditto –: The Meeting of the Assembly of the United Nations*		18 Aug.
157.		– Ditto –		25 Aug.
158.	General Overseas	London Forum: Why Do We Travel? (unscripted with 1 other speaker)	1830–1905	27 Aug.
159.	North American	London Commentary: Recent Events in Morocco*	2035	1 Sept.
160.		– Ditto –: The Election Results in Germany*		7 Sept.
161.		– Ditto – : The Question of Trieste*		15 Sept.
162.		– Ditto – : The European Defence Community*		22 Sept.
163.	European	London Calling Europe: European Letter Box (4 speakers, and chairman; unscripted discussion)	1845–1915	27 Sept.
164.	North American	London Commentary: Foreign Affairs	2035	29 Sept.

		at Margate*		
165.		– Ditto – : Political Prospects in France and Germany*		6 Oct.
166.		– Ditto – : Stalin and Yugoslav views on Trieste*	1935	15 Oct.
167.		– Ditto – : The Suez Canal and the Middle East*		22 Oct.
168.		– Ditto – : The Bermuda Meeting*		12 Nov.
169.		– Ditto – : The Present State of the Trieste Question*		26 Nov.
170.		– Ditto – : Verdict on Bermuda*	1330	10 Dec.
171.	London Calling Asia	The Long View: Reason and Unreason* (18 mins followed by questions)		19 Dec.
				1954
172.	North American	London Commentary: *The British Conference* by Robert McKenzie*	2035	28 Jan.
173.		– Ditto – : The French Crisis over Indo-China*		13 May.
174.		– Ditto – : Can Mendes-France succeed?		15 Jul.
175.		– Ditto – : London Forum:	1715–1745	25 Jul.

		Communism in under-developed countries*		
176.	London Calling Asia	Question Time (unscripted; with W.J. Brown and another speaker, and Harold Ingrams in the chair) 2 parts	1430–1500	28 Jul. & 11 Aug.
177.	North American	London Commentary: Mr. Eden's Tour of Europe*	2035	16 Sept.
178.	London Calling Asia	Ideas and Events: Review of *The Interregnum 1923–4*, Vol. 4 of E.H. Carr's *A History of Soviet Russia**	?	3 Nov.
179.		Question Time (with Hugh Gaitskell and Lady Astor) 2 parts	1330–1400	22 Dec. 5 Jan. 1955
180.	North American	London Commentary: Looking Back at 1954*	1935	29 Dec.
				1955
181.	North American	London Commentary: The Prospect for Western Europe*		13 Apr.
182.	General Overseas	London Forum: Does Civilisation Depend Upon the Middle Classes? (unscripted discussion with 2 other speakers and a chairman)	?	28 Aug.
183.	North	London Commen-	1830	14 Sept.

	American	tary: Dr. Adenauer's Visit to Moscow*		
				1956
184.		New World: Bunking and Debunking (unscripted discussion) (24 minutes)		(rec. 10 Jan.)
185.	General Overseas	London Forum: The Red Brick Universities (unscripted with Professor A.L. Goodhart and John Wain; Bruce Miller in the chair)	1715–1745	18 May.
186.	European	Book Review: *Documents on German Foreign Policy*, March-August 1939 (13 minutes)	1745	18 Jul.
187.	General Overseas	London Forum: Wine and Food Snobbery (unscripted discussion) (30 minutes)	?	(rec. 19 Dec.)
				1957
188.		A Study In Opposition: Charles James Fox*	1615–1630	8 Mar.
189.		The English Gentleman* (unscripted discussion with A.P. Ryan) (7–10 minutes)	2030	4 Dec.
				1958
190.		London Forum: The	1715–1745	10 Aug.

		Patterns of Revolution (unscripted discussion)		
				1961
191.		The World Today: The Trial of Adolf Eichmann (7 minutes)	2200	10 Apr.
192.	North American	World Report, 14: Divided Germany. Interviewed by Andrew Gardner ($9\frac{1}{2}$ minutes)	?	(rec. 8 Dec.)
				1964
193.	General	Dateline London, 85: Effects of the First World War		(rec. 8 Jun.)
194.		World Report: Churchill's 90th birthday		(rec. 16 Nov.)
				1965
195.	German	Bismarck in the Perspective of History		1 Apr.
				1967
196.	World	Outlook: Debtor to his Profession		(rec. 19 Nov.)
197.	Overseas Regional	World Report: Xmas edition – a feature on the past year		(rec. 27 Nov.)
198.	World	Outlook: The Beaverbrook Library		26 Nov.

			1970
199.	World	Larger Than Life: A.J.P. Taylor	13 Dec.
	(i)	Repeat	14 Dec.
	(ii)	Repeat	16 Dec.
			1971
200.	African	Postmark Africa: The Causes of the Second World War	13 Mar.
			1972
201.	Overseas Regional	Report from London: the release of the Cabinet Papers for 1941–5	3 Jan.
202.	World	Candidates for Greatness: Lord Beaverbrook	14 Jan.
	(i)	Repeat	15 Jan.
	(ii)	Repeat	18 Jan.
			1973
203.	Overseas Regional	World Report	(rec. 3 Jan.
			1975
204.	Central European Directive	Thirty Years After the War	3 Apr.
			1976
205.	World	Outlook: The Press Barons	19 Feb.

206.		Patterns of the Past: Overlord Embroidery, Britain in World War Two		31 Aug.
				1977
207.	German	The Monarchy		(rec. 14 Feb.)
208.	Overseas	John Wilkes		(rec. 15 Aug.)
209.	World	Interview on *The Lords*		(rec. 13 Dec.)

(c) *Television (BBC)*

	Programme		*Time*	*Date of Broadcast*
				1950
1.	In The News		2125	25 Aug.
2.			2212	6 Oct.
3.			2132	13
4.			2129	3 Nov.
5.			2036	24
6.			2121	8 Dec.
7.			2149	15
8.			2118	29
				1951
	(i)	repeated	1501	3 Jan.
9.			2120	5
	(i)	repeated	1501	10
10.			2133	19
	(i)	repeated	1501	24
11.			2147	26

12.			2100	2 Feb.
13.			2152	16
14.			2115	23
15.			2100	2 Mar.
16.			2116	9
	(i)	repeated	1501	14
17.			2100	30
	(i)	repeated	1501	4 Apr.
18.			2114	6
	(i)	repeated	1501	11
19.			2118	20
	(i)	repeated	1501	25
20.			2117	27
	(i)	repeated	1501	2 May.
21.			2150	4 May.
	(i)	repeated	1531	9
22.			2131	11
	(i)	repeated	1501	16
23.			2146	25
	(i)	repeated	1501	30
24.			2030	7 Sept.
25.			2046	28
26.			2148	28 Oct.
27.			2132	2 Nov.
28.			2152	23
29.			2046	30
30.			2151	28 Dec.
				1952
31.			2134	4 Jan.
	(i)	repeated	1501	9
32.			2116	25
	(i)	repeated	1501	30
33.			2132	1 Feb.
34.			2132	29
	(i)	repeated	1500	5 Mar.
35.			2153	7
	(i)	repeated	1500	12
36.			2145	4 Apr.
	(i)	repeated	1500	9

37.		2049	18
(i)	repeated	1500	23
38.		2157	2 May.
(i)	repeated	1500	7
39.		2209	30
40.		2121	17 Oct.
41.		2136	14 Nov.
42.		2140	12 Dec.
			1953
43. Private Opinion		2111	24 Jul.
44. In The News		2044	30 Oct.
45.		2145	27 Nov.
			1954
46. Any Questions		2103	9 Mar.
47. In The News		2215	30 Apr.
48.		2129	14 May
49.		2208	10 Dec.
			1960
50. Omnibus 1850–1960		2204	28 Aug.
			1961
51. Did Hitler Cause the War? A discussion about *The Origins of the Second World War*, with H. Trevor Roper (Repeated on radio, Home Service; *see* Appendix (a) 57).		2212	9Jul.
			1962
52. The Twenties:		2241	3 Feb.

	(1) The New World Pub. as 'A New World?', *Li.* 67,1715. 8 Feb. pp 247–50		
53.	(2) The Irish Troubles Pub. in *Li.* 67, 1716. 15 Feb. pp 283–6	2245	10
54.	(3) Peace Making Pub. in *Li.* 67,1717.22 Feb. pp 331–4	2246	17
55.	(4) The General Strike Pub. in *Li.* 67, 1719. 8 Mar. pp 409–12	2303	3 Mar.
56.	(5) The Baldwin Years Pub. in *Li.* 67, 1720. 15 Mar. pp 466–8	2243	10
57.	(6) The Great Depression Pub. in *Li.* 67, 1721. 22 Mar. pp 505–8	2252	17
58.	The Court of Last Resort – Summit Meetings	2127	13 Jun.
			1963
59.	Men of the 1860's: (1) Napoleon III Pub. in *Li.* 69, 1784. 6 Jun. pp 955–7	2216	27 May.
60.	(2) Francis Joseph Pub. in *Li.* 69,1785. 13 Jun. pp. 993–5	2218	4 Jun.
61.	(3) Lord Palmerston Pub. in *Li.* 69,1786. 20 Jun. pp 1033–5	2216	10
62.	(4) Alexander II Pub. in *Li.* 69, 1787. 27 Jun. pp 1069–71	2234	17
63.	(5) Karl Marx Pub. in *Li.* 70, 1788. 4 Jul. pp 13–15	2222	24
64.	(6) Bismarck Pub. in *Li.* 70, 1789. 11 Jul. pp 47–9.	2216	1 Jul.

65.	Tonight. Feature on the morals of famous people in the Victorian period	1850	20 Sept.
66.	Tonight. Interviewed by Dereck Hart on the book *The Reichstag Fire, Legend and Truth*	1905	18 Nov.
67.	Panorma. Reviewing the highlights of 1963	2115	23 Dec.
			1964
68.	The Hour Approaches	2128	5 Jun.
69.	Beaverbrook Tribute	2225	9 Jun.
70.	First Impressions: celebrity	1830	27 Oct.
71.	Tonight: The Two Faces of Taylor. Discussing C.P. Snow's *Corridors of Power*	1855	9 Nov.
	(i) Repeated in The World of Tonight	1555	15 Nov.
			1965
72.	Guest	2215	6 Oct.
			1966
73.	Plunder. Taking part in the programme, including a conversation with Malcolm Muggeridge	1930	28 May.
74.	Whoosh. On H.G. Wells	2125	15 Sept.
			1967
75.	Dee Time. Participant in this 'talk show'	1800	28 Oct.
			1968
76.	Dee Time. Participant	1715	8 Jun.

			1969
77.	Nationwide. Discussion on British Standard Time	1800	23 Oct.
			1971
78.	24 Hours Special: The Great Decision. Interviewed on the results of the referendum on Britain joining the EEC	2210	28 Oct.
			1972
79.	Tuesday's Documentary: The Uncrowned King. Discusses King Edward VIII and Mrs. Simpson Extracts in *Li.* 87, 2254. 8 Jun. pp 759	2120	30 May.
80.	Parkinson. Interviewed by Michael Parkinson	2230	10 Jun.
81.	24 Hours. Discusses Lord Beaverbrook	2240	26 Jun.
			1973
82.	Crosstalk. (1) In discussion with Rt. Hon. Richard Crossman MP Pub. in *Li.* 89, 2288. 1 Feb. pp 148–9	2313	7 Jan.
83.	Week In Week Out. Discusses Lloyd George	2323	12 Feb.
84.	One Pair of Eyes: The Road to Ruritania	2215	25 Oct.
			1974
85.	Read All About It. Discusses new paper-back books	2219	24 Jun.

86.	Newsday. Interviewed by Robin Day	1930	19 Sept.
87.	Nationwide. Interviewed about what role Hitler planned for the Duke of Windsor	1758	14 Oct.
88.	Nationwide. Interviewed about Rudolph Hess	1759	20 Nov.
			1975
89.	Newsday. Interviewed about the wider implications for British politics of the revolt of Tory MPs	1930	13 Feb.
90.	The Book Programme. Discussion with Arthur Marwick	1944	22 Apr.
91.	Midweek. Discussion on his *The Second World War* with Ludovic Kennedy Pub. in *Li.* 93, 2404. 1 May. p 579		(Apr.)
			1976
92.	Newsday. Discussion with Lord Blake about the coming year	1930	2 Jan.
93.	Nationwide. Interviewed about St George's feast day and the lack of attention paid to it.	1800	1 Mar.
94.	Tonight. Interviewed about the remaining candidates for the Labour leadership	2222	29
95.	Nationwide. Interviewed about King Edward VIII's abdication	1758	18 Jun.
96.	The War Lords. (1) Mussolini	2254	4 Aug.
	Pub. in *Li.* 96, 2469. 5 Aug. pp 132 – 4 and A22, pp 15–42	2254	4 Aug.
97.	(2) Hitler Pub. in *Li.* 96, 2470. 12 Aug. pp 165–8 and A22, pp 43–70	2250	11 Aug.

98.	(3) Churchill Pub. in *Li.* 96, 2471. 19 Aug. pp 196–8 and A22, pp 71–98	2250	18 Aug.
99.	(4) Stalin Pub. in *Li.* 96, 2472. 26 Aug. pp 233–5 and A22, pp 99–126	2250	25 Aug.
100.	(5) Roosevelt Pub. in *Li.* 96, 2473. 2 Sept. pp 265–7 and A22, pp 127–56	2250	1 Sept.
101.	(6) War Lords anonymous Pub. in *Li.* 96, 2474. 9 Sept. pp 301–3 and A22, pp 157–86	2310	6 Sept.
102.	Fabric of an Age. On the rise of Manchester Extracts in *Li.* 96, 2475. 16 Sept. pp 333–4 The programme won the Manchester Socicty of Architects' Award for Architectural Initiative, 1976	2010	16 Sept.
	(i) Repeat	2055	13 Sept. 1978
			1977
103.	(BBC 2) The Book Programme. One of a panel	?	20 Jan.
104.	How Wars Begin. (1) The Modern War – from French Revolution to French Empire Pub. in *Li.* 98, 2517. 14 Jul. pp 44–6	2315–2345	11 Jul.
105.	(2) Two Contrasting Wars Pub. in *Li.* 98, 2518. 21 Jul. pp 72–4	2254–2324	18 Jul.
106.	(3) Bismarck's Wars Pub. in *Li.* 98,2519. 28 Jul. pp 106 – 8	2315–2345	25 Jul.
107	(4) The First World War	2315–2345	1 Aug.

	Pub. in *Li.* 98, 2520. 4 Aug. pp 138 – 40 (omitting his concluding warning that weapons might fail to deter again in the future: 'And so it will be again')		
108.	(5) The Second World War Pub. in *Li.* 98, 2521. 11 Aug. pp 175–7	2310–2340	8 Aug.
109.	(6) The Cold War Pub. in *Li.* 98, 2522. 18 Aug. pp 200–2	2308–2338	15 Aug.

1978

110.	Revolution. (1) The First Revolution, Modern Style Pub. in *Li.* 100, 2568. 13 Jul. pp 40–2	2304–2334	10 Jul.
111.	(2) The Revolution That Never Was Pub. in *Li.* 100, 2569. 20 Jul. pp 78 – 80	2315–2345	13 Jul.
112.	(3) 1848 – The Year of Social Revolution Pub. in *Li.* 100, 2570. 27 Jul. pp 106–8	2250–2320	17 Jul.
113.	(4) 1848 – The Year of National Revolutions Pub. in *Li.* 100, 2571. 3 Aug. pp 142–4	2325–2355	20 Jul.
114.	(5) Revolutionaries Without A Revolution Pub. in *Li.* 100, 2572. 10 Aug. pp 177–9	2302–2332	24 Jul.
115.	(6) The Last Great European Revolution Pub. in *Li.* 100, 2573. 17 Aug. 204–6	2316–2346	27 Jul.

INDEX